An interpret
AMERICAN FOREIGN RELATIONS

THE DORSEY SERIES IN HISTORY

AN INTERPRETIVE HISTORY OF AMERICAN FOREIGN RELATIONS

Wayne S. Cole
University of Maryland

1974 · Revised Edition
THE DORSEY PRESS   Homewood, Illinois 60430
Irwin-Dorsey International   London, England WC2H 9NJ
Irwin-Dorsey Limited   Georgetown, Ontario L7G 4B3

Revised Edition

First Printing, January 1974

ISBN 0-256-01413-2
Library of Congress Catalog Card No. 73–82311
Printed in the United States of America

To Fred Harvey Harrington

Preface

This history of American foreign relations differs from other books on the subject in at least three ways. First, in this volume I advance a hypothesis for interpreting the history of American foreign relations which tries to answer the "whys" rather than simply add fact upon fact. This hypothesis gradually evolved in my thinking during more than 25 years of study, teaching, and research on the subject. For me and for many of my students this interpretive approach helps to make the history of American foreign affairs more meaningful. I summarize my hypothesis in the first chapter of this book and apply it in succeeding chapters. Second, this book is briefer and less detailed than other volumes on the history of American foreign relations. Its brevity makes it more adaptable to one-term courses on that subject. It also makes it easy to use in combination with books of readings, documents, and monographs. Finally, without making it a bibliographical survey, I introduce readers to some of the leading scholars and their interpretations of American diplomatic history.

In this revised edition I have tried to refine, correct, and update the distinctive features of the original volume. I have retained the basic interpretive hypothesis, but have applied it more clearly and consistently throughout. In contrast to the common practice of permitting "compacts" to grow, I have further shortened this edition by eliminating repetition and less important material. In addition I have updated the references to recent scholars and their interpretations. In this connection I have substantially rewritten the final part on American foreign relations since World War II, updating it to 1973 and incorporating new data, perspectives, and interpretations.

My intellectual debts to teachers, scholars, and students who influenced my thinking are so numerous that it is impossible for me to acknowledge them properly. Six scholars, however, must be singled out for special emphasis: Fred W. Wellborn of the University of Maryland; Thomas A.

Bailey of Stanford University; Herbert Butterfield of Cambridge University; Hans J. Morgenthau of the University of Chicago; the late Charles A. Beard; and especially Fred Harvey Harrington of the University of Wisconsin. The six men differ widely in their points of view and interpretations. Nevertheless, all contributed to my intellectual development and to the approach I have used in this book.

Many of those who aided in the preparation of the first edition continued their help and encouragement on this edition. I am grateful to colleagues and students who pointed out errors and suggested improvements. Among those to whom I am indebted are Kenneth E. Folsom, Donald C. Gordon, Horace S. Merrill, Leland L. Sage, Graham Shanks, E. B. Smith, and Terry G. Summons. I am particularly grateful to Harold Larson, who carefully read the entire volume and made numerous suggestions for improvements. Kinley J. Brauer of the University of Minnesota and Paul A. Varg of Michigan State University read the revised manuscript for the publisher, and their constructive suggestions improved the final product. Mrs Gaenor Willson generously helped with the index. My wife, Virginia Rae Cole, read proof. She also provided the quiet encouragement and patient tolerance that made my task more pleasant.

December 1973   WAYNE S. COLE

Contents

PART III. PRELUDE TO IMPERIALISM, 1861–1898

PART IV. AGE OF IMPERIALISM, 1899–1917

PART V. FROM WORLD WAR TO WORLD WAR, 1918–1941

PART VI. THE NUCLEAR AGE, 1942–1973

List of maps

1

An approach to the study of American foreign relations

International relations in the last third of the twentieth century challenge human capacities for wisdom, creativity, and survival. Power imbalances arouse fears for national security. Economic activities provide both bonds and friction between peoples. The self-righteousness and intolerance of conflicting ideologies make accommodation difficult. Emotions attached to the symbols of state, nation, ideology, race, or religion immeasurably complicate the task of obtaining international order. Thermonuclear weapons make "power politics" a decidedly deadly "game." The explosiveness of contemporary world affairs urgently requires statesmen and citizens to demonstrate more wisdom, judgment, and self-discipline than did those of previous generations. No tool of thought or action should be neglected if it contributes, however slightly, to the understanding and responsible control of world affairs.

One such tool is history. Knowledge about the past inevitably is fragmentary and imperfect. Facilities for measuring causes, consequences, and wisdom are pitifully crude and imprecise. Consequently, students should not expect any historical interpretation or approach to provide perfect truth or "solutions." The finest of historical interpretations can be no more than aids in the search for understanding. Nevertheless, perceptive study of history can throw meaningful light on patterns of the past, realities of the present, and the possibilities for the future. That conviction underlies this book.

The general organizational and interpretive approach in this volume may be stated very briefly: *America's role in world affairs has been the product of both international and domestic influences—both external and internal forces. The results of those two categories of influences have varied widely, but one of the frequent and important characteristics of those results has been American expansion in one form or another.* This hypothesis has three parts—external influences, internal influences, and expansion. Each of these requires elaboration.

EXTERNAL INFLUENCES

The foreign policies of the United States (and all other states) were designed partly to cope with the actions of other countries in the international community. The United States (like other states) has had two primary objectives in dealing with external conditions. One of those has been peace. Peace, however, was rarely if ever the only goal or even the dominant one. No state would have to go to war if it were determined that avoiding war was its sole or dominant objective. Any state could avoid war by refraining from making demands and by yielding to all demands by others. Such a course, however, would not be consistent with national survival. Wars begin when people and their governments decide that there are certain things more important than peace. America has been involved in every major world war fought since the first permanent English colony was established in the Western Hemisphere in 1607. In addition, the United States has fought regional wars and engaged in military actions without the formality of a declaration of war.

The second objective of the United States (and other states) in dealing with external conditions is variously called national security, self-preservation, or survival. The government of every state has an obligation to protect its security and insure survival of the state. National security has always been a fundamental objective of the United States. The pursuit of that goal may have a peaceful and "live-and-let-live" quality about it. But the drive for security can easily be converted into something that is aggressive, expansionist, and warlike. It can be used to justify expansion to get more defensible boundaries or to prevent another state from seizing strategic positions. Conceivably the drive for national security could even be used to justify a "preventive war." And if national security is defined very broadly—including preservation of domestic institutions, economic prosperity, ideological and religious beliefs, and the power of particular leaders and groups—then the drive for security conceivably could be used to justify almost any kind of action in world affairs.

Power plays a more conspicuous and crude role in the relations between states in the international community than it normally plays in the relations between individual humans. Idealists often urge the abandonment of "power politics." The fact remains, however, that power has played a conspicuous role in international affairs, it does play such a role, and in one way or another it will continue to play a role in the future. It is not possible to eliminate power from human affairs. The need is to so organize and use power as to render maximum benefits for the people of the world. The absence of an effective world government capable of enforcing order among states partly accounts for the prominent role of national power in international affairs. Despite the United Nations, there is no policeman on the corner to regulate relations between states and to protect the weak against the strong. In the relative international anarchy that prevails, ultimately a sovereign state's survival, its success or failure, is dependent upon its power relative to that of the states with which it is dealing. One might wish it were not so, but it is, and will continue to be so long as the multistate system prevails and so long as there is no world government.

Military forces are essential for national power. But a state's power involves much more than simply the size and effectiveness of its armed forces. The power of a state in international affairs includes everything that helps it to achieve its goals minus everything that inhibits its efforts to obtain its objectives. The elements of national power include geography, natural resources, industrial capacity, military preparedness, population, national character, national morale, quality of government, and quality of diplomacy. National power is always relative to that of the states with which it is dealing. A state's power may vary on different issues and in different parts of the world. Today the United States is one of the two strongest states, but during the first century of its independent history America was not powerful relative to the major states of Europe. In a direct confrontation the United States could not match such giants as Britain or France. Fortunately for the United States, however, the great powers in the eighteenth and nineteenth centuries were often preoccupied with their problems in Europe and elsewhere. Consequently, the power they brought to bear in their dealings with the United States was distinctly limited, particularly in the Western Hemisphere. "Europe's distresses spelled America's successes" often in the early diplomatic history of the United States. In any event, America's role in world affairs becomes meaningful partly in terms of its efforts to protect peace and security in the face of actions by other states in the international community.

INTERNAL INFLUENCES

In addition, American foreign policies (and those of other states as well) were partly the result of internal influences. Undoubtedly statesmen, diplomats, and military leaders often wish those domestic influences did not operate. They sometimes contend that domestic matters should not intrude into foreign affairs. But such views are essentially unrealistic. Internal conditions have affected American foreign affairs in the past, they do now, and they will in the future. It is not possible (even in a dictatorship) to eliminate domestic considerations completely. The most one might do is to guide such influences in directions that are not inconsistent with national welfare. Domestic affairs and foreign affairs are intimately related to each other. Numerically the overwhelming majority of the contacts between people in different countries are the extension of the day-to-day economic, social, and cultural activities of those people. Many of the policies of every state in international affairs grow partly out of the needs, desires, and ambitions of the dominant individuals and groups within that country. The specific objectives and actions of the United States in foreign affairs might be quite different if another group with different values, interests, or ambitions were in power at a particular time.

Countless domestic considerations may affect foreign policy views. Politics may be involved—the hope that a particular foreign policy may win votes or weaken political opponents. Economic interests may be important. One cannot explain all human attitudes and actions exclusively in economic terms. But individuals and groups may be more attracted by foreign policies that might benefit them financially than by policies restricting their opportunities for economic gain. Groups have not been reluctant to seek government help for their economic activity in foreign affairs. Various economic groups may have quite different views on foreign affairs, partly because of their diverse interests. Ethnic ties may be important. Sympathies of immigrants or descendants of immigrants (i.e., "hyphenated Americans") for their original mother country or their hostility for enemies of their mother country may greatly affect their attitudes on particular issues. Even religious beliefs and affiliations may cause Americans of one particular faith or another to take stands on foreign policies that may differ from the attitudes of people of different faiths. Missionary activities may directly affect their views. Ideas represent another powerful domestic influence. One cannot explain all foreign policies in ideological terms, but neither can one get an accurate understanding if ideological considerations are omitted. And finally, the emotions and psychological makeup of individual Americans and groups of Americans represent a particularly significant category of domestic influences. Leaders with different psychological and reaction patterns might follow quite different policies in the same situations. Once emotions are aroused, they can be extremely powerful influences on foreign affairs. In any event, foreign affairs and domestic affairs are intimately related, and America's role in world affairs becomes meaningful partly in terms of these internal influences.

In at least two ways power plays a fundamental role in domestic influences, just as it is basic to external considerations. First, power in its broadest sense determines which individuals and groups become dominant within a state, which are able to make their views prevail in shaping domestic and foreign policies. The internal struggle for power often is conducted politely and legally. The methods may be quite moral and ethical. Normally it is accomplished without physical violence. But the struggle goes on just the same, and its outcome determines whose interests and wishes will best be served in both domestic and foreign affairs. Second, just as a state's security in international relations cannot be assured without power, so the desires of domestic groups cannot prevail abroad without effective supporting power.

AMERICAN EXPANSION

Unfortunately, historians do not have facilities for measuring historical forces with the accuracy of a physicist. But if they had that capacity, they might explain much of American foreign relations in terms of external and internal influences. The approach may be visualized in geometric terms. That is, if the external and internal influences are the forces acting on foreign affairs (i.e., the vectors in a parallelogram), then America's policies and actions in foreign affairs represent the resultant of those two categories of influences. It might be diagramed in the following manner:

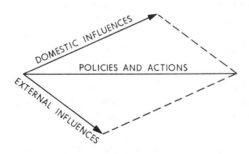

Historians cannot measure either the force or direction of these influences (vectors) or actions (resultants) with such precision. But if they could, they might throw much additional light on America's role in world affairs.

In at least one extremely important aspect, however, this geometric figure is not satisfactory. The use of the parallelogram implies a determined or fixed resultant. Such may be the case. But those forces operate through living human beings who presumably have a capacity for choice among alternative courses of action. Particular conditions (domestic and foreign) may greatly affect their choices, but those conditions may not absolutely determine one particular choice. Consequently, in some respects the language of the statistician may be more appropriate than that of the geometrician. The statistical term "probability" seems relevant. Given certain influences (external and internal) operating on an individual or group of individuals, there may be a high degree of probability that one alternative may be selected in preference to others and quite improbable that other alternatives will be chosen. Emphasis on impersonal forces should not obscure the role of the individual personality. At the same time, however, recognition of the importance of "freedom of the will" should not hide the fact that conditions (external and internal) increase tremendously the probability that certain alternatives may be chosen in preference to others.

The exact nature of the internal and external influences has changed constantly. Consequently, the direction and force of the resultant (i.e., the policies and actions) varied widely. Nevertheless, among others one particular characteristic of that resultant stood out prominently and frequently. One of the most constant themes in the history of American foreign affairs was expansion in one form or another. From the time of the first permanent English colony in 1607 until the present moment, American history has been characterized by almost continuous expansion. Expansion included every activity by which the United States increased its influence or control in other parts of the world. Sometimes that was territorial and colonial expansion—including the movement across the North American continent and the acquisition of colonies and protectorates overseas. But often American expansion was nonterritorial. Sometimes it was expansion of trade and investments. Sometimes it was expansion through religious organizations and missionary activities. There was intellectual, cultural, and ideological expansion. The tremendous diplomatic power of the United States in the world today and the presence of American military forces in many parts of the earth are evidences of that expansion. There were times when the United States did not expand rapidly. Nevertheless, one of the most consistent and important patterns in the history of American foreign affairs was the steady growth of American power, influence, and control in other parts of the world in one way or another. And that expansion was the result of both external influences in the drive for peace or security and internal influences.

The chapters that follow are organized and presented in terms of the interpretive approach outlined in this first chapter. The history of American foreign relations is, for the purpose of convenience, divided into six chronological periods. The first chapter in each of these six sections describes briefly the general patterns of world affairs in that period—that is, describes some of the external influences. The next chapter of each section surveys briefly the domestic conditions affecting American foreign relations at that time. Then several chapters follow in each section tracing America's actual role in world affairs in terms of the external and internal influences, with particular emphasis on the ways those influences contributed to American expansion.

SUPPLEMENTARY READINGS

Almond, Gabriel A. *The American People and Foreign Policy.* New York: Frederick A. Praeger, Inc., 1960.

Bailey, Thomas A. *The Man in the Street: The Impact of American Public Opinion on Foreign Policy.* New York: Macmillan Co., 1948.

Beard, Charles A. *The Idea of National Interest: An Analytical Study in American Foreign Policy.* New York: Macmillan Co., 1934.

Butterfield, Herbert. *Christianity, Diplomacy and War.* New York: Abingdon-Cokesbury Press, 1953.

————. *History and Human Relations.* New York: Macmillan Co., 1952.

Carr, Edward H. *The Twenty Years' Crisis, 1919–1939: An Introduction to the Study of International Relations.* London: Macmillan & Co., Ltd., 1940.

Lasswell, Harold D. *World Politics and Personal Insecurity.* New York: McGraw-Hill Book Co., 1935.

Morgenthau, Hans J. *In Defense of the National Interest: A Critical Examination of American Foreign Policy.* New York: Alfred A. Knopf, Inc., 1952.

————. *Politics Among Nations: The Struggle for Power and Peace.* 4th ed. New York: Alfred A. Knopf, Inc., 1967.

Northrop, F. S. C. *The Taming of the Nations: A Study of the Cultural Bases of International Policy.* New York: Macmillan Co., 1952.

Van Alstyne, Richard W. *The Rising American Empire.* Oxford University Press, 1960.

Weinberg, Albert K. *Manifest Destiny: A Study of Nationalist Expansionism in American History.* Baltimore: Johns Hopkins Press, 1935.

Wright, Quincy. *A Study of War.* Chicago: University of Chicago Press, 1942.

PART I

The new nation in an age of
revolution and war
1775-1815

2

Rivalry, revolution, and war: External influences on American foreign relations to 1815

Conceived in 1607 and delivered in 1776, the United States was born in a world environment so violent and insecure that the infant state's survival was by no means assured. But from 1775 to 1815, that environment provided not only threats but opportunities as well for the new nation. Both successes and failures of the United States foreign policies were, to a considerable extent, determined by developments abroad. As Samuel Flagg Bemis, the leading scholar on the diplomacy of the American Revolution, phrased it: "It was this bitter cut-throat international rivalry which was to make American independence possible." It also made possible national survival, commercial gains, and territorial expansion, and it tempted Americans to try for even more. The results of American foreign policies in those early years were due partly to the qualities of American statesmen, diplomats, generals, and citizens—their skill and ineptness, their wisdom and ignorance, their courage and cowardice, and their needs and desires. But the results were due also to the rivalries and circumstances that prevailed among the major states of Europe and their empires.

During the centuries from 1492 to 1815 the Western world was plagued by recurrent friction and war among the various European states. The specific causes for each of the many wars varied. Some (particularly in the sixteenth and seventeenth centuries) resulted partly from religious controversies. Many were dynastic quarrels about who should rule where. Survival of the state was involved. Some, after 1789, had ideological bases with countries identifying with ideas of the French Revolution or with defense of monarchies. All of the wars were struggles for power.

Some of the conflagrations resulted partly from conflicting commercial ambitions couched in terms of the prevailing mercantilistic theories. Mercantilists considered economic self-sufficiency essential for a state's wealth, power, and security. They stressed the need for a favorable balance of trade—that is, a pattern in which a state exported more than it imported, with the difference made up by shipments of gold into the country. Gold was the ultimate measure of a state's wealth. Colonies were an essential part of the successful operation of the system. They were expected to provide sources for food and raw materials, markets for manufactured products, and quantities of gold and silver. Mercantilism was not a laissez-faire system; it was a form of economic nationalism, with the government regulating economic patterns by means of tariffs, quotas, navigation acts, and trade bans.

In that connection, many European wars were partly the result of efforts to build, protect, and expand colonial empires in Asia and America. Colonies were justified in religious terms, in mercantilistic terms, in the name of security, or were the product of lust for power, adventure, and glory. Whatever the reasons (or justifications), the drives for empire often led to conflict and war.

The belligerents varied from war to war. On the Continent, France battled against the Hapsburgs in Spain, Austria, and the Netherlands through two and one-half centuries before the Diplomatic Revolution of 1756. Pursuing its balance-of-power policies, England warred first against the Spanish Hapsburgs and then against Bourbon France.

Partly because of its geographic location in the search for new routes to the East, the first country to achieve distinction so far as expansion outside of Europe was concerned was Portugal. Through Prince Henry, Bartholomeu Diaz, Vasco da Gama, and others, Portugal moved south along the coasts of Africa, around the Cape of Good Hope, and on to Asia. Pedro Cabral, by touching South America, established the Iberian country's claims in the New World. But Portugal could not prevail when greater powers got under way. It was united with Spain in 1581, and its independence after 1640 depended heavily upon English support, first against Spain and then against France. Portugal retained Brazil until the 1820's and other colonies longer, but that tiny country was weak long before the first permanent English colony was established in North America.

The second state to rise to dominance in the struggle for power and empire was Spain. Spain completed its unification between 1469 and 1516, early in the history of modern Europe, and in 1492 Spain crushed the last of Moorish resistance on the Iberian Peninsula. Christopher Columbus sailed for Spain, and through the daring exploits of conquistadores who followed after him Spain built the largest empire ever constructed in the

Western Hemisphere. Under Charles V (1516–1556) and Philip II (1556–1598), Spain extended and consolidated its holdings in Europe and America. When Philip II took over Portugal and its empire in 1581, Spain was at the peak of its power and prestige. And Spain established its great empire roughly a century before either Britain or France began to build theirs.

No sooner did Spain triumph, however, than its power began to crumble, and most Western European states got in on the exciting task of tearing away at Spanish power and holdings. France, England, the Netherlands, and others shared in the adventure. Hatred of Spain became intense. The defeat of the Spanish Armada by the English under Queen Elizabeth in 1588 was the most dramatic event in the collapse of Spanish power, and with that episode Spain began its long, slow decline. Thus, by the time of the first permanent English colony in America at Jamestown in 1607, Spain was already past its peak. Through rearguard tactics, Spain desperately tried to retain what it had and to delay the disintegration of its vast holdings. In those efforts Spain was remarkably successful. It kept most of its overseas empire until the 1820's, and some of it even longer.

Spain's weakness, its difficulties in retaining its empire, and its ideological hostility to revolution and republics account for its coolness to the American War for Independence beginning in 1775. After the United States won its independence, Spanish colonies bordered the new nation on two sides—Florida to the south and the Louisiana Territory to the west. Spain controlled the mouths of the Mississippi and other rivers used by Americans. In such a context, the fast-fading old European state feared and obstructed the growing power and ambitions of the vigorous new nation in America. Finally, when France under Napoleon overran Spain, and Napoleon's brother Joseph was placed on the throne in 1808, the Spanish empire in America began to disintegrate. By the middle of the 1820's, most of its colonies in Latin America had won their independence.

A third country to play its brief role at the center of the international stage was the Netherlands. In the first half of the seventeenth century, Dutch merchants and bankers were active all over the world. The Dutch built colonies in many places, particularly as trading centers. New Netherlands, founded in 1624, settlements in Brazil, and the Dutch East Indies were products of that activity. But the Netherlands, like Portugal earlier, lacked an adequate home base for world power. France assailed it on the Continent. In the third quarter of the seventeenth century, England fought three Anglo-Dutch wars in which the Dutch colonial challenge was broken. In 1664 England seized New Netherlands, which became New York. The Netherlands continued to be important as a trading and financial center—and aided the United States in that capacity a bit during the American Revolution. Nevertheless, from 1688 onward the political and military power of the Netherlands was slight. It (like Portugal) depended upon

England for the protection of its security against France and other continental powers.

Thus by 1688 the two principal contenders remaining in the European struggle for power and supremacy were France and England. From 1688 to 1815 France and England (and states bound to them) engaged in a long, bitter struggle for supremacy. That period roughly coincided with the last century of American colonial history and the first generation in the history of the independent United States.

Details varied from war to war, but certain contrasting patterns stood out in the strategies of the English and French. Except for the French and Indian War, France was concerned primarily with maintaining dominance on the continent of Europe. Again excepting the French and Indian War, maritime and overseas colonial considerations generally were secondary in French strategy. England tried to maintain a balance of power in Europe by marshaling the lesser states on the Continent to block French dominance there. But England did not center its efforts on the Continent nearly so much as France did. England was more concerned with maintaining control of the seas through its navy, bases, and merchant fleet. It sought control of world commerce—particularly with colonies in America and Asia. England attached greater importance than France did to colonial empires administered according to the canons of mercantilism.

For purposes of convenience, the seven Anglo-French wars from 1689 to 1815 may be divided into two broad groups. The first of those series (sometimes called the "second Hundred Years' War") included five wars between 1689 and 1783. European matters were very much involved in each of those wars (often they were the primary concern), but those five wars were partly struggles to control colonial empires in America and Asia. The War of Spanish Succession (in America called Queen Anne's War) from 1701 to 1713 resulted in substantial colonial gains for England. By means of the Treaty of Utrecht that ended the war, England gained Hudson's Bay Territory, Nova Scotia, and Newfoundland in North America, plus Gibraltar and other territories elsewhere. England also gained the asiento or slave trade monopoly from France's ally, Spain.

The French and Indian War began in America in 1754 and two years later spread to Europe as the Seven Years War. In that conflagration England triumphed and shattered France's overseas empire in America and Asia. In the Treaty of Paris that ended the war in 1763, France lost all of its remaining colonies on the mainland of North America. Important unintended consequences of the French and Indian War helped lead to American independence in the following decade. Elimination of the French from North America made colonists feel less need for English protection. Colonists, for the first time in the Anglo-French wars, played major roles in the fighting and gained confidence in their own martial skills while discovering that the British were not invincible. The vast territories acquired by the English led them to institute administrative innovations displeasing to colonists, who had long enjoyed the mother country's "salutary neglect." And finally, the financial burden of the wars plus the costs of administering and defending the enlarged empire moved the English to impose new taxes in the Colonies that were most unwelcome.

In a very real sense, then, the American Revolution beginning in 1775 was one of the indirect consequences of the English victory in the French and Indian War. And the success of America in establishing its independence in the America Revolution from 1775 to 1783 was possible because of the last in the first series of Anglo-French wars. The American Revolution was not simply a war between America and England. France became a belligerent in 1778, Spain in 1779, and the Netherlands in the next year. European statesmen were moved by self-interest: hatred of England, desire for revenge, determination to seize on the opportunity to weaken England and enhance their own power positions, and the hope for gains in Europe and elsewhere. Spain, for example, wanted Gibraltar—not American independence. But European rivalries worked to America's advantage. The United States could not have won its independence when it did had it not been for the French aid. England established its imperial supremacy in the Anglo-French colonial wars, but one of the by-products of those wars was independence for the United States.

For a decade, from 1783 to 1793, England and France were at peace with each other. During that time the United States struggled unsuccessfully to make its government under the Articles of Confederation work effectively. In 1789 the French Revolution began in Europe. In that same year America abandoned the Articles and replaced them with the present Constitution. George Washington, as the first President under that Constitution, tried to lead the nation to unity and strength. Peace in Europe endured until near the end of Washington's first term, but war on the Continent began in 1792 and involved Britain the following year.

The second of the two series of Anglo-French wars began in 1793 and did not finally end until 1815. That second series included both the French Revolutionary Wars in the last decade of the eighteenth century and the Napoleonic Wars in the first decade and a half of the nineteenth century. Though colonial matters were involved, they primarily concerned European and continental matters. They included virtually every European country at one time or another. Great Britain organized and led four coalitions against France. In a variety of ways the French Revolution and Napoleon upset the European balance of power and endangered the security of European states—including Great Britain. The wars were life-and-death struggles with no holds barred. In part they were struggles between the greatest land power in the world (France) and coalitions led by the greatest naval power in the world (Great Britain). With Napoleon's military victory at Austerlitz in 1805, France was supreme on the continent of Europe. Lord Nelson's naval victory at Trafalgar in the same year confirmed Britain's supremacy on the seas. Eventually Britain and its allies triumphed, with the defeat of France under Napoleon at Waterloo in 1815.

The French Revolution (1789–1799) and its wars corresponded chronologically to the Federalist Period of American history when George Washington and John Adams were Presidents of the United States. The Napoleonic Era (1799–1815) and its wars corresponded chronologically to the Jeffersonian Era of American history when Thomas Jefferson and James Madison were Presidents. The United States became involved in both the Wars of the French Revolution and the Napoleonic Wars. Understandably, the European belligerents wanted to limit the right of neutrals to trade with their enemies. Through its Orders-in-Council, enforced by its powerful navy, Britain determined to control all trade with Napoleon's Europe. And in his Berlin and Milan Decrees, Napoleon tried to use his control of continental ports to prevent trade with Britain. The United States as a neutral understandably wanted maximum freedom to trade with belligerents on both sides in the wars. Partly as a consequence of the conflicts of interests over neutral rights, the United States entered an undeclared naval war with France from 1798 to 1800, during the last years of the Wars of the French Revolution. And partly as a result of the neutral rights controversy, the United States entered the War of 1812 against Britain near the end of the Napoleonic Wars.

That second series of Anglo-French wars, then, had certain harmful results for the United States. Americans lost ships, cargoes, and seamen. The British captured the nation's capital and burned the White House during the War of 1812. But those European wars also had beneficial results for the United States. Jay's Treaty of 1794–1795 with Great Britain was one result, and it included some provisions desired by the United States. The wholly favorable Pinckney Treaty of 1795 with Spain was another indirect result. The Louisiana Purchase of 1803 was possible partly because of the developments among European states. American merchants enjoyed profits (as well as losses) from trading with the European belligerents. And the Napoleonic Wars, by inadvertently promoting political independence for the Latin-American states, made it easier for Americans to expand commercially and territorially in that region.

America's role in world affairs in 1815 was not shaped alone by external developments, however. Domestic conditions within the boundaries of the United States also provided part of the explanation.

SUPPLEMENTARY READINGS

Bourne, Edward G.   *Spain in America, 1450–1580.* New York: Harper & Bros., 1904.

Brinton, Crane.   *A Decade of Revolution, 1789–1799.* New York: Harper & Bros., 1934.

Bruun, Geoffrey. *Europe and the French Imperium, 1799–1814.* New York: Harper & Bros., 1938.

Buffington, Arthur H. *The Second Hundred Years War, 1689–1815.* New York: Henry Holt & Co., Inc., 1929.

Dorn, Walter L. *Competition for Empire, 1740–1763.* New York: Harper & Bros., 1940.

Gershoy, Leo. *From Despotism to Revolution, 1763–1789.* New York: Harper & Bros., 1944.

Mowat, Robert B. *A History of European Diplomacy, 1451–1789.* New York: Longmans, Green & Co., Inc., 1928.

Newton, Arthur P. *The European Nations in the West Indies, 1493–1688.* London: A. & C. Black, Ltd., 1933.

Parkman, Francis. *France and England in North America.* 9 vols. Boston: Little, Brown & Co., 1910.

Roberts, Penfield. *The Quest for Security, 1715–1740.* New York: Harper & Bros., 1947.

Thwaites, Reuben G. *France in America, 1497–1763.* New York: Harper & Bros., 1905.

Wrong, George M. *The Rise and Fall of New France.* 2 vols. New York: Macmillan Co., 1928.

3

The new nation: Domestic influences on American foreign relations to 1815

The United States before 1815 differed radically from twentieth-century America. And those distinctive internal characteristics helped account for the foreign policies of the young nation.

THE PEOPLE

With only about 2.5 million people when the Revolution began in 1775, the population was considerably less than that of the present city of Chicago. Even at the close of the War of 1812, with less than 8.5 million, the United States had a smaller population than New York City has today. By 1815 there were approximately 1.5 million blacks in the United States—most of them in the South and most of them slaves. Indians generally were outside organized white society. Very few Americans were of Latin or Slavic descent. Most people were immigrants or descendants of immigrants from the Anglo-Saxon and Germanic countries of northern and western Europe—England, Scotland, Ireland, and Germany. And Anglo-Saxons dominated politically, economically, and culturally.

Reflecting the ethnic composition, most Americans with religious affiliations then were Protestants. The Irish and some of the Germans were Roman Catholic, and there were a few Americans of Jewish faith. The great influx of Catholic and Jewish immigrants, however, did not begin until much later.

Geographically, most Americans lived east of the Appalachian Mountains—generally very close to the Atlantic coast. In the eighteenth century, Scotch-Irish and German settlers moved down the valleys of the Appalachians, and some began to locate west of the mountains during the Revolution. Vermont, Kentucky, and Tennessee became states while Washington was President. Ohio became a state in 1803 and Louisiana in 1812—making a total of eighteen by the close of the period. But most of the present area of the United States was not settled by whites when the War of 1812 ended.

Before 1815 most Americans lived on farms, on the frontier, or in small towns—in striking contrast to the highly urbanized society of the United States in the twentieth century. The first census in 1790 classified 95 percent of Americans as rural. Even the so-called urban people lived in cities tiny by present standards. The largest city during the American Revolution was Philadelphia with about 30,000 people. Despite its growth and influence, New York City had fewer than 150,000 inhabitants as late as 1815.

THE ECONOMY

The American economy before 1815 also differed greatly from that of today. For purposes of analysis most individuals in those years may be divided into two broad categories: the shipping-commercial group and the farmer-agrarian group.

The smaller of the two—the shipping-commercial group—included merchants and traders who owned their own ships, fishermen (particularly from New England), shipbuilders, and the bankers and creditors who helped finance the trading and shipping enterprises. Before 1815 that group included little commercial manufacturing. Geographically the shipping-commercial group was most numerous in New England and in eastern portions of the Middle Atlantic states. It was present on a smaller scale in the southern coastal cities such as Charleston and New Orleans. Politically the members tended to work through the Federalist Party. Among its many able political spokesmen were John Adams of Massachusetts, and Alexander Hamilton and John Jay of New York.

American foreign trade before 1815 differed strikingly from the patterns today. Foreign trade played a relatively larger role in the economy before 1815 than in any other major period of American history. Since the United States had little commercial industry of its own, most imports consisted of manufactured and semimanufactured products. Since most Americans were farmers, exports consisted largely of agricultural commodities such as wheat, flour, tobacco, and cotton. Most foreign trade was conducted with Europe, and particularly with Great Britain. The China trade began in the 1780's and was lucrative to some merchants.

Despite legal obstructions, trade with the West Indies continued active and profitable. United States trade with Latin America began while Spain still had its empire, and it expanded after Latin America won independence. Nevertheless, Europe and particularly Great Britain continued to receive most American exports and send most of its imports. England manufactured products that Americans wanted, while England needed many of the commodities that American farmers produced. The United States before 1815 generally had an "unfavorable" balance of trade—that is, it imported more products than it exported. Most foreign trade was carried in ships owned and operated by Americans. The United States had one of the leading merchant fleets in the world. Those ships not only transported products in American trade but also engaged in the carrying trade between other countries. The profits from the carrying trade helped fill the gap left by the unfavorable balance of trade. Until the beginning of the War of 1812, American foreign trade, and the profits from that trade, generally increased—in spite of (and partly because of) the European wars and the interference by European belligerents with American ships.

Throughout those years the United States had a debtor status in international finance—that is, foreigners loaned and invested much more money in the United States than Americans loaned and invested abroad. Private lenders and investors from Great Britain provided most of the foreign capital. The influx of capital helped fill part of the gap left by the unfavorable balance of trade and also helped finance America's rapid economic growth.

The interests and activities of members of the shipping-commercial group directly affected their attitudes toward foreign policies. Understandably, the members of that group supported policies that would promote and protect American foreign trade. They wanted commercial treaties, an efficient consular service, and a large and effective navy. Many of them wanted protection and subsidies for the fishing industry. They considered peace with Great Britain essential at almost any price. Since most trade was with Britain, war with that country would have disastrous direct effects on American foreign trade. Britain's powerful navy could, in the event of war, destroy America's trade with other countries as well. Generally the group opposed westward territorial expansion by the United States. Most of them would not profit directly from western expansion. New lands in the West might drain off the labor supply in the East and increase its cost. Westerners might buy fewer European products and produce less for export (at least at first) than if they remained in the East. And politically, westward expansion might lead to the creation of more agrarian states that would weaken the relative political power of the shipping-commercial interests. A few merchants and traders supported the westward movement, but they were exceptions.

The second (and by far the larger) of the two broad economic categories before 1815 was the farmer-agrarian group. It included small farmers, planters, fur traders, and land speculators. A very large percentage of Americans engaged in land speculation, from small farmers to city financiers. Patrick Henry, Benjamin Franklin, and George Washington, among others, were in various land speculation schemes. Geographically farmer-agrarians were in every section of the country. But they were most numerous and powerful in the South and West ("West" meaning the Piedmont, valleys of the Appalachians, and the Ohio-Mississippi Valley in those years). Politically they generally supported the Anti-Federalist, Democratic-Republican, or Jeffersonian Republican Party. Their greatest political spokesman was Thomas Jefferson of Virginia.

The interests and activities of the farmer-agrarian group directly affected foreign policy attitudes. Farmers (then and now) needed foreign trade. They bought manufactured products from abroad, and many of their farm commodities eventually reached other parts of the world. Foreign interference with ships flying the American flag aroused their patriotism. In general, however, farmers attached much less importance to the expansion and protection of foreign trade than did the shipping-commercial group. The China trade and the fishing industry had little appeal to most of them. Members of that group tended to be anti-British and pro-French. The farmer-agrarian group generally urged American westward territorial expansion. Some hoped for additional cheap lands. They wanted the United States to control the mouths of rivers (such as the Mississippi) through which their products went to markets. Territorial expansion might facilitate control or defeat of hostile Indians. Some hoped to benefit from land speculation in the West. And still others wanted to expand their fur-trading operations. In general they favored low tariffs on the manufactured products they had to buy. And most of them wanted the Indians ruthlessly controlled, driven out, or (if need be) killed off.

POLITICAL PATTERNS

For purposes of convenience the political history of the United States to 1815 may be divided into four distinct periods. The first was the American Revolution, from 1775 to 1783. The Second Continental Congress and its appointees and committees provided such central government as there was during the Revolution before 1781. But that Continental Congress (though it got the job done) amounted to little more than a meeting of representatives of sovereign states.

The Articles of Confederation, from 1781 to 1789, provided the second period of American political history. That first constitution authorized relatively weak, decentralized authority with sovereignty residing in the states. Committees and department secretaries performed the executive functions. The Articles provided for a one-house legislature representing the states, with equal voting powers for all states and extremely limited power for the legislature.

During the Revolution various factions struggled inconclusively for dominance and for control of domestic and foreign policies. In the 1780's the shipping-commercial group (in alliance with large southern planters) gradually gained the upper hand. One result was the drafting and adoption of the present Constitution of the United States by 1789.

The next period in American political history (the first under the new Constitution) was the Federalist Era, from 1789 to 1801. Two men served as President in that period—Washington from 1789 to 1797, and John Adams for one term from 1797 to 1801. The dominant party became the Federalist Party, with Alexander Hamilton as its greatest leader. It was strongest in the Northeast and drew its most important support from the merchant-trader-creditor groups in the cities, with additional support coming from the wealthiest of the southern planters. It tended to be conservative, pro-business, pro-English, "elitist," and somewhat undemocratic on the issues of the day. Dominant from 1789 to 1801, the Federalist Party provided vigorous minority opposition after 1801 until it disappeared with its defeat in the elections of 1816.

The next period in American political history (the second under the Constitution) was the Jeffersonian Era, from 1801 to 1817. Two men served as President—Thomas Jefferson from 1801 to 1809, and James Madison from 1809 to 1817. The party they led was the Democratic-Republican or Jeffersonian Republican Party. It drew its greatest support from farmers and small planters of the South and West. Under Jefferson's leadership it represented (in comparison with the Federalist Party) a relatively democratic, pro-farmer, pro-French, and territorial expansionist point of view. Its sympathies did not extend very much to the small urban working class. For most of sixty years (from 1801 to 1861) the farmer-agrarian group, working first through Jefferson's Republican Party and later through Jackson's Democratic Party, controlled both the domestic and foreign policies of the United States.

IDEOLOGICAL PATTERNS

The challenging and exhausting tasks of conquering a new land, of surviving and making a living in the New World, were not conducive to systematic philosophizing. Widespread illiteracy, limited news media, and poor transportation and communication facilities inhibited the distribution of ideas and information. Preoccupation with personal, local, and state problems was commonplace for the upper classes and the masses alike.

The extent of public apathy should not be exaggerated, however. Most people were innocent of the reflective thought and great learning of a

Jefferson. But even the illiterate were not without conceptions of the true, the good, the beautiful, and the possible—however unsophisticated those conceptions may have been. Furthermore, those views, whether eloquently expressed or crudely "felt," affected the attitudes that men and women took toward America's relations with the rest of the world.

To some degree the ideas of Americans (then and now) were rooted in their own experiences and interests—experiences and interests that helped them to see truth in certain ideas and not in others. One of the ideas present from the beginnings of American colonial history and deeply rooted in experience has come to be called "isolationism." Most immigrants came partly to escape evils in Europe—religious persecution, economic hardships, wars, or personal problems. And most of them hoped for something better in America. Thus from the beginning there was implicit the assumption (or at least the hope) that the New World was better than the Old. Many literally saw America as a Promised Land reserved by God for His chosen people. The long and arduous trip to America magnified the geographic (and moral) separateness of America.

During the American Revolution the belief that America should keep out of Europe's wars was common. Thomas Paine wrote that America should "steer clear of European contentions." In 1785 Jefferson suggested that America should "practice neither commerce nor navigation, but . . . stand with respect to Europe precisely on the footing of China. We should thus avoid war, and all our citizens would be husbandmen." At the same time John Adams wrote that "If all intercourse between Europe and America could be cut off forever, if every ship we have were burnt, and the keel of another never to be laid, we might still be the happiest people upon earth, and, in fifty years, the most powerful." Both Jefferson and Adams knew that the commercially active United States could not actually follow the policies they described. But President Washington was advancing an old and widely held view when, in his "Farewell Address" in 1796, he urged: "The great rule of conduct for us, in regard to foreign Nations is in extending our commercial relation to have with them as little *political* connection as possible." He did, however, approve "temporary alliances for extraordinary emergencies." If informed Americans had such thoughts, it is understandable that the views appealed to the semiliterate frontiersman working from dawn to dusk to clear fields in the forest and to coax the virgin soil to produce a crop so that he and his family might survive.

So-called isolationist views may have seemed a bit less valid to the merchant whose ships touched distant ports or to the family in a coastal city whose husband or father traveled the world over as a merchant seaman. The oceans not only separated the New World from the Old, they also served as avenues linking the New and the Old. Personal memories, family ties, trade, learning, tradition, and personal experience bound many to Europe. And even those who would have preferred isolation found that the violence, ideologies, and passions of the Wars of the French Revolution and the Napoleonic Wars made it impossible for America to turn its back on Europe completely.

Some in those years had interests, ideas, and emotions that made them sympathetic with England and hostile to its enemies. Anglophiles were most numerous in the Federalist Party and its forerunners and included such able Americans as Alexander Hamilton and John Jay. Some had been Loyalists or Tories during the Revolution and had never wanted to separate from the British Empire in the first place. Some conservatives had not been enthusiastic about the War for Independence but had gone along with it to prevent it from going to extremes contrary to their interests and ideas. Most Anglophiles were of English descent and had ethnic, cultural, family, and emotional ties with England. Many merchants were moved partly by economic considerations. Many Federalists had not been enthusiastic about the advanced ideas in the Declaration of Independence—including the idea that "all men are created equal," the natural rights of man, and the compact theory of government. They believed the Articles of Confederation were too democratic and did not sufficiently restrain the "excesses" and "passions" of the masses. Most Federalists did not want to return to divine right monarchy, but many feared democracy and wanted some form of constitutional government that could be controlled by an "aristocracy of talent"—or at least by men of property. They were less than enthusiastic about the French Revolution.

At the same time, many other Americans sympathized with France as opposed to Britain. The Francophiles and Anglophobes generally were Anti-Federalists and later Jeffersonian Republicans. They were most numerous and vocal in the agrarian South and West. Their attitudes were influenced by the Enlightenment or "Age of Reason" as it extended from Europe to America. The Enlightenment in Western civilization frowned on reliance on traditional authority. It minimized the supernatural and inclined toward Deism in theology. It stressed the essential goodness and dignity of man. It included a belief in the inevitability of progress. The Enlightenment included a faith in the capacity of man through reason, science, and education to understand and control his environment for the betterment of himself and society. Emphasis was on practical progress for mankind on earth rather than on life after death. In politics it embraced the natural rights theory, the compact theory of government, and belief in the right of revolution.

The views of Anglophobes resulted partly from the American Revolution itself. Wartime hatred of the British continued long after independence. Though the French acted out of self-interest, some Americans realized that French assistance had made independence possible. Since America gained its independence through revolution and the Declaration of Independence endorsed the right of revolution, it was easy for Americans to view foreign revolutions with sympathy and even enthusiasm. Struggles to overthrow monarchy seemed intrinsically moral and right— whether the tyrant was George III or Louis XVI. Idealistic enthusiasm for the French was cooled rapidly by the antics of Edmond Genêt, the execution of the King, the bloodletting in the Reign of Terror, and by the rise of a new tyranny in the person of Napoleon Bonaparte. In general, however, the intellectual and political followers of Thomas Jefferson found more common ideological ground with the French after 1789 than with the British.

Furthermore, some Republicans either lacked the ethnic ties to England or had ethnic origins that predisposed them to hate the English. For example, Germans living in Pennsylvania (the so-called "Pennsylvania Dutch") may have had no overpowering reason to hate the British, but neither did they have any strong reasons for liking them. Scotch-Irish frontiersmen had substantial reasons for hating England. They or their ancestors had suffered discrimination and hardship at the hands of the British before they fled from North Ireland to America.

The importance of economic ties with England was felt less keenly by farmers in the South and West than by merchants in the Northeast. Many farm products were sold to Britain, and farmers needed English manufactures. But many in the West were subsistence farmers or sold largely on local markets. And even those whose products eventually found their way to England were less directly aware of the importance of foreign markets until those markets were cut off by British, French, or American actions.

Politics also entered into consideration for many. It was easy to be anti-British and pro-French when political opponents, the Federalists, were such Anglophiles. The Federalists, for their part, found it expedient to charge Republicans with being more enamored of France than of America.

Concern with Anglophobes and Anglophiles, with Francophobes and Francophiles, should not be overemphasized, however. Most Americans were preoccupied largely with their own personal welfare, and with that of their state and nation—not with Britain, France, or any other foreign country. With only rare exceptions, even the most fervent Anglophiles did not want to rejoin the British Empire or submerge America's future in that of England. And all but the most ecstatic supporters of the French Revolution did not wish to endanger American security and interests by waging war on behalf of the French.

That was true even though a real spirit of American nationalism developed only very slowly. Up to 1815 most Americans were much more attached emotionally to their particular locality, state, or section than they were to the United States as a nation. Gradually, however, the emotions and symbols of nationalism began to emerge. Some of the roots of that nationalism could be traced to the fact that Americans or their ancestors had originally fled evils in Europe to make their way in the New World, where they hoped to find greater opportunities or freedom. The pride many felt in a local area or state was broadened into a pride in America. Common problems, struggles, and accomplishments in winning independence and conquering the frontier gave many a feeling of unity that evolved into nationalism.

Some writers and intellectuals added their influence. The geography books published in 1784 and after by New England's Jedediah Morse put America at the center and emphasized the superiority of American soil, climate, and resources. In his spelling books, first published in 1783, and in his dictionary, Noah Webster encouraged use of distinctly American words, spelling, and usage. Historians described the American Revolution as a struggle by valiant Americans against the evil tyranny that was George III's Britain. Parson Mason Weems wrote so-called biographies of American leaders that had as much fiction as truth. Weems's story of young George Washington and his cherry tree contributed nothing to knowledge of the nation's first President, but helped magnify America's heroes into godlike figures. In sermons and essays many clergymen encouraged the belief that Americans were a chosen people and that the hand of God was guiding the nation inevitably toward a sacred destiny.

Political bases for American nationalism were provided by the Constitution adopted in 1789, by Alexander Hamilton's economic policies, by the new capital city separate from any state, and by the Supreme Court's decisions under Chief Justice John Marshall. Many politicians in their quest for votes helped stimulate chauvinism. Despite the military reverses on land and sea, the War of 1812 aroused the spirit of nationalism— and even provided what later became the national anthem. Foreign visitors noted the boastfulness of Americans, their boundless faith in the nation's future, and their belief in the superiority of all things American.

That growing American nationalism reenforced the ideological and emotional bases for both isolationism and expansionism. The belief in America's moral superiority encouraged the conviction that little but harm could come from involvement with the corruption and tyranny of monarchical Europe. At the same time, however, chauvinism and its intrinsic self-righteousness inspired the belief that the United States had an almost divine destiny to lead the world toward democracy, freedom, and the good life. Most Americans in those years would have restricted the nation's leadership to the power of example outside of North America. By developing democracy, freedom, and economic prosperity, the United States might serve as a beacon for less fortunate peoples to follow out of their misery and darkness. Few Americans before 1815 would have had the United States commit its military, diplomatic, or economic resources to accomplish that utopia in foreign lands. Confidence in American superiority and faith in the power of example were not inconsistent with so-called isolationist attitudes as they evolved.

MILITARY FORCES

The United States won its independence in war with Great Britain and maintained it in undeclared naval wars with France and the Barbary States, and in the War of 1812 against Britain. Nevertheless, the armed forces of the young nation before 1815 were tiny and weak relative to those of the major European countries. A professional military caste, traditional in Europe, did not exist in America. Financial and industrial resources for raising and equipping military forces were severely limited. Localism and state pride opposed efforts to build national military forces. State militia generally were badly trained, inadequately equipped, and poorly led. Faith in democratic "citizen soldiers" sometimes was misplaced. "The spirit of 1776" moving men to heroic sacrifices in battle often was conspicuous by its absence. The flamboyant confidence and nationalism of Henry Clay's congressional War Hawks in 1812 generally was not reflected in enlistments or victories after war began. Generalship in the Revolution rarely was better than adequate; in the War of 1812 it was often miserably incompetent. In peacetime (for example, under the Articles of Confederation) national military forces sometimes almost ceased to exist. Anti-Federalists and Jeffersonian Republicans in the agrarian West and South greatly feared the dangers to democracy posed by a permanent military establishment. They doubted the necessity for a navy adequate for more than coastal defense. President Jefferson's fleet of more than 150 one-gun, 45-foot "gunboats" symbolized that agrarian attitude—and was inadequate even for the task it was supposed to serve.

At the same time, however, a multitude of circumstances prevented that military weakness from having the disastrous consequences one might have anticipated. Supply and command difficulties for European military forces operating across the Atlantic were considerable. Military targets in America were so scattered and decentralized, transportation and communication facilities were so poor, and the populace in the countryside was so hostile, that it was hard for foreign forces to strike decisive blows. European overconfidence was a liability at times. Furthermore, Britain had to contend with European belligerents while fighting America. The United States could not have prevailed in the Revolution without French economic, military, and naval support. Napoleon (not the United States) absorbed most of Britain's military resources from 1812 to 1814. Lack of popular enthusiasm and political support for war with America inhibited Britain during both the Revolution and the War of 1812. Furthermore, if "citizen soldiers" were inadequate at times, they were not always so. If there were incompetent generals, there were also Washingtons and Jacksons. Coastal Federalists pushed successfully for naval appropriations in 1794 and after, and created a separate Navy Department in 1798. Jefferson's administration founded the United States Military Academy at West Point. Even state militia occasionally performed superbly—as under Andrew Jackson at New Orleans in January, 1815, after the peace treaty with Britain had been signed. American diplomacy was handicapped by military weakness, but special circumstances in Europe and America prevented that weakness from being as damaging as it might have been.

ADMINISTRATION AND CONDUCT OF FOREIGN AFFAIRS

The colonial period before 1775 provided Americans with very little practical experience in the administration and conduct of foreign affairs. Merchants and shipowners negotiated in their commercial dealings with officials and businessmen in foreign lands. Benjamin Franklin, Arthur Lee, Silas Deane, and others obtained useful experience when they served as colonial agents in London. But the British government reserved to itself authority for formal diplomatic matters of its empire.

During the Revolution the Second Continental Congress was responsible for conduct of foreign affairs until 1781. The Congress in 1775 created a Committee of Secret Correspondence under the initial chairmanship of Franklin to conduct correspondence with friendly Europeans. In 1777 the Committee's name was changed to Committee for Foreign Affairs. The change reflected official American independence. Perhaps it was also a tacit admission that there was very little "secret" about the Committee and its agents. The combined effectiveness of the British Navy, spies, and cooperative Loyalists in America rendered the term inappropriate. The personal secretaries of America's representatives in France often were British spies. Most famous and successful of those agents was Dr. Edward Bancroft of Massachusetts. As secretary first to Silas Deane, then to Franklin, and later to the joint commission in France, he had access to the most secret information. He lived in the same house with Franklin and Deane, and even worked for Franklin during the peace negotiations in 1782–1783. Arthur Lee, a member of the commission, suspected and distrusted Dr. Bancroft—but did not know that his own personal secretary was also a British spy. The enemy commonly obtained copies of secret American documents before they reached the intended American hands.

American diplomats during the Revolution were inexperienced "shirt-sleeve diplomats" and were essentially political appointees. Some were inept, some failed, and Silas Deane even deserted to the enemy. Others, such as John Jay, John Adams, the naturalized Dutchman Charles

Dumas, and Benjamin Franklin, proved to be impressively able. As always, though, success came most easily (even for the talented) when the circumstances were right.

The powers of the central government under the Articles of Confederation were severely limited, but it did have exclusive authority for the conduct of foreign affairs—including power to send and receive ambassadors, make peace or war, and make treaties, subject to approval by a vote of at least nine in the legislature. Under the Articles, the Congress in 1781 created a Department of Foreign Affairs to administer foreign relations. The first man chosen to head the Department as Secretary of Foreign Affairs was Robert R. Livingston, Jr. He was succeeded by the able and strong-willed John Jay in 1784. Since under the Articles the secretaries were appointed by and responsible to Congress, the British pattern of ministerial responsibility might have evolved had not the Articles been abandoned.

Under the new Constitution adopted in 1789 the federal government had exclusive authority for control of foreign affairs. The President was given primary responsibility for foreign affairs, but his powers under the Constitution were distinctly limited. He was authorized to receive ambassadors and (subject to approval by the Senate) to appoint them. Following the precedent set by the first Secretary of State, Thomas Jefferson, the United States consistently followed the "*de facto* theory of recognition" until early in the twentieth century. That is, the United States based its decision to recognize on the foreign government's effective control of the state and its capacity to bind that state in its dealings in international affairs. The decision to extend recognition was not based on the morality or legality of the government or the means by which it came to power. The Constitution gave the President authority to make treaties with the advice and consent of the Senate, providing two thirds of the senators present concurred. Washington sought the advice of the Senate on certain treaties but found the procedure difficult. Since then Presidents generally have not sought the "advice and consent" and have simply submitted treaties to the Senate for approval or rejection after they were signed. Under the Constitution the President was commander in chief of the armed forces. Conceivably he could use that power to reinforce diplomatic negotiations. He could (as Polk did in 1846) use the power to make war inevitable. Presidents even conducted undeclared wars—as Adams did against France and as Jefferson did against the Barbary States. The President had the power to issue state of the union and other messages. The Monroe Doctrine, for example, originated in a message to Congress. And finally, the President executed laws and treaties—and diplomacy is essentially an executive function.

Presidential authority in foreign affairs was not only very limited, but the Constitution also gave important negative powers to Congress. Under the Constitution the Senate could refuse to approve diplomatic appointments. Treaties were not binding until approved by a two-thirds vote of the Senate. Congress (both houses, by a simple majority) had exclusive power to declare war. Congress had the power to levy taxes and make appropriations—increasingly important for American foreign policies. Congress might pass other legislation affecting foreign affairs—neutrality legislation, for example—and could adopt advisory resolutions.

The Constitution is a living document, and practices under it have changed as circumstances and leaders changed. The long-term tendency has been for presidential power in foreign affairs to increase relative to that of Congress. That tendency is most striking in the twentieth century, however, and was much less conspicuous before 1815. A combination of circumstances (including the temperaments and philosophies of the men who were President) inhibited the growth of presidential authority in foreign affairs.

In contrast to the President and Congress, the United States Supreme Court played only a minor role in American foreign affairs. Conceivably the Court could declare treaties or foreign policy legislation unconstitutional as it did domestic legislation. In practice, however, the Supreme Court seemed to assume that control of foreign affairs was outside its jurisdiction. The Supreme Court did not exercise any significant restraining influence over the President or Congress in foreign affairs.

Under the President the main responsibility for the actual conduct of foreign affairs rested with the Department of State under the Secretary of State. Before 1815 and throughout the nineteenth century, it was extremely small. In 1790 it had a staff of only five, and as late as 1820 it employed only fourteen persons in Washington in addition to the Secretary of State. The Secretary of State, the top position in the President's Cabinet, was always a political appointee, but generally he was selected from among the more able and respected leaders of the majority party. John Jay served briefly until Thomas Jefferson took over as Secretary of State in Washington's first Cabinet. The importance of the Secretary of State in foreign affairs relative to that of the President varied depending upon the abilities and personalities of the two men involved. Until the late 1820's the position was often a stepping-stone to the Presidency. Jefferson, Madison, Monroe, and John Quincy Adams all served in that Cabinet post before they gained the Presidency. Most of those early secretaries had had diplomatic experience—a pattern that did not generally prevail during the rest of the nineteenth century.

Two general categories of foreign service officers served the United States overseas—diplomats and consuls. Diplomats were the official representatives from one government to another and normally resided in the capital city of the foreign state. Traditionally there were four grades of diplomats: ambassadors (residing in an embassy), envoys extraordinary and ministers plenipotentiary, ministers resident (residing in legations), and chargés d'affaires (subordinate or temporary officers). Americans commonly distrusted diplomats, and some early congressmen did not even wish to maintain permanent diplomatic posts abroad. Even President Washington did not wish to send many diplomats and, for a time, preferred only chargés. Since the ambassador traditionally was the personal representative of a monarch, the United States sent only ministers and chargés during the first century of its constitutional history—providing American representatives with less status than those of other countries. Not until the 1890's did the United States begin to use the rank of ambassador.

In the eighteenth and nineteenth centuries the United States did not have a professional career foreign service. Generally American diplomats were political appointees; often they were little qualified by experience or ability for their responsibilities. Commonly they did not know the language of the country to which they were assigned. Salaries were too low to support diplomats at major posts, so the best appointments went to men who were wealthy enough to be able to accept them—often planters or businessmen. Some able and distinguished men represented the United States in diplomatic posts before 1815—Jay, Franklin, Jefferson, Madison, John Quincy Adams, and others but many other American diplomats were inadequate. At the same time, foreign diplomats did not consider appointments to the United States particularly appealing. Before 1815 the dusty, drab, unsophisticated town of Washington, D.C., did not compare favorably with the major European capitals. Nor did the power or status of the new nation impress foreign statesmen. Consequently, foreign governments often sent third-rate diplomats to represent them in America.

In addition to diplomats, consuls were economic and social agents of a government sent to serve the interests of their compatriots living, traveling, or doing business abroad. Consuls were assigned to major population and business centers—not simply to capital cities. Traditionally there were four grades: consul general, consul, vice consul, and consular agent. Before 1815 the United States relied largely on consular agents. In those years the nation had a very inferior consular service. The predominantly agricultural society did not attach very high priority to business or travel abroad. Often American agents were simply businessmen who performed consular duties on the side. Others were political appointees. Until 1855 they were paid only on a fee basis. In general, despite important exceptions, neither the diplomats nor the consuls of the United States before 1815 were equal to their counterparts from other lands.

SUPPLEMENTARY READINGS

Adams, Henry. *History of the United States during the Administrations of Jefferson and Madison.* 9 vols. New York: Charles Scribner's Sons, 1889–1891.

Bailey, Thomas A. *The Man in the Street: The Impact of American Public Opinion on Foreign Policy.* New York: Macmillan Co., 1948.

Beard, Charles A. *Economic Origins of Jeffersonian Democracy.* New York: Macmillan Co., 1915.

————. *The Idea of National Interest: An Analytical Study in American Foreign Policy.* New York: Macmillan Co., 1934.

Curti, Merle. *The Roots of American Loyalty.* New York: Columbia University Press, 1946.

Gilbert, Felix. *To the Farewell Address: Ideas of Early American Foreign Policy.* Princeton, N.J.: Princeton University Press, 1961.

Jensen, Merrill. *The New Nation: A History of the United States During the Confederation, 1781–1789.* New York: Alfred A. Knopf, Inc., 1950.

McCamy, James L. *The Administration of American Foreign Affairs.* New York: Alfred A. Knopf, Inc., 1950.

Millis, Walter. *Arms and Men: A Study in American Military History.* New York: G. P. Putnam's Sons, 1956.

Plischke, Elmer. *Conduct of American Diplomacy.* 3d ed. New York: Van Nostrand Reinhold, 1967.

Savelle, Max. *The Origins of American Diplomacy.* New York: Macmillan Co., 1967.

Strout, Cushing. *The American Image of the Old World.* New York: Harper & Row, Publishers, 1963.

Van Alstyne, Richard W. *Genesis of American Nationalism.* Waltham, Mass.: Blaisdell Publishing Co., 1970.

Weinberg, Albert K. *Manifest Destiny: A Study of Nationalist Expansionism in American History.* Baltimore: Johns Hopkins Press, 1935.

Williams, Benjamin H. *Economic Foreign Policy of the United States.* New York: McGraw-Hill Book Co., 1929.

4

The diplomacy of the
American Revolution

The United States had two related foreign policy objectives during the American Revolution from 1775 to 1783. First, it sought recognition and aid from continental European states. Second, the United States required a peace treaty with Britain recognizing American independence and territories.

EUROPEAN AID

Most American attempts to win recognition and assistance from European states failed or met with only meager success. Nevertheless, the aid that American diplomacy did get—notably from France—was vital to the success of the Revolution. Those essential accomplishments resulted partly from the talents of American diplomats. More important, however, were conditions in Europe that determined the policies of continental governments. National self-interest—not ideology or pro-American sympathies—provided the key to European policies toward the American Revolution.

Most European leaders had no sympathy for the Americans and had not the slightest intention of recognizing the independence of the new state. The efforts of American agents failed in most European countries. For example, Arthur Lee's attempts to win recognition from Frederick the Great of Prussia in 1777 met with no success. South Carolina's Ralph Izard had identical results as commissioner to the Grand Duchy of Tuscany.

William Lee tried his talents on Austria in 1778—and failed. A vivid illustration was provided by the experiences in Russia of Francis Dana from Massachusetts. Seeking recognition, aid, a commercial treaty, and membership in the so-called "Armed Neutrality," young Dana arrived in St. Petersburg in August, 1781. For nearly two years, however, the would-be diplomat suffered frustration and failure. He neither spoke nor read either Russian or French (though his fourteen-year-old secretary, John Quincy Adams, had a schoolboy knowledge of French). Dana was instructed to make no move vis-à-vis Russia without approval by the French Minister there—who was under orders not to support any American diplomatic approaches to the Russian government. Catherine II had no ideological interest in the American cause. By the time Dana arrived, Catherine had proposed to mediate between Britain and America—an offer she would not jeopardize by recognizing the United States. Her enthusiasm for the "Armed Neutrality" had evaporated to the point where she even referred to it as the "Armed Nullity." Not until the summer of 1783 did Dana see real hope of obtaining an audience at the Russian court. By that time, with the Revolution in America already won and with other interests in Russia negligible, the mission did not seem worth further effort—either to Dana or to the American government. Acting on instructions from Congress, Dana gladly left St. Petersburg in August, 1783. The United States did not finally win formal diplomatic recognition from Russia until twenty-six years later.

Two other European states (Spain and the Netherlands) gave a little assistance to America—but it was of minor significance and was not inspired by any sympathy for the United States. Spain under Charles III did not want the idea of revolution and independence to spread to its huge empire. An independent and expansionist United States might endanger Spanish holdings in North America, particularly in the lower Mississippi Valley. On June 21, 1779 (after urgings from France and in alliance with France), Spain declared war on Britain. Through Beaumarchais in France, the Spanish government from 1776 to 1779 gave the equivalent of nearly $400,000 in grants to America. Spain also loaned an additional $250,000 to the United States in 1778 and 1781–1782. But that limited assistance was the product of French pressure and, more importantly, of Spanish determination to regain Gibraltar and other territories. Indeed, the American cause was tied to Gibraltar when France promised Spain not to make peace with Britain until Spain regained Gibraltar. Spanish forces took West Florida in the fighting but failed to win Gibraltar. In spite of Spanish belligerency and financial aid, Spain was never an ally of the United States against Britain. And in Madrid, neither Arthur Lee in 1777 nor John Jay from 1780 to 1782 was able to win diplomatic recognition from Spain.

American aid from the Netherlands was not much greater. During most of the Revolution the Netherlands was not a belligerent, and Dutch merchants profitably traded with all sides in the war. That carrying trade was helpful to America—particularly via the Dutch colony of St. Eustatius in the West Indies. Believing that military involvement would destroy the profitable war trade, the Netherlands clung tenaciously to official neutrality. Britain, on the other hand, considered the Dutch carrying trade more damaging than Dutch belligerency. Consequently, Great Britain deliberately forced the Netherlands into the war. In September, 1780, the British had captured Henry Laurens, an American diplomat on his way to the Netherlands. Among the documents they seized with him was a rough draft for a possible treaty between America and Holland. It had no official status and did not represent Dutch wishes. Nevertheless, the British used the document as an excuse for declaring war on the Netherlands in December, 1780. The British Navy quickly swept Dutch ships off the seas and seized St. Eustatius—essentially ending Holland's carrying trade with Britain's enemies.

Unable to avoid war, the Netherlands and its bankers did, then, give a little support to America—though largely after the fighting of the Revolution had ended. In 1782 Holland recognized American independence and officially received American diplomats—first John Adams and later Charles F. Dumas. The Netherlands was the only country other than France to do so during the Revolution. On October 8, 1782, John Adams signed a treaty of friendship and commerce with the Netherlands. Furthermore, Dutch bankers (not the government) loaned about $3.6 million to the United States government from 1782 through 1788. Dutch assistance was not unimportant, but it was inspired by the drive for profits, not by sympathy for America. And probably the Dutch neutral carrying trade with America and France until 1780 was more helpful than anything Holland did after Britain forced it into the war. If America had had to depend for outside aid only on that obtained from Spain and the Netherlands, the struggle for independence would have been lost.

Only in France did American diplomats win substantial assistance. Some of the Americans negotiated skillfully with the French, but French national interests (not American diplomatic talents) provided the key to French policies. The government under King Louis XVI had no ideological sympathy for the Americans. French leaders hoped that the new United States would be a weak state, dependent upon France. Individual idealists aside, France aided the American Revolution because of a desire for revenge against Britain for defeats suffered in the French and Indian War and because of a determination to reduce British power and prestige relative to France.

Beginning in 1776 (even before the Declaration of Independence) France gave secret aid to America. Those subsidies (including munitions) were given through a fictitious trading company called "Rodrigue Hortalez and Company" headed by the French playwright, Caron de Beaumarchais, who had been won to the cause by Arthur Lee. The subsidies continued even after France recognized the United States in 1778 and were granted as late as 1784. Altogether the gifts totaled nearly $2 million—something of a small-scale French foreign aid program.

Silas Deane represented the United States in Paris as early as July, 1776, and late that year the United States appointed a three-man commission to seek recognition, aid, and a military alliance from France. The commission included men from the different sections of America: Deane from Connecticut in New England, Arthur Lee from Virginia in the South, and Franklin from the Middle Atlantic state of Pennsylvania. It also represented various political views: Lee was a radical who shared the ideas in the Declaration of Independence, while Franklin, and particularly Deane, were more conservative. Of the three Benjamin Franklin was the most able and effective. Born in Boston, the youngest son of a candlemaker, Franklin became a printer, publisher, scientist, philosopher, and diplomat. He was seventy years old when he reached France in December, 1776, but his faculties were in no way diminished by his years. Intellectually a product of the Enlightenment, he was pragmatic, undoctrinaire, and realistic. Though learned and cosmopolitan, he affected the simple and rustic appearance that Parisians expected of Americans. Good-humored, detached, and at ease in almost any setting, Franklin set a standard for American diplomacy that few have equaled since. He was the only member of the commission to France who was later included in the five-man commission that negotiated the peace treaty with Great Britain.

Though increasingly willing to give secret assistance, France was not prepared to recognize the United States or go to war against Britain until American military forces demonstrated in combat that they might win the war. That military demonstration occurred when American forces under General Horatio Gates forced the surrender of General John Burgoyne at Saratoga, New York, on October 17, 1777. The news of that dramatic surrender reached France in December and, by itself, might have ended France's hesitation. In addition, however, it made the Lord North Ministry in Britain more conciliatory toward America. Encouraged by the American victory and determined to prevent reconciliation between Britain and its colonies, France moved quickly to support the American cause openly and effectively. Early in 1778 France formally recognized United States independence. On February 6, 1778, France and the United States entered into a treaty of friendship and commerce, and at the same time signed a defensive alliance. It provided that if France and Britain went to war, neither the United States nor France would make peace without the consent of the other. In the alliance France also promised not to stop fighting until American independence was assured. That alliance endured twenty-two years, until 1800. Furthermore, in addition to subsidies, the French government began to make loans to the United States that, by the end of the Revolution, totaled the equivalent of $6,350,000. In June, 1778, without a formal declaration, France drifted into war with Britain. A French expeditionary force arrived in America in 1780, and the combination of French troops and navy along with General George Washington's military forces brought the surrender of General Cornwallis at Yorktown on October 17, 1781. As Samuel Flagg Bemis phrased it: "The French Alliance was decisive for the cause of American independence."

THE PEACE TREATY

The negotiation of the Treaty of Paris ending the American Revolution was not simply an Anglo-American matter, isolated from the concerns of other states. It was part of broader European negotiations and settlements affecting other European countries. And partly because of circumstances in Europe and within Britain, the results were more favorable for America than one might have expected from the power and military situation in the New World.

For reasons of their own, individual European states in 1779 and 1780 offered to mediate between Britain and its American colonies. At one time or another Spain, Russia, and Austria were parties to such proposals. Even America's ally, France, under the foreign policy direction of the Count de Vergennes, was willing to consider the offers. They all failed, however, because British leaders did not want foreign intervention in what they considered an essentially domestic matter within the British Empire. The failure was fortunate for the cause of American independence, because the mediation proposals pointed to a settlement that would have kept America within the British Empire.

In 1779 Congress appointed John Adams as commissioner with responsibility for negotiating a peace settlement directly with Britain. Circumstances blocked progress, however, and in June, 1781, Congress issued new instructions and expanded the mission to a five-man peace commission. The commission included representatives of all sections of the country and spokesmen for both commercial and agrarian sectors of the American economy. The shipping-commercial interests of New England and the Middle Atlantic area were represented by three diplomats: John Jay of New York, Benjamin Franklin of Pennsylvania, and John Adams of Massachusetts. Adams in particular was alert to the needs and desires of the New England commercial and fishing interests. The provisions in the final treaty covering fishing rights and liberties were due particularly to Adams' concern. Southern agrarian interests were represented on the commission by two men: Thomas Jefferson of Virginia and Henry Laurens of South Carolina. In the actual negotiations, however, the agrarians were less adequately represented than the commercial and urban interests. Thomas Jefferson arrived in Europe too late to participate in the negotiations. Henry Laurens had been captured at sea by the British but was released before negotiations began. Nevertheless, he procrastinated and took no part in the discussions until near their close. He was responsible for a clause in the treaty that required the British to evacuate without taking their Negro slaves with them. The main American negotiators, however, were Jay, Franklin, and Adams, and they displayed impressive diplomatic skill in their dealings with both Britain and France.

Growing opposition to the war in England forced the resignation of Lord North in March, 1782. A new ministry was formed under Lord Rockingham, and with his death in July, Lord Shelburne became Prime Minister. The new government concluded a peace settlement with America. A note from Benjamin Franklin to Shelburne (then Secretary of State) in March, 1782, opened the way to conversations. The British sent Richard Oswald to meet with Franklin. Oswald symbolized the growing British eagerness for peace. He was an elderly Scottish merchant whose wealth had been accumulated partly through the slave trade. In that unsavory business he had had dealings with Laurens, now one of the American commissioners. Oswald had once lived in Virginia for a time and had friends and property in America. Furthermore, he was influenced by Adam Smith's laissez-faire economic theories and was skeptical of the mercantilism implicit in the colonial relationship. Such a spokesman could not be expected to drive a hard bargain with the Americans.

Negotiations between Oswald and the Americans proceeded rapidly. On November 30, 1782, the preliminary terms were agree to and signed in Paris. France was not represented in the negotiations, and Vergennes was not even informed of the preliminary articles until after they were signed. Both Jay and Adams were skeptical of French dedication to American interests, and Franklin, too, favored negotiating independently of France. The distrust of France was justified. That European ally wanted to weaken Britain by means of the American struggle but preferred to make the United States a weak satellite of France. The preliminary articles were not to be binding, however, until France and Britain had also agreed on peace terms. In January, 1783, both the French and the Spanish agreed on preliminary peace terms with the British, and the final treaties, including the Anglo-American Treaty of Paris, were signed on September 3, 1783.

The peace treaty between Britain and the United States was almost identical to the preliminary articles. Britain recognized American independence in the treaty. It provided that the boundaries of the United States extended to the Mississippi River in the West, even though American forces did not have effective military supremacy in much of the area west of the Appalachians. To the south the boundary was at the thirty-first parallel and St. Mary's River (that is, the northern boundary of East and West Florida, which went to Spain). The Great Lakes separated the United States from British Canada in the North. The agreement gave Americans the "Right" to fish in the Newfoundland fishing banks, the

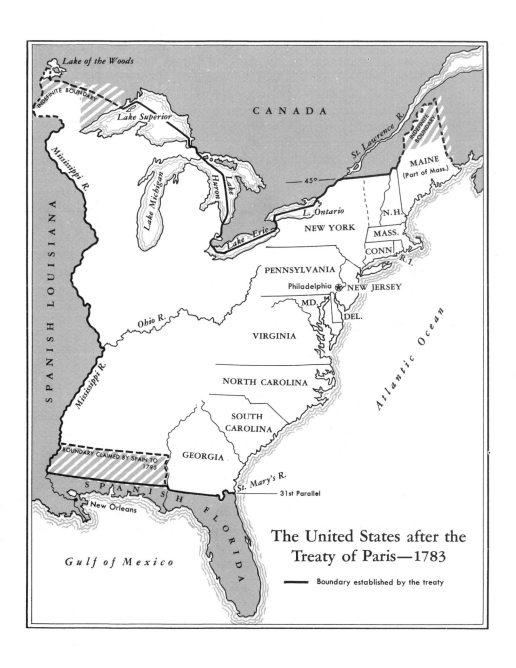

Lake of the Woods

INDEFINITE BOUNDARY

Lake Superior

CANADA

Mississippi R.

St. Lawrence R.

INDEFINITE BOUNDARY

MAINE
(Part of Mass.)

SPANISH LOUISIANA

Lake Michigan

Huron

Lake

45°

L. Ontario

Lake Erie

N.H.

NEW YORK

MASS.

CONN.

R.I.

PENNSYLVANIA

Philadelphia ✪ NEW JERSEY

Ohio R.

MD.

DEL.

Mississippi R.

VIRGINIA

Atlantic Ocean

NORTH CAROLINA

SOUTH
CAROLINA

BOUNDARY CLAIMED BY SPAIN TO
1795

GEORGIA

S P A N I S H   F L O R I D A

St. Mary's R.

31st Parallel

New Orleans

Gulf of Mexico

The United States after the
Treasury of Paris—1783

Boundary established by the treaty

"Liberty" to fish in territorial waters of Newfoundland, and the "Liberty" (under certain conditions) to dry and cure fish on unsettled portions of Nova Scotia and Labrador. The treaty required the United States Congress to "recommend" that state legislatures protect Loyalists in America and compensate them for property lost through confiscation during the Revolution. Creditors in England and America were to meet no legal impediments to the collection of pre-Revolutionary debts.

In reviewing the negotiations and treaty, Samuel Flagg Bemis concluded that one could "have nothing but praise" for the work of the American diplomats in Paris. He called the treaty the "greatest victory in the annals of American diplomacy." That victory was due in part to American and French military successes, especially at Saratoga in 1777 and at Yorktown in 1781, and in part to the talents of American diplomats. To a certain extent the treaty reflected economic interests and sectional attitudes in America. It was also due to external conditions, including war-weariness in Britain and European power politics.

SUPPLEMENTARY READINGS

Bemis, Samuel Flagg.   *The Diplomacy of the American Revolution*. Bloomington: Indiana University Press, 1957.

Corwin, Edward S.   *French Policy and the American Alliance of 1778*. Princeton, N.J.: Princeton University Press, 1916.

Darling, A. B.   *Our Rising Empire, 1763–1803*. New Haven, Conn.: Yale University Press, 1940.

Morris, Richard B.   *The Peacemakers: The Great Powers and American Independence*. New York: Harper & Row, Publishers, 1965.

Stourzh, Gerald.   *Benjamin Franklin and American Foreign Policy*. Chicago: University of Chicago Press, 1954.

Van Alstyne, Richard W.   *Empire and Independence: The International History of the American Revolution*. New York: John Wiley & Sons, Inc., 1965.

5

Foreign relations under the Articles of Confederation

Externally the period of the Articles of Confederation after the Revolution was characterized by relative peace in international affairs. Minor episodes aside, there were no major threats to American security in the Western Hemisphere from 1783 to 1789.

On the domestic scene, within the United States the American people, state governments, and the weak central government struggled to shift from a wartime to a peacetime footing and to set the United States on its course as an independent, self-governing country. Those efforts provoked heated controversy between the conservative shipping-commercial group with some planter support and the more democratically inclined farmer-agrarian group. The two factions battled evenly during the early part of the era. By the last half of the decade the urban shipping-commercial group gained the upper hand.

In foreign affairs, however, the shipping-commercial group was more powerful and better served than in domestic affairs. The objectives that group sought were easier to get than those desired by the agrarians. Conditions abroad (external influences) facilitated the attainment of certain shipping-commercial goals and tended to obstruct the accomplishment of agrarian goals. The attitudes and role of John Jay, Secretary of Foreign Affairs from 1784 to 1789, reinforced those patterns. He was one of the more able and distinguished men in America. A member of a well-to-do New York family, Jay was reared in comfortable circumstances and educated at King's College, was admitted to the bar in New York, married the beautiful daughter of a prominent New Jersey family, and served with distinction in various political and legal posts in America. His missions to Spain and France gave him valuable diplomatic experience. With his keen mind, powerful personality, unquestioned integrity, and unlimited self-confidence, Jay exercised great influence over Congress under the Articles of Confederation. But no man, whatever his abilities, is wholly divorced from his environment. And Jay was a product of urban-commercial-creditor-conservative-upper class circles in New York City. Like most of his friends, Jay found it easy to appreciate the importance of commercial and creditor interests. At the same time, like his associates, he distrusted Westerners and was skeptical of the wisdom of American westward territorial expansion. He worked devotedly for the "national interests" as he understood them. Given his scale of values, however, he found it more essential to serve eastern commercial interests than the agrarian interests of the South and West.

For purposes of analysis, the history of American foreign affairs under the Articles after the Revolution may be divided into two categories: first, diplomacy related to the needs and desires of the shipping-commercial group of the Northeast; and second, diplomacy related to the needs and desires of the farmer-agrarian group of the South and West.

COMMERCIAL DIPLOMACY

American merchants after independence wished to continue the old trade privileges with Britain and its colonies. At the same time, they wanted to open new trade channels with other countries and their colonies on at least an equal footing with the merchants of other parts of the world. To obtain those goals, American merchants and shippers of the Northeast sought trade treaties with leading countries.

Most scholars, following the lead of John Fiske's interpretation in *The Critical Period of American History*, emphasize the diplomatic failures of United States commercial diplomacy under the weak Articles of Confederation. The United States suffered a commercial depression in the middle of the 1780's. At the close of the Revolution, in 1783, Great Britain barred American ships from direct trade with the British West Indies—an extremely valuable part of pre-Revolutionary trade. Despite earnest efforts the United States Minister to Great Britain, John Adams of Massachusetts, was not able to get a commercial treaty during the period. American attempts to win a trade treaty with Spain also failed. The United States had to contend with certain restrictions and prohibitions in direct trade with the colonies of all European states. The difficulties caused by the North African Barbary States for shipping in the Mediterranean were not satisfactorily resolved. And in the last years of the decade, negotiations for additional trade treaties came to a standstill.

Nevertheless, the leading historian on the Articles of Confederation, Merrill Jensen, has urged that the difficulties be put in a broader context and the failures be balanced by the accomplishments. Depressions are a common aftermath of wars. It is unlikely that any government of the new nation could have prevented one then. Prosperity revived before the Constitution replaced the Articles. Furthermore, in a time when mercantilism was still dominant and before Adam Smith's laissez-faire theories gained substantial political support, legal obstructions to trade with the colonies of European states inhibited merchants from other countries as well as Americans. United States difficulties with the Barbary States were shared by European shippers. And the suspension of negotiations on trade treaties was a natural product of the political uncertainty as the United States shifted from the Articles to the new Constitution. The pattern probably would have been similar in any major political transition, whatever the qualities of the governments involved.

Moreover, merchants from continental Europe wanted the profits from trade with America, so the United States found it relatively easy to negotiate commercial treaties with several countries. The trade treaty with France dated from 1778 in the midst of the Revolution. A similar trade treaty was concluded with the Netherlands in October, 1782, after the Articles of Confederation went into operation. The United States got a commercial treaty with Sweden in 1783, another with Prussia in 1785, and still another with Morocco in 1787. Denmark, Portugal, and others sent agents to explore trade possibilities. American shippers began their trade with China in that decade.

Even with Britain, trade developments were not wholly unfavorable for American merchants. According to Professor Jensen, "so far as direct trade with England was concerned," American merchants after 1783 "had the same privileges they had had as colonists." Most goods could legally be traded between the United States and the British West Indies— provided they were carried in British ships. And Americans regularly ignored the legal restrictions. Needing the products and wanting the profits, many in the West Indies were eager to cooperate with American shippers in violating the prohibitions. Consequently, under the Articles of Confederation the overwhelming bulk of American foreign trade (both import and export) continued to be with Great Britain and the British Empire, much as it had been before the Revolution.

Despite many irritating restrictions and diplomatic reverses, American efforts to promote foreign trade under the Articles of Confederation were more successful than was generally conceded. Again to quote Jensen, "Most of the ports of the world were open, not closed, to American citizens." Internally, the ingenuity of American merchants and the political pressures from commercial interests were important. Secretary of Foreign Affairs John Jay and many American diplomats were from the Middle Atlantic and New England commercial centers and attached high importance to serving the needs of merchants and shippers abroad. In addition, external influences facilitated the accomplishments. Other countries were eager to expand profitable trade and to get trade treaties with the United States. Mutual economic interests made diplomatic negotiations relatively easy.

AGRARIAN TERRITORIAL DIPLOMACY

If commercial interests in foreign affairs were served reasonably well under the Articles of Confederation, agrarian interests were not. Farmer-agrarians of the South and West were particularly concerned with the outcome of negotiations with America's immediate neighbors on the North American continent, that is with Great Britain to the north and with Spain to the south and west. None of those negotiations succeeded in the 1780's.

For more than sixty years after the Revolution, the United States had boundary and territorial disputes with Britain in Canada on America's northern border. The difficulties affected frontiersmen, farmers, land speculators, and fur traders, but were of little direct interest to the shipping-commercial group. Ambiguities and errors in the Treaty of Paris of 1783 caused some of the disputes. Others developed as America expanded further west. And an immediate major controversy arose from Britain's clear violation of certain peace terms.

With the close of the Revolutionary War, Britain retained control of seven fortified posts along the northwest border of the United States and within American territory. Those Northwest posts included forts as Oswego, Niagara, Detroit, Michilimackinac, and others. In the peace treaty Britain had promised to evacuate them "with all convenient speed," but at the same time the British government ordered its forces in America to hold the posts. They did so for thirteen years after the Revolution. The British even barred American ships from the Great Lakes. Britain justified its action on the ground that the United States had failed to live up to certain provisions of the peace treaty. Specifically Britain pointed to legal obstructions to the collection of pre-Revolutionary debts and to the failure of states to restore property confiscated from former Loyalists. It had grounds for complaint, but Britain determined to retain control of the Northwest posts even before American violations were apparent. Much more important was the desire of Canadian traders to maintain British control as long as possible to protect fur-trading profits in the area. Military commanders feared that evacuation would arouse Britain's Indian allies in the region and might result in widespread Indian warfare and violence. American diplomacy under the Articles of Confederation failed to dislodge the British from the Northwest posts. And none of the boundary disputes with Britain was settled.

Equally serious were American territorial difficulties with Spain, difficulties that were not resolved successfully under the Articles either. The peace settlements ending the American Revolutionary War left Spain with both East and West Florida on the southern border of the United States, and with the Louisiana Territory on the western border. Those arrangements gave it control of New Orleans and both sides of the Mississippi River from its mouth for a considerable distance inland. Spain worried about the American threat posed to its holdings and tried various methods to protect its territories against American encroachments.

Two principal controversies disrupted Spanish-American relations in the South and West at the close of the American Revolution. The first concerned location of the boundary between Spanish Florida and the United States. Britain and the United States had agreed secretly in the preliminary peace negotiations that if Britain got Florida the boundary would be at approximately 30°30′ north latitude, where the Yazoo River flowed into the Mississippi River at Vicksburg. On the other hand, if Spain got Florida the boundary would be at the thirty-first parallel, 165 miles farther south. Since Florida went to Spain, the United States claimed the latter boundary. In transferring Florida to Spain, however, Britain did not define the boundaries, and there was precedent since 1764 for the Yazoo River line. Since the Anglo-American treaty did not bind Spain, since there was strong precedent for the Yazoo River boundary, and since Spanish troops held the disputed territory, Spain understandably objected to placing the boundary farther south.

The second major controversy concerned the American right to navigate on the Mississippi, including those three or four hundred miles that flowed through Spanish territory. The Anglo-American peace treaty declared that such navigation "from its source to the Ocean shall for ever remain free and open to the Subjects of Great Britain and the Citizens of the United States." Again, however, Spain was not a party to that treaty. In 1784 Spain closed the Mississippi to American shipping. That closing was of no great interest to New England fishermen or New York merchants, but it was of vital concern to the people in Kentucky, Tennessee, and Ohio west of the Appalachians. Approximately 50,000 Americans lived there in the 1780's, and the number was growing rapidly. Most of them saw the Ohio-Mississippi system as their lifeline to the sea, the only practicable route for shipping their products to market. The Spanish government, concerned for the security of its empire and fearful of the restless energies of western frontiersmen, tried to check American expansion by closing the Mississippi to American use and by persuading commercially oriented Americans in the Northeast to concur in that action.

Those problems and influences in Spanish-American relations culminated in the fruitless Jay-Gardoqui negotiations of 1785–1786. John Jay of New York represented the United States, while Diego de Gardoqui, an experienced diplomat, served Spain. They negotiated on all the major outstanding issues dividing the countries, including the Florida boundary, navigation on the Mississippi, and trade relations. On the thorny issue of navigation, however, the instructions of the two diplomats irreconcilably conflicted. Congress told Jay not to give up the right of navigation on the Mississippi, while Spain instructed Gardoqui not to allow the right of navigation. That deadlock precluded agreement unless one or the other of the governments altered its instructions. Through weeks of hard work, Jay and Gardoqui hammered out a tentative agreement, but it depended upon Congress' willingness to change its instructions on the matter of navigation. If the United States would give up (Jay used the word "forbear") the use of the Mississippi River for twenty-five or thirty years, Spain would agree to certain other matters, including a favorable treaty for direct trade with Spain.

Jay's willingness to seek the necessary change of instructions generally is credited to Gardoqui's skill in capitalizing on Jay's particular weaknesses. Gardoqui had observed Jay's vanity, his devotion to his lovely wife, Mrs. Jay's vulnerability to gifts and attention, and her great influence on her husband. Consequently, Gardoqui played up to Jay's self-esteem and showered Mrs. Jay with flattery and presents. The Spanish diplomat wrote to his government early in 1786: "Notwithstanding my age, I am acting the gallant and accompanying Madame to the official entertainments and dances, because she likes it and I will do everything which appears to me for the King's best interest." His tactics were effective.

Of at least equal significance in explaining Jay's course, however, was the fact that he, like most of his peers in the urban Northeast, did not consider westward expansion terribly important or even desirable. Rufus King of Massachusetts in 1786 believed "that every Citizen of the Atlantic States who emigrates to the westward of the Allegany is a total loss to our Confederacy." Many in the East (including Jay) shared King's general attitude or milder variants of it. Gardoqui used flattery and a generous commercial treaty to persuade Jay and eastern urban shipping-commercial groups to abandon western interests in 1786—and Jay went for the bait.

The request for the change in Jay's instructions provoked a heated debate that absorbed most of the attention of congressmen during the summer of 1786. The final vote in Congress was seven to five in favor of allowing Jay to sign the agreement that would have included a commercial treaty and closed the Mississippi to Americans for twenty-five or thirty years. The vote was along strictly sectional lines. Seven northern states voted for the change and five southern states opposed (Delaware was not present). It was a hollow victory for Jay, however, because the Articles required a vote of nine states to approve a treaty. After the debate it was apparent that southern opposition would block any treaty that did not allow Americans free navigation on the Mississippi. Gardoqui stayed on in the United States until October, 1789, but the negotiations had collapsed long before.

Despite their failure, the Jay-Gardoqui negotiations had enduring consequences and are highly significant. The episode warned agrarians in general and Southerners in particular of the danger (from their point of view) of allowing any constitutional arrangement that might enable commercial groups to control foreign policy to the detriment of the South and West. The two-thirds rule protected agrarian interests in 1786, and Southerners made certain it was included in the new Constitution drafted in 1787. In addition, the Jay-Gardoqui negotiations dramatized how the interests of the two major economic-sectional groups in America could cause them to take radically different positions on an important foreign policy matter. Both Jay and his opponents were dedicated to the "national interests," but their respective values, rooted in quite different needs and goals, led them to conflicting definitions of the "national interests."

At just the moment when Gardoqui's efforts floundered, the Spanish government shifted its tactics in the West. In December, 1788, Spain relented and began to allow Americans to use the Mississippi River through Spanish territories under certain conditions—including payment of duties. The shift did not mean that Spain's fears of American expansion had evaporated. Instead, Spain simply was taking a different approach to the problem. By the end of the decade it was attempting to lure Americans in the Southwest to break away from the United States. Perhaps the West might establish an independent country closely bound to Spain, or it might actually become part of the Spanish Empire, to assure use of its lifeline to the sea. The idea grew partly out of the antics of an unprincipled American general by the name of James Wilkinson, who sold it to Spanish officials in 1787. At one time Wilkinson was on the payroll of three governments—the United States, Spain, and Great Britain—but he could be depended upon to serve no one but himself. The General did his best to lead Kentucky out of the Union but got little support from Americans there. His scheme failed, but the United States did not finally get a satisfactory agreement with Spain until 1795, in the Federalist Era.

In conclusion, American diplomacy under the Articles of Confederation met with much success in its efforts to get trade opportunities beneficial to eastern shipping-commercial interests (though they were not content with what they got). At the same time, the government under the Articles failed to settle any of the boundary and river controversies with Britain and Spain that concerned farmer-agrarians of the South and West. Those results were due both to domestic and to international circumstances. Internally Jay and other diplomats battled vigorously for commercial interests but were prepared, under certain circumstances, to sacrifice agrarian interests. Externally, foreign countries wanted the profits from trade with the United States, so American accomplishments were easy. On the other hand, Britain and Spain, for reasons of self-interest, would not yield on boundary matters, the Northwest posts, and use of the Mississippi. And the United States, under the Articles of Confederation, was too weak and divided to compel them to yield.

SUPPLEMENTARY READINGS

Bemis, Samuel Flagg. *Jay's Treaty: A Study in Commerce and Diplomacy.* New York: Macmillan Co., 1923.

————. *Pinckney's Treaty: America's Advantage from Europe's Distress, 1783–1800.* New rev. ed. New Haven, Conn.: Yale University Press, 1960.

Burt, Alfred L. *The United States, Great Britain, and British North America: From the Revolution to the Establishment of Peace after the War of 1812.* New Haven, Conn.: Yale University Press, 1940.

Darling, Arthur B. *Our Rising Empire, 1763–1803.* New Haven, Conn.: Yale University Press, 1940.

Fiske, John. *The Critical Period of American History, 1783–1789.* Boston: Houghton Mifflin Co., 1888.

Jensen, Merrill. *The New Nation: A History of the United States during the Confederation, 1781–1789.* New York: Alfred A. Knopf, Inc., 1950.

Monaghan, Frank. *John Jay.* Indianapolis: Bobbs-Merrill Co., Inc., 1935.

Whitaker, Arthur P. *The Spanish-American Frontier, 1783–1795.* Boston: Houghton Mifflin Co., 1927.

6

Foreign relations in the Federalist Era

The abandonment of the Articles of Confederation and the adoption of the new Constitution in 1789 represented a sharp break in American political history. Though the government under the Constitution represented much that was new in both domestic and foreign affairs, it also continued certain earlier patterns—including the growing political power and influence of the urban-creditor-commercial interests in domestic and foreign affairs. President George Washington from 1789 to 1797 wanted to be above factions and included representatives of both agrarian and commercial groups in his Cabinet. The top Cabinet post went to Thomas Jefferson, who returned from his position as Minister to France to serve as Washington's Secretary of State. The Virginia planter and author of the Declaration of Independence was America's most able spokesman for agrarian democracy. The position of Secretary of the Treasury went to thirty-four-year-old Alexander Hamilton of New York, an Anglophile and the greatest conservative spokesman for urban business interests. Of the two men, however, Hamilton exerted the greater influence on both the domestic and foreign policies of the Washington administration. Insofar as foreign policies under Washington reflected domestic interests, they were largely the product of the needs and desires of urban-shipping-creditor interests—particularly after the resignation of Jefferson in December, 1793. Despite the cleavages between Hamilton and John Adams, a comparable tendency prevailed during Adams' term as President from

49

1797 to 1801. Consequently, reflecting those dominant domestic groups, American foreign policies in the Federalist Era aimed at two related goals; first, the promotion and protection of foreign trade; and second, the maintenance of peace with Great Britain—the country with which most American trade was conducted, which commanded needed foreign capital, and whose powerful navy controlled the seas. Federalists did not completely ignore agrarian interests (some of the largest southern planters were Federalists) provided they did not conflict with trader interests and provided they did not require too much effort, cost, or risk. Nevertheless, the Federalist scale of priorities ranked agrarian needs well below commercial needs.

External influences also affected foreign policies under the Federalists. The French Revolutionary Era coincided chronologically with the Federalist Era in the United States. War began on the continent of Europe in 1792 and involved Britain in February, 1793. Americans almost unanimously opposed United States involvement in the Wars of the French Revolution in Europe, and (whatever their political views and economic interests) they determined to guard national security in the face of those wars. The attitudes of individual Americans toward specific foreign policies varied considerably, however, depending on their own particular needs and philosophies. The Wars of the French Revolution provided both threats to American interests abroad and opportunities to win goals. Paradoxically, though Federalists gave priority to commercial interests, the Wars of the French Revolution gave the government easy opportunities to win objectives desired by agrarians. Because of external circumstances, agrarians got as much from the diplomacy of the Federalist Era as merchants did, or even more.

COMMERCIAL POLICIES

Both before and during the Wars of the French Revolution the administrations of Washington and Adams took steps to promote and protect American merchants and shipbuilders. Hamilton's efforts to improve relations with Britain, in opposition to Jefferson's pro-French biases, were part of that pattern. Furthermore, the federal government gave bounties or subsidies to the fishing industry. It discriminated against foreign shipbuilders by not allowing their products to be registered as American ships. Coastal shipping between American ports was limited to American ships, and foreign vessels were barred. A federal law in 1789 levied a higher tonnage duty or harbor tax on foreign than on American ships in United States ports. The Tariff of 1789 provided that rates would be 10 percent higher if the products were brought to the United States in foreign ships than if they were brought in American vessels. Federalist administrations expanded the consular service so that it could more effectively seek out business opportunities for American merchants. Expansion of the Navy was only partly inspired by the requirements of national security. It was also designed to win better treatment for American shipping. The administrations also negotiated treaties with three of the North African Barbary States to reduce interference with American trade in the Mediterranean. Algiers in 1795, Tripoli in 1796, and Tunis in 1797 all signed treaties with the United States. Each of the three treaties required the United States to give cash payments and "presents" to the Barbary rulers. The results were not satisfactory, but the government did try to help American merchants in that part of the world. Those commercial policies of the United States during Federalist administrations (like those of European governments at the same time) were not examples of laissez-faire, free trade, or equality of opportunity. They gave government support to American merchants and discriminated against foreign competitors.

AMERICA AND THE WARS OF THE FRENCH REVOLUTION

For nearly a decade after the American Revolution no general wars swept Europe or endangered American security. That happy situation ended near the close of Washington's first term, and for almost a quarter of a century Europe and the world rocked under the impact of the Wars of the French Revolution and the Napoleonic Wars. Since overseas empires were of only marginal interest in those wars, American national security was less directly endangered than it might have been. Nevertheless, wars of that magnitude could not fail to affect the United States. At least three general categories of effects may be identified: commercial, territorial, and emotional. First, American merchants profited from war trade with both sides. They also suffered financial losses when belligerents tried to prevent or control trade with their enemies. Second, by altering international power balances the wars sometimes endangered American territorial security (Napoleon in the Louisiana Territory, for example). Other power changes seemed to offer the United States opportunities to expand when North American neighbors were weakened or preoccupied in Europe. And third, the wars aroused Americans ideologically and emotionally, with sympathy or hostility toward one or another of the European powers. American nationalism grew in response to European challenges. Eventually the United States became involved in the fighting, but initially Americans were almost unanimous in their determination to keep the United States out of the European wars. That attitude was shared by Federalists and Anti-Federalists alike.

President Washington sought the advice of his cabinet members by submitting thirteen foreign policy questions to them on April 18, 1793. The first question asked whether the United States should issue a neutrality proclamation. Both Jefferson and Hamilton wanted the United States to remain neutral, and Hamilton strongly urged a proclamation. Jefferson initially objected. He doubted whether the Constitution gave the President authority to declare neutrality. He also hoped to use official neutrality as a bargaining weapon to win diplomatic concessions from the belligerents—particularly from Britain. After discussion, however, the cabinet voted unanimously in favor of the Proclamation. In deference to Jefferson's reservations, the word "neutrality" was not included in the final document issued on April 22, 1793, but the meaning was clear. On June 5, 1794, Congress also adopted a Neutrality Act.

It was one thing to desire and proclaim neutrality, but it was quite a different thing to maintain it. The wars in Europe were life-and-death struggles, and both sides used every conceivable method to crush opponents—including interference with neutral trade. Both sides obstructed shipping and seized American ships and cargoes. Americans who sought them could easily find justifications for war against either Britain or France. In general, the agrarian Anti-Federalists led by Jefferson were sympathetic with France and favored economic coercion to force concessions from Great Britain. The Federalists headed by Hamilton, however, were anti-French and considered peace with Britain essential at almost any cost. Given the interests and attitudes of the dominant groups, it is not surprising that in the Federalist Era the United States successfully avoided war with Britain and drifted into an undeclared naval war with France in 1798. For purposes of convenience, the main patterns may be traced in terms of United States relations with each of three leading European belligerents: Great Britain, Spain, and France.

Great Britain and Jay's Treaty

Relations between the United States and Great Britain had been strained since the Revolution; the European war brought them close to the breaking point. Problems growing out of the Treaty of Paris remained— including British occupation of the Northwest posts, boundary disputes, pre-Revolutionary debts, treatment of former Loyalists, and British evacuation with southern slaves. Frontiersmen accused Britain of inciting the Indians against them and were alarmed at British support for an Indian buffer state in the Northwest. American ministers failed to get a commercial treaty. England did not even bother to send a minister to the United States until the fall of 1791, when young George Hammond filled the post. After war erupted in 1793, British policies toward neutrals made an already bad situation much worse.

When the French Revolutionary Wars began, American shippers profitably expanded their carrying trade with belligerents on both sides. Many traded directly between the French West Indies and France, commerce previously reserved exclusively for French shippers. Reflecting self-interest, Americans supported a broad interpretation of neutral rights. The United States insisted that neutrals could legally trade with belligerents in noncontraband goods and that contraband should be defined narrowly.

Great Britain understandably objected to America's booming trade with its enemy. Reflecting its self-interest as a belligerent whose most powerful weapon was its navy, Britain defined belligerent rights broadly and rejected America's sweeping definition of neutral rights. Consequently, in a series of Orders-in-Council in 1793–1794, the British government cracked down on neutral commerce with France and the French colonies. In particular, Britain invoked its "Rule of 1756" that said trade prohibited in time of peace could not be opened in time of war. It was to prevent American trade between France and the French West Indies that had been closed to American vessels before the war. When American merchants attempted to evade the "Rule" by taking products from the French West Indies to the United States before going on to France, Britain invoked the "Doctrine of Continuous Voyage," allowing action against American ships sailing from the French West Indies whether going directly to France or indirectly by way of the United States. Britain not only issued its Orders-in-Council but its navy enforced them vigorously against American merchant ships. Britain seized hundreds of ships and cargoes, and impressed seamen from American ships. American pride and pocketbook suffered. War seemed imminent.

Americans agreed on the need for neutrality and objected to violations of "neutral rights" as the United States defined them. Nevertheless, they differed sharply about the best methods for guarding American interests.

Thomas Jefferson, James Madison, and their agrarian followers favored a tough line in dealing with Britain. They wanted to use trade concessions as the carrot and economic coercion as the stick to cause Britain to relax or revoke its Orders-in-Council. Consequently, in March, 1794, Congress imposed an embargo against foreign shipping that lasted two months.

The Federalists, however, controlled the government. Although British policies angered them, most Federalists vehemently opposed the Jefferson-Madison methods. They feared such tactics would move the United States into the French camp and lead to war with Britain. Hamilton believed an Anglo-American war would destroy American commerce, wipe out revenue sources essential to his domestic financial program, and undercut the economic bases for the Federalist-controlled government under the new Constitution. He believed those developments would destroy American power and security. Though Federalists wanted British concessions, they opposed economic coercion and considered peace with Britain absolutely essential. And the Hamiltonian (not the Jeffersonian) approach won out. Indeed, Secretary of State Jefferson became so irritated at Hamilton's constant interference in foreign affairs that he resigned from the Cabinet in December, 1793.

Federalists blocked further economic pressures and persuaded President Washington to send a special emissary to Britain. At Hamilton's suggestion, Washington named John Jay, Chief Justice of the Supreme Court, for the mission. Qualified by ability, experience, and reputation, Jay also shared Hamilton's views. Despite Anti-Federalist objections, the Senate approved the appointment in April, 1794. Jay's instructions, drafted by Hamilton, allowed him great discretion in the negotiations. He was to try to settle problems growing out of the peace treaty (including British occupation of the Northwest posts), win British recognition of American neutral rights, get compensation for ships and property seized by Britain, and negotiate a commercial treaty. He was not to violate America's agreements with France. But his main responsibility was to prevent war between the United States and Great Britain.

With Hamilton's pro-British party in control, with a dedicated Federalist serving as the special emissary, and with the new nation contending with one of the most powerful states in the world, the chances for a striking American diplomatic victory were not good. Jay had little in the way of inducements to offer. Federalists rejected economic coercion, and the government lacked both the power and the will for military coercion. Jay's principal bargaining weapon was the threat that if Britain did not yield, the United States might join a new "Armed Neutrality." Hamilton destroyed that feeble weapon, however, when he injudiciously told the British Minister, Hammond, that the Administration would not join. In such circumstances, Jay might preserve peace, but the possibilities for gaining substantial British concessions were slight.

The treaty signed by Jay on November 19, 1794, fell far short of American hopes. Britain did not revoke the Orders-in-Council or accept the American definition of neutral rights, though it did agree to pay for goods seized under the Orders. Britain made no concession on impressment, definition of contraband, paper blockades, or the Rule of 1756. The treaty did not include a satisfactory general commercial agreement. Article XII, which would have opened the British West Indies to limited trade in small American vessels (less than 70 tons), was so unsatisfactory that the Senate rejected it and the article never went into effect. British demands concerning the rights of former Loyalists were dropped, but so were southern claims arising from British evacuation with American slaves. In Jay's Treaty, Britain did promise to evacuate the Northwest posts by June 1, 1796. Nevertheless, that important concession (so desired by Westerners) was not due to the vigor of Jay's negotiations. Growing American military strength in the area under General "Mad Anthony" Wayne led Lord Grenville to decide to evacuate the posts. Even then the treaty allowed

Britons and Canadians to conduct fur trade within the American territory served by the posts.

An interesting and significant feature of Jay's Treaty was the provision for four mixed commissions to handle certain specified Anglo-American disputes. With no outside party included and with no provision for binding awards, they were not arbitral commissions. One was to determine the location of the St. Croix River boundary in northern Maine. A second was to locate the northwestern boundary of the United States. A third mixed commission was to decide the amount owed to Britain for pre-Revolutionary debts—debts the United States government promised to (and did) pay if the private American debtors (largely Southerners) did not. And finally, the treaty provided for a mixed commission to fix damages arising out of seizure of American ships by the British and seizure of British ships by privateers fitted out in American ports. Only the last of the four commissions was completely successful. It awarded $10,345,200 to Americans and $143,428 to Britain. The other three commissions either failed completely or had only limited success. The problems they represented had to be handled by regular diplomacy later.

President Washington was greatly disappointed in the treaty when it reached the United States in March, 1795. He even considered not submitting it to the Senate, and he tried to keep its provisions secret for a time. They soon leaked out, however, and public response was highly critical. Even some Federalists condemned it. Anti-Federalists vehemently attacked the treaty. Jay, once highly respected, was denounced and burned in effigy. The repercussions destroyed his promising political future. Secretary of State Edmund Randolph opposed ratification. Nevertheless, Hamilton and his followers defended it, and in June the Senate voted 20 to 10 for approval. Washington ratified it in August, 1795.

Jay had failed to win most of the concessions he sought from Britain. Nevertheless, Jay's Treaty did help preserve peace between the United States and Great Britain. And that, after all, was the primary objective of Hamilton and the Federalists. Furthermore, despite the commercial orientation of the Federalists, the treaty benefited agrarians in the United States. It got the British out of the Northwest posts. The unpopularity of the treaty weakened the Federalist Party and enhanced the political strength of the agrarian Anti-Federalists. And the negotiations with Britain helped persuade Spain to make diplomatic concessions desired by Americans in the Southwest.

Spain and the Treaty of San Lorenzo

In the 1790's United States relations with Spain continued to be plagued, as they had been under the Articles, with a variety of irritating problems:

boundary disputes, disagreements on use of the Mississippi River, and restrictions in trade policies. The relations were further complicated by Spain's roles in the Wars of the French Revolution. Fortunately, in the Federalist Era most of those problems were resolved satisfactorily for the United States.

Internally, United States relations with Spain were affected by the persistent flood of energetic American pioneers into the Southwest. After the Jay-Gardoqui negotiation in 1786, most Federalists realized that it would be politically dangerous to consider compromise on American use of the Mississippi River. At the same time, if Spanish holdings in North America were to be safeguarded, Spain would either have to appease the advancing frontiersmen with concessions, block them with diplomacy and force, or "divide and conquer" by offering concessions on the use of western rivers to persuade the West to separate from the United States. Spain attempted all of those tactics, including continued plotting with separatist leaders in the West. The Treaty of San Lorenzo in 1795 used the first of the three tactics.

Externally, the changing roles of the two countries in European power struggles, and particularly their changing relations with Britain, affected the policies of each toward the other. In 1793–1794, with Britain and Spain allied and warring against France, and with Anglo-American relations approaching the breaking point, Spain felt no need to make concessions to the United States. Spanish procrastination and delay frustrated the diplomatic efforts of William Carmichael and William Short, America's representatives in Madrid. But when Jay's negotiations in 1794 seemed to point to an Anglo-American rapprochement, and when Spain made peace with France in the summer of 1795, Spain found it expedient to seek an accord with the United States.

Even before the changes in Europe opened the door to Spanish concessions, President Washington appointed a special emissary to Spain, much as he had earlier sent Jay to Britain. Chosen for the mission was Thomas Pinckney, from a distinguished South Carolina family. He had lived in England for nineteen years as a boy and young man and studied at Oxford and in France. He fought with honor in the American Revolution and filled major government posts in America and abroad. Pinckney was not one of the great men of his day, but he was cosmopolitan, intelligent, and responsible. He was, like Jay, a Federalist, and at different times both of them negotiated with Spain. Nevertheless, they represented different sections of the country and different segments of the economy. The Spanish treaty proposed by Jay in 1786 contrasted with the Treaty of San Lorenzo negotiated by Pinckney ten years later, partly because conditions abroad were different and the population (and political) pressure in the Southwest had increased in the interval. In addition, the results differed because of the contrasting values of the New Yorker and the South Carolina planter. Pinckney was dedicated to defense of the right of navigation on the Mississippi. In any event, he arrived in Spain in June, 1795, just at the right moment to accomplish a major diplomatic victory.

Pinckney's Treaty (or the Treaty of San Lorenzo) was signed on October 27, 1795. In it Westerners and Southerners at no cost gained all they had sought from Spain. The Spanish Minister, Manuel de Godoy, at first hoped to use concessions in the West to buy an alliance with the United States. But that was a price that the United States would not pay. In the treaty Spain and the United States agreed to the thirty-first parallel and St. Mary's River as the boundary between the United States and Spanish Florida, exactly the line claimed by the United States from the beginning. Spain thus abandoned its strong claims to the Yazoo boundary. Pinckney's Treaty also opened the Mississippi to Americans from its source to the ocean with no time limit. Spain gave Americans the duty-free right of deposit in New Orleans. That enabled American products to be moved from river boats to ocean-going vessels. At the end of three years the right of deposit could be continued there or assigned by Spain to some other spot on the Mississippi shore. Both countries agreed to control Indians within their territories. Spain even endorsed the definition of neutral rights to which the United States was committed. Though it did not open Spanish colonies to American merchants, Pinckney's Treaty was a striking diplomatic victory for the United States. The Senate promptly and unanimously approved it. The United States obtained that highly favorable settlement largely because of conditions in Europe and Spanish fears in Europe and the Southwest, not because Hamilton and his Federalists attached high priority to the boundary and river matters in the Southwest.

Difficulties with Revolutionary France

Though the United States maintained peace with Britain and concluded a satisfactory treaty with Spain, relations with France, America's ally, went through a succession of spasms that finally brought the two states to blows. The French Revolution in 1789 evoked widespread sympathy in the United States. Nevertheless, leading Federalists had serious misgivings about the French Revolution, even in its early moderate stages. As the Revolution became more violent and extreme, growing numbers in the United States began to have doubts. Execution of King Louis XVI in 1793, France's war against its European neighbors, and the bloodletting of the Reign of Terror in 1793–1794 alienated many Americans, particularly in Federalist circles. When Citizen Genêt and then Jay's Treaty were added in the Federalist Era, the results were highly inflammatory.

America's alliance with France posed serious problems when that ally declared war on Britain and Spain in 1793. Twelve of the questions President Washington submitted to his Cabinet on April 18, 1793, dealt with policies toward France and the Alliance. On only one of the twelve did Jefferson and Hamilton agree. They both advised Washington to receive the new minister en route to Philadelphia from the First French Republic, though Hamilton would have qualified that reception. So far as the Alliance was concerned, Hamilton argued that since it had been concluded with the government under the now deposed and dead King, it was "temporarily and provisionally suspended." He also pointed out that the Alliance was only a defensive agreement and that France was waging an offensive war. In contrast, Jefferson correctly insisted that treaties bound nations, not just governments, and that those with France were still in force. He urged delaying a final decision, hoping that the United States might never be called upon to aid its ally. Washington followed the advice of his Secretary of State. Jefferson's recommendation was sound, for France did not urge the United States to enter the war. Its leaders were not impressed by American military potential. The United States could be more helpful, the French believed, as a neutral with pro-French sympathies than as a belligerent.

Edmond Charles Genêt, the colorful and brash new Minister to the United States, was from a distinguished French family. He was only thirty years old, but he was already a talented linguist and an experienced diplomat. He was also a dedicated, crusading republican. He interpreted the instructions from his government broadly and was strikingly uninhibited in his efforts to make the neutral United States essentially into a base of operations against Britain and Spain. Arriving in Charleston, South Carolina, on April 8, 1793, Genêt aroused a tumultuous welcome that encouraged the impulsive young diplomat. His overland journey to Philadelphia took him through rural areas where pro-French enthusiasm assured warm receptions. Indeed, the enthusiasm he inspired had anti-Federalist connotations that were not overlooked by American political leaders. Even the frigid reception President Washington gave Genêt in Philadelphia did not discourage him. In American ports he outfitted privateers to raid British shipping and recruited seamen to war against France's enemies. He authorized French consuls in America to serve as admiralty courts for the disposal of prizes brought into port by French privateers. He planned a three-pronged attack from American soil against Spain in Florida and the Louisiana Territory. He commissioned the American Revolutionary hero, George Rogers Clark, to organize and lead an expedition against Spanish New Orleans. And he even had designs on Canada.

Nevertheless, the combination of Genêt's own rashness plus conditions both in Europe and in America destroyed the young diplomat's mission. Genêt failed to get essential financial support from his government. In June, 1793, when the Jacobins overthrew the Girondins in France, Genêt fell from favor at home. The Reign of Terror that followed not only shocked conservative Federalists but disillusioned previously sympathetic

Republicans as well. Later Jay's Treaty that got Britain out of the Northwest posts and Pinckney's Treaty that resolved boundary and river difficulties with Spain weakened western willingness to aid France against
its enemies.

In addition, domestic political patterns in the United States checked
Genêt. America's unwillingness to make advance payment on its debt to
France blocked that source of funds for Genêt's projects. Probably most
Americans were pro-French, but the anti-French Federalists controlled
the government. Hamilton, Jay, and other Federalist leaders spared no
efforts to discredit Genêt with the President and the American people.
Federalist sources charged Genêt with plans to appeal directly to the people over the head of President Washington, charges that Genêt failed to
disprove. In a choice between Washington and Genêt, partisan American
criticism of the President increased, but the effects damaged the French
diplomat much more. In August, 1793, the President's Cabinet decided to
demand Genêt's recall. Jefferson's resignation from the Cabinet on December 31 left Genêt without a sympathetic voice in Administration circles.
When, in February, 1794, Joseph Fauchet arrived as new French Minister,
he had instructions to arrest his predecessor and return him to France
for trial and perhaps execution. Washington prevented this, however, and
Genêt lived out his life in the United States, marrying an American girl
and, in 1804, becoming an American citizen.

While Genêt's mission strained relations between the two countries, the
antics of America's ministers further widened the breach. The United
States diplomatic representative to France from 1792 to 1794 was Gouver-
neur Morris of New York, an aristocratic conservative. His hostility to
the French Revolution pleased his fellow Federalists almost as much as
it displeased the new French leaders. His slanted reports to America
reinforced the anti-French Federalist biases. His royalist sympathies led
him to use the American legation as an asylum for French nobles fleeing
the Revolution. He plotted unsuccessfully to help King Louis XVI and
Marie Antoinette escape. Consequently, when Washington asked for
Genêt's recall, France obliged but demanded Morris' recall at the same
time.

His successor from 1794 to 1796 erred in the opposite direction. James
Monroe of Virginia warmly sympathized with the French Revolution and
was so eager to improve relations with France that he quickly alienated
Federalists in America, annoyed Britain, and exceeded his authority in
efforts to ease French alarm about possible Anglo-American accord. When
President Washington sent John Jay on a special mission to England,
Monroe assured the French that the action would not undermine America's
ties with France. When they finally learned the contents of Jay's Treaty,
French leaders insisted that they undermined American neutrality and
conflicted with America's treaties with France. Only with great difficulty

did Monroe prevent more drastic French response to the treaty. But his efforts did not satisfy either the French or the Federalists (who thought he was hopelessly pro-French). Consequently, in 1796 President Washington terminated Monroe's mission, and France ended its diplomatic relations with the United States.

Near the close of his administration, President Washington tried to restore normal relations by sending Charles C. Pinckney of South Carolina (a brother of Thomas Pinckney) to represent the United States in Paris. The effort failed. The French Directory not only refused to receive Pinckney but warned him that if he did not leave France he would be subject to arrest. Pinckney promptly fled to the Netherlands. As diplomatic relations deteriorated, French interference with American ships and cargoes sharply increased.

Such was the state of American relations with its French ally at the close of Washington's administration. It was little wonder that Washington, in his Farewell Address, urged America "to steer clear of permanent alliances" and warned against "inveterate antipathies against particular nations and passionate attachment for others." He used general terms that could apply to all foreign states, but America's only alliance was with France, and it was the attachment to France by his political opponents that particularly disturbed the President. Put in that context, he was warning against close ties with France as much as he was calling for an independent foreign policy. Attachments and sympathy for Britain did not particularly worry him (or Hamilton, who wrote the "Farewell Address"). To that extent the speech was a political document directed against France's Anti-Federalist friends in America who supported Jefferson's unsuccessful candidacy for President in 1796.

President John Adams tried to reestablish relations with France by sending a three-man commission. Composed of two Federalists (Charles C. Pinckney and John Marshall of Virginia) and one Anti-Federalist (Elbridge Gerry of Massachusetts), it included persons of distinction from both political parties and from both the North and the South. Like Pinckney's earlier effort, however, the mission failed. Under instructions from Talleyrand, three French agents (Hottinger, Bellamy, and Hauteval) approached the American envoys and insisted on gifts and loan of large sums of money before France would receive them. The commissioners had neither the money nor the authority to accede to the demand, and they eventually returned to the United States. As subsequently publicized in the United States, the so-called "XYZ" affair inflamed public opinion. The incident, combined with French seizure of American ships and the anti-French biases of Federalist leaders, aroused patriotic considerations of national honor and even war fervor. Congress appropriated funds for military and naval preparations. Washington agreed to lead the Army in the event of war, and Hamilton eagerly volunteered to be second in command. Indeed, had it not been for the tenacious stand by President Adams, war with France almost certainly would have ensued. As it was, the United States and France waged a spirited undeclared naval war from 1798 to 1800. Moved by the international crisis (and by the growing political power of Republicans), Federalists pushed through the Alien and Sedition Acts that, in practice, were used more against political opponents than against subversives. Not until 1800 did the United States conclude an agreement with Napoleon's France that ended the alliance and stopped the undeclared war. The agreement did not provide for payment of spoliation claims by either France or the United States. Federalists in the Senate blocked the treaty on the first vote in 1800, but in modified form it won approval the following year.

CONCLUSIONS

During the Federalist Era the government successfully preserved American national security in the face of the Wars of the French Revolution. It also followed policies designed to protect and expand American foreign trade. Among those policies was the determined aim of avoiding war with Great Britain—America's most valuable customer. Though both Britain and France provided cause for war, the United States maintained peace with Britain and drifted into an undeclared war with France. That pattern fairly well reflected the interests and values of the merchant-shipper groups as interpreted by Federalist leaders.

At the same time, developments abroad during the Wars of the French Revolution made it easy for the Federalists to accomplish goals desired by agrarians in foreign affairs. Those accomplishments included Jay's Treaty that got Britain out of the Northwest posts and the generous provisions of Pinckney's Treaty. Furthermore, the unpopular Jay's Treaty and the despised Alien and Sedition Acts helped to weaken the Federalist Party. President Adams' successful efforts to avoid war with France won approval from agrarians in both parties. But by splitting the Federalist Party (Hamiltonians against Adams followers, and merchant-shipper group against agrarians) his policies made it easier for the agrarian-dominated Jeffersonian Republican Party to win political dominance in the election of 1800.

SUPPLEMENTARY READINGS

Beard, Charles A. *Economic Origins of Jeffersonian Democracy.* New York: Macmillan Co., 1915.

Bemis, Samuel Flagg. *Jay's Treaty: A Study in Commerce and Diplomacy.* New York: Macmillan Co., 1923.

————. *Pinckney's Treaty: America's Advantage from Europe's Distress, 1783–1800.* New rev. ed. New Haven, Conn.: Yale University Press, 1960.

Chinard, Gilbert. *Honest John Adams.* Boston: Little, Brown & Co., 1933.

62   *An interpretive history of American foreign relations*

Combs, Jerald A. *The Jay Treaty: Political Battleground of the Founding Fathers.* Berkeley: University of California Press, 1970.

Dauer, Manning, J. *The Adams Federalists.* Baltimore: Johns Hopkins Press, 1953.

DeConde, Alexander. *Entangling Alliance: Politics and Diplomacy under George Washington.* Durham, N.C.: Duke University Press, 1958.

————. *The Quasi-War: The Politics and Diplomacy of the Undeclared War with France, 1797–1801.* New York: Charles Scribner's Sons, 1966.

Handler, Edward. *America and Europe in the Political Thought of John Adams.* Cambridge, Mass.: Harvard University Press, 1964.

Perkins, Bradford. *The First Rapprochement: England and the United States, 1795–1805.* Philadelphia: University of Pennsylvania Press, 1955.

Thomas, Charles M. *American Neutrality in 1793: A Study in Cabinet Government.* New York: Columbia University Press, 1931.

Varg, Paul A. *Foreign Policies of the Founding Fathers.* East Lansing: Michigan State University Press, 1963.

Whitaker, Arthur P. *The Mississippi Question, 1795–1803: A Study in Trade, Politics, and Diplomacy.* New York: D. Appleton-Century Co., 1934.

————. *The Spanish-American Frontier, 1783–1795.* Boston: Houghton Mifflin Co., 1927.

7

Thomas Jefferson and the Louisiana Purchase

The defeat of John Adams in the election of 1800 marked the end of the Federalist Era and of shipping-commercial control in American foreign affairs. The inauguration of Thomas Jefferson as President in 1801 marked the beginning of a long era of farmer-agrarian-planter dominance in American politics. The Jeffersonian Republican Era proper included only two presidential administrations: Jefferson's from 1801 to 1809 and James Madison's from 1809 to 1817. Except for two brief Whig interludes, however, agrarians and their political spokesmen generally controlled the federal government and foreign policies for six decades, from the time Jefferson was inaugurated until Abraham Lincoln became President in 1861.

Of all the Presidents in that long era, Thomas Jefferson best personified farmer-agrarian attitudes on both domestic and foreign affairs. To be sure, he became meaningful partly in terms of his great intellect, his patriotism, his pragmatism, and his personal temperament. Probably the most learned man to be President of the United States, Jefferson was an intellectual product of the Enlightenment. Not skilled as a public speaker, Jefferson was most effective with his pen, as witnessed by his personal letters and by the almost poetic Declaration of Independence that he composed. His experiences as United States Minister to France under the Articles of Confederation strengthened his Francophile tendencies, but they also intensified his nationalism and his distrust of Europe. His scholarship was not of the ivory tower variety. He was pragmatic, not doctrinaire. "What is practicable must often control what is pure theory," he wrote. In temperament he disliked controversy and was sensitive to criticism. Consequently, as President he preferred compromise to avoid unnecessary conflict.

Nevertheless, as a slave-owning planter from the Virginia piedmont, Jefferson's great learning and varied experiences in America and abroad never really separated him from the soil and the men who cultivated it. He once wrote, "Those who labor in the earth are the chosen people of God, if ever He had a chosen people, whose breasts He has made his peculiar deposit for substantial and genuine virtue." He made his main appeal and drew his greatest support from the agricultural areas of the South and West. He believed a democratic republic could be founded securely only on agriculture accompanied by wide distribution of land ownership. It was easy for him to have confidence in majority rule in that day when most Americans were farmers. He was not an equalitarian, however. Reflecting his status as a big planter, Jefferson believed the common people (i.e., the farmers) should elect, but the government officials should be people of superior talent and intellect. He had much faith in the contributions of education and a free press to the effective operation of republican institutions. He did not, however, envisage the same education for all. The extent and kind of education should depend, he believed, on the abilities of the individual.

Jefferson distrusted city people, including merchants, financiers, and the urban working class. He favored development of enough commerce and industry to serve domestic needs and national security, but no more than that. He worried about that day in the remote future when land in America would be so filled that the people would be "piled up upon one another in large cities, as in Europe." He doubted that democracy could long survive in such a setting. That unfortunate day could be postponed, he believed, by American expansion into additional territories in the West (including the Louisiana Territory that the United States acquired under his leadership).

As President, Jefferson worked to guard American national security in foreign affairs. And he did not ignore the wishes of the shipping-commercial groups. Insofar as his definitions of national security were affected by domestic considerations, however, they reflected the values and interests of rural America. And where the interests of commercial and agricultural groups conflicted in foreign affairs, Jefferson could be depended upon to throw his weight with the farmers.

The external influences on American foreign affairs in the Age of Jefferson revolved around the Napoleonic Wars. Napoleon Bonaparte became First Consul in 1799 and Emperor of France in 1804. The Napoleonic Wars began in 1803 and were not finally ended until after the defeat of

Napoleon at Waterloo in 1815. The Napoleonic Wars ("Europe's distresses"), and uprisings in the Caribbean led to the Louisiana Purchase. Those wars gave American merchants opportunities for profitable war trade. And many agrarians *believed* that those wars gave them opportunities to annex Canada and Florida in the War of 1812 against Great Britain —though the efforts to get those territories in the Jeffersonian Era failed.

THE REPUBLICANS AND AMERICAN FOREIGN TRADE

Jefferson was not uninterested in foreign trade. Indeed, commercial farmers generally realized that their prosperity was affected by foreign markets for their products and by foreign sources of manufactured products. Nevertheless, Jeffersonian Republicans were not particularly interested in promoting the profits of American merchants and shippers. The Republican administrations were willing to promote and protect American foreign trade and shipping if it did not hurt the farmers, if it did not cost too much money or effort, if it appeased merchants and thereby reduced political opposition, if it enhanced farm prosperity, and if the defense of trade was tied to patriotism and national honor. Those attitudes were reinforced by President Jefferson's temperament. Practical, reasonable, and disliking heated controversy, Jefferson (as Hamilton correctly predicted) did not choose to destroy all that the Federalists had built. He modified some of his predecessors' policies and reversed others, but most of Hamilton's economic program was allowed to stand with little change under Republican leadership. Jefferson did reduce the size of the Navy and undertook the ineffective gunboat policy. At the same time, however, he continued discriminatory tonnage duties, subsidies to the fishing industry, excluding foreign ships from coastal trade, and new consulates abroad.

Jefferson's policies toward the continuing difficulties with the North African Barbary States demonstrated how the Republicans would protect foreign trade provided it did not hurt farmers, did not require too much effort or risk, and was tied to patriotic considerations. The problem grew out of raids on American commerce in the Mediterranean by ships from Morocco, Algiers, Tripoli, and Tunis after British protection ended with American independence. Under the Articles of Confederation and later under the Federalists, the United States had sought safety through treaties that called for expensive "presents" or payments to the Barbary leaders. Nevertheless, the difficulties continued. In 1800 the ruler of Algiers forced an American frigate, the *George Washington*, to take his ambassador to Constantinople along with a large and varied cargo. In 1801 Tripoli abruptly declared war on the United States. Without a formal declaration of war, President Jefferson sent a small American naval squadron against Tripoli. Individual Americans displayed daring and imagination in the dramatic fighting in North Africa. Jefferson's effort, however, was lim-

ited. American ships established a feeble and ineffective blockade of Tripoli. The United States reached an agreement with that country partly because of an American conspiracy with a competing ruler of the state. And
even that treaty with Tripoli in 1805 was not very satisfactory. The United
States had to pay a $60,000 ransom for captured American seamen, and
each new American consul was to bring a "present." In return the ruler
of Tripoli promised not to molest American merchant ships in the Mediterranean. Jefferson's administration had made a minor effort with meager
results. And he withdrew American naval units from the Mediterranean
in 1807. Not until 1815, under President James Madison, did the United
States take any further forceful action on the problem.

THE LOUISIANA PURCHASE

A major episode much more directly affecting the interests of Jefferson's constituents involved the Louisiana Territory. That huge area between the Mississippi River in the east and the Rocky Mountains to the
west had changed hands several times. In the independent history of the
United States, it belonged to Spain until 1800. Spain was too weak to be
a serious threat to American national security or to block American expansionist ambitions in the future. And in Pinckney's Treaty of 1795,
Spain instituted generous policies on American use of the Mississippi
River.

The secret Treaty of San Ildefonso of October, 1800, that Napoleon imposed on Spain radically altered that satisfactory situation. The treaty
gave the Louisiana Territory to France. Napoleon wanted it to serve as
the food basket for his sugar-producing holdings in America centered in
Santo Domingo in the Caribbean. In return France promised to give territory in Italy to the Duke of Parma, son-in-law of the Spanish ruler. France
also solemnly promised not to transfer the Louisiana Territory to a third
power. Napoleon did not keep either of those promises. Furthermore, in
1802 (after the Treaty of San Ildefonso but before the French took control
of the Territory) Spain suspended the American right of deposit at New
Orleans (east of the Mississippi but part of the Louisiana Territory).

The response in the United States to those developments was highly
inflammatory, particularly in the West. Spain was no serious threat to
American security and interests, but France (the most powerful state
on the European continent) could be. The Louisiana Territory in French
hands could stop American territorial expansion, destroy the prosperity
of Westerners who depended on the Ohio-Mississippi River system, and
even threaten the security of the United States within its existing boundaries. Westerners who had been alarmed earlier by Spanish obstructions
now urged drastic actions to guard their interests. Some urged military
solutions and even war.

At the same time, Federalists tried to capitalize on the crisis politically by supporting the Ross Resolution that would have authorized the United States to take New Orleans by force. Federalist antipathy for France was well known, but so was Federalist lack of sympathy for western interests. Political advantage rather than immediate national interest inspired the ineffective Federalist support for the warlike Resolution in the Senate.

President Jefferson was the key figure so far as official United States reaction was concerned. Despite his pro-French sympathies, Jefferson believed that French command of New Orleans, controlling commercial egress via the Mississippi River, would constitute an intolerable threat to American vital interests and security. As he wrote to Robert R. Livingston, United States Minister to France: "There is on the globe one single spot, the possessor of which is our natural and habitual enemy. It is New Orleans, through which the produce of three-eighths of our territory must pass to market, and from its fertility will ere long yield more than half of our whole produce, and contain more than half of our inhabitants." He contended that the moment France took possession of New Orleans "we must marry ourselves to the British fleet and nation." He considered military action to block such a French move. The President instructed the aged Livingston to try to purchase New Orleans and Florida from France. Early in 1803 he appointed James Monroe of Virginia as special envoy to negotiate, along with Livingston, for the purchase of New Orleans. If France refused to sell or to make some other acceptable arrangement that would safeguard America's use of the river, Monroe was to cross the channel and seek an alliance with Britain.

The explanations for Jefferson's course were many. Partly they grew out of his personal conviction that France in control of New Orleans represented a serious external threat. Domestically the dramatic appointment of Monroe was designed to quiet the more warlike people in his own party in the West. Furthermore, he hoped by sending Monroe to prevent the Federalists from gaining political advantage from their militant appeals to Westerners on the issue.

Fortunately, developments in Europe and the Caribbean caused Napoleon to abandon his ambitious plans in the Western Hemisphere even before Monroe reached Paris. French troops had not been able to suppress the Negro insurrection led by Toussaint L'Ouverture in Santo Domingo, the center for Napoleon's New World empire. The revolt could not be crushed without greater expenditure of men and money than Napoleon was able to allocate for the purpose at that time. He had more essential needs in Europe for his resources in the approaching war against Britain and its coalitions. Napoleon did not attach much weight to United States power, but he did not wish to drive America into the arms of Great Britain. In the face of such an Anglo-American combination the Louisiana Territory could be a vulnerable Achilles heel for France. Furthermore, money derived from the sale of the Territory could be put to use for the wars in Europe.

Consequently, on April 11, 1803, Talleyrand surprised Livingston by offering to sell all of the Louisiana Territory (not just New Orleans) to the United States. Neither Livingston nor Monroe (who arrived soon after the initial offer) had authority to make such a purchase. Rather than miss the opportunity, however, the diplomats worked out the terms of the treaty that was dated April 30, 1803. It provided that the United States should pay $15 million for the Territory—though Napoleon would have accepted less. The exact boundaries were not clearly defined. The purchase could not be consummated, however, until and unless the Senate approved the treaty, Congress appropriated the money, and the President exchanged ratifications.

Earlier, Jefferson had defended a "strict constructionist" interpretation of the Constitution in attacking Hamilton's economic program. He had contended that the powers of the federal government in general and the President in particular were limited to those explicitly spelled out in the Constitution. All other powers, he believed, were reserved to the states or to the people. When he first learned of the Louisiana Purchase Treaty he believed it would require a constitutional amendment before the government would have the necessary authority to act. Such a course would have taken much time, however, and the whole project might have collapsed. Confronted with a practical situation affecting, in his opinion, national security and vital interests, Jefferson did not hesitate. In October, 1803, he submitted the treaty to the Senate and urged approval. During two days of debate Republicans from agricultural states in the South and West defended the treaty. At the same time, most Federalists from New England and the Middle Atlantic states, who had been loose constructionists, now opposed the treaty, partly on the grounds that it exceeded the constitutional authority of the federal government. They also doubted that France had the right to sell, since it had not fulfilled the commitments it had made to Spain to get the territory. Federalists worried that an agricultural society would develop in the new lands to the west that would strengthen Republican political dominance and endanger the interests of the urban and commercial Northeast. Nevertheless, the Senate approved the treaty, with the vote following party lines: Republicans for it and Federalists opposed. After a similar but longer debate, the House of Representatives adopted the necessary financial legislation. Ratifications were promptly exchanged, and on December 20, 1803, American officials and troops officially took over the Territory from the French (who had replaced Spanish officials in New Orleans only twenty days before).

The Louisiana Purchase provided an excellent illustration of the way American foreign affairs were the product of both external and internal influences, and the way those influences contributed to American expan-

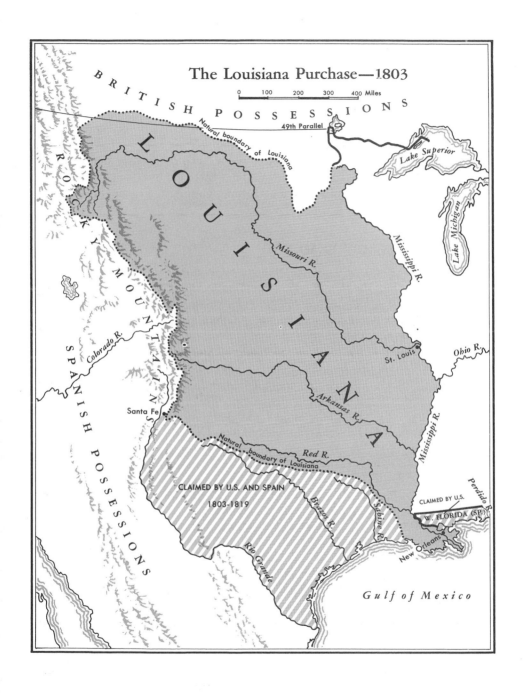

The Louisiana Purchase—1803

sion. Externally, Napoleon did not decide to sell the Louisiana Territory because of American power or diplomatic skill. He decided to sell because impending war in Europe and insurrection in Santo Domingo made it expedient for him to do so. Internally, the United States government vigorously sought New Orleans and quickly seized the opportunity to buy the whole Territory because the administration and party in power were sympathetic to the interests of agrarians in the West and South who would benefit from the Purchase. The Louisiana Territory nearly doubled the size of the United States at a cost of about three cents an acre. The Territory equaled the combined area of Britain, Germany, France, Spain, Portugal, and Italy.

SUPPLEMENTARY READINGS

Adams, Henry. *History of the United States during the Administrations of Jefferson and Madison.* 9 vols. New York: Charles Scribner's Sons, 1889–1898.

Beard, Charles A. *Economic Origins of Jeffersonian Democracy.* New York: Macmillan Co., 1915.

Brant, Irving. *James Madison: Secretary of State, 1800–1809.* Indianapolis: Bobbs-Merrill Co., Inc., 1953.

Chinard, Gilbert. *Thomas Jefferson: The Apostle of Americanism.* 2d ed. rev. Ann Arbor: University of Michigan Press, 1957.

Field, James A., Jr. *America and the Mediterranean World, 1776–1882.* Princeton, N.J.: Princeton University Press, 1969.

Irwin, Ray W. *The Diplomatic Relations of the United States with the Barbary Powers, 1776–1816.* Chapel Hill: University of North Carolina Press, 1931.

Kaplan, Lawrence S. *Jefferson and France: An Essay on Politics and Political Ideas.* New Haven, Conn.: Yale University Press, 1967.

Lyon, E. W. *Louisiana in French Diplomacy, 1759–1804.* Norman: University of Oklahoma Press, 1934.

Perkins, Bradford. *The First Rapprochement: England and the United States, 1795–1805.* Philadelphia: University of Pennsylvania Press, 1955.

Tansill, Charles C. *The United States and Santo Domingo, 1798–1873.* Baltimore: Johns Hopkins Press, 1938.

Whitaker, Arthur P. *The Mississippi Question, 1795–1803: A Study in Trade, Politics, and Diplomacy.* New York: D. Appleton-Century Co., 1934.

Wright, L. B. and MacLeod, J. H. *The First Americans in North Africa: William Eaton's Struggle for a Vigorous Policy Against the Barbary Pirates, 1799–1805.* Princeton, N.J.: Princeton University Press, 1945.

8

The War of 1812

The most difficult problems facing the United States in foreign affairs during the administrations of Presidents Thomas Jefferson and James Madison grew out of the Napoleonic Wars from 1803 to 1815. The War of 1812 was the name given to American participation in those wars. The Napoleonic Wars focused primarily on the European continent; they were not much concerned with struggles for empire. Until the United States became a belligerent, they did not directly endanger American territorial security. Indeed, by absorbing the energies of European states, the wars seemed to give the United States temporary power advantages in the Western Hemisphere that encouraged expansionist ambitions. The Napoleonic Wars were all-out efforts, however, and each side used every possible method to crush its enemies—including control of ocean commerce in neutral ships.

For purposes of analysis, the causes for the War of 1812 may be divided into two categories corresponding to the two broad socioeconomic interest groups in the United States. First, there were maritime causes growing out of impressment, interference with United States shipping, and America's defense of "neutral rights." And second, there were territorial causes growing out of the expansionist ambitions of many Americans in the agricultural South and West.

NEUTRAL RIGHTS AND MARITIME GRIEVANCES

The Napoleonic Wars enabled American shippers to make substantial profits trading with belligerents. Neither side, however, was waging war for the profit of American businessmen. Both Britain and France tried to control or block American trade with their enemies.

In the first decade of the nineteenth century, France under Napoleon conquered or neutralized most of Europe. Napoleon tried to use his control of European ports to prevent neutrals from trading with England and to deny Britain a European market. He proclaimed his so-called "Continental System" through a series of decrees. In the Berlin Decree of 1806 he prohibited trade with Britain and ordered seizure of all ships that touched Britain or British colonial ports. His even more drastic Milan Degree of 1807 ordered seizure of all ships that even allowed themselves to be searched or taxed by the British. The Continental System never completely prevented American trade with England, but it led to the loss of hundreds of American ships at the hands of the French.

British interference with American commerce was even more irritating and effective, however, because of the greater size and power of the British Navy. That was particularly true after the victory at Trafalgar in 1805. The British counterpart to the Napoleonic Decrees was a succession of Orders-in-Council designed to control all trade with Napoleon's Europe. Neutral ships en route to France and other continental countries had to stop first in England. Those noncontraband cargoes that were allowed to continue on their way did so only after conforming to British duty and licensing requirements. The Orders-in-Council were part of the general effort to crush Napoleon. In addition, they were mercantilistic efforts to force British products and ships on Europe. In effect Britain told Napoleon: "If you will not have *our* trade, as far as we can help it you shall have *none;* and as to so much of any trade as you can carry on yourselves, or others carry on with you through us, if you admit it you shall pay for it. The only trade, cheap and untaxed, which you shall have shall be either direct from us, in our own produce and manufactures, or from our allies, whose increased prosperity will be an advantage to us."

Furthermore, Britain continued to invoke its Rule of 1756 against American trade between France and its colonies. American traders tried to avoid the "Rule" by taking cargoes from the West Indies to the United States before going on to France. The *Polly* decision of 1800 seemed to put ships outside the purview of the Rule of 1756 and the Doctrine of Continuous Voyage if they paid duty in the United States. With the *Essex* decision of 1805, however, the British found it much easier to use the Doctrine of Continuous Voyage to prevent evasion of the Rule of 1756. Thereafter even payment of duties in the United States did not, by itself, exempt American ships from seizure.

Britain also stepped up its impressment of seamen from American ships. Impressment was a product of a variety of related circumstances: the urgent need for large numbers of seamen in the Royal Navy; the higher pay and less demanding conditions aboard American ships; the ease with which Englishmen could obtain American citizenship (or fraudulent citizenship papers); and the refusal of Britain to release naturalized American citizens from their obligations as British citizens. Several thousand Englishmen served on American ships during the Napoleonic era, and many of them had deserted from the British Navy. Britain was determined to regain their services, by force if necessary. Estimates vary widely, but Britain probably impressed more than six thousand seamen from American ships. Most of them were Englishmen, but some were Americans or Englishmen who had legally changed their citizenship. Britain took most from merchant ships, but in the highly inflammatory *Chesapeake* incident in June, 1807, the British *Leopard* forced removal of four sailors from an American frigate. Only one was a British citizen (he was promptly hanged), but all had deserted from service in the Royal Navy.

Dealing with those maritime difficulties during the Napoleonic Wars fell to the Republican administrations of Jefferson and Madison. As agrarians they attached less direct importance to ocean commerce and trading profits than Federalists generally did. At the same time, however, they were patriotic nationalists determined to protect American rights and honor. Though their enthusiasm for France had long since cooled, they had no love for the British. Furthermore, they were political realists who, in some degree, responded to chauvinistic, economic, and expansionist influences among their agrarian constituents. Their pacifist inclinations (and awareness of the weakness of the United States relative to the European powers) made them reluctant to attempt military solutions. Jefferson and Madison preferred diplomatic and economic methods. But when nonviolent methods appeared to fail, war seemed to provide the only acceptable solution.

Jefferson and Madison were attracted by the possibilities of using economic pressures and inducements as substitutes for military coercion in foreign affairs. They experimented with economic methods briefly in 1806. From 1807 to 1812 the Republican administrations inaugurated a series of three major economic schemes. They were designed to persuade Britain and France to recognize "neutral rights" as the United States defined them and to stop "illegal" interference with American ships and seamen. More fundamental, they were designed to keep the United States out of the European wars by removing maritime irritations that might project the nation into war.

The first (and most drastic) of the three schemes was the Embargo Act adopted by Congress and signed into law by President Jefferson on December 22, 1807. The Embargo was a delayed response to the *Chesapeake* incident. It prohibited any American ships and cargoes from leaving the United States for any foreign port. Ships engaged in coastal trade were heavily bonded to prevent them from sailing abroad. Hopefully the

Embargo might compel Britain or France to revoke their damaging maritime policies.

Both external and internal conditions caused the Embargo to fail. It was aimed more against Britain than against France. Indeed, in effect it supplemented Napoleon's Decrees in obstructing American trade with Britain. Consequently, the Embargo did not cause the French Emperor to abandon his Continental System. It hurt Britain, but not so much as the Republicans expected or hoped. Britain turned to other parts of the world (including Latin America) for trade to replace that lost because of the Embargo. Furthermore, the law could not be enforced effectively, and many American ships continued to trade with Britain. Britain was hurt and annoyed by the Embargo, and—if it had continued longer—might have been persuaded to make concessions. Nevertheless, in practice the Embargo did not force either Britain or France to yield to American demands.

Furthermore, on the domestic scene the Embargo hurt Americans more than it did the British or French. Federalist spokesmen for commercial New England and the Middle Atlantic states vigorously objected to the policy. Those American shippers who did not violate the law were hurt by it more than they had been by the British Orders-in-Council and the Napoleonic Decrees. The Embargo also harmed those Americans whose interests Jefferson most wanted to serve, the farmers and planters. Loss of foreign markets sharply reduced the prices they could get for their agricultural products. Consequently, as the months passed, the domestic uproar against it (from Republicans as well as from Federalists) reached a crescendo. The unpopular Embargo led to a Federalist political revival in the elections of 1808. The failure of the Embargo to win concessions abroad, and its harmful economic and political consequences at home, killed it in March, 1809, just as Jefferson's Presidency ended.

The Non-Intercourse Act of March 1, 1809, was the second major economic effort to win concessions and avert war. It was more moderate than its predecessor but operated from the same general assumptions. It allowed American trade with all countries except Britain and France and ports controlled by them. If either Britain or France revoked its trade restrictions, the United States would resume trade with that particular belligerent.

The second experiment failed when the British government repudiated the Erskine Agreement of 1809. Young David M. Erskine, Britain's representative in Washington, earnestly tried to smooth relations between Great Britain and the United States. His lack of diplomatic experience and his eagerness to preserve peace, however, caused him to exceed his instructions. In an agreement concluded in April, 1809, Erskine promised that Britain would revoke its Orders-in-Council in return for an American commitment to reopen trade with Britain while keeping it closed with

France. Though it did not cover impressment or the Rule of 1756, the Erskine Agreement seemed to be a clear victory for the Non-Intercourse Act. Delighted with the quick success, President Madison promptly authorized American ships to sail for England. His action was premature, however. George Canning, British Foreign Secretary, had not authorized Erskine to make such an unqualified concession. His instructions called for more conditions, including American acceptance of the Rule of 1756 and British authority to seize American ships trading with France. The agreement that Canning wanted would have required a major retreat by the United States; the agreement that Erskine negotiated was tantamount to a substantial British concession. Canning therefore disavowed the Erskine Agreement, and in August Madison reimposed the ban on trade with Britain.

The Non-Intercourse Act was also unsuccessful in ending Napoleon's Continental System. During the interval when American trade with Britain was reopened briefly in the summer of 1809, Napoleon considered making concessions to the United States. But Canning's repudiation of the Erskine Agreement ended that possibility.

The third economic scheme in the series was the weakest of all and, like its predecessors, it failed. The Macon Bill No. 2 of May, 1810, allowed trade with all countries, including Britain and France. It provided, however, that if either Britain or France revoked its commercial restrictions (and the other belligerent failed to do so within three months), the United States would stop trading with that country's enemy. That is, if Britain revoked its Orders-in-Council, the United States would close trade with France; if France revoked the Napoleonic Decrees, the United States would stop trading with Britain.

Napoleon promptly seized on the new policy and tricked the United States into ending its trade with Britain. The Emperor directed his Foreign Minister, the Duke of Cadore, to inform the United States of France's willingness to end the Napoleonic Decrees on November 1, 1810, providing Britain also revoked its Orders-in-Council or that the United States persuaded Britain to respect its neutral rights. The conditions deliberately made the Cadore letter confusing and meaningless. Nevertheless, President Madison again acted precipitously. Though France continued to enforce the Napoleonic Decrees against American ships, in 1811 Madison banned further American commerce with Britain.

Despite their efforts, Jefferson and Madison were unable to protect American neutral rights and to avoid war through diplomacy and economic methods. Two days before the United States declared war in June, 1812, Great Britain decided to revoke its Orders-in-Council, but the news arrived in America too late to prevent war.

Many variables accounted for the failure of Administration tactics. The Embargo hurt Britain, but not so severely as many Americans expected or hoped. Britain's access to resources in its colonies, among its allies, and in Latin America was sufficient to make it economically independent of the United States if necessary. Many American merchants continued to trade with the belligerents in violation of the American laws. Also, Britain attached much greater importance to defeating Napoleon and controlling English economic access to the Continent than it did to any inconveniences caused by American policies. And finally, American diplomacy and economic pressures were not backed by any substantial military or naval power. The United States did not carry as much weight with the leading belligerents as Americans at the time liked to believe.

British maritime policies played a major role in causing the War of 1812. But ironically, British interference with American shipping did not, for the most part, arouse enthusiasm for war among the merchants and traders whose ships and cargoes were being seized. British and French actions angered and hurt merchants and traders from New England and the Middle Atlantic states. They wanted the interference to stop and wanted American neutral rights preserved. They did not, however, favor the use of economic coercion against their European customers. And they did not want to go to war to protect neutral rights. Commercial and creditor interests from northeastern coastal areas and their Federalist political spokesmen generally opposed the declaration of war. After Congress declared war they gave little or no support to the nation's war effort. Many continued to trade with the enemy.

Part of the explanation for Federalist opposition to Republican foreign policies was partisan politics. The Federalists opposed almost anything their political opponents favored. Furthermore, in coastal cities their homes, properties, and lives were more vulnerable to attacks in the event of war than were those in rural areas of the South and West. They also feared that war might add more territory to the United States that might eventually strengthen the Republicans politically and further weaken the relative power of the Federalists. But most important, American shippers had made profits from war trade (even though some of their ships and seamen were seized), so they opposed any policies or war that disrupted that profitable commerce. Besides, Britain often paid for cargoes it seized. It is one of the ironies of American history that the Embargo and War of 1812 that ostensibly were designed to protect American commerce actually hurt American merchants and trade more than the British and French restrictions. The Embargo hurt New England merchants severely (at least those who did not violate it). And by the end of the War of 1812, British warships had nearly swept the American merchant fleet from the oceans. British and European shippers took over American commerce all over the world, particularly in Latin America. Furthermore, the Treaty of Ghent that ended the War of 1812 did not include any provisions to protect American neutral rights on the high seas in the event of any future general wars. The main support for war with Britain did *not* come from the urban commercial-creditor groups in the Northeast or from their Federalist spokesmen.

Nevertheless, British interference with American shipping did play a key role in bringing on the War of 1812. It angered most Americans and intensified Anglophobia (even among many Federalists). Though farmers and planters did not particularly care about shipping profits, many of them (particularly in the South) realized that their prosperity was affected by foreign markets for their cotton, tobacco, and wheat. More specifically, from 1808 to 1812 American agriculture suffered depression and hard times. Seeking an explanation for their economic difficulties, many farmers and planters blamed the British commercial obstructions. Even more important was the nationalistic response to British actions. The United States had won its independence only recently. British and French obstructions struck at the pride, dignity, and honor of the new nation. Assaults on American ships, lives, and flag aroused patriotic emotions. Patriots and partisans determined to defend the American republic (and the Republican Party) against monarchist challenges from the English and French abroad and from the Federalists at home. Such feelings were at least as important in leading to war as any detached calculations of self-interest or national interest. France gave the United States almost as much cause for war as Britain did, but the habit of Anglophobia in the South and West made their chauvinistic responses to British policies particularly belligerent. That was especially true when those responses coincided with sectional ambitions.

EXPANSIONIST AMBITIONS

The Twelfth Congress, elected in 1810, brought to the fore a group of Republican congressmen, largely from rural constituencies in the South and West, who played leading roles in the decision for war. The most vociferous of these "War Hawks" were from the Northwest, the West, and the South. They included, among others, John A. Harper of New Hampshire; Peter B. Porter from western New York; Henry Clay and Richard M. Johnson of Kentucky; Felix Grundy of Tennessee; John C. Calhoun, William Lowndes, and Langdon Cheves of South Carolina; and George M. Troup of Georgia. The circumstances behind the election of those and other War Hawks varied widely. Some had no real opposition. Personalities and local and state issues were decisive in some races. Few if any of the contests turned clearly on foreign policy considerations. Nevertheless, the War Hawks played key roles in the congressional decision for war in 1812. The Federalists representing urban, commercial, and creditor interests in the Northeast generally opposed economic coercion and war, while the most vigorous leadership for war came from Republican representatives of the agricultural West and South.

Some of the more important reasons for the attitudes of Republicans toward Britain have already been suggested: their long-time Anglophobia; their tendency to blame the agricultural depression on British trade restrictions; their chauvinistic responses to impressment, seizure of ships, and challenges to American pride and honor. Without impressment and the Orders-in-Council the congressmen from the South and West would not have been for war. In addition, however, they and their constituents were angered by British policies (or alleged policies) on the North American continent. Part of the support for war grew out of the determination to punish Britain, guard agrarian interests, and satisfy agrarian ambitions through the conquest of Britain's Canada to the north and its Spanish ally's Florida to the south. Fundamentally the sectional alliance between the South and West, both agrarian and Republican and moved partly by the desire for territorial expansion, accomplished the declaration of war on Britain.

Many in the South and Southwest had long wanted Spanish Florida. Some lusted for farmlands there. More were attracted because it controlled the mouths of southern rivers useful for getting products to the sea and thence to markets. Spain's failure to maintain effective control there made it a refuge for renegade whites, blacks, and Indians, whose occasional forays across the border endangered life and property. National security might benefit by eliminating a European state from that border.

To the north, interest in Canada predated American independence. Though land speculators like Peter Porter were attracted, the "land-hunger" explanation for American expansionist interest in Canada has long been discredited. More important, fur traders and farmers welcomed Canada as an outlet to the sea by way of the St. Lawrence River. American fur traders hoped to eliminate British competitors. Increased national security to be obtained by eliminating powerful Britain from America's borders affected the thinking of some. Conquest of Canada might be the easiest way to wage war against Britain in retaliation for its violation of neutral rights on the high seas. And of immediate concern for Westerners was the Indian menace that they blamed on the British in Canada. An exceptionally talented Shawnee, Tecumseh, and his half brother, the Prophet, energetically organized western Indians to block further white encroachments. Westerners were easily convinced that the British encouraged and armed the Indians. The problem reached a crisis in the Battle of Tippecanoe on November 7, 1811, between American military forces under William Henry Harrison and Indians from Prophet's Town in Indiana. Most frontiersmen were convinced that driving the British

out of Canada would end the Indian difficulty. Furthermore, many Westerners thought the task would not be very difficult. Henry Clay once
boasted that "the militia of Kentucky are alone competent to place
Montreal and Upper Canada at your feet."

In summary, the War of 1812 was a product of both external and internal influences, and within the United States both commercial and agrarian considerations were involved. Externally, British and French interference with American ships, cargoes, and seamen aroused American
hostility on both economic and patriotic grounds. The belief that Britain
incited Indians against settlers in the West further aroused war sentiment. At the same time, British preoccupation with war in Europe invited
the hope that the United States might be able to triumph against that
great power. On the domestic scene a variety of circumstances, including
economic self-interest, led Federalist commercial interests in the Northeast to favor peace with Britain at almost any price. On the other hand,
Republicans from the agricultural South and West were angered by in-
sults to the national honor at the hands of the European belligerents.
They blamed the agricultural depression on British trade restrictions.
And they hoped that conquest of Canada and Florida might satisfy agrarian desires and solve the Indian problem. In the war message that
James Madison of Virginia reluctantly submitted to Congress on June 1,
1812, the President cited both maritime and continental grievances
against the British. The vote (79 to 49 in the House and 19 to 13 in the
Senate) was the closest war vote in American history. While there were
individual exceptions in the voting patterns, the decision for war was
accomplished largely by the sectional alliance between the agricultural
South and West working through the Republican Party. The Federalist
stronghold in the urban and commercial Northeast tended to oppose
the decision.

WAR AND PEACE

In military terms, America's performance in the War of 1812 fell far
short of the more optimistic expectations and was inadequate for the
goals ostensibly sought in the war. There were bold plans for a three-
pronged invasion of Canada. Some American warships won spectacular
individual victories on the high seas. By the end of the war the United
States controlled key northern lakes. General Andrew Jackson won an
impressive victory over Britain's finest troops at New Orleans after the
peace treaty was signed. And the United States did avoid defeat at the
hands of the world's most powerful state.

Nevertheless, for the most part the United States was strikingly ineffective militarily and was fortunate to emerge with a draw. The attempted invasions of Canada failed. The plans to take Florida accom-

plished little. By the end of the war the American Navy and merchant fleet were swept from the seas. And the British even captured and burned the nation's capital and sent the President and his household scurrying for safety.

The Treaty of Ghent, signed December 24, 1814, ended the war, but it gave the United States none of the objectives sought in the conflagration. It simply restored the status quo ante bellum. The United States won no assurances for the protection of neutral rights in the event of any future general war. The treaty did not mention impressment. The United States did not get Canada or any part of it. Nor did it get Florida in that treaty. The only territory obtained by the United States during the war was Mobile, Alabama in West Florida, taken from the Spanish by American troops under General James Wilkinson.

Part of the explanation for the failure must be found in the power of America's adversary. Britain was handicapped by the priorities of the war in Europe, the vast distances involved, and by the lack of enthusiasm in Britain for the war. Furthermore, England's rapidly growing industry was beginning to make its mercantilism obsolete and hint at the triumph of laissez-faire in Victorian England later. A generation passed before Britain abandoned its Corn Laws, but premonitions of the transition could be seen in British acceptance of the Treaty of Ghent. In that agreement Britain, in effect, attached greater importance to expanding markets in America for its manufactured products than it did to the mercantilistic needs of England's traders. Nevertheless, Britain was a formidable adversary. Were it not for circumstances within Britain and Europe, the United States might have fared even less well than it did in the peace settlement.

In addition, part of the explanation for America's ineffectiveness may be found in conditions within the United States. American military preparations were inadequate before and during the war. Many of the military leaders were relics from the American Revolution. They had not been particularly able in the earlier contest, and they had not improved with age. The regular army had fewer than 7,000 men when war was declared, and most of them were not available for use in Canada. State militia were badly trained, equipped, and led. And contrary to predictions, few (even in Kentucky) were eager to volunteer for military service. The Navy was better prepared than the Army, but it had to battle the most powerful fleet in the world. And even during the war Congress did not provide adequate financial support for the forces.

Another important and related internal explanation for America's failure lay in divided public opinion. Congress and the American people were strikingly unenthusiastic about war. Opposition to war from Federalists, especially in commercial New England, was particularly serious. State governments in New England openly discouraged enlistments in the regular army. Governors of Massachusetts and Connecticut refused to allow federal use of their state militias. New England banks were among the richest in the nation, but their Federalist managers loaned more to the English during the war than to the United States government. So many New England shippers continued to trade with England that Britain did not even bother to blockade New England until 1814. The antiwar sentiment from Federalist-commercial New England culminated with the Hartford Convention in 1814, attended by representatives from Massachusetts, Connecticut, and Rhode Island. The delegates denounced the war and Madison's administration. The Convention urged adoption of amendments to the Constitution designed to protect sectional interests and states' rights. Its proposals reached Washington just as news of the peace treaty and Jackson's victory at New Orleans arrived. That coincidence and its earlier antiwar activities helped provide the *coup de grâce* for the Federalist Party.

If the sectional disaffection had been limited only to the Northeast, however, it would have been less serious than it was. The declaration of war in June, 1812, had been accomplished basically by the sectional alliance between the planter South and the farming West. But the alliance then promptly fell apart. The South would not help the North invade Canada. Even President Madison and his Secretary of State James Monroe (both Southerners from Virginia) were not enthusiastic about the conquest of Canada. At the same time, the North and West would not help in Florida. Throughout American history, continental territorial expansion was possible only when the South and West worked together to accomplish their goals. When that sectional alliance temporarily broke down during the War of 1812 (and with New England unwilling to help either section), both sections failed to get what they wanted.

The War of 1812 did, however, have certain consequences, many of them unintended. It ended Indian difficulties for a time. It paved the way for the annexation of Florida later. It confirmed America's independence of Britain. It aroused American nationalism. It helped kill the Federalist Party. And, ironically, it triggered the industrial revolution in the United States that eventually triumphed over the agricultural society that Jefferson, Madison, and their fellow Republicans represented in both domestic and foreign affairs.

SUPPLEMENTARY READINGS

Adams, Henry. *History of the United States during the Administrations of Jefferson and Madison.* 9 vols. New York: Charles Scribner's Sons, 1889–1898.

Brant, Irving. *James Madison.* 6 vols. Indianapolis: Bobbs-Merrill Co., Inc., 1941–1961.

Brown, Roger H.   *The Republic in Peril, 1812.* New York: Columbia University Press, 1964.

Burt, Alfred L.   *The United States, Great Britain, and British North America: From the Revolution to the Establishment of Peace after the War of 1812.* New Haven, Conn.: Yale University Press, 1940.

Coles, Harry.   *The War of 1812.* Chicago: University of Chicago Press, 1965.

Dangerfield, George.   *The Era of Good Feelings.* New York: Harcourt, Brace & Co., 1952.

Engelmann, F. L.   *The Peace of Christmas Eve.* New York: Harcourt, Brace & Co., 1962.

Horsman, Reginald.   *The Causes of the War of 1812.* Philadelphia: University of Pennsylvania Press, 1962.

Mayo, Bernard.   *Henry Clay: Spokesman of the New West.* Boston: Houghton Mifflin Co., 1937.

Perkins, Bradford.   *Prologue to War: England and the United States, 1805–1812.* Berkeley: University of California Press, 1963.

Pratt, Julius W.   *Expansionists of 1812.* New York: Macmillan Co., 1925.

Sapio, Victor A.   *Pennsylvania and the War of 1812.* Lexington: University Press of Kentucky, 1970.

Sears, Louis M.   *Jefferson and the Embargo.* Durham, N.C.: Duke University Press, 1927.

White, Patrick C. T.   *A Nation on Trial: America and the War of 1812.* New York: John Wiley & Sons, Inc., 1965.

Zimmerman, James F.   *Impressment of American Seamen.* New York: Columbia University Press, 1925.

PART II

Manifest Destiny
1816–1860

9

Conservatism and order in a world of change: External influences on American foreign relations, 1816–1860

From the close of the Napoleonic Era until the Crimean War in 1854, international relations in Europe were unusually peaceful. Even the Crimean War did not become a world war. In those decades Latin America successfully completed revolutions and struggled less successfully with the problems of independence. The combination of stability in Europe and independence in Latin America made it relatively easy for the United States to guard its security and continue its expansion.

EUROPE

During the forty-five years after the final defeat of Napoleon in 1815, many dynamic ideas and influences pointed to far-reaching changes in Europe and the world. Liberalism, with its origins in the Enlightenment, the French Revolution, and the Industrial Revolution, was one of those ideological forces for change. Nationalism, a child of the French Revolution and of the Age of Napoleon, was another. The Industrial Revolution had started in England in the eighteenth century and spread to Western Europe and the United States in the first decades of the nineteenth. It caused quiet but revolutionary economic, social, political, intellectual, and international changes whose effects have been felt the world over.

Nevertheless, from 1815 to 1860 those who wanted to restore the old order, resist change, and promote stability were even more powerful. In the Age of Metternich, Austria and Russia successfully blocked liberalism and nationalism. They were scarcely touched by the Industrial Revolution. In the West, France appeared restrained and moderate as it regained its place in the European community. Preoccupation with postwar problems and domestic markets encouraged continental Europe to look inward more than abroad. Great Britain commanded industrial, financial, and naval supremacy, and it slowly turned toward liberalism and laissez-faire. At the same time, it wanted peace and stability so it could import raw materials and profitably export its industrial products and capital.

The Congress of Vienna in 1814–1815 drafted a general blueprint for the period. Czar Alexander I of Russia, Lord Castlereagh of Britain, and Talleyrand of France all played leading roles there. But Prince Metternich of Austria was the dominant figure. The statesmen at Vienna determined to prevent France from threatening European peace and security in the future. But they did not destroy either France or the old multistate system. Instead, they tried to restore the old order and to guard it against challenges from inside and out. To that end, the statesmen at Vienna restored legitimate monarchs to European thrones. They compensated the victorious powers with territorial concessions. And they created the Quadruple Alliance to safeguard the arrangements. That Alliance originally consisted of Austria, Russia, Prussia, and Great Britain. France was added in 1818. The parties to the Quadruple Alliance (or Concert of Europe) were not wholly united on its purposes. Metternich and other continental statesmen wanted it to protect peace and security against any French revival. But they also wanted to guard the Vienna settlement against revolutionary challenges from the heresies of liberalism and nationalism. Britain, on the other hand, objected to intervention in the internal affairs of European states. Britain's Castlereagh wanted the Concert of Europe limited to peace-keeping functions in Europe. Nevertheless, conferences at Troppau-Laibach (1821) and Verona (1822) authorized Austrian suppression of uprisings in Italy and comparable French actions later in Spain. Those patterns displeased Britain. Furthermore, Britain was never comfortable when committed too rigidly on continental matters. Consequently, under George Canning it withdrew from the Concert of Europe in 1822. Though the formal organization ended in the 1820's, the continental powers continued to contribute to European stability and order. And in the United States a British suggestion and President Monroe's exaggerated fear of Quadruple Alliance intervention in Latin America led to the Monroe Doctrine in 1823.

Britain's withdrawal from the Concert of Europe did not end its concern about developments in Europe. Independence, not literal "isolation," characterized British foreign policies in the middle half of the nineteenth century. British balance-of-power policies helped prevent any state or group of states from challenging the equilibrium that prevailed in Europe and elsewhere. Britain particularly determined to keep the Netherlands, Belgium, and Luxembourg across the English Channel free from domination by any major continental state. But it did not limit its balance-of-power policies to the Low Countries, and the system worked impressively well.

Many variables account for the success of the balance of power. National power was widely distributed among several European countries, so that no state had enough power to overcome the power of those likely to combine against it. It was a fluid and flexible system, with all major European states and many lesser ones playing roles in its operation. Particularly important, however, was the diplomacy and power of Great Britain.

With the defeat of France in 1815, Great Britain emerged as the most powerful state in the world. It was blessed with political stability and able leadership at home. It had the most productive industrial system in the world. London was the banking and financial center of the world. Britain had the world's greatest merchant fleet. The Royal Navy ruled the oceans. The British Empire was smaller than it had been and not so large as it was to be, but it was still great and wealthy. Britain, its leaders, its diplomats, its seamen, and its businessmen commanded unequaled prestige everywhere. No government took any significant move in international affairs without considering possible British reactions. Not without cause has the nineteenth century been called the British century, or the absence of general world wars between 1815 and 1914 been referred to as the "Pax Britannica." Britain contributed much to the stability and order that prevailed.

Like all states, Britain shaped its policies primarily to serve its own self-interest. Ambitious states were often frustrated by Britain, as Russia was in the Crimean War. The United States objected to British activity in Oregon, Texas, California, and Central America. Nevertheless, many countries (including the United States) were as secure as they were in the nineteenth century partly because of Britain's balance-of-power policies.

Britain's influence on world affairs was not limited to the balance of power. It also encouraged free trade, discouraged European colonial expansion, and opposed the African slave trade. Britain in the nineteenth century became the leading advocate of the removal of economic barriers to the free flow of goods and capital in international affairs. Britain's laissez-faire policies corresponded to the growing skepticism about mercantilism and to the increasing acceptance of the economic theories of Adam Smith. But British leaders found Smith's theories so appealing partly because they suited British interests. England's industrial and financial supremacy assured its competitive advantage if other states did not discriminate with tariffs and other restrictions. Continental European states generally were less efficient in trade, manufacturing, and finance and did not wholly share Britain's free-trade enthusiasm. American manufacturers needed tariff protection to compete with British producers even in their own home markets. Their self-interest combined with nationalism in the Era of Good Feelings to build high protective tariffs in the United States for fifteen years following the War of 1812. But commercial farmers and planters in the United States were almost as dependent upon world markets for their agricultural products as British manufacturers were for their capital and industrial exports. Consequently, from 1833 until the Civil War the United States, like Britain, followed low-tariff policies. The United States tariff policies, however, grew out of its agricultural economy, while Britain's resulted from its efficient industrial system.

European preoccupation with domestic and continental matters inhibited overseas activity from 1816 to 1860. In addition, British power also helped check European expansion in Africa, Asia, and Latin America. For a variety of reasons, including Britain's influence, there was not as much European territorial expansion in the middle decades of the nineteenth century as there had been earlier or as there was to be later. That pattern worked to America's security and territorial advantage in the Western Hemisphere.

Britain also became the leading opponent of slavery and the international slave trade in the nineteenth century. Most countries cooperated with Britain's crusade. The United States, however, was still sensitive about any possible British interference with American shipping (even in the slave trade), and the South was defensive about any interference with slavery. Consequently, despite strong antislavery agitation by many Americans, the United States did more than any other country to reduce the effectiveness of Britain's crusade against the African slave trade.

In sum, European international developments from 1816 to 1860 were characterized by much stability and peace, and by very little colonial expansion. Those circumstances made it relatively easy for the United States to guard its national security, concentrate on internal development, expand westward, and increase its foreign trade. The United States was not secure primarily because of its military forces; they were quite weak. The United States was not secure because its national power was so great; several European states were more powerful. The United States was not secure because of its moral pronouncements such as the Monroe Doctrine; they were words that could not check any major European state at any time. The United States was as secure as it was largely because of the balance of power that prevailed among the major

European countries. Furthermore, the European balance of power and the lack of colonial expansion enhanced America's opportunities for territorial expansion. If the balance of power had not inhibited European states, and if Britain had not attached such great importance to the American market for its capital and manufactured products, the United States might have encountered much more effective European opposition to its westward territorial expansion.

LATIN AMERICA

Until the Napoleonic Era Spain controlled most of Latin America, Portugal governed Brazil, and Britain, France, the Netherlands, and other European states had much smaller holdings. Under the Bourbon monarchs Spain had managed to keep its vast American empire only with much difficulty. Merchants from many countries (particularly from Britain and the United States) had aggressively expanded their trade with Spain's American colonies. But the Napoleonic Wars opened the door to independence.

In 1808 Napoleon placed his brother, Joseph Bonaparte, on the Spanish throne. Spain's colonies generally refused to acknowledge the new ruler. Around 1810 they organized local revolutionary juntas that took over political power in the New World. Ostensibly the juntas did not seek independence. They generally professed loyalty to Ferdinand VII of Spain. Nevertheless, Spanish control ended temporarily and the possibility of independence (like that already won by the United States) appealed to many in Latin America. By 1813 British military forces under the Duke of Wellington ousted Joseph Bonaparte from power, and Ferdinand VII resumed the throne. Latin Americans, however, found Ferdinand harsh and oppressive. Their brief taste of independence made them restive under European rule of any sort. Consequently, between 1816 and 1825 the struggle for independence went forward aggressively. In Argentina, Chile, and to a degree in Peru, the leading figure in the revolution was José de San Martín. In Venezuela, Colombia, Ecuador, and Peru, Simon Bolivar led the drive for independence. After earlier failures under Hidalgo and Morelos, Mexico finally won its independence in 1821 under Augustín de Iturbide. By 1825 the last of Spanish troops were ousted from South America. Spain retained Cuba and Puerto Rico in the Caribbean for another three quarters of a century, but its great empire in the Western Hemisphere was largely ended.

In Brazil the patterns were different. Napoleon's invasion of Portugal in 1807 forced King John VI and the royal family to flee to their American colony. The King returned to Portugal in 1821 but left his son, Dom Pedro, as regent in Brazil. Under his leadership Brazil declared independence in 1822, but unlike the rest of South America it remained a monarchy. Pedro I ruled until forced to abdicate in 1831. His five-year-old son then became King Dom Pedro II. After a regency, Dom Pedro II reigned until ousted in 1889.

Though most of Latin America successfully threw off European control, it was less successful in building orderly democracy after independence. A variety of circumstances complicated the task: the continued control by the landed aristocracy during and after the revolutions; social and economic inequities, with the few having much and the many enduring extreme poverty; widespread illiteracy; inhospitable climate; concentrated Indian populations in some countries; and authoritarian traditions and institutions. Most Latin-American states in the nineteenth century alternated between authoritarian regimes (generally military dictatorships) on the one hand, and revolutions that sometimes verged on anarchy on the other hand. Order generally was obtained at the price of freedom, while democracy often was accompanied by chaos and disorder.

In a different era the Latin-American difficulties might have brought sweeping European intervention. Indeed, Britain and France, among others, did intervene from time to time in Argentina, Mexico, and elsewhere. But Latin America was not carved into European colonies in the nineteenth century, and that was not because of the Monroe Doctrine. The weakness of Latin-American states and the instability of their governments, however, encouraged outside influences. In South America the most powerful outside state in the nineteenth century was Great Britain. It did not establish colonies in South America, but it dominated trade and finance. In North America the United States was the main expansionist power (particularly in Mexico), and by the middle of the century United States power almost approached that of Britain in Central America. The balance of power and anti-imperialism in Europe combined with weakness and instability in Latin America provided external circumstances highly favorable for United States territorial and commercial expansion in Latin America. It was not entirely surprising that by the mid-nineteenth century Mexico had lost about two thirds of its original area to the United States.

SUPPLEMENTARY READINGS

Albrecht-Carrié, René. *A Diplomatic History of Europe Since the Congress of Vienna.* New York: Harper & Bros., 1958.

Artz, Frederick B. *Reaction and Revolution, 1814–1832.* New York: Harper & Bros., 1934.

Binkley, Robert C. *Realism and Nationalism, 1852–1871.* New York: Harper & Bros., 1935.

Langer, William L. *Political and Social Upheaval, 1832–1852.* New York: Harper & Row, 1969.

Madariaga, Salvador de. *The Fall of the Spanish American Empire.* London: Hollis & Carter, Ltd., 1947.

Mowat, Robert B. *A History of European Diplomacy, 1815–1914.* London: E. Arnold, 1922.

Nicolson, Harold G. *The Congress of Vienna: A Study in Allied Unity, 1815–1822.* New York: Harcourt, Brace & Co., 1946.

Schenck, Hans G. *The Aftermath of the Napoleonic Wars: The Concert of Europe, An Experiment.* New York: Oxford University Press, 1947.

Seton-Watson, Robert W. *Britain in Europe, 1789–1914: A Survey of Foreign Policy.* Cambridge: University Press, Inc., 1937.

10

Agriculture, nationalism, and sectionalism: Domestic influences on American foreign relations, 1816–1860

During the four and one-half decades that preceded the Civil War, many of the earlier domestic characteristics of the United States remained little changed. As always, however, the new intermixed with the old.

THE PEOPLE

When the War of 1812 ended there were just over eight million Americans. By the time Lincoln was elected in 1860, the population had increased 400 percent, to nearly thirty-two million. If one excluded their overseas colonies, neither Britain nor France equaled America's population by 1860. America's role in world affairs was less than its population might suggest. Nevertheless, the population growth relative to that of European states suggested America's increasing importance in world affairs, particularly in the Western Hemisphere. Many Irish and Germans immigrated in the period, but Anglo-Americans remained dominant. Slavery was more widely established in the South than ever before. By 1860 there were over four million blacks in the United States, most of them slaves.

The westward movement continued at an accelerated rate. By 1860 the frontier line ran from Texas through eastern Kansas and Nebraska to central Minnesota. There were also substantial settlements on the far western coast. In 1816 there were nineteen states in the union; by 1860 there were thirty-three. They included all of the states east of the Missouri River as well as Texas, California, and Oregon. The vast area between the Missouri to the east and California and Oregon to the west, however, was little settled by whites.

The United States continued to be overwhelmingly rural. About 80 percent of the people lived on farms or in small towns in 1860. Urban population increased at three times the rate of rural growth, but the great era of American cities came after the Civil War.

Reflecting ethnic patterns, most Americans before the Civil War were Protestant in their religious affiliations. In general, the foreign policy views in religious groups tended to correspond to the dominant attitudes in the sections of the country in which the denomination was strong. For example, New England and the Middle Atlantic states generally opposed the War of 1812 and the Mexican War; religious denominations that were strong in the Northeast (such as Congregationalists, Unitarians, and Quakers) also opposed those wars. In contrast, the South and West supported the War of 1812 and the Mexican War; the denominations strongest in those sections (such as Methodists, Presbyterians, and Baptists) usually supported those wars. As the sectional controversy over slavery intensified and the Civil War approached, denominations whose followings were largely in the North (including Congregationalist, Unitarian, Quaker, and Catholic) united in opposition to the South and slavery. Denominations with substantial followings in both the North and the South (Methodist, Baptist, and Presbyterian) literally split in two on the issue. Southern clergymen had no difficulty finding biblical sanction for slavery, and northern clergymen frequently cited the Bible to demonstrate that slavery was contrary to Christianity. Religious views frequently intensified existing attitudes and emotions on foreign affairs.

THE ECONOMY

The American economy from 1816 to 1860 continued to be predominantly agricultural, and farmer-agrarian groups continued to dominate economic, political, and foreign policies. Cotton production, however, was much greater and more widespread than it had been, and spokesmen for southern cotton planters became more powerful in agrarian leadership. The sectional alliance between the planting South and the farming West within the Democratic Party controlled the federal government most of the time and was responsible for low tariffs and territorial expansion. Differences on the issue of extending slavery into western territories gradually divided the South and West and eventually destroyed the sectional alliance in the 1850's. That ended agrarian political dominance, but it did not occur until the very end of that period.

American foreign trade generally increased despite the inability of the shipping-commercial group to regain the political dominance it had had in the Federalist Era. Imports continued to consist largely of manufactured products. Most exports continued to be agricultural products. With the growth of the textile industry in Europe, however, and with the spread of southern cotton production, raw cotton increasingly dominated American exports. Cotton was the largest single export item between 1816 and 1860, generally accounting for more than half of the dollar value of all sales abroad each year. With Latin-American independence, and with the ports of China and Japan gradually opened, American traders became increasingly active in those areas. Nevertheless, Britain and Europe continued to receive most of America's exports and provide most of its imports. The United States still had an unfavorable balance of trade. Most American commerce continued to be carried by its own large and efficient merchant fleet. Particularly colorful were the beautiful clipper ships that outraced most competitors in the 1840's and 1850's. Despite the continued importance of the American merchant fleet, however, in the 1850's it began to decline. Profits from shipping were often less than other investments provided. New capital was not attracted to commerce as it had been, and in some cases entrepreneurs shifted their investments to railroads, industry, or land.

The United States continued weak industrially. The annual value of American manufactured products increased 800 percent from 1816 to 1860. But even in 1860 only about 4 percent of Americans were employed in manufacturing, and the total value of manufactured products was considerably less each year than the output in England or even in France.

Between 1816 and 1860 the United States continued to have a debtor balance in international finance, and as before, most of the foreign capital came from Britain. The federal government borrowed little, but state governments borrowed heavily from foreign creditors in the 1820's and 1830's to construct canals and finance state banks. Defaults by many state governments after the Panic of 1837 hurt the American credit rating for a time. In the 1840's and 1850's little foreign capital went to governments, and most was invested in business enterprises, including railroads. Americans with capital generally invested at home rather than abroad.

Despite slumps in 1819, 1837, and 1858, a central theme in American economic development from 1816 to 1860 was expansion. Farm production expanded; foreign trade increased; industrial production grew; and canals, river steamboats, and railroads kept pace with the rest of the economy. That economic growth partially accounted for America's expansion in foreign affairs at the same time.

POLITICAL PATTERNS

For purposes of analysis American political history from 1816 to 1860 may be divided into three chronological periods. The first was the Era of Good Feelings from 1816 to 1827. The period was not characterized by an absence of political controversy. It was an Era of Good Feelings largely in the sense that there was no battling between separate political parties. There was only one national party, the old Jeffersonian Republican Party, and political battles occurred within its framework. The Federalist Party died after its defeat in 1816. The merchants, traders, creditors, and big planters who had worked through it now generally became Republicans. That remaining party included (and attempted to represent and serve) both the farmer-agrarian and the shipping-commercial group.

The Era of Good Feelings was more conservative politically than the earlier Jeffersonian Era. The conservatism was due partly to the absorption of so many former Federalists by the Republican Party and to the efforts of Republican leaders to please both merchants and agrarians. The influence of both factions was symbolized by the two men who were President during the period: James Monroe of Virginia (1817–1825), an agrarian who had no difficulty acting like a moderate Federalist; and John Quincy Adams of Massachusetts (1825–1829), whose New England antecedents did not prevent him from favoring westward territorial expansion. The influence of both merchants and agrarians manifested itself in foreign affairs, notably in the Monroe Doctrine.

With the breakdown of the one-party system and the emergence of a new two-party arrangement late in the 1820's, a new period in American political development began that lasted until the 1850's. One of the parties that emerged was the National Republican Party, soon to be named the Whig Party. It was the political descendant of the Federalist Party and the parent of the present Republican Party. The Whig Party, like the earlier Federalist Party, drew strong support from merchants and shippers, from bankers and creditors, and from the wealthiest of southern planters. Manufacturers generally were Whigs, though they were weaker than they were to be in the later Republican Party. The Whig Party won more support from western farmers than the Federalist Party had, particularly from those who followed Henry Clay's leadership. It tended to favor protective tariffs, a national bank, federal aid for internal improvements, and fair treatment of the Indians. It opposed westward territorial expansion. Its most famous leaders were Henry Clay of Kentucky and Daniel Webster of Massachusetts, though both of them failed in their several efforts to win the Presidency. Only two Whigs were ever elected President. Both of them were Westerners; both were military heroes; and both died in office. William Henry Harrison of Tippecanoe fame was elected in 1840 and died of pneumonia a month after he was inaugurated in 1841. The Vice President who replaced him, John Tyler, was really a southern Democrat in background and convictions. General Zachary Taylor was elected on the Whig ticket in 1848 but died in 1850 and was replaced by Millard Fillmore.

The other party that emerged in 1828 was the Democratic Party. It was the successor to Jefferson's Republican Party and has a continuous history to the present. The Democratic Party drew its main support from farmers everywhere, from the smaller southern planters, and from small business entrepreneurs. It won more support from urban workers than Jefferson's party had, but it was predominantly a political alliance between the farming West and the planting South. It generally opposed protective tariffs and federal aid for internal improvements. It favored forcing Indians out of land desired by whites and generally wanted to make it easy for farmers to get land. It enthusiastically urged westward territorial expansion. Among its more famous leaders before 1860 were Andrew Jackson of Tennessee, John C. Calhoun of South Carolina, Thomas Hart Benton of Missouri, and Stephen A. Douglas of Illinois. Except for the two brief Whig interludes, all American presidents were Democrats from 1829 when Jackson was inaugurated until 1861 when Lincoln replaced Buchanan. Andrew Jackson served two terms from 1829 to 1837. His protégé, Martin Van Buren of New York, floundered on the economic panic that ruined his administration from 1837 to 1841. James K. Polk served only one term (1845–1849) but successfully accomplished his goals of tariff reduction and territorial expansion. The handsome but ineffective Franklin Pierce of New Hampshire served from 1853 to 1857. The bachelor President, James Buchanan, after a long political and diplomatic career, served from 1857 to 1861, as the sectional controversy moved toward Civil War.

The 1850's inaugurated a new phase in party history. The Democratic Party continued but was divided and weakened by the slavery controversy and by its growing identification with the South and slavery. The Whig Party split and died in the wake of the Kansas-Nebraska controversy. It was replaced by a new Republican Party in 1854. Unlike its predecessors, the Republican Party drew all of its support from the North and none from the South. It was backed by merchants and shippers, though they were not as powerful as they had been in either the Federalist or Whig parties. More important were financial and creditor groups, the rising industrial and manufacturing classes, and thriving railroad entrepreneurs. More than its predecessors, the Republican Party had substantial support from middle western farmers. Its economic programs were similar to those of the earlier Federalists and Whigs, but in the 1850's it was fundamentally a sectional alliance between the urban-business Northeast and the agricultural Middle West, bound together by common opposition to extension of slavery in the territories.

It first ran a candidate for president in 1856 and won that office with the election of Lincoln in 1860.

IDEOLOGICAL PATTERNS

Many ideological currents could be identified in the United States between 1816 and 1860. Three may be singled out for particular attention: nationalism, sympathy for foreign revolutions, and Manifest Destiny.

Nationalism is the complex body of ideas, emotions, and interests developed around the modern state or nation. It includes feelings of patriotism, loyalty, and pride in one's country, and a willingness to sacrifice (even life itself) for one's country. It places loyalty to state above other secular loyalties. It includes symbols such as the flag, rituals such as the pledge of allegiance, and a glorification of early heroes. Before the War of 1812 localism and sectionalism were more prevalent than nationalism, but the roots of American nationalism were developing even before the War of 1812 and they flowered in the Era of Good Feelings and the Age of Jackson. Americans quickly forgot the many military and naval defeats in the war. They glorified and glamorized the few victories the United States managed to win. During the war, "Yankee Doodle" became almost an official national anthem, and "Uncle Sam" was already emerging as the cartoonists' personification of the United States. The war even provided what eventually became the national anthem, "The Star-Spangled Banner," composed by Francis Scott Key while aboard a British ship during the bombardment of Fort Mc-Henry near Baltimore.

The Era of Good Feelings was characterized by a high degree of nationalism. The protective Tariff of 1816, the Second Bank of the United States chartered in the same year, Henry Clay's "American System," the drive to improve domestic transportation facilities, were all expressions of and forces for nationalism. So were Supreme Court decisions under Chief Justice John Marshall, the poetry of Walt Whitman, and the histories by George Bancroft. The fiery warrior, Andrew Jackson, appealed to and aroused spirited nationalism both through his proud military feats and by his presidential opposition to the Bank and to nullification.

Nationalism again had dual effects on American foreign policy attitudes. It provided an emotional and ideological basis for isolationism as Americans tried to preserve the purity and glory of America from the evil and corruption of European monarchies. It also encouraged expansionism and Manifest Destiny. Americans felt obliged to spread the glories of their freedoms to less fortunate peoples elsewhere, either by the power of example or through military force. Sectionalism and localism were also present and grew more intense in the 1840's and

1850's. What passed for nationalism was often a generalizing of sectional interests and ambitions. Nevertheless, nationalism was a powerful domestic influence of foreign affairs.

Americans generally sympathized with foreign revolutions from 1816 to 1860. The United States had won its independence by revolution. It was easy to favor revolutions that were directed against European monarchies. Insofar as revolutions abroad weakened or immobilized other states, they might enhance the relative power and security of the United States. Sometimes foreign revolts led to American territorial expansion, as they did in West Florida in 1810 and in Texas later. Since change was expected to be away from the old order and toward the democracy and freedom that America represented, many believed revolutions would lead to a more desirable world.

Sympathy for foreign revolutions before 1860 did not include positive United States government assistance to revolutionaries. Groups and individuals might encourage or assist revolts, but the role of the government was limited to example, sympathetic pronouncements by individual leaders, and to prompt diplomatic recognition.

Latin-American wars for independence had many appealing qualities for Americans: they were against Old World domination; they were against monarchies; they were not generally class struggles; and they opened opportunities for commercial and territorial expansion by the United States. The United States government maintained official neutrality, but many individual Americans openly sympathized. In 1810–1811 the United States sent more consular agents into Latin America, and trade there increased. Henry Clay vigorously urged diplomatic recognition as early as 1818, but it was delayed until independence was clearly established (and until Spain ratified the Adams-Onís Treaty of 1819 that transferred East Florida to the United States). In 1822 the United States recognized Colombia and Mexico. Recognition was accorded Argentina in 1823, Brazil and Central America in 1824, and Peru in 1826. Two of the new governments (Mexico and Brazil) were monarchies at the time.

There were also numerous revolutions in Europe in 1820, 1830, and 1848 that were variously inspired by liberalism, nationalism, or both. Most Americans gave little attention to the upheavals, but many approved. Two of the revolts aroused much American enthusiasm: the Greek struggle against the Turks in the 1820's and the Hungarian uprising against Austria beginning in 1848. A few Americans participated in the Greek revolt, and many greeted Louis Kossuth enthusiastically when he toured the United States seeking financial support. Nevertheless, the United States government did not become involved, and popular enthusiasm was not sufficient to affect the outcome of the uprisings.

Another expression of sympathy for foreign revolutions was the "Young America" movement within the Democratic Party in 1852. It backed Stephen A. Douglas and later Franklin Pierce for President. It contended that the United States had a mission to perform and that the mission could be accomplished by active participation in world affairs. It was particularly sympathetic to European movements for republican self-government and national independence. Kossuth's movement in Hungary won its approval. It did not affect government policies, but it did reveal a widespread American sentiment.

Many conservatives (particularly Whigs) were not optimistic about revolutions abroad. The enthusiasm of others cooled when the results were different than they had been in the United States. Nevertheless, before 1860 most Americans sympathized with foreign revolutions and hoped that through those revolts others would follow the footsteps of the United States to independence and freedom.

Manifest Destiny was a particularly powerful ideological influence on American foreign affairs in the 1840's. It was the belief that the United States was destined, perhaps by a higher power, to spread the blessings of its civilization and democratic institutions westward to the Pacific and to other parts of the world. The phrase was first popularized in 1845 by the journalist, John L. O'Sullivan, but the attitudes covered by it existed long before.

Professor Frederick Merk has distinguished between Manifest Destiny and Mission. He viewed Manifest Destiny as selfish, acquisitive, aggressive, parochial, and atypical of American ideals and practices. In contrast he saw the concept of Mission as idealistic, self-denying, responsible, compassionate, and a "truer expression" of the American spirit.

Another scholar on the subject, Albert K. Weinberg, made it clear that Manifest Destiny took many different forms over the years. During the American Revolution, when natural-rights ideas were popular, it included the belief that the United States had a natural, God-given right to security and to defensible boundaries. That reasoning was used when the American negotiators pressed successfully for the land between the Appalachians and the Mississippi River in the peace treaty with Britain. Jefferson and others also used the idea at the time of the Louisiana Purchase.

Manifest Destiny also took the form of "geographical predestination" or the quest for "natural boundaries." Geographic predestination took at least three different forms: nearness of a territory (like Cuba); enclosure by the same natural barrier, such as a river, a mountain range, or the ocean; and the existence of a common territorial feature such as a river in a valley. As Weinberg phrased it, "The pragmatic effect of this triple character of the criterion of the natural boundary was all to the advantage of expansionism." For example, in the negotiations ending the American Revolution diplomats contended that the Mississippi River was the more natural boundary than the Appalachian Mountains, even though most Americans lived east of the mountains. Then, in urging approval of the Louisiana Purchase west of the river, expansionists said the Mississippi was really the central feature of the whole Mississippi Valley as far west as the Rocky Mountains. In any event, the mountains were more of a natural boundary than the river. As Americans became interested in California and Oregon, however, it became obvious that the ocean, not the mountains, provided America's natural boundary. And later, similar reasoning was used to urge annexation of Hawaii, and even the Philippines in the western Pacific. If desirable lands lay beyond, "the geographically justified terminus of one expansion movement became the point of departure for a subsequent one."

"The destined use of the soil" also affected Manifest Destiny. God intended the soil to be cultivated, and it should not be left to those who did not use it productively. Such reasoning seemed appropriate in taking lands from Indians, and even from Mexicans in the Southwest and from fur-trading Englishmen in Oregon. Manifest Destiny often called for extending freedom and democracy and for preventing extension of the power of foreign states that Americans believed did not represent freedom and democracy. It was a bit ironic that in the 1840's the United States extended the area of freedom by annexing territories that were then opened to slavery. "True Title" was a variation of Manifest Destiny used when America's legal claim was weaker than that of a competing country, as in much of the Oregon Territory. In justifying efforts to annex all of Mexico in 1848, some defined Manifest Destiny to include the "mission of regeneration of unfortunate people." They believed that the United States had an almost sacred duty to help the unfortunate Mexicans by bringing them into the shrine of American democracy, even if the Mexicans had to be forced in by military conquest. And finally, Manifest Destiny included the idea of "natural growth," the belief that it was as normal and natural for a young nation to grow as it was for a child or a young plant. To frustrate growth would stunt and cripple the healthy nation. That belief was advanced by Young America in 1852, and in the following year by Secretary of State Edward Everett when he urged purchase of the Gadsden Territory.

This brief summary of Manifest Destiny may invite the cynical suspicion that the ideas were no more than conscious rationalizations used to justify seizure of territories desired for selfish reasons. Undoubtedly that was true in individual instances. But if that were all, Manifest Destiny would have been less powerful than it actually was. Many

Americans (particularly in the South and West) sincerely believed those ideas, and the intensity of their beliefs strengthened the expansionist movement. As Professor Weinberg phrased it: "Moral ideology was the partner of self-interest in the intimate alliance of which expansionism was the offspring."

MILITARY FORCES

American land and sea forces dwindled after the War of 1812. The Army was reduced to about 6,000 men, hardly adequate for garrison duty and Indian fighting. State militia deteriorated further in size and quality. The Navy, too, shrank from its wartime levels and was inadequate for even the modest responsibilities assigned to it (protecting trade, apprehending pirates and slave traders, and providing coastal defense).

During the Mexican War from 1846 to 1848 a flood of volunteers from the South and West swelled the Army to nearly 100,000 men. Mexican weakness made the American military task less difficult, and the able professional military officers produced by the Military Academy at West Point provided effective leadership for United States forces. Robert E. Lee, Ulysses S. Grant, Thomas J. Jackson, Joseph E. Johnston, William T. Sherman, and George McClellan were among the many young officers whose combat experience during the Mexican War was valuable training for their greater responsibilities later in the Civil War. The United States did not lose a battle during the Mexican War. But when it ended the Army was reduced to about 10,000 men.

United States armed forces generally proved adequate for the missions assigned to them from 1816 to 1860. Nevertheless, American diplomacy was not backed by military power as great as that commanded by the major European states at that time.

CONCLUSION

The Industrial Revolution and urbanization had not gone far enough before 1860 to alter substantially the domestic influences on American foreign affairs. Agrarians of the South and West working through the Democratic Party provided the dominant domestic influence on foreign affairs, with shipping and trade playing a lesser role. Both groups encouraged American expansion, but of different kinds generally. The dominant agrarians were largely responsible for westward territorial expansion in North America; the commercial groups encouraged trade expansion overseas. The great era of urban industry and finance was still beyond the horizons of the future.

SUPPLEMENTARY READINGS

Bailey, Thomas A.   *The Man in the Street: The Impact of American Public Opinion on Foreign Policy.* New York: Macmillan Co., 1948.

Beard, Charles A.   *The Idea of National Interest: An Analytical Study in American Foreign Policy.* New York: Macmillan Co., 1934.

Binkley, Wilfred E.   *American Political Parties: Their Natural History.* Rev. ed. New York: Alfred A. Knopf, Inc., 1945.

Curti, Merle.   *Peace or War: The American Struggle, 1636–1936.* New York: W. W. Norton & Co., Inc., 1936.

———.   *The Roots of American Loyalty.* New York: Columbia University Press, 1946.

Dangerfield, George.   *The Era of Good Feelings.* New York: Harcourt, Brace & Co., 1952.

Merk, Frederick.   *Manifest Destiny and Mission in American History.* New York: Alfred A. Knopf, Inc., 1963.

Millis, Walter.   *Arms and Men: A Study in American Military History.* New York: G. P. Putnam's Sons, 1956.

Sprout, Harold H. and Sprout, Margaret.   *The Rise of American Naval Power, 1776–1918.* Princeton, N.J.: Princeton University Press, 1939.

Strout, Cushing.   *The American Image of the Old World.* New York: Harper & Row, Publishers, 1963.

Turner, Frederick Jackson.   *Rise of the New West, 1819–1829.* New York: Harper & Bros., 1906.

———.   *The United States, 1830–1850: The Nation and Its Sections.* New York: Henry Holt & Co., Inc., 1935.

Weinberg, Albert K.   *Manifest Destiny: A Study of Nationalist Expansionism in American History.* Baltimore: Johns Hopkins Press, 1935.

Williams, Benjamin H.   *Economic Foreign Policy of the United States.* New York: McGraw-Hill Book Co., 1929.

11

Foreign relations in the Era
of Good Feelings

External conditions affecting American foreign relations from 1816 to 1828 included Spanish weakness and the disintegration of Spain's New World empire. They included the determination by the Concert of Europe to preserve peace, stability, and the Old Order. And they included the power of Great Britain, its balance-of-power policies, and the beginnings of its gradual transition toward laissez-faire, free trade, and anti-imperialism. Within the United States, foreign policies were shaped by a government attempting to serve both agrarian and commercial interests, a pattern symbolized in the White House by Virginia's neo-Federalist James Monroe and by Massachusetts' nationalistic expansionist John Quincy Adams.

More than any other individual, Adams guided American foreign policies during the Era of Good Feelings, first as Secretary of State from 1817 to 1825 and then as President from 1825 to 1829. His experience in foreign affairs began at the age of eleven, when he accompanied his father to France in 1778. While still a boy, John Quincy Adams served as secretary to Francis Dana on his unsuccessful diplomatic mission to Russia. He was his father's secretary during negotiation of the peace treaty with Great Britain ending the American Revolution. After taking time out to get a degree from Harvard and to win admission to the Massachusetts bar, Adams held diplomatic posts in the Netherlands, Russia, England, and elsewhere. He helped negotiate the Treaty of Ghent ending the War of 1812. Scholarly, conscientious, and multi-lingual, Adams was a man of integrity and independence. He won respect from most but rarely inspired warm affection. Like his father, he was too aloof and inflexible for the requirements of practical politics. Like his father, his deficiencies in the political arts inhibited his effectiveness as President. Nevertheless, he was one of America's greatest Secretaries of State.

Many details of American foreign relations during the Era of Good Feelings may be examined under three headings: Anglo-American relations; Spanish-American relations and the Adams-Onís Treaty; and the Monroe Doctrine.

ANGLO-AMERICAN RELATIONS

The United States and Great Britain have never fought against each other since the Treaty of Ghent ended the War of 1812. Great Anglo-American diplomatic accord developed much later, but the Era of Good Feelings provided early portents of that later cooperation.

Friction occurred, of course, and Anglophobia was common among Americans. Continued British mercantilism blocked United States efforts to open British West Indian ports to American traders. Certain enumerated American products could be sold legally in the British West Indies, but only if carried in British ships. John Quincy Adams tried repeatedly to open British colonial ports to American ships. When diplomacy failed, he tried economic coercion by closing American ports to British ships coming from colonies that were not open to United States merchants. By 1822, under pressure from West Indian planters and from British industry, Great Britain was willing to grant limited concessions. That was not enough for Adams. Not content with "half a loaf," he got nothing. His unyielding stand may have resulted from his inflexible temperament and from his tenacious dedication to the trading interests of his native New England. But perhaps, as George Dangerfield suggested in his able study of the Era of Good Feelings, he may have been affected by the beginnings of protectionism emerging from Massachusetts' new "infant industries," an influence that soon added Daniel Webster to the protectionist fold. For its part, the United States in 1816, 1824, 1828, and 1832 irritated British manufacturers and merchants by enacting protective tariffs. American and British interests also conflicted enough in the Oregon Territory to make a boundary settlement there impossible (though not enough to cause either country to force a showdown in the territory).

Despite irritations, however, there were substantial bases for and evidences of developing Anglo-American accord. British industrialists considered the United States a most important market for their products and were determined not to allow minor matters to close it. American merchants considered peace with Britain essential to their prosperity, since Britain was still the leading country in American foreign trade. Various considerations prevented a more serious clash in Oregon, including the still limited agrarian activity there, the restraining influence of shipping-commercial interests on American territorial expansionists, and in England the role of liberal-industrial interests in checking the imperialists. Both Britain and the United States favored the Latin-American wars for independence. Britain welcomed the expanded markets for its industrial products that an independent Latin America provided. American merchants had similar views on trade opportunities there. Independent Latin-American states might be even less dangerous to American security (and less of a barrier to expansionist ambitions) than Spain had been. The Monroe Doctrine did not wholly please Britain. But it grew out of an initial British suggestion and to a degree reflected interests and desires of statesmen and economic groups in both countries.

The improved relations between the United States and Great Britain led to several specific agreements. In 1815 they signed a convention on direct trade between each other. The Rush-Bagot executive agreement of 1817 (soon made into a treaty) limited naval armaments on the Great Lakes between the United States and British Canada. The Convention of 1818 extended the trade agreement of 1815, dealt with the North Atlantic fisheries problem, established the forty-ninth parallel as the northern boundary of the Louisiana Territory, and provided for joint occupation of the Oregon Territory for ten years (an arrangement that was extended in 1827). And in 1830, when Britain had edged even further away from mercantilism, the United States under President Andrew Jackson finally got a treaty that opened British West Indian ports to American ships under certain conditions.

The Era of Good Feelings, then, saw substantial improvement in relations between the United States and Great Britain. That improvement resulted from the fact that in certain respects the interests of the dominant groups in the two countries either coincided or did not seriously conflict.

SPAIN AND THE TRANSCONTINENTAL TREATY

In Spanish-American relations the Adams-Onís Treaty of 1819–1821 was comparable in importance to the earlier Pinckney's Treaty. It has often been called the Transcontinental Treaty, since it literally traced the boundary between the United States and Spanish territory across the North American continent. Beginning on the Atlantic, the treaty transferred East Florida from Spain to the United States. In return the

United States assumed responsibility for claims by American citizens against Spain to the amount of $5 million—though none of that was paid to the Spanish government. The boundary between the United States and the remaining Spanish holdings in America began on the Gulf coast at the mouth of the Sabine River west of Louisiana, and zigzagged north and west until it followed the forty-second parallel to the Pacific Ocean (the northern boundary of the present states of Utah, Nevada, and California). By accepting that line the United States, in effect, yielded any claim it might have had to Texas, and Spain yielded its claims to the Oregon Territory.

Both internal and external circumstances contributed to the settlement. Within the United States the provisions appealed to both wings of the agrarian sectional alliance that was responsible for American westward territorial expansion. Southerners had long wanted Florida. With encouragement from Madison's administration, part of West Florida revolted against Spain in 1810 and successfully sought admission to the United States. During the War of 1812, American forces under General James Wilkinson seized the area controlled by the Spanish garrison at Mobile. President Monroe ordered General Andrew Jackson in 1818 against Seminole Indians who had raided Americans along the border. Jackson promptly seized East Florida and even executed a couple of British citizens there. He insisted that he had acted under orders. Monroe denied that he had authorized the conquest and he removed American troops from Spanish Florida. But at the urging of John Quincy Adams, the President did not repudiate or punish the fiery General. Southern agitation for Florida, Spanish weakness and difficulties, and the growing power of the United States, all capped by Jackson's spectacular military triumphs, clearly revealed that Spain's days in Florida were numbered. Jackson's successes enabled Secretary of State Adams to win points in his diplomatic negotiations that the Spanish Minister, Don Luis de Onís, had been resisting tenaciously for months.

At the same time as the annexation of East Florida pleased Southerners, Westerners liked that part of the treaty that strengthened America's claims to the Oregon Territory. The United States yielded on Texas, but only a handful of Americans lived there in 1819, and President Monroe was not much interested in it. Pressures for claiming the area were not as powerful as they were to become later. Besides, time was on the side of American expansionists, who had not ruled out the possibility of getting Texas later.

Externally, with Latin-American Wars for Independence causing the Spanish Empire in America to crumble, Spain was more willing to reach a boundary settlement with the United States than it might have been in less trying times. Furthermore, neither Great Britain nor France was willing to support Spain against the United States. Even the execu-

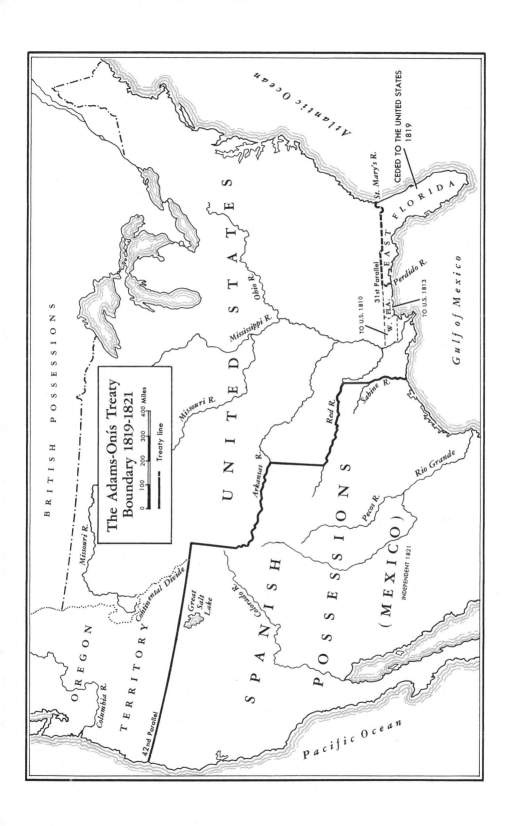

Atlantic Ocean

CEDED TO THE UNITED STATES 1819

St. Mary's R.

FLORIDA

31st Parallel

EAST

Perdido R.

Gulf of Mexico

TO U.S. 1810

W. FLA.

TO U.S. 1813

U N I T E D   S T A T E S

Ohio R.

Mississippi R.

Missouri R.

Red R.

Sabine R.

Arkansas R.

Rio Grande

Pecos R.

S P A N I S H

P O S S E S S I O N S

(M E X I C O)

INDEPENDENT 1821

The Adams-Onís Treaty
Boundary 1819-1821

0 100 200 300 400 Miles

Treaty line

B R I T I S H   P O S S E S S I O N S

Missouri R.

Continental Divide

Colorado R.

Great
Salt
Lake

O R E G O N

T E R R I T O R Y

Columbia R.

42nd Parallel

Pacific Ocean

tion of two British citizens by Jackson in Florida in 1818 did not arouse Britain to block American ambitions there. Several considerations affected British attitudes, but as Dangerfield phrased it, "Asked to choose between Arbuthnot and Ambrister [the men Jackson hanged] on the one hand, and the North American market on the other, the British government did not hesitate." With its American empire disintegrating, and with Britain and France unwilling to support it, Spain found it expedient to yield to American demands. The treaty was signed on February 22, 1819, and the Senate unanimously approved it two days later. Political turmoil in Spain, and procrastination to delay United States recognition of the independence of its Latin-American colonies, postponed Spanish approval for nearly two years. But ratifications were finally exchanged in 1821. And as expected, United States recognition of the newly independent Latin-American states followed soon after.

THE MONROE DOCTRINE

No policy statement in the history of American foreign affairs captured such an enduring and revered hold on American thought as President James Monroe's statement in 1823. The Monroe Doctrine was not a treaty, not an executive agreement, not an act of Congress, not a multilateral inter-American policy, and not international law. Its principles were not original with Monroe. It was not effectively enforced by the United States for many years. And it was not even called the Monroe Doctrine until long after Monroe left the Presidency. It was simply a statement of policy included in the President's message to Congress on December 2, 1823.

In its original form it had three main premises. First, it warned the Quadruple Alliance against extending European political systems to the Western Hemisphere:

> The political system of the allied powers is essentially different . . . from that of America. . . . we should consider any attempt on their part to extend their system to any portion of this hemisphere as dangerous to our peace and safety. With the existing colonies or dependencies of any European power we have not interfered and shall not interfere. But with the Governments who have declared their independence and maintained it, and whose independence we have, on great consideration and on just principles, acknowledged, we could not view any interposition for the purpose of oppressing them, or controlling in any other manner their destiny, by any European power in any other light than as the manifestation of an unfriendly disposition toward the United States.

Second, Monroe advanced the noncolonization principle:

> . . . the American continents, by the free and independent condition

which they have assumed and maintain, are henceforth not to be considered as subjects for future colonization by any European powers.

And third, Monroe endorsed the American policy of nonintervention in Europe:

> In the wars of the European powers in matters relating to themselves we have never taken any part, nor does it comport with our policy so to do. . . . Our policy in regard to Europe . . . remains the same, which is, not to interfere in the internal concerns of any of its powers; to consider the government *de facto* as the legitimate government for us; to cultivate friendly relations with it, and to preserve those relations by a frank, firm, and manly policy, meeting in all instances the just claims of every power, submitting to injuries from none.

Monroe's statement was aimed against two apparent external threats to American interests in the Western Hemisphere and was triggered by a British proposal to the United States. First, the Monroe Doctrine was aimed against the danger that the Concert of Europe might use its power (as it had in Italy and Spain) to put down the Latin-American revolutions and reestablish monarchical governments there. Second, the Monroe Doctrine was aimed against Russian colonial expansion south into the Oregon Territory. In 1821, under Czar Alexander I, Russia issued a ukase that, in effect, extended the southern boundary of its Alaskan colony to the fifty-first parallel. In the Ukase of 1821 Russia claimed exclusive trading and navigation rights down to 51° north latitude. It also barred foreign ships from approaching within 115 miles of that coast on pain of seizure.

Like the United States, Great Britain preferred an independent Latin America and objected to efforts by the Quadruple Alliance (or one of its members) to reestablish European control there. In August, 1823, the British Foreign Secretary, George Canning, suggested to Richard Rush, the United States Minister in London, that Britain and the United States issue a joint declaration. That statement would have questioned Spain's ability to recover its colonies; it would have renounced any desire by the United States or Britain to seize Latin America; and it would have opposed the transfer of any part of Latin America to any other state. The idea appealed to Rush, who promptly transmitted it to his government in Washington. President Monroe, too, was favorably disposed, as were the two former Presidents, Jefferson and Madison, that he consulted. Secretary of State John Quincy Adams, however, objected. He did not believe the European powers would intervene in Latin America and, in any event, he opposed a joint statement with Britain. He believed it would be more dignified for the United States to act unilaterally rather "than to come in as a cock-boat in the wake of the British man-of-war." Consequently, the United States rejected

Canning's proposal, but his suggestion led directly to Monroe's statement in his message to Congress.

Not only did external challenges and a foreign proposal lead to the Monroe Doctrine, but developments abroad also prevented the threats from materializing. Contrary to American mythology, neither the Quadruple Alliance nor Russia actually endangered the Western Hemisphere at the time Monroe issued his message. So far as the Concert of Europe was concerned, neither Austria nor Prussia had any interest in Latin America or any plans to intervene. Russia had not formulated its policies on the matter by December, 1823, and ironically Czar Alexander I did not even toy with the possibility of intervention until after Monroe's message. Even then it was just a passing consideration unaffected by United States opposition. France had considered the possibility of establishing independent Bourbon monarchies in Latin America but had not acted on the idea. In October, Canning discussed the matter with the French Ambassador to Britain, the Prince de Polignac. As a result, in the so-called Polignac Memorandum of October 12, 1823, France "disclaimed . . . any intention or desire . . . to appropriate to Herself any part of the Spanish Possessions in America. . . . She adjured, in any case, any design of acting against Colonies by force of arms." Thus British diplomacy and power checked the slight possibility of French intervention nearly two months before the Monroe Doctrine.

So far as Russian colonial expansion in the Northwest was concerned, Secretary of State Adams had protested against the Ukase of 1821 through regular diplomatic channels long before Monroe's message. Alexander I had no colonial ambitions in America. He was not impressed by the United States, but he did view America as a potential adversary of Britain and did not want to antagonize America. The Czar decided to yield on the boundary matter as early as July, 1822, a year and a half before the Monroe Doctrine. In 1824, in the first treaty between Russia and the United States, Russia accepted 54°40′ north latitude as the southern boundary of Alaska and agreed to freedom of seas in the North Pacific. That favorable treaty, however, was not due to the Monroe Doctrine. As Dexter Perkins, the leading scholar on the Monroe Doctrine, phrased it: "From the standpoint of its immediate results, it was close to futility."

In addition to external influences, the Monroe Doctrine was consistent with the dominant domestic patterns within the United States. Its antiforeign, anti-European, and antimonarchical tenor reflected American chauvinism in the Era of Good Feelings. The Doctrine's unilateralism and noninterventionism (the central ingredients of isolationism) expressed American nationalism.

Furthermore, the Monroe Doctrine was consistent with the desires of both the shipping-commercial interests on the one hand and the

farmer-agrarian interests on the other. That was symbolized in its authorship. President Monroe of planter Virginia was responsible for the statement aimed against intervention by the Quadruple Alliance in Latin
America. He was also responsible for presenting the policy in his message to Congress. Secretary of State Adams, from commercial Massachusetts, was responsible for the noncolonization principle, for emphasizing
nonintervention in Europe, and for making it a unilateral policy rather
than a joint statement with Britain. That dual authorship symbolized
the temporary political alliance of planter and merchant during the
Era of Good Feelings.

The Monroe Doctrine appealed to both wings of that political alliance by keeping the door open for continued expansion by both commercial and agrarian interests. American merchants wanted to increase
trade in Latin America. They feared that reestablishment of Spanish
control, intervention by the Quadruple Alliance, or any European
colonial expansion in Latin America, would conflict with their commercial ambitions there. The noncolonization principle did not apply to
the United States (unlike Canning's original proposal). It opposed
only European competitors of American territorial expansion. It would
have been difficult to formulate any foreign policy that appealed more
neatly to the interests and ambitions of the two main economic groups
in the United States than did the Monroe Doctrine.

It did not, however, get nearly so much attention in 1823 as it won
subsequently. European and Latin-American leaders were not awed
by it. Colombia in 1824 and Brazil in 1825 responded by seeking defensive alliances with the United States. The United States rebuffed their
approaches, however, and for more than a century the Monroe Doctrine
remained a unilateral United States policy, not a multilateral policy
shared with other states in the Western Hemisphere.

Simon Bolivar organized a Pan-American Conference in Panama in
1826. He envisaged a confederation of Spanish-American states, but
the United States was invited to the meeting. John Quincy Adams, then
President, and his Secretary of State, Henry Clay, did not object to
accepting the invitation. Many congressmen, however, feared entangling
alliances and involvement in Latin-American affairs. The Senate finally
approved the two delegates named by Adams, but one died on the way
and the other arrived after the conference ended. Only Colombia,
Mexico, Peru, and Central America were represented at Panama, though
Britain and the Netherlands had observers on hand. The Conference
approved a treaty of confederation, but only Colombia ratified it.

Not only did the Monroe Doctrine win little attention but European
states frequently violated it with impunity. Britain seized the Falkland
Islands off Argentina in 1833. In 1838 France blockaded Mexico at Vera
Cruz and invaded and blockaded Argentina. Britain extended the

boundaries of British Honduras and seized one of the Bay Islands off Honduras in 1838. From 1845 to 1849 Britain and France jointly intervened in Argentina. The United States government either ignored each of those episodes or made only token protests. In no case did the United States compel the European state to withdraw.

The failure to invoke the Monroe Doctrine effectively before the Civil War was the result of America's limited interests and limited power. The agrarians who controlled the government most of the time before 1861 were interested in those parts of Latin America adjoining the United States, including Florida, Texas, New Mexico, and California. Some were even attracted by Cuba and Central America. But they had no interest in South America. New England traders might be affected by developments in Argentina, but generally they did not control American foreign policies. Argentina was farther from the United States than Great Britain was. With the relatively limited mobility of nineteenth-century military forces, and with no isthmian canal to defend, European intervention in Argentina did not seem to represent as much of a threat to American security as it would have in the twentieth century. United States relations with Latin-American states generally were not very close before the Civil War.

In addition to America's limited interests in South America, the United States also lacked the power necessary to enforce the Monroe Doctrine effectively. In those parts of Latin America that adjoined the United States, American power was adequate. In South America, however, and in much of the Caribbean and Central America, the United States was not strong enough to make its will prevail, even if its interests there had been much greater than they were. In the nineteenth century, Great Britain, not the United States, was the most powerful outside state in South America.

Nevertheless, as Dexter Perkins wrote of the Monroe Doctrine, ". . . we must not . . . err on the side of too complete a depreciation of its place in the history of American foreign policy. . . . it became in later years an American shibboleth, powerful in its appeal, and far-reaching in its influence." It obtained that greater importance as both the interests and the power of the United States grew in Latin America.

SUPPLEMENTARY READINGS

Bemis, Samuel Flagg. *John Quincy Adams and the Foundations of American Foreign Policy.* New York: Alfred A. Knopf, Inc., 1949.

Brooks, Philip C. *Diplomacy and the Borderlands: The Adams-Onís Treaty of 1819.* Berkeley: University of California Press, 1939.

Cox, Isaac J. *The West Florida Controversy, 1798–1813: A Study in American Diplomacy.* Baltimore: Johns Hopkins Press, 1918.

Dangerfield, George. *The Era of Good Feelings.* New York: Harcourt, Brace & Co., 1952.

Griffin, Charles C. *The United States and the Disruption of the Spanish Empire, 1810–1822.* New York: Columbia University Press, 1937.

Perkins, Bradford. *Castlereagh and Adams: England and the United States, 1812–1823.* Berkeley: University of California Press, 1964.

Perkins, Dexter. *A History of the Monroe Doctrine.* Boston: Little, Brown & Co., 1955.

————. *The Monroe Doctrine, 1823–1826.* Cambridge, Mass.: Harvard University Press, 1927.

Rippy, J. Fred. *Rivalry of the United States and Great Britain over Latin America, 1808–1830.* Baltimore: Johns Hopkins Press, 1929.

Tatum, Edward H. *The United States and Europe, 1815–1823.* Berkeley: University of California Press, 1936.

Whitaker, Arthur P. *The United States and the Independence of Latin America, 1800–1830.* Baltimore: Johns Hopkins Press, 1941.

12

Territorial expansion: Annexation of Texas

One of the most consistent themes in the history of American foreign affairs was expansion in one form or another. Until 1853 the most conspicuous form was territorial expansion westward to the Pacific. The details varied, but that continental expansion grew out of the needs and ambitions of the farmer-agrarian group in the United States. Traders wanted West Coast ports, but the territorial expansion could not have been accomplished without the sectional alliance between the planting South and the farming West. That alliance first worked through Jefferson's Republican Party and later through Jackson's Democratic Party. When the alliance split for any reason neither section got what it wanted. When the issue of slavery in the territories completely divided the West from the South in the 1850's, American contiguous territorial expansion ended.

In addition to domestic bases for westward expansion, the United States also acquired new territories to cope with foreign threats (real or imagined). That is, the United States annexed Texas, Oregon, and California partly to prevent Britain and France from controlling them to the disadvantage of the United States. The fact that Britain and France were interested in Texas and California primarily to block American growth did not make that external explanation any less genuine.

In terms of domestic politics, the presidential election of 1844 paved the way for the annexation of Texas, Oregon, and California. Foreign

114

policy issues generally were not conspicuous in presidential contests, and elections have not thrown much light on American foreign policy views. In 1844, however, foreign affairs did play a major role. The Whig Party nominated Henry Clay of Kentucky for President. Fearful of splitting his heterogeneous party (and losing the election), Clay tried to avoid the controversial issues of expansion and slavery. The Democratic candidate, however, was an enthusiastic and outspoken expansionist, James K. Polk of Tennessee. He unequivocally urged tariff reduction and territorial expansion. Specifically he advocated annexation of Texas and all of Oregon. He also determined to get California, but he did not reveal that ambition to the voters. Contrary to mythology the Democrats did not use the slogan "Fifty-four forty or fight" in 1844; Whigs tried to discredit the Democrats later by charging them with using it. Nevertheless, Polk's Democrats did urge "the reoccupation of Oregon and the reannexation of Texas." That drive for Texas in the Southwest and for Oregon in the Northwest was ideal for keeping the South and West politically aligned. That alliance was essential both for the political success of Polk's Democrats and for westward territorial expansion. Ironically, votes for the antislavery, antiexpansionist Liberty Party weakened Clay enough in New York to throw that state's electoral votes to the proslavery, expansionist Polk and helped give him the victory nationally in an extremely close contest. The results were so close that the election could not properly be called a foreign policy mandate, but Polk chose to interpret his victory in those terms.

Polk was an exceptionally talented politician and an underrated President. Born in North Carolina of Scotch-Irish parents, he graduated from the University of North Carolina and passed the bar in Tennessee. He became a friend of Andrew Jackson there and during seven terms in the House of Representatives (two as Speaker of the House) he vigorously led political support for Jackson's policies. Governor of Tennessee in 1839–1841, he twice failed to win reelection. As a "dark horse" he gained the Democratic presidential nomination in 1844 with Jackson's support. He was quiet, intense, and reserved, often keeping his thoughts and plans from those about him. Always frail physically, Polk literally worked himself to death during his four years as President. Unlike most of his predecessors and successors in the White House, he successfully accomplished the major goals he set for his administration (including tariff reduction and territorial expansion). Unfortunately, his impressive successes revived the divisive issue of slavery in the territories. To that extent he weakened his own Democratic Party and helped point America on its way toward the Civil War.

Polk's first territorial objective was accomplished largely before he was inaugurated. Texas had been part of the Spanish Empire until the 1820's, when it was included in the newly independent country of

Mexico. A few Americans were interested in Texas as early as the 1780's or 1790's. Some even contended that the Louisiana Purchase included Texas. The number of Americans there in the first two decades of the nineteenth century was small, however, and in the Adams-Onís Treaty the United States yielded its flimsy claims.

In the 1820's American activity and interest in Texas sharply increased. The new Mexican government encouraged settlers in Texas with generous land grants and substantial local self-government. It required that settlers become Mexican citizens, be Roman Catholics, and accept Mexican laws. Even those conditions were not enforced effectively.

At the same time, many Americans (particularly from the South) became interested in Texas. Soil exhaustion on overworked farms drove some to seek productive lands further west. Planters wanted lands for younger sons while keeping their home estates intact for the eldest. Small farmers hoped to become planters with abundant cheap western lands. Slave owners in the Southeast may have seen Texas as a profitable market for their surplus slaves. From a political point of view, many saw Texas as a potential slave state (or states) to maintain voting equality for the South in the United States Senate. And there were always the adventurous whose quest for the unknown, and the unfortunate whose escape from the known, drove them to the challenge and refuge that was Texas.

The combined effect of favorable Mexican policies and southern expansionist tendencies led many to migrate to Texas in the 1820's. Most famous were the Austins, father and son. An unsuccessful businessman from Connecticut, Virginia, and Missouri, Moses Austin sought a land grant for a settlement in Texas. He died in 1821, but his talented twenty-seven-year-old son, Stephen, carried the project to fruition. As early as 1825 some 1,800 persons lived in the Austin settlement, of whom over 400 were slaves. Other similar projects were attempted, though they were less successful and less well led. By 1830 perhaps 20,000 people lived in Texas, most of them from the United States.

By that time the Mexican government questioned the wisdom of its earlier generous immigration policies. Most of the settlers in Texas came from the United States and were not assimilated into the Mexican culture. They continued to speak English and retained their attachments to the United States. Most of them became Catholic in name only, if that. They often were critical and contemptuous of Mexicans and their government. Some were a rough lot, not amenable to law and order (Mexican or any other kind). In Nacogdoches in 1826 Benjamin Edwards led a tiny uprising and proclaimed the independence of a short-lived Republic of Fredonia. Government forces easily crushed him, and even Austin helped Mexican officials in the episode. But it alarmed Mexicans and further convinced them that their earlier policies had been too lenient.

To make matters worse from the Mexican point of view, the United States government under Presidents John Quincy Adams and Andrew Jackson tried to buy Texas. Adams and Secretary of State Clay instructed South Carolina's Joel R. Poinsett, the first United States Minister to Mexico, to buy all or part of Texas. The Mexican government would not sell and eventually demanded the recall of Poinsett, who had conspired in Mexican politics in efforts to accomplish his mission. When Jackson became President in 1829 he sent Anthony Butler with instructions to buy Texas for $5 million. During the next six years that indiscrete "diplomat" intrigued in Mexico's internal politics and even tried bribery. His meddling failed to get Texas for the United States, but it further alarmed Mexicans concerning the expansionist intentions of their neighbor to the north. Historian Samuel Flagg Bemis has argued that "If Mexico had been willing to sell she would have avoided the whole later Texas question, and the Mexican War that resulted from it, and the ensuing great territorial cession of 1848." Such reasoning, understandably, did not appeal to most Mexicans at the time.

Thoroughly alarmed, the Mexican government enacted the Colonization Law of 1830 designed to block the flow of Americans into Texas and to control those already there. It prohibited citizens of countries adjoining Mexico (that is, the United States) from settling there. Mexico also banned further introduction of slaves. It restricted local self-government and imposed new tariffs. But Mexico did not enforce the new policies effectively, and Americans continued to come. They brought more slaves. Austin's efforts to persuade the Mexican government to alleviate Texas' grievances accomplished little. Tensions mounted, emotions flared, and extremists won increased support both in Texas and in Mexico City. The result was the Texas War for Independence in 1835–1836.

The Texans did not have an easy task, as the slaughter at the Alamo in San Antonio tragically revealed. The commander-in-chief of the Texas army was Sam Houston, the tall, broad-shouldered, former governor of Tennessee, and close friend of President Jackson. Houston defeated and captured Mexico's General Santa Anna at San Jacinto in April, 1836, assuring success for the revolution. Despite later clashes, Mexico could not regain control over the Lone Star Republic.

Americans overwhelmingly sympathized with Texas, and many individuals actively aided the revolution. President Jackson's long interest in acquiring Texas for the United States was well known. Nevertheless, the United States did not plot the revolt. The federal government under Jackson carefully refrained from taking sides in the fray. The President made no move to annex Texas during the revolt and did not even recognize its independence until March, 1837, just before he left office. More than ten months after San Jacinto, his action could not justly be called precipitous.

Though there were differences of opinion, Texas expected and sought annexation by the United States. Most Americans, particularly from Democratic circles in the South and West, expected and wanted the same thing. For a variety of reasons, however, annexation was long delayed, and Texas was independent for more than nine years. The urban Northeast with its Whig, commercial, and antislavery orientation generally opposed the idea. Indeed, Jackson and later Tyler urged that annexation of Texas be coupled with the acquisition of California's fine ports to appease eastern trading interests. Many Northerners feared that annexation might lead to an unwanted war with Mexico. The depression that followed the Panic of 1837 absorbed American attentions for a time. Jackson's hand picked successor for the Presidency, Martin Van Buren of New York, represented the urban part of the Democratic Party. Unlike his political mentor, Van Buren opposed both territorial expansion and the slavery that went with it. The election of 1840 placed a western military hero, William Henry Harrison, in the White House, but for a fleeting instant it also put the urban business interests of the Northeast and their Whig Party in a stronger position to block territorial expansion than they had had in four decades.

Harrison's death shortly after inauguration in 1841 brought John Tyler of Virginia to the Presidency. Though elected on a Whig ticket, Tyler was at heart an anti-Jackson southern Democrat. His elevation gave annexationists their best opportunity since Jackson had left office. The new Secretary of State, Tyler's fellow Virginian Abel P. Upshur, made good progress negotiating a treaty of annexation until his accidental death in February, 1844. Tyler's next Secretary of State, John C. Calhoun of South Carolina, signed the completed treaty but bungled by publicly linking the annexation of Texas with the defense of slavery. Calhoun seized on a British statement that Britain was dedicated to "the abolition of slavery throughout the world." He insisted that annexation was essential to guard against the British antislavery threat. Calhoun's approach was popular in the South, but it alienated many all over the Northeast and Middle West. By tying expansion to slavery in his case for the treaty, Calhoun began to wreck the alliance between the South and West. The Senate rejected the treaty of annexation in June, 1844, by a vote of sixteen for and thirty-five against.

Nevertheless, conditions both inside and outside the United States made certain that Texas would be annexed. Southerners and their political spokesmen, of course, provided continued support for annexation. The election of 1844 was interpreted as an indication of widespread approval for Polk's determination to get Texas (and Oregon). It stimulated Manifest Destiny sentiment in the West. Linking Oregon in the Northwest with Texas in the Southwest enabled many in the Middle West to look more kindly on the acquisition of Texas (despite their moral scruples about slavery). The lame-duck President John Tyler was a Southerner and an expansionist. After the election of 1844 he was more determined than ever to add Texas to the United States before he left office. Furthermore, many in the United States had invested in stock of Texas land speculation companies. Still others held Texas bonds. If they hoped to realize a gain (or avoid a loss), they needed to get Texas in the Union. The combination of southern expansionists, a Southerner in the White House, northern creditors with financial interests in Texas, the Oregon sop to the Middle West, election of the expansionist Polk in 1844, and the vibrant spirit of Manifest Destiny, all added up to an impressive domestic alignment for annexation.

In addition, there were external conditions that encouraged annexation, specifically the activity of Britain in Texas and the skillful maneuvers by the Texas President, Sam Houston. Great Britain and, to a lesser extent, France were interested in Texas. Britain wanted it as an open market for its manufactured products. As an independent cotton-producing country, Texas would make British textile industries less dependent on the United States for their raw cotton than they had been. An independent Texas might be more receptive to Britain's antislavery crusade than the United States was. Emancipation in Texas might undermine slavery in the United States. As a part of its balance-of-power policies, Britain welcomed a strong and independent Texas to block the expansion and power of the United States in the Western Hemisphere. Though individual Englishmen were more ambitious, the British government did not plan to annex Texas. It did, however, envisage an independent Texas closely bound to Great Britain. To that end, Britain proposed that Mexico recognize Texas' independence, with that independence to be guaranteed by Britain, France, Mexico, and perhaps by the United States.

Texas leaders deliberately encouraged the belief that an Anglo-Texan accord would be the alternative if the United States did not annex Texas. President Sam Houston wanted annexation. After the United States rebuffed Texan overtures, however, he subtly encouraged American fears that Britain was gaining the upper hand in Texas. American fear of Britain's intentions (often exaggerated in the United States) was fundamental in the annexation of Texas.

President Tyler eagerly devised a political maneuver that converted those circumstances into effective action. Unable to get the two-thirds Senate vote required for a treaty, Tyler decided to accomplish his goal through a joint resolution of Congress. Such a course needed only simple majorities in both Houses of Congress. The tactic worked. Voting along party lines, both Houses approved the joint resolution by the end of February, 1845, and President Tyler signed it on March 1, just before he left office. It provided that Texas would come in as a state, not as a territory. In effect, it allowed Texas to come in as a slave state. Texas was to keep its public lands but would be responsible for its public debts. With the consent of Texas, it could be divided into as many as five states.

The joint resolution frightened Mexico into belated action. In May, 1845, Britain and France persuaded Mexico to recognize Texas' independence provided Texas would not allow itself to be annexed by any other country (that is, by the United States). Texas, thus, had the opportunity to choose continued independence recognized by Mexico, or annexation as a slave state by the United States. The Texas legislature voted unanimously in June for the latter alternative. In December, 1845, under President Polk, Texas formally became a part of the United States.

SUPPLEMENTARY READINGS

Adams, Ephraim D. *British Interests and Activities in Texas, 1838–1846.* Baltimore: Johns Hopkins Press, 1910.

Barker, Eugene C. *The Life of Stephen F. Austin.* Nashville: Cokesbury Press, 1925.

————. *Mexico and Texas, 1821–1835.* Dallas: P. L. Turner Co., 1928.

Binkley, William C. *The Texas Revolution.* Baton Rouge: Louisiana State University Press, 1952.

Goetzman, William H. *When the Eagle Screamed: The Romantic Horizon in American Diplomacy, 1800–1860.* New York: John Wiley & Sons, Inc., 1966.

Reeves, J. S. *American Diplomacy under Tyler and Polk.* Baltimore: Johns Hopkins Press, 1907.

Sellers, Charles G. *James K. Polk: Continentalist, 1843–1846.* Princeton, N.J.: Princeton University Press, 1966.

Smith, Justin H. *The Annexation of Texas.* New York: Baker & Taylor, 1911.

Wiltse, C. M. *John C. Calhoun: Sectionalist, 1840–1850.* Indianapolis: Bobbs-Merrill Co., Inc., 1951.

13

Territorial expansion: Oregon and the Canadian border

The United States had border conflicts from the beginning of its independent history. Those problems arose not only with Spain and Mexico to the South but also with Great Britain to the North. Both the Revolutionary War and the War of 1812 involved that border. The earlier problems were treated in several agreements, including the Treaty of Paris in 1783, Jay's Treaty of 1794, the Rush-Bagot Agreement, the Convention of 1818, and others. Britain and the United States resolved the remaining territorial differences in the Webster-Ashburton Treaty of 1842 and in the Oregon Treaty of 1846.

Both treaties of the 1840's involved territorial problems, but the self-interest of the countries (and of the dominant groups in them) made both amenable to compromise. Canada on the border was, in effect, a vulnerable American "hostage" that inhibited British policies toward the United States. Equally important by the 1840's was Britain's highly efficient industrial and financial system. Reflecting that economy, Britain was well into its laissez-faire phase. Colonies overseas were not as essential as they had been earlier. They were not nearly so essential as the American market for British industrial products and capital.

So far as the United States was concerned, the treaty in 1842 was the work of New England's Daniel Webster. He was responsive to the needs of Massachusetts' "infant industries," but he also reflected the same commercial Anglophile considerations that had moved Jay and the Federalists earlier. Westerners wanted all of the Oregon Territory, but neither the Northeast nor the South shared that view. In any event, neither was willing to risk war with Great Britain to get all of Oregon. Consequently, the West had to settle for less than it wanted. Reflecting those circumstances to some degree, the personal roles of conciliatory statesmen and diplomats both in Britain and in the United States affected the outcome.

THE WEBSTER-ASHBURTON TREATY

Disagreements about the location of the Canadian-American boundary, and incidents resulting from that uncertainty, occurred from the beginning of American independence. During Martin Van Buren's administration provocative episodes increased, and the passions aroused on both sides endangered the peace between Great Britain and the United States. Britain easily crushed the Canadian rebellion in 1837, but the rebels won much sympathy in the United States. One of the defeated rebel leaders, William Lyon Mackenzie, fled to the United States, recruited funds and men, and then set up headquarters on Navy Island on the Canadian side of the Niagara River. A private American steamboat, the *Caroline,* carried supplies to him. The British sent a small military force to seize the vessel in Canadian waters. When the officer found the ship had moved to the American side, he continued his mission there. The British force captured, burned, and sank the *Caroline.* In the process the military unit killed one American and wounded others. The United States protested British invasion of American jurisdiction. Britain held, however, that it was justified in self-defense when the United States failed to control those who were aiding the rebels from American soil.

American sympathy for the Canadian rebels (a sympathy that some combined with a desire to add Canada to the United States) extended to the organization of secret societies designed to aid the Canadians. Hunters' Lodges along the northern border recruited thousands and even attempted feeble military invasions of Canada. The Lodges and raids were more of an annoyance than a danger to Britain. Most American leaders disapproved of them, and President Van Buren sent General Winfield Scott to restrain them. Nevertheless, they revealed substantial Anglophobia, and they complicated British problems in Canada.

In 1840 a Canadian named Alexander McLeod was arrested in New York and charged with the murder of the American who died in the *Caroline* incident three years earlier. Britain protested that a man could not properly be tried for an act committed under orders as a member of an organized military unit. The United States rejected that reasoning.

Harrison's Secretary of State Daniel Webster said that the state of New York had jurisdiction over the case and that the federal government could not intrude. Webster did secure assurances that if McLeod were convicted, Governor William H. Seward of New York would pardon him. Fortunately, the court acquited McLeod in the fall of 1841.

In the middle of Van Buren's term, near-violence erupted between Canadian and American lumbermen in the Aroostook River Valley in Maine, an area claimed by both Britain and the United States. They averted violence, however, and President Van Buren sent General Scott, who arranged a truce in 1839. The episode further inflamed Anglo-American relations.

Despite the tradition of Anglophobia within their Democratic Party, Presidents Jackson and Van Buren both worked to smooth relations with Britain. The Whig Party that won the Presidency with the election of William Henry Harrison included some Western Anglophobes, as well as tariff protectionists, among its new manufacturers from the Northeast. Nevertheless, like the Federalists earlier, Whigs generally were more pro-British than their political opponents. Those tendencies were well served when Harrison appointed two New Englanders to the key posts affecting Anglo-American relations. Edward Everett, Minister to Britain from 1841 to 1845, was a Harvard Professor of Greek. He hit it off well with British leaders and won their respect and affection. Daniel Webster, Secretary of State from 1841 to 1843, had been given the red-carpet treatment on his visit to England in 1839. That experience strengthened his already Anglophile inclinations. He suggested that the United States and Great Britain resolve their differences through direct high-level negotiations, and he then stayed on in Tyler's Cabinet to see the negotiations to successful completion.

Those who shaped British foreign policies at the time shared the Whig hopes for resolving Anglo-American differences. Lord Aberdeen, British Foreign Secretary from 1841 to 1846, was conciliatory and responded promptly to Webster's suggestion. He sent Lord Ashburton, Alexander Baring, as special emissary to represent Britain in the negotiations with Webster. Lord Ashburton was not a professional diplomat. He was a distinguished businessman with substantial experience and interests in the United States. He had visited America as early as 1795 and had traveled widely there. He had much trade and large investments in the United States, and he was persuaded of the importance of the United States to British prosperity. Ashburton had even married a Philadelphia socialite. The frank and amiable negotiations between Webster of commercial New England and Ashburton of entrepreneurial England got on splendidly. They signed their Webster-Ashburton Treaty in August, 1842. Webster's skilled propaganda campaign, secretly financed

The Webster-Ashburton Treaty Boundary of 1842

━━━━━━ Treaty line

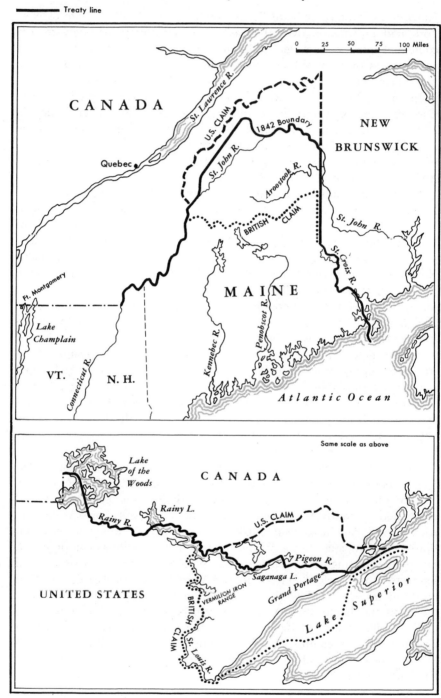

by federal funds, and the payment of $150,000 to Maine and Massachusetts, overcame opposition. The treaty won quick approval in the Senate, with only a handful of Democrats and one Whig voting against it.

The treaty compromised on the Maine boundary, with some 7,000 square miles of the disputed territory going to the United States and about 5,000 to Great Britain. It gave Britain the route it wanted for a military road from New Brunswick to the St. Lawrence, while the United States got the Aroostook Valley. They compromised partly because each of the countries had different maps that, unbeknown to the other, supported the other's claims. Webster had two maps that supported the British territorial claim, while the British Foreign Office had a map that coincided with America's claims to the whole area. Later research revealed that the British map was correct and that the United States should have had all of the disputed territory. Webster, of course, had no way of knowing that at the time. The United States kept Fort Montgomery north of Lake Champlain, which, due to a faulty survey line made earlier, had been constructed on land belonging to Britain. The treaty also clarified the boundary between Lake Superior and the Lake of the Woods in northern Minnesota. Many years later, Americans discovered and developed the fabulously rich Vermilion iron ore range in the area that Ashburton yielded to the United States there. America lost timber resources in northern Maine, but it gained the vastly more valuable iron ore reserves. There was a happy but unintended symbolism in the fact that Daniel Webster, who was beginning to speak the language of industrial America, obtained territory for the United States that was rich in the iron ore that was to undergird the spectacular development of America's heavy industry in the twentieth century. The treaty also included provisions dealing with African slave trade, extradition, and lesser matters. The treaty was not popular, particularly in Democratic circles of the South and West and in Maine. Nevertheless, the dominant interests at that moment in both Great Britain and the United States brought to the fore governments and diplomats who could and would compromise. The compromises were not popular, but they did not undermine the vital interests or security of either country. And they did resolve conflicts that had long disturbed relations.

THE OREGON TERRITORY

The Oregon Territory in the far Northwest was bounded on the east by the Rocky Mountains, on the south by the forty-second parallel, on the west by the Pacific Ocean, and on the north by the line 54°40′ north latitude. It included the present states of Washington, Oregon, and Idaho, as well as British Columbia and adjoining areas.

Before 1819 four countries claimed the Oregon Territory: Spain, Russia, Great Britain, and the United States. Two of them were eliminated without difficulty before 1825. Spain yielded its rights to the United States in the Adams-Onís Treaty of 1819. Czar Alexander I decided as early as July, 1822, not to press Russian jurisdiction south of 54°40′. That decision was confirmed in treaties with the United States in 1824 and with Great Britain in 1825. The task of reconciling British and United States claims was not accomplished so easily nor so quickly.

Both countries had substantial bases for their claims. Britain's Captain James Cook touched the Oregon coast in 1778. A British naval officer, Captain George Vancouver, explored the area in 1792. By the 1820's Britain's Hudson's Bay Company had major fur-trading operations north of the Columbia River under the direction of Dr. John McLoughlin. By the 1840's the Company had around 3,000 employees in the Territory, and Dr. McLoughlin provided the only effective government. Most whites living, trading, and farming north of the Columbia in 1840 were British, not Americans.

The United States also had strong claims to the Territory, particularly the area south of the Columbia River. A New England shipper and trader, Captain Robert Gray, explored the Oregon coast in 1788–1789 and in 1791–1792. He discovered and named the Columbia River. He also demonstrated the value of Oregon to the China trade by taking profitable cargoes of otter skins from Oregon to China. Other New England shippers soon used Oregon as a stopping point in the China trade. Those approaches from the sea were supplemented by explorations by land, particularly by Meriwether Lewis and William Clark in 1805–1806. John Jacob Astor's American Fur Company established a trading post at the mouth of the Columbia in 1811, though the British forced him to sell out during the War of 1812. American claims were strengthened by the Adams-Onís Treaty. In the 1830's American missionaries became active there, including the Methodist Jason Lee and the Presbyterian Dr. Marcus Whitman. Not until the middle of the 1840's did many settlers from the United States move to Oregon, and most of them located south of the Columbia in the fertile Willamette Valley.

The variety of domestic groups that shared American expansion into Oregon was significant. Shipping-commercial groups, fur traders, and missionaries all had interests there. Agrarians were represented by the Lewis and Clark expedition that President Jefferson sent and, belatedly, by the frontiersmen and farmers who traveled the Oregon Trail in the 1840's. The Democratic Party in 1844 saw political advantage in expansion as it offered Oregon for the West along with Texas for the South. Through it all, nationalism and Manifest Destiny provided ideological and emotional bases for American interests.

Though both Britain and the United States had strong claims in Oregon, before 1844 neither insisted on the whole Territory. Britain's interests and activity were largely north of the Columbia River, and it offered repeatedly to divide the Territory at the Columbia. Americans, on the other hand, were active largely south of the Columbia. The United States offered several times to divide Oregon at the forty-ninth parallel. Consequently, domestic politics notwithstanding, the area in dispute essentially was that part of the Oregon Territory located between the Columbia River to the south and the forty-ninth parallel to the north.

For more than a quarter of a century after the Convention of 1818 the United States and Great Britain could not agree on a boundary line, and neither felt strongly enough to force the issue to a showdown. In 1827 they renewed and extended indefinitely the original ten-year joint-occupation agreement. Either country could end the arrangement by giving a one-year notice. The large influx of American settlers in Oregon beginning around 1843 finally moved the politicians and diplomats to action.

Polk's Democratic campaign in 1844 to annex all of Oregon got a little support in the South and even a bit in the East. But the politicians and journalists who trumpeted most loudly for all of Oregon were largely from such middle western states as Ohio, Indiana, Illinois, and Missouri. The campaign for all of Oregon was not based on occupation, settlement, legal rights, or on a realistic analysis of the diplomatic possibilities. And neither Polk nor most of his supporters (even in the West) wanted war with Great Britain to get all of the Territory.

Suddenly in 1846 the Oregon controversy that had plagued Anglo-American relations so long was resolved peacefully. President Polk forced the issue by persuading Congress to pass a resolution in April, 1846, authorizing him to give the required twelve-month notice ending joint occupation. The British Foreign Secretary, Lord Aberdeen, responded by suggesting that the Territory be divided at the forty-ninth parallel, with Great Britain keeping Vancouver Island. Since the United States had repeatedly proposed that boundary, President Polk without hesitation forwarded the British offer to the United States Senate for its advice. The Senate urged acceptance—and in effect freed Polk from his campaign commitment to get all of Oregon up to 54°40′ north latitude. The Oregon Treaty was signed in June, 1846, and won quick approval from both governments.

On the surface the settlement appeared to represent a retreat by both countries. Polk abandoned his crusade for all of Oregon, and Britain retreated from its demand for the Columbia River line. In diplomatic terms, however, it was Britain (not the United States) that made the real concession. Despite the Democratic platform and campaign in 1844,

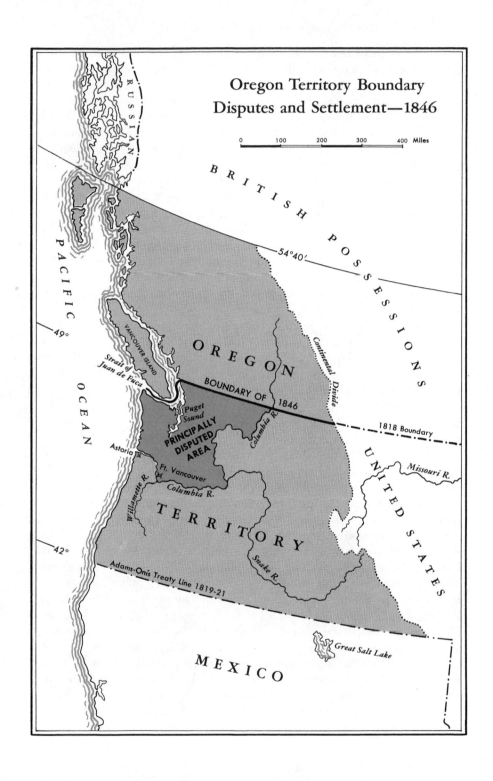

Oregon Territory Boundary
Disputes and Settlement—1846

0   100   200   300   400 Miles

RUSSIAN

BRITISH POSSESSIONS

54°40'

PACIFIC

49°

OREGON

VANCOUVER ISLAND

Strait of
Juan de Fuca

BOUNDARY OF 1846

Continental Divide

Columbia R.

1818 Boundary

OCEAN

Puget
Sound

PRINCIPALLY
DISPUTED
AREA

Astoria

Ft. Vancouver

Columbia R.

UNITED STATES

Missouri R.

Willamette R.

TERRITORY

42°

Snake R.

Adams-Onís Treaty Line 1819-21

Great Salt Lake

MEXICO

in diplomacy the United States had never actually tried to get anything north of the forty-ninth parallel. On the other hand, by accepting the division Britain abandoned the area between the Columbia and the forty-ninth parallel that was settled and controlled largely by the British. The boundary that Britain accepted was, for the most part, the one urged all along by the United States.

Several considerations affected Britain's decision. The large influx of American settlers threatened the British position and was one of the reasons the Hudson's Bay Company in 1845 moved its Oregon headquarters to Vancouver Island. Fur trade in the disputed area was becoming less profitable. Britain was fully into its laissez-faire, free-trade era at the same time as the United States under Polk was reducing tariffs. Consequently, Britain considered peaceful trade with the huge American market far more valuable than the disputed territory in Oregon. A sandbar made the Columbia River of little value as a port, but by drawing a line on the forty-ninth parallel and keeping Vancouver Island Britain gained access to Puget Sound via the Strait of Juan de Fuca. In other words, the Oregon Treaty of 1846 gave Britain access to the best port in the Territory. And finally, Britain did not want war with the United States. In such a war Canada would be difficult to defend, and Britain's profitable market in the United States would be lost.

At least three related considerations affected the decision of the United States under President Polk to accept the forty-ninth parallel rather than insist on 54°40′ north latitude. In the first place, most Americans, including Polk, did not want war with Britain, the most powerful state in the world. And the United States could not get all of Oregon without war. Second, Professor Norman Graebner has advanced the port theory explaining Polk's expansionist goals. According to his analysis, Polk's primary objective in the Northwest was access to the best port in the Oregon Territory. By tracing the boundary down the middle of the Strait of Juan de Fuca the United States, like Britain, got access to Puget Sound. So far as ports were concerned, nothing would be gained by moving the boundary further north. And third, though the West wanted all of the Oregon Territory, most people in the South and East did not. Most Southerners (including President Polk of Tennessee) had no enthusiasm for annexing all of Oregon at the risk of war with Britain. Commercial interests in the East could get what they wanted (that is, access to the best port in Oregon) by compromising on the forty-ninth parallel. Leaders in both sections insisted that the northern part of the Territory was of little value either for farming or for trade. With the South and East willing to compromise, the West was without the sectional allies that were essential for the accomplishment of its more extensive territorial objective. In a sense, so far as the United States was concerned, the Oregon Treaty of 1846 was the result of a sectional alliance between opponents of the acquisition of all of Oregon. With southern Democrats and eastern Whigs unwilling to support the West, that section had to acquiesce in the more limited settlement.

SUPPLEMENTARY READINGS

Corey, Albert B.   *The Crisis of 1830–1842 in Canadian-American Relations.* New Haven, Conn.: Yale University Press, 1941.

Fuess, Claude M.   *Daniel Webster.* 2 vols. Boston: Little, Brown & Co., 1930.

Graebner, Norman A.   *Empire on the Pacific: A Study in American Continental Expansion.* New York: Ronald Press Co., 1955.

Jacobs, Melvin C.   *Winning Oregon: A Study of an Expansionist Movement.* Caldwell, Idaho: Caxton Printers, Ltd., 1938.

Jones, Wilbur D.   *Lord Aberdeen and the Americans.* Athens: University of Georgia Press, 1958.

McCormac, Eugene I.   *James K. Polk: A Political Biography.* Berkeley: University of California Press, 1922.

Merk, Frederick.   *The Oregon Question: Essays in Anglo-American Diplomacy and Politics.* Cambridge, Mass.: Belknap Press of Harvard University Press, 1967.

Reeves, Jesse S.   *American Diplomacy under Tyler and Polk.* Baltimore: Johns Hopkins Press, 1907.

Sellers, Charles G.   *James K. Polk: Continentalist, 1843–1846.* Princeton, N.J.: Princeton University Press, 1966.

14

Territorial expansion: California and the Mexican War

Americans did not have sufficient interests in northern Oregon to justify war with mighty Britain. The attractions of California in the Southwest, however, were much greater, and Mexico's power was not adequate to deter America's acquisitiveness there. Substantial American interests in California, combined with America's power advantage there, made the United States and President Polk less conciliatory than they had been in dealing with Great Britain in the Northwest. The result was the Mexican War of 1846–1848.

External explanations for the war came from Mexico, Great Britain, and France. Though Mexico had not been able to regain control of Texas during its decade of independence, annexation of Texas in 1845 led the Mexican government to break diplomatic relations with the United States. Many Mexicans urged war with the United States over Texas. Boundary disputes and border incidents disrupted Mexican-American relations. Mexico failed to pay claims and damages owed to American property owners along the border, despite an arbitral award on the matter in 1840. California had deteriorated economically under Mexico, and the government did not exercise effective control there. Indeed, Mexico's ineffectiveness in California created a power vacuum that almost invited outside intervention. In any event, Mexico did not avoid war with the United States. With Americans divided on the issue, and with the hope for British and French support, many Mexicans believed they could win such a war.

British and French seamen and shippers in California were attracted by the splendid harbors at San Diego and San Francisco. French interests there were extremely limited, however, and the French government had no plans for seizing California. British interests and activities were greater, and some bondholders hoped that Mexican financial obligations might be maneuvered into a British territorial foothold in California. Nevertheless, the British government did not try to annex California. Such interest as the British government displayed was inspired largely by the desire to prevent the United States from annexing California. The fact that the British and French governments had no plans to annex California was not terribly relevant. President Polk and many other Americans *believed* that they were a threat in California, and they acted on the basis of that belief.

In addition to external influences, the Mexican War and the annexation of California resulted from a multitude of domestic considerations. Both commercial and agrarian groups hoped to benefit from California. The shipping-commercial groups were active in California long before the agrarians. American shippers in the China trade stopped in California for supplies and cargoes. Prior to the 1820's they particularly sought sea otter skins to trade in China. American whalers also visited there. New England ships in the 1820's and later profitably bought cattle hides for America's shoe industry. Many eastern Whigs, including Daniel Webster, were attracted by the commercial importance of California's harbors. Even agrarians, for reasons of their own, wanted California's windows to the Pacific. Professor Norman A. Graebner has advanced the hypothesis that the principal goal of President Polk and other expansionists in California was its great ports, particularly at San Francisco and San Diego. Commercial interests there were personified by the vigorous activities of Boston's Thomas O. Larkin. But commercial interests alone did not result in annexation, and they declined in the 1840's.

More important by the 1840's were agrarian interests. In addition to the earlier approach from the sea, in the 1840's many American pioneers were making the long overland trek from the Mississippi Valley to California. None of the key steps leading directly to the annexation of California could have been accomplished without support won from the agricultural sections of the country. The Democratic South and West accomplished the election of Polk in 1844, the declaration of war on Mexico in 1846, and the approval of the Treaty of Guadalupe Hidalgo that transferred California and New Mexico to the United States. Visions of transcontinental railroads to the Pacific Coast excited the imagination of politicians and entrepreneurs in both the North and the South. And through it all was the vibrant spirit of Manifest Destiny, aroused by newspaper editorials and political orations in a people that needed little urging.

President Polk provided the leadership and political talents that converted those circumstances and influences into action. He did not publicly urge annexation of California before his election in 1844, but that goal became his overwhelming obsession. He hoped he could get it peacefully, perhaps by purchase. But even if peaceful methods failed or moved too slowly for the one-term President (and they did), he was determined to get California.

Late in 1845 Polk initiated two peaceful (or short-of-war) efforts to get California, and at the same time American naval and military forces in the West got orders that contemplated possible forceful solutions. Polk sent John Slidell, an expansionist from New Orleans, as United States Minister to Mexico. As a minimum he was to obtain Mexican recognition of the Rio Grande boundary in return for American assumption of claims by its citizens against Mexico. He was authorized to pay as much as $20 million more for a boundary that would give San Francisco to the United States, or $25 million if it included Monterey.

Slidell's mission failed. Officially the Mexican government under President Herrera refused to receive Slidell because it had agreed only to receive a "commissioner" to settle the Texas controversy. Slidell, however, was sent as a minister. To receive him in that capacity would be tantamount to reestablishing normal diplomatic relations with the United States, a course that Mexico would not follow until it was satisfied on the Texas matter. In January, 1846, after Herrera fell, the same reasoning was used by his successor. But it was more of an excuse than a reason. The more fundamental explanation was the government's difficulty staying in power. If it became known that it considered acquiescing in American control of Texas or, worse still, selling California to the United States, it would quickly be ousted from power. The Slidell mission was blocked by political and emotional conditions within Mexico. The United States sought more than existing Mexican governments would or could provide. Polk even toyed with the possibility of a secret million-dollar subsidy to help the new Mexican government keep the support of its army (and stay in power) until a satisfactory treaty could be concluded. Domestic political problems associated with the idea in the United States led Polk to abandon it.

At the same time, the Polk administration initiated a second effort to get California through Thomas O. Larkin. A New England merchant active in California trade, Larkin served as United States Consul in Monterey. In October, 1845, Secretary of State James Buchanan sent an interesting set of instructions to Larkin. The central theme of the document directed Larkin to "exert the greatest vigilance in discovering and defeating any attempts which may be made by foreign governments [particularly by Great Britain] to acquire control over" California. Buchanan insisted that the United States had "no desire to extend our federal system over more territory than we already possess, unless by the free and spontaneous wish of the independent people of adjoining territories." Nevertheless, the underlying tone of the instructions pointed to ultimate annexation by the United States. Buchanan warned that "emigration to it of people from the United States" would make it "impossible" for any European power to hold California as a colony. In dealing with Californians, Larkin was "to arouse in their bosoms that love of liberty and independence so natural to the American continent." Buchanan made it clear that if Californians "should desire to unite their destiny with ours, they would be received as brethren, whenever this can be done without affording Mexico just cause of complaint." Confident of future trends, he recommended letting "events take their course, unless an attempt should be made to transfer them without their consent either to Great Britain or France." Larkin was to make it clear that "should California assert and maintain her independence, we shall render her all the kind offices in our power, as a sister Republic."

Despite protestations to the contrary, Larkin's instructions could be interpreted by that dedicated expansionist as encouraging him to promote developments in California like those earlier in West Florida and Texas and those later in Hawaii that led to annexation by the United States. Americans might use the word "subversion" to describe such patterns if they were directed against the United States by a foreign agent. Since Larkin's enthusiastic desire to add California to the United States was well known, Polk's administration could not have been surprised when he interpreted his instructions broadly and worked imaginatively to accomplish his goal. He might have succeeded if he had had more time, but war erupted before his efforts were consummated.

As early as 1842 an overeager American naval officer heard reports of war between the United States and Mexico and promptly seized Monterey. The mistake was soon corrected, but it was a portent of things to come. In June, 1845, America's naval commander in the Pacific was ordered to seize San Francisco if he "ascertained with certainty" that Mexico and the United States were at war. Those orders were subsequently repeated and the Navy strengthened in the Pacific. President Polk also sent Colonel John C. Frémont on an exploring expedition in California (that is, in Mexican territory), and that impulsive officer soon got into difficulties with Mexican authorities there. In January, 1846, after Slidell's mission failed, Polk ordered American forces in Texas under General Zachary Taylor to leave the Nueces River and advance through disputed territory to the Rio Grande. Under Spain and Mexico the area between the Nueces and the Rio Grande had not been part of Texas, though the Republic of Texas claimed it in 1836. The troop movement was ordered despite (or because of) the possibility that it might lead to clashes with Mexican forces in the disputed area. For more than a month, however, no incident occurred.

Polk grew impatient. After consulting his Cabinet on May 9, 1846, the President decided to ask Congress to declare war. He planned to base his request primarily on Mexico's financial irresponsibility and on its refusal to receive Slidell. Before Polk could prepare his war message, however, news reached him that Mexican troops on April 25, 1846, had crossed the Rio Grande and had killed or captured all members of a small United States cavalry patrol.

In the dramatic message that Polk submitted to Congress on May 11, 1846, the President asserted:

> Mexico has passed the boundary of the United States, has invaded our territory and shed American blood upon the American soil. She has proclaimed that hostilities have commenced, and that the two nations are now at war. As war exists, and, notwithstanding all our efforts to avoid it, exists by the act of Mexico herself, we are called upon by every consideration of duty and patriotism to vindicate with decision the honor, the rights, and the interests of our country.

He did not mention his continued determination to annex California. Congress quickly responded to his appeal and voted overwhelmingly to declare war on Mexico. Even Whigs momentarily gave their support, with only two in the Senate and fourteen in the House voting against war.

Observers then and since have differed widely in their evaluation of America's responsibility for the war. Many have defended the United States. They pointed out that Mexico did not try to avoid the war and thought it could win. Nowhere in his writings or statements did President Polk say that he wanted war or confess that he deliberately provoked Mexico into war. After the conflict began he repeatedly insisted that he sought only a just and honorable peace, with an unspecified indemnity. The instability and weakness of the Mexican government endangered the interests, property, and lives of many Americans, and made the Southwest vulnerable to European intervention. Professor Samuel Flagg Bemis wrote: "Certain it is that no countryman of President Polk today would desire to undo either the annexation of Texas or the Mexican purchases of 1848 and 1853."

Others have been less generous. An obscure Whig congressman from Illinois by the name of Abraham Lincoln gained a bit of attention when he introduced "Spot Resolutions" asking where on American soil American blood had been shed. Clearly he believed it was shed on Mexican, not American, soil. If Mexico made no effort to avoid war, neither did it seek it. Mexico, France, and Britain did not in fact endanger American vital interests or security in 1846. Polk *was* determined to get a very large part of Mexico, including California. He did not publicize that resolve, but he recorded it in his diary and revealed it to his political confidants. Democratic Senator Thomas Hart Benton of Missouri, who was close to the Administration, later wrote:

> It is impossible to conceive of an administration less warlike, or more intriguing, than that of Mr. Polk. They were men of peace, with objects to be accomplished by means of war; so that war was a necessity and an indispensability to their purposes. They wanted a small war, just large enough to require a treaty of peace, and not large enough to make military reputations, dangerous for the presidency. Never were men at the head of government less imbued with military spirit, or more addicted to intrigue.   .

Polk may have preferred peaceful methods, but he was determined to get California even if peaceful methods seemed inadequate. And finally, no country is likely to want to yield any of its territory, no matter what methods it may have used to get it. Whether others would find that continued desire to retain the territory to be sufficient justification for the methods used in all cases may be doubted.

The United States military forces defeated Mexico quickly in 1846–1847. Indeed, Polk found the political aspects of the conflict more difficult than the military tasks. The leading generals, Winfield Scott and Zachary Taylor, were both Whigs, and Polk did not wish to enhance their political potential by giving them opportunities to become national heroes. He was unable to find qualified Democrats to take their places, however, and his political fears were realized. Taylor won the Presidency on the Whig ticket in 1848, and Scott was the Whig Party's unsuccessful candidate for President in 1852.

The California Bear Flag movement, John C. Frémont, and the United States Navy were too much for Mexican forces on the West Coast. They largely completed the conquest of California during the summer of 1846 before the United States Army under Stephen W. Kearny arrived. Even before Congress declared war, General Zachary Taylor's troops checked Mexican advances at the Texas border, and in February, 1847, turned back General Santa Anna's much larger force in the Battle of Buena Vista. Taylor could have crushed Mexico, but Polk feared that the Whig General might gain too much political stature from his victories. In a vain effort to check Taylor politically, most of his best troops were siphoned off for use under General Winfield Scott. After an amphibious landing near Vera Cruz in March, 1847, General Scott ably commanded the dramatic drive inland against Santa Anna's army. When Mexico City fell to Scott's attackers in September, 1847, organized Mexican military resistance ended.

The negotiation of the Treaty of Guadalupe Hidalgo of 1848 ending the Mexican War was one of the most unusual episodes in American diplomatic history. With much accuracy a contemporary wrote that the treaty was "negotiated by an unauthorized agent, with an unacknowledged government, submitted by an accidental President to a dissatisfied Senate." For a variety of reasons, President Polk in April, 1847, sent Nicholas P. Trist of Virginia to accompany Scott's army. In that way Polk hoped to make certain that the fighting would not end until he got a treaty transferring California and New Mexico to the United States. The President considered Trist the right man for the job. Though arrogant, he had a good mind and much energy. He spoke Spanish and French fluently and had had experience as United States Consul in Cuba. From Polk's point of view Trist's political assets were even more impressive. He had been President Andrew Jackson's secretary, had married Thomas Jefferson's granddaughter, and was a long-time Democrat. If his negotiations succeeded, they would bring credit to the Democratic Party, not to the Whigs as the victories by Taylor and Scott did. As chief clerk in the State Department, Trist was not prominent, so his appointment did not provoke factional jealousies. He was sent as an executive agent, so if he failed Polk could easily discard him without embarrassment and appoint a regular diplomat. If he succeeded, he was not likely to divert much acclaim away from the President.

At first, Trist and Scott feuded furiously and inundated the Administration with emotional letters denouncing each other. They soon patched up their differences, however, and became warm, cooperative friends. Suddenly, in October, 1847, Polk and Secretary of State Buchanan ordered Trist's recall. Trist's accord with Scott did not entirely please the President. Furthermore, Trist had considered a Mexican peace offer that would have put the boundary at the Nueces River and would have left San Diego in Mexican hands. Polk believed Trist's performance was far too generous both to the Mexicans and to the Whigs. And it would not have given the United States one of the major ports that the President wanted in California.

With encouragement from Scott, the British legation, and the Mexicans, Trist decided to ignore his recall. Though he was no longer authorized to do so, he skillfully seized an opportunity to negotiate a peace treaty in accord with his original instructions. The Treaty of Guadalupe Hidalgo signed on February 2, 1848, transferred to the United States all of the territory of the present states of California, Nevada, and Utah; most of New Mexico and Arizona; and parts of Colorado and Wyoming. The treaty placed the boundary at the Rio Grande and Gila Rivers and gave the United States the splendid harbors at San Francisco and San Diego. In return the United States was to pay Mexico $15 million and assume the claims of Americans against Mexico up to $3,250,000.

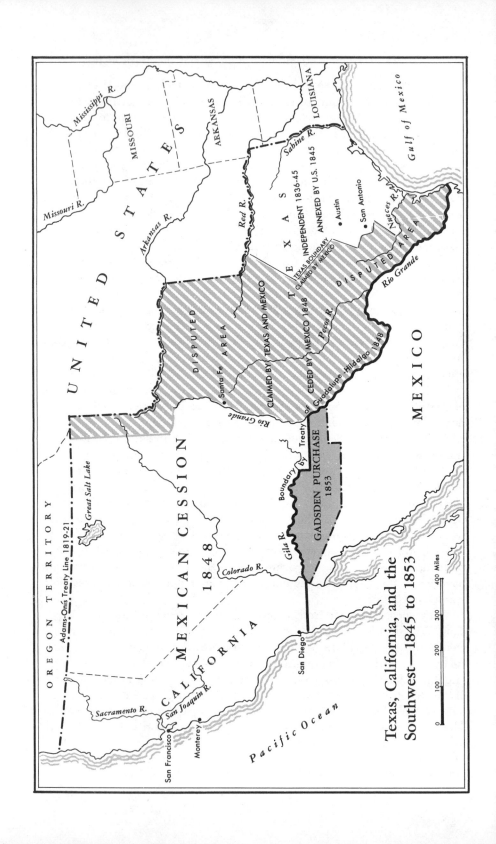

Texts, California, and the
Southwest—1845 to 1853

UNITED STATES

MISSISSIPPI R.

MISSOURI

ARKANSAS

LOUISIANA

Gulf of Mexico

Missouri R.

Missouri R.

Arkansas R.

Red R.

Sabine R.

TEXAS

TEXAS INDEPENDENT 1836-45
ANNEXED BY U.S. 1845

Austin

San Antonio

Nueces R.

DISPUTED AREA

TEXAS BOUNDARY
CLAIMED BY MEXICO

CLAIMED BY TEXAS AND MEXICO

CEDED BY MEXICO 1848

Pecos R.

Rio Grande

1848

MEXICO

DISPUTED

AREA

Santa Fe

by Treaty of Guadalupe-Hidalgo

Rio Grande

Boundary

Gila R.

GADSDEN PURCHASE
1853

OREGON TERRITORY

Adams-Onís Treaty Line 1819-21

Great Salt Lake

MEXICAN CESSION
1848

Colorado R.

CALIFORNIA

Sacramento R.

San Joaquin R.

San Francisco

Monterey

San Diego

Pacific Ocean

Miles
0 100 200 300 400

Polk's break with Trist (and Scott) was complete. Trist was ousted from the government service and was not even paid his salary and expenses in Mexico until twenty years later. Nevertheless, his treaty had the provisions that Polk wanted, including California and its ports. And Polk's term was nearing its close. Consequently, the President submitted the Treaty of Guadalupe Hidalgo to the Senate, and it won approval in March, 1848.

Mexican weakness and instability, combined with American fear of British and French intentions, led President Polk and the agricultural South and West to wage a war that (with Texas and Oregon) added nearly one million square miles to the area of the United States. During the 1840's the United States acquired over half of Mexico's original territory.

SUPPLEMENTARY READINGS

Bemis, Samuel Flagg. *The Latin American Policy of the United States: An Historical Interpretation.* New York: Harcourt, Brace & Co., 1943.

Fuller, John D. P. *The Movement for the Acquisition of all Mexico, 1846–1848.* Baltimore: Johns Hopkins Press, 1936.

Graebner, Norman A. *Empire on the Pacific: A Study in American Continental Expansion.* New York: Ronald Press Co., 1955.

Merk, Frederick. *Manifest Destiny and Mission in American History: A Reinterpretation.* New York: Alfred A. Knopf, Inc., 1963.

Pletcher, David M. *The Diplomacy of Annexation: Texas, Oregon, and the Mexican War.* Columbia: University of Missouri Press, 1973.

Reeves, Jesse S. *American Diplomacy under Tyler and Polk.* Baltimore: Johns Hopkins Press, 1907.

Rives, George L. *The United States and Mexico, 1821–1848.* 2 vols. New York: Charles Scribner's Sons, 1913.

Sellers, Charles G. *James K. Polk: Continentalist, 1843–1846.* Princeton, N.J.: Princeton University Press, 1966.

Singletary, Otis A. *The Mexican War.* Chicago: University of Chicago Press, 1960.

Smith, Justin H. *The War with Mexico.* 2 vols. New York: Macmillan Co., 1919.

15

The end of agrarian
territorial expansion

The last contiguous continental territory obtained by the United States was the Gadsden Territory, purchased from Mexico for $10 million in 1853. The Gadsden Territory, in the present states of Arizona and New Mexico, was south of the Gila River between El Paso, Texas, on the east and Yuma, Arizona, on the west. It was purchased for a projected southern railroad route to the West Coast. In addition, that desert area proved to contain rich ore deposits, particularly copper in the Ajo area. With that purchase American contiguous continental territorial expansion ended.

That did not mean that agitation for more territory ceased. Patriotic, security, and commercial considerations aroused expansionist interests in both the North and the South. In the 1850's, however, Southerners particularly wanted expansion. They hoped in that way to head off foreign antislavery crusades. And they wanted territories that could be made into slave states so that the South could regain its voting equality in the United States Senate. Voting equality, they believed, was essential to protect southern institutions, economy, way of life, and slavery from northern assaults.

Expansionists in the 1840's and 1850's considered several alternatives. One was to divide Texas into five states. But the joint resolution of 1845 required the consent of Texas for such a division, a consent that was not forthcoming. Another possibility was the annexation of more of Mexico, perhaps all of Mexico. Many, including some Whigs, had urged that course during the Mexican War. Nevertheless, Polk and most Southerners opposed taking all of Mexico. They believed that most of it was not suited for cotton production and was not likely to become slave territory. Some Southerners wanted areas in Central America. But in the 1850's Southerners focused particularly on the Spanish colony of Cuba.

Cuba inspired a multitude of expansionist appeals. Manifest Destiny in the form of propinquity and natural growth pointed to its eventual acquisition by the United States. National security at the very least required that it be kept out of British and French hands; at the most some insisted that American security necessitated annexation of Cuba. Merchants from New York as well as from New Orleans traded profitably there. And to all of those considerations Southerners added the defense of slavery, their "peculiar institution."

The Polk Administration in 1848 tried to buy Cuba for $100 million, but Spain made it clear that it would rather see "the Pearl of the Antilles" sunk in the ocean than yield it to the United States. Filibustering expeditions to Cuba led by Narciso López won substantial support from Southerners in the United States. López sought Cuban independence, but he organized, recruited, and financed his expeditions in the United States. His first attempt failed in 1849 when federal authorities under Whig President Taylor seized his two ships in New York harbor. His second expedition sailed from New Orleans in 1850, but Cubans did not rally to his cause. López fled to Key West, was arrested, and was later released. The following year the adventurer led 400 men on a third attempt, again sailing from New Orleans. The Spanish easily crushed the invasion; López and many of his followers were executed. The unfortunate man got more support among Southerners in the United States than he won in Cuba.

Whigs generally denied any desire to annex Cuba. Usually they urged only that its ports be open without discrimination to American traders and that it not be transferred from Spain to any other European power. Nevertheless, even some Whigs revealed less limited ambitions there. In 1852 Great Britain and France (as they had twice before) invited the United States to enter a convention in which the three states would individually and collectively renounce any intentions to annex Cuba. Secretary of State Edward Everett of Massachusetts replied that Cuba was "mainly an American question." He would not rule out the possibility of American annexation in the future.

President Franklin Pierce in 1853 named Pierre Soulé to be United States Minister to Spain. That injudicious Democratic politician from Louisiana was a dedicated expansionist and was obsessed with a determination to gain Cuba for the United States. He had scarcely assumed his duties in Madrid when Spanish authorities in Havana used a technicality to justify seizing a cargo of cotton from the American steamship, the *Black Warrior*. The government instructed Soulé to demand disavowal of the act, and an indemnity of $300,000. Soulé on his own initiative demanded a satisfactory reply within forty-eight hours. Tensions mounted and some expansionists hoped the episode might lead to war, with Cuba as the victor's prize. Instead, Spain bypassed Soulé by dealing directly with the government in Washington, and the shipowners worked out a settlement in direct negotiations with officials in Cuba.

Pierce's Secretary of State, William L. Marcy, also authorized Soulé to buy Cuba from Spain for as much as $130 million. If Spain rejected the offer, Marcy made it clear to Soulé that the United States would welcome and assist Cuban independence from Spain, presumably as a prelude to annexation by the United States.

A particularly famous expression of expansionist desires for Cuba was the so-called Ostend Manifesto of 1854. Secretary of State Marcy suggested that Soulé confer about Cuba with John Y. Mason, Minister to France, and James Buchanan, Minister to Great Britain, and submit their recommendations to the Department of State. The three met at Ostend, Belgium, and concluded their conversations at Aix-la-Chapelle. Since it was not signed at Ostend, and since it was not a manifesto, the document was misnamed. Both its contents and its bold style reflected the dominant role of Soulé. The diplomats listed reasons why they believed the United States should annex Cuba and reasons why they thought Spain would be wise to yield it. They recommended that the United States offer to buy Cuba for not more than $120 million. If Spain refused to sell, the Ministers were convinced that the United States would "be justified in wresting it from Spain." The document was supposed to be confidential, but it was soon publicized. Political expediency forced Marcy to reject the recommendations. Repudiated by his government, Soulé resigned before the end of the year. Many Americans in the 1850's, particularly in the South, wanted to annex Cuba. But they failed.

The activities of Americans in Central America's Nicaragua provided a remarkable miniature symbolizing the patterns of domestic influences on nineteenth-century expansion. William Walker from Tennessee and Louisiana personified southern agrarian expansionism in Nicaragua. Trader expansion took the form of Cornelius Vanderbilt from New York. Walker's defeat in his contest with Vanderbilt symbolized the frustration of southern expansionism in the 1850's. And finally, Vanderbilt's later decision to shift his investments from shipping to railroads within the United States was part of the movement of American capital from foreign trade to domestic railroads and industry in the last half of the nineteenth century.

Cornelius Vanderbilt was the "big name" in early United States trade with Nicaragua. In 1849 he and his business associates got permission from Nicaragua to build an isthmian canal there, but they quickly discovered that the project was beyond their financial and technical resources. Vanderbilt then organized the Accessory Transit Company, which got authority for a transportation system across Nicaragua, including exclusive rights to steam navigation on the waters of that Central American country. Vanderbilt's firm operated steamboats on the San Juan River and Lake Nicaragua and completed the remaining twelve miles across the isthmus by land (eventually by carriage on a macadamized road Vanderbilt constructed). That ingenious arrangement linked with Vanderbilt's steamships going to New York in the Atlantic and to San Francisco in the Pacific.

William Walker then entered the picture. That restless proslavery soldier of fortune had earlier led an unsuccessful filibustering expedition into northern Mexico. A political faction in Nicaragua invited the southern "grey-eyed man of destiny" to lead a mighty army of fifty-eight adventurers in 1855 to help the so-called Liberals against the Conservative government there. Surprisingly, his motley band prevailed, and Walker was promptly named commander in chief of the Nicaraguan army. The following year he became President of the country.

Walker's success aroused opposing factions in Nicaragua, alarmed leaders of other Central American states, and displeased the British and United States governments as well. Vanderbilt initially helped Walker with transport and funds, but the filibusterer then made a fatal mistake. He was persuaded to cooperate with Charles Morgan of New York and C. K. Garrison of San Francisco, who were attempting to seize control of Vanderbilt's firm. Walker found Vanderbilt to be a much more formidable adversary than his Nicaraguan opponents had been. Through his control of shipping, Vanderbilt cut off Walker's sources of supplies and reinforcements. At the same time, he saw to it that arms reached Walker's enemies in Nicaragua and Costa Rica. As a result, Walker fell from power in 1857. Walker tried three times to regain control in Central America, but he failed. On his final attempt in 1860 he was captured by the British, turned over to Honduras, and promptly executed.

But Vanderbilt no sooner crushed Walker than he began to seek more profitable business opportunities elsewhere. Late in the 1850's he sold his interests in Nicaragua and began to invest in American railroads. Nevertheless, when Secretary of State William H. Seward in 1867 completed a treaty that gave the United States control of the transit route in Nicaragua, he was building on ground already prepared partly by Walker's activities and, more importantly, by Vanderbilt's commercial enterprises.

Just as American activities in Nicaragua symbolized changing patterns of domestic influences on American expansion, so the circumstances surrounding the history of the Clayton-Bulwer Treaty of 1850 with Great Britain threw light on America's changing power position in Latin America. Britain's power supremacy in South America prevailed throughout the nineteenth century, and Britain was more active in Central America than any other European state. Nevertheless, the challenge from the United States was great enough north of the equator to win a *modus vivendi*. Just as the earlier joint-occupation agreement for the Oregon Territory served as a tolerable interim arrangement until American interests and power grew enough to win a favorable settlement, so the Clayton-Bulwer Treaty served as a tolerable (though controversial and unpopular) interim arrangement in Central America.

In addition to its trade and investments in Central America, Great Britain had long controlled Belize and later all of British Honduras. Britain also claimed the nearby Bay Islands and established a protectorate over the Indians on the Mosquito Coast. Britain seized Greytown at the mouth of the San Juan River in 1848. American diplomats sent to Nicaragua by Presidents Polk and Taylor in 1849 only succeeded in heightening Anglo-American tensions. The negotiations moved to London and then to Washington, where the Whig administration, through Secretary of State John M. Clayton, eagerly sought a settlement in negotiations with Britain's Minister, Sir Henry Lytton Bulwer. In the Clayton-Bulwer Treaty that they signed in April, 1850, each country agreed not to obtain exclusive control or fortification of an isthmian canal. They guaranteed the neutrality of any such canal. They promised not to "colonize, or assume, or exercise any dominion over Nicaragua, Costa Rica, the Mosquito Coast, or any part of Central America." In a supplementary declaration Britain insisted that the Treaty did not apply to its "settlement at Honduras or to its Dependencies." The United States did not wholly endorse that interpretation. The treaty was deliberately obscure. American and British interests and power were so evenly balanced in Central America at that time that agreement was possible only when the treaty was ambiguous enough to allow each country to believe (or pretend) that it won a favorable settlement.

Throughout the 1850's the United States and Great Britain bickered about the meaning of the treaty. The United States insisted that Britain was obligated to withdraw from the Bay Islands and the Mosquito Coast. Britain, in contrast, maintained that those holdings were not affected by the treaty, that it prohibited only *further* colonization in Central America. By the end of the decade Britain assuaged the United States through treaties with Nicaragua and Honduras that relinquished Britain's protectorate over the Mosquito Indians and acknowledged the jurisdiction of Honduras over the Bay Islands. Greytown became a free port. Britain's course arose partly from its deference to the growing power of the United States and from its increasing awareness of the significance of that power for British interests in the future. It was also due to the declining importance that British leaders attached to colonies in the middle of the nineteenth century. Nevertheless, Great Britain continued to be a major obstacle to American expansion. Externally Spanish and Latin-American opposition were weak and ineffective, but British and French opposition to American expansion were not to be treated lightly.

In addition, there were domestic explanations for the end of agrarian continental expansion. Whigs had political reasons for opposing further acquisitions. Shipping-commercial interests could satisfy their needs in the areas without actual annexation. But most important, agrarian territorial expansion ended because the slavery controversy broke the sectional alliance between the farming West and the planting South. Without that alliance no further territorial acquisitions were possible until new economic, sectional, political, and ideological bases for an expansionist coalition could be formed. From 1783 to 1848 each stage in the history of American continental expansion was accomplished with the support of the South and West: the original territory in 1783; the Louisiana Territory; Florida and Oregon; Texas and Oregon; and California and the Southwest. When the alliance broke, as it did during the War of 1812 and over the drive for all of Oregon, the United States failed to get territory. In the decade before the Civil War the South wanted more, but the West (actually the whole North) opposed further territorial expansion. Some Northerners, particularly in the Democratic Party, wanted more. Franklin Pierce, James Buchanan, and Stephen A. Douglas, among others, favored territorial expansion in the 1850's. They were moved partly by patriotism and Manifest Destiny. They were also northern Democratic politicians who needed the support of southern Democrats if their political ambitions on the national level were to be realized.

For the most part Northerners in both political parties, in the Northeast and the Middle West, opposed further territorial expansion in the 1850's. The Whig opposition was consistent with its political heritage, going back to Federalist days, but the western opposition reversed its earlier tendencies. By the 1850's Westerners had plenty of unsettled land to occupy within American boundaries. Furthermore, to the north the United States could only go into British Canada. Additional expansion in that direction would almost certainly lead to an unwanted war with Britain. More important, Westerners began to oppose further territorial acquisitions (and Easterners intensified their opposition) when the issue of expansion was tied to the issue of slavery. That had happened earlier occasionally, for example in Calhoun's abortive treaty for the annexation of Texas in 1844. But the Wilmot Proviso of 1846 accomplished it more decisively. It would have prohibited slavery in all territory acquired in the Mexican War. The House of Representatives adopted it repeatedly, but it never won approval in the Senate and never became law. The

Wilmot Proviso, and later the Kansas-Nebraska Act, dramatically bound territorial expansion to the spread of slavery. By doing so they divided western and southern agrarians. The South wanted both slavery and expansion, but if territorial expansion meant further spread of slavery most western agrarians would have no more of it. At the same time, the issue of slavery in the territories made possible a new northern sectional alliance between the farming West and the urban-commercial-industrial-financial Northeast. The slavery issue, in effect, drove the Middle West to change sides in the sectional controversies. Without sectional allies the South's chances for gaining more territory for the United States (and for slavery) ended.

SUPPLEMENTARY READINGS

Caldwell, Robert G. *The Lopez Expeditions to Cuba, 1848–1851.* Princeton, N.J.: Princeton University Press, 1915.

Ettinger, Amos A. *The Mission to Spain of Pierre Soulé, 1853–1855.* New Haven, Conn.: Yale University Press, 1932.

Garber, Paul N. *The Gadsden Treaty.* Philadelphia: University of Pennsylvania Press, 1924.

Greene, Lawrence. *Filibuster: The Career of William Walker.* Indianapolis: Bobbs-Merrill Co., Inc., 1937.

Nichols, Roy F. *Advance Agents of American Destiny.* Philadelphia: University of Pennsylvania Press, 1956.

Perkins, Dexter. *The Monroe Doctrine, 1826–1867.* Baltimore: Johns Hopkins Press, 1933.

Rauch, Basil. *American Interest in Cuba, 1848–1855.* New York: Columbia University Press, 1948.

Scroggs, William O. *Filibusters and Financiers: The Story of William Walker and His Associates.* New York: Macmillan Co., 1916.

Williams, Mary W. *Anglo-American Isthmian Diplomacy, 1815–1915.* Washington, D.C.: Lord Baltimore Press, 1916.

16

American commercial expansion

Even in the agrarian era before the Civil War, the United States did not limit itself to continental territorial expansion. Throughout its history the United States also expanded through trade and shipping abroad. Trader expansion generally was not as spectacular as westward territorial expansion. Before the Civil War it did not result in the acquisition of overseas possessions. It got very little direct support from the federal government during the first sixty years of the nineteenth century, except when the Whigs were in power briefly. Nevertheless, that relatively inconspicuous trading activity was an important part of American expansion before 1860. And it helped pave the way for a more active and powerful role for the United States in world affairs later.

Though it increased in absolute terms, foreign commerce declined relative to the total American economy from 1816 to 1860. Profits from foreign trade and shipping tended to be lower than they had been at the beginning of the century. British, French, and Dutch competition challenged the American carrying trade. Many American investors became convinced that returns on capital invested in shipping and trade were lower and more risky than returns from lands, railroads, and manufacturing within the United States. After the middle of the century even the beautiful clipper ships found it harder to compete with British iron steamships. America's merchant fleet began to decline even before the Civil War.

Nevertheless, American merchants and shippers were extremely active all over the world; they were an important part of American expansion before the Civil War. Furthermore, their expansive tendencies were supplemented by the related activities of whalers, missionaries, and the Navy. American foreign commerce, and the expansion related to it, may be examined in each of the major regions of the world.

GREAT BRITAIN AND EUROPE

Two thirds of American foreign trade before the Civil War was with Europe, and more than half of that was with Great Britain. That huge commerce resulted from established business contacts and buying habits. Europeans, and particularly the British, provided the credit essential for trade. In those decades both the United States and Great Britain, for different reasons, gradually lowered tariff barriers. Britain's industrial and financial supremacy made it easy for its leaders to embrace Adam Smith's laissez-faire theories. At the same time, the United States, led by the planting South, favored low tariffs or free trade to enable rural America to buy industrial goods at the lowest possible price.

Fundamentally the North Atlantic trade thrived because each country produced commodities that the others needed. The United States sold agricultural products to Britain and France, particularly raw cotton. Cotton was by far the largest single item in the American export trade with Europe, often exceeding the value of all other exports combined. British and French textile industries became increasingly dependent on cotton produced by southern planters. At the same time, American manufacturers could not satisfy the domestic market for industrial goods. Americans needed and wanted the products turned out by factories in Great Britain. The complementary economies of agricultural America on the one hand and industrial Britain and Western Europe on the other assured a steady and profitable flow of goods both ways across the Atlantic to the benefit of millions of people on both continents.

LATIN AMERICA

Much of United States expansion into northern Latin America resulted from agrarian territorial interests, for example, in Louisiana, Florida, Texas, California, and the Southwest. In addition, American expansion in Latin America grew out of commercial activities. United States trade with Latin America before 1860 was second only to trade with Europe. During the War of 1812 the British Navy nearly destroyed United States trade with Latin America, but it quickly revived after the war. When the Wars for Independence disrupted Latin-American agriculture, the United States sold wheat, flour, and other farm products there.

Despite its importance, in the nineteenth century American trade in Latin America was second to that of Great Britain. Latin America fitted into United States trade with the West Coast of North America and with China. The United States had a splendid merchant fleet and active commercial agents. Central America and the Caribbean were geographically close to the United States, especially to southern ports such as New Orleans. Early in the century Latin America welcomed American agricultural products, and by the 1850's the United States even sold small but growing quantities of manufactured items there.

British merchants, however, had even more impressive advantages in commercial competition in Latin America. Britain had the world's greatest industrial capacity. Its businessmen had abundant capital with which to finance trade. Britain had the largest merchant fleet in the world and the biggest navy to guard it (and to win deferential treatment for its merchants). Britain's consular service was vastly superior to that of the United States. Consequently, Americans were only second to the British in Latin-American trade. They were, however, a vigorous and aggressive second.

United States trade was not evenly distributed in Latin America. In South America, British leadership, influence, and commerce far exceeded those of the United States throughout the nineteenth century and on into the twentieth. American merchants were most active north of the equator, particularly in the Caribbean and Central America.

American West Indian trade in the Caribbean extended back to the seventeenth and eighteenth centuries, and it continued in the nineteenth. The European states that controlled those islands used discriminatory regulations to inhibit trade, but gradually the United States got commercial treaties and concessions that opened wider the trade opportunities. Spain allowed American merchants to trade directly with Cuba and Puerto Rico after 1823. Britain relaxed its restrictions on American trade with the British West Indies in 1830. The Netherlands opened the ports of its American colonies to direct United States trade in 1852. The commercial treaty with France allowed Americans to trade with the French West Indies from 1778 until it was revoked in 1800. During the Napoleonic Wars the United States again traded with the French West Indies. In 1815 France closed its colonies to American ships, and they were not opened to them again until 1866. Only Sweden allowed Americans to trade directly between its Caribbean colony and the European mother country.

The annexation of Oregon and California and the California gold rush beginning in 1849 increased American interests in Central America, since many went to the West Coast by way of Central America. As the population increased on the Pacific Coast, trade expanded, and much of it passed through the isthmus. The new territories and population on the

West Coast imposed additional security responsibilities on the United States Navy. Territorial acquisitions, population movement, trade, and national security all increased American interest in a railroad or canal route across Central America. Vanderbilt was a part of those patterns in Nicaragua.

Until 1903 Panama was a part of Greater Colombia. For a time Colombia encouraged the United States in an effort to counteract British interests there. Consequently, in the Treaty of New Granada of 1846, Colombia promised that any transportation or communication system across the Isthmus of Panama would "be open and free to the Government and citizens of the United States." The United States, for its part, guaranteed "the perfect neutrality" of the isthmus for unobstructed transit from sea to sea. The United States also guaranteed Colombian sovereignty over Panama.

More important than the government in promoting American expansion in Panama before the Civil War were certain entrepreneurs and shippers. Notable was William H. Aspinwall, a New York businessman who founded the Pacific Mail Steamship Company in 1848, linking Panama with San Francisco. At the same time, George Law and Marshall O. Roberts of New York organized the United States Mail Steamship Company between Panama and New York. Both companies won mail subsidies from the federal government. Aspinwall then helped organize the Panama Railway Company to connect the two lines. The 47-mile railroad was completed in January, 1855. At first it won huge profits, as much as 44 percent a year on the original investment, but they soon declined. Competition from the transcontinental Union Pacific hurt after 1869. French interests bought the railroad in 1880. Both the government (through the Treaty of 1846 and its mail subsidies) and businessmen (notably Aspinwall and Law) expanded American influence in Panama. They helped pave the way for the later American dominance there and for the interocean canal itself.

AFRICA

For Europeans and Americans before 1860, Africa was still the "Dark Continent." Traders touched the coasts of that huge, mysterious area, but they were ignorant of the lands, people, and resources that lay beyond sight of water. Americans had traded along the Mediterranean coast of North Africa in the eighteenth century, and they did not finally resolve their difficulties with the Barbary States there until after the War of 1812.

The American Colonization Society, with southern support, began taking freed slaves from the United States to Liberia in West Africa in 1822. Even Abraham Lincoln approved the effort, but it did not solve the race problem. The Society colonized only a few thousand blacks as compared with the four million blacks in the United States. Liberia became a protectorate of the United States, and in the twentieth century the Firestone Tire and Rubber Company converted part of it into huge rubber plantations.

The slave trade was the most sordid part of the American commercial relations with Africa before 1861. Though illegal most of the time, traders brought perhaps four million Africans to the New World (mainly to Central America, the West Indies, and Brazil) in the nineteenth century alone, many times more than were colonized in Africa. American shippers or ships flying the American flag handled much of the African slave trade. Furthermore, though they often sold to Southerners, the urban Northeast provided most of the American slave traders. It was ironic that the section that had the leading abolitionists also included many of the African slave traders. Many slaves were brought directly to the United States, but more were sold in Latin America. Slave traders used ships built for speed, often the clipper ship type, so they were difficult to catch. They built the decks close together so they could crowd as many Africans into them as possible. Conditions on board were horrible in the extreme and invariably many slaves died en route. But those who survived brought good prices, and traders won substantial profits.

As early as the 1770's some states outlawed the importation of slaves. The Constitution specified that the federal government could not prohibit the importation of slaves before 1808, but in 1807 Congress passed a law banning slave imports as soon as the Constitution allowed. By 1820 Congress had adopted legislation declaring the international slave trade a piracy punishable by death. Great Britain outlawed the slave trade in 1807, and abolished slavery in its empire in 1833. Britain also conducted a worldwide crusade to end the traffic in slaves. Most Latin-American and European countries agreed to allow the British Navy to apprehend any of their ships engaged in slave trading.

The United States, however, failed to enforce its own laws on the matter, and it refused to cooperate effectively with Britain's efforts. Consequently, in effect, the American flag shielded slave traders in their illicit traffic. Anglophobia helped account for the refusal to cooperate with Britain. Southerners feared that Britain ultimately sought the extinction of slavery everywhere, even in the United States. Slave traders wanted to guard their profits. And Americans determined to continue their long struggle for freedom of the seas. The United States had fought one war with Britain partly to protect its rights on the high seas, and it had no intention of allowing the British Navy to "visit and search" American ships, even in a cause so worthy as stopping the African slave trade.

In the Treaty of Ghent ending the War of 1812 both countries agreed to continue their separate efforts to stop the slave trade, but American efforts were extremely limited. In 1819 Congress appropriated $100,000 for the Navy to enforce the slave trade ban, but by 1834 it appropriated only $5,000, and it provided no funds from 1835 to 1842. The Webster-Ashburton Treaty of 1842 required each country to maintain a fleet of not less than eighty guns to suppress the slave trade. Both promised to try to close markets buying African slaves. In practice the United States failed to keep an adequate fleet off Africa. Navy ships generally were too slow to catch slave traders. They were not authorized to seize them en route to Africa. When the Navy managed to overtake and capture slave traders with their illegal cargoes, American courts failed to convict them. Consequently, the United States did not execute any slave trader until 1862, after the Civil War began. In that same year the United States finally signed an agreement with Great Britain that allowed either country to seize British or American slave traders, who were then to be tried in joint Anglo-American courts. With Southerners absent, the Senate quickly approved the treaty, and the American slave trade with Africa ended.

THE PACIFIC AND FAR EAST

There were beginnings in the 1780's, but American shippers were not very active in the Pacific before the nineteenth century. American trade in the Pacific and Far East was always small relative to that with Europe or even Latin America, but the hopes and dreams for the future were boundless. And the trade grew in the first half of the nineteenth century.

From the start Hawaii was important to Americans active in the Pacific. Before the 1820's the so-called Sandwich Islands were important to the United States only as a stopping place for ships trading with China. Shippers got supplies there, as well as sandalwood that they later sold in China. Before the Civil War, Americans led the whaling industry in the North Pacific, and by the 1830's Hawaii was the headquarters for American whaling fleets. In addition, some Americans settled in Hawaii and became businessmen and planters. Most of them had been (or were descendants of) traders, whalers, or missionaries. The Dole family, for example, had originally gone to Hawaii as missionaries. Gradually Americans got the best sugar and planting lands in Hawaii and also became politically powerful.

The first American missionaries went to Hawaii around 1820. They came particularly from New England, the same section that provided most of the traders and whalers there. Some of those missionaries (notably Hiram Bingham) became very powerful. They opposed French Catholic missionaries and to that extent obstructed French expansion there. Letters, articles, books, and sermons by missionaries helped arouse the interest of Americans at home. Missionaries often criticized traders and whalers for exploiting and corrupting native Hawaiians. For their part, traders and whalers disliked the missionary influence. Nevertheless, both the economic groups and the missionaries increased American influence in Hawaii.

As compared to economic groups and missionaries, the United States government and its Navy were not very active in Hawaii before the Civil War. An occasional Navy ship stopped in Hawaii, but the Navy did not appear in force and not often enough to please the merchants. President John Tyler, reflecting trader influence in the Whig Party, extended the Monroe Doctrine to include Hawaii in 1842. Appropriately, his Secretary of State Daniel Webster, from commercial New England, wrote the President's statement on the matter. It had little effect, however. In 1854 the United States negotiated a treaty calling for the annexation of Hawaii, but the Senate never approved it. A reciprocity treaty met the same fate. The United States did not annex Hawaii until 1898, but the activities of American traders, whalers, businessmen, planters, and missionaries early in the century prepared the way for annexation.

The most challenging (and disappointing) part of American activity in the Pacific was in China. America's earliest interests there grew out of trade. The first American merchant ship to make the voyage and return was the *Empress of China.* It sailed from New York in 1784 with a cargo of ginseng and other products, and returned the following year loaded with tea. Its backers got 25 percent profits on their investment. Very quickly dozens of other American merchants and ships began to trade with China.

Nevertheless, China trade before 1860 was only a small part of the total American foreign commerce. It never developed as much as the more optimistic Americans hoped and expected. The United States was a poor second to the British in China. The federal government did not provide much help. Merchants had difficulty finding commodities that the Chinese would accept. The first ship carried ginseng, supposed to have medicinal value. Many traders stopped in California and Oregon for furs. Some got sandalwood in Hawaii that was used for incense and ornamental carvings. Even before the Civil War the China trade began to decline relative to the total American economy and foreign trade.

Despite the difficulties and disappointments, many merchants from New England and the Middle Atlantic states found the China trade to be extremely profitable. Americans specifically developed the clipper ships in the 1840's and 1850's for the China trade. The cargo space in their sleek hulls was limited, but it was adequate for the tea and silk they carried. Their unprecedented speed was ideal for the vast distances of the Pacific. But after the middle of the century even they could not match the British iron steamships.

The first two American Protestant missionaries reached Canton in

1830; by 1860 there were eighty-eight scattered in all of the Chinese cities that were open to foreigners. They did not win many converts among the masses, but some of their converts in the upper classes held positions of influence. Often the only Americans who knew the Chinese language, missionaries served as interpreters for merchants and diplomats. Peter Parker of Massachusetts was the first medical missionary there; he introduced Western medical methods. Through their letters, articles, books, and sermons, missionaries increased the knowledge and interest of Americans at home about China. They were more vigorous than traders in urging the United States government to help and protect them. By spreading Western ideas they contributed a bit to the later downfall of the Manchu Dynasty. It was more than a coincidence that New England, the headquarters for many China traders, also provided much of the money and personnel for American missionary activity.

The American government followed after the traders and missionaries in China but was less aggressive than many of them wished. The dominant agrarians in the United States had little interest in the Far East. Nevertheless, in response to commercial and missionary agitation, the federal government did involve itself a little, particularly during the Whig administrations. One American warship visited Canton in 1819 and another made a longer visit in 1830. President Jackson sent Edmund Roberts of New Hampshire on a partially successful mission to seek commercial treaties with Cochin China, Siam, Muscat, and Japan.

More significant was Cushing's Treaty or the Treaty of Wanghia of 1844. Externally, it resulted from Britain's successful use of military and naval force against China in the Opium War of 1839–1842. Britain wrung from the reluctant Chinese the favorable Treaty of Nanking of 1842 that opened five port cities to the British and relaxed some of the annoying restrictions. The United States remained neutral but gained by diplomacy most of what Britain got through force. China made concessions to play the United States off against Britain. Internally, the Cushing Treaty resulted from the efforts of merchants and their Whig spokesmen. Abbott Lawrence, a Whig Representative from Massachusetts, submitted a memorial from American merchants in China asking Congress to provide naval protection and a trade treaty with China. Secretary of State Daniel Webster of Massachusetts wrote President Tyler's message urging Congress to appropriate the necessary funds. The chairman of the Committee on Foreign Affairs who led the move in the House of Representatives was John Quincy Adams of Massachusetts. The man appointed to lead the mission was Caleb Cushing, the son of a shipowner from Newburyport, Massachusetts. In addition to commercial interests, even some agrarians were attracted. A representative from South Carolina mused aloud about the potential market if the Chinese millions would chew tobacco instead of using opium.

Except for an indemnity and the island of Hong Kong, the United States got everything in Cushing's Treaty that Britain had won by force. Previously Canton had been the only Chinese port open to foreigners, and that only part of the year. Now to Canton were added Amoy, Foochow, Ningpo, and Shanghai. The United States got the same treatment on customs duties and trade regulations that Britain got. The United States gained the right to maintain consuls and establish homes, businesses, hospitals, and churches in the treaty ports. Furthermore, except for violators of the bans on opium trade and trade with other port cities, the United States obtained extraterritoriality rights. That is, except for those specific offenses, Americans charged with crimes committed in Chinese territory would be tried before American officials. The treaty won prompt and unanimous approval in the United States Senate.

During the fantastically destructive and bloody Taiping Rebellion against the Manchu Dynasty from 1850 to 1864, many Americans sympathized with the rebels. Many of the early leaders of the revolt professed forms of Christianity. Nevertheless, American merchants began to fear that the alternative to the Manchu Dynasty might be anarchy and dismemberment of China. The adverse results for Americans and their property might be worse than the annoyances from the autocratic and arrogant Manchus. Most Americans in China were pleased when the revolt failed.

Merchants and missionaries in China further improved their status through the Treaty of Tientsin of 1858. As with Cushing's Treaty, the United States obtained that favorable agreement by peaceful diplomacy after Britain and France had used force against China. Indeed, the American Minister, William B. Reed, actually followed close behind as the British and French forces defeated the Chinese defenders. The treaty opened more ports to Americans. It provided more binding guarantees for the protection of American lives and property. It authorized full toleration in treaty cities for missionaries and their converts. Through the most-favored-nation clause American traders gained all the privileges that Britain and France got from China.

In addition to California, Oregon, Hawaii, China, and many small Pacific islands, Americans became interested and active in Japan in the 1850's. Again traders and their Whig spokesmen in the government played the key roles. Japan had closed its ports to foreigners for more than two centuries, but domestic politics and internal changes were beginning to point to an end to the isolation. Growing pressures from Britain and Russia also were involved. But an American naval force under Commodore Matthew C. Perry accomplished the initial crack in the door. The Perry expedition, like the earlier Cushing mission to China, was conceived during a Whig interlude while old Daniel Webster was again Secretary of State in 1852. Born in the commercial state of Rhode Island, Perry vigorously urged naval activity to promote and protect American foreign trade. Perry's show of force in 1853 and 1854, changing conditions within Japan, and other foreign challenges in the western Pacific, led Japan to conclude a treaty with the United States. It guaranteed decent treatment for shipwrecked seamen. And it permitted an American consul in Japan. It was not much of a treaty, but it was a beginning. Four years later Townsend Harris, a New York merchant serving as consul in Japan, skillfully concluded a general commercial treaty with Japan that opened the way for rapid expansion of American trade there.

The powerful role that the United States was to play in the Pacific and the Far East was still far in the future. But traders and missionaries, backed with a little naval activity and diplomacy, began to prepare the way for that greater role.

SUPPLEMENTARY READINGS

Bradley, Harold W.   *The American Frontier in Hawaii: The Pioneers, 1789–1843.* Stanford, Calif.: Stanford University Press, 1942.

Dennett, Tyler.   *Americans in Eastern Asia.* New York: Macmillan Co., 1922.

Dulles, Foster Rhea.   *America in the Pacific.* Boston: Houghton Mifflin Co., 1932.

————.   *China and America: The Story of Their Relations Since 1784.* Princeton, N.J.: Princeton University Press, 1946.

————.   *The Old China Trade.* Boston: Houghton Mifflin Co., 1930.

Kuykendall, Ralph S.   *The Hawaiian Kingdom, 1778–1854.* Honolulu: University of Hawaii Press, 1938.

Latourette, Kenneth S.   *The History of Early Relations between the United States and China, 1784–1844.* New Haven, Conn.: Yale University Press, 1917.

Stevens, Sylvester K.   *American Expansion in Hawaii, 1842–1898.* Harrisburg: Archives Publishing Co. of Pennsylvania, Inc., 1945.

Swisher, Earl.   *China's Management of the American Barbarians: A Study of Sino-American Relations, 1841–1861, with Documents.* New Haven, Conn.: Yale University Press, 1953.

Tong, Te-kong.   *United States Diplomacy in China, 1844–1860.* Seattle: University of Washington Press, 1964.

Treat, Payson J.   *Diplomatic Relations between the United States and Japan, 1853–1895.* 2 vols. Stanford, Calif.: Stanford University Press, 1932.

Walworth, Arthur C.   *Black Ships off Japan: The Story of Commodore Perry's Expedition.* New York: Alfred A. Knopf, Inc., 1946.

PART III

Prelude to imperialism
1861–1898

17

Quiet erosion of an enduring stability: External influences on American foreign relations, 1861-1898

On the surface, the years from 1861 to 1898 appeared to continue the stability and order of the preceding decades. No general war swept Europe or the world. Bismarck led Prussia into wars (including the Franco-Prussian War of 1870–1871), but they were carefully localized conflicts for limited goals. Japan and China clashed in the 1890's, but the fighting ended quickly. There was friction in Africa. But there were no world wars.

Great Britain continued to be the leading world power and its balance-of-power policies had stabilizing effects. Britain still led the movement for laissez-faire and free trade. The "Little England" movement of the 1860's was not popular with everyone, but there was not much imperialism in the 1860's and 1870's. Even Bismarck, after the unification of Germany in 1871, did not seek overseas colonies. Until the 1880's international affairs seemed much as they had been for half a century. Even in 1898 few would have predicted the international holocausts that followed in the twentieth century.

Nevertheless, quiet changes were underway that were to have world-shaking consequences. The Industrial Revolution accelerated and spread further east in Europe. By midcentury it reached Germany, where it developed very rapidly. By the 1890's it even extended a bit into Russia. Some areas in southern and eastern Europe persisted in old ways that had not changed much for centuries. Elsewhere the rapid growth of

159

industry had intense domestic effects. It moved millions from rural areas to the cities. It built a more powerful bourgeoisie. It was responsible for a larger and more restive urban working class. The Industrial Revolution created greater wealth and more material goods for many, but it also intensified urban slums, unemployment, business cycles, class conflicts, and population pressures. Inevitably there were domestic political repercussions as the new bourgeoisie challenged the old landed aristocracy, and as the urban working classes grew increasingly dissatisfied with the policies of both the landed elite and the new middle class.

But the effects of the Industrial Revolution were not limited to the domestic scene. The dislocations and changing opportunities drove many millions of Europeans to seek better things in the New World. By the 1880's and 1890's increased productivity encouraged entrepreneurs and their governments to look abroad more aggressively for cheap raw materials and expanded markets for industrial products. The huge capital accumulations resulting from industrialization encouraged financiers to seek profitable places to lend and invest abroad. Industry increased the power of some states relative to others. The impact on military technology seemed to make the negotiation of precautionary alliances more essential. Railroads threatened to outflank Britain's sea power. All of that increased international distrust and insecurity. The Industrial Revolution also played a role in the further growth of nationalism.

The French Revolution and the Napoleonic Era had aroused nationalism in Western Europe, but it intensified and spread to Central and Eastern Europe during the nineteenth century. In Italy the workings of European power politics and the varied efforts of idealistic Mazzini, realistic Cavour, and dashing Garibaldi united most of the peninsula by 1861. Taking advantage of Austria's defeat at the hands of Bismarck's Prussia, Italy gained Venetia in 1866. When French troops were withdrawn during the Franco-Prussian War, Italy seized Rome in 1870, and its unification was complete.

More significant for world politics was German unification under the leadership of Otto von Bismarck. That master of *Realpolitik*, after careful diplomatic and military preparations, led Prussia to war against Denmark in 1864, Austria in 1866, and France in 1870–1871. In each case Bismarck's diplomacy made certain that his victim would not get outside help. In each case he conducted limited wars for limited goals. In each case Prussia triumphed quickly and decisively. Bismarck treated Austria gently after the Seven Weeks' War, but the harsh Treaty of Frankfurt in 1871 inspired Frenchmen to want revenge. The new German Empire under Kaiser William I was too powerful for the shaky Third French Republic to manage alone, however, and Bismarck's limited goals and skillful diplomacy made it impossible for France to win allies so long as the Iron Chancellor steered Germany's course.

The growing weakness of the Hapsburg Empire in Austria was essential to the unification of both Italy and Germany. And the survival of Austria-Hungary after 1867 was chronically endangered by the nationalism of ethnic groups within its heterogeneous population. The Dual Monarchy of Francis Joseph might have been less threatened if other states had not been so eager to take advantage of the nationalistic movements. Czarist Russia had problems enough of its own, but it hoped to capitalize on nationalism in the Balkans to advance its own goals there and in the Dardanelles.

In addition to industrialization and nationalism, a multitude of psychological and ideological currents began to undercut the status quo. The relative peace and stability in Europe had much to commend it. But like the British who set the dominant tone for the century, like Queen Victoria who gave her name to the era, and like the smoky factories of England's industrial Black Country, the century was something less than exciting for most. The statesmanship of Britain's William Gladstone and Benjamin Disraeli often was of a high order, but it was short on heroics. Napoleon III was an artful politician for bourgeois France, but he was a pale substitute for his more famous namesake. Many in Europe wearied of what Americans later might have called "Babbittry."

The developing technology, nationalism, and power changes in world affairs helped inspire ideologies that promoted (or rationalized) more adventuresome foreign policies. Some applied the biological theories of Charles Darwin to human relations. They used "Social Darwinism" to justify international conflict, imperialism, and even war in the name of "the struggle for survival" and "the survival of the fittest." Some began to think of the "White Man's Burden," while others worried about the "Yellow Peril," and some Germans spoke of the *Drang nach Osten*.

Industry, nationalism, ideology, and international power changes rapidly fermented in the last decades of the nineteenth century. And some of their international effects were becoming visible to the more perceptive observers. Germany in Europe, Japan in the Far East, and the United States in the Western Hemisphere were beginning to develop impressive power in their respective parts of the world. Each had a stable government with an energetic population. Each was building an industrial system capable of challenging or surpassing Britain's. Each began to build a modern navy, not nearly so large as Britain's but large enough to be formidable in its home waters. Each by the 1890's began to display imperialistic tendencies. None of the three was a world power in 1898, but each was a regional power strong enough to challenge Britain's dominance in its particular part of the world. By the close of the century each was strong enough to strain Britain's capacity to maintain the balance of power in opposition to it. The developments were disturbing enough to provoke an armaments race, a scramble for colonies, and to lead Britain to seek accords of one sort or another with each of the rising states.

Nevertheless, to a surprising degree the surface of international developments was little ruffled in the last third of the century. Economic statistics revealed the industrial gains being made by Germany, Japan, and the United States relative to Great Britain. But most Englishmen were unaware, unpersuaded, or unworried. Britain and France had been adversaries too often and too long to allow Englishmen to shed many tears over France's difficulties at the hands of Prussia. Bismarck so successfully limited Germany's ambitions in Central Europe that it was easy for Englishmen to view Germany as a satiated state. And if Germany blocked French or Russian designs in Europe, few in Britain would regret it. Bismarck did not attempt to challenge Britain's imperial supremacy or its command of the seas. Even after young Kaiser William II "dropped the pilot" by ousting Bismarck in 1890, the British were slow to take alarm. At the turn of the century Britain unsuccessfully explored the possibility of making an alliance with Germany. For a decade the alliance of 1894 between Russia and France operated as much against Britain as it did against Germany. So far as Japan was concerned, not many in the West were impressed before the Sino-Japanese War of 1894–1895, and despite Japan's quick military successes few were seriously alarmed about Japanese power after the war ended.

From 1861 to 1898 fundamental changes occurred within and among the European states. Nevertheless, in the 1860's and 1870's the international implications of those changes were little noted. Stability and order generally prevailed in world affairs. While that stability lasted, the United States continued to benefit from it. America could survive a terrible Civil War, reconstruct itself after that war, conquer the last American frontier, exploit its vast resources, and build an impressive industrial system, all without having to concern itself very much about threats from abroad. By the 1890's, however, changing power and policy patterns in Europe and elsewhere provided challenges and opportunities that were to tempt the United States into a more adventuresome role in world affairs.

SUPPLEMENTARY READINGS

Albrecht-Carrié, René. *A Diplomatic History of Europe Since the Congress of Vienna.* New York: Harper & Bros., 1958.

Binkley, Robert C. *Realism and Nationalism, 1852–1871.* New York: Harper & Bros., 1935.

Hayes, Carlton J. H. *A Generation of Materialism, 1871–1900.* New York: Harper & Bros., 1941.

Langer, William L. *European Alliances and Alignments, 1871–1890.* New York: Alfred A. Knopf, Inc., 1939.

Mowat, Robert B. *History of European Diplomacy, 1815–1914.* London: E. Arnold, 1922.

Sontag, Raymond J. *European Diplomatic History, 1871–1932.* New York: D. Appleton-Century, 1933.

————. *Germany and England: Background of Conflict, 1848–1894.* New York: D. Appleton-Century Co., 1938.

Taylor, Alan J. P. *The Struggle for Mastery in Europe, 1848–1918.* Oxford, England: Clarendon Press, 1954.

18

The triumph of industry: Domestic influences on American foreign relations, 1861-1898

The American Civil War beginning in 1861 was the terrible tragedy of a "Brothers' War." It was a struggle to preserve the union. It resolved a constitutional controversy over federal authority and states' rights. It freed the slaves. And in their classic work, *The Rise of American Civilization*, Charles and Mary Beard saw it as "The Second American Revolution." They referred to the successful revolution in which northern business, with the support of urban workers and free farmers, overthrew the agrarian political dominance that had long been led by the southern planter aristocracy and its spokesmen. The North's victory assured the political triumph of industrial, financial, urban America over rural America.

In the decades after the Civil War many of the foreign policy implications of that revolution were cushioned and obscured by the tremendous opportunities within the United States for both businessmen and farmers—opportunities in its burgeoning cities and in the vast reaches and resources of the West. But that preoccupation with internal economic challenges only temporarily diverted attention away from more enduring foreign policy consequences of the rise of industry and finance. To an impressive degree, America's increasingly active, powerful, and expansionist role in world affairs during the twentieth century is a product of the triumph of industry and finance during the second half of the nineteenth century.

THE ECONOMY

The farmer-agrarian group that was dominant before the Civil War continued to be important after 1861. Encouraged by the Homestead Act and railroads, farmers put more new land under cultivation during the last third of the nineteenth century (especially on the Great Plains) than had been opened to cultivation during the first 250 years of American history. From the beginning of the Civil War until the Spanish-American War of 1898, rural population (including both farm and small-town) increased nearly 80 percent. Agricultural production increased spectacularly.

Nevertheless, agricultural population, production, and income increased more slowly than the urban figures. Furthermore, farm production (at home and abroad) increased more rapidly than the market could absorb gracefully. Consequently, prices for farm products declined, and agriculture suffered an increasingly severe depression. Droughts and other natural hazards on the Great Plains made a bad situation worse. Agrarian protest and reform movements like the Grange, the Farmers' Alliances, and the Populist Party won enthusiastic support but accomplished little. The defeat of William Jennings Bryan and his Populist and Democratic parties in 1896 symbolized the declining power of the farmer in America.

Similarly, the American merchant marine began to decline even before the Civil War, and from 1861 to 1898 it carried a shrinking proportion of American foreign trade. The shipping-commercial group never ruled the economy or government in the last half of the nineteenth century.

Instead, since 1861 industry and finance have had the upper hand. In the last third of the nineteenth century industry grew to impressive proportions. By 1898 the United States was the leading manufacturing state in the world, surpassing even Great Britain. Germany, too, lagged well behind the United States. Furthermore, through consolidations many American firms became giants and near-monopolies with great wealth and power. The United States Steel Corporation organized in 1901 was America's first billion-dollar combination, but business geniuses such as John D. Rockefeller and Andrew Carnegie had already created huge enterprises in the last decades of the nineteenth century.

The growth of industry was paralleled by the accumulation of huge quantities of fluid capital in American hands. The rise of financial and investment giants like the House of Morgan and Kuhn, Loeb, and Company lagged only slightly behind the rise of industry.

By the 1890's many American industrialists, railroad builders, and financiers looked abroad hopefully for raw materials, markets, and profits. But for a quarter of a century after the Civil War most businesses found ample economic opportunities within the boundaries of the United States. Manufacturers got most of the raw materials they needed at low cost from the farms and mines of America. The rapidly expanding population and economy, carefully guarded from foreign competition by ever higher tariffs, consumed most of the products turned out by American industrialists. The burst of railroad construction, including the exciting transcontinental lines, absorbed much of the output of America's iron and steel industries. Furthermore, despite their growth many American industries in the 1870's and 1880's still could not compete on the open market with older British businesses.

Financiers, too, generally found ample opportunities for profitable investment within the boundaries of the United States without having to look abroad. They invested in railroads, western lands, and manufacturing. Rockefeller turned to oil, Charlemagne Tower to the iron deposits of Minnesota. Consequently, the combination of external peace and order and ample economic opportunities within the United States helped reduce American interest and activity in foreign affairs to a minimum during the 1870's and 1880's.

At the same time, however, those economic changes were laying the groundwork for expansion overseas in the 1890's and after. The completion of the transcontinental and trunk railroads, and the ending of the western frontier as a continuous line by 1890, symbolized the contraction (or believed contraction) of economic opportunities within the United States. America's Minister to Austria-Hungary, John A. Kasson, wrote in 1881: "We are rapidly utilizing the whole of our continental territory. We must turn our eyes abroad, or they will soon look inward upon discontent." Though most businesses continued to win all or most of their profits at home, more and more manufacturers and investors by the 1890's began to look abroad for low-cost raw materials, for markets, and for profitable investments. And more of them (while still insisting on tariff protection at home) found that they could compete profitably on the world market if they did not encounter discriminatory policies abroad.

The rise of industry and finance significantly altered American economic relations with other parts of the world. Before the Civil War most exports were agricultural products, particularly raw cotton. That continued to be true after the Civil War. But by 1898 the United States sold a growing proportion of manufactured commodities abroad (though not until World War I did manufactured exports exceed the annual value of agricultural exports). Before the Civil War most imports were manufactured commodities, particularly from England. That was also true later, but after 1861, Americans bought increased quantities of raw materials to be processed in factories, and tropical and semitropical food products such as sugar and coffee.

Industrialization tended, in degree, to change the direction of foreign trade. Before the Civil War most American trade was with its natural markets in England and Western Europe. The United States needed and bought their manufactured goods while they absorbed America's agricultural and mineral products. After the Civil War the greater part of American trade continued to be with Britain and Europe. But as the United States industrialized, a growing proportion of its commerce was with Latin America, Canada, and Asia. Those less industrialized economies supplied raw materials and semitropical food products while they bought manufactured goods from the United States. By 1900 the non-European parts of the world accounted for only one fourth of American foreign trade, but that was more than in 1861 and it was growing.

Beginning in the middle of the 1870's, the United States shifted from an unfavorable to a favorable balance of trade. That is, earlier the United States generally imported more than it exported, but in the 1870's the rapidly growing exports surpassed the value of imports. That favorable balance of trade has continued in most years since 1875.

And finally, industrialization and the rise of finance capitalism encouraged Americans to invest and lend more capital in other parts of the world. The United States retained its debtor balance in international finance until World War I (that is, foreigners had loaned or invested more in the United States than Americans had loaned or invested abroad). By the 1880's and 1890's, however, Americans began to invest and lend more in Canada, Latin America, Hawaii, China, and even in Europe. Those foreign investments were relatively small in the nineteenth century, but they were the advanced guard for the huge investments and loans of the twentieth century.

In summary, the dominant groups in the United States from 1861 to 1898 were no longer the farmer-agrarian or the shipping-commercial groups. They were the industrial and financial interests of the cities. Abundant economic opportunities within the United States for farmers, manufacturers, railroad entrepreneurs, and financiers, when combined with world peace and order abroad, reduced American interest and activity in world affairs to a minimum. The greatest era of American economic activity abroad came in the twentieth century rather than the nineteenth. Nevertheless, the industrialization of the United States, the rise of finance capitalism, the completion of the transcontinental railroads, and the end of the western frontier as a continuous line, all combined to help prepare the way for American expansion overseas, particularly in the less industrialized areas of Latin America, the Pacific, and the Far East.

THE PEOPLE

The high birth rate and massive immigration continued America's impressive population growth. When the Civil War began, there were thirty-two million people in the United States. During the Spanish-American War in 1898 the population exceeded seventy-three million, more than any European country except Russia.

Furthermore, between 1861 and 1898 the movement westward to the frontier and the migration to the cities accelerated. The movement west of the hundredth meridian progressed so rapidly that much of the tillable soil on the Great Plains was settled, and by 1890 the Census Bureau could no longer trace a continuous frontier line. Even more important was the movement to the cities. In 1861 only about 20 percent of Americans lived in cities of 2,500 or more. By 1898 (despite the great movement west to the Last American Frontier), over 40 percent lived in cities of 2,500 or more. The urban population increased nearly 500 percent while the rural population increased only 80 percent. And despite the continued majority position of rural and small-town America, the urban population exercised an influence on economic, intellectual, and foreign affairs that exceeded its proportion of the total population.

In addition to population growth, the westward movement, and urbanization, there were significant increases and changes in immigration patterns. The earlier immigration from countries of northern and western Europe (Britain, Germany, and Ireland) continued in the last third of the nineteenth century and was reinforced by a large movement of Scandinavians. In addition, beginning particularly in the 1880's, many immigrants came from the countries of southern and eastern Europe (Italy, Russia, Poland, Greece, and the Balkans). Some became farmers, but acute poverty forced most of them to seize the more readily available opportunities in the cities. Consequently, a growing minority in the United States was of Latin or Slavic descent. The new immigration patterns exerted little direct influence on American foreign affairs before 1898. They had negative effects, however, in arousing nativist opposition and ethnic bigotry among those people already living in the United States. In any event, the Anglo-Saxon and Germanic peoples remained numerically, culturally, economically, and politically dominant.

Irish-Americans require special mention so far as foreign affairs were concerned. They came throughout the nineteenth and twentieth centuries, but they shared two characteristics of the new immigration: they generally settled in the cities, and they were Roman Catholics. They came in such huge numbers that there are now more people of Irish descent living in the United States than there are in Ireland. Like the earlier Scotch-Irish, the Irish-Americans bitterly hated the English. Irish Fenians in the United States even planned and attempted unsuccessfully to invade Canada in the 1860's. Elections in the last decades of the nineteenth century were often so close that a few thousand votes in key states could determine the results. Consequently, politicians from both parties found it expedient to appeal to the politically active Irish-Americans in the cities of the Northeast by denouncing the British. Irish-Americans prolonged and intensified Anglophobia and probably slowed the development of Anglo-American diplomatic accord.

Like the Irish-Americans and some German-Americans, the immigration from southern and eastern Europe included millions of Roman Catholics. It also included many Orthodox Catholics and people of Jewish faith from Russia and Eastern Europe. But just as the new immigrants did not gain dominance in other areas of activity, so their religious ties exerted little direct influence on American foreign affairs before 1898. Most Americans with religious affiliations were Protestants. The influx of Catholics, however, did have the negative effect of intensifying anti-Catholic sentiment and to that extent may have made many Protestants more enthusiastic about war with Catholic Spain in 1898.

POLITICAL PATTERNS

The two major political parties today were also the major parties from 1861 to 1898. The Democratic Party of Jefferson and Jackson had been weakened by sectional tensions and the Civil War, but it was by no means dead. Other than Andrew Johnson (elected with Lincoln on a Union Party ticket in 1864), the only Democrat to win the Presidency during the half century following the start of the Civil War was Grover Cleveland, who served two separate terms, 1885–1889 and 1893–1897. The presidential elections were always close, however, and sometimes (for examples, Rutherford B. Hayes and Benjamin Harrison) the victorious Republican got only a minority of the total popular vote. Frequently Republican Presidents had to contend with one house of Congress controlled by a Democratic majority.

Despite the continued strength of the Democrats, the Republican Party generally controlled national politics from 1861 to 1898. Every President except Cleveland during the period won election on a Republican ticket. All except Ulysses S. Grant (and Cleveland) served less than two terms. The Republican Party represented a political alliance between the agricultural Middle West and the business Northeast. Most urban workers in those years also voted Republican. Despite farmers and workers, however, the policies and actions generally reflected the interests and desires of the business, manufacturing, and financial wing.

Both major parties included reformers of one sort or another, but neither party demonstrated much compassion for farmers or workers. Pro-business conservatives dominated both parties. They spoke of laissez-faire policies limiting the government's role in the economy. In practice they only limited the government's regulation of business, not its aid. Government efficiency and honesty were not considered as essential as business freedom from government restraints. At the same time, business sought and got government help and subsidies. Land grants to railroads and high protective tariffs were only two of the more obvious forms of government aids to business. Even most reformers would only have made business competition more gentlemanly and ethical; they would not have put the government on the side of labor or the farmer. As a few businesses gained efficiency and looked abroad for markets, even tariff reforms were not wholly devoid of business self-interest.

During the last third of the nineteenth century, men with ability and imagination were more likely to enter business than politics. Many congressmen and state legislators could be and were bought by railroads and others who wanted favors and could afford to pay for them. Demagoguery was common. Republicans "waved the bloody shirt" by blaming Democrats for slavery, the Civil War, and treason. Chauvinism, antiforeign bigotry, and "twisting the British lion's tail" were effective political tactics.

IDEOLOGICAL PATTERNS

After the Civil War most Americans were too busy conquering the last American frontier, building railroads, and developing businesses and industries to give much attention to the philosophical bases for their actions. The absence of foreign threats and the adequacy of economic opportunities at home reinforced already well-established isolationist tendencies. The peace and security enjoyed by the United States from 1865 to 1898 were (then and later) credited by many to the policies of nonentanglement and nonintervention in Europe. Few in those years traced the peace and security to the British Navy, to the balance of power, or to world peace generally. Americans gave the credit to geography and to their own wisdom and virtue. They distrusted foreigners in general and the British in particular. Nativist hostility toward Orientals and toward the new immigration reinforced xenophobia. Most Americans embraced isolationist views more than the sophisticated ideological themes that were to undergird American imperialism and internationalism.

Nevertheless, in the last decades of the nineteenth century and on into the twentieth century there were subtle but fundamental shifts in American foreign policy attitudes, particularly toward Latin America, the Pacific, and the Far East. Earlier most Americans viewed the world from the frame of reference of a weak, have-not, rising state. There were elitist philosophies, but most Americans were not sympathetic with the dominant powers. As the United States became richer and more powerful, with territory to guard and vested interests to defend, leadership groups became a bit more sympathetic with the defense of authority, property, and order. They became a little less convinced that all men were created equal, a little less impressed by the right of revolution, and a bit less persuaded that the democratic will of the people should prevail if it endangered property rights and business profits. If might did not make right, at least America was mighty because it was right. Even in their compassion for the weak and oppressed, many Americans viewed themselves as superior people stooping to help those who were not (and perhaps could not be) equals. The attitudes often were those of *noblesse oblige* rather than those of democracy. Populists in the 1890's attacked privileged classes and worshiped "the will of the people," but they were too "radical" to win acceptance in dominant circles. And even Populists did not always extend their compassion to people abroad with yellow or black skins. As the poor boy from the other side of the tracks prospered, got a big house on the hill, and began to win acceptance in ruling circles, his empathy with the poor and the "outs" slowly dissipated.

Among those who envisaged a larger role for the United States in world affairs, some hoped that international organization and arbitration might provide peace and security. Pacifists particularly lauded such methods. They won relatively little support, however, among Americans. Even many who approved arbitration did so only when the circumstances made it advantageous for the United States. Arbitration appealed most to Americans when the United States was not a party to the dispute. Sometimes it was acceptable when dealing with Great Britain, which was too powerful to be downed easily in direct diplomatic or military confrontations. Furthermore, late in the nineteenth century British leaders were so eager to win American cooperation that they acquiesced in arbitral arrangements that were rigged to the advantage of the United States. But where American security, honor, or vital interests were involved (or, more accurately, where Americans said that security, honor, or vital interests were involved), where the United States dealt with a weaker state, or where the United States might gain more through power (or by diplomacy backed by power), most Americans considered arbitration unacceptable and even dishonorable. In most circumstances Americans (like nationalists in other countries) glorified national sovereignty, insisted on freedom of action, and urged uncompromising defense of national honor and interests as the chauvinist defined them. In those respects the "isolationist" and the "imperialist" were one and the same.

Just as the rise of industry and finance built economic bases for American imperialism overseas, so also late in the nineteenth century Americans began to perfect ideological justifications for that colonial expansion. Biology, history, geography, race, religion, and sea power all found their ways into the ideology of American expansionism. England's Charles Darwin demonstrated scientific restraint and intellectual self-discipline when he advanced his biological theories in *The Origin of*

Species, published in 1859. But laymen who applied his evolution theories to human relations were not so inhibited. Popularizers such as the historian John Fiske used Darwin's ideas to explain and justify American overseas imperialism. The struggle for survival was as inevitable in international affairs, Fiske believed, as it was in the biological world. In that struggle the fittest would inevitably survive. Fiske and his fellow American spokesmen for Social Darwinism never doubted that the Anglo-Saxon states led by the United States were the fittest. Their triumph was not only inevitable, Fiske believed, but was positively desirable for both the United States and for lesser peoples who would benefit from the extension of American institutions, government, products, and religion. In Fiske's thinking Social Darwinism as applied to American foreign affairs took on a "white man's burden" pattern.

No less persuasive was the Reverend Josiah Strong's widely read book, *Our Country,* first published in 1885. That Congregational clergyman was influenced by Social Darwinism and became a spokesman for the Social Gospel movement. He urged an "imperialism of righteousness" and advocated American Protestant missionary activity to Christianize the world. At the same time, he worried about the economic and social significance of contracting opportunities at home, the rise of industry and finance, and the dangers of socialism. Foreign markets for American dollars and industrial products were a conspicuous part of his expansionist message.

While Strong approved the use of power to advance spiritual and humanitarian goals, Captain Alfred Thayer Mahan added moralistic trimmings to sweeten his essentially power justification for American imperialism. An Annapolis graduate with little experience at sea, Mahan advanced his geopolitical theories in numerous books and articles beginning with *The Influence of Sea Power upon History, 1660–1783,* published in 1890. He believed that control of the seas was vital to national power, survival, and prosperity. He also called for strategically located naval bases, an isthmian canal, an active merchant marine, and flourishing foreign trade. His was a world view, not a continentalist approach. And industry, commerce, shipping, and colonies were essential to his scheme.

In 1893 the University of Wisconsin's young historian, Frederick Jackson Turner, explained America's historical evolution in terms of the frontier and the westward movement. If, as Turner suggested, American democracy and prosperity grew out of the frontier experience, the almost inevitable question was whether they could endure when the frontier ended (as the Census Bureau said it had in 1890). In different terms Thomas Jefferson had raised a similar question a century earlier. Turner inspired a generation of historians, but many businessmen and politicians worried about the question too. Could American institutions, democracy, freedom, and prosperity survive when the frontier was gone and the West was filled? Turner himself saw expansion overseas as a not unexpected aftermath of the ending of the continental frontier. He did not formulate an imperialistic ideology, but many did who followed the implications of his frontier hypothesis.

For example, in numerous articles and in *The Law of Civilization and Decay,* published in 1895, Brooks Adams (like his brother, Henry Adams) worried about the deterioration of the society that his great ancestors had helped guide. The depression that followed the Panic of 1893 intensified his fears. He predicted revolution, chaos, and decay if some new outlet were not found for America and its economy. He saw overseas expansion as the salvation for American institutions and democracy at home. Brooks Adams had close personal contacts with many in America's eastern urban leadership elite. His convincing reasoning reinforced the imperialistic enthusiasms of Theodore Roosevelt, John Hay, Henry Cabot Lodge, and other expansionists.

The specifics varied in the approaches of these and other spokesmen for American imperialism near the end of the nineteenth century. But certain themes recurred frequently. Each reflected "racist" views in his emphasis on Anglo-Saxon superiority. Each urged imperialism in the righteous terms of benefiting mankind by spreading the glories of a superior civilization. But each was prepared to use American power to accomplish that expansion. Most of them urged Anglo-Saxon cooperation, but they saw the United States as the leader of the partnership. In the ending of the western frontier and in the rise of cities each saw growing problems endangering American institutions, prosperity, freedom, and democracy. Each was aware of both the problems and the possibilities of a highly productive urban industrial economy. And each found solutions for American problems at home, as well as opportunities for the fulfillment of America's mission, through expansion overseas. Each approved American acquisition of colonies abroad. Each spoke primarily to the educated leadership elites of urban America. And their ideas, activities, and influence extended into the "age of imperialism" from the 1890's into the early years of the twentieth century.

MILITARY FORCES

During the Civil War both the North and the South built their armed forces to unprecedented size and effectiveness. Nearly 900,000 men served in Confederate armed forces, with a maximum strength of more than 250,000 men reached in 1863. At one time or another 1.5 million men served in the Union forces, with over 600,000 in uniform when the fighting ended in April, 1865. Total casualties (North and South) exceeded one million dead and wounded. In its industrial technical aspects and in its total war characteristics, the Civil War marked a transition toward modern warfare. With the end of the Civil War, however, the Confederacy and its armed forces were gone, and the Union armies quickly demobilized.

During most of the generation between the Civil War and the beginning of the Spanish-American War the regular Army had around 25,000 men widely scattered in small units for garrison duty and Indian warfare. There was no general staff and no planning facility. The Army benefited from some technical improvements, including the breech-loading Springfield rifle. In the 1880's it also began to use breech-loading cannon. But the Army was tiny and weak compared to forces of European states then. The state militia or National Guard deteriorated to negligible military significance. Except briefly, when it was inflated with 225,000 volunteers for the 1898 adventure in Cuba, the Army made little progress in the last third of the nineteenth century. Even in that "splendid little war" only the weakness and ineffectiveness of the Spanish allowed the United States to prevail so quickly and easily.

The Navy, too, languished after the Civil War. In the 1860's and 1870's its obsolete ironclads and sailing ships continued to stress coastal defense and potential commerce raiding. It is doubtful, if put to the test, whether they would have been adequate even for those assignments. Most civilians were not interested in the Navy, and professional naval officers comfortably preferred old ways.

In the 1880's, however, the government began to build a modern steel-hulled, steam-powered Navy. In 1883, under President Chester Arthur, Congress appropriated funds for three light cruisers and a dispatch boat. Grover Cleveland's administration added three ships, including two second-class battleships, the *Maine* and the *Texas*. In 1890, under President Benjamin Harrison, Congress authorized construction of three first-class battleships, the *Indiana, Massachusetts,* and *Oregon*.

That same year saw the first of Captain Mahan's books on the importance of sea power. Though not original, he brought together and popularized ideas for a general theory of national security through sea power. Rather than coastal defense and commerce raiding with emphasis on cruisers, Mahan called for concentrated fleet power and control of the seas with priority to battleships. More broadly he stressed the need for naval bases, coaling stations, colonies, an isthmian canal, a subsidized merchant marine, and a thriving foreign trade. In his thoughtful study, *Arms and Men,* Walter Millis suggested that "Mahan's major impulse was simply to produce an argument for more naval building." In providing a rationale for sea power in time of peace as well as war, Mahan's ideas suited the needs of "the rising nationalists, the armament manufacturers, the ship and engine builders, military men hoping to enlarge their careers, bankers looking for foreign investment, merchants interested in colonial markets, investors in the 'banana republics.'" Despite security considerations, it probably was more than a coincidence that the beginnings of the modern American Navy coincided chronologically with the rise of steel manufacturing and with the leveling off and decline of railroad construction.

During much of the last third of the nineteenth century, American foreign policies were not backed by large military and naval forces. But national power involved much more than military forces in being. American power increased spectacularly in the last third of the century. American population exceeded that of any European state except Russia. The United States developed its huge resources rapidly. The Civil War assured national unity and the supremacy of the federal government. American industrial capacity outstripped that of any other country by the end of the century. By 1898 the United States was a regional power and was fast becoming a world power. The new Navy was part of that development. But nonmilitary elements—including industrial and financial capacity—were more fundamental to that power growth.

SUPPLEMENTARY READINGS

Bailey, Thomas A. *The Man in the Street: The Impact of American Public Opinion on Foreign Policy.* New York: Macmillan Co., 1948.

Beard, Charles A. *The Idea of National Interest: An Analytical Study in American Foreign Policy.* New York: Macmillan Co., 1934.

———— and Beard, Mary R. *The Rise of American Civilization.* Rev. ed. New York: Macmillan Co., 1934.

Curti, Merle. *Peace or War: The American Struggle, 1636–1936.* New York: W. W. Norton & Co., Inc., 1936.

Higham, John. *Strangers in the Land: Patterns of American Nativism, 1860–1925.* New Brunswick, N.J.: Rutgers University Press, 1955.

Hofstadter, Richard. *Social Darwinism in American Thought, 1860–1915.* Philadelphia: University of Pennsylvania Press, 1944.

Kirkland, Edward C. *The Coming of the Industrial Age: Business, Labor and Public Policy, 1860–1897.* New York: Holt, Rinehart & Winston, Inc., 1960.

LaFeber, Walter. *The New Empire: An Interpretation of American Expansion, 1860–1898.* Ithaca, N.Y.: Cornell University Press, 1963.

Livezey, William E. *Mahan on Sea Power.* Norman: University of Oklahoma Press, 1947.

Millis, Walter. *Arms and Men: A Study in American Military History.* New York: G. P. Putnam's Sons, 1956.

Pratt, Julius W. *Expansionists of 1898: The Acquisition of Hawaii and the Spanish Islands.* Baltimore: Johns Hopkins Press, 1936.

Shannon, Fred A. *The Farmer's Last Frontier: Agriculture, 1860–1897.* New York: Farrar & Rinehart, Inc., 1945.

Sprout, Harold H. and Sprout, Margaret. *The Rise of American Naval Power, 1776–1918*. Princeton, N.J.: Princeton University Press, 1939.

Strout, Cushing. *The American Image of the Old World*. New York: Harper & Row, Publishers, 1963.

Turner, Frederick Jackson. *The Frontier in American History*. New York: Henry Holt & Co., Inc., 1920.

Weinberg, Albert K. *Manifest Destiny: A Study of Nationalist Expansionism in American History*. Baltimore: Johns Hopkins Press, 1935.

Williams, Benjamin H. *Economic Foreign Policy of the United States*. New York: McGraw-Hill Book Co., 1929.

Williams, William Appleman. *The Roots of the Modern American Empire: A Study of the Growth and Shaping of Social Consciousness in a Marketplace Society*. New York: Random House, 1969.

19

The Civil War and foreign relations

The Civil War and its diplomacy may be studied in terms of the personalities who played their varied roles. One may also view the contest and its consequences in terms of coincidence and chance that conceivably could have given victory to either side depending upon the outcome of a multitude of unpredictable circumstances. In addition, however, the Civil War was a struggle between different kinds of societies with all the economic, ideological, and power variations that those societies represented.

The North increasingly represented an urban business society, while the South was largely rural. Economically the North was becoming oriented predominantly in terms of industry and finance. In contrast the South continued to concentrate on agricultural production, with emphasis on cotton. Ideologically in the minds of many Europeans the North represented democracy, social mobility, opportunity, and aggression. They generally identified the South with slavery, landed aristocracy, social stratification, and a struggle for independence. In foreign affairs (as on the battlefield) the Civil War was partly a contest between the resources and policies of a predominantly urban industrial society and those of an agricultural society.

The central goal of the Confederacy in foreign affairs was to win European recognition and intervention. Its hopes were based on European desires for a divided and weakened America, and on British and

French needs for southern cotton. Northern diplomacy aimed at preventing European intervention. In both military combat and diplomacy (they were part of the same struggle), northern business and its allies commanded greater power, and they triumphed. The success of northern foreign policies contributed substantially to the North's ultimate victory in the Civil War. At the same time, its military accomplishments assured success in foreign affairs, and guaranteed failure for Confederate diplomacy.

KING COTTON DIPLOMACY

The Confederacy was less fortunate in the caliber of its foreign policy statesmen and diplomats than it was in the quality of its military leaders. Some, including Henry Hotze in England and Juan A. Quintero in Mexico, served effectively in difficult circumstances. Nevertheless, from President Jefferson Davis and Secretaries of State Robert Toombs and Judah P. Benjamin on down, the Confederates responsible for foreign affairs generally were not as able as their Union counterparts.

Confederate foreign policies aimed to win European intervention, particularly by Great Britain and France. Southern leaders would have welcomed any of several forms of intervention. They sought diplomatic recognition. They wanted loans, credit, shipping, and trade. They needed warships, rams, and other military equipment from British and European sources. They hoped that Britain and France might repudiate and defy the North's blockade of Confederate ports. And they would have welcomed any mediation proposal that might assure Confederate independence. Depending on the degree of intervention, conceivably the success or failure of southern diplomatic efforts could mean the survival or death of the Confederacy. And in 1861–1862 special circumstances allowed optimism for the Confederacy in foreign affairs.

The stick and the carrot (in that order) that the Confederacy used to try to force or attract European intervention was cotton. An Arkansas planter boasted that cotton was "the king who can shake the jewels in the crown of Queen Victoria." And there was convincing evidence to support his view. Cotton textile manufacturing was Britain's largest industry. It consumed 50,000 bales of cotton each week, more than the United States and continental Europe combined. Approximately one fifth of the English population depended for a living directly or indirectly on cotton. France was less involved, but its cotton textile industry was one of its largest. Around 700,000 Frenchmen based their livings upon cotton. And both Great Britain and France got most of their raw cotton from America.

Southerners determined to create a cotton famine in England and France by preventing the export of cotton. The Confederate government never formally enacted an embargo, lest Europeans blame the South for their difficulties. Instead, through local, state, and private efforts the South accomplished an almost complete embargo. Planters did not send their crops to market; merchants and exporters did not load the cotton on ships; and shippers did not carry it away from Confederate ports. Citizens organizations, with almost unanimous public approval, brought pressure where and when it was needed. Until the spring of 1862 only insignificant quantities of cotton escaped from the Confederacy. At the same time, the Confederacy sent agents abroad to remind Europeans that only a Confederate success could reopen and safeguard their main source for that essential raw material.

When the embargo failed to force European intervention, the Confederacy in 1863 began to use its raw cotton as a basis for credit with which to buy the products it needed from European suppliers. Initially, private shippers handled the export of cotton, and the financial and material gains for the Confederacy were disappointing. By 1864–1865, however, the government assumed exclusive authority over the export and disposal of southern cotton in Europe. The results were modest and too late to be decisive. But they were more helpful to the Confederacy than any previous foreign policy tactics in the use of the South's leading agricultural commodity.

THE NORTH AND FOREIGN AFFAIRS

Just as the Confederacy sought foreign intervention on its behalf, so the Union aimed to prevent intervention. President Abraham Lincoln's statesmanship and sound judgment were fundamental to the North's success, but he focused most of his attention on domestic matters and on winning the war.

The main responsibility for directing foreign affairs fell to Lincoln's Secretary of State, William H. Seward. A highly successful Whig and Republican politician from New York, Seward believed that he, rather than Lincoln, deserved the Presidency. Like most who served as Secretary of State during the last three quarters of the nineteenth century, Seward had had no previous experience in foreign affairs. Lincoln chose him to head the Cabinet because of his political prominence in the Republican Party, not because of any apparent diplomatic qualifications. Initially, Seward was contemptuous of Lincoln. He arrogantly envisaged himself in the role of a "prime minister" for Lincoln, whom Seward saw as grossly indecisive and ineffective.

In the spring of 1861 Seward even advised the President to provoke war with Spain or France on the grounds that a foreign war might drive the North and the South together and avert Civil War. Lincoln quietly ignored Seward's drastic recommendation. Fortunately for the Union,

Seward grew to recognize Lincoln's greatness, and he became one of the President's more able and trusted subordinates. His outstanding performance was among the variables that prevented European intervention.

In addition to Lincoln and Seward, the North's cause abroad was well served by Charles Francis Adams of Massachusetts, the United States Minister to Great Britain. Son of one President and grandson of another, Adams performed with impressive tact, firmness, and skill in countering Confederate moves in England and in preventing intervention.

Without minimizing the talents of Lincoln, Seward, Adams, and others, however, their common task was made easier by the economic power and military successes of the North. Antietam, Gettysburg, and Vicksburg were as essential to the success of northern foreign policies as Lincoln, Seward, and Adams were. Furthermore, northern diplomatic successes were not won without difficulty. There was much uncertainty and concern about the diplomatic outcome, particularly in 1861–1862. Externally, the delicate balance of power in Europe left France and even England less free to act independently in the American Civil War than they or the Confederacy might have preferred.

President Lincoln, in effect, invited limited British intervention when he proclaimed a blockade of Confederate ports in April, 1861. He might have closed southern ports, but a blockade under international law could only be directed against a foreign state. Consequently, when Great Britain proclaimed its neutrality in May, 1861 (also an action relevant to a war between belligerent states), it followed logically the path pointed to by Lincoln's prior action.

More sensational was the *Trent* affair. In November, 1861, the U.S.S. *San Jacinto*, under Captain Charles Wilkes, stopped the British mail-steamer, the *Trent*, on the high seas and seized two Confederate commissioners, James M. Mason of Virginia and John Slidell of Louisiana. Mason was en route to England while Slidell was bound for duties in France. Northerners enthusiastically applauded Wilkes' action. Britain, of course, protested vigorously. Emotions flared on both sides of the Atlantic. The possibility of war between Great Britain and the United States seemed very real. Such a war would have assured survival of the Confederacy and would have destroyed Lincoln's chances for restoring the union. Lincoln and Seward did not approve of Wilkes' unauthorized action, but its popularity made it risky for them to repudiate the naval hero. It would have been particularly dangerous politically if it appeared that the Administration were backing down before British demands. The possibility of war with Britain, however, had sobering effects on northern public opinion. Lincoln's Cabinet approved release of the two Confederate agents and allowed them to continue on their way. Seward's note to the British government explaining the decision was couched in terms that seemed to be "talking back" to the British. His words were aimed more toward the American public than toward the British. By mid-January, 1862, the danger of war with Britain over the incident had passed.

There were also sharp differences over private construction and sale of ships in Britain for the Confederacy. British spokesmen insisted that it was consistent with international law, provided the ships were not armed. The United States strongly disagreed. Seward and Adams protested repeatedly against construction and sale of ships and rams to the Confederacy, with or without armaments. The British government was moved less by legal considerations than by the desire to avoid war with the United States. Furthermore, it did not wish to set precedents that might be harmful to Britain in future wars. Two ships, the *Alabama* and the *Florida*, escaped from British shipyards in 1862 and were armed elsewhere. They caused substantial damage to northern shipping throughout the remainder of the war. But the British government yielded to Adams' firm protests and prevented two Laird rams and other vessels from falling into Confederate hands. The Confederacy also failed to get fighting ships from France.

On that matter, as on the blockade and other considerations involving neutral rights, Seward and Adams held out for a broad definition of belligerent rights and a narrow definition of neutral rights. Great Britain, in the unusual posture of a neutral, acquiesced in the Union interpretation of neutral rights during the Civil War. In taking that course, British leaders were looking ahead to the time when Britain, as the world's greatest naval power, could use American precedents to sustain its long-term preference for a narrow definition of neutral rights. Long-range interests of the great naval power, rather than sympathy for the North, led the British to concur in the positions advanced by Seward and Adams on neutral rights during the Civil War.

European and British opposition to slavery handicapped Confederate diplomacy. But Lincoln consistently insisted that the North was fighting to preserve the union, not to free the slaves. His approach reduced the sympathy the North might have won in other parts of the world. Lincoln never changed his fundamental goal in the war. The Emancipation Proclamation issued on September 22, 1862, and put into effect on January 1, 1863, was designed for domestic politics and foreign affairs. At Seward's suggestion Lincoln delayed the Proclamation until after the North had checked Lee's military forces at Antietam, Maryland. That success in checking General Lee's penetration of the North increased European doubts about the future of the Confederacy. And that military engagement, by triggering the Emancipation Proclamation, made it easier for the North to persuade the British that its eventual triumph would end slavery in America. Legally the Proclamation did not free any slaves that had not already been freed by earlier congressional action. It was a political move, a war measure, and a diplomatic tactic.

Despite the crises and problems, northern efforts to prevent European intervention succeeded. By the middle of 1863 there was no further real danger that Great Britain, France, or any other country would recognize the Confederacy or intervene effectively. Some of the reasons for the success of northern foreign policies have already been suggested. Others become meaningful in an examination of the policies of the major European states.

RUSSIA AND THE CIVIL WAR

The leading state that clearly favored the North over the Confederacy from the first was Czarist Russia under Alexander II. There never was the slightest possibility that Russia would recognize the Confederacy or intervene. The Czar freed the serfs in Russia at about the same time that Lincoln freed the slaves. A few Russians even fought in the Union armies. In 1862, when France sought Russia's cooperation in an offer of mediation in the Civil War, Russia refused. Units of the Russian Navy dropped anchor in San Francisco and in New York in the fall of 1863. Americans interpreted those visits as friendly gestures, and they received the Russians enthusiastically. Secretary of the Navy Gideon Welles exclaimed, "God bless the Russians." And long afterwards Oliver Wendell Holmes wrote of Russia "who was our friend when the world was our foe."

National self-interest generally is responsible for most expressions of friendship between states. And so it was with Russia's attitudes toward the North during the Civil War. Both Russia and the United States had long considered Great Britain to be the leading barrier to their separate expansionist ambitions. Their common opposition to Great Britain had given them a community of interest that continued during the Civil War. The Russian Minister to the United States, Baron Edouard de Stoeckl, wrote that Anglo-American rivalry was "the best guarantee against the ambitious projects and political egotism of the Anglo-Saxon race." Just as America feared Anglo-French intervention in the Civil War, so Russia feared the involvement of Britain and France when Russia in 1863 again suppressed an uprising in Poland. Indeed, fear of war with Britain was the real reason for the Russian fleet's visits to America. Russian leaders wanted their ships in neutral ports so that they would not be bottled up by the British in the event of war. Scholars did not find proof of that motivation, however, until they got access to the Russian archives a half century later. Whatever the motives, Russia's friendship was most welcome in the North.

FRANCE AND THE CIVIL WAR

Napoleon III of France favored the Confederacy, but French public opinion divided and patterns changed from time to time. At the beginning of the Civil War, antislavery and anti-British attitudes aroused much French sympathy for the North. In 1862–1863 opinion shifted toward the South, and near the end of the war it changed slightly back toward the North.

Circumstances in the nineteenth and twentieth centuries often made it expedient for France to cooperate with Great Britain in world affairs. But France had fought too many wars against the British to waste much affection on them. Like the Russians, the French rather liked the idea of a strong United States to contest the British. At the same time, however, the success of Napoleon's Mexican venture depended partly on the inability of a divided and weakened United States to enforce the Monroe Doctrine. Those conflicting considerations, along with Napoleon's sensitivity to public opinion, affected his policies.

Napoleon III favored some form of European intervention, particularly in 1862–1863. In October and November, 1862, he formally urged Russia and Great Britain to join with France in a joint mediation offer. Russia flatly rejected the proposal. Great Britain under Lord Palmerston seriously considered mediation but finally vetoed the idea.

To protect his Mexican scheme Napoleon III favored a joint mediation benefiting the Confederacy. But he would not risk unfavorable political repercussions at home, and he would not undertake mediations alone without Britain's cooperation. Consequently, the key to the outcome of the struggle between Confederate King Cotton diplomacy and Seward's opposing policies lay in Great Britain.

GREAT BRITAIN AND THE CIVIL WAR

Britain's policies toward the Civil War could affect the course of other states on the matter. The dominant view among English leaders was both sympathetic and optimistic about the future of the Confederacy. Emotionally, Englishmen resented the boastful crudeness and pretensions of Americans. It was easy to see the North as an oppressive bully and the Confederacy as the underdog fighting for its freedom. It was pleasing to see upstart Yankees have their comeuppance. Ethnically, southern whites were mostly of Anglo-Saxon descent, while the North had a large non-English population (including German-Americans and English-hating Irish-Americans). Socially, upper classes in England found the stratified society of the South with its landed aristocracy more appealing than the fluid and democratic social patterns of the North.

Ideologically, many conservatives in both the Tory and Whig parties saw in the American Civil War persuasive evidence of the imperfections and dangers of democracy. They considered it a violent warning against extending the franchise beyond the limits set in the British Reform Bill of 1832. The Confederacy had slavery, but by 1861 England's antislavery crusade had lost some of its fervor. Besides, Lincoln repeatedly denied that he was fighting to free the slaves. And many of those who were most repelled by a slave labor system did not have the vote in England anyway. In terms of power politics a divided and weakened America would pose less of a challenge to Canada and to Britain's interests in Latin America, to say nothing of Britain's supremacy on the world scene.

Economically, the North's developing industry clashed with Britain's economy, while the South's agriculture supplemented it. Yankees competed with British manufacturers, financiers, and traders. Furthermore, their protectionist Morrill tariff interfered with British sales and profits in America. In contrast, southern cotton planters supplied Britain with an essential industrial raw material, borrowed British capital, and bought British manufactured products. The South's low-tariff predilections provided an open market for British industry and capital. While the British did not have to have anything the North produced (not even its wheat), they did need the South's cotton. The inability of England to get southern cotton during most of 1861–1862 caused acute difficulties in textile cities in the Midlands. Mills began to shut down and by the end of 1862 two million Englishmen suffered real hardship and destitution because of the cotton famine there. In brief, Englishmen shed few tears over America's turmoil in 1861–1865. And most of them believed that the Confederacy would make good its attempt to go its separate and independent way. Most assumed that sooner or later Britain would recognize the Confederacy with no misgivings or regrets. But, confident of the outcome, British leaders felt they could bide their time until Confederate success was a *fait accompli.*

Great Britain proclaimed its neutrality, in effect recognizing Confederate belligerency. Its leaders conferred unofficially with Confederate agents. They worried about the danger of revolutionary disturbances and harmful political repercussions resulting from the cotton famine in 1862. Britain formally considered the possibility of joint mediation in the fall of 1862.

Despite its sympathies with the South, however, and despite toying with the possibility of recognition and mediation, Great Britain under Prime Minister Palmerston and Foreign Secretary John Russell never intervened. It never formally recognized the Confederacy, it did not offer to mediate, and it did not repudiate the northern blockade.

There may have been some ideological bases for the British course; there were important economic explanations for its policies; and there were decisive military explanations. Antislavery considerations may not have been terribly important, since the laboring classes who felt strongly on the issue were not, at that time, an effective political voice. Nevertheless, after the Emancipation Proclamation it did appear to many Englishmen that a northern victory was likely to have the desired effect of freeing the slaves. By the time the South in 1865 tried to get British support by offering to free the slaves, it was too late. Furthermore, English radicals led by John Bright saw a relationship between their own crusade to broaden the franchise and the effort by the North to make "government of the people, by the people, and for the people" prevail in America.

Several considerations prevented King Cotton from being as effective in England as the Confederacy had hoped. Unfortunately from the South's point of view, Britain had a huge surplus of raw cotton on hand when the Civil War began. Consequently, the cotton famine did not become acute until the middle of 1862. Even then, though workers suffered, the owners did not. The inability to get southern cotton actually increased the value of the cotton supplies on hand in England. If the blockade were broken and raw cotton became easily available, the owners of existing supplies would have suffered financial losses. And the owners, not the hard-pressed workers, carried weight with the British government. Furthermore, as the war dragged on, English manufacturers found alternate sources of raw cotton in India, Egypt, and Brazil, so they were not as dependent on the South as they had been earlier. At the same time, linen and woolen textile industries thrived as they took up the slack left by the languishing cotton manufacturing. Other sectors of the British economy also prospered as they shipped and sold manufactured products, including munitions, to both sides in the Civil War. War trade with both North and South was more than enough to offset losses suffered by cotton textile workers so far as the total British economy was concerned. British shippers also gained at the expense of Americans in the worldwide carrying trade. Britain could get along without northern wheat; it could get supplies from Russia and elsewhere. But the war trade was far more valuable to the British economy than southern cotton supplies.

In addition to ideological and economic considerations, the relative power of the North and the South determined Britain's course. Initially, Britain assumed that the Confederacy would succeed without British intervention. But as the South's military fortunes waned, so did the possibility of British intervention. Union forces checked and turned back General Robert E. Lee's invasion of Maryland in the Battle of Antietam in September, 1862. That crucial engagement occurred just as the cotton famine reached its most critical stage, and just before France made its strongest bid to win British cooperation with a mediation proposal. But the Confederate failure at Antietam encouraged Britain to reject mediation. And the Union victories at Gettysburg and Vicksburg in July, 1863, killed any lingering possibility of British recognition, mediation, or intervention of any sort. Great Britain had hoped for Confederate success, but not if that could only be accomplished at the cost of a major Anglo-American war. When Confederate troops were unable to destroy the Union forces, Confederate diplomacy failed as well.

In the final analysis the industrial North, with the support of free farmers and workers of the North, commanded greater power than the planter-farmer South. And that power prevailed both on the battlefield and in foreign affairs. The success on each front contributed to the success on the other.

SUPPLEMENTARY READINGS

Adams, Ephraim D.   *Great Britain and the American Civil War.* 2 vols. New York: Longmans, Green & Co., Inc., 1925.

Bancroft, Frederic.   *The Life of William H. Seward.* 2 vols. New York: Harper & Bros., 1900.

Callahan, James M.   *The Diplomatic History of the Southern Confederacy.* Baltimore: Johns Hopkins Press, 1901.

Case, Lynn M., and Spencer, Warren F.   *The United States and France: Civil War Diplomacy.* Philadelphia: University of Pennsylvania Press, 1970.

Duberman, Martin B.   *Charles Francis Adams.* Boston: Houghton Mifflin Co., 1961.

Harris, Thomas L.   *The Trent Affair.* Indianapolis and Kansas City: Bowen-Merrill Co., 1896.

Jordan, Donaldson, and Pratt, Edwin J.   *Europe and the American Civil War.* Boston: Houghton Mifflin Co., 1931.

Monaghan, Jay.   *Diplomat in Carpet Slippers: Abraham Lincoln Deals with Foreign Affairs.* Indianapolis: Bobbs-Merrill Co., 1945.

Owsley, Frank L. and Harriet C.   *King Cotton Diplomacy: Foreign Relations of the Confederate States of America.* 2d ed. Chicago: University of Chicago Press, 1959.

Van Deusen, Glyndon G.   *William Henry Seward.* New York: Oxford University Press, 1967.

Villiers, Brougham, and Chesson, W. H.   *Anglo-American Relations, 1861–1865.* London: T. F. Unwin, Ltd., 1919.

Winks, Robin W.   *Canada and the United States: The Civil War Years.* Baltimore: Johns Hopkins Press, 1960.

20

The United States and Europe, 1865-1898

During the generation that followed the Civil War the United States devoted less attention to Europe than usual. No European states endangered United States security. Americans were preoccupied with their own domestic economic and political concerns. If unilateralism, nonintervention in Europe, and nationalism were hallmarks of American isolationism, then the United States generally was isolationist in the decades following the Civil War. America's most spectacular dealings with European states resulted from conflicts of interests in Asia, the Pacific, and the Western Hemisphere.

Nevertheless, the United States has never literally isolated itself, and it did not do so during the so-called "nadir of diplomacy" that followed the Civil War. Americans continued to trade more with Britain and Western Europe than with other areas. British financiers loaned and invested heavily in the United States. American cultural ties were still primarily with Britain and Europe. Immigration provided personal and family links with Europe. Long-range patterns in dealings with particular states began to appear. The United States was a party to treaties with European states. It participated in multilateral conferences and conventions. And from time to time individual diplomatic crises forced official and public attention on Europe.

187

NAPOLEON III AND MEXICO

During the last quarter of the nineteenth century most Americans and their leaders gave little thought to France, its people, or its policies. But a major crisis in Franco-American relations emerged from Napoleon III's ambitions in Mexico. Chronic instability and disunity in Mexico almost invited foreign intervention. That possibility increased in the summer of 1861 when President Benito Juárez suspended payment on Mexico's foreign debts. France, Spain, and Great Britain decided to intervene jointly to force payment. They invited the United States to join them, but Seward declined. The European troops took Vera Cruz in January, 1862, but Britain and Spain soon withdrew and disassociated themselves from the venture.

Napoleon III persisted on a scale that clearly revealed that his goals were not limited to collecting debts. Despite stubborn Mexican resistance, French troops took Mexico City by the summer of 1863. In cooperation with the French, conservative Mexicans who opposed Juárez organized a Council of Notables that invited the Austrian Archduke Maximilian to assume the Mexican throne. Eager to reign, encouraged by the invitation and a plebiscite, and assured of the support of Napoleon's troops, the handsome, idealistic Archduke and his beautiful, ambitious wife, Carlota, arrived in Mexico in the middle of 1864.

Emperor Napoleon III may have had in mind the grandeur of his more famous namesake when he undertook the adventure. If it succeeded it might bring political advantage at home. The chaos in Mexico while the United States was torn by Civil War seemed to provide him with the perfect moment for his move. It might prevent United States hegemony in the Western Hemisphere. Whatever his motives, the venture was an alarming European challenge to United States interests and security in the Western Hemisphere.

When the initial three-power intervention seemed to have only limited and temporary objectives, the United States did not formally object. Even after Napoleon's more extensive ambitions became apparent, the Civil War prevented the United States from opposing the French effectively. Nevertheless, Secretary of State William H. Seward kept the record clear by indicating American objections to French actions. In 1863–1864, as the North gained the upper hand in the Civil War, Seward's objections became firmer. He never explicitly mentioned the Monroe Doctrine, but he clearly implied it. With Lee's surrender at Appomattox, Seward was free to step up his pressures on France. He was careful, however, not to move so rapidly that France could not extricate itself without fighting the United States. By the end of 1865 France promised to withdraw its troops, and the last of them left Mexico in the spring of 1867. Maximilian foolishly elected to remain in Mexico, and he died bravely before a Mexican firing squad. Carlota personally appealed to Napoleon III and to the Pope for support for her husband. When her desperate efforts failed, the high-strung young woman went mad and was confined in a chateau near Brussels during the rest of her long life.

Circumstances in Europe and in Mexico were of major importance in causing Napoleon to abandon his unfortunate puppets in Mexico. The whole episode had cost more money and troops than he had expected or intended. It proved to be unpopular in France and was a political liability for him there. He worried about Bismarck's Prussia in Central Europe. Furthermore, Mexican resistance showed no signs of ending. Maximilian's liberalism had alienated Mexican conservatives, and French troops could not down Juárez' guerrilla fighters. The whole venture was proving to be a fiasco for Napoleon. He had misgivings about it as early as 1863, and conceivably he might have withdrawn his troops, with or without Seward and the Monroe Doctrine.

Nevertheless, Seward did perform skillfully in gradually stepping up his pressures on France. And with the close of the Civil War his diplomacy was backed by more power than Napoleon was prepared to concentrate in America. The combination of difficulties in Europe and Mexico, plus America's protests and power, made it expedient for Napoleon to abandon his scheme. Understandably, most Americans were not displeased when Napoleon III fell from power after his defeat in the Franco-Prussian War of 1870–1871.

Americans objected when a private French company under Ferdinand de Lesseps attempted to build a canal across the Isthmus of Panama in the 1880's. The French company found the technical, financial, and health problems too great for its resources, however, and it failed by the end of the decade. There was friction between French Catholic missionaries and American Protestant missionaries in East Asia. And American trade and financial ties with France were weak compared to those with Britain or even Germany.

GERMANY AND THE UNITED STATES

Except for certain hyphenated groups, most Americans were little interested in Central Europe. The states in Central Europe did not affect American security or vital interests. Unlike Britain and France, they did not consider intervention during the Civil War, and Prussia's policies at that time were as satisfactory to the North as those of any European state except Russia. Just as the Civil War directed American attention inward, so unification under Mazzini, Cavour, and Garibaldi concentrated Italian attention inward in Central Europe. Similarly, Prussia's Bismarck focused on Europe before, during, and after his successful unification of the German Empire in 1871. Italy after unification had neither the interests nor the power to disturb the United States in the Western Hemisphere or elsewhere. Germany's power and industry grew rapidly, but so long as Bismarck was at the helm Germany did not challenge the United States directly outside of Europe. Many American scholars studied in Germany, and the German influence on higher education in the United States was very great. After young Kaiser William II ousted Bismarck in 1890, German-American relations cooled a bit, but by 1898 neither Germany nor Italy could accurately be labeled a major opponent of the United States in world politics.

Certain incidents, however, did disrupt United States relations with Germany late in the nineteenth century. The unified German Empire was a new element in the European and world power structure. Germany's increasingly productive industry competed with America's urban economy. Furthermore, America's expanding agricultural production and exports alarmed farmers in Prussia and Bavaria. Like France and other European states, Germany in the 1880's imposed discriminatory restrictions on the import of pork products from the United States.

Kaiser William II's militant speeches, his naval building program, his colonial ambitions in Samoa and elsewhere, and the beginnings of the German challenge to British supremacy provoked some misgivings in the United States in the 1890's. But Anglophobia, the affection of German-Americans for their fatherland, and continuing American isolationism, prevented acute or chronic friction between the United States and Germany before 1898. Clear trends pointing to war between the United States and Germany in the twentieth century did not exist before 1898.

ANGLO-AMERICAN RELATIONS

Great Britain has played a larger role than any other country in the history of American foreign relations. Despite the inflammatory efforts of Irish-Americans and other Anglophobes, the United States and Great Britain peacefully resolved various differences during the generation following the Civil War. By the 1890's leaders in both countries consciously guided the two states toward cooperation in world affairs.

Canada was directly and indirectly involved in Anglo-American relations. Its location made it an American hostage for British good conduct. The American example may have encouraged Canadian agitation for autonomy or independence. At the same time, American expansionist ambitions alarmed Canadians and made them more reluctant to lose Britain's protective cover than they might otherwise have been. During the last half of the nineteenth century and the first years of the twentieth, there were annoying border incidents, as well as persistent disputes over fishing rights and pelagic sealing. In those incidents Great Britain was torn between its responsibilities to Canada and its need for

United States cooperation in world affairs. Canadians often felt, not without justification, that Britain's desires for American support took precedence over Canada's interests.

Confederate agents in Canada caused various border incidents, including a small raid on St. Albans, Vermont, in 1864. Irish nationalists in the United States viewed Canada as a convenient place to strike at the hated English. Their Fenian Brotherhood raised funds, recruited and trained "armies," and twice attempted military assaults on Canada. Canadians easily crushed a Fenian raid across the border at Buffalo in 1866, and a similar attempt in 1870 was even more futile. The United States government acted against the Fenians, but probably moved less swiftly and decisively than it might have if the Irish-American vote had been less important politically.

A major problem in Anglo-American relations concerned claims growing out of northern losses during the Civil War brought about by ships built in England for the Confederacy. Estimates of the damages caused by the *Alabama,* the *Florida,* and the *Shenandoah* varied widely, as did opinions on Britain's legal responsibility for the losses. American protests and Britain's desire to avoid harmful precedents had led Britain during the last half of the Civil War to prevent any more such ships from falling into Confederate hands. British misgivings on the matter, however, did not go far enough to satisfy American extremists. Charles Sumner of Massachusetts, chairman of the Senate Foreign Relations Committee, insisted that the British policies had prolonged the Civil War by two years at a cost of more than $2 billion. Though he did not explicitly say so, he clearly implied that Britain could fulfill that obligation by transferring Canada to the United States. Even the anti-imperialist "Little England" movement in the 1860's was not prepared for such a drastic course, certainly not to the advantage of the United States. Canadians objected to the idea even more than the English did.

Fortunately for Anglo-American relations, moderation eventually prevailed. Secretary of State Fish, with the willing cooperation of Prime Minister William Gladstone and Lord Clarendon in England, and Sir John Rose and Prime Minister John Macdonald of Canada, arranged for a Joint High Commission to negotiate a settlement of differences. The result was the Treaty of Washington signed in May, 1871. It covered many problems in relations between the United States, Great Britain, and the Dominion of Canada. It provided for arbitration by the German Emperor of the claims of Britain and the United States to the San Juan Islands in the Strait of Juan de Fuca, an award that eventually went to the United States. The treaty also tried to reconcile continuing differences between Canadians and Americans on fishing rights and liberties in territorial waters. The fishing provisions were more generous to Americans than to the Canadians and British. The treaty provided for a joint commission to arbitrate general claims between the parties. That commission eventually awarded nearly $2 million to the British and nothing to Americans. Most important, the Treaty of Washington called for arbitration of the *Alabama* claims by a tribunal composed of appointees of Great Britain, the United States, Brazil, Italy, and Switzerland. Britain expressed regret that the *Alabama* and the other ships had escaped its ports, and for the damage caused by those ships. The treaty laid down rules for the arbitrators, including one that emphasized a neutral's responsibility for allowing fighting ships to escape its ports for use against a belligerent. In other words, the treaty was "rigged" in favor of the general American position on the direct *Alabama* claims. The treaty neither acknowledged nor denied responsibility for indirect damages. In general the Treaty of Washington was more favorable to the United States than it was to Great Britain and Canada, and it won quick approval in the United States Senate. Even Sumner voted for it.

The arbitral tribunal met in Geneva in 1871–1872 with Charles Francis Adams representing the United States. Under instructions from Secretary Fish, the United States presented claims for both direct and indirect damages. That move shocked the British and threatened to scuttle the arbitration effort. But at Adams' suggestion the tribunal ruled out the indirect claims, and eventually awarded $15.5 million to the United States.

The whole controversy over the *Alabama* claims had poisoned Anglo-American relations for a decade. In the final analysis, however, skillful and responsible diplomacy prevailed. The peaceful resolution of the disputes laid the groundwork for the calculated efforts to promote Anglo-American diplomatic cooperation later. And the settlement reflected the growing power of the United States relative to Great Britain.

Political appeals to Anglophobia by "twisting the British lion's tail" were almost standard in American political campaigns during the latter part of the nineteenth century. But when the Democratic incumbent, Grover Cleveland, contested with Republican Benjamin Harrison for the Presidency in 1888, the British Minister, Sir Lionel Sackville-West, blundered into that political game. A Californian, who pretended to be a naturalized American citizen of British descent, wrote to the British Minister asking his advice on voting in the election of 1888. Sackville-West in a private letter replied that he thought Cleveland might be more favorable to Britain than his opponent. Republican newspapers promptly published the letter throughout the country, and Anglophobes (and Republicans) set out to defeat Britain's alleged lackey, Cleveland. To stave off defeat, Cleveland demanded that Britain recall Sackville-West. When the British Foreign Office procrastinated, the injudicious Englishman was given his passport and sent on his way. Annoyed by the incident, Britain did not send a successor until the defeated Cleveland left office in 1889. The incident hurt, but did not do irreparable damage (except, possibly, to Cleveland's chances for a second consecutive term as President). Sackville-West's successor, Sir Julian Pauncefote, ably served the cause of Anglo-American accord until his death in the United States in 1902.

A more persistent difficulty, one that was not handled satisfactorily from the American frame of reference in the nineteenth century, concerned the killing of seals. The great seal herds located on and near America's Pribilof Islands in the Bering Sea were threatened with extinction by pelagic sealing, that is killing seals in the open seas. That procedure led to heavy destruction of females and their pups. Since pelagic sealing occurred outside the conventional territorial waters, national legislation seemed inadequate for the problem. Furthermore, no treaty covered the matter. In a desperate effort to save the herds, the United States in the 1880's began to seize Canadian ships engaged in sealing on the high seas. The United States justified its course on the questionable grounds that the Bering Sea, partly enclosed by American-owned Alaska and the Aleutian Islands, was a closed sea subject to United States jurisdiction. British leaders may have sympathized with the American objective, but doubted the lawfulness of its methods. Canadians rejected both the goal and the methods. By agreement in 1892 the dispute was arbitrated, and the decision went against the United States. Eventually the United States paid $473,151 for damages caused by seizure of Canadian ships. Not until the negotiation of a four-power treaty in 1911 was satisfactory protection arranged for the seal herds.

On seal killing the United States seemed morally correct but legally wrong, and the United States was downed. In the more inflammatory Venezuelan boundary dispute the United States position was less defensible, and the legal aspects were not so clear. Nevertheless, world politics and national power served the American wishes. The boundary between British Guiana and Venezuela had been disputed at least since the 1840's. Control of the mouth of the Orinoco River was involved, and discovery of gold inland expanded and intensified the territorial claims of both parties. In a straight power contest Britain was certain to triumph; conversely, arbitration with its tendency to "split the difference" might have favored Venezuela. Britain had many boundary disputes in its far-flung empire. To accept arbitration of each dispute would certainly trim its territory and sacrifice the advantages its power provided. In such a situation, understandably Venezuela urged arbitration and Britain opposed it. Lacking sufficient power of its own, Venezuela sought United States support for its stand.

With the approval of President Cleveland, the new Secretary of State, Richard Olney, on July 20, 1895, demanded that Britain agree to arbitration. The former railroad lawyer charged that Britain's territorial claims threatened American interests and violated the Monroe Doctrine. He climaxed his note with the boast: "Today the United States is practically sovereign on this continent, and its fiat is law upon the subjects to which it confines its interposition. . . . its infinite resources combined with its isolated position render it master of the situation and practically invulnerable as against any or all other powers." Olney was a sincere and dedicated spokesman for American expansion, including economic expansion in Latin America. Furthermore, with the depression of the 1890's eroding support for the Administration, Olney's chauvinistic challenge to Great Britain was good politics.

Britain's Lord Salisbury delayed his reply for four months and then calmly demolished Olney's analysis, denied that the Monroe Doctrine was relevant on the matter, and flatly rejected arbitration. Thoroughly aroused, Cleveland in December, 1895, sent a message to Congress requesting appropriations for a commission to study the claims of the two states. The President said that when those findings were reported it would "be the duty of the United States to resist by every means in its power as wilful aggression upon its rights and interests the appropriation by Great Britain of any lands or the exercise of governmental jurisdiction over any territory which after investigation we have determined of right belongs to Venezuela." Emotions flared and firebrands, both in the United States and in Great Britain, talked of war. But moderates spoke out as well.

In the midst of the tempest, Germany's Kaiser William II sent a telegram to President Paul Kruger of Transvaal congratulating him on the Boer success against Britain's Jameson. The Kruger telegram dramatized Britain's difficulties elsewhere and its need for peace with the United States in the Western Hemisphere. By November, 1896, Britain and the United States agreed to arbitration of the boundary dispute. The arbitral award handed down in 1899 generally supported the British claims, except that Venezuela got control of the important Orinoco River.

The whole episode aroused more passions than its importance justified, either for the United States or for Great Britain. Through it all, even the United States acted more for its own self-interest than out of any real concern for Venezuela. The incident was a disturbing crisis in Anglo-American relations. But coming at a time when the Boer War and a German challenge occupied Britain's main attention, the incident helped to emphasize Britain's need for good relations with the United States.

By 1898 Anglo-American accord had progressed to the point where British sympathy for the United States in the Spanish-American War could hardly have been unexpected. Britain generally approved American policies toward the Spanish in Cuba, and its benevolent neutrality helped prevent any European intervention on behalf of Spain. Britain also encouraged American annexation of Hawaii and the Philippines. In 1898 the British government even suggested an alliance with the United States to guard their common interests in China. Tradition caused the United States to reject a formal alliance, but leaders in both states recognized their similar interests and often pursued parallel policies in Asia.

THE UNITED STATES AND CZARIST RUSSIA

Americans generally had little interest in Eastern Europe, and only a few were active there or informed about the area. The United States and Russia established formal diplomatic relations in 1809 when President James Madison and Czar Alexander I headed the two states. The controversy over the southern boundary of Alaska in the early 1820's was resolved without major difficulty. The two countries concluded a commercial treaty in 1832, but very little trade developed. Russia seemed to be the North's best friend abroad during the Civil War. That so-called "friendship," however, was rooted more in an absence of contacts than in any positive affection. More important was the fact that both Russia and the United States viewed Great Britain as an adversary and as a barrier to their separate expansionist ambitions. Except for their common opposition to Great Britain, the term "indifference" more accurately described the early relations between Russia and the United States. The purchase of Alaska by the United States from Russia in 1867 occurred within the framework of the "tradition" of friendship. But that was one of the last episodes in that phase of Russian-American relations.

As early as the 1850's Russian leaders began to consider selling Alaska. The fur-bearing sea otter was being exterminated, and the Russian-American Company that controlled the area faced bankruptcy. If Alaska were to be retained as a colony, the Russian government would either have to subsidize the company heavily or take over administration of the territory. Many feared that Great Britain or the United States might seize it, particularly after it became known that gold existed there. Russia preferred to sell rather than have it seized by another state. And if it were to yield it, it would rather have it go to the United States than to Great Britain. The Russian government under Czar Alexander II decided in 1866 to try to sell Alaska to the United States for a minimum of $5 million. The sales assignment went to the Russian Minister, Baron Edouard de Stoeckl.

Fortunately for the Russians, Secretary of State William H. Seward was as eager to buy as Russia was to sell. He sought territories for the United States both in the Western Hemisphere and in the Pacific, gen-

erally without success. The purchase of Alaska was the greatest coup
in his expansionist efforts.

Stoeckl asked $7 million for Alaska; Seward offered $5 million; and
the Russian Minister expected the final price to fall somewhere between
the two figures. Instead, the United States paid Russia's full asking price
and in addition, at Seward's suggestion, added $200,000 more to get it
free of any claims. Though the area has been worth many times its
original purchase price, the negotiations were not a high point in the
history of American bargaining. When Stoeckl got approval of the terms
from his government, he notified Seward that same evening and suggested they sign the treaty next day. Instead, Seward eagerly urged that
the treaty be drafted and signed that very night. And it was, at four
o'clock in the morning on March 30, 1867. President Johnson submitted
it to the Senate that same day.

There had been no publicity about the negotiations, so the treaty
surprised Americans. Most of them knew little and cared less about
Alaska. Newspapers and political opponents derided "Seward's Folly"
and "Johnson's Polar Bear Garden."

Nevertheless, Seward of New York and Senator Charles Sumner of
Massachusetts set about selling the idea to the Senate and the American
people. They pointed to Alaska's rich natural resources, its potential
commercial importance in the Pacific, and its strategic location. They
cited Russia's support during the Civil War and suggested that America
should buy Alaska as a gesture of friendship. They also warned that if
the United States did not buy it, Alaska might fall into the hands of
Great Britain or some other "hostile" state.

Their vigorous campaign succeeded, and the Senate voted 27 to 12
to approve the treaty. That vote by no means assured favorable action
by the House of Representatives on the essential appropriation for the
purchase. Stoeckl appears to have tried to help things along by dis-
tributing funds to receptive congressmen and by financing favorable
propaganda. Furthermore, by the time the vote was taken the American
flag was already flying in Alaska. As one patriotic congressman phrased
it, "Palsied be the hand that would dare to remove it." The necessary
funds were voted in the summer of 1868. The purchase of Alaska, however, was one of the last major evidences of Russian-American
friendship.

Beginning slowly in the 1880's and 1890's the friendship cooled and
gradually was replaced by growing friction and hostility. The patterns
had an ideological aspect as the autocracy and oppression of Alexander
III and Nicholas II contrasted with the democratic reform sentiments
of Populists and Progressives in the United States. George Kennan
traveled in Russia in the 1880's and on his return wrote of the imprisonment and persecution of political dissenters there. The anti-Semitic

pogroms and violent persecution of Jews in Czarist Russia shocked Americans. When naturalized Americans of Russian descent and of Jewish faith attempted to visit Russia, they encountered the same abuses and discrimination that native Russian Jews suffered. Some Americans blamed radical unrest in the United States on the new immigration, including immigrants from Russia.

Changing relations between the United States and Great Britain undermined the earlier Russian-American friendship. The opposition of Russia and the United States to Great Britain had been the main basis for their mutual sympathy and cooperation during much of the nineteenth century. As Great Britain and the United States drew closer to each other by the close of the century, however, that basis for Russian-American accord disappeared.

And finally, their expansionist interests and activities brought Russia and the United States into conflict with each other. Both countries had had long histories of expansion. But previously they had moved in different parts of the world. Russia concentrated on Eastern Europe, the Balkans, and Asia. The United States moved west across the North American continent. By the 1890's, however, their expansionist interests met in North China, Korea, and Manchuria. Abraham Lincoln's Secretary of State, William H. Seward, had predicted that development with remarkable foresight in 1861 when he wrote: "Russia and the United States may remain good friends until, each having made the circuit of half the globe in opposite directions, they shall meet and greet each other in the regions where civilization first began."

There were remnants of friendly attitudes in both countries. But only rarely since the 1890's have the United States and Russia dropped their mutual distrust. The Bolshevik revolution in the fall of 1917 and the subsequent Communist regime in the Soviet Union greatly intensified that friction. But it began to develop significantly late in the nineteenth century, long before the Communists came to power.

THE UNITED STATES AND EUROPEAN CONFERENCES

In addition to specific episodes with individual European states, the United States participated in a growing number of multilateral conferences and signed multilateral conventions. Conspicuous as a United States representative in some of those negotiations was a Middle Westerner, John A. Kasson, a former Republican congressman from Iowa. When voters rejected him at the polls, he won various political appointments, particularly in foreign affairs. For example, in 1863 he represented the United States in the negotiation of an international postal agreement. He headed the American delegation at the Congress of Berlin that Bismarck called in 1884 to deal with problems in the African

Congo. President Cleveland did not submit the resulting treaty to the Senate, but Americans shared in its drafting. Four years later Kasson again was in Berlin, where, with British and German representatives, he hammered out a three-power protectorate over Samoa. In the 1890's he negotiated reciprocity treaties, though they failed to win Senate approval.

Under Clara Barton's prodding, the United States in 1882 joined the International Red Cross, and in 1896 Americans participated in the first modern Olympics in Athens, Greece. During the fifteen years between 1883 and 1898 the United States approved five multilateral treaties with European states covering such matters as cables, exchange of official publications, protection of industrial property, suppression of African slave trade, and publication of tariffs. Most of the multilateral conferences and agreements involving the United States dealt with nonpolitical matters, but they did represent American participation in matters of common concern with European states.

SUPPLEMENTARY READINGS

Allen, H. C.   *Great Britain and the United States: A History of Anglo-American Relations, 1783–1952.* New York: St. Martin's Press, Inc., 1955.

Bailey, Thomas A.   *America Faces Russia: Russian-American Relations from Early Times to Our Day.* Ithaca, N.Y.: Cornell University Press, 1950.

Blumenthal, Henry.   *France and the United States: Their Diplomatic Relations, 1789–1914.* Chapel Hill: University of North Carolina Press, 1970.

————.   *A Reappraisal of Franco-American Relations, 1830–1871.* Chapel Hill: University of North Carolina Press, 1959.

Callahan, James M.   *American Foreign Policy in Canadian Relations.* New York: Macmillan Co., 1937.

Dulles, Foster Rhea.   *The Imperial Years.* New York: Thomas Y. Crowell Co., 1956.

————.   *Prelude to World Power: American Diplomatic History, 1860–1900.* New York: Macmillan Co., 1965.

————.   *The Road to Teheran: The Story of Russia and America, 1781–1943.* Princeton, N.J.: Princeton University Press, 1945.

Grenville, John A. S., and Young, George B.   *Politics, Strategy, and American Diplomacy.* New Haven: Yale University Press, 1966.

Nevins, Allan.   *Hamilton Fish: The Inner History of the Grant Administration.* New York: Dodd, Mead & Co., 1937.

Perkins, Dexter.   *The Monroe Doctrine, 1826–1867.* Baltimore: Johns Hopkins Press, 1933.

————.   *The Monroe Doctrine, 1867–1907.* Baltimore: Johns Hopkins Press, 1937.

Pletcher, David. *The Awkward Years: American Foreign Relations under Garfield and Arthur*. Columbia: University of Missouri Press, 1963.

Stolberg-Wernigerode, Otto. *Germany and the United States during the Era of Bismarck*. Reading, Pa.: Henry Janssen, 1937.

Tansill, Charles C. *Canadian-American Relations, 1875-1911*. New Haven, Conn.: Yale University Press, 1943.

Shippee, Lester B. *Canadian-American Relations, 1849–1874*. New Haven, Conn.: Yale University Press, 1939.

Williams, William A. *American-Russian Relations, 1781–1947*. New York: Rinehart & Co., Inc., 1952.

Younger, Edward. *John A. Kasson: Politics and Diplomacy from Lincoln to McKinley*. Iowa City: State Historical Society of Iowa, 1955.

21

Harbingers of American imperialism

Exciting and profitable opportunities at home turned American attention inward during the decades following the Civil War. The stable and peaceful international situation enabled the United States to survive its neglect of foreign affairs without damage. Nevertheless, little-noticed changes at home and abroad during the "nadir of diplomacy" quietly eroded those bases for "isolationism" and "continentalism." Aggressive political leaders tried to guide the United States toward more ambitious policies abroad, particularly in Latin America and the Pacific. Sometimes they tried to get colonies, but more often they sought friendly governments and economic opportunities. Until the nineteenth century neared its close, those precursors of American overseas imperialism generally failed. They could not arouse enough enthusiasm among the American people, and the United States lacked the power commanded by Great Britain in South America and the western Pacific. But those leaders, rather than their less expansionist compatriots, were in tune with things to come.

The advance agents of American overseas imperialism represented domestic influences fundamentally different from those represented by the leaders who had guided American continental expansion westward across North America. The agrarians who followed the footsteps of Thomas Jefferson and James K. Polk generally were not impressed by the need for overseas expansion, except when they were aroused by appeals to patriotism, national honor, and national security. The spokesmen for overseas expansion in the last third of the nineteenth century more often talked the language of urban commerce, industry, and finance. They fitted the general economic, social, political, ideological, and foreign policy traditions of John Jay, Alexander Hamilton, and Daniel Webster. Among the "John the Baptists" of American overseas imperialism were politicians as diverse as William H. Seward, Ulysses S. Grant, and James G. Blaine, Republicans all. America's dominance in Alaska, Samoa, Hawaii, and the Pan American Union were partially products of their energies.

SEWARD AND AMERICAN EXPANSIONISM

William H. Seward's standing as one of America's greatest Secretaries of State did not rest only on his success in preventing European intervention in the Civil War and on helping to get the French out of Mexico. He was also an early major spokesman for American expansion overseas. Like those of the more successful imperialists later, Seward's expansionist views were within the framework of traditional "isolationism." That is, like most Americans he opposed involvement in alliances, and he opposed intervention in European affairs. At the same time, however, Seward vigorously urged American expansion in the Western Hemisphere and the Pacific. The New Yorker included agriculture in his expansionist analysis, but he spoke more in terms of security, industry, commerce, finance, and destiny. He wanted colonies in the Caribbean and he sought Alaska. He assumed that Canada, too, would one day be a part of the United States. Seward's imperial ambitions included Hawaii. In China, where America's power was negligible, Seward urged an Open Door policy a generation before John Hay. In his conception of civilization expanding westward across America and the Pacific, he saw Asia as "the chief theatre of events in the world's great hereafter." Except in Alaska and Midway Island, his colonial schemes failed. Seward was ahead of his time; neither the domestic nor the external situation was quite ready. But he, rather than his critics, correctly anticipated the future.

In 1867 Seward signed a treaty for the purchase of the Danish West Indies (Virgin Islands) for $7.5 million. Denmark wanted to sell, provided the people in the Islands approved the transfer. After a favorable plebiscite, Denmark ratified the treaty. But Congress, absorbed in its reconstruction feud with President Andrew Johnson's administration, was in no mood to cooperate. The House of Representatives made it clear that it would not appropriate funds for the purchase whether the Senate acted or not. The Senate did not even bother to vote on the treaty, and the whole effort failed. Seward's desire to annex Haiti or Santo Domingo in the Caribbean did not even reach the treaty-signing stage.

His ambitions also exceeded his accomplishments in the Pacific. He engineered the extremely important purchase of Alaska from Russia in 1867. In that same year the United States annexed Midway Island, a thousand miles west of Hawaii. It had not previously been occupied and was expected to serve as a coaling station for American shipping in the area. Seward instructed the American Minister to explore the possibility of annexing Hawaii, but he failed to get such a treaty. Even a reciprocity agreement with Hawaii signed in 1867 failed to win Senate approval.

In China, Seward had the benefit of an unusually able diplomat, Anson Burlingame from Massachusetts. An antiforeign Know Nothing politician earlier, as Lincoln's Minister to China in 1861 he dropped his nativist views. Burlingame was the first United States Minister to reside at Peking. He earnestly and effectively sought friendly relations with China. He cooperated with other states to discourage them from seeking special privileges that might weaken or dismember China. Respect for Chinese territorial integrity and sovereignty might win deference for American traders and missionaries (many of whom were from his native New England) that could not be obtained with America's limited power in East Asia. Unlike other spokesmen for the Open Door, however, Burlingame was genuinely interested in the welfare of China and the Chinese, not just in serving American ambitions there.

When Burlingame planned to return to the United States, the Chinese government demonstrated its confidence in him by inviting that foreigner to head a goodwill mission in 1868 to America, Europe, and around the world. He agreed to do so.

Americans enthusiastically received the Chinese mission wherever it traveled in the United States. Burlingame spoke movingly of Chinese progress and desire for friendly relations (conveniently ignoring the continued anti-Western sentiments in China and in the Imperial Government). Burlingame for China and Seward for the United States signed a treaty in 1868 that strengthened provisions of the earlier Treaty of Tientsin. The United States again rejected any intention of intervening in China's internal affairs. And in Burlingame's Treaty each state agreed to admit immigrants from the other. Seward wanted that provision for the labor supply it would provide in the United States, particularly for the construction of railroads in the West. The Burlingame Mission then continued on to London, Paris, Berlin, and St. Petersburg, where Burlingame died of pneumonia in 1870.

GRANT AND SANTO DOMINGO

Ulysses S. Grant from 1869 to 1877 was America's worst President in the nineteenth century. He had a talent for making bad appointments. One of his rare able appointees was his Secretary of State, Hamilton Fish of New York. Fish did not wholly share Seward's enthusiasm for expansion, and he restrained some of President Grant's more injudicious impulses. The United States did not add more territory during Grant's administration.

Nevertheless, like Seward, Grant proved to be an advance agent for American overseas imperialism. A Middle Westerner and a successful professional military officer, Grant was not personally a part of the urban, business community. But he was awed by men of wealth and flattered by their attention and generosity. His responsiveness to their suggestions, his deference to congressional authority, and his failure to provide much positive presidential leadership made him acceptable to much of the urban, business wing of the Republican Party. The partnership of business and military that his administration symbolized was not without significance in the history of American expansion since the Civil War.

President Grant's obsession for annexing Santo Domingo sprang from his own concern for American military security and from his responsiveness to individuals with financial interests there. Involved was "Colonel" Joseph W. Fabens, a New England-born soldier of fortune whose tactics won him friends, influence, and property in Santo Domingo. One of his cohorts was General Buenaventura Baez, whose tottering government of Santo Domingo required help. Completely sold on the idea, Grant concluded a treaty in 1869 calling for annexation. Fish did not favor the project, and Charles Sumner, chairman of the Senate Foreign Relations Committee, vehemently opposed it. Rumors of skulduggery and corruption cast a shadow over the effort. With no isthmian canal in being, and with European states making no major moves in the area, it was impossible to persuade most Americans of the security need for the colony. Domestic interests were too limited, too weak, and too unsavory to prevail. In 1870–1871 Grant threw the full weight of his office behind the treaty, citing security, commerce, markets, and freedom as reasons for annexation. But he failed; the Senate rejected his treaty.

At the same time, revolution swept Cuba, one of Spain's few remaining colonies, from 1868 to 1878. During that Ten Years War the Cubans won much sympathy, encouragement, and financial help in the United States. Secretary of State Fish favored Cuban independence, but he opposed war with Spain. And he did not want to annex Cuba. Grant's goals were not so limited, but Fish successfully kept the President in check.

In 1873 the Spanish seized the *Virginius*, a ship flying the American flag and carrying supplies to the Cuban rebels. The Spanish promptly tried and shot fifty-three of the crew and passengers (including eight Americans). Fish protested very strongly, though his case was weakened by evidence that the ship was Cuban-owned and was illegally flying the American flag. The Spanish agreed to pay an indemnity to families of the Americans who had been executed. They also promised to return the ship to the United States, though it sank on the way. Spain crushed the rebellion by 1878 and promised certain reforms. But the attitudes of the Spanish, Cubans, and Americans all began to take the forms that were to lead to the Spanish-American War two decades later and to the American colonial expansion resulting from that war.

In the Pacific, Grant and Fish helped pave the way for American expansion in Hawaii and Samoa. In 1875 the United States concluded a reciprocity treaty with Hawaii that lowered tariff rates and allowed Hawaiian sugar into the United States duty free. The trade privileges were explicitly limited to the United States (no Open Door policy for others). Hawaii also promised not to lease or transfer territory to any other country. The treaty encouraged sugar production in Hawaii and greatly increased trade between the two states. Consequently, Hawaiian economic prosperity became almost wholly dependent upon the United States and, to a large extent, was controlled by Americans.

On the route to Australia, Samoa attracted the interest of American land speculators, shippers, and naval officers. Commander Richard W. Meade negotiated an agreement with Samoan leaders in 1872 giving the United States use of the harbor at Pago Pago for a naval base, in return for American good offices in the event of international difficulties there. Grant and Fish approved the agreement, but the Senate did not.

For Grant, as for Seward earlier, expansionist ambitions exceeded accomplishments. But the interest and efforts pointed to the Age of Imperialism.

BLAINE'S PAN-AMERICANISM

James G. Blaine of Maine served as Secretary of State briefly under President James Garfield in 1881. He had a longer tour in that office under President Benjamin Harrison from 1889 to 1892. Blaine's role in Republican politics (and foreign affairs) in the last third of the nineteenth century was similar to that of Daniel Webster and Henry Clay in Whig Party politics earlier. Highly ambitious, the "Plumed Knight" repeatedly sought the Presidency. He never won it, but he was better known and more powerful in his party than most who did. Like Clay, his personal magnetism and charm made him a hero to many. Allegations of corruption marred that portrait, however, even in an era when certain peccadillos were more tolerated (and even admired) than in most of American history. Like Clay and Webster, Blaine supported protective tariffs. But like his fellow New Englander, Daniel Webster, Blaine eagerly sought trade opportunities abroad for American businessmen. He believed that domestic markets alone could not absorb America's increasing industrial and agricultural output. Large and growing foreign markets were essential. In a day when most American industry was not yet efficient enough to compete profitably on the open market with British manufacturers, Blaine sought preferential treatment for American products abroad. He believed, however, that some industries needed protection less than others.

Blaine expected Canada to become part of the United States eventually, and he wanted naval bases and coaling stations abroad. But he did not seek colonies so much as he wanted trade expansion. He was interested in the Pacific, but he particularly looked to Latin America for markets. He envisaged an American-controlled isthmian canal for national security, but he was more interested in commercial advantages that such a canal might provide on the west coast of South America and in the Pacific. Though he favored agricultural exports, he was even more eager to find markets for industry. In fathering the Pan American Union, Blaine spoke largely of peace and trade. President Harrison generally shared Blaine's foreign policy views, but the President was more militant and chauvinistic than his colorful Secretary of State.

In 1881 Blaine issued invitations to Latin-American states for an Inter-American Conference in Washington. He did not invite European states, their American colonies, or Canada. Blaine hoped the conference would develop peace machinery for the Western Hemisphere, but he particularly wanted to bind the states together commercially. With the assassination of Garfield and the elevation of Chester A. Arthur to the Presidency, however, Blaine resigned and the invitations were canceled. Later, in 1889–1890, when Blaine again served as Secretary of State, the Inter-American Conference (called by Cleveland) finally met, with eighteen countries represented. Blaine tried to impress the Latin Americans by prefacing the formal sessions with a 6,000-mile tour of the United States in a special train. The Conference failed to approve either Blaine's arbitration proposals or his plans for an inter-American customs union. It did create the Bureau of American Republics, which became the Pan American Union in 1910. And it recommended reciprocity treaties.

Blaine seized on the reciprocity proposal as a way of redirecting Latin-American trade away from Europe and toward the United States. Congress did not share his enthusiasm for reciprocity. Only a major political effort enabled him to get a reverse kind of reciprocity included in the McKinley Tariff of 1890. Under that legislation sugar was placed on the tariff-free list. If other countries discriminated against American exports in their tariff policies, the administration could ban the import of sugar, coffee, and other products from those states. In other words, if other states discriminated against American products, the United States would discriminate against theirs. That coercive tactic persuaded most Latin-American countries to sign reciprocity treaties with the United States.

A major crisis in United States relations with Chile in 1891–1892 was less characteristic of Blaine's approach in Latin America. It was more in tune with Harrison's temperament and with foreign policy patterns that evolved around the turn of the century. President José Balmaceda faced opposition and rebellion in Chile. United States Minister Patrick Egan, a fervent Anglophobe, blamed the uprising on European influences. Balmaceda became identified with the United States, while the Congressionalist rebels benefited from anti-Yankee prejudices. Those patterns were reinforced when the United States prevented a rebel ship, the *Itata*, from landing a cargo of munitions that it had got in California. Despite American support (or because of it), Balmaceda fell from power in the summer of 1891.

In an emotion-packed atmosphere in October, 1891, Captain Winfield S. Schley of the U.S.S. *Baltimore* allowed his men to go on shore leave in Valparaiso, Chile. A saloon brawl erupted, and a mob attacked the American sailors. Two Americans were killed, several were wounded, and more were arrested and imprisoned. Captain Schley demanded release of his men, apologies, and indemnities. Officials in Chile were unresponsive, and protests from Washington evoked an indignant response from the Chilean Minister to the United States. President Harrison and his Cabinet were emotionally prepared for war if a satisfactory response were not forthcoming quickly. Handicapped by ill-health, Blaine restrained his President, but Harrison laid the matter before Congress for action. Jingoes (like young Theodore Roosevelt) shouted for war. Chile reluctantly backed down, apologized, and eventually paid a $75,000 indemnity for the loss of lives.

Throughout the incident Blaine shared the President's desire to protect American interests and to reduce British influence (and trade) in Chile. He did not want war, and he did not believe Harrison's militant approach would serve the cause of either peace or trade. Nevertheless, both Blaine and Harrison (though differing on methods) wanted American activity and expansion in Latin America, including South America, where British power and commerce retained the upper hand. The Harrison-Blaine administration also demonstrated its expansionist ambitions in Samoa and Hawaii in the Pacific.

THE UNITED STATES AND SAMOA

Though Americans had visited Samoa in the southwest Pacific early in the nineteenth century, little activity developed. Under President Rutherford B. Hayes the United States in 1878 concluded a treaty that allowed an American naval base at the beautiful harbor of Pago Pago in the island of Tutuila. In return the United States made its good offices available to Samoa in the event of international difficulties. Great

Britain and Germany promptly negotiated similar treaties. Samoa interested only a handful of Americans; its economic value to the United States was slight, its strategic significance negligible.

Nevertheless, the few Americans there (traders, consuls, and naval officers) did not limit their goals and efforts to modest levels. The splendid harbor at Pago Pago aroused acquisitive instincts, particularly among navy and shipping people. They clashed with ambitious agents of competing governments and economies, particularly from Germany and Great Britain. The Europeans in Samoa (particularly the Germans) were more aggressive than their governments, but their activities alarmed Americans there. If the United States did not act decisively, Samoa might fall under German control. The Samoans were so divided and politically unstable that they, in effect, invited foreign intervention. In brief, the attractiveness of the islands, the weakness and instability of the native population, and the competing intrigues of foreigners there aroused imperialist efforts by Germans, Englishmen, and Americans. Instead of improving the situation, the treaties of 1878 and 1879 further encouraged intrigue among the consuls and others from the three competing states.

From the American viewpoint the German consul seemed most aggressive and dangerous. President Cleveland and Secretary of State Thomas F. Bayard protested in 1885 when German activities became particularly alarming. Chancellor Bismarck's response seemed conciliatory, so in 1887 the United States invited Great Britain and Germany to resolve their differences at a conference in Washington. The negotiations there failed, however. Congress appropriated $500,000 to protect lives and property in Samoa, and provided $100,000 more to build a naval base at Pago Pago. A timely typhoon in March, 1889, may have prevented an armed clash between German, American, and British naval vessels in the harbor at Apia in Samoa. The storm destroyed all three German ships and all three American ships there. Only the lone British naval vessel successfully escaped to the open sea. The tragedy caused heavy loss of life, and provided a somber atmosphere for a conference called by Bismarck to deal with Samoa. In Berlin, representatives from the three countries (including Kasson for the United States) concluded a tripartite agreement. The Berlin General Act of 1889 recognized Samoan independence, but provided for a three-power protectorate over the islands. Despite its entangling characteristics, the Senate approved the agreement. It never worked well. Intrigue with native leaders, violence, and jockeying for power continued among representatives of the three states.

Not until 1899 did the governments successfully resolve their differences. By that time the Spanish-American War had removed American inhibitions about annexing distant colonies. Bismarck's hand no longer restrained Germany's colonial ambitions. Britain's interests in Africa and its conciliatory attitudes toward the United States made it cooperative. At the suggestion of Germany, the three states signed a partition treaty in 1899. It gave Germany the two largest Samoan Islands. The United States got Tutuila and its harbor at Pago Pago. Britain obtained no part of Samoa, but won certain concessions from Germany in Africa and elsewhere. In 1914 New Zealand took over Germany's Samoan Islands.

THE UNITED STATES AND HAWAII

More important were the influences and developments that led to annexation of Hawaii by the United States in 1898. Though official efforts to get Hawaii failed earlier, the groundwork for annexation was prepared long before 1898. Shippers, whalers, and missionaries all increased American interest and influence in Hawaii. They and their descendants often stayed on to become planters and businessmen there. The Dole family, for example, first went to Hawaii as missionaries and remained as increasingly wealthy planters, businessmen, and politicians.

Under agrarian leadership in the first six decades of the nineteenth century, the United States government did not provide much support for Americans in Hawaii. Even Seward's expansionist enthusiasm for Hawaii in the 1860's could not prevail against public disinterest and congressional opposition.

The Reciprocity Treaty concluded during the Grant administration in 1875 bound Hawaii to the United States economically. The Cleveland administration in 1887 won exclusive use of Pearl Harbor as a naval base, and also extended the reciprocity agreement. Consequently, Hawaiian sugar production increased many fold. Hawaii bought nearly all of its imports from the United States, while the United States took most of Hawaii's exports. By 1893 Americans owned about two thirds of the productive property in Hawaii. Nominally Hawaii continued to be a sovereign independent kingdom; in reality it was intimately bound to the United States. The power of those ties was revealed in the early 1890's by an expansionist American diplomat, an American tariff revision, a nationalistic Hawaiian Queen, an American cabal in Hawaii, and a tiny revolution.

In 1889 John L. Stevens of Maine became the United States Minister to Hawaii. He enthusiastically urged annexation of Hawaii. He did not keep his feelings secret either from Americans in Hawaii or from his sympathetic superiors in Washington, Secretary of State Blaine and President Harrison. Stevens deliberately encouraged the fear that Britain, Germany, or some other state might seize Hawaii if the United States failed to do so.

The McKinley Tariff Act adopted by the United States Congress in

1890 removed the duty on sugar and awarded a bounty to American sugar producers. Under the reciprocity treaties of 1875 and 1887 Hawaiian sugar had been admitted free of duty to the United States, giving it preferential treatment over sugar from Cuba and other Latin-American areas. Furthermore, the arrangement had not compelled Hawaiians to compete with subsidized American producers. The reciprocity agreements had greatly encouraged Hawaiian sugar production and had made Hawaii dependent on the American market for its prosperity. The McKinley Tariff destroyed that preferential arrangement and forced Hawaiians to compete on an equal footing with Caribbean sugar producers and with subsidized American growers. The result was a major crisis in the Hawaiian economy that helped lead to the revolutionary upheaval in 1893.

In 1891, on top of Stevens's expansionism and the dislocating tariff revision, came a new Hawaiian monarch, Queen Liliuokalani. Talented, educated, strong-willed, and Christian, Queen Liliuokalani was a dedicated Hawaiian nationalist. She denounced foreign (i.e., American) dominance in Hawaii. She wanted "Hawaii for Hawaiians." She encouraged native Hawaiian customs, and used lotteries to reduce her government's dependence on American sources of revenue. Unfortunately for her cause, she was not subtle or tactful.

The efforts of the American Minister, the economic dislocation caused by American tariff policies, the anti-American Hawaiian nationalism personified by the new Queen, and the growing concern among annexationist-minded American planters and missionaries in Hawaii, all came to a premature climax in the Hawaiian Revolution of 1893. On January 4, 1893, Stevens left Honolulu on the U.S.S. *Boston* for a cruise off the islands. That seemed to be the appropriate moment for the Queen to make her move (Stevens may have hoped his absence would have that response). On January 14, 1893, Queen Liliuokalani announced her plan to proclaim a new Hawaiian constitution to replace the constitution of 1887. The earlier document had given substantial power in the legislature to the foreign element, mostly Americans. The new constitution would restore lost power to the crown. It would have removed property qualifications for voting, thus reducing the advantage of property-owning Americans and increasing the power of propertyless Hawaiians. The plan probably appealed to most natives, but it thoroughly alarmed the Americans, who promptly staged a rebellion.

That frightened the Queen into abandoning her proposal, but it was too late to stop the uprising. The Queen's army of 496 men was three times the size of the rebel force and was better equipped. If there had been no outside interference she could have crushed the revolt. But the rebels appealed to Stevens (who conveniently returned at that crucial moment) to provide protection. Stevens promptly sent United States troops ashore on January 16. They were stationed across the street from the government building and near the royal palace. Clearly they challenged the monarchy more than they protected lives and property. The following day the revolutionary Committee of Public Safety abolished the monarchy and organized a Provisional Government to serve until annexation could be accomplished. On that same day Stevens recognized that Provisional Government, just thirty hours after the rebels had indicated they were so weak they needed American protection. Queen Liliuokalani did not abdicate until after Stevens recognized the Provisional Government. In doing so she correctly said that she yielded "to the superior force of the United States of America."

The following day a five-man commission (none of them native Hawaiians) left to negotiate a treaty of annexation with the United States. That treaty was signed on February 14, 1893, less than a month after the revolt began. President Harrison urged Senate approval and insisted that "the overthrow of the monarchy was not in any way promoted by this Government."

Before the Senate acted, however, Grover Cleveland again became President of the United States. While not entirely innocent of expansionist sentiments, Cleveland did not favor colonial expansion, and he had a moralistic conception of what was and was not proper for a government. He withdrew the treaty from Senate consideration, and sent James H. Blount to conduct an investigation. Blount's report in July, 1893, severely indicted Stevens for his role in the developments. It concluded that the Hawaiians overwhelmingly opposed the Provisional Government and annexation.

Consequently, President Cleveland sent Albert S. Willis as the new Minister to Hawaii with instructions to get guarantees from Queen Liliuokalani that she would grant amnesty to the rebels. Then he was to explore the possibility of peacefully restoring her to the throne. At first the Queen insisted "as the law directs that such persons should be beheaded and their property confiscated." When she reluctantly relented, Willis was blocked by the refusal of the Provisional Government under Sanford B. Dole to step down.

Cleveland then turned the matter over to Congress. In February, 1894, the House of Representatives adopted a resolution denouncing Stevens and opposing annexation or a protectorate. The Senate later voted to allow Hawaii to maintain its own government without American interference. On July 4, 1894, the Provisional Government organized on a permanent basis. Nevertheless, its constitution authorized the President of Hawaii to conclude a treaty of union with the United States whenever possible. Not until William McKinley replaced Cleveland as President, and not until jingoes and imperialists gained the upper hand during the Spanish-American War, did the United States finally annex Hawaii by joint resolution in July, 1898. That annexation was an anticlimax when compared with the developments of 1893. It was a logical culmination of a century of growing American influence in Hawaii. The processes by which the United States acquired Hawaii were not very different from the methods by which it got West Florida in 1810, Texas in 1845, and the Panama Canal Zone in 1903.

SUPPLEMENTARY READINGS

Dennett, Tyler. *Americans in Eastern Asia: A Critical Study of the Policy of the United States with Reference to China, Japan, and Korea in the Nineteenth Century.* New York: Macmillan Co., 1922.

Dulles, Foster Rhea. *China and America: The Story of Their Relations since 1784.* Princeton, N.J.: Princeton University Press, 1946.

————. *Prelude to World Power: American Diplomatic History, 1860–1900.* New York: Macmillan Co., 1965.

Grenville, John A. S., and Young, George B. *Politics, Strategy, and American Diplomacy.* New Haven, Conn.: Yale University Press, 1966.

LaFeber, Walter. *The New Empire: An Interpretation of American Expansion, 1860–1898.* Ithaca, N.Y.: Cornell University Press, 1963.

May, Ernest R. *Imperial Democracy: The Emergence of America as a Great Power.* New York: Harcourt, Brace & World, Inc., 1961.

Perkins, Dexter. *The Monroe Doctrine, 1867–1907.* Baltimore: Johns Hopkins Press, 1937.

Plesur, Milton. *America's Outward Thrust: Approaches to Foreign Affairs, 1865–1890.* DeKalb: Northern Illinois University Press, 1971.

Pletcher, David M. *The Awkward Years: American Foreign Relations under Garfield and Arthur.* Columbia: University of Missouri Press, 1963.

Pratt, Julius W. *Expansionists of 1898: The Acquisition of Hawaii and the Spanish Islands.* Baltimore: Johns Hopkins Press, 1936.

Ryden, George Herbert. *The Foreign Policy of the United States in Relation to Samoa.* New Haven, Conn.: Yale University Press, 1933.

Stevens, Sylvester K. *American Expansion in Hawaii, 1842–1898.* Harrisburg, Pa.: Archives Publishing Co., 1945.

Tyler, Alice Felt. *The Foreign Policy of James G. Blaine.* Minneapolis: University of Minnesota Press, 1927.

Williams, William Appleman. *The Roots of the Modern American Empire: A Study of the Growth and Shaping of Social Consciousness in a Marketplace Society.* New York: Random House, 1969.

22

The Spanish-American War

Despite the important Pinckney's Treaty of 1795 and the equally important Adams-Onís Treaty of 1819–1821, Spain and the United States had never been warmly attracted to each other. American attitudes were part of the general New World distrust and hostility toward the Old World. Democratic America objected to monarchical Spain. Protestant America reacted negatively to Catholic Spain. Furthermore, from the beginning Spain had colonies in the Western Hemisphere that the United States wanted. On the other side, Spain distrusted the radical challenge of democratic America. Catholic Spain had no love for Protestant America. And America's lust for Spanish territories was matched by Spain's determination to retain its colonies. By the 1890's Spain had lost most of its empire, but in the Caribbean it still had Cuba and Puerto Rico. In the Pacific it retained the Philippines and Guam.

The Spanish-American War in 1898 was part of Spain's continuing efforts to keep what remained of its empire. It was a product of Cuba's efforts to win its freedom. It expressed American determination to throw off Old World control in the Western Hemisphere and to win independence for the Cubans. It included a self-righteous paternalism that implied the United States could straighten things out for the inferior Latins —Spanish, Cubans, and Latin Americans generally. It was a part of the growing nationalism and imperialism that swept the United States. It was a spring (and summer) adolescent lark for the muscular and confident young United States. It was consistent with the growing efforts of American businessmen to find profitable markets abroad for their industrial products and investment capital. And it was a dramatic preview of the burgeoning power that the United States was to command in the twentieth century. Conceivably Spain's presence in the Caribbean and the chronic disturbances there endangered American security. Many said so, anyway. Others then and later doubted whether the war was essential for the preservation of America's national security and vital interests. In any event, like the Mexicans in the 1840's, the Spanish provided provocations that invited action by the United States. But unlike the Mexicans earlier, the Spanish did not want war and almost desperately tried to avoid it. In both cases the United States gave their Latin adversaries no acceptable alternative; the United States forced war on a reluctant Spain, as it had a half century before forced war on a willing Mexico.

American sympathy for Cuban efforts to win independence, and American acquisitive ambitions there (the two attitudes were not always entirely separate and unrelated), developed early in American history. The various uprisings against Spanish rule in Cuba, particularly the Ten Years War beginning in 1868, aroused emotions in the United States. By 1878 Spain crushed the rebels, and many of their leaders fled to the United States. Spain appeased Cubans with promises of reforms, but little changed there. Renewed revolt awaited only the proper circumstances. They came by 1895.

On top of Spanish misrule and Cuban suffering, the United States played a central role in providing the circumstances for renewed Cuban revolt and its successful outcome. During Grover Cleveland's second term as President, the United States again revised its tariffs. The McKinley Tariff of 1890 had put sugar on the free list. That hurt Hawaiians but helped Cubans. The Wilson-Gorman Tariff of 1894 ended reciprocity and put a tariff back on sugar. That suited Hawaiian sugar producers but struck a staggering blow at the Cuban economy that already depended heavily on its markets in the United States. The McKinley Tariff helped provoke the Hawaiian Revolution of 1893; the Wilson-Gorman Tariff helped provoke the Cuban Revolution in 1895.

Most of the leaders, money, supplies, and plans for the Cuban uprising in 1895 originated in the United States. Leaders of the Ten Years War fled to the United States and spent the intervening years organizing followers, arousing enthusiasm, raising funds, and laying plans in their various headquarters in New York, Washington, and elsewhere. Some became naturalized American citizens. Some, including José Martí, had not been in Cuba for many years. He was killed soon after the revolt began, in 1895. Others, such as Maximo Gomez of Santo Domingo, were not even Cubans. In any event, all of them based their hopes upon funds, support, and intervention from the United States. They deliberately disrupted the island's economy and resources to provoke American intervention on their behalf. And they succeeded. Cuba might have won its independence eventually under other circumstances, but it gained its independence when it did because of the United States.

Understandably, Spain tried to suppress the revolt and retain its prized colony. In that effort Spain used both concessions to the Cubans and military force. Neither method succeeded. Spanish misrule continued. The rebels were not content with promised reforms in Spanish administration of the colony; they considered greater autonomy under continued Spanish hegemony to be quite inadequate. Nothing short of complete independence would do. Spanish military efforts were both costly and ineffective. By 1898 Cuban rebels and disease had cost Spain the death of 50,000 of its soldiers and the wounding or disabling of 50,000 more. The difficulty of distinguishing between friend and foe led General Valeriano Weyler to inaugurate a reconcentration policy. That is, he confined noncombatants to towns and cities, while ravishing the rebels (and everyone else) in the countryside. Both combatants and noncombatants suffered terribly, as they do in all contested mass uprisings. The Spanish committed atrocities, just as the Cuban rebels did. But the fighting and guerrilla warfare continued. Most in the United States found Spanish concessions inadequate and saw in the Spanish military actions increasing justification for war.

Not everyone in the United States wanted to go to war against Spain to free the Cubans. Some newspapers, such as E. L. Godkin's New York *Evening Post,* opposed war, though generally their circulation and advertising were not as great as those of the more militant newspapers. Professor Julius W. Pratt has emphasized that big business in the United States generally did not want war. The American economy had only recently recovered from the severe depression that followed the Panic of 1893; war might disrupt that renewed prosperity. Business and the Republicans had just successfully downed the inflationary challenge posed by William Jennings Bryan's free silver campaign in 1896; they did not want to admit inflation through the back door of war. Americans whose businesses and property in Cuba were endangered or destroyed by the revolution wanted peace restored to the island. Some favored war to protect their direct interests there, but many did not. Grover Cleveland, President until 1897, sympathized with the Cubans and insisted on Spanish concessions, but he opposed war with Spain. Mark Hanna, an Ohio industrialist and a powerful United States senator, led the campaign to elect McKinley. He did not favor intervention in Cuba. President McKinley's Secretary of State, John Sherman of Ohio, too old and senile to lead, did not work for intervention. Nor did Assistant Secretary William R. Day, who became Secretary of State when war began. Speaker of the House Thomas B. Reed opposed war, and so did Senate leaders.

William McKinley of Ohio, inaugurated President in 1897, was more able and less reactionary than his subsequent reputation would indicate. He was a talented politician and a popular President. He warmly sympathized with the Cubans and secretly contributed $5,000 of his own funds for humanitarian relief in Cuba. But like the businessmen whose interests he served so often, McKinley did not initially want war to free the Cubans.

The United States Minister Stewart L. Woodford earnestly tried to persuade Spain to grant concessions that might satisfy the Cubans and make war by the United States unnecessary. Spain's inability to crush the uprising, along with growing pressure from the United States, forced the Spanish government to grant ever more sweeping concessions. In the fall of 1897 Spain promised the Cubans self-government except for control of foreign affairs, the army, the navy, and the administration of justice. Spain relieved General Weyler of his command. In March, 1898, after the sinking of the U.S.S. *Maine* increased war fervor in the United States, Spain revoked the reconcentration decrees, promised financial aid, and authorized an autonomous Cuban congress. Early in April, 1898, Spain agreed unconditionally to suspend hostilities and grant an immediate armistice. Whether such concessions would have satisfied the rebels at any time may be doubted, but they might have been acceptable to the United States earlier. By April, 1898, neither the Cubans nor the United States would be content with anything short of complete independence for that Caribbean island.

Important individuals and groups in the United States opposed war; Spain did not want war; and Woodford successfully persuaded Spain to promise every concession except complete independence. Why then did war erupt between the United States and Spain? A combination of general influences, aroused emotions, and inflammatory incidents made it possible.

The Navy, personified by Captain Alfred Thayer Mahan, saw the strategic significance of Cuba for American security. Some officers were not entirely innocent of an eagerness to try out their shiny new warships.

In his analysis of economic bases for expansion, Professor Walter LaFeber has contended that American business began to drop its opposition to war in the early spring of 1898 *before* the President and Congress acted. Business suffered harmful effects from the international uncertainties, and some felt growing interest in foreign markets and investments. Those patterns, according to LaFeber, erased much business opposition to war in March and early April, 1898. And McKinley was keenly alert to business needs and wishes at home and abroad.

Aggressive politicians, led particularly by urban Republicans, would be content with nothing less than the fruits of war. And some, like Theodore Roosevelt of New York, would be disappointed if the fruits were gained without war. Roosevelt, Henry Cabot Lodge of Massachusetts, Albert J. Beveridge of Indiana, and others were moved by honest patriotism, genuine compassion for the Cubans, and by very real considerations of national security. But their jingoism was also good politics in 1898. With an aristocratic background and a Harvard education, Theodore Roosevelt felt a strong sense of *noblesse oblige*—of responsibility to serve his nation. His aggressively masculine love for the out-of-doors and for a life of action made him contemptuous of more effete or sensitive tastes. Mahan's big-navy ideas won Roosevelt's enthusiastic support. In the 1890's his enthusiasm for war (any war with almost any country) reached its climax. He believed that only cowards would avoid a just war and that most wars were just. "No triumph of peace is quite so great as the supreme triumphs of war," he wrote in 1897. He was disdainful of efforts to maintain peace with Spain. He served as Assistant Secretary of the Navy under President McKinley. Roosevelt was more warlike than most, but his sentiments were shared by other politicians at the time.

Newspapers, the "Yellow Press," contributed to the war spirit. Genuine crusading idealism on behalf of the Cubans combined with business determination to gain advertising, increase circulation, and make money. Jingoism was by no means limited to large-circulation urban newspapers; similar patterns prevailed in papers all over the country. The New York *Tribune*, published by Whitelaw Reid, already favored the active American foreign policies it was to support during the next seventy years. But Joseph Pulitzer's New York *World* and William Randolph Hearst's New York *Journal* outdid most newspapers (and tried to outdo each other) in their inflammatory efforts. Balance, objectivity, and accuracy were neither desired nor obtained in their columns. All "news" aimed at damning the Spanish and arousing sympathy for the Cubans. Whole battles were invented. Atrocities by Cubans were justified or ignored; atrocities by the Spanish were exaggerated and given banner headlines. Illustrators combined artistic talent and imagination to build hatred of Spain.

Jingoes and the Yellow Press fed on the inevitable violence and suffering in revolutionary Cuba. And in February, 1898, their cause was served by two incidents so inflammatory that they would have required a stronger President than McKinley to resist their warmaking influence. First was the publication of the de Lome letter on February 9, 1898. The Spanish Minister, Dupuy de Lome, was not an admirer of the United States, but he was an experienced diplomat and he did not want war. In a personal letter to a Spanish friend in Cuba, de Lome described President McKinley as "weak and a bidder for the admiration of the crowd." He called him "a would-be politician who tries to leave a door open behind himself while keeping on good terms with the jingoes of his party." The letter was stolen at its destination in Havana and published sensationally by Hearst's *Journal* and other newspapers throughout the country. Many Americans in both parties had made similar observations about the President. But when the Spanish Minister, even in private correspondence, used such words it was interpreted as further proof of the evil qualities of the Spanish. De Lome promptly resigned his post, and the Spanish government apologized, but the damange could not be repaired.

Far more inflammatory was the sinking of the U.S.S. *Maine* in Havana harbor on February 15, 1898, less than a week after publication of the de Lome letter. The *Maine*, a fairly new second-class battleship, was ordered to Havana in January, 1898, on an ostensibly friendly visit. In the tense atmosphere that prevailed, however, its arrival was not without precautionary and even coercive connotations. Within three weeks an explosion destroyed the warship. It sank very rapidly. Of the 350 men and officers on board at the time, 260 lost their lives.

Captain Charles Sigsbee, commander of the ship, in his telegram to Washington advised that "Public opinion should be suspended until further report." But few in the United States followed that recommendation. A Spanish inquiry indicated that it was destroyed by an internal explosion; a United States Navy court of inquiry blamed it on an external submarine mine. Neither could fix responsibility for the disaster. The ship was raised in 1911, and a second inquiry produced evidence that the sinking was due to an external explosion. The ship was then towed to deep water and sunk. The responsibility and cause for the explosion remain unknown. No responsible Spanish official would have wanted the ship sunk. Cuban insurrectionists might have welcomed the incident but probably would have lacked the technical requirements for the task. It may have been an accident. But the American people overwhelmingly concluded that the Spanish had done the evil deed. The jingoes and Yellow Press gave hysterical assurances of Spanish responsibility. "Remember the Maine" became the slogan for war, even though no one knew in fact what or who caused it to sink.

With the de Lome letter and the sinking of the *Maine*, both countries moved rapidly toward war. Spain sought intercession by Europe and the Pope to prevent war. Europeans sympathized with Spain, but not enough to oppose the pro-American attitudes of Great Britain, and not enough to antagonize the increasingly powerful United States. Meaningful help from that quarter was not forthcoming; Spain was on its own in coping with its rebellious colony and with the difficult giant in North America.

At the President's request, Congress, on March 9, voted $50 million for military preparations. McKinley submitted his message to Congress on April 11, asking authority to force an end to the war in Cuba. In his message the President briefly mentioned Spain's final concessions of April 9, promising to extend further reforms and suspending hostilities. In forwarding those Spanish concessions, Woodford urged the President:

"I hope that nothing will now be done to humiliate Spain as I am satisfied that the present Government is going and is loyally going to go as fast and as far as it can." But most of the President's message to Congress was warlike. On April 20, 1898, Congress declared Cuba free, demanded Spanish withdrawal, and authorized the President to use force to accomplish that end. At the same time it adopted the Teller resolution renouncing any intention by the United States "to exercise sovereignty, jurisdiction, or control" over Cuba. Most who voted for that self-denying resolution undoubtedly did so on idealistic grounds, but Senator Teller was also concerned about the economic interests of the beet sugar industry in his home state of Colorado. On April 25, 1898, Congress formally declared war, backdating the resolution to April 21.

Externally, the Spanish-American War grew out of the Cuban insurrection and efforts by the rebels to win American intervention. It resulted from Spanish misrule and from the suffering and deaths its actions wrought in Cuba. Pride and political circumstances made the Spanish government unable or unwilling to grant the Cuban independence that, by April, 1898, was the only way to prevent war. It grew out of the pro-American policies of Great Britain that helped prevent European intervention on behalf of Spain. And it emerged from the very real significance of the Caribbean and Cuba for the national security of the United States.

Internally, the Spanish-American War developed from genuine ideological and humanitarian sympathies for the Cubans and out of intense hostility to all that Catholic, monarchical Spain represented. It resulted partly from the inflammatory efforts of the Yellow Press and jingoes. It was a product of America's burgeoning power. It was possible because of the ideological and diplomatic premises from which President McKinley operated and because he lacked the political courage or determination to resist the pressures for war. And it was not unrelated to America's rapidly expanding industrial and capital-surplus economy.

Evaluations of the American decision for war depend partly on the circumstances from which one views it. In 1898 it did not seem a very terrible thing. The horrors of the Civil War had faded from the memories of most; a new generation looked to a glorious future, not to an earlier conflict. Like Theodore Roosevelt, most Americans went off like knights on a medieval crusade with its self-righteousness, its limited military commitment, and its opportunities for individual heroism. One could contemplate war more lightly in 1898 (at least against a "has-been" like Spain), than would be possible in the second half of the twentieth century.

The war was a most unequal contest. Spain was doomed to defeat, though one might not have thought so to look at the military chaos in the United States. The American Navy had been preparing for years, but the regular Army was smaller than the present New York City police force. There was no quartermaster general, no general staff, and no planning facility. The regular Army was scattered widely in small garrisons. The national guard was hardly better than nothing. Political favoritism and profiteering made a bad situation worse. Orders were made, revised, canceled, remade, and contradicted.

In the final analysis, however, Spain was no match for American power and resources. Spain had a population of eighteen million; the United States had seventy-five million. Spain was nearly bankrupt; the United States was a leading financial center. Spain's economy was not far out of the Middle Ages; the United States was the leading industrial nation in the world. America had five battleships and numerous cruisers and smaller vessels; Spain's one battleship was laid up and saw no service. Spain had one good cruiser, though its main guns were not mounted. It had three smaller cruisers. The rest were little more than junk. Only in the size of its army did Spain have an advantage, and American volunteers quickly changed that. Spain could not win; it went through the motions in the name of national pride and honor.

The first military engagement with the Spanish did not occur in Cuba but took place thousands of miles further west, in the Philippines. There on May 1, 1898, America's Pacific fleet under Commodore George Dewey destroyed the Spanish Navy in Manila Bay. In two hours of fighting the Spanish fleet was reduced to shambles. Of 1,200 men, the Spanish lost 381 killed and wounded. None of the six American ships was seriously damaged. Two American officers and six men were wounded slightly. Only one American died, and he was an engineer who died of heat prostration in the hold of his ship. Though the Spanish fleet there was destroyed in Manila Bay, the United States did not take the city of Manila until August 13, nor the rest of the Philippines until later.

In the Atlantic the Spanish Navy under Admiral Cervera sailed from the Azores and quietly slipped into the harbor at Santiago, Cuba, without being intercepted by the Americans. Efforts to immobilize the Spanish fleet there by blocking the harbor failed. But when American ground forces approached Santiago, Cervera on July 3 led his ships out of the harbor, where the waiting American fleet under Winfield Scott Schley destroyed or grounded every one of the Spanish ships. The Spanish lost 400 men killed and wounded; for the United States one man was killed and another was wounded.

Eager to fight, Theodore Roosevelt quickly resigned from the Navy Department and volunteered in the Rough Riders. Though one skeptic suggested that Roosevelt's account of his role should have been called "Alone in Cuba," he was only second in command of his regiment under Colonel Leonard Wood. Field Command of American forces in Cuba fell to the competent but unexciting General William R. Shafter. He weighed nearly 300 pounds and suffered from the gout. A wooden platform facilitated mounting the "stout-hearted mule" that he rode. Little wonder that the press and public preferred to identify with the more dashing Theodore Roosevelt. Despite blunders, American forces under Shafter advanced, and after victories at El Caney and San Juan Hill on July 1 and 2, they closed in on Santiago. The Spanish there surrendered on July 17. General Nelson A. Miles hurriedly took Puerto Rico eight days later. The United States and Spain concluded an armistice on August 12. Rarely has any war wrought so little damage in battle to the combatants as the Spanish-American War. Americans suffered more from yellow fever than they did from Spanish bullets.

Though Spanish diplomats did the best they could, the United States and its President decided for themselves what terms they would require in the peace settlement. With nominal Cuban independence already assured, the main issue concerned the future of the Philippines. Public opinion, the peace commission, and even the President were torn on the matter. Three of the five men whom McKinley named to the peace commission (Whitelaw Reid of the New York *Tribune;* Senator Cushman K. Davis of Minnesota, chairman of the Senate Foreign Relations Committee; and Senator William P. Frye of Maine) wanted the United States to keep all of the Philippine Islands. One of the commissioners (Senator George Gray, a Democrat from Delaware) was an anti-imperialist who opposed taking any part of the Philippines. And the head of the delegation (former Secretary of State William R. Day) was on the fence. He wanted to keep only part of the Philippines at most.

Anti-imperialists drew support from many sources and vehemently opposed annexing the Philippines. William Jennings Bryan of Nebraska, an agrarian free silver advocate and a former and future Democratic presidential candidate, opposed annexation in 1898. Some farm groups such as sugar, tobacco, and hemp producers feared competition from the Philippines. Most of organized labor, including the American Federation of Labor under Samuel Gompers, opposed colonial expansion, partly because they feared competition from immigrant labor and from products of cheap labor in the colonies. A few businessmen and industrialists, such as Andrew Carnegie, supported the anti-imperialists, though they were only a small minority of the business community. Intellectuals and educators, such as William James and William Graham Sumner, were anti-imperialists, as were writers such as Mark Twain and Finley Peter Dunne, creator of Mr. Dooley. Many political and social reformers, such as the Liberal Republicans Carl Schurz and E. L. Godkin, were anti-imperialists as was the pacifist social worker, Jane Addams.

Politically the issue cut across party lines, but most Democrats (both gold and silver Democrats) were anti-imperialists. A few Republicans, particularly older antislavery Republicans, opposed keeping the Philippines. Those and others organized an Anti-Imperialist League in 1898–1899 as a pressure group to advance the cause. It established headquarters in Chicago, organized units in a dozen major cities, and by May, 1899, had around 30,000 members. The anti-imperialists did not emphasize commercial, religious, constitutional, or humanitarian arguments for the most part. They opposed annexing the Philippines largely on the grounds that it would be contrary to American belief in government by the consent of the governed and contrary to the ideals in the Declaration of Independence.

In 1898–1899, however, the imperialists were even more powerful. Most Republican leaders supported annexation, including such able young men as Senator Henry Cabot Lodge, Senator Albert J. Beveridge, and Theodore Roosevelt (though Roosevelt later viewed the Philippines as America's Achilles heel). Big-navy spokesmen, including Captain Mahan, supported annexation. Expansionist newspapermen, including Whitelaw Reid, William Randolph Hearst, and others, wanted the colony. Leading businessmen and business associations urged annexation. Chambers of Commerce and *The Wall Street Journal* hoped for expanded markets and for profits from foreign investments in overseas colonies. Most Filipinos were already Christians, but under Spanish guidance they were Roman Catholics. That did not seem quite satisfactory to Methodists, Baptists, Presbyterians, Congregationalists, Episcopalians, and other American Protestants. The challenging opportunities for missionary efforts in the Philippines inspired their expansionist inclinations.

President McKinley made the final decision, but that talented politician was certainly not unaware of public and group opinion on the issue. In explaining his decision to a group of clergymen later, however, the President preferred to credit God's guidance:

> I went down on my knees and prayed Almighty God for light and guidance more than one night. And one night late it came to me this way—I don't know how it was, but it came: (1) That we could not give them back to Spain—that would be cowardly and dishonorable; (2) that we could not turn them over to France or Germany—our commercial rivals in the Orient—that would be bad business and discreditable; (3) that we could not leave them to themselves—they were unfit for self-government—and they would soon have anarchy and misrule over there worse than Spain's was; and (4) that there was nothing left for us to do but to take them all, and to educate the Filipinos, and uplift and civilize and Christianize them, and by God's grace do the very best we could by them, as our fellow-men for whom Christ also died. And then I went to bed and went to sleep and slept soundly.

With Spanish military forces hopelessly beaten, the desperate efforts by

Spanish diplomats to retain the Philippines failed. The wishes of the President and other American imperialists prevailed.

The Treaty of Paris ending the Spanish-American War, signed on December 10, 1898, provided for Cuban independence. It also gave the Philippines, Guam, and Puerto Rico to the United States. As a sop to the Spanish it provided for payment of $20 million by the United States for Spanish public works and improvements in the Philippines.

Even the President's support, however, did not assure favorable Senate action on the treaty. It might not have won approval had not William Jennings Bryan of Nebraska unexpectedly thrown his weight behind it. With his backing the treaty won the necessary two-thirds vote on February 6, 1899, two days after fighting erupted in the Filipino insurrection against the United States.

It was one thing for the United States to annex the Philippines; it was quite a different thing to get the seven million Filipinos to like it. At first their leader, Emilio Aguinaldo, had cooperated with Dewey, believing that the United States would assure independence. When that hope was not realized, Aguinaldo fought against the United States as furiously as he had earlier fought the Spanish. Now the Americans, rather than the Spanish, were charged with committing atrocities (and the charges were not always false). More American lives were lost in suppressing the insurrection than in fighting the Spanish-American War. Finally, the United States captured Aguinaldo in March, 1901, and persuaded him to urge his followers to stop fighting. By 1902 the insurrection was crushed. The whole affair left a bad taste in the mouths of most Americans. The United States' brief orgy of overseas colonial expansion largely ended. But most of the external and internal forces for nonterritorial expansion persisted and grew more powerful in the twentieth century.

SUPPLEMENTARY READINGS

Beale, Howard K.   *Theodore Roosevelt and the Rise of America to World Power*. Baltimore: Johns Hopkins Press, 1956.

Beisner, Robert L.   *Twelve Against Empire: The Anti-Imperialists, 1898–1900*. New York: McGraw-Hill Book Co., Inc., 1968.

Freidel, Frank.   *The Splendid Little War*. Boston: Little, Brown & Co., 1958.

Healy, David F.   *The United States in Cuba, 1898–1902*. Madison: University of Wisconsin Press, 1963.

Jenks, Leland Hamilton.   *Our Cuban Colony: A Study in Sugar*. New York: Vanguard Press, Inc., 1928.

LaFeber, Walter.   *The New Empire: An Interpretation of American Expansion, 1860–1898*. Ithaca, N.Y.: Cornell University Press, 1963.

Leech, Margaret.   *In the Days of McKinley*. New York: Harper & Row, Publishers, 1959.

May, Ernest R. *Imperial Democracy: The Emergence of America as a Great Power*. New York: Harcourt, Brace & World, Inc., 1961.

_____. *American Imperialism: A Speculative Essay*. New York: Atheneum Publishers, 1968.

Millis, Walter. *The Martial Spirit*. Cambridge, Mass.: Literary Guild of America, 1931.

Morgan, H. Wayne. *America's Road to Empire: The War with Spain and Overseas Expansion*. New York: John Wiley & Sons, Inc., 1965.

_____. *William McKinley and His America*. Syracuse, N.Y.: Syracuse University Press, 1963.

Pratt, Julius W. *America's Colonial Experiment: How the United States Gained, Governed, and In Part Gave Away a Colonial Empire*. Englewood Cliffs, N.J.: Prentice-Hall, Inc., 1950.

_____. *Expansionists of 1898*. Baltimore: Johns Hopkins Press, 1936.

PART **IV**

Age of imperialism
1899–1917

23

Imperialism and world war: External influences on American foreign relations, 1899-1917

During most of the nineteenth century the United States thrived in a relatively secure world environment. Seers might identify disturbing clouds on the distant international horizons, but few expected the destructive storms they would bring.

Nevertheless, changes underway pointed to a far less safe and stable world situation for the twentieth century. Japan's military victories, over China in 1894–1895 and over Russia ten years later, dramatized both its growing power and its expanding ambitions. The United States triumph in the Spanish-American War of 1898 was similarly revealing. And Germany's Kaiser William II seemed more bellicose than Bismarck had been. Germany may have designed its new navy to defend its security in the North Sea, but it disturbed Britain, whose survival depended on control of the seas. Furthermore, the Kaiser did not seem to limit Germany's goals to Central Europe as much as the Iron Chancellor had.

One should not conclude that World War I was inevitable. Britain did not immediately consider Germany and its navy to be vital threats to its survival. The centuries-old enmity between Britain and France made accord between them unlikely. Similarly, Britain's chronic opposition to Russia's expansionist efforts made an Anglo-Russian rapprochement unlikely. The Franco-Russian Alliance of 1894 was aimed more against Britain than against Germany. The Kaiser was not eager to alienate Great Britain; and British leaders tried three times around the turn of the century for an alliance or formal arrangement with Germany. The British agreements with France in 1904 and with Russia in 1907 resolved certain differences, but they were not alliances and were not designed to be. Europe and the world stumbled into their most disastrous war in the summer of 1914. In the aftermath it is possible for statesmen and scholars to identify steps that led to that terrible conflagration. But leaders considered many alternatives along the way. The fact of war did not necessarily mean that it was inevitable. But it came.

Changes in the power of individual states enhanced the ambitions of the growing states and aroused feelings of insecurity among others. New groupings of states aimed to preserve security and prevent war, but they provoked emotions of insecurity among those that were not party to the arrangements. Drives for empire and military might ostensibly enhanced power and security, but they alarmed other states and led to comparable efforts by them. Repeated crises in North Africa, in the Balkans, and elsewhere inflamed emotions. They encouraged rigidity of institutions and thinking when flexibility might have served the international community and its members better. When the alliances were sufficiently firm, when national dogmas were sufficiently rigid, and when fears and pride were sufficiently aroused, a tiny spark could set off an explosion. That spark came with the assassination of the Austrian Archduke Francis Ferdinand at Sarajevo on June 28, 1914. There had been many earlier sparks that had not resulted in general war. World War I erupted when the explosive compound was properly prepared. Included in that compound were industrialization, imperialism, armaments, alliances, nationalism, strategic doctrines, and the insecurity born of uncertainty. It also included the element of personal leadership (and personal bungling and miscalculation).

In many ways the further rise and spread of industrialization contributed to international difficulties in the twentieth century. Power shifts closely paralleled the relative development of industry. Great Britain's industrial head start made its preeminence possible in the nineteenth century. But industrialization also enhanced the power of the young giants (Germany in Europe, Japan in Asia, and the United States in the Western Hemisphere) that challenged or surpassed British power in the twentieth century. Austria's decline and Italy's continued weakness were related to their industrial backwardness. The tremendous productivity of industrial systems made national boundaries inadequate, even obsolete, in economic terms. The voracious appetite of modern industry encouraged the search abroad for secure access to low-cost raw materials. The awesome productivity of modern industry required ever-expanding markets. Industrial states found some of those markets at home, but unobstructed foreign markets seemed essential as well.

Furthermore, the huge capital accumulations created by industrialization promoted lending and investing in other parts of the world.

Industrialization also had revolutionary effects on military technology. By producing railroads, telephones, telegraphs, steel-hulled steamships, cars and trucks, tanks, radios, and even flimsy airplanes, industry provided greater military speed and mobility than ever before. And it increased the destructive capability of those forces many fold. That mobility and destructiveness seemed to require the negotiation of alliances before wars began. To wait until the fighting started might be too late. At the same time, the tremendous productivity of industry made states capable of sustaining the insatiable material requirements of total war. The specific effects of industrialization varied in each country. By way of example, the ouster of the Prussian Junker Bismarck and the development of German imperialism symbolized the rise of industry in Germany.

During the last two decades of the nineteenth century and on into the early twentieth century, there was a new wave of imperialism and colonial expansion. It was so striking that the period has been called the Age of Imperialism. All major states got in on the exciting race for colonies, including Germany under Kaiser William II, France under the Third Republic, Great Britain, Russia under Czar Nicholas II, Japan, Italy, Belgium, the Netherlands, and the United States. Those and other states scrambled for colonies in most of the major underdeveloped areas of the world, including Africa, Asia, and the Caribbean. The new wave of imperialism was the product of many influences. Restless men sought adventure and exciting challenges. Industrial economies and the entrepreneurs who guided them sought raw materials, markets, and places for profitable investments. Nationalism and appeals to national pride and glory played powerful roles.

Social Darwinism, White Man's Burden ideas, and the determination to spread Christianity through missionary activity provided ideological justifications for imperialism as a positive good. And partly the new wave of imperialism grew out of feelings of national insecurity aroused by the rise of new states that challenged the old balance of power. When one state got a colony, other states became fearful and felt compelled to do so as well. States sought colonies for strategic naval and military bases deemed essential for national survival. They wanted colonies to provide natural resources vital to national power and war efforts. And sometimes they sought territories in order to prevent some other expansionist state from seizing them. Whatever the reasons, world affairs around the turn of the century were characterized by imperialism and expansion by all of the major states and many lesser ones.

Related to power changes, industrialization, and imperialism was the armaments race. In the 1880's and 1890's Germany, Japan, and the United States all began to modernize and enlarge their navies. The new navies were chauvinistic expressions of the growing power of those states. They justified the naval expansion in the name of the defense of national security, vital interests, and national honor. Each of those states was capable of building new navies because of the productivity of its heavy industries. And each justified and used its navy to bind its growing empire to the home state. No matter how innocent and persuasive the justifications, however, that naval expansion disquieted the older dominant states.

Great Britain became particularly alarmed by the new German Navy in European waters. Consequently Britain and France stepped up their naval building programs. In the changing circumstances Great Britain was no longer able, as it had been earlier, to maintain its navy larger than the next two largest in the world. Britain did, however, have by far the largest navy and did keep it larger than the next two largest in Europe. Furthermore, in 1906 Britain developed the powerful dreadnoughts. They increased its naval power, but they also made many of its older ships obsolete. Germany, more nearly starting from scratch, therefore had almost as good a chance to build future naval power as Britain had. In any event, British naval expansion inspired Germany, Japan, and the United States to further construction, and a heated naval building race developed. It was more than a coincidence that the naval armaments race erupted mainly between those countries that had steel and shipbuilding industries capable of building (and profiting from building) modern warships. That naval race extended into a general armaments race, including land armies as well. The armaments were supposed to enhance national security and preserve peace; but they also aroused feelings of insecurity that helped lead down the road to war. They also played a role in another element of the compound, the alliance systems.

Bismarck accomplished the unification of Germany by means of successful wars against Austria and then France. For France he dictated the punitive Treaty of Frankfurt in 1871, with its heavy indemnity and the transfer of all of Alsace and part of Lorraine to Germany. Bismarck hoped the punitive settlement, following on the heels of French military defeat and the collapse of the government under Napoleon III, would leave France too weak for successful revenge. In addition, Bismarck guarded against retaliation by isolating France diplomatically. He did that through a system of alliances that made certain that in the event of a Franco-German war other states would either remain neutral or fight on the side of Germany. Through that diplomacy Bismarck obtained the Dual Alliance with Austria in 1879, the Triple Alliance with Italy and Austria in 1882, and the Reinsurance Treaties with Russia in 1881 and 1887. He did not get an alliance with Great Britain, but he maintained good relations with that great power. In his successful diplomatic isolation of France Bismarck demonstrated his genius quite as impressively as he had earlier in accomplishing German unification.

When young William II became Kaiser in 1888 he was not content to let the old Chancellor run things. In less than two years he "dropped the pilot" and chose advisers less likely to upstage a young monarch. Kaiser William II and his new ministers were not as evil as the Allies insisted during World War I, but neither were they as wise and able as the Iron Chancellor. Their goals for Germany were not as limited as Bismarck's had been. Bismarck maintained friendly relations with European states and tried to avoid frightening them; the Kaiser often made blustering, saber-rattling statements that increasingly alarmed Britain and continental powers. Bismarck generally opposed German expansion overseas; the Kaiser aggressively sought colonies abroad. Under Kaiser William II most of Bismarck's alliance system fell apart, and Germany, in effect, drove Russia and Great Britain into France's waiting arms.

The conflicts of interests between Russia and Austria-Hungary in the Balkans made it difficult for Bismarck to keep both of them within his alliance system; the task was quite beyond the capacities of his successors. Germany and Russia did not renew their Reinsurance Treaty in 1890, the first major rift in Bismarck's system. Nominally the Triple Alliance lasted until World War I began in 1914. Italy's power, however, was not very great in or out of alliances. Its course shifted as its particular interests and the balance of power shifted. As Bismarck's system fell apart and as the opposing forces formed and gained in power, Italy's attachment to Germany and Austria weakened. On the ground that Austria was not fighting a defensive war, Italy never joined the Central Powers during World War I. Instead, attracted by the promises and power of Germany's enemies, Italy became a belligerent on the side of France, Russia, and Great Britain in 1915. Consequently, other than accords with lesser states, the only major alliance that held together for Germany in World War I was the Dual Alliance with Austria-Hungary. And if Germany had given less sweeping assurances to that ally, the little Balkan war in the summer of 1914 might not have started or might not have become a general war.

At the same time as Germany's alliance system faltered, the Kaiser's antics and blunders began to alarm Britain and other states. France eagerly seized on the resulting opportunities to build its own system and got an alliance with Russia in 1894. A decade later France and Great Britain formed the Entente Cordiale. It was not an alliance, but a friendly understanding resolving various differences between the two states, particularly in Africa. By removing some sources of friction, however, it paved the way for closer accord later. When Russia and Great Britain reached an agreement in 1907 on their respective spheres of influence, particularly in Persia, the Triple Entente of France, England,

and Russia was accomplished. Like the Entente Cordiale, it was an informal understanding, not an alliance. Nevertheless, by removing sources of discord it made closer cooperation possible later. Both France and Russia had been long-time British adversaries. But Russia's conflicts with Austria-Hungary in the Balkans, France's conflicts with Germany in Africa and elsewhere, and Britain's growing alarm about the German Navy, all helped drive those unlikely partners together (contrary to German expectations and intentions). Successive crises, particularly in Morocco and the Balkans, gradually tightened the bonds between France, Russia, and Great Britain. Not until Germany violated Belgian neutrality in August, 1914, however, did Britain finally commit its forces to war on the French side.

At the same time that France built its power grouping, Great Britain drew closer to Japan in Asia and to the United States in the Western Hemisphere. The 1902 alliance between Great Britain and Japan served both to guard British interests in Asia and to reduce its military requirements there. The United States and Great Britain did not become formal allies, but leaders in both countries around the turn of the century assiduously cultivated improved diplomatic relations. Britain's slipping relative power and the growing German naval threat gradually turned Great Britain away from its traditional "splendid isolation." Former adversaries became essential friends. The Anglo-Japanese alliance, the growing accord with the United States, and the tightening bonds of the Triple Entente seemed essential to enable Britain's still great but overextended power to meet its commitments and guard its interests, particularly against the German challenge.

The specific objectives of the individual states in the several alliances varied widely. In general, however, they were designed to protect the security and interests of the states, prevent war if possible, and assure that if war erupted the states would have either friendly neutrals or helpful cobelligerents. The alliances, by themselves, did not cause World War I. But neither did they prevent it. Furthermore, they helped make Austria-Hungary and Serbia bold enough to contemplate a local Balkan war. More serious, the alliances converted that regional war into a world war.

No single state or leader was responsible for the general circumstances, the compound, that exploded when the spark ignited at Sarajevo on June 28, 1914. Similarly, no single state or leader was solely responsible for the sequence of events that led from the assassination of Francis Ferdinand to World War I. Nevertheless, in the dramatic summer days that followed that incident, each state hoped to advance or defend certain national objectives, each state bore part of the responsibility for what followed, and each might have prevented the conflagration if it had pursued different policies.

Serbia and its nationalists wanted to create a Greater Serbia. To accomplish that goal required some territory and people then within Austria-Hungary. It also necessitated overcoming Austro-Hungarian opposition. Serbia might have prevented war if it had restrained its extremist nationals, if it had used the information available to prevent the assassination, and if it had yielded to Austria-Hungary's admittedly drastic ultimatum of July 23.

Given the divisive impact of its heterogeneous ethnic composition, Austria-Hungary considered Serbian nationalism a threat to its survival. It determined to use the assassination as the excuse for a local war to crush the Serbian challenge once and for all. Austria-Hungary under Emperor Francis Joseph might have prevented war if it had taken more adequate precautions to protect the heir to its throne on his visit to Bosnia, if its demands on Serbia after the incident had been more reasonable, and if it had accepted Serbia's conciliatory response to its ultimatum. Austria-Hungary was the first to act when it declared war on Serbia on July 28, 1914.

The Versailles Treaty blamed the war on Germany. But in his careful study Sidney B. Fay concluded that "Germany did not plot a European War, did not want one, and made genuine, though too belated efforts, to avert one. She was the victim of her alliance with Austria and of her own folly." With its other alliances evaporating and consequently with its power slipping, Germany resolved to support Austria-Hungary, its only dependable ally. Like Austria-Hungary, Germany hoped the war could be localized. Nevertheless, Germany's "blank check" assurances of support for Austria-Hungary made its ally recklessly bold and daring. If Germany had limited and qualified its assurances, Austro-Hungarian demands on Serbia might not have been so warlike and Austria-Hungary might have been more willing to accept Serbia's response. In the event of a general conflagration, the geographic and diplomatic situation forced Germany to anticipate a two-front war. The German military leaders resolved to use the Schlieffen plan to cope with that problem. It called for striking swiftly through Belgium to knock out France on the Western Front before turning east to meet the Russians. Successful operation of the plan required action quickly against France and could not permit delay sufficient to allow Russian mobilization. The doctrinaire attachment of the military to that strategy triggered Germany's declaration of war on Russia on August 1, when Russia mobilized. It also caused Germany to force a decision on France. Furthermore, military adherence to the Schlieffen plan, with its drive through neutralized Belgium, brought Great Britain into the war on August 5, and provoked anti-German emotions in the United States.

Russia under Czar Nicholas II sought assured access to the sea through control of Constantinople and the Straits. These goals caused chronic conflicts of interest with Austria-Hungary in the Balkans. Russia might have prevented war if it had not encouraged Serbian drives for national unity, and had not backed Serbia against Austria-Hungary. Furthermore, according to Fay "it was primarily Russia's general mobilization, made when Germany was trying to bring Austria to a settlement, which precipitated the final catastrophe, causing Germany to mobilize and declare war." If Russia had yielded to German demands not to mobilize there might not have been a general war.

France welcomed opportunities for revenge against Germany and was determined to regain Alsace-Lorraine. Furthermore, France needed to keep its alliance system intact to guard against German power. France might have prevented war if it had not given Russia firm assurances of its support in the crisis. France's backing strengthened Russia's support for Serbia against Austria-Hungary. It also hardened Russia's resolve to continue mobilization in the face of German protests. And when Germany on July 31 asked France's intentions, the firm French reply led Germany to mobilize and, on August 3, 1914, to declare war on France.

Great Britain wanted to maintain its dominance and the balance of power. To that end Britain wanted to check the German naval and military challenge. During the summer crises, British leaders tried to preserve peace. Nevertheless, Britain might have averted war if it had made its probable course more clear from the beginning. If it had warned France that Britain would not fight, France might not have given such firm assurances to Russia, Russia might have been more responsive to German protests against mobilization, and Russia might not have backed Serbia so resolutely. Conversely, if Great Britain had made it clear from the beginning that it would fight on France's side in a general war, Germany and Austria-Hungary might not have been so bold in the courses they pursued. And though it was a more remote consideration at that time, a clear indication of America's future course might have had some effects.

Emotions, national goals, doctrines, blunders, and miscalculations brought Europe and the world to war in July and August, 1914. The Central Powers in World War I included Germany, Austria-Hungary, Turkey, and Bulgaria. The Allies included France, Russia, Great Britain, Japan, Italy, and many other states.

Several variables blocked success for Germany's Schlieffen plan: Belgium's surprisingly tenacious resistance, France's heroic military defenses in the First Battle of the Marne, and Russia's unexpectedly rapid mobilization and advances in the East. When Germany's drives faltered, the war settled down to a dreary, bloody, and costly stalemate. Despite unprecedented expenditures of men and material, neither side on the western front could move the lines of trenches and barbed wire more than a few miles (or a few hundred yards).

Millions of deaths later, two major states in different ways threatened to break the stalemate. Neither of those states (Russia in Eastern Europe and Asia, and the United States in the Western Hemisphere) was in Western or Central Europe. Internal difficulties and military reverses proved too much for the government of Czarist Russia. Revolution in March, 1917, brought a provisional government under Prince Lvov and later under Alexander Kerensky. When it was no more effective than its predecessor, a second revolution in November, 1917, brought the Bolsheviks under Nikolai Lenin and Leon Trotsky to power. They took Russia out of the war by agreeing to the Treaty of Brest-Litovsk in March, 1918. That relieved the Central Powers on the Eastern Front and enabled them to concentrate more of their forces in the West.

At the same time, however, a succession of events and circumstances culminating with Germany's unrestricted submarine warfare brought the United States into the war on the side of the Allies on April 6, 1917. With Russia out of the war and American power not yet fully available, Germany made a desperate final effort to crush the Allies in the spring and early summer of 1918. That effort failed. One by one the Central Powers fell, and on November 11, 1918, Germany signed the armistice and the fighting ended. With ten million military deaths and twice that many wounded, it was the most destructive war in human history up to that time.

Those developments undermined or reduced the national security of the United States. American security never has been dependent only upon its own power and policies. It has always been affected by developments outside its boundaries. The new challenges to the balance of power, the new wave of imperialism, the armaments race, and the eruption of World War I threatened American national security. Or, at the very least, those developments caused many Americans and their leaders to believe that American security and interests were endangered.

The United States actions in foreign affairs from 1899 to 1917 fitted in with and coincided with the general trends and tendencies on the world scene. Like most European countries, the United States was imperialistic and successfully sought colonies and protectorates overseas. Like the major European countries, the United States was actively involved in the naval armaments race. The United States also became a part of the new power alignments, though it did not formally join any alliance. As a belligerent in World War I, America was only an associate power, not a member of a formal alliance. Nevertheless, it did take sides long before 1917. In the 1890's and after, the United States drew closer to Great Britain in diplomatic and security matters. Friction between the United States and Germany tended to increase. By 1917 there was much debate about whether to enter World War I or not, but if it entered it was already certain that the United States would enter on the side of Great Britain and against Germany. The United States, like the European states, was a part of the new power groupings.

And finally, from 1899 to 1917 the United States played the role of a major world power. From the moment it won its independence until roughly the 1880's, European states and statesmen viewed America as weak. By the 1890's the United States was sufficiently powerful to exert real influence of major proportions on world politics, even when dealing with the leading European states. The United States did not win World War I by itself; its total military contribution was small compared to those of France, Britain, and Italy. Nevertheless, given the deadlock in the European war, America's economic might, its men and materiel, were sufficient to help swing the balance toward an Allied victory. America's role in world affairs after 1898 was that of a major state. And, unlike Great Britain and France, the United States emerged from World War I more powerful than ever before.

SUPPLEMENTARY READINGS

Albertini, Luigi. *The Origins of the War of 1914.* 3 vols. London and New York: Oxford University Press, 1952–1957.

Albrecht-Carrié, René. *A Diplomatic History of Europe since the Congress of Vienna.* New York: Harper & Bros., 1958.

Barnes, Harry Elmer. *The Genesis of the World War: An Introduction to the Problem of War Guilt.* New York: Alfred A. Knopf, Inc., 1929.

Fay, Sidney Bradshaw. *The Origins of the World War.* 2d ed., rev. 2 vols. in one. New York: Macmillan Co., 1935.

Langer, William L. *The Diplomacy of Imperialism, 1890–1902.* 2d ed. New York: Alfred A. Knopf, Inc., 1951.

Mowat, Robert B. *A History of European Diplomacy, 1815–1914.* London: E. Arnold, 1927.

Schmitt, Bernadotte E. *The Coming of the War, 1914.* New York: Charles Scribner's Sons, 1930.

———. *Triple Entente and Triple Alliance.* New York: Henry Holt & Co., Inc., 1934.

Seton-Watson, Robert W. *Britain in Europe, 1789–1914: A Survey of Foreign Policy.* New York: Macmillan Co., 1937.

Sontag, Raymond J. *European Diplomatic History, 1871–1932.* New York: Century Co., 1933.

Taylor, A. J. P. *The Habsburg Monarchy, 1815–1918: A History of the Austrian Empire and Austria-Hungary.* London: Macmillan & Co., Ltd., 1941.

———. *The Struggle for Mastery in Europe, 1848–1918.* Oxford, England: Clarendon Press, 1954.

Woodward, Ernest L. *Great Britain and the German Navy.* Oxford, England: Clarendon Press, 1935.

24

Industry and finance in the Progressive Era: Domestic influences on American foreign relations, 1899–1917

The years immediately before entry into World War I were commonly called the Progressive Era in American history. Both urban and rural reformers tried to identify and root out corruption and abuses in government and business. That progressive reform movement swept the nation in an atmosphere of economic prosperity and substantial faith in the inevitability of progress in the United States. The reform movement and the continued influence of agriculture may have inhibited American overseas expansion a bit. But the movement's emphasis on democratic control of public policies, its crusading idealism, and the dramatic leadership of men such as Theodore Roosevelt and Woodrow Wilson helped arouse mass emotions for aggressive crusades abroad.

More fundamental, however, was the continued growth, productivity, and power of urban industry and finance. Contrary to conservative fears, the progressive movement did not inhibit the growth of business. The long-term trends toward increased industrial productivity, control of the economy by big finance, and concentration of population and power in the burgeoning cities continued. And those patterns within the United States affected foreign affairs more than the progressive reform movement did. Like the developments on the world scene at the same time, those domestic tendencies generally encouraged American activity and expansion abroad.

THE ECONOMY

By the end of the 1890's the United States had recovered from the depression that had followed the Panic of 1893. The economy suffered a jolt in the Panic of 1907, but it did not last long. The nation seemed headed for a major slump in 1913–1914, but the stimulus provided by war in Europe helped restore prosperity in 1915–1916. And while the United States was a belligerent in 1917–1918, it prospered as never before. Most Americans, in varied degree, shared in the prosperity of the Progressive Era.

Farmers did share, but their production, income, and population increased more slowly than did urban business and industry. Political spokesmen for rural America continued to affect national policies; William Jennings Bryan of Nebraska symbolized that role on both domestic and foreign policy issues. Farmers influenced Congress and controlled many state legislatures. Nevertheless, farmers did not generally control American policies, either domestic or foreign.

Similarly, the merchant-shipper group was weaker relative to the total economy than it had been a century before. The decline of the American merchant marine reversed temporarily during World War I, but shippers did not dominate economically or politically.

The number of urban wage earners increased substantially. There were numerous organizations of skilled workers, notably the American Federation of Labor under Samuel Gompers and the Railroad Brotherhoods. Unions won sympathetic policies from Woodrow Wilson's administration before and during World War I. Most wage earners were not members of unions, however, and labor organizations were not nearly as powerful as they became later. Despite some exceptions such as the Industrial Workers of the World, most workers and their unions were conservative in the sense that they wanted to improve their lot within the framework of the capitalistic system. The interests and attitudes of workers, when projected into foreign affairs, generally coincided with those of their employers. Developments in foreign affairs that helped management often held potential benefits for employees in that same business. On foreign policy issues the interests and attitudes of labor were more likely to coincide with those of their employers than with those of farmers. In any event, despite their growing numbers and organization, wage earners and unions did not dominate in the United States before World War I. The middle class, not the workers, reigned in the Progressive Era. Neither labor, nor shippers, nor farmers controlled economically from 1899 to 1917. Instead, industry, finance, and business held the upper hand.

The United States had surpassed both Great Britain and Germany in steel production before the end of the 1890's. The volume of American industrial production roughly doubled between 1899 and 1917. At the same time, businesses combined into ever larger units. United States Steel Corporation, organized in 1901, was America's first billion-dollar combination, but other giant businesses appeared, such as Standard Oil, International Harvester, and General Motors. Antitrust agitation had little effect. Those increasingly huge and productive industries exercised tremendous influence directly and indirectly on American life, including foreign affairs.

The rise of finance capitalism followed and roughly paralleled the growth of manufacturing. Before the 1890's the United States had a shortage of domestic developmental capital; foreign financiers, particularly from England, filled the void. By the 1890's Americans had accumulated huge quantities of developmental capital of their own. Large banking houses emerged; the House of Morgan was greatest of all. Financiers provided much of the capital needed for the industrial mergers and consolidations. Consequently, control of industry tended to pass from the hands of the manufacturer into those of the financier. Probably at no time before or since have financiers commanded so much power in the American economy as they did during the two decades following the Spanish-American War.

Those economic patterns had at least two general effects on American foreign relations: first, they increased American interest, activity, and expansion in other parts of the world; and second, they tended to alter the character of American economic relations with the rest of the world. Each of those effects deserves elaboration.

After the Civil War the conquest of the last American frontier, the building of the transcontinental railroads, and the adequacy of domestic raw materials and markets for industry, all encouraged Americans to look inward rather than abroad. By the 1890's, however, and continuing on into the twentieth century those patterns changed. The closing of the frontier as a continuous line, the completion of the American railroads, the increased production of American industry, and the growing size and power of American capital, all tended to increase interest in other parts of the world and to promote expansion.

Between 1899 and 1917 most American manufacturers continued to find both their raw materials and their markets within the boundaries of the United States and sought protection behind tariff walls. But as industrial production increased, more manufacturers began to look abroad for raw materials and markets. As they tried to expand markets abroad, and as some of them became more efficient than their foreign competitors, industrialists in some lines became as eager to eliminate foreign-trade discriminations as they were to maintain tariff protection at home. Those that developed a comparative cost advantage began to consider equal opportunities abroad (that is, the "Open Door") more essential than a privileged position in the home market. Similarly, between 1899 and 1917 American creditors continued to lend and invest in the United States. But with the closing of the frontier, the completion of the railroads, and the spectacular growth of capital accumulations, American financiers increasingly looked to other parts of the world for profitable places to lend or invest. Among the domestic influences that contributed to American interest, activity, and expansion abroad from 1899 to 1917 was the growing efficiency and power of industry and finance.

In addition, the rise of industry and finance continued to change the nature of American economic (and political) relations with other parts of the world. Because of industrialization a growing proportion of American exports consisted of manufactured products. Between 1899 and 1917 the value of manufactured and semimanufactured commodities exported from the United States greatly exceeded the value of raw material and agricultural exports. As the United States industrialized, an ever growing proportion of imports consisted of either raw materials to be processed in factories, or tropical and semitropical food products such as sugar, bananas, and coffee. The United States maintained its favorable balance of trade. That pattern provided an exchange surplus available for purchases or investments abroad. The rise of industry and finance encouraged Americans to invest and lend more abroad. Between 1899 and 1917 Americans loaned and invested heavily in Hawaii, Canada, Mexico, and Cuba. When the United States became a belligerent in World War I, even the federal government (in addition to private individuals and firms) loaned to the Allied governments. During World War I the United States for the first time achieved a creditor balance in international finance. That is, by the end of World War I Americans had loaned or invested more abroad than foreigners had loaned or invested in the United States.

Finally, the rise of industry and finance tended to change the direction of American economic (and diplomatic) interests overseas. As the United States became an industrial and financial center its economy seemed to compete with, rather than complement, those of Great Britain and Europe. More and more industrialists and financiers began to look toward so-called underdeveloped areas of the world (Latin America, Canada, the Pacific, and the Far East) for opportunities. Those areas supplied raw materials and semitropical food products that Americans wanted. They in turn desired American manufactured commodities. And their undeveloped resources attracted American investments. Many businessmen became extremely optimistic about economic opportunities in Latin America and China in the 1890's and the first decade of the twentieth century. That optimism provided part of the explanation for American foreign policy preoccupation with Latin America, the Pacific, and the Far East in those years. Nevertheless, that refocus of economic activity away from Europe should not be overemphasized. Most American trade continued to be with Europe. Furthermore, the high hopes for gains in Latin America and China proved to be exaggerated. The difficulties often were greater than the gains. Needs and desires did not, by themselves, assure markets. In Europe political stability, going institutions, and established contacts and tastes continued to attract more American products than did Latin America or Asia. As Professor Fred Harvey Harrington has pointed out, America's "Asia first" emphasis in the decade following the Spanish-American War partly reflected optimistic hopes for economic gains there. But the "Europe first" emphasis of American foreign policies after 1910 resulted partly from disappointment in the results of economic efforts in China and the Pacific.

THE PEOPLE

American population totals, composition, and distribution reflected and reinforced the general patterns. Due to a high birth rate, low death rate, and massive immigration, the population increased from less than 75 million in 1899 to over 100 million in 1917. Throughout those years the United States had more people within its boundaries than any European state except Russia.

At the same time, the society became increasingly urbanized. In 1899 roughly 40 percent lived in cities of 2,500 population or more; by 1917 the proportion was about half. That urban population greatly influenced the American economy, intellectual patterns, political actions, and foreign affairs. With the exception of William Jennings Bryan, all of the Secretaries of State from 1899 to 1917 spoke for the eastern, urban, financial and business sectors of the population rather than for rural and small-town America.

More people immigrated to the United States between 1899 and 1917 than in any other period of American history, reaching an all-time peak of one and a quarter million immigrants in 1907. Thousands of them came from the states of Northern and Western Europe, including Great Britain, Ireland, Germany, and the Scandinavian countries. But most were from Southern and Eastern European states such as Italy, Russia, Poland, and the Balkans. Most of the immigrants settled in the growing cities of the Northeast and the Great Lakes, and initially most of them became part of the urban labor force. Thus a growing minority, particularly in the cities, was of Latin or Slavic descent, though the Anglo-Saxon and Germanic peoples continued their dominance in both domestic and foreign affairs.

That immigration had many effects on America's role in world affairs. For example, the muscles, minds, and talents of those millions increased the productivity and power of the United States. Without their contributions, and those of their descendants, the power of the United States in world affairs would not have increased as rapidly as it did. Furthermore, the flood of immigration provoked more antiforeign nativist agitation within the United States. Those nativist patterns were in tune with American nationalism and isolationism. Late in the nineteenth century, Congress by law barred certain categories of diseased persons, paupers, and criminals. Treaty and domestic law restricted Chinese immigrants beginning in the 1880's, and Japanese workers could not come after the Gentlemen's Agreement of 1907 under Theodore Roosevelt. During World War I Congress, over President Woodrow Wilson's veto, enacted a literacy requirement for immigrants. The most discriminatory restrictions did not come until the 1920's, but the restrictions and bigoted agitation irritated other countries. And finally, many of those transplanted ethnic groups retained Old World hatreds and attachments. Irish-Americans continued their anti-British biases; they probably retarded the development of Anglo-American accord and strengthened isolationist opposition to entering World War I on the side of Great Britain. At the same time, German-Americans also reinforced isolationist or noninterventionist sentiments. Many of them retained cultural, linguistic, and sentimental ties with Germany and were proud of their German backgrounds. Generally they did not urge the United States to enter World War I on the side of Germany, but they did favor neutrality and nonintervention. In contrast to the Irish-Americans, who usually lived in cities, the isolationism of German-Americans was reinforced by the fact that many of them lived in rural areas.

In terms of religious affiliations, the United States continued to be predominantly Protestant. But a growing minority, particularly in the cities, was of Orthodox, Roman Catholic, or Jewish faith. The foreign policy attitudes and influence of religious groups tended to coincide with ethnic patterns. For example, despite many exceptions Roman Catholics tended to be noninterventionist toward World War I, but that tendency may not have been due to theological or church considerations. Irish-Americans and many German-Americans were Roman Catholic, and their ethnic ties (rather than their religious affiliations) may have guided their foreign policy inclinations.

On the other hand, many clergymen, particularly Protestants, helped arouse enthusiasm for waging war on Germany. Some clergymen portrayed "Kaiser Bill's" Germany as the agent of the devil and saw war against Germany as a holy crusade in the name of righteousness. The evangelist Billy Sunday insisted that "If you turn hell upside down, you will find 'Made in Germany' stamped on the bottom." Most clergymen did not take such extreme stands. Many were Christian pacifists. Nevertheless, by extending conventional moral values and religious sentiments into international controversies, many of them intensified the enthusiasm and self-righteousness of American participation in World War I.

Organized religious groups, particularly Protestants, also continued to encourage American expansion overseas through missionary activities. Missionaries and the churches that supported them particularly influenced American attitudes and policies in the Pacific and Far East. Missionaries not only brought Christianity, they also brought their way of living and their material goods. To that extent they encouraged markets for American products. Often descendents of missionaries stayed on in the areas as businessmen or diplomats. Like businessmen, missionaries wanted to eliminate foreign barriers and restrictions on their activities. To that extent they, like businessmen, encouraged Open Door policies. When missionaries got into difficulties abroad they, like businessmen, sought the support and protection of the American government. Sometimes they demanded military protection. And sometimes they wanted the United States to acquire colonies or protectorates to facilitate missionary activities.

POLITICAL PATTERNS

Neither the Republican Party nor the Democratic Party presented a united front on either domestic or foreign policy issues. Both were alliances of dissimilar groups with diverse views that were drawn together to get into office and control the government. Most government policies, domestic and foreign, obtained support from some in both parties. The progressive movement, for example, won important support from both the Republican Party under Theodore Roosevelt and others and the Democratic Party under Woodrow Wilson. Nevertheless, between 1899 and 1917 the two parties may have had slightly different tendencies on foreign affairs. The Republican Party represented greater interest in Asia and Latin America, while the Democratic Party had somewhat more of a "Europe first" focus. The Republican Party was a bit more willing (or eager) to promote and protect the interests of American businessmen overseas than the Democratic Party. The Republican Party may have been a bit more imperialistic and a little more willing to use strong-arm tactics in its dealings with other states. The Republican Party may have been more anit-British and pro-German than the Democratic Party. And there may have been slightly more internationalism in Democratic circles, while Republicans may have been a bit more nationalistic and determined to maintain American sovereignty and freedom of action. Insofar as those tendencies prevailed, however, the differences between the parties were only matters of degree. The similarities on foreign policy were more striking than the differences.

As before, foreign affairs generally were not major issues in presidential or congressional campaigns between 1899 and 1917, and they did not determine the election results. In three of the presidential races and in all of the congressional contests in those years foreign affairs played no significant role. Two of the presidential elections were among those rare ones in which foreign affairs got much attention.

Imperialism was a conspicuous issue in the presidential campaign of 1900. The Republican Party and its candidate William McKinley approved annexation of the Philippines after the Spanish-American War. They were believed to approve American colonial expansion abroad. Though he supported the Treaty of Paris in 1899, William Jennings Bryan, the Democratic candidate in 1900, criticized annexation of the Philippines and opposed expansion overseas. In that stand he reflected and spoke for agrarian radicals from the upper Mississippi Valley. But imperialism was not the only issue in the campaign. Domestic considerations such as monetary policy, free silver, anti-trust policies, personalities, and prosperity were far more important in deciding the outcome. Professor Thomas A. Bailey, who carefully studied the foreign policy aspects of the election, concluded that "about all that can be said with certainty is that McKinley polled more votes than Bryan." Despite McKinley's victory, Professor Bailey believed that if the question had been put to a direct vote the people would have voted for turning the Philippines free, at least eventually.

Foreign affairs were prominent in the presidential campaign of 1916 between Republican Charles Evans Hughes and the Democratic incumbent Woodrow Wilson. Democratic party leaders appealed for votes with the slogan, "He kept us out of war." But there were many other domestic considerations in the campaign. In an extremely close contest, Hughes's accidental snubbing of Hiram Johnson in California probably had more to do with the outcome than foreign affairs. It is doubtful whether any national election from 1899 to 1917 was won or lost on the grounds of foreign policy. And it is impossible to determine from the elections what the people favored or opposed on foreign affairs.

Three Republicans and one Democrat served as President between 1899 and 1917. William McKinley, who was assassinated in 1901, was a popular but not a strong President. He was highly responsive to political currents and public opinion. The colorful, aggressive, militant Vice President Theodore Roosevelt of New York became President with the death of McKinley. After an election victory on his own in 1904, he served until 1909. He was far more interested in foreign affairs than most of his predecessors, and he favored an active role for the United States in world affairs. More than most, Roosevelt was acutely alert to the role of power in international affairs. His actions on behalf of expansion and imperialism became associated with the phrase "Big Stick policy," and with the Roosevelt Corollary to the Monroe Doctrine. With Roosevelt's backing, William Howard Taft won the Presidency as a Republican and served one term from 1909 to 1913. Big, fat, jovial, intelligent, earnest, and legal-minded, Taft was politically inept and bungling. American imperialism during his administration was associated with the phrase,

"Dollar Diplomacy." His policies focused more on the Far East than on Europe.

Following the succession of Republicans, the Democrat Woodrow Wilson won the Presidency and served two terms from 1913 to 1921. Born in the South, he was the son of a Presbyterian minister. He got a doctorate in history and government, and was a professor and president of Princeton University before becoming Governor of New Jersey. Idealistic, moralistic, and doctrinaire, he tended toward self-righteousness and inflexibility. He criticized the imperialism of his predecessors, but in practice his moralism and idealism drove him to policies not greatly different from those of the Republicans who preceded him in the White House. Despite the party, temperament, background, and physical differences between those four Presidents, the policies they followed in foreign affairs were more similar than one might have expected. All in different ways guided the United States toward active and expansionist roles in world affairs.

IDEOLOGICAL PATTERNS

Many of the ideological roots for American activity and expansion overseas in the Progressive Era and the Age of Imperialism may be traced to two general attitudes. First, most Americans had a tremendous optimistic faith in the inevitability of progress toward some more perfect society and world. Much of that faith later was dampened by the tragedy of the Great Depression in the 1930's, and still later by the specter of a suicidal nuclear World War III. By the last third of the twentieth century many were less certain that the future would be better than the past. But from 1899 to 1917 American faith in the future was at its peak. The progressive movement reflected that optimism, as reformers hoped to build the good society by correcting abuses that had crept into America's otherwise splendid system. That optimism extended into foreign affairs. Most believed that progress was natural and inevitable and that the world was nearer to the achievement of enduring peace than ever before. World War I challenged that optimism, but under Wilson's leadership even America's role in that war was played within the atmosphere of optimism and utopianism.

In addition, Americans had confidence that the United States (its people and leaders) knew or could find the solutions, that Americans had the wisdom and ability to lead the world toward that more perfect condition. In their attitudes toward foreign affairs Americans generally had not been overburdened with feelings of humility or self-doubt, and they were not in those years. They had various theories about how the United States might most effectively provide that leadership. Some, in the isolationist tradition, believed the United States should lead by the power of example. That is, if the United States perfected its democratic system at home, others might be so favorably impressed that they would attempt, without coercion, to follow America's steps. William Jennings Bryan saw American leadership in those terms. Others, in the imperialistic pattern, believed the United States would have to exercise its economic, diplomatic, and military power to move people in Latin America, the Pacific, and Asia toward the better life. Theodore Roosevelt, Henry Cabot Lodge, Alfred Thayer Mahan, and others fitted that general pattern. Still others, in the internationalist vein, believed the United States should cooperate with other Western states (particularly with Great Britain) to build world peace and order through international organization. Woodrow Wilson symbolized and spoke for that general approach. Whatever the method, most Americans were confident of their wisdom and ability to lead the world toward that better way.

Those general attitudes of faith in progress and confidence in America's capacity to lead appeared in a variety of more specific ideological patterns. They included the White Man's Burden idea, Social Darwinism, and eventually the idea of fighting in World War I to help make the world safe for democracy. Captain Mahan, historian John Fiske, Brooks Adams, and President Woodrow Wilson were among the better known and more effective spokesmen for ideas of expansion in the Age of Imperialism.

MILITARY FORCES

Between the Spanish-American War and World War I the United States Army was much smaller and less powerful than those of other comparable states. Nevertheless, in the twentieth century the Army was never allowed to become as small as it was when Congress declared war on Spain in 1898. America required troops to suppress the Filipino insurrection, to occupy Cuba, and to guard its expanded empire. Though it did not generally reach authorized levels, the Army generally had 75,000 men or more between the Spanish-American War and World War I.

More important were organizational and planning innovations under such able Secretaries of War as Elihu Root (1899–1904) and Henry L. Stimson (1911–1913). Both of those men later served with distinction as Secretaries of State. Both were elitist and conservative on domestic issues. Their talents won top administrative appointments but did not inspire (and were not inspired by) mass appeal among voters. And both of them (like most of the Secretaries of State in the period) emerged from eastern, urban, upper-class backgrounds. Both had been highly successful corporation lawyers in New York City.

Under Root's leadership the Army War College was created and a General Service and Staff College organized at Leavenworth, Kansas. He persuaded Congress to adopt the Dick Act in 1903 that created a

General Staff Corps (modeled on the German General Staff) as a planning agency. The position of Commanding General of the Army was abolished, and a newly created Chief of Staff advised the President and Secretary of War. The Dick Act also reorganized the National Guard and provided greater uniformity in equipment, training, and organization. Within limits, Congress authorized the President to call the National Guard into federal service to maintain internal order and to check invasion. Secretary of War Stimson began reorganizing the Army by brigades and divisions. As Chief of Staff from 1910 to 1914 General Leonard Wood aggressively crusaded for a more massive preparedness program.

Congress did not adopt Selective Service until May, 1917, after it had declared war, and American ground forces played no significant role in the European war that year. Nevertheless, building on the earlier reforms and drawing forces from the regular Army, the National Guard (16 divisions), volunteers, and draftees, the Army expanded to some 3.5 million men during World War I. Of those, 1.4 million served in the American Expeditionary Force under General Pershing. Despite the speed with which it was recruited and trained, it played a vital role in checking Germany's final drives and in the decisively successful Allied offensives in the late summer and fall of 1918.

The movement to build an American Navy worthy of a great power had started earlier and was well advanced by 1899. The furious naval building race between Great Britain and Germany, combined with congressional economy efforts, allowed the United States to slip from second to third place by 1914. Nevertheless, with Mahan and his followers loudly trumpeting for naval power, and with heavy industry and chauvinists reinforcing the effort, the Navy continued to win larger appropriations than the Army. With the advent of the dreadnought, the United States rapidly built its own versions to replace its obsolete warships. Despite the vulnerability of the Philippines in the face of the power Japan demonstrated in the Russo-Japanese War of 1904–1905, preparedness advocates generally focused their propaganda against the growing might of the British and German navies in Europe. In 1915–1916 Congress authorized the position of Chief of Naval Operations under the Secretary of the Navy. Provided with planning staff and authority, the role of the Chief of Naval Operations was roughly comparable to the Chief of Staff created for the Army a dozen years before. By the time the United States entered World War I many urged an American Navy "second to none." The American Navy, along with the British, played an important role in preventing German military leaders from fulfilling their boasts that unrestricted submarine warfare could bring the Allies to their knees before the United States could make its power felt in Europe.

Naval power appealed to many isolationists on the assumption that it could guard the Western Hemisphere against foreign threats. But Mahan and his followers were by no means isolationists or "continentalists."

Their conception of the Navy's role encompassed far wider horizons than simply hemispheric defense. When President Theodore Roosevelt (himself a big-navy advocate and a disciple of Captain Mahan) sent his fleet around the world in 1907–1909, he dramatized the growing power of the United States and its expanded interests.

The size of the United States Army from 1899 to 1917 lagged behind America's new status in world affairs. And some believed that even the Navy was not commensurate with America's new role. Nevertheless, the Army reforms and the new Navy were parts of America's growing power and expansion in world affairs.

The changing power relations on the world scene, the new wave of imperialism and armaments, and finally World War I, all made the United States less safe and secure than it had been during much of the nineteenth century. That increasingly unsettled international situation seemed to require more active foreign policies if the United States were to guard its interests and security. At the same time, the rise of urban industry and finance and the decline of rural and small-town America reinforced the same tendencies. Even the progressive movement, with its idealistic crusading reform spirit, encouraged optimism about the possibility of building a better world abroad. Both external and internal circumstances encouraged an increasingly active and expansionist role for the United States in world affairs between the Spanish-American War and World War I.

SUPPLEMENTARY READINGS

Bailey, Thomas A.   *The Man in the Street: The Impact of American Public Opinion on Foreign Policy.* New York: Macmillan Co., 1948.

Beard, Charles A.   *The Idea of National Interest: An Analytical Study in American Foreign Policy.* New York: Macmillan Co., 1934.

Faulkner, Harold U.   *The Decline of Laissez Faire, 1897–1917.* New York: Rinehart & Co., Inc., 1951.

Hofstadter, Richard.   *The Age of Reform: From Bryan to F.D.R.* New York: Alfred A. Knopf, Inc., 1955.

Link, Arthur S.   *Woodrow Wilson and the Progressive Era, 1910–1917.* New York: Harper & Row, Publishers, 1954.

May, Ernest R.   *American Imperialism: A Speculative Essay.* New York: Atheneum, 1968.

Merrill, Horace S. and Marian G.   *The Republican Command, 1897–1913.* Lexington: University Press of Kentucky, 1971.

Millis, Walter.   *Arms and Men: A Study in American Military History.* New York: G. P. Putman's Sons, 1956.

Mowry, George E. *The Era of Theodore Roosevelt.* New York: Harper & Row, Publishers, 1958.

Sprout, Harold, and Sprout, Margaret. *The Rise of American Naval Power, 1776–1918.* Princeton, N.J.: Princeton University Press, 1939.

Strout, Cushing. *The American Image of the Old World.* New York: Harper & Row, Publishers, 1963.

Weinberg, Albert K. *Manifest Destiny: A Study of Nationalist Expansionism in American History.* Baltimore: Johns Hopkins Press, 1935.

Williams, Benjamin H. *Economic Foreign Policy of the United States.* New York: McGraw-Hill Book Co., 1929.

25

The Big Stick policy in Latin America

From 1899 to 1917 American interest, activity, and expansion in Latin America varied according to three overlapping criteria. First, they depended upon the size and strength of the particular Latin-American countries. The United States dominated several of the smaller and weaker states and converted them into protectorates. Such was the case with Panama, Cuba, Santo Domingo, Haiti, and Nicaragua. In contrast, the United States did not dominate any of the five largest Latin-American countries: Brazil, Mexico, Argentina, Colombia, and Chile. Second, American activity and influence varied according to the distance of the country from the United States. American dominance was greatest in the nearby Caribbean and Central America. The United States did not win control below the equator in South America, where Great Britain continued to be the leading outside state. And finally, America's activity and influence varied according to the intensity of its interests there.

In terms of external security interests, the United States determined to prevent any non-American state from gaining a dominant position in Latin America, especially in the Caribbean and Central America. Proximity to the United States made it imperative that no aggressive power gain a foothold there. The isthmian route and the approaches to it (particularly after completion of the Panama Canal in 1914) were vital to American security and essential for naval movements from one ocean and coast to the other. The economic and political instability of many

Latin-American states in effect invited foreign intervention. And the weakness of Latin-American states made most of them incapable of preventing such intervention through their own military efforts. They were, in other words, tempting places for European actions that might endanger United States security and interests. Furthermore, the major states of the world from 1899 to 1917 were in fact seeking colonies and protectorates abroad, so there was the real possibility that they might seek them in the Western Hemisphere.

In actual practice no European or Asiatic state seriously attempted to establish or increase holdings in Latin America during the early years of the twentieth century. Germany tried to protect investments of its citizens in the Dominican Republic and in Venezuela, and the Zimmermann note in 1917 hinted at bigger things. But there is no evidence that the German Empire under Kaiser William II actually plotted colonial expansion in Latin America before or during World War I. Some Japanese businessmen were hopeful, but the Japanese government did not make any expansionist moves there. France, Italy, and Russia were not threats in Latin America. Despite its continued dominance in South America and its importance elsewhere, Great Britain generally cooperated with the United States in Latin America. Sometimes Britain even urged the United States to be more aggressive in guarding their common interests there. It did not endanger the United States in the Western Hemisphere between 1899 and 1917.

Nevertheless, the determination to protect security against possible outside threats was one of the most important reasons or justifications for American activity and expansion in Latin America. It is at least conceivable (indeed probable) that if the major powers had not been aware of the opposition of the United States they might have moved into Latin America as they did into Africa and Asia. Furthermore, even though there were no concrete outside security threats by way of Latin America, many Americans *believed* that there were dangers from that quarter. And acting on the basis of those convictions they urged activity and expansion to guard against that possibility.

In addition to external security interests, there were also important domestic interests that promoted American activity and expansion in Latin America. Ideological desire to spread freedom, democracy, and the American way of life was an influence for some. Under President Wilson and Secretary of State Bryan those ideological considerations took on the characteristics of what Professor Arthur S. Link has called secular "missionary diplomacy." In addition, Protestant religious groups were interested, though missionary considerations were not nearly as great as they were for American Asiatic policies. Politicians sought political gain through chauvinistic appeals for the protection of American rights and honor in Latin America. Particularly important among the domestic influences were urban economic interests. Businessmen wanted to promote their trade, investments, and loans in Latin America. And they wanted to discourage or eliminate European competitors.

Historians have differed widely in their assessment of the relative importance of the various influences accounting for American activity and expansion in Latin America. In the 1920's and 1930's many anti-imperialist historians emphasized economic bases for imperialism in Latin America. During World War II and the cold war the prevailing view stressed security explanations and minimized economic considerations. In the 1960's and 1970's New Left historians reemphasized economic interpretations, and their critical analyses gained popularity in the atmosphere of discord and alienation that developed with the shock and frustrations of the Vietnam war. Vogues in historical interpretation will doubtless continue to shift in the future.

The United States used many methods to accomplish its goals and guard its interests in Latin America from 1899 to 1917. Generally it relied upon conventional peaceful diplomacy. Most official dealings with Latin America were through normal diplomatic channels. The United States participated in inter-American conferences and in the Pan American Union. Secretary of State Elihu Root made a goodwill tour of Latin America in 1906. In his 1913 Mobile address Woodrow Wilson emphasized the friendly intentions of his administration.

Nevertheless, the diplomacy was overshadowed by less common but more spectacular techniques. When amicable methods seemed inadequate, and when Americans believed their interests were sufficiently important to justify more drastic actions, the United States resorted to coercion, particularly north of the equator. The phrase "Big Stick Policy" described those actions, and it was identified particularly with President Theodore Roosevelt. In actual practice, however, all of the administrations from 1899 to 1917 brandished the big stick in Latin America.

The coercion took political, economic, and military forms. Nonrecognition was a common political method, that is, withholding diplomatic recognition from governments that did not meet the approval of the United States. That use of nonrecognition as a weapon was contrary to the *de facto* recognition policies followed by the United States ever since Thomas Jefferson became the first Secretary of State in 1790. The United States also used economic pressure. The popular phrase to describe the economic methods was "Dollar Diplomacy." It was identified particularly with the Taft administration that wanted to substitute "dollars for bullets," but the methods covered by the phrase were used by all of the administrations in the period. Dollar Diplomacy was a two-edged sword: it was the use of government facilities to promote American trade and investments, and it was the use of trade expansion and investments to advance diplomatic objectives. One particular device under that heading was the "customs receivership." It was an arrangement whereby United States officials collected the tariffs of a Latin-American state and controlled the allocation of those tax revenues. Through the customs receivership the United States controlled the financial lifeline of that country's government and assured its cooperation. It also safeguarded private American loans to that government.

If political and economic methods seemed inadequate, the United States sometimes resorted to force or threat of force. At one time or another each of the presidential administrations between 1899 and 1917 sent military forces into one or another of the Caribbean or Central American countries. In some cases the United States set up military regimes in small Latin-American states. In still other instances where the United States did not actually intervene with military force it got what it wanted because of the threat of force. Those methods helped the United States become the dominant power in the Caribbean and Central America. They protected the various interests of the United States and its citizens there. But the coercive methods also won for the United States the intense hatred of millions of Latin Americans then and later.

CUBA AND THE PLATT AMENDMENT

The United States had warred against Spain to win independence for Cuba, and in the Teller Resolution had renounced any intention of annexing Cuba. Nevertheless, it quickly became apparent that the United States had no intention of keeping its hands off of that Caribbean country. Security, economic, and chauvinistic considerations determined otherwise. After the Spanish-American War, United States military forces stayed on. Under General Leonard Wood's leadership they repaired the physical ravages of revolution and war. They made constructive improvements in sanitation, education, and public works. Wood authorized preliminary steps toward Cuban self-government, including the drafting of a constitution.

At the same time, however, American troops remained until the Cubans formally agreed to a special relationship with the United States. That dependent relationship was spelled out in the Platt Amendment. Introduced in Congress by Senator Orville H. Platt of Connecticut, it was the work of Secretary of War Elihu Root. Congress adopted it as an amendment to the Army appropriation bill of 1901, and the Cubans reluctantly attached it to their new Constitution in 1902 before the United States would withdraw its military forces. Cuba and the United States also concluded a treaty in 1902 embodying the same provisions. Under the Platt Amendment Cuba promised not to enter into any agreement that would impair its independence or give a foreign power (other than the United States) a foothold. Cuba agreed not to go into debt beyond its ability to repay from ordinary revenues. The Platt Amendment gave the United States the right to intervene if necessary "for the preservation of Cuban independence, the maintenance of a government adequate for protection of life, property, and individual liberty." And it allowed the United States to establish coaling or naval bases in Cuba. The Platt Amendment remained in force for a generation, until most of it was abrogated in 1934. And the United States interpreted its rights under the Platt Amendment broadly and invoked it repeatedly.

Charging corruption in the election of 1905, Liberals revolted against the Cuban government. President Tomás Estrada Palma was unable to crush the uprising and urged the United States to intervene. Reluctantly Theodore Roosevelt agreed to do so. In 1906 Charles Magoon as provisional governor, with the support of American Marines, took over direction of Cuban affairs before turning the reins over to the newly elected President José Miguel Gómez in 1909. In 1911, under President William Howard Taft, the United States again sent in the Marines to help crush a black rebellion in eastern Cuba. When another contested election led to uprisings against the government of President Mario Menocal, the Woodrow Wilson administration sent in the Marines in 1917. In each of those instances the practical effect of American military intervention was to sustain the government in power and help crush rebellions.

America's political and military dominance of Cuba under the Platt Amendment was reinforced by economic ties. The two states concluded a Reciprocity Treaty in 1902. The United States was the principal market for Cuba's leading export, sugar. American exports to Cuba doubled between 1900 and 1910, while private American investments there increased nearly 400 percent in the same period. Those economic patterns were by no means unrelated to political and military developments. It was significant that Menocal, Cuba's President from 1912 to 1921, was a wealthy planter and the managing director of the Cuban American Sugar Company.

Cuba and Cubans undoubtedly benefited from close ties with the United States. The United States contributed to stability, order, and prosperity in Cuba and encouraged constitutional government there. Complete withdrawal of American influence would not have resulted in utopia, either politically or economically. Nevertheless, the United States sharply limited Cuba's independence and sovereignty. American policies seemed to attach greater importance to stability, order, and property than to individual freedom and democracy. Even if one views American policies as "benevolent paternalism," countless Cubans understandably resented and even hated the Yankees. Americans would have felt the same way if the United States had been under the dominance of a foreign power, however benevolent. Furthermore, it is not entirely clear that American national security would have been endangered if it had played a less active role in Cuba.

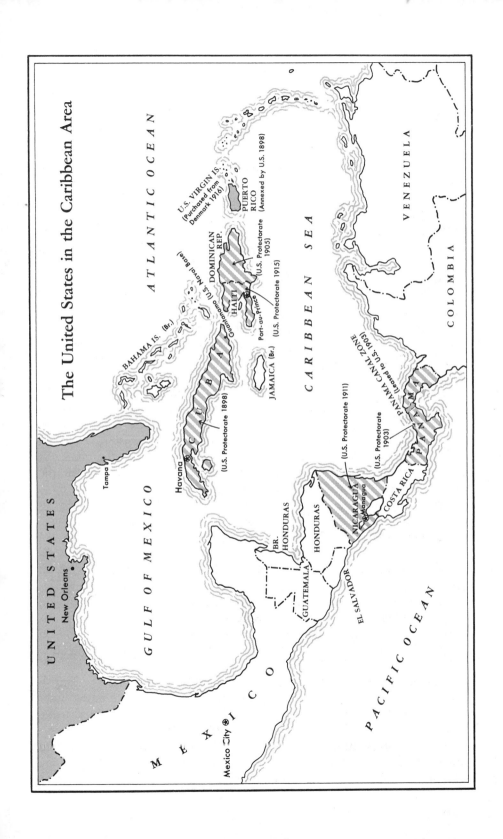

The United States in the Caribbean Area

UNITED STATES

New Orleans

Tampa

GULF OF MEXICO

M E X I C O

Mexico City ⊛

PACIFIC OCEAN

ATLANTIC OCEAN

BAHAMA IS. (Br.)

Havana ⊛

C U B A
(U.S. Protectorate 1898)

Guantánamo (U.S. Naval Base)

HAITI
(U.S. Protectorate 1915)

Port-au-Prince

DOMINICAN REP.
(U.S. Protectorate 1905)

JAMAICA (Br.)

U.S. VIRGIN IS.
(Purchased from Denmark 1916)

PUERTO RICO
(Annexed by U.S. 1898)

CARIBBEAN SEA

BR. HONDURAS

HONDURAS

GUATEMALA

EL SALVADOR

NICARAGUA
(U.S. Protectorate 1911)

Managua

COSTA RICA

PANAMA

PANAMA CANAL ZONE
(leased to U.S. 1903)

(U.S. Protectorate 1903)

COLOMBIA

VENEZUELA

"I TOOK PANAMA"

American interest and activity in Panama had assumed substantial proportions early in the nineteenth century. The acquisition of California and Oregon on the West Coast in the 1840's provided a major stimulus to American trade and transportation schemes in Central America. That activity languished with the completion of the transcontinental railroads after the Civil War, but it never disappeared. The Spanish-American War dramatically revived interest. In 1898 a worried American public impatiently followed the slow progress of the U.S.S. *Oregon* from the West Coast around the tip of South America to the Caribbean, where it could engage the enemy. A Central American canal would have shortened its journey substantially and would have made its guns available much sooner. The annexation of additional territories in both the Pacific and the Caribbean made it even more essential that the United States Navy have secure access to a canal for speedy movement from one ocean to the other. An isthmian canal was an important part of Captain Mahan's increasingly popular sea power ideas. American businessmen hoped a canal might facilitate trade with the countries on the west coast of South America. And the chauvinists never found it difficult to see reasons for raising the stars and stripes over additional territory, particularly in the Western Hemisphere. At least four problems or obstacles had to be resolved, however, before an American-controlled isthmian canal could become a reality. They included the Clayton-Bulwer Treaty, the choice of a route, the rights of earlier canal builders, and permission from the Latin-American country involved.

The Clayton-Bulwer Treaty provided that neither the United States nor Great Britain would build or control a Central American canal alone. If undertaken jointly, the treaty required that such a canal should not be fortified. When signed in 1850 the treaty was, in effect, a *modus vivendi* that reflected the relative power of the two countries in Central America at that time. During the half century that followed, however, United States power and interests outstripped those of Great Britain in Central America. With more pressing concerns elsewhere, Britain was prepared to relinquish most of its security responsibilities in the region to the United States. British leaders sought the favor and cooperation of the United States.

Secretary of State John Hay and Sir Julian Pauncefote, the British Ambassador to the United States, fully shared a determination to build Anglo-American accord. Consequently, they had little difficulty drafting an agreement in 1900 to amend the outdated Clayton-Bulwer Treaty. That first Hay-Pauncefote Treaty would have permitted the United States to build and control a canal in Central America without doing it jointly with Great Britain. But it continued the ban on fortifications, and because of that the United States Senate amended the treaty to death. Decidedly elitist in his inclinations, Hay generally was not enthusiastic about the products of elective democracy. The Senate's audacity in destroying his diplomatic masterpiece infuriated him. But he and the British Ambassador returned to their task and negotiated a second Hay-Pauncefote Treaty in 1901 that met the Senate objections. It replaced the Clayton-Bulwer Treaty and allowed the United States unilaterally to build, control, and fortify such a canal, requiring only that the United States assure equal treatment for the shipping of all countries in the use of the canal. That second treaty won quick Senate approval. It was a concrete expression of Britain's determination to build Anglo-American accord, and it removed the first obstacle to an American canal.

A second problem was to decide on the route for a canal. Some considered the Isthmus of Tehuantepec across southern Mexico, but the main contest was between Nicaragua and Panama. Each won enthusiastic support. Led by Senator John T. Morgan of Alabama, advocates of construction through Nicaragua pointed out that it was closer to the United States than Panama and that Lake Nicaragua and the San Juan River provided natural waterways part of the distance. Two government commissions recommended the Nicaraguan route in the 1890's.

Panama also had its advantages and its advocates. The Central American Isthmus was narrowest in Panama. The French company of which Ferdinand de Lesseps was president was believed to have completed about two fifths of the necessary excavations before it failed. In 1894 a newly organized New Panama Canal Company took over the rights of the older French company. Incorporated in New York, the ownership of its stock was never made public. Its rights were to expire in 1904, thus giving an incentive for moving quickly on the matter. Its capacity to construct a canal was never demonstrated, but the propaganda and lobbying skill of two of its agents proved impressively effective. The leading spokesmen for the new company were Philippe Bunau-Varilla and William Nelson Cromwell. Bunau-Varilla, a Frenchman, had been a chief engineer for the earlier de Lesseps effort, and he was a stockholder in the New Panama Canal Company. Cromwell, an attorney, was legal counsel for the company. Bunau-Varilla was a talented and persistent propagandist; Cromwell was a master at the art of behind-the-scenes manipulations. Neither was interested primarily in serving American national interests in the episode; both could win substantial financial gains if the United States built through Panama.

Instructed by Congress, President McKinley appointed an Isthmian Canal Commission to determine the best canal route. Under Rear Admiral J. G. Walker, that "Second Walker Commission" generally preferred Panama. Nevertheless, in November, 1901, it recommended building through Nicaragua because of the excessive price the New Panama Canal Company asked for its rights. The Commission thought $40 million might be a reasonable sum to pay the company, but considered the company's asking price of $109 million to be excessive.

Confronted with the alternatives of $40 million or nothing, the New Panama Canal Company unhesitatingly chose the former and dropped its price to the figure suggested by the Commission. Consequently, in January, 1902, the Commission changed its recommendation from Nicaragua to Panama, provided Colombia gave permission to build there.

In the meantime the new President, Theodore Roosevelt, was so persuaded of the advantages of the Panama route that he would not consider any other alternative. Bunau-Varilla also convinced many senators of the destructive dangers of volcanos to any canal in Nicaragua (he placed a Nicaraguan postage stamp on the desk of each senator showing a smoking volcano). The combination of the activities of Cromwell and Bunau-Varilla, the Second Walker Commission's recommendations, the President's strong preferences, the volcano scare, and the price reduction by the New Panama Canal Company, had its intended result. In June, 1902, Congress adopted the Spooner Amendment to the Isthmian Canal Act, authorizing construction through Panama if the necessary arrangements could be made with the New Panama Canal Company and with Colombia.

At that point the third problem was easily resolved. The United States paid the New Panama Canal Company $40 million through the House of Morgan. One may reasonably assume that Bunau-Varilla did not lose financially in the transaction. Cromwell later submitted a bill of $800,000 for his services to the company. But just exactly who got what part of the $40 million was never made public.

The final obstacle to overcome was Colombia, whose territory included Panama. Colombians wanted the advantages that a canal would bring, but they worried about the effects of American control of their territory. The difficulty of dealing with Colombia was increased by the weakness of its government and by internal political instability. After earlier attempts had failed, the United States and Colombia signed the Hay-Herran Convention in January, 1903. It would have allowed the United States to use a 6-mile zone across Panama for a canal. It guaranteed Colombian sovereignty over the zone. The United States agreed to pay Colombia $10 million and, after a nine-year interval, $250,000 a year. The United States Senate quickly approved the treaty. In Colombia it did not fare so well. Eventually the Colombian Senate unanimously rejected the treaty and made it clear that it wanted more money. Its course was the product of chauvinism, anti-American fears, greed, and politics. But it was also perfectly legal under both domestic and international law. President Roosevelt alertly defended American sovereignty, but he was not able to appreciate the exercise of sovereignty by foreign states whose wishes conflicted with his. He was infuriated by the action of the Colombian senators and privately referred to them as "contemptible little creatures" and "foolish and homicidal corruptionists."

Given the power of the United States and its interest in the canal, the impatient and bellicose President would not allow the weak state of Colombia to block him long. It only remained to be determined which of several methods he might use to overcome Colombia's objections. He might have renegotiated the treaty to meet the demands for more money. If that had been done after the New Panama Canal Company's rights expired in 1904, it would not have increased the final cost for the United States. He might have shifted to the Nicaraguan route. But he does not seem to have seriously considered either of those alternatives. He chose, instead, to capitalize on more dramatic and violent developments in Panama itself, developments that he did not plot but certainly welcomed and used.

Even before Colombia rejected the Hay-Herran Convention, Panamanians began to plan a revolution. Since Colombia had, with American cooperation, easily suppressed earlier uprisings, those plans by themselves may not have succeeded. This time, however, they won the active support of the New Panama Canal Company and the tacit cooperation of the United States. Bunau-Varilla promised the conspirators $100,000 to finance the revolution. The Frenchman in conferences with the President and his Secretary of State persuaded himself that the United States would not allow Colombia to crush a revolt in Panama. Roosevelt did not conspire with the rebels or with Bunau-Varilla, but he correctly anticipated developments. The government sent American naval vessels to both sides of the isthmus with orders to "maintain free and uninterrupted transit" across Panama. They also were ordered not to allow Colombian troops to land. Those orders were justified under the provisions of the Treaty of New Granada of 1846. The United States had invoked that Treaty before, but always to sustain Colombian control. This time the President chose to interpret the agreement to the disadvantage of Colombia.

The nearly bloodless revolt occurred on November 3, 1903, and Panama declared its independence that same day. Judicious bribes (with money Bunau-Varilla had provided) kept local police and troops from suppressing the uprising. American ships blocked Colombian efforts to send reinforcements. The United States extended diplomatic recognition to the government of the new state on November 7, four days after the revolt. Less than a week later President Roosevelt received the first Panamanian Minister to the United States, none other than Bunau-Varilla, the Frenchman who financed the revolt to safeguard the financial interests of his company. On November 18, 1903, two weeks after the revolt, the two countries signed the Hay Bunau-Varilla Treaty, giving the United

States the canal rights it sought. Its provisions were similar to those of the ill-fated Hay-Herran Convention but were more favorable to the United States. It gave the United States use of a 10-mile zone for its canal. Though Panama was nominally sovereign in the zone, the United States could exercise all authority there as though it were sovereign. The treaty made Panama a protectorate of the United States, even to the extent of allowing intervention under certain circumstances. The United States agreed to pay Panama $10 million immediately and, after a nine-year interval, $250,000 a year. The methods used by the United States to obtain the Canal Zone were somewhat similar to those that earlier gave it West Florida, Texas, and Hawaii.

The United States government did not plot the revolution in Panama, and it had no great difficulty finding justifications for its course in treaty, international law, and national interest. Roosevelt later insisted that "No one connected with the American Government had any part in preparing, inciting, or encouraging the revolution." Nevertheless, Colombians understandably took a different view of the matter. Many Americans shared their misgivings. As an anti-imperialist, agrarian Democrat, William Jennings Bryan denounced Roosevelt's tactics. Secretary of State Bryan in 1914 signed a treaty that would have expressed American regrets and paid Colombia the extra $25 million it had sought in 1903. Roosevelt's defenders successfully blocked the treaty in the Senate. Not until 1921, after Roosevelt's death, did the United States finally make its peace with Colombia by paying $25 million. There was no official apology, but it was clearly implied. It would have been no more costly in dollars, and much less costly in goodwill, if the United States had paid the sum two decades earlier. The settlement in 1921 may have been inspired partly by conscience and the desire for improved diplomatic relations. But American oil companies wanted the settlement so that the Colombian government would not discriminate against them in granting oil concessions there. Construction of the Panama Canal was completed by 1914 in time for use during World War I. The canal greatly increased American determination to guard the Caribbean approaches to that vital waterway.

THE VENEZUELAN INCIDENT

General Cipriano Castro's dictatorship in Venezuela from 1899 to 1908 was financially irresponsible. In 1902–1903 three European countries (Great Britain, Germany, and Italy) blockaded and bombarded Venezuelan ports to force payment of debts and claims. None of the three European states actually sought territory there. Under Roosevelt's leadership the United States did not officially object to the blockade so long as the European states did not try to get territory in the Western Hemisphere.

Finally, at the suggestion of Venezuela, and with some tactful pressure from Roosevelt, the four countries agreed to submit the controversy to arbitration by the Hague Tribunal in 1903. Later (when anti-German statements were more in vogue) Roosevelt boasted that he had threatened war on Germany if the Kaiser refused arbitration. Historians, led by Dexter Perkins and others, generally have believed that Roosevelt's later account was not correct. After thoroughgoing research, however, Professor Howard K. Beale concluded that though Roosevelt acted tactfully and subtly, the President did bring firm pressure on the Kaiser to accept arbitration.

Domestic influences behind the American course in the incident were limited but important. American investments in Venezuela were negligible, and trade there was not great. There was little or no missionary interest. Most obvious among the domestic influences were the personality and temperament of the President and the ideological influences represented by the Monroe Doctrine.

External influences were more numerous and conspicuous. They included the financial irresponsibility of the Castro government, the determination of Europeans to force a settlement, and the resolve to guard American security and approaches to the isthmus by preventing European states from getting footholds.

At least four related variables led to arbitration of the dispute. First was the great power of the United States in the Caribbean. Second, none of the three blockading powers had any intention of trying to use the incident as a cover for territorial expansion. Third, both Germany and Great Britain were anxious to maintain friendly relations with the United States at that time. And finally, there was the diplomatic skill of the President. Partly as the result of the incident, he formulated and enunciated his Roosevelt Corollary to the Monroe Doctrine in a comparable incident involving the Dominican Republic.

THE DOMINICAN REPUBLIC AND HAITI

Located on the east end of the island of Haiti, the Dominican Republic was and is important to the security of the Caribbean, the isthmus, and the canal. Throughout the nineteenth century it had been plagued with dictatorships, revolution, turmoil, and disorder. It also worked itself deeply into debt to European and American creditors. Some foreign creditors urged intervention to assure repayment.

That situation plus the earlier Venezuelan incident led the President in 1904 to enunciate his Roosevelt Corollary to the Monroe Doctrine. In that Corollary the President said that Latin-American countries that conducted themselves responsibly, maintained order, and paid their debts, could count on American friendship. But when Latin-American states were guilty of chronic wrongdoing and impotence, some foreign intervention might become necessary. Under the Monroe Doctrine the United States would not allow European intervention. Consequently, the United States must assume responsibility for intervention when it became necessary in the Western Hemisphere. That Roosevelt Corollary was used many times to justify diplomatic, economic, or military intervention by the United States in the internal affairs of Latin-American states from 1904 to 1930.

In 1905 the Roosevelt administration concluded an executive agreement with the Dominican Republic allowing the United States to set up a customs receivership in which Americans collected the tariffs and distributed the revenues to the Dominican government and its creditors. The arrangement was put in treaty form in 1907 and, in modified form, endured until after World War II. The arrangement resolved the financial difficulties of the government, but political instability continued.

Confronted with growing disorder and violence there, the Democratic Woodrow Wilson administration urged the Dominican Republic to increase American authority over its internal affairs. Specifically the United States demanded the appointment of an American financial adviser, placing the constabulary under American officers, and giving the United States control of internal taxes in addition to the customs. The newly elected President of the Dominican Republic rejected the proposals and was ousted by revolution. In the face of recalcitrance and violence, Secretary of State Robert Lansing urged American military intervention, and President Wilson reluctantly consented. In 1916 America sent in the Marines, who proceeded to set up a military dictatorship under the United States Navy Department. The Dominican President was ousted, the legislature suspended, Marine officers assumed cabinet posts, and the press was severely censored. American military control was responsible for improving roads, bridges, sanitation facilities, and schools. It provided stability and order. Atrocities by American troops were punished with courts-martial. But the American military government there was no more consistent with freedom and democracy than military regimes elsewhere under other auspices. Beginning in 1922 the United States began to permit a bit of self-government, but the Marines were not withdrawn until 1924, eight years after they were sent in. And the customs receivership and other controls in American hands endured much longer.

A similar though slightly milder pattern evolved in Haiti, the black republic on the west end of that same Caribbean island. Haiti had been plagued by chronic political disorder and violence that reached a particularly horrible extreme in 1915, when President Guillaume Sam was murdered and torn limb from limb by a mob. In that environment of anarchy and terror, the United States under President Wilson sent in the Marines to restore order, protect life and property, and prevent European intervention. For all practical purposes the United States determined the next President of Haiti, and then required him to accept a treaty giving the United States extensive control there. Signed in 1915 and ratified in 1916, it combined features of the Platt Amendment with a customs receivership and the internal controls soon to be imposed on the Dominican Republic. Haitians continued to fill public offices, but only because they submitted to American demands. Though United States control was slightly less direct than in the Dominican Republic, it was not democracy and freedom for the Haitians. As Professor Julius Pratt phrased it: "The result was a reasonably efficient dictatorship dominated by the United States treaty officials with the support of the navy and Marine Corps." Journalists there who criticized American actions quickly found themselves in jail. The Marines committed what most Americans would call atrocities if they had been done by troops of any other country. American banks strengthened their hold on Haiti's economy. The Marines were not finally withdrawn until 1934, nearly twenty years after they were originally sent in. And other American controls continued much longer.

NICARAGUA

As in other areas, both external and internal influences affected United States policies toward Nicaragua in Central America. In terms of external security considerations Nicaragua represented a possible alternative canal route. Its proximity to Panama made it imperative that it be kept out of unfriendly hands. Most important among the domestic influences were economic interests. American trade there was not great, and investments totaled only about $2.5 million in 1912, less than in most other Latin American states. But the size of the holdings was not as significant as the influence of the people involved and the effectiveness of their efforts. Philander C. Knox, Secretary of State under President William Howard Taft from 1909 to 1913, had been legal counsel for the largest American firm active in Nicaragua, the United States–Nicaraguan Concession.

From 1893 to 1909 Nicaragua was under the dictatorship of José Zelaya. By 1909 Zelaya canceled a concession to one American company and threatened to cancel the United States–Nicaraguan Concession. High taxes and heavy duties fell on American companies. In 1909 Zelaya was overthrown by revolution. That upheaval won the support of many Nicaraguans, but it also was backed by Americans, including officials of the United States–Nicaraguan Concession. The State Department under Secretary of State Knox in a harsh diplomatic note broke relations with Zelaya's government during the revolution. American troops landed at Bluefields to help prevent the crushing of the uprising. Adolfo Díaz, who became President in 1911, had been the local secretary for a large United States mining company in Nicaragua. The United States set up a customs receivership in the country in 1911. At the request of President Díaz the United States sent in over 2,000 Marines to crush a revolt against him in 1912. A small unit of Marines remained in the country for the next thirteen years. In 1916 the United States concluded the Bryan-Chamorro Treaty, which gave America exclusive rights to build a canal through Nicaragua in return for a payment of $3 million. President Calvin Coolidge removed the Marines briefly in 1925, but sent them back in to quell an uprising in 1927. They were not finally removed until 1933, just before President Herbert Hoover left office.

"WATCHFUL WAITING" IN MEXICO

Though the United States never completely dominated any of the larger Latin-American states, it did intrude on its nearest neighbor, Mexico. The complications there were a direct result of the Mexican Revolution beginning in 1910. Porfirio Díaz had been President of Mexico most of the time from 1876 to 1911. He was a powerful dictator who had actively encouraged and protected foreign investors in lands, railroads, oil, and mining. Though earlier he had cooperated with Americans, such as Edward L. Doheny, by 1910 the aging dictator seemed to favor British oil interests, headed by Lord Cowdray. Consequently, American oil entrepreneurs favored the overthrow of Díaz in 1910–1911, and may even have contributed financially to the revolution. The United States government promptly recognized the new revolutionary regime headed by Francisco Madero. An advocate of honest elections, Madero appealed to Americans who hoped for representative democracy there. But the joys were short-lived. In 1913 General Victoriano Huerta seized power and arranged the murder of Madero. President Taft's Ambassador to Mexico, Henry Lane Wilson, had actively opposed Madero and encouraged his overthrow by Huerta. But President Woodrow Wilson's moral sensitivities and his dedication to constitutional government were shocked by Huerta's methods. Furthermore, Huerta (like Díaz earlier) was unsympathetic with American oil interests and favored the British group led by Lord Cowdray.

The phrase "watchful waiting" was used to describe Wilson's policies toward Huerta. But that phrase implied a more passive role than America actually played. The United States threw its weight against Huerta's government, and his ouster was due partly to the United States. Wilson used a political weapon when he refused to extend diplomatic recognition on the grounds that Huerta had come to power through force and unconstitutional means. Wilson also used economic coercion. He allowed the private sale of arms and munitions to Huerta's opponents in Mexico but not to Huerta's government. American diplomacy helped prevent Huerta's government from getting loans it sought in Europe. And the United States even intervened with military force at Tampico and Vera Cruz in 1914.

The military intervention grew out of an incident over the arrest of American sailors there. The Americans were quickly released and the Mexicans apologized. But Admiral Mayo of the U.S.S. *Dolphin* demanded an apology and a twenty-one-gun salute to the American flag. Mexico wanted a simultaneous gun-for-gun American salute or written promises to return the salute. That the Americans would not give. When a German merchant ship, the *Ypirango*, carrying military supplies for Huerta arrived, President Wilson ordered the Navy and Marines to seize Vera Cruz. That military blow cut off the dictator's best source of imports and customs revenue. The ABC countries, Argentina, Brazil, and Chile, offered to mediate the dispute, an offer that both Mexico and the United States accepted. The mediation effort at Niagara Falls, Ontario, failed, but it gave the United States the occasion for withdrawing its troops from Vera Cruz.

At the same time, American businessmen in Mexico, including the Doheny oil interests, threw their weight against Huerta. They stopped payment of taxes to his government, and they contributed substantial sums to his opponents in Mexico.

General Huerta finally got the impression that he was not wanted. He resigned in July, 1914, and fled from Mexico. Not an appealing figure, he fell partly because of the widespread violent opposition from competing Mexican leaders and their followers. But he also fell because of active opposition from the United States government and American businessmen.

In the turmoil that followed, Venustiano Carranza gained control of the Mexican government and eventually won recognition from the United States in October, 1915. At the same time, the Wilson administration banned further sale of arms to Carranza's opponents. Carranza was a dedicated Mexican nationalist and was highly critical of United States interference. But among contending leaders he became the most acceptable to the United States.

One of the losing Mexican leaders, Pancho Villa, showed his displeasure at America's course by murdering American citizens on both sides of the border in 1916. With Carranza's grudging acquiescence, President Wilson ordered troops under General John J. Pershing across the Mexican border to capture Pancho Villa. Pershing's expedition failed to get its man, but it thoroughly aroused the Mexicans. Carranza's objections to the invasion of Mexican soil grew increasingly strident. Given the growing danger of American involvement in World War I in Europe, the objections from Carranza's government, and the difficulty of catching the wily Villa in the deserts of northern Mexico, most were relieved when the United States removed its troops in February, 1917.

In that same year Mexico drafted the most important constitution in Latin-American history, one that wrote into enduring forms the social and economic goals of the continuing Mexican Revolution. Article 27 of the Constitution of 1917 was to strain Mexican-American relations for a quarter of a century. It forbade foreign ownership of land near the Mexican borders, and it gave ownership of all subsoil mineral rights to the government. If it were made retroactive, Article 27 would pose a threat to American property and business interests in Mexico.

Throughout the developments there, both external and domestic considerations affected the policies of the United States toward Mexico. External influences included the political instability, revolutionary violence, and nationalistic hostility in Mexico toward interference by the United States. They also included the favoritism of Díaz and Huerta for British businessmen over Americans. Among the domestic influences were the moralistic-legalistic attitudes of President Wilson; the economic interests of investors in minerals, oil, and lands of Mexico; and nationalistic responses to the abuse and murder of American citizens at Mexican hands.

CONCLUSIONS

The policies of the United States toward Latin America from 1899 to 1917 may have stimulated the growth of American trade and investments there. They discouraged European or Asiatic countries from trying to gain territory in the Western Hemisphere. American troops and dollars built roads and bridges, and they improved sanitation facilities. The policies gave the United States the economically and strategically important Panama Canal.

At the same time, however, the "Big Stick" policies were seriously criticized then and later. Though the area was and is of major importance to American security, it does not appear that there was any real threat by any non-American state from 1899 to 1917. Furthermore, the United States could have obtained the right to build the canal without the questionable methods it used. American methods did not build democracy in Latin America; often American support went to dictators who promised stability and order. And the methods built a tremendous amount of hatred and fear of the United States in the minds and emotions of millions of Latin Americans, attitudes that still persist.

SUPPLEMENTARY READINGS

Beale, Howard K.   *Theodore Roosevelt and the Rise of America to World Power*. Baltimore: Johns Hopkins Press, 1956.

Beard, Charles A. *The Idea of National Interest: An Analytical Study in American Foreign Policy.* New York: Macmillan Co., 1934.

Bemis, Samuel Flagg. *The Latin American Policy of the United States: An Historical Interpretation.* New York: Harcourt, Brace & Co., 1943.

Callcott, Wilfred H. *The Caribbean Policy of the United States, 1890–1920.* Baltimore: Johns Hopkins Press, 1942.

Cline, Howard F. *The United States and Mexico.* Cambridge, Mass.: Harvard University Press, 1953.

Fitzgibbon, Russell H. *Cuba and the United States, 1900–1935.* Menasha, Wis.: George Banta Publishing Co., 1935.

Healy, David F. *The United States in Cuba, 1898–1902: Generals, Politicians, and the Search for Policy.* Madison: University of Wisconsin Press, 1963.

Hill, Howard C. *Roosevelt and the Caribbean.* Chicago: University of Chicago Press, 1927.

Link, Arthur S. *Wilson: Confusions and Crises, 1915–1916.* Princeton, N.J.: Princeton University Press, 1964.

————. *Woodrow Wilson and the Progressive Era, 1910–1917.* New York: Harper & Row, Publishers, 1954.

Miner, Dwight C. *The Fight for the Panama Route: The Story of the Spooner Act and the Hay-Herran Treaty.* New York: Columbia University Press, 1940.

Munro, Dana G. *Intervention and Dollar Diplomacy in the Caribbean, 1900–1921.* Princeton, N.J.: Princeton University Press, 1964.

————. *The United States and the Caribbean Area.* Boston: World Peace Foundation, 1934.

Nearing, Scott, and Freeman, Joseph. *Dollar Diplomacy: A Study in American Imperialism.* New York: Viking Press, 1925.

Parks, E. Taylor. *Colombia and the United States, 1765-1934.* Durham, N.C.: Duke University Press, 1935.

Perkins, Dexter. *A History of the Monroe Doctrine.* Boston: Little, Brown & Co., 1963.

————. *The Monroe Doctrine, 1867–1907.* Baltimore: Johns Hopkins Press, 1937.

Pratt, Julius W. *America's Colonial Experiment: How the United States Gained, Governed, and in Part Gave Away a Colonial Empire.* Englewood Cliffs, N.J.: Prentice-Hall, Inc., 1950.

Quirk, R. E. *An Affair of Honor: Woodrow Wilson and the Occupation of Veracruz.* Lexington: University of Kentucky Press, 1962.

Scholes, Walter V. and Marie V. *The Foreign Policies of the Taft Administration.* Columbia: University of Missouri Press, 1970.

26

The Open Door policy in the Far East

American interest and activity in the Pacific and Far East increased from 1899 to 1917 (and particularly until 1910). The extent of interest, activity, and control varied widely in different areas. It was greatest in the eastern Pacific and declined as one moved westward away from North America and across the continent of Asia. The United States completely dominated in the area bounded by Alaska in the north, purchased from Russia in 1867; the Hawaiian Islands in mid-Pacific, annexed in 1898; and the Panama Canal Zone, leased in 1903. The United States did not rule the western Pacific but was an important power there through its Navy and its island colonies, including Midway, occupied in 1867; the Philippines and Guam, acquired in the Spanish-American War; Wake Island, occupied in 1899; and the Samoan Islands, which the United States divided with Germany in 1899.

In East Asia, including China, Korea, and Japan, Americans were interested and active but not dominant. In most parts of East Asia other states were stronger, even to the extent of controlling spheres of influence, protectorates, or colonies there. Starting in the south, the French were dominant in Indochina and in the Yunnan province of southern China. The British were active everywhere, but were most powerful in the Yangtze Valley of east central China, and in Hong Kong and Shanghai. Germany won a leasehold in the Shantung Peninsula. Japan had Formosa and gained control in Korea, southern Manchuria, and Inner

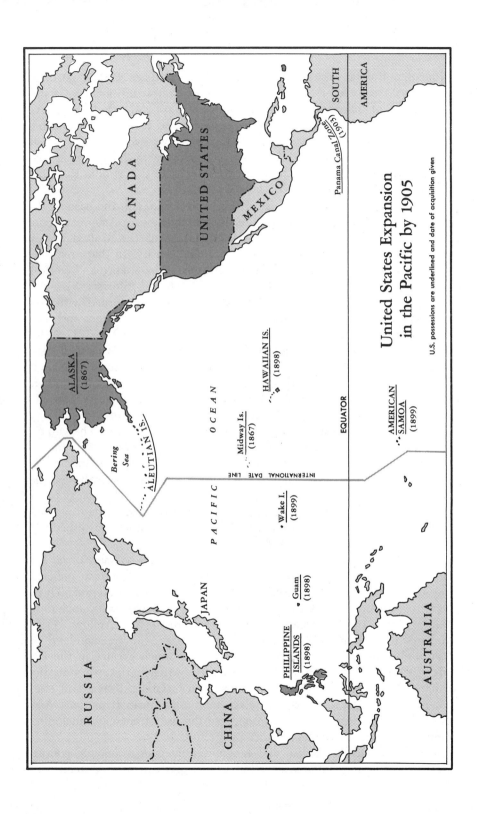

United States Expansion
in the Pacific by 1905

U.S. possessions are underlined and date of acquisition given

Mongolia. Russia was particularly active in northern China, northern Manchuria, and Outer Mongolia. The United States did not have a formal sphere of influence, but Americans were most interested and active in those parts of East Asia where the Japanese and Russians were strongest: northern China, Manchuria, and Korea. Those overlapping interests helped account for America's growing friction with both Russia and Japan. Americans had little interest or influence in the Middle East and Central Asia before 1917.

The external security interests of the United States in the eastern Pacific were clear and unequivocal. As in the Caribbean, Americans considered the area bounded by the West Coast of the United States, Alaska, Hawaii, and Panama vital to national security. In that area they did not brook the slightest challenge to American dominance and control. In the western Pacific and in East Asia the external interests were different. Before 1898 the United States was primarily concerned with protecting the lives, property, and activities of American traders and missionaries there. That continued to be important from 1899 to 1917. With the annexation of the Philippine Islands after the Spanish-American War, however, the United States had to defend that huge group of islands 8,000 miles from the American shores. Theodore Roosevelt and others saw them as a vulnerable "Achilles heel" in American security arrangements. Then and later, military authorities questioned America's ability to defend them against a major power in the western Pacific. The vulnerability of that colony increased with the growing power and ambition of Japan and Germany in the area. To protect business and missionary interests and to guard the Philippines and other island possessions, the United States developed a generalized desire to prevent any state or group of states from gaining an upper hand in East Asia to the disadvantage of the United States and Great Britain. Again, Americans especially worried about Russia, Japan, and Germany.

The categories of domestic influences on American policies in the Pacific and Far East were similar to those on its Latin-American policies, but the relative weight of the several categories was different. There were, of course, ideological and nationalistic considerations, including White Man's Burden ideas. Some worried about the "Yellow Peril." Mahan's theories grew to include need for bases on the mainland of Asia. Religious and missionary influences were much greater in the Pacific and Far East than in Latin America. Missionaries were in the vanguard of American activity and expansion in China, Korea, and elsewhere. They did not limit themselves to purely spiritual matters. And they were not always reluctant to endorse the use of coercion, including military force, to guard and advance their efforts.

In addition to ideological and religious influences, economic considerations encouraged American activity and expansion in the Pacific and

Far East. The magnitude of trade and investments there was not as great as in Latin America. But in the 1890's and the first decade of the twentieth century many American traders, railroad builders, manufacturers, and financiers were tremendously hopeful about the possibilities for business triumphs in the Pacific and Far East. The actual number of men and firms was not great, and the financial returns were often disappointing. Sometimes businessmen and financiers moved in reluctantly under government prod. By 1910 many financiers and entrepreneurs were so disappointed in the returns that they began to refocus away from Asia toward the Western Hemisphere and Europe. Nevertheless, those disappointments should not obscure the expansive influence of the earlier economic optimism.

America's methods in the Pacific and Asia varied according to the magnitude of its interests and power relative to those of other states there. In its Pacific colonies, where its interests (external and internal) were great and where its power was supreme, the United States followed a "closed door" policy similar to that in the Caribbean. In East Asia, where its interests were more limited and where it was not strong enough to dominate, the United States attempted more subtle tactics.

Leaders held widely varying views on the best methods for the United States in East Asia. Some anti-imperialists, such as William Jennings Bryan, insisted that American interests and power in East Asia were so limited and the risks so great that the United States ought to pull out of the Philippines and leave the power struggles in the Far East to others. At the other extreme, some wanted the United States to use Big Stick methods in East Asia as it did in the Caribbean. The desire for naval bases on the China coast and the American military participation in crushing the Boxer uprising reflected that view. In practice, however, the United States lacked the power and will for such an approach before 1917. Some hoped that America might safeguard its interests by urging the states to adhere to an Open Door policy giving equal opportunities to citizens of all states in the several spheres of influence in China. Secretary of State John Hay advanced that view in his Open Door note of 1899. Unsupported by effective power, such an appeal could not prevail against the interests of the major states active in East Asia. Some also hoped to keep China intact and powerful so that it could resist expansionist states that threatened to tear it apart and so Americans could continue to trade and invest there. Hay urged that approach in his second Open Door note of 1900. But internal cleavages and upheavals, combined with antiquated ways, made China quite unable to match the power of modern industrial states active there.

Some hoped to protect American interests in East Asia by cooperating with other interested states in some combination or another. John Hay, for example, urged close cooperation with Great Britain. Dr.

272 *An interpretive history of American foreign relations*

Horace N. Allen, a missionary and diplomat in Korea, urged cooperation with Czarist Russia to block Japanese ambitions in northeast Asia. Jacob Schiff of Kuhn, Loeb, and Company favored working with Japan, where Americans had much trade and many investments, in opposition to Russian expansion in Asia. At times and up to a point Theodore Roosevelt shared that view. Others, including Secretary of State Philander C. Knox, wanted the United States to work with all the competing states to restrain them and assure Americans a share. By 1905 President Roosevelt felt that American interests could best be protected by balancing Japan off against Russia to prevent either state from gaining the upper hand to the disadvantage of the United States. Each of the several methods was proposed, and most of them were attempted. None of them worked well. Insofar as American interests in East Asia were served at all before 1917, it was largely because of an accidental, unintentional, shaky balance of power among the competing states.

CHINA AND THE OPEN DOOR POLICY

At no time in American history was there more optimism about the opportunities for businessmen and missionaries in China, and more determination to capitalize upon those supposed opportunities, than in the 1890's and the first decade of the twentieth century. Manufacturers speculated on the possible markets for their products among the 400 million Chinese. Financiers and railroad builders ruminated hopefully on the investment opportunities in the economically underdeveloped reaches of China. Church leaders and missionaries had high hopes about the possibilities for converting the Chinese to Christianity. Naval officers wanted bases on the China coast. Utopian idealists dreamed of letting the Chinese in on the glories of democracy and freedom, though the Chinese were under the impression that they (not the Westerners) had the superior civilization. The actual number of Americans actively interested in China was not great—but their enthusiasm and vigor was considerable. And they were not without influence.

At the same time, developments within China and international developments in East Asia threatened to close China to Americans and aroused fears for the defense of the Philippines. Despite Chinese confidence in their own cultural superiority, the British and French had clearly demonstrated their military superiority over the Chinese in the Opium Wars earlier in the nineteenth century. The hold of the Manchu Dynasty in China had been severely shaken by the unbelievably bloody Taiping Rebellion of the 1850's and early 1860's. The weakness of China under the Manchus was further dramatized by its military defeat at the hands of Japan in 1894–1895. The combination of internal turmoil in China, the ineffectiveness of the Manchu Dynasty, the demonstrated military weakness of China, and the imperialistic ambitions of the major states, resulted in the creation of "spheres of influence" in China by most of the states active in East Asia. By the end of the 1890's it seemed entirely conceivable that the imperial powers might completely dismember China and close that land to American economic, missionary, naval, and idealistic interests. If that happened America's position in the Philippines might be endangered.

The most famous of the efforts by the United States to protect its interests in China were represented by the Open Door notes of 1899 and 1900. The idea was by no means original in 1899. Daniel Webster, Anson Burlingame, and William H. Seward had all urged the general view earlier in the nineteenth century. The British, in different terms, had advocated such policies for many years. Both British and American businessmen had favored an Open Door in China long before Secretary of State John Hay issued his notes.

Numerous American businessmen were concerned. They included tobacco interests, notably the James B. Duke interests; cotton textile manufacturers; kerosene producers, largely Rockefeller's Standard Oil; and financiers such as E. H. Harriman, James Stillman, Jacob Schiff, and George F. Baker. In their concern for equal opportunities in China such businessmen could find common ground with American church and missionary groups. Many of those interests worked through the American Asiatic Association, organized in 1898 under the leadership of Clarence Cary, John Foord, and others. It brought together many of the leading Americans who were directly interested in preventing the dismembering of China and in keeping China open. That pressure group, the interests it represented, and its propaganda were extremely important domestic influences behind the Open Door notes.

Externally, China's weakness, intense antiforeign sentiments among the Chinese, and encroachment by imperialistic states endangered American interests sufficiently to force a search for policies to meet the challenge. Great Britain, in a different way, was also part of the external background of the Open Door policies. With its power beginning to slip and with growing challenges to meet elsewhere, Great Britain was beginning to turn away from the Open Door idea it had supported so long. But the shift was not abrupt or complete, and the message did not always reach (or persuade) subalterns in British business and diplomatic circles. In 1898 Britain had suggested the possibility of an Anglo-American alliance to guard the status quo and commercial opportunities for all in China. The McKinley administration rejected the British suggestion, but unilaterally the United States pursued a course designed to have similar effects.

A British citizen, Alfred B. Hippisley, played an important role in the origin of the note of 1899. Married to an American, Hippisley had served on the staff of the Chinese Imperial Maritime Customs Service and was extremely interested in promoting trade in China. He suggested the idea for a note to an American friend of his, William W. Rockhill. Cold and formal, Rockhill was an expert on Asia. He knew oriental languages, had traveled in Tibet, and had served in the American legation in Peking. He was pro-British, anti-Russian, and enthusiastic about American expansion in Asia. In Washington he served informally as Hay's adviser on Asian policies. He revised Hippisley's draft and urged it on the Secretary of State. Thus the first Open Door note had its origins externally in Chinese weakness and in an idea long urged by the British. Internally, it grew out of interests represented by a private pressure group. It was first drafted by a British citizen, revised by an American citizen, and was issued almost unchanged by Hay in 1899 as a statement of United States policies in China.

Sophisticated, suave, and aristocratic, John Hay was a writer, a former secretary of Lincoln, and had held several diplomatic posts before becoming McKinley's Secretary of State in 1898. Hay's wealth and his wife's fortune brought him close to important eastern business interests. He was a friend of leading imperialists, including Theodore Roosevelt, Henry Cabot Lodge, Henry and Brooks Adams, Captain Alfred Thayer Mahan, and W. W. Rockhill. The British had received him and his writings warmly during his tour as Ambassador to Great Britain. In turn Hay was a passionate Anglophile who enthusiastically worked for Anglo-American cooperation in world affairs, including those of East Asia. Hay did not draft the first Open Door note, but he was wholly receptive to the views it represented and issued it over his name in the fall of 1899.

Sent to Great Britain, Germany, Russia, France, Japan, and Italy, the note was not designed to protect China or the Chinese people; it was designed fundamentally to serve the interests of Americans in China. It did not object to spheres of influence in China; indeed, it acknowledged and accepted their existence. It did no more than urge states that held spheres of influence not to discriminate against citizens of other states with regard to tariffs, harbor dues, and railroad rates within their particular spheres.

None of the six countries to which the note was sent unequivocally promised to support the Open Door policy. England, Germany, and Japan in general approved with some reservations and qualifications. France acquiesced with some reluctance, but Russia essentially rejected the idea. Hay bluffed, however, and publicly announced in March, 1900, that all of the states had accepted the Open Door policy. No one called his bluff, and it has been cited as a great diplomatic coup by the Secretary of State. His note and his bluff may have had certain political benefits for the McKinley administration in an election year when the Filipino insurrection was raging and when Republican imperialism was under attack. But they had no practical influence in China and East Asia. Despite the adoration by Americans then and since, the Open Door policy was not international law. It was not a binding treaty. The policy did not end spheres of influence and was not designed to. Furthermore, it did not even end discrimination within spheres of influence. The United States had neither the power nor the will to enforce the Open Door policy, and at times it even participated in departures from the Open Door. Its effects on popular imagination in the United States were far greater than its influence on world politics and China. As a simple slogan it became a powerful and relatively inflexible domestic influence on American Far Eastern policies in the twentieth century.

New Left scholars, following the lead of Professor William Appleman Williams, advance a different view. Williams sees the Open Door as "the central feature of American foreign policy in the twentieth century" and as "a brilliant strategic stroke which led to the gradual extension of American economic and political power throughout the world." It was a method by which the highly productive American economy attempted to sustain itself at home by expanding into an "informal empire" abroad. "Open Door Imperialism" is a central feature in New Left critical analyses of American expansion in the twentieth century.

In the midst of the Open Door episode, the Boxer rebellion of 1900 in China provided the United States and other Western states with a violent expression of the antiforeign and anti-Western passions that have so complicated relations with Asia in the twentieth century. The Boxer uprising was not directed against the Chinese government. It aimed at foreign influences in China, including business and missionary activities. The crafty old Dowager Empress Tz'u Hsi secretly encouraged the Boxers, hoping they might oust foreign influences and strengthen the Manchu Dynasty. With the lives of hundreds of foreigners endangered, the interested powers sent 19,000 troops to crush the uprising. Most of the troops were Japanese and Russian, but there were also British, French, and Germans. The United States provided 2,500 men for the expedition. Against such a force the Boxers were helpless, the foreign colony was relieved, and order was restored. The Boxers had been brutal, but the foreign troops were at least as bad. They looted, burned, and pillaged, thus further inflaming xenophobia in China.

The incident officially closed with the negotiation of the Boxer Protocol of 1901. W. W. Rockhill represented the United States in the negotiations. That executive agreement provided for punishment of the ringleaders, guarantees against further incidents, and imposed a heavy indemnity on the Chinese government for the loss of lives and property. It gave the powers the right to maintain troops in Peking, in Tientsin, and on the railroad between the two cities. The negotiators, in effect, pretended that the Manchu Dynasty had had nothing to do with the uprising. Throughout the affair the United States wanted to protect American lives and property. But it also tried to restrain the demands of the other states and to prevent them from using the incident as an excuse for further weakening or dismembering China. That course by the United States was not inspired by any great love of China and the Chinese. It grew out of concern for American self-interest.

That same concern and reasoning led Secretary of State Hay to issue his second Open Door note in July, 1900. It expanded on his earlier note by expressing the American desire for the preservation of Chinese territorial and administrative integrity. Coming in the midst of the Boxer crisis, the second note neither called for nor received replies from the other states.

In the decade and a half that followed enunciation of the Open Door policy, the United States and its citizens suffered numerous frustrations, disappointments, and failures in China. Those reverses occurred in investment schemes and trade patterns. They were aggravated by the revolution in China beginning in 1911, and by Japan's growing power in East Asia.

Various American entrepreneurs and bankers played roles in the financial schemes in China before the first World War. E. H. Harriman, a major railroad promoter and the father of Averell Harriman, dreamed of building a transportation system around the world, and to that end he sought a railroad through southern Manchuria. J. P. Morgan and the banking interests he controlled were active. So were Rockefeller's Standard Oil Company and Jacob Schiff of Kuhn, Loeb, and Company. Those and other financial groups generally worked in cooperation with the Department of State and key government officials. Sometimes the initiative for the projects came from the financiers, who sought government support. Other times the initiative came from the government, which urged the financiers into China. Often it was difficult to tell which was the moving force, or even which influence an individual served. For example, Willard Straight sometimes performed as a government official and sometimes as an agent for financial interests. He was a newspaper correspondent in the Far East and had served as an American consular agent there. He cooperated with financiers such as Morgan and Harriman, and he considered himself an advance agent for American investment and trade expansion in China. But he was also chief of the Far East Division of the Department of State in 1908–1909. Both as a business agent and as a government official he pushed American expansion in Asia and sought to strengthen China against Japan's growing power. He made no great effort to distinguish between his private and government roles and probably saw them both as part of the same great effort. Philander C. Knox, President Taft's Secretary of State, also saw the government and business as sharing common interests in Asia. By the time he assumed responsibility for guiding America's foreign policies in 1909, however, American business enthusiasm for projects in China was waning.

Most of the investment projects in East Asia failed or met with meager success. One such venture involved the American China Development Company. When organized in 1895 it involved several American financiers, but it came to be dominated by J. P. Morgan. It got a concession from the Chinese government to build 840 miles of railroad from Hankow to Canton between the Russian and French zones in China. But the whole project was badly managed. The company violated its concession agreement frequently. It only built 28 miles of railroad. It appeared more interested in financial manipulation than in constructing railroads. Confronted with such mismanagement the Chinese government canceled the concession in 1905 and settled with the American China Development Company on terms so favorable that the Americans got nearly twice the amount they had invested. The project collapsed largely because of bungling and irresponsible performance by the company. President Roosevelt shared China's disgust with the company, though he supported its claims in the final settlement.

E. H. Harriman was also involved in various complicated projects for a railroad in China. He never got authority for his schemes, however, and he had not yet won success for his plans when he died in 1909.

With the death of Harriman, Secretary of State Knox then proposed a so-called Neutralization Plan in 1909. It was designed to have financiers from all major interested states, including the United States, Great Britain, Japan, Russia, Germany, and France cooperate in the financing, administration, and profits of a Manchurian railroad. Knox hoped in that way to expand American investments and to prevent Japanese and Russian dominance in Manchuria. All of the powers concerned, even Great Britain, rejected the Knox proposal, and it failed to win acceptance. Britain and France were more interested in getting Japanese and Russian support against Germany. Neither Britain nor France was as interested in northeast Asia (or in Russian and Japanese expansion there) as the United States was. And the scheme backfired by driving Russia and Japan closer together against the American challenge to their ambitions. Failure of Knox's scheme ended American railroad investment efforts in Manchuria, and Americans refocused their attention farther south in China.

In 1909 a combination of bankers from France, Germany, and Great Britain was about to get a concession from China to build a major railroad in southern and western China from Canton to Hankow and then west. But President Taft and Secretary Knox used firm diplomatic pressure to get American bankers included in that banking consortium in 1911. The American group included Morgan; Kuhn, Loeb, and Company; First National Bank; and National City Bank. Morgan lost interest in the combination, however, and when the new President, Woodrow Wilson, ended the government's official support the American group withdrew from the first consortium in 1913. The optimism of American financiers and government officials about the possibilities for loans and investments in China was not realized.

Americans were no more successful in expanding trade there than they were in promoting investments. Americans traded in China, of course, as they had for more than a century. They sold particularly tobacco, kerosene, and cotton textiles. But the trade was always small relative to America's total foreign trade and was always less than 3 percent of the value of America's foreign trade.

The Chinese Revolution of 1911 further complicated the situation. After the revolt erupted, Sun Yat-sen quickly returned to his country to attempt to assume leadership of the revolt, an effort that he never completely accomplished. With the Manchu Dynasty ousted, a Republic emerged under a former Manchu official, Yüan Shih-k'ai. He had no interest in democracy or reform and envisaged making himself the equivalent of an emperor. When Yüan Shih-k'ai died in 1916, China degenerated into violence and disorder, in spite of the efforts of Sun Yat-sen to form an effective government. American officials, businessmen, and missionaries generally preferred order to the instability and violence of the revolution. Many of them were sorry when the revolt began and were glad when Yüan gained power and promised order. The United States was the first major state to recognize the Yüan Shih-ka'i government in 1913. On top of all those disappointments and difficulties, the United States faced the expansion and growing power of Japan in China and East Asia.

THE RISING SUN IN EAST ASIA

For half a century after Perry's expedition to Japan in 1853–1854, Americans generally viewed Japan sympathetically. Japan adopted certain Western ways and "modernized" more rapidly than China or any other Asian state. It quickly became the leading non-Western trading country and built a large and efficient merchant fleet. The Industrial Revolution started late but progressed very rapidly, until Japan's light manufactured goods competed effectively with those made in Britain, Western Europe, and the United States. At the same time, Japan began to modernize its military forces. Under the leadership of commercial-industrial-military interests the Japanese consolidated national political power. When Western states moved into the Age of Imperialism, Japan was not far behind. Like Germany, Japan eventually challenged the dominant states led by Great Britain and the United States. But before 1905 most did not see Japan in that role.

At first the Japanese (like the British and Americans) seemed to like the Open Door idea. They needed raw materials and markets, and the Open Door seemed consistent with that need. The Anglo-Japanese Alliance of 1902 came at the same time that Anglo-American cooperation developed. Japanese interests and ambitions clashed with those of Russia in northern China, Manchuria, and Korea at a time when anti-Russian views increased in the United States. Some envisaged an Anglo-American-Japanese accord in opposition to Russian expansion in Asia. In contrast to Russia, Japan was not a Christian state, but American missionaries encountered less official opposition from the Japanese than from the Russians.

One of the earliest Americans to sound warnings against Japan's growing power in Asia was Dr. Horace N. Allen, the first Presbyterian medical missionary in Korea. The tall redheaded physician saved the life of the Korean queen's nephew and in 1885 became physician for the royal family of Chosen. Allen's aggressive temperament and considerable political ability enabled him to influence royal policy and made him an important agent for American business and diplomatic expansion there. From 1887 to 1889 he even served as adviser for the first Korean diplomatic mission to the United States. In 1897 he became American Minister to Korea, a post he filled until 1905, just before Japan took over there. In his several capacities (missionary, business agent, and diplomat) Allen grew alarmed at the increasing power of the Japanese in the Hermit Kingdom. In a personal conference with President Roosevelt and W. W. Rockhill in 1903, Dr. Allen warned against the Japanese menace and urged cooperation with the Russians against Japan. But Roosevelt was not persuaded, and Allen's days in Korea (like those of the United States there) were numbered.

The turning point in Japanese-American relations came with the Russo-Japanese War of 1904–1905. A product of their conflicting ambitions in Manchuria (and Korea and North China), war erupted with a surprise Japanese attack on the Russian fleet at Port Arthur in February, 1904. Russia won French sympathy and financial backing. Japan found encouragement from the British, and London bankers helped finance the Japanese war. Initially, Americans sympathized with tiny Japan against the giant Russian bear. President Roosevelt wrote that "Japan is playing our game." On Wall Street the House of Morgan, with its English background and ties, helped finance the Japanese effort. Similarly, Jacob Schiff of Kuhn, Loeb, and Company was a moving force in American loans to Japan. He was shocked by the anti-Semitic pogroms in Czarist Russia.

It was easier for Americans to sympathize with Japan in the role of an underdog than it was after Japan surprised most observers by winning impressive military and naval triumphs over the Russians. Russian dominance in northeastern Asia endangered American interests, but dominance by a powerful and aggressive Japan might be equally harmful. Moved by that consideration (and by secret entreaties by the Japanese, whose resources were as exhausted in victory as Russia's were in defeat), President Theodore Roosevelt offered to mediate a settlement between the two belligerents. In persuading the powers to accept his invitation, and in guiding them to an acceptable peace treaty, Roosevelt performed with impressive tact, skill, and effectiveness. Despite his earlier and later bellicose actions, the President received the Nobel Peace Prize for his part in ending the Russo-Japanese War. In the Treaty of Portsmouth, signed in September, 1905, the Japanese won a free hand in Korea. Russia yielded the south half of Sakhalin Island and its leased territory in Liaotung Peninsula to Japan. Russia kept its hold on northern Manchuria but gave up its railroad holdings in southern Manchuria. The Japanese had demanded an indemnity but did not get it. Consequently, the Japanese severely denounced Roosevelt and the United States. Nevertheless, the balance that Roosevelt sought between Japan and Russia in northeast Asia did not prevail during the forty years that followed the Treaty of Portsmouth. In spite of (and partly because of) Roosevelt's diplomatic intervention, Japan had the upper hand. At the same time, relations between the United States and Japan deteriorated.

Roosevelt thought it was futile to make moralistic pronouncements against Japanese dominance where the United States lacked the power to force Japan to withdraw. Consequently, he tried to make the best of a bad situation by recognizing the Japanese position in exchange for certain Japanese guarantees affecting American interests in East Asia and the western Pacific. In the Taft-Katsura executive agreement of 1905, Japan renounced any aggressive ambitions in the Philippines, and in return the United States acquiesced in Japanese suzerainty in Korea. Japan established a protectorate over Korea before the end of 1905 and annexed it five years later. When California discriminated against Orientals, President Roosevelt won concessions from Californians and at the same time concluded a Gentleman's Agreement with Japan in 1907 barring Japanese workers from the United States. In 1907 he also sent an American Navy fleet around the world, including a major stop at Tokyo. The visit went off nicely with proper courtesies on both sides. But Roosevelt designed the whole episode partly to remind Japan of American power and to suggest tacitly that there were limits to America's patience in East Asia. Whether the visit of the fleet inhibited Japanese moves may be doubted; it may have encouraged Japanese leaders to see the necessity for further building of their naval power in the Pacific. In 1908 Roosevelt's Secretary of State concluded another executive agreement with Japan, the Root-Takahira Agreement. In it both states promised to maintain the status quo in the Pacific. They endorsed the Open Door policy in China, and both promised to respect each other's possessions in the region. The United States saw this as a self-denying agreement for Japan; the Japanese saw it as endorsement of their already special position in East Asia. In any event, as Japan's power increased, Americans found its actions out of tune with the Open Door, and the United States could not do anything about it.

When World War I erupted in Europe, Japan entered the war on the side of Great Britain, France, and Russia. Japan determined to use the European conflagration as the occasion for further strengthening its position in East Asia. It seized German holdings there and in the Pacific. In 1915 Japan presented its famous Twenty-One Demands to the Chinese government under Yüan Shih-k'ai. Japan did not get all it sought, but China had to acquiesce in the Japanese take-over of Germany's Shantung leasehold and to further consolidation of Japanese dominance in Manchuria. Secretary of State William Jennings Bryan applied the nonrecognition policy to Japanese demands in China, indicating that the United States would not recognize changes accomplished there in violation of existing treaties or in violation of the Open Door. Unbacked by effective power and the will to use it, the method was ineffective. In 1917 Secretary of State Robert Lansing concluded an executive agreement with the Japanese Ambassador Viscount Ishii in which the United States recognized Japan's "special interests in China" and at the same time both states endorsed the Open Door there. Since the two premises seemed to contradict each other, the agreement was an expression and source of continuing friction between the two states.

By 1917 Japanese ambitions posed a direct challenge to American interests in the western Pacific and East Asia and to the Open Door policy. But the United States was neither willing nor able to check that challenge effectively. Despite appealing policy statements and expansionist ambitions, the United States could not effectively defend its interests where its power was deficient.

SUPPLEMENTARY READINGS

Bailey, Thomas A. *Theodore Roosevelt and the Japanese-American Crises.* Stanford, Calif.: Stanford University Press, 1934.

Beale, Howard K. *Theodore Roosevelt and the Rise of America to World Power.* Baltimore: Johns Hopkins Press, 1956.

Campbell, Charles S. Jr. *Special Business Interests and the Open Door Policy.* New Haven, Conn.: Yale University Press, 1951.

Dennett, Tyler. *Americans in Eastern Asia.* New York: Macmillan Co., 1922.

_____. *John Hay: From Poetry to Politics.* New York: Dodd, Mead & Co., 1934.

_____. *Roosevelt and the Russo-Japanese War.* Garden City, N.Y.: Doubleday & Co., Inc., 1925.

Dulles, Foster Rhea. *China and America: The Story of Their Relations since 1784.* Princeton, N.J.: Princeton University Press, 1946.

Esthus, Raymond A. *Theodore Roosevelt and International Rivalries.* Waltham, Mass.: Ginn-Blaisdell, 1970.

_____. *Theodore Roosevelt and Japan.* Seattle: University of Washington Press, 1966.

Griswold, A. Whitney. *The Far Eastern Policy of the United States.* New York: Harcourt, Brace & Co., 1938.

Harrington, Fred Harvey. *God, Mammon and the Japanese: Dr. Horace N. Allen and Korean-American Relations, 1884–1905.* Madison: University of Wisconsin Press, 1944.

Irige, Akira. *Across the Pacific: An Inner History of American-East Asian Relations.* New York: Harcourt, Brace & World, Inc., 1967.

McCormick, Thomas J. *China Market: America's Quest for Informal Empire, 1893–1901.* Chicago: Quadrangle Books, 1967.

Neu, Charles E. *An Uncertain Friendship: Theodore Roosevelt and Japan, 1906–1909.* Cambridge, Mass.: Harvard University Press, 1967.

Neumann, William L. *America Encounters Japan: From Perry to MacArthur.* Baltimore: Johns Hopkins Press, 1963.

Scholes, Walter V. and Marie V. *The Foreign Policies of the Taft Administration.* Columbia: University of Missouri Press, 1970.

Trani, Eugene P. *The Treaty of Portsmouth: An Adventure in American Diplomacy.* Lexington: University of Kentucky Press, 1969.

Treat, Payson J. *Diplomatic Relations between the United States and Japan, 1895–1905.* Stanford, Calif.: Stanford University Press, 1938.

Varg, Paul A. *Open Door Diplomat: The Life of W. W. Rockhill.* Urbana: University of Illinois Press, 1952.

_____. *The Making of a Myth: The United States and China, 1897–1912.* East Lansing: Michigan State University Press, 1968.

Vevier, Charles. *The United States and China, 1906–1913.* New Brunswick, N.J.: Rutgers University Press, 1955.

Zabriskie, E. H. *American-Russian Rivalry in the Far East, 1895–1914.* Philadelphia: University of Pennsylvania Press, 1946.

27

The United States and World War I

United States relations with Latin America, the Pacific islands, and the Far East in the 1890's and in the first decade of the twentieth century were more spectacular than its relations with Europe. Nevertheless, the United States and its citizens were more affected by Europe than by other parts of the world. And in the second decade of the twentieth century the United States took a Europe-first emphasis in foreign affairs that has prevailed most of the time since then.

In terms of external considerations, the most powerful states (the ones strong enough to endanger American security) were in Europe. What they did or did not do could affect American vital interests. In addition, there were many domestic considerations. Family, ethnic, cultural, and linguistic ties directed attention toward Europe. Intellectual, ideological, scientific, and institutional patterns had similar effects. There were religious and church bonds. Financially, first as a debtor and later as a creditor, America looked to Europe. The value of commerce with Europe exceeded the value of American trade with all the rest of the world before 1917. The role of the United States in World War I dramatized the continued importance of Europe for America. It also highlighted America's increasing power relative to the European states.

Historians have advanced widely varying interpretations of American entry into World War I. The so-called revisionists, led by Charles C. Tansill, contended that American entry into World War I was neither necessary nor wise. They believed that involvement was not the product of influences essential to American national security or vital interests. The revisionist view won wide support in the 1930's, but it is rejected by most scholars today. Opposed to the revisionists were historians who believed that under the circumstances the United States had no satisfactory alternatives to the policies it followed. They concluded that entry into World War I could not have been avoided without sacrificing American honor, vital interests, and security. Charles Seymour, Arthur S. Link, and Ernest R. May shared that general view.

For purposes of analysis, American policies toward World War I from the time it began in 1914 until the United States became a belligerent in 1917 may be examined in terms of the domestic and external circumstances. The domestic influences included both those opposing and encouraging American involvement. Many of the external considerations became meaningful through United States relations with two of the leading belligerents, Great Britain and Germany.

DOMESTIC INFLUENCES

Certain domestic influences encouraged "isolationism," and opposed involvement in the European war. Most German-Americans, while not urging participation on the side of Germany, wanted neutrality and did not wish to fight against their fatherland. Irish-Americans opposed entering the war on the side of the hated English.

Many progressives and reformers opposed involvement in the war. Those noninterventionist reformers represented both rural and urban points of view. Most western agrarian progressives were "isolationists" on foreign affairs. They included Senators Robert M. LaFollette of Wisconsin, William E. Borah of Idaho, George W. Norris of Nebraska, and Hiram Johnson of California. They also included William Jennings Bryan of Nebraska, Secretary of State during the first two and one-half years of Woodrow Wilson's administration. To a degree even President Wilson shared their inclinations. His academic and political careers evolved in the urban Northeast, particularly in New Jersey. And in practice his domestic and foreign policies increasingly conformed to urban patterns. Nevertheless, Wilson was born and reared in the South and was not entirely innocent of agrarian values and sentiments. In addition, some urban reformers and radicals (though not most urban progressives) embraced the noninterventionist position. Some of them, such as Jane Addams in Chicago, operated from a pacifist frame of reference.

Rural and urban reformers differed in their conceptions of the good society, but they shared certain general attitudes on foreign affairs. They feared that war would shatter the domestic reform movement within the United States. They distrusted big business and finance. They blamed big business for most of the social and political evils in the

United States. And they also blamed imperialism and war on the business drive for profits. Urban radicals often saw socialism as the solution; agrarian progressives generally preferred inflation and trust-busting. But both believed international bankers and munitions makers to be villains responsible for leading the United States into foreign conflagrations. Neither groups of noninterventionists considered business profits to be a valid part of America's vital interests abroad.

In addition, many businessmen opposed entering World War I. Such business isolationists were most numerous in retail and service lines, in light-goods industries, and in small towns.

Indeed, the vast majority of Americans (including the President) hoped the United States could stay out of the European war. President Wilson sympathized with the Allies, but he tried to be neutral in thought and action. And his biographer, Arthur S. Link, believes that he succeeded remarkably well in that effort. In sending Colonel Edward M. House on his various missions in 1915–1916, the President hoped to prevent American involvement by bringing an early peace in Europe.

At the same time, other domestic influences encouraged involvement on the side of the Allies. American ethnic, cultural, ideological, intellectual, and institutional ties with Great Britain were greater than comparable bonds with Germany or any of the other Central Powers.

There were significant economic influences that moved the United States closer to the Allies. The United States was not dragged into World War I by conspiring munitions makers and international bankers to protect their profits and loans. Economic factors, even in a much broader sense, represented only part of the compound. During the first year of the war Secretary of State William Jennings Bryan advised American financiers not to make loans to the Allied governments, though they did extend credits. In response to an inquiry from J. P. Morgan and after consulting the President, in August, 1914, Bryan informed financiers that private loans to belligerents would be "inconsistent with the true spirit of neutrality." Even the revisionist historian Charles C. Tansill concluded that there was "not the slightest evidence that during the Hundred Days that preceded America's entry into the World War the President gave any heed to demands from 'big business' that America intervene in order to save investments that were threatened by possible Allied defeat."

But one may emphasize that economic influences were not the only cause and still recognize them as among several important domestic variables moving the United States closer to the Allies. To quote Tansill again:

The real reasons why America went to war cannot be found in any single set of circumstances. There was no clear-cut road to war that the President followed with certain steps that knew no hesitation. There were

many dim trails of doubtful promise, and one along which he traveled
with early misgivings and reluctant tread was that which led to American
economic solidarity with the Allies.

From the beginning of the war in 1914 the Allies bought increasing
amounts in the United States, including agricultural products, manufactured commodities, and war goods. In 1915 the House of Morgan became
the official purchasing agent in the United States for the British and
French governments. Those growing Allied purchases helped to rescue
the United States from an economic slump and contributed to an expanding prosperity shared in varying degree by most Americans, not just by
bankers and munitions makers.

When the British and French found it increasingly difficult to pay for
American products, the United States government, in the fall of 1915, reversed Bryan's earlier stand and approved private loans to the Allies.
Secretary of the Treasury William Gibbs McAdoo had strongly urged
that policy change to sustain American trade and prosperity. It occurred
after Bryan had resigned and was replaced as Secretary of State by
Robert Lansing of New York. Lansing worried that continuation of the
loan ban would cause "restriction of outputs, industrial depression, idle
capital, financial demoralization, and general unrest and suffering
among the laboring classes." Even Professor Link, who minimizes the
importance of economic influences, concluded: "American material well-
being was in large measure dependent upon foreign trade, and particularly upon trade with the Allied world. . . . The credit embargo and the
war trade could not both survive." According to Professor Daniel M.
Smith, "Trade with the Allies increased 184 percent over peacetime. A
virtually new munitions industry was created by Allied purchases, and
by 1917 America had exported over one billion dollars' worth of explosives and arms to Europe."

By April, 1917 private loans to the Allied governments totaled more
than $2 billion. At the same time, loans to the Central Powers were neg-
ligible and American trade with them dwindled. Though the entire country felt the economic effects, they were most striking in the northeastern urban industrial and financial sectors. Economic considerations, by
themselves, did not cause the United States to enter the war. Nevertheless, they were among the important domestic influences moving the
United States closer to the Allies.

Despite diversity and mixed feelings, many Americans in and out of
government had strong pro-British and anti-German biases from the
beginning. Most major newspapers and foreign correspondents were pro-
British. Anglophiles were numerous among intellectuals and academi-
cians. With the conspicuous exception of William Jennings Bryan, most
of the President's key advisers were distinctly pro-British and anti-Ger-

man. They included Colonel Edward M. House, Robert Lansing, and Walter Hines Page, the American Ambassador to Great Britain.

President Wilson shared the pro-British views of his advisers. The son of a Presbyterian minister, Wilson was one of the most learned men ever to serve as President of the United States. With a doctorate in history and government, he had a career as a university professor and as president of Princeton University before entering politics. But his learning and knowledge focused largely on domestic matters, not foreign affairs, before he became President in 1913. Wilson sincerely wanted to keep the United States out of World War I, and he tried to be neutral in thought and action. He objected to British violations of American neutral rights. Nevertheless, he had long admired the British and their parliamentary system of government. Though he urged "peace without victory," he saw no threat to American security and interests in an Allied victory; he did not take the same view toward the possibility of a German victory. He earnestly wanted neutrality and peace, but the President believed that "England is fighting our fight."

Finally, Americans ideologically and emotionally drew closer to the Allies. Despite their preference for nonintervention and peace, millions became persuaded that the Kaiser and the "Huns" were evil and that a victory for Germany would mean the ascendancy of autocrats, militarists, treaty violators, and perpetrators of brutal atrocities. Despite much Anglophobia and Czarist Russia's presence on the Allied side, most Americans sincerely believed that democracy and freedom were more likely to prevail if the Allies triumphed than if the Central Powers won.

GREAT BRITAIN AND AMERICAN NEUTRAL RIGHTS

Substantial Anglo-American diplomatic cooperation had developed around the turn of the century. Nevertheless, there was much friction between the two states from 1914 to 1917. That friction grew out of the understandable determination of the British to use their control of the seas to block as much neutral trade with the Central Powers as possible. Foreign Secretary Sir Edward Grey explained Britain's policies in these words: "Blockade of Germany was essential to the victory of the Allies, but the ill-will of the United States meant their certain defeat. . . . The object of diplomacy, therefore, was to secure the maximum of blockade that could be enforced without a rupture with the United States." Conversely, Americans understandably wanted to protect their rights to trade with belligerents within the limits of international law as the United States interpreted it. Despite its temporary lapse during the Civil War, the United States had long urged a broad definition of "neutral rights." Britain had backed a narrow interpretation of neutral rights and a broad conception of belligerent maritime rights. Efforts to codify international law on neutrality had floundered. Consensus prevailed on certain matters, but in practice "might made right." The strong determined which of several possible definitions of neutral rights would prevail. United States efforts to defend a broad definition of neutral rights were not likely to prevail unless Americans were willing to risk a major break with Great Britain. Neither the Administration nor the majority of the American people seriously considered that course.

The United States and Britain disagreed on their definitions of contraband. Absolute contraband consisted of actual arms, munitions, and war implements. All countries agreed that a belligerent had the legal right to confiscate absolute contraband and the ship carrying it to the enemy. Controversy arose over definitions of limited or conditional contraband. It consisted of nonmilitary supplies useful to armies in the field. Conditional contraband could be seized, but the belligerent had to compensate the owner and release the ship. Britain insisted that since Germany was practically an armed camp most goods, including food, were limited contraband. The United States, in contrast, wanted a much more restricted definition of conditional contraband. In practice Britain steadily lengthened the list of commodities it treated as contraband.

The United States also objected to British practices in the exercise of the right of visit and search. International law recognized the right of a belligerent to stop and search neutral vessels on the high seas to check for contraband. The British, however, took neutral ships to their ports to search them. They contended that that was necessary if they were to search the huge cargoes of modern ships thoroughly without undue risk from submarine attacks.

British interpretation of the doctrine of continuous voyage also displeased the United States. Under conventional international law a belligerent could seize contraband going from one neutral port to another neutral port if the ultimate destination of the cargo were an enemy port. Previously the doctrine applied when both legs of the voyage were by sea. In World War I, however, the British applied it to neutral shipments to the Netherlands and Denmark where the second leg would be by land.

In its Orders in Council of March, 1915, Britain, in effect, proclaimed a blockade of Germany. Conventional international law required that to be legal a blockade must be effective and must apply to all neutrals alike. By closing the approaches to the North Sea the British made their pseudo blockade effective against the United States but not against Norway and Sweden.

To those and other British practices the United States protested repeatedly and ineffectively. Unlike its course on German submarine warfare, the United States did not hold Britain to "strict accountability" for violation of American neutral rights. The British sometimes apologized.

They sometimes yielded on minor points. They generally compensated Americans for losses and damages. But the British did not yield to the American definition of neutral rights, and they did not stop interfering with American shipping. In spite of the very real friction on the matter, the United States drew closer to Britain and finally entered the war on the Allied side.

A multitude of variables accounted for American willingness to acquiesce in British practices. Part of the explanation lay in the pro-British sentiments of American leaders and many of their followers. Retaliation with an embargo or financial coercion would have hurt American profits and prosperity more than the British tactics did. The British handled the United States skillfully and tactfully. Britain did not invoke all its restrictions abruptly; only gradually did it tighten the economic screws on Germany. When Britain in 1915 blocked the flow of raw cotton to Germany, it eased the blow by absorbing the American exports itself. British propaganda in the United States was effective. The British controlled direct cable access to the United States. They understood American thinking and emphasized emotional appeals rather than legalistic arguments in their propaganda. They sometimes timed propaganda to coincide with British replies to American diplomatic protests on neutral rights. Part of the explanation lay in the fact that the British practices resulted only in the loss of property (that Britain often paid for) while the German practices on the seas caused the loss of lives as well. By 1914–1917 Anglo-American diplomatic accord already had years of development behind it. And finally, the United States drew closer to Britain in spite of friction because American leaders and citizens became convinced that a British defeat would increase the difficulty of guarding American national security; at the same time a British victory would not be a threat to American security, interests, or ideals.

GERMAN SUBMARINE WARFARE

German unrestricted submarine warfare in 1917 was the immediate cause for American entry into World War I. But that external spark ignited a highly explosive compound composed of both internal and external elements.

There was more explicit pro-German sentiment in the United States (particularly among German-Americans) than there was to be twenty-five years later before Pearl Harbor. Nevertheless, a multitude of variables brought the United States and Germany closer to war. Some friction and hostility had been building since the "pork controversy" of the 1880's and the rise of Kaiser William II to power. Long before 1914 Americans began to worry about economic competition from German industry and finance. The United States feared German colonial ambitions in Latin America and the Pacific. Even before World War I, Germany strained Britain's capacity to maintain the balance of power that the United States increasingly endorsed.

The German High Command, enslaved by its doctrinaire attachment to the Schlieffen plan, insisted on the military necessity for pushing through neutralized Belgium in 1914. That action brought Britain into the war against Germany. It also shocked millions of Americans. They sympathized with Belgium as the underdog, and they saw the German action as a shameless treaty violation. The inevitable atrocities (publicized, dramatized, and exaggerated by British propaganda) further inflamed American emotions and began to paint a portrait of the Germans as little better than subhuman beasts.

At the same time, the Germans bungled their propaganda efforts in the United States. Language difficulties, cultural differences, and lack of direct cable access handicapped the Germans. Emphasis on legal arguments and logic proved less effective than the emotional appeals of British propaganda. Sabotage activities were traced to German agents and further aroused anti-German sentiments.

But it was German use of the submarine that ultimately brought the United States into the war. Britain's command of the seas made certain that American neutral trade would benefit the Allies against the Central Powers. Germany's hopes for combating that Allied advantage would have been served if the United States had successfully compelled British respect for neutral rights as America defined them. In 1914–1915 there was no real possibility that Britain would yield enough to destroy the effectiveness of its most powerful weapon. Furthermore, there was no real likelihood that the United States under President Wilson would risk a break with Great Britain on the issue. Far more hopeful (particularly in the opinion of the German admirals) was submarine warfare.

Because it was new and unique, international law had not yet developed to govern submarine warfare. Hidden beneath the surface, submarines could strike devastating blows at both warships and merchant vessels. Ever confident of their favorite weapon, German naval leaders believed that unrestricted submarine warfare would quickly bring Britain and the Allies to their knees. Kaiser William II, Chancellor Bethmann-Hollweg, and some German generals were not so sanguine. In any event, effective use of the submarine seemed to require surprise. Conventional international law required that warships should not sink merchant vessels without warning and without providing for the safety of passengers and crews. But, in contrast to surface warships and to present-day submarines, the submarines of World War I were tiny, fragile craft. If they surfaced and gave advance warning, they could be rammed or sunk by guns carried on belligerent merchant ships. To make warning even more risky, Britain used so-called Q ships that looked like conventional merchant ships but were actually heavily armed decoys designed to invite attacks with the expectation that the submarine could not survive the contest. Exempting neutral ships from submarine attack simply encouraged belligerents to use neutral flags and markings on their merchant vessels.

The Germans insisted that they first used the submarine against merchant shipping only after it became essential in retaliation for British mining of North Sea approaches to German ports late in 1914. The Germans also insisted that submarines could not give advance warning unless Britain agreed to disarm its merchant ships. Britain would not do that. Interestingly, despite the alarm caused by submarines, at first Germany was not able to put more than a dozen submarines into action at one time.

In 1915 Secretary of State William Jennings Bryan almost desperately sought a compromise that might keep the United States out of the war. He contended that the United States should balance its diplomatic protests against German submarine warfare with equally firm protests against British violations of neutral rights. He wanted to warn Americans not to travel on belligerent ships in war zones, but President Wilson said that would abandon American rights. Bryan also favored forcing Britain into a more moderate posture by banning armed merchant ships from American ports. Robert Lansing vigorously objected to those proposals. President Wilson shared Bryan's desire for peace, but he was unwilling to compromise American prestige and rights (as he defined them) to accomplish that end.

German submarine warfare may be described in terms of three cycles: one in 1915, one in 1916, and the last in 1917. The first two called for limited submarine warfare in European waters; the last called for unrestricted submarine warfare. Each was urged on the Kaiser and his advisers by the German admirals and their supporters. The Kaiser had serious doubts about the wisdom of the proposal. Chancellor Bethmann-Hollweg feared it would bring the United States into the war and thereby cause a German defeat. But neither he nor the Kaiser could provide an alternative promising an early German victory. And neither was willing or able to stand up against the naval leaders' optimistic predictions of a quick triumph if their weapon were unleashed. In each cycle German submarines caused loss of American lives and property. In each case the United States vigorously protested. As a result Germany yielded and temporarily stopped or severely restricted its use of submarines against merchant ships in the fall of 1915 and again in 1916, but not in 1917. Germany undertook its course in 1917 with the full realization that it would bring the United States into the war. Its leaders hoped, however, that Germany could crush the Allies before the United States could make its power felt effectively. That hope was not realized.

The first cycle began on February 4, 1915, when Germany proclaimed limited submarine warfare in a zone around Great Britain and Ireland effective February 18. German submarines would destroy enemy merchant ships in the zone. Though not directed against neutral ships, Germany warned neutrals to stay out of the zone to prevent unintentional incidents. In announcing the action the German government urged neutrals to "show no less consideration for the vital interests of Germany than for those of England."

In Bryan's absence and after consulting the President, Robert Lansing sent a very strong protest to Germany and warned that the United States would hold Germany to "strict accountability" for the loss of American lives and property resulting from German submarines. The protests by the United States and other neutrals, along with divided counsels and misgivings in the German government, slowed moves to implement the submarine warfare.

Nevertheless, inevitably there were incidents involving Americans. An American died when a submarine sank the British ship *Falaba* late in March. German aerial bombs damaged the *Cushing,* an American freighter. Two Americans died when a submarine attacked the *Gulflight,* an American tanker. But the climax in the first cycle came when submarine U-20 sank the huge British liner, *Lusitania,* off Ireland on May 7, 1915. The captain of the *Lusitania* had neglected to follow course and speed precautions that might have prevented a submarine attack. One well-placed torpedo was sufficient to sink the ship within eighteen minutes. Of the nearly 2,000 persons on board 1,198 died. Among the dead were 128 Americans.

All administration leaders agreed on the necessity for a formal protest. Secretary of State Bryan, however, differed from Lansing and the President's other advisers on the severity of the protest and on the use of arbitration, compromise, and delay in dealing with Germany. Torn by conflicting advice and by the potential consequences of the possible alternatives, Wilson finally rejected the advice of his Secretary of State. Bryan reluctantly signed the strong note of protest to Germany on May 13. Germany regretted the loss of American lives, but insisted that the *Lusitania* was an auxiliary cruiser of the British Navy, was armed (actually the guns were not mounted), and carried munitions contraband (it did). Bryan's almost desperate efforts failed to win the President to a more conciliatory course. The Nebraskan resigned from the Cabinet rather than sign the second *Lusitania* note on June 9, 1915. Bryan hoped his resignation and subsequent speaking crusade might arouse enough antiwar sentiment to force the administration to change its policies. But most Americans supported the President's defense of American rights and honor against the German menace.

In that crisis Germany hesitated, faltered, and finally yielded temporarily. The firm stand by the Wilson administration increased the misgivings of the Kaiser, Chancellor, and many generals about the wisdom of submarine warfare. Additional incidents occurred, notably the sinking of the *Arabic* on August 19, with the loss of two Americans. German diplomatic notes and orders to submarine commanders reflected the divided counsels and mixed feelings. By September, 1915, Germany decided not to sink passenger ships without warning and without providing for the safety of passengers. Germany suspended submarine activity on the West Coast of England and in the English Channel. Though lesser incidents occurred, the German retreat on the issue in September, 1915, ended the first cycle and provided a brief lull.

In February, 1916, German admirals and their supporters forced resumption of limited submarine warfare. After notifying neutral governments, Germany on February 29, 1916, renewed submarine attacks on armed belligerent merchant ships in the war zone. Again there were incidents involving Americans. Most inflammatory was the attack on the French *Sussex* in the English Channel on March 24, though no Americans lost their lives. With Colonel House and Secretary of State Lansing urging the President on, the administration, on April 18, sent a strong protest threatening to sever diplomatic relations if Germany did not abandon its attacks on merchant ships. Once again the German Chancellor Bethmann-Hollweg successfully prevailed over the admirals in winning the Kaiser's backing. Consequently, orders went to submarine commanders severely restricting their activities and, soon after, withdrawing U-boats from the war zone. And in the *Sussex* pledge of May 4, 1916, Germany promised not to attack unresisting merchant ships (whether armed or not) without warning and without provision for passenger safety. The pledge included a condition specifying that it would be binding only if the United States also compelled Allied respect for neutral rights and freedom of the seas. Though the United States did not obtain such assurances from Great Britain and the Allies, the United States accepted the pledge, and Germany operated within its framework during the ten months that followed. The *Sussex* pledge ended the second cycle of submarine warfare. Wilson's firmness and patience had helped Chancellor Bethmann-Hollweg carry the day against the German admirals and their supporters.

Nevertheless, in the last half of 1916 the German advocates of unrestricted submarine warfare won growing support from generals, politicians, and public opinion. The failure of the offensive at Verdun in 1916 dramatized the need for drastic innovations if Germany were to break the military deadlock. The admirals conceded that unrestricted submarine warfare would bring the United States into the war against Germany. But they argued that the U-boats could crush the Allies before American military power could make itself felt in Europe. Moreover, the admirals were skeptical of American military capacity anyway. Kaiser William II shared his Chancellor's reluctance to use unrestricted submarine warfare. But with the failure of peace efforts and in the absence of viable military alternatives that might promise victory, the Kaiser wavered. On January 9, 1917, with Chief of Staff Field Marshal Paul von Hindenburg supporting the admirals on the issue, the Kaiser approved unrestricted submarine warfare. Chancellor Bethmann-Hollweg still doubted the wisdom of the course, but he no longer had power enough to prevent it. On January 31, 1917, Germany announced that beginning the next day its submarines would sink all ships (belligerent and neutral, armed and unarmed) in the war zones surrounding Britain. Only one American ship would be allowed into Britain each week under careful restrictions.

With urgings from Lansing and House, and with the full approval of his Cabinet, President Wilson severed diplomatic relations with Germany on February 3, 1917. Soon the expected incidents occurred. Americans died on both belligerent and American ships sunk by the submarines. The intercepted Zimmermann telegram revealed German efforts to organize Mexico and Japan against the United States in the event of war.

EFFORTS FOR PEACE AND DECISION FOR WAR

Long before German unrestricted submarine warfare forced the United States into the conflagration, Wilson tried to mediate an end to the war. Colonel Edward M. House encouraged and served that effort. The President had earnest humanitarian motives for trying to end the bloodshed. The possibility of being acclaimed the world's peacemaker appealed to his ego and messianic temperament. A negotiated settlement in Europe might provide a more enduring peace than decisive victory by either side. Most important, prolonged conflict abroad threatened to involve the United States as a belligerent. The President's efforts to end the war were part of his continuing desire to keep the United States out of the holocaust.

President Wilson's peace efforts failed, both because of domestic influences within the United States and because of external circumstances. Internally, most Americans and their leaders envisaged peace in terms of an Allied victory. Few really wanted "peace without victory" and even fewer were willing to consider a settlement more favorable to Germany than to its enemies. With the exception of Bryan, those views prevailed among Wilson's top advisers. Lansing and Page generally opposed all peace efforts. They were nearly as dedicated to the defeat of the Central Powers as the Allies were. Colonel House encouraged peace negotiations,

but he did so on the assumption that if they succeeded they would benefit the Allies. Wilson was less partisan than his advisers (particularly
late in 1916), but he shared their general sentiments. Given those biases
(or definitions of American interests relative to the European war), their
peace moves were not likely to succeed unless Germany were so close
to defeat that it would grasp at anything better than complete surrender. But in such a situation the Allies might not have seen any particular advantage in mediation over militarily imposing a victor's peace.

Externally, neither side in the war was willing to acquiesce in any
peace settlement that did not give it the fruits of victory. Some of the
states may have blundered into war rather than entering it with precise
aggressive designs. But once at war, and particularly after pouring vast
resources and manpower into the conflict, they were not willing to settle
for less than victory. Britain and France wanted peace—provided such
a settlement would give them all or most of what they might gain from
a decisive military triumph. Germany wanted peace—provided it was a
victor's peace. Neither side was able to break the military deadlock, but
neither was yet so exhausted that it would accept a settlement reflecting
that deadlock. The collapse of Russia in 1917 and the glowing promises
by the admirals about the effectiveness of submarine warfare encouraged Germany to hope for victory. The possibility of American involvement on their side encouraged the Allies to hope for triumph. Neither
was willing to consider mediation or peace that did not give the results
of victory. Domestic politics in most of the states reinforced those attitudes. Such expectations on both sides, when combined with the continued military stalemate, doomed Wilson's peace efforts to failure.

Wilson had offered his good offices in 1914, shortly after war began.
In the spring of 1915 he sent Colonel House to Europe to consult the belligerent governments on seeking some avenue to peace. At that time
each state seemed willing to consider peace only on a victor's terms.

Early in 1916 Colonel House once again visited Europe to explore the
possibilities of peace. That mission resulted in the secret House-Grey
memorandum initialed on February 22, 1916. It provided that:

> President Wilson was ready, on hearing from France and England that
> the moment was opportune, to propose that a Conference should be sum-
> moned to put an end to the war. Should the Allies accept this proposal,
> and should Germany refuse it, the United States would probably enter
> the war against Germany. . . . if such a Conference met, it would secure
> peace on terms not unfavorable to the Allies; and, if it failed to secure
> peace, the United States would leave the Conference as a belligerent on
> the side of the Allies, if Germany was unreasonable.

On House's return to the United States the President accepted the memorandum, except that he added another "probably" in the last sentence
about leaving the conference as a belligerent on the side of the Allies.

Despite the qualifications, the memorandum was highly favorable to Britain: Britain and France were to decide the time for the conference; they were assured of favorable terms; and they were encouraged to believe that German recalcitrance would bring the United States into the war. Britain never put the plan into operation, but it encouraged British hopes for eventual American belligerence on the side of the Allies.

On December 18, 1916, with time rapidly running out, President Wilson sent notes to each of the belligerents inviting them to state the terms on which they would be willing to make peace. The Allies responded by listing a victor's terms. Germany did not list its terms. It expressed willingness to enter into direct negotiations with the Allies but would not include neutrals. In a major address to the Senate on January 22, 1917, the President made a final try for peace. But his "peace without victory" theme in that address did not appeal to either the Allies or the Central Powers. A few days later the German announcement of unrestricted submarine warfare doomed all hopes for a negotiated settlement and for continued American neutrality.

Germany began its unrestricted submarine warfare on February 1. The United States severed diplomatic relations on February 3. Britain revealed the intercepted Zimmermann note before the end of the month. In March, Americans died when U-boat torpedoes sank belligerent and American merchant ships. At the same time, the federal government authorized the arming of American merchant ships. On April 2, the President addressed a special joint session of Congress urging a declaration of war on Germany. Congress responded willingly (82 to 6 in the Senate, and 373 to 50 in the House). On April 6, 1917, the United States and Germany were officially at war.

SUPPLEMENTARY READINGS

Buehrig, Edward H.   *Woodrow Wilson and the Balance of Power.* Bloomington: Indiana University Press, 1955.

Cooper, John M., Jr.   *The Vanity of Power: American Isolationism and World War I, 1914–1917.* Westport, Conn.: Greenwood Publishing Corporation, 1969.

Curti, Merle E.   *Bryan and World Peace.* Northampton, Mass.: Smith College Studies in History, 1931.

Link, Arthur S.   *Wilson the Diplomatist: A Look at His Major Foreign Policies.* Baltimore: Johns Hopkins Press, 1957.

————.   *Wilson: The Struggle for Neutrality, 1914–1915.* Princeton: N.J.: Princeton University Press, 1960.

————.   *Wilson: Confusions and Crises, 1915–1916.* Princeton, N.J.: Princeton University Press, 1964.

————. *Wilson: Campaigns for Progressivism and Peace, 1916–1917.* Princeton, N.J.: Princeton University Press, 1966.

May, Ernest R. *The World War and American Isolation, 1914–1917.* Cambridge, Mass.: Harvard University Press, 1959.

Millis, Walter. *Road to War: America, 1914–1917.* Boston: Houghton Mifflin Co., 1935.

Notter, Harley. *The Origins of the Foreign Policy of Woodrow Wilson.* Baltimore: Johns Hopkins Press, 1937.

Perkins, Bradford. *The Great Rapprochement: England and the United States, 1895–1914.* New York: Atheneum Publishers, 1968.

Peterson, Horace C. *Propaganda for War: The Campaign Against American Neutrality, 1914–1917.* Norman: University of Oklahoma Press, 1939.

Seymour, Charles. *American Neutrality, 1914–1917.* New Haven, Conn.: Yale University Press, 1935.

Smith, Daniel M. *The Great Departure: The United States and World War I, 1914–1920.* New York: John Wiley & Sons, Inc., 1965.

————. *Robert Lansing and American Neutrality, 1914–1917.* Berkeley: Univeristy of California Press, 1958.

Tansill, Charles C. *America Goes to War.* Boston: Little, Brown & Co., 1938.

Wittke, Carl. *German-Americans and the World War.* Columbus: Ohio State Archaeological and Historical Society, 1936.

PART **V**

From world war to world war
1918-1941

28

Aggression, appeasement, and war: External influences on American foreign relations, 1918-1941

World War I, the peace settlements following that war, and the Great Depression of the 1930's provided much of the soil out of which World War II emerged. The war, the peace settlements, and the depression helped make people in many states dissatisfied with the status quo and determined to change existing conditions, by war if necessary. That dissatisfaction became particularly acute in Germany, Italy, and Japan. Though World War I, the peace settlements, and the Great Depression hurt and embittered citizens of those states, they did not completely crush them. Desperation and demagoguery persuaded many that they had enough power to correct the conditions they did not like. Those illusions thrived on the fact that the war, the peace settlements, and the depression had seriously weakened the dominant states. Britain, France, and Russia either could not or would not effectively defend the status quo against all possible challenges. The United States was the only country powerful enough to sustain Anglo-French dominance and to block the dissatisfied states. During the 1920's and 1930's, however, the United States refused to assume that responsibility. In the final analysis it did so only when the Axis powers overwhelmed most of their European and Asiatic adversaries and threatened to leave America an island in an armed, aggressive, and hostile world.

EFFECTS OF WORLD WAR I

Few areas were unaffected by World War I and the peace settlements that followed it. Victor and vanquished, belligerent and neutral, European and non-European, colonial powers and colonies—all felt the effects directly or indirectly. And so far as Europe was concerned most of the effects were harmful.

Despite later denials, Germany was beaten when it signed the armistice on November 11, 1918. The Versailles Treaty imposed by the victors was harsh enough to anger and hurt the Germans but not harsh enough to destroy them. Germany lost all of its overseas colonies. It lost some European territory, notably Alsace-Lorraine. The Versailles Treaty disarmed Germany except for a 100,000-man army, ostensibly adequate for little more than maintaining internal order. In the "war guilt" clause Germany had to accept complete responsibility for starting the war. The victors required Germany to pay reparations for direct and indirect damages caused by the war. Those reparations later were set at approximately $33 billion.

The Versailles Treaty was not nearly as severe as the Treaty of Brest-Litovsk that Germany had imposed on communist Russia in 1918. And it was not as harsh as the treaties suffered by other Central Powers at the close of World War I. Nevertheless, it was harsh enough to embitter Germans. It became the scapegoat on which they blamed their difficulties. Even moderate German politicians attacked it. Extremist demagogues used hatred of the treaty to inflame German nationalism, militarism, and xenophobia. Adolf Hitler and his National Socialists won support by promising to right the wrongs of the Versailles settlement.

Germany's Weimar Republic was cursed from its beginnings in 1919. Though it had no alternative, many denounced it for accepting the Versailles Treaty. As Chancellor briefly in 1923 and as Foreign Minister until his death in 1929, Gustav Stresemann set the tone for German foreign policies in the 1920's. Like all German leaders, he wanted to restore German power and prestige. But he realized that his country's weakness and isolation made the methods of Bismarck or William II inappropriate at that time. Instead, he tactfully conciliated former enemies and won for Germany an increasingly influential place in the counsels of Europe. While assuaging fears of Germany, Stresemann's policies helped Germany regain a bit of the status it had lost in military defeat. They also encouraged some (particularly in Great Britain and the United States) to favor easing the more punitive provisions of the peace settlement. The Dawes Plan of 1924, the Locarno Pact of 1925, and admission of Germany to the League of Nations were hopeful products of the new image that Stresemann tried to create for Germany. But even Stresemann, the symbol of moderation in foreign affairs, determined to ease the burdens and indignities of the despised Versailles Treaty, even to the extent of favoring German rearmament. Despite Stresemann's talents in foreign affairs and despite other able leaders, the Weimar Republic faced problems in the 1920's and early 1930's that it could not resolve satisfactorily in terms of the desires of the German people.

Furthermore, World War I and its aftermath aroused the fear of a communist take-over in Germany. That fear did not disappear with the failure of communist coups in 1919, and it played into the hands of extremists who insisted that nazism was the only viable alternative to communism. Hitler's promises to save Germany from communism helped win followers even before the world depression strenghtened the appeal of those promises.

In Russia the autocratic and corrupt government of Czar Nicholas II could not satisfy either the demands of the war or of the people. It fell in the March Revolution in 1917 and was replaced by a provisional government under Prince Lvov and later under Alexander Kerensky. That provisional government, too, was unable to accomplish the dual tasks of satisfying the Russian people and defeating the Central Powers on the Eastern Front. It fell before the bolshevik or communist revolution under Nikolai Lenin and Leon Trotsky in November, 1917. Russia's military defeats in World War I, the successful revolutions there, and the turmoil as the bolsheviks consolidated their position, weakened Russia in international affairs. But the revolutions provoked widespread alarm about the possible spread of communism elsewhere. And the accomplishments under the new leadership laid the groundwork for the rise of the Soviet Union to world power during and after World War II.

The effects of World War I were nearly as unsatisfactory for some of the victors as they were for the vanquished. Moved by Allied promises, Italy had turned away from Germany and entered the war on the side of the Allies. But Italy did not get all that the British and French had promised. It was acutely dissatisfied with the peace settlements, particularly the Fiume arrangements. Moreover, the Italians suffered heavy casualties in the war, and it had imposed severe strains on an already shaky economy. The postwar government could not meet the challenges. In the crises and dissatisfactions, Benito Mussolini and his fascists gained power in 1922. The first of the fascist dictators, he gained control legally and at first did not seem to threaten drastic innovations. In the 1920's Mussolini's Italy shared Britain's lack of enthusiasm for France and its sympathy for some of the German desires to revise the peace settlements. But disappointments with the results of World War I, chronic economic problems, lack of power, and Mussolini's nationalism and fascism pointed to the possibility of more aggressive policies when future economic and power changes provided the opportunities.

Even more important were the effects of World War I on Great Britain and France. They had long been the leading powers in European and world affairs. They were the dominant states in the League of Nations between the two world wars. Nevertheless, World War I severely hurt Britain and France. Like the Central Powers, both suffered terrible casualties that cost them the lives and talents of many of their ablest young men. Much of the war was fought on French soil, with the resulting destruction of property and productive facilities. Britain liquidated many of its investments abroad to finance the war effort, and businessmen from the United States and other countries took over foreign trade that the British had once controlled. The war weakened the relative power of both France and Britain and made them less capable than before of maintaining world order and security. Furthermore, the horrors of World War I made many in Britain and France so fearful of another war that they were unwilling to risk actions that might have prevented World War II. World War I and the subsequent peace settlements increased the danger that some states such as Germany might provoke a war to change the results to their advantage. At the same time, World War I reduced the capacity of Britain and France to oppose such aggression effectively.

With the exception of the United States, the only major state to emerge from World War I significantly stronger than before was Japan. It had little direct interest in European aspects of the war. Japan entered World War I on the Allied side because of the opportunity to improve its position in the Pacific area and Far East. As a result, Japan gained mandates over former German colonies in the Pacific. It also strengthened its position on the mainland of Asia at the expense of China and Russia. Those gains and the prosperity of the 1920's helped keep Japan relatively quiet in world politics during the decade following World War I. Baron Shidehara as Foreign Minister from 1924 to 1927 and again from 1929 to 1931 played a role in Japanese foreign affairs much like that of Stresemann in Germany. But like Stresemann, Shidehara's conciliatory methods hid essentially nationalistic and expansionist goals. And they faced opposition from extremists and military officers who preferred more direct methods. Neither the gains of World War I nor the moderation of Shidehara's foreign policies were sufficient to prevent the Great Depression from driving Japan to renewed aggression and war.

THE GREAT DEPRESSION

The Great Depression of the 1930's was worldwide, and its economic, social, psychological, political, and foreign policy effects extended into every state. Hundreds of millions suffered acute hardships and became dissatisfied with their existing leaders, governments, systems, and policies (domestic and foreign). In that depression-fed atmosphere of desperation and paranoia many were willing to follow extremist dema-gogues if they promised to lead them out of the wilderness of the Great Depression. Many sought scapegoats for their difficulties. Generally the scapegoat was the government in power at the time, regardless of whether that government was responsible for the depression or its dura-tion. Often the scapegoat was a minority group within the country, as when Hitler's Nazis blamed and persecuted the German Jews. Sometimes the scapegoat was a foreign state or group of states. Germany, for ex-ample, blamed its troubles on the victors in World War I and on the Ver-sailles Treaty and reparations that the victors imposed. Though people in the Soviet Union did not suffer the depression (as a new thing, any-way), their Communist leaders blamed many of Russia's domestic and foreign difficulties on the capitalist countries.

The specific patterns varied widely. In those states with well-estab-lished democratic traditions and institutions, the people tried to end the depression through democratic methods. That was the general pattern in Great Britain, France, the United States, the Low countries, and the Scandinavian states. Nevertheless, the fact that they were preoccupied with domestic problems in the 1930's diverted some of their attention and energies away from equally important problems in world affairs. And even in Britain, France, and the United States there were extremists. There were those who feared and opposed domestic reforms. Many pre-ferred to meet the challenge of the depression through nationalism, mili-tary preparedness, and active foreign policies.

In Latin America, where democratic traditions and institutions were weak or nonexistent, in the 1930's nearly every state suffered revolu-tions or *coups d'état* that brought new strong men or military dictators to power. In the Soviet Union the Communists under Joseph Stalin pushed industrialization and collectivization in the first three five-year plans. Early in the decade millions died as the Communists broke agri-cultural resistance to collectivization. When the international situation grew more menacing late in the decade, Stalin's five-year plans (like the policies of noncommunist states) were refocused to stress production for military purposes. In Italy the Fascists under Benito Mussolini fur-ther consolidated their position, became increasingly chauvinistic and militaristic, and found a partial outlet for their energies in the conquest of Ethiopia in 1935–1936.

In Germany the Great Depression was the death blow for the flounder-ing Weimar Republic, and it gave Adolf Hitler and his National Social-ists their opportunity to get control of the government. Though not a majority in the Reichstag, the Nazis had the strongest party when Presi-dent Hindenburg named Hitler to be Chancellor in January, 1933. Had it not been for the Great Depression, Hitler probably could not have gained power at that time. Hitler and the Nazis appealed to and aroused all that was worst in the German people. He appealed to feelings of racial superiority. He and his Nazis aroused anti-Semitism and were responsible for fantastically cruel persecution of the Jews. Hitler capitalized on the German authoritarian tradition and respect for authority as he built a totalitarian system. He took advantage of the German fear and hatred of communism. He appealed to and aroused the spirit of German nationalism and militarism. He blamed Germany's difficulties on the Versailles Treaty and on the countries responsible for that settlement. Hitler and his Nazis promised to restore Germany to power, glory, and prosperity by suppressing the Jews, uniting Germanic peoples, securing *Lebensraum* (living space), rebuilding German military might, and wiping out the Versailles settlement, including those parts dealing with disarmament, reparations, colonies, war guilt, and European territories. When Hitler could gain his goals by diplomacy or bluff, he did so. But he had no inhibitions about using force if other methods seemed inadequate.

A somewhat comparable pattern evolved in Japan. The Great Depression hit Japan's economy severely. With a large population in a small area with few resources, Japan depended heavily on foreign trade for essential raw materials and for markets for its industrial products and capital. With the Great Depression its foreign trade dropped abruptly, with corresponding economic, political, and foreign policy repercussions at home. Motivated by fear of communism, economic desperation, nationalism, militarism, and the drive for national security, Japan attempted to solve its difficulties by expansion in East Asia and the western Pacific. That goal later was dignified with the name, "Greater East Asia Co-Prosperity Sphere." That is, Japan hoped to serve as the industrial, financial, and military leader for that area in East Asia and the western Pacific. Establishment of the sphere would free Japan from the vagaries of dependence on world markets outside of its control. It would also enhance Japanese military security in that part of the world. Many in Japan preferred peaceful methods in building the arrangement. But when peaceful methods were inadequate, many in Japan (particularly the military who, in tradition and in practice, were not under effective civilian control) had no inhibitions about using military force. When Japanese leaders became convinced that United States opposition threatened their plans in China and East Asia, they attacked Pearl Harbor in an attempt to knock out American resistance long enough to enable Japan to complete its defeat of China and establish its Greater East Asia Co-Prosperity Sphere.

The Great Depression of the 1930's was not the only cause for World War II. But if the various governments and national economies had been able to prevent the depression, or had been able to end it more quickly and effectively, World War II might not have erupted when it did.

THE QUEST FOR PEACE

The methods urged and used by leaders of the several states to preserve peace and security varied widely. Nevertheless, certain broad general patterns could be identified.

The methods of the Soviet Union fell roughly into three periods. From the time the Bolsheviks gained power in 1917 until the early 1920's, many Russian leaders sought peace through communist world revolution. Leon Trotsky became the symbol and spokesman for that approach. As the ultimate path to peace it affected the attitudes of all Communist leaders. By the early 1920's, however, it was apparent to most that successful world revolution was not going to be a reality in the immediate future, so they improvised interim approaches. In the 1930's until the Munich Conference in 1938, Russian leaders sought peace through collective security arrangements with the West aimed at blocking aggression by Fascists in Italy and Spain, by the Nazis in Germany, and by the militarists in Japan. Among the major powers in the 1930's, the Soviet Union was the leading advocate of collective security.

Most leaders of Western countries, however, were as distrustful and fearful of Russia as they were of Italy, Germany, and Japan. They did not cooperate effectively among themselves against the Axis; they certainly would not work effectively with communist Russia. When the British and French would not block Hitler's move west in remilitarizing the Rhineland in 1936, Stalin's already dim hopes for winning Western cooperation dwindled. After Russia's advice and cooperation were rejected and ignored at Munich in the fall of 1938 (Russia was not included in the conference), Soviet leaders abandoned their efforts to build a collective security system with the West against the Axis. From October, 1938, until June 22, 1941, when Hitler's forces attacked Russia, the Soviet Union tried to preserve its peace and security by appeasing Germany to postpone war, by desperately building its military defense forces, and by welcoming hostilities between the Axis and the West that would weaken Russia's potential enemies and postpone the day when the forces of the Axis (or the West) might be directed against the Soviet Union.

The French path to peace focused on the understandable determination to keep Germany weak and to guard against any revived German menace. Fear of Germany lay at the root of most French foreign policies between the two world wars. The harshness of the Versailles Treaty was due in large part to the French determination to crush Germany and keep it weak. Even the conciliatory policies of Aristide Briand in the Locarno Pacts of 1925 and the Pact of Paris of 1928 became meaningful within that framework. France sought alliances to guard against a possible future war with Germany. It opposed disarmament and revision of the peace treaties unless those actions were accompanied by binding commitments by the United States and other countries to come to France's aid in the event of war with Germany. France viewed the League of Nations primarily as a vehicle for preserving the international status quo, and particularly to prevent a revived Germany from altering the status quo to the disadvantage of France. The French Army (reputed to be the best in the world) and the Maginot fortifications aimed to make France impregnable if Germany ever again attempted war against France. Dig far enough in French foreign policies between the two world wars and one finds the French obsession for security against Germany.

On many issues the British approach coincided with that of France. Nevertheless, there were significant differences, at least in degree. Though circumstances put them on the same side against Germany in the two world wars, the French and British generally were not warm admirers of each other. Symbolically the English Channel appeared much wider when viewed from France or England than it seemed from the western shores of the Atlantic. In the 1920's the British (like many Americans) were inclined to feel sympathy for the Germans. Many British leaders agreed with moderate Germans that the Versailles Treaty had been too harsh and that its more punitive provisions should be revised. In terms of self-interest the British saw a revival of the German economy as essential for the economies of Europe and Great Britain. Though the British, like the French, saw the League of Nations as a vehicle for preserving Anglo-French power dominance, there was a difference in their attitudes. More than the French, many British leaders saw the League partly as an instrument for peaceful changes that might reduce the dangers of war.

Prime Minister Neville Chamberlain's appeasement of Hitler was rooted partly in a determination to avoid the destruction and terror of a World War II. It may have been based partly on the hope that the revival of Germany would provide a barrier against communist Russia in Eastern Europe. But in addition, Chamberlain's appeasement policies grew out of the hope that if peaceful changes were made, and if the harshness of the Versailles settlement were corrected, Germany (even under Hitler) might become satiated and content with its lot. Peace might be preserved. Despite sporadic cooperation on some earlier issues, not until after Hitler violated the promises he made at Munich did Britain and France draw together in the common conviction that Germany must not be allowed to expand further and must be stopped by force if necessary. Unfortunately the British and French governments reached that conclusion at a time when the policy could not be implemented effectively, that is, when Hitler determined to turn east against Poland. After World War II began in September, 1939, and particularly after the fall of France and during the Battle of Britain, the British under Winston

Churchill determined to resist Nazi military assaults and to win effective aid from the United States that could make possible the defeat of the Axis powers in Europe.

STEPS TO WAR

World War II started in Asia before it began in Europe. The Japanese military used a minor railroad explosion as the excuse for taking over Manchuria in 1931–1933 and for establishing the puppet empire of Manchukuo there. In 1937 Japan began an undeclared war against China that did not end until the final defeat of Japan in August, 1945. European developments gave Japan unusual opportunities for expansion in Asia. With the fall of France in 1940, Japanese forces moved into northern French Indochina. After the beginning of the Russo-German War in 1941 safeguarded Japan's northern flank, the Japanese swept over the rest of Indochina. With Europe embroiled in its own war, only the United States seemed in a position to block Japan's expansion. Japanese leaders hoped that the attack on Pearl Harbor and the Philippines would destroy America's capacity to check Japan. They hoped then to sweep over China, Southeast Asia, and the southwest Pacific, take what they wanted, and dig in so securely that the United States could not dislodge them.

At the same time, a whole series of frightening crises moved Europe down the road to war. Hitler and his Nazis came to power in Germany in January, 1933. The following year they consolidated their position, eliminated opposition parties, and converted Germany into an absolute dictatorship. In 1935 Hitler began to rebuild German military might in violation of the Versailles Treaty. In 1935–1936 Italy under Mussolini conquered Ethiopia in Africa. The League of Nations failure in that crisis virtually ended that organization's significance in the struggle to preserve peace. Germany remilitarized the Rhineland in 1936 in violation of existing treaties. The Spanish Civil War from 1936 to 1939 brought the Fascists to power there under Francisco Franco. With Russia helping the Loyalist government and with Italy and Germany helping Franco, the Spanish Civil War was a prelude to the bigger war to come.

Using bluff and threat of force, Hitler in March, 1938, engineered the *Anschluss*, the incorporation of Austria into greater Germany. In October, 1938 (after Chamberlain's appeasement of Hitler at Munich), Nazi Germany seized the Sudetenland of Czechoslovakia and Chamberlain spoke of "peace in our time." Despite his promises to the contrary, in March, 1939, Hitler dismembered the rest of Czechoslovakia. The Russo-German Non-Aggression Pact of August 23, 1939, assured Hitler that he could move east against Poland without opposition from the Soviet Union, the only major state in a position to resist there with any chance of success. On September 1, 1939, Hitler invaded Poland, and France and Britain finally decided to yield no further. They declared war on Germany, and World War II in Europe was formally under way.

Despite its successes, Japan bogged down in huge China without destroying Chinese resistance. But Hitler's blitzkrieg demonstrated terrifying effectiveness in European fighting. German forces crushed Poland in less than a month. There was a lull in the fighting (a "phony war" or "sitzkrieg") during the winter of 1939–1940, when headlines went to the Russo-Finnish War in Eastern Europe. But in the spring of 1940, Nazi German forces overran Denmark, Norway, the Netherlands, Luxembourg, and Belgium. In May at Dunkirk they drove the British forces off the European mainland. France surrendered on June 22, 1940. Even before the fall of France the *Luftwaffe* assaulted Britain from the air and German submarines attacked its supply lines from beneath the seas. In the Battle of Britain that Churchill correctly labeled Britain's "finest hour," the British fought alone against the Nazi onslaught. The Royal Air Force, the British Navy, the English Channel, and the British people under Churchill's leadership successfully defended the United Kingdom. But Hitler retained command of Western and Central Europe. Checked in the West, Hitler turned east to the Balkans and finally struck massively at the Soviet Union on June 22, 1941.

CONCLUSIONS

In summary, World War I and the postwar peace settlements seriously undermined the prewar balance of power. They left Germany defeated and angered—but not destroyed. They left Italy, Russia, and Japan dissatisfied with existing arrangements. And they left France and Great Britain weakened and less capable, by themselves, of enforcing the peace settlements and preserving the status quo.

The Great Depression of the 1930's made a bad situation worse. It increased the willingness of many to follow extremist leaders in aggressive actions. It decreased the capacity of Britain and France to enforce order and security in the face of the Axis challenges. The various efforts by the European states to preserve peace and security failed, partly because of American unwillingness to share effectively in those efforts. By September, 1939, the most destructive war in human history was underway both in Europe and in Asia.

In the middle of the nineteenth century the United States was secure partly because the power balances abroad prevented any serious challenges to American survival. But World War I, the postwar settlements, and the Great Depression all helped to destroy those earlier balances and security arrangements. Much of what the United States did and did not do in foreign affairs from 1918 to 1941 became comprehensible in terms of America's efforts to protect and preserve its peace and security in the face of disturbing and dangerous developments in other parts of the world.

SUPPLEMENTARY READINGS

Albrecht-Carrié, René. *A Diplomatic History of Europe Since the Congress of Vienna.* New York: Harper & Bros., 1958.

Birdsall, Paul. *Versailles Twenty Years After.* New York: Harcourt, Brace & World, Inc., 1941.

Bullock, Alan. *Hitler: A Study in Tyranny.* London: Odhams Press, Ltd., 1960.

Carr, Edward H. *The Twenty Years' Crisis, 1919–1939.* 2d ed. London: Macmillan & Co., Ltd., 1946.

Churchill, Winston S. *The Second World War: The Gathering Storm.* Boston: Houghton Mifflin Co., 1948.

———. *The Second World War: Their Finest Hour.* Boston: Houghton Mifflin Co., 1949.

———. *The Second World War: The Grand Alliance.* Boston: Houghton Mifflin Co., 1950.

Gatzke, Hans W. *Stresemann and the Rearmament of Germany.* Baltimore: Johns Hopkins Press, 1954.

Kennan, George F. *Russia and the West under Lenin and Stalin.* New York: Little, Brown & Co., 1961.

Shirer, William L. *The Rise and Fall of the Third Reich: A History of Nazi Germany.* New York: Simon and Schuster, Inc., 1960.

Thomas, Hugh. *The Spanish Civil War.* London: Eyre & Spottiswoode, Ltd., 1961.

Taylor, A. J. P. *English History, 1914–1945.* New York and Oxford: Oxford University Press, 1965.

———. *The Origins of the Second World War.* New York: Atheneum Publishers, 1962.

29

Boom and bust: Domestic influences on American foreign relations, 1918–1941

THE PEOPLE

The combination of immigration restrictions, birth control, and the depression temporarily reduced the rate of population growth in the United States from 1918 to 1941. Nevertheless, the population continued to increase. At the beginning of the period there were approximately 100 million Americans in the continental United States; by 1941 the figure reached 133 million. Both totals were greater than those for any European state except the Soviet Union.

If the rate of growth declined, however, the rate of urbanization did not. A growing proportion of the American people lived and worked in the cities rather than in rural areas. By 1941 approximately 58 percent lived in cities of 2,500 population or more. And that urban population exercised an influence in America that exceeded its proportion of the total population. The urbanization of the United States (with the accompanying economic, ideological, ethnic, and political developments) was the most important domestic influence making twentieth-century foreign policies different from those earlier in American history. So far as domestic influences were concerned, the rise of American internationalism closely related to the rise of the city with all that represented.

From World War I to World War II the United States radically altered its immigration policies. In a succession of laws during the 1920's

Congress established a quota system based on national origins. By the end of that decade the United States admitted a maximum of 150,000 quota immigrants each year. Each country got a quota based on the proportion of that country's descendents living in the United States in 1920. Under that arrangement the largest quotas went to Great Britain, Germany, and Ireland. The states of eastern and southern Europe got very small quotas, while Japan and China got none at all. That system sharply limited the number of immigrants admitted each year. It also discriminated against Orientals and the Slavic and Latin immigration from eastern and southern Europe. Moreover, the Great Depression and the administrative policies of immigration officials resulted in admitting fewer immigrants in some years than left the country as emigrants. Nevertheless, partly because of the comparative birth rates, the proportion of Latins and Slavs in the population increased during the period. And they increased their economic, cultural, and political influence, particularly in urban areas.

Diversity prevailed in all ethnic groups, but Irish-American anti-British biases continued. Generally Irish-Americans opposed the Versailles Treaty and the League of Nations because they considered them too favorable to England. Their opposition to aid to Britain encouraged isolationist tendencies among Irish-Americans before Pearl Harbor. Similarly, German-Americans tended to oppose the Versailles settlement because they considered it too harsh on Germany. As Samuel Lubell has emphasized, German-Americans tended to be more isolationist than the population as a whole. Their attitudes helped account for isolationism in the Middle West, where German-Americans were numerous. Only a tiny proportion of German-Americans were pro-Nazi, however. Though Italian-Americans divided among themselves, they tended to sympathize with the isolationist or noninterventionist view in the decade before Pearl Harbor. Americans of English descent were scattered and often less conscious of their ethnic origins, but they were a bit more favorable than others toward the Versailles Treaty, the League of Nations, internationalism, and aid to Britain. That tendency was one of the variables causing the South to be more interventionist than any other section of the country before Pearl Harbor.

So far as organized religion was concerned, the majority of Americans with religious affiliations continued to be Protestants. Despite the discriminatory immigration restrictions and their continued minority status, however, the proportions of Roman Catholics and Jews tended to increase, especially in the cities. No religious group was completely homogeneous in its foreign policy views. Furthermore, the foreign policy influence of religious groups from 1918 to 1941 overlapped with ethnic influences. Roman Catholics, for example, tended to be more isolationist than the population as a whole. That was largely because of the substantial Irish-American, German-American, and Italian-American ethnic base for Roman Catholicism. After the start of the Russo-German War in June, 1941, Catholic opposition to communism probably strengthened that noninterventionist inclination. Lutherans (including German-Americans and Scandinavian-Americans) were more isolationist than the population as a whole. One study concluded that Methodists in the decade before Pearl Harbor tended to be "noninterventionist internationalists." The terms may have been contradictory but not necessarily inaccurate. The Methodists (like many others) were torn by irreconcilable sentiments as war drew nearer.

In contrast to their counterparts in the Spanish-American War and World War I, most church leaders were less idealistic about entering World War II and less inclined to view the war as a crusade for righteousness. Many religious leaders supported the League of Nations. Doctrinaire pacifism was widespread among them in the 1930's. Nevertheless, missionaries in China promoted anti-Japanese sentiments in the United States. At the same time ethnic, institutional, theological, and educational ties encouraged many Episcopalian leaders to be internationalists and in favor of aid to Britain. Similarly, the Nazi persecution of the Jews and the predominantly urban orientation of the Jewish population in the United States encouraged them to be more internationalist and interventionist than the population as a whole. Whatever their prewar views, with the attack on Pearl Harbor religious groups gave almost united support to the nation's war effort.

THE ECONOMY

Many of the characteristics of the American economy from 1918 to 1941 were similar to those earlier in the century. In the 1920's the farm bloc won support from many Democrats and Republicans in Congress on certain measures. President Franklin D. Roosevelt required the support of agrarian progressives for the adoption of his New Deal domestic program. Nevertheless, agriculture was not dominant economically or politically. Similarly, despite the Reciprocal Trade Agreements program beginning in 1934, the shipping-commercial group was not dominant. In the 1920's the number of urban wage earners increased while union membership declined; in the 1930's the number of wage earners in private employment decreased while union membership increased. But in both decades the attitudes of wage earners toward foreign affairs tended to reflect the economic interests of that portion of the business economy of which they were a part.

Even more than before, the United States between the world wars had a predominantly urban-business-industrial-creditor economy. And American foreign policies, in part, reflected the interests, needs, and desires of labor, management, and capital operating and dependent upon that industrial-financial economy. Throughout that period the United States was the leading financial center of the world and the leading industrial state. As before, industrialization and the rise of finance capitalism increased American interest and activity in other parts of the world. A growing proportion of American exports consisted of manufactured products. Imports increasingly consisted of raw materials and tropical and semitropical food products. The United States continued to maintain the favorable balance of trade it had had most of the time since the 1870's. And as a result of America's industrial-financial economy and favorable balance of trade, the United States continued to have a creditor balance in international finance.

In terms of the general level of prosperity, the years from 1918 through 1941 may be divided roughly into three periods. From 1918 to 1929 (except for the sharp but brief slump in 1920–1921) the United States enjoyed booming economic prosperity and expansion. Farmers were in a relative depression in the 1920's, and wage earners did not benefit as much as business did, but there was widespread industrial and financial prosperity and expansion. From 1929 through 1938 the United States suffered the worst economic depression in its history. Those "hard times" hit nearly everyone, including farmers, workers, and businessmen. There was some improvement under Roosevelt's New Deal from 1933 to 1937, but the economy suffered a serious recession in 1937. There were still nearly ten million unemployed or on relief at the close of the New Deal era in 1938. In the early years of World War II, before the United States became a formal belligerent (that is, from 1939 to 1941), the economy slowly regained prosperity. That recovery was more rapid in coastal cities than in rural and small-town America.

One extremely important feature of the American economy from 1918 to 1941 (indeed, throughout the twentieth century) was that industries and farms consistently produced more than the available market within the United States absorbed. A basic (and continuing) problem was to find adequate markets at home and abroad for all the goods, services, and capital created by the economy. The problem was handled partly by devices to increase demand within national boundaries. Such methods included protective tariffs, credit and installment buying, advertising, higher wages, tax inducements for capital expansion, and lowering interest rates. Nevertheless, the domestic market has never absorbed all the American goods, services, and capital. Consequently, the methods used to sustain domestic prosperity by expanding markets have had fundamental effects on American foreign policies.

For purposes of convenience in examining some of the methods used by the United States to secure markets for its output, one may divide the years from 1918 through 1941 into three broad periods. The first ran from 1918 through 1932. In those years two major methods related to foreign affairs. First, the United States tried to guard the domestic market for its own producers by enacting ever higher protective tariffs. Second, the United States, in effect, subsidized foreign purchases of American products by lending and investing private capital abroad. Those private (not government) loans and investments, in effect, provided the dollars foreigners could and did use to buy American goods and services. The system made it difficult for foreign producers who needed American markets. And it caused problems for foreign governments that owed war debts to the United States. But so far as American businessmen were concerned, the system worked quite well during the prosperity decade from 1918 to 1928. Late in the decade, for a variety of reasons, (including the attractiveness of speculation on the stock exchange) Americans began to reduce the rate at which they loaned or invested abroad. During and after the financial collapse in 1929, Americans virtually stopped lending and investing abroad. Consequently, the private subsidy to foreign purchases of American goods and services practically disappeared during the depression decade. To make matters worse, the Smoot-Hawley Tariff of 1930, the highest in American history, made it even more difficult for foreigners to pay for goods and services by selling their own products in the United States.

The second period in an analysis of American methods to secure markets for its output was less clear-cut, but it corresponded roughly to the early New Deal era. In the "First New Deal" of 1933–1934 many in the administration of President Franklin D. Roosevelt envisaged restored prosperity through government-directed planning relying primarily on domestic markets within the United States. That approach appealed to such early "brain trusters" as Raymond Moley, Hugh S. Johnson, and George N. Peek. With some reservations it was in tune with the emphases of western agrarian progressives such as George W. Norris, Gerald P. Nye, and Robert M. LaFollette, Jr. Though they would have used different methods, urban socialists had some hopes for those efforts at national planning. Charles A. Beard's optimism about the Roosevelt administration in both domestic and foreign affairs was greatest at that time. He sketched his ideas along those lines in his book, *The Open Door at Home,* published in 1935. Professor Lloyd C. Gardner and other recent New Left historians have regretted that that "self-containment" phase of the New Deal was so incomplete and transitory.

Despite diversity and contradictions, supporters of the First New Deal hoped that if, with government help, business received high prices and workers got high wages, the effective domestic demand could absorb most of the goods, services, and capital produced by the economy. Prosperity would revive. The National Industrial Recovery Act and the first Agricultural Adjustment Act in 1933 fit that pattern. That general approach was consistent with and encouraged the growth of isolationism in those years. But that phase of the New Deal did not last long, and it was not implemented as fully as people like Peek, Beard, and Nye would have preferred. The New Deal instituted many needed reforms; its relief programs reduced human suffering; and its recovery programs contributed to limited economic revival. But the New Deal did not develop sufficient markets either at home or abroad to absorb all the goods, services, and capital that the American economy could turn out. It did not end the depression.

The third period ran from the latter part of the 1930's through 1941 (or, more accurately, to the present). In those years, so far as foreign affairs were concerned, the United States, in effect, expanded the markets for its products in three ways. First, through the reciprocal trade agreements program beginning in 1934 under Secretary of State Cordell Hull's leadership, the United States tried to increase markets by multilateral tariff reductions. Congress authorized the negotiation of executive trade agreements in which the United States could alter existing tariff rates as much as 50 percent in return for comparable adjustments in the customs duties of the foreign state. Each reciprocal trade agreement included an unconditional most-favored-nation clause that extended the tariff reductions to all other states that did not discriminate against American products. In other words, the program tried to encourage multilateral trade expansion. But despite many such agreements, it was less effective in solving America's economic difficulties than Hull had hoped.

Second, the United States government increased the demand for American goods and services through large expenditures for military preparedness, defense, and war. President Roosevelt began his naval building program with Public Works Administration funds as early as 1934. Between 1939 and 1941 the government vastly increased its expenditures for military forces in the face of Axis aggression and World War II. Even before Pearl Harbor federal expenditures for military preparedness exceeded New Deal expenditures. Whether intended or not, defense appropriations were a more massive (and less criticized) "pump priming" operation for the economy than the New Deal had been.

And finally, the government expanded markets by lending or giving capital and goods to foreign states. These subsidies for foreign purchases differed from those of the 1920's in that they consisted of government capital rather than private capital as before. Government subsidies for exports developed on a small scale in the 1930's with the Export-Import Banks, but they assumed major proportions with the enactment of Lend-Lease in March, 1941. The combination of the reciprocal trade program, growing military defense expenditures, foreign aid programs, and older conventional domestic and foreign markets provided sufficient effective demand directly and indirectly to restore the economy to nearly full prosperity by the end of 1941. Urban business and industry felt the stimulating effects earliest and most, but eventually the beneficial economic effects extended to nearly everyone, including farmers.

POLITICAL PATTERNS

Five men served as Presidents of the United States from 1918 to 1941. Democratic Woodrow Wilson completed his second term in 1921, though he was a sick man the last year and one-half of his administration. Republican Warren G. Harding of Ohio was President from 1921 until his death in August, 1923. He failed as President and he knew little about foreign affairs. Secretary of State Charles Evans Hughes and Secretary of Commerce Herbert Hoover largely guided the government's foreign policies for the President. With Harding's death, Calvin Coolidge of Vermont took over the reins of the Presidency, completing that term and serving another before leaving office in 1929. Though more able than Harding, Coolidge was no more informed about foreign affairs than his predecessor. His Secretaries of State, Hughes and Frank B. Kellogg, along with Secretary of Commerce Hoover, played the dominant roles in shaping the government's foreign policies.

Herbert Hoover, Republican President of the United States from 1929 to 1933, had had much experience in foreign affairs. He had become a multimillionaire through his international mining engineering operations. He administered food relief in Belgium during World War I and advised Wilson at the peace conference. As Secretary of Commerce in the 1920's he actively promoted foreign trade and investments. A Quaker in his religious beliefs, Hoover was not attracted by the use of force in international affairs. His Secretary of State, Henry L. Stimson of New York, was a product of the same general urban-financial-legal background that had produced such people as John Jay, Alexander Hamilton, Elihu Root, Robert Lansing, and Charles Evans Hughes. Like those men, Stimson favored an active, expansionist role for the United States in world affairs, a role consistent with the urban business interests with which he (and they) were closely identified. Stimson's considerable ability and strong views, when combined with Hoover's preoccupation with the depression that ruined his administration, enabled the Secretary of State to play a major role in American foreign affairs from 1929 to 1933. But Hoover was far more able and interested in foreign affairs than either of the two men who preceded him as President. Consequently, he actively influenced foreign affairs; Stimson was by no means a free agent.

The fifth President in the period was the Democrat, Franklin D. Roosevelt of New York. Inaugurated in 1933, Roosevelt was in his fourth term when he died in April, 1945. His Secretary of State during most of that time was Cordell Hull of Tennessee. An internationalist, Hull particularly influenced American policies on foreign trade, Latin America, and the Far East. Nevertheless, President Roosevelt was tremendously interested in foreign affairs and played an increasingly influential role in shaping the nation's foreign policies, particularly from 1937 onward and especially toward Europe.

As usual, foreign affairs were not conspicuous in most of the congressional and presidential elections in those years. Foreign policy issues were negligible in the congressional and presidential campaigns and elections from 1922 through 1938 inclusive. In one congressional campaign and in two presidential races foreign policy issues were prominent, that is, in the congressional elections of 1918 and in the presidential contests of 1920 and 1940. But even in those instances the significance of foreign affairs in the outcome was not clear-cut or decisive.

During World War I President Wilson had urged an adjournment of politics, an appeal that was imperfectly honored on both sides of the political fence. In the fall of 1918, however, his political advisers urged the President to call for the election of a Democratic Congress. In his public appeal Wilson said that Democratic majorities were essential for the development of a sound peace program. Republicans interpreted his statement as a gratuitous slap at them and as a violation of the "no-politics" truce while the war was still in its final phases. In any event, they took off their kid gloves and battled aggressively against their Democratic opponents (and the President). The elections gave the Republicans slim majorities in both houses of Congress. They also gave the Republicans majorities and the chairmanships in Senate and House committees.

In the case of the Foreign Relations Committee, Senator Henry Cabot Lodge of Massachusetts became chairman. An imperialist and a big-navy spokesman, he also was a personal and political enemy of the President. The election results left Wilson the leader of a minority party at the time of the Versailles Conference. Those results partly accounted for the failure of the Senate to approve the Versailles Treaty. Nevertheless, it was by no means certain that foreign affairs had much to do with the election results. Most of the contests turned on personalities and on domestic, state, and local issues—not on foreign affairs. Furthermore, both parties were so divided within themselves on foreign affairs that it was impossible to determine from the election what the people did or did not favor in a postwar peace settlement.

Foreign affairs were prominent in the presidential election of 1920. Wilson and the Democratic candidates, James M. Cox of Ohio and Franklin D. Roosevelt, hoped to make the election a mandate on the League of Nations. They campaigned clearly on a platform urging American membership in the League. The Republicans and their nominees, Harding and Coolidge, straddled on the issue. They endorsed adherence to an association of states, but not to Wilson's League. Some Republicans said that a vote for Harding would be a vote for the League; others said it would be a vote against it. Probably most Americans wanted what Harding called "normalcy" and a cessation of reform crusades both at home and abroad. The election of Harding and the defeat of Cox did not clearly reveal American attitudes on the League of Nations one way or the other.

Similarly the presidential race of 1940 failed to provide a meaningful picture of American foreign policy views. The fall of France and the Battle of Britain cast alarming shadows over the conventions and campaigns that year. The critical international situation led Franklin D. Roosevelt to seek an unprecedented third term. The Republicans nominated a dark-horse candidate, Wendell Willkie. He hailed from Indiana, but by 1940 was more accurately identified with Wall Street in New York. His nomination was a victory for the eastern-urban-business-internationalist wing of the Republican Party. The presidential nominations of both parties were urban (rather than rural and small-town) victories.

In his personal convictions, neither candidate was an isolationist; each was an internationalist. Each, however, feared isolationist strength in what could be a close contest; each feared defeat if he took an unequivocal internationalist stand. As the campaign wore on, Willkie's attacks on Roosevelt increasingly aimed to win the isolationist vote. And Roosevelt felt compelled to respond in kind. In Boston he said: "And while I am talking to you mothers and fathers I give you one more assurance. I have said this before, but I shall say it again and again and again: Your boys are not going to be sent into any foreign wars." Roosevelt won reelection, but the margin was not great. Probably most isolationists voted for Willkie, though he was not an isolationist. Probably most internationalists voted for Roosevelt, though many conservative Republican business internationalists voted against him. It was not a clear mandate on foreign policies.

In the 1920's and through much of the 1930's there was powerful isolationist sentiment in all sections of the country and in both parties. During the early New Deal era and for much of his domestic reform program, President Roosevelt relied heavily on the sectional alliance of the urban Northeast and the rural and small-town West. Urban liberals were sometimes pacifists and often internationalists. But western agrarian liberals who supported the New Deal generally were isolationists. A strong internationalist approach by the President would have shattered the sectional alliance so essential for his domestic program. And that New Deal program won top priority from the Administration in the middle of the decade. With Roosevelt's overwhelming election victory over Republican Alf M. Landon in 1936, the President no longer felt so obliged to cater to the wishes of western progressives on either domestic or foreign affairs.

In the latter part of the New Deal and after Roosevelt began to shift his emphasis to internationalism, the President won his main support from the sectional alliance of the South and Northeast. Conservative southern Democrats had not liked the New Deal, but they led the most interventionist section of the country on foreign affairs. In the Northeast most urban liberals continued to follow the President when he shifted from domestic reform to foreign affairs. In addition, with that shift Roosevelt won powerful support from conservative businessmen and financiers who had previously opposed his New Deal. The House of Morgan, Henry L. Stimson, Dean G. Acheson, the *New York Herald Tribune,* the Henry Luce publications, and columnists such as the Alsop brothers generally had opposed Roosevelt on New Deal issues. They rallied to his support when he began to lead in the direction of internationalism and aid to the allies. Consequently, the coalition that Roosevelt led by 1940–1941 was more conservative, urban, and internationalist than the one he had depended on in 1933–1934. Given the decline of rural and small-town America, the growing conservative criticism of the New Deal, and the threatening international situation, President Roosevelt was moving with the political tides (rather than against them) after 1938 when he refocused his attention away from domestic reforms toward internationalism, national defense, and aid to Britain.

IDEOLOGICAL PATTERNS

Many of the views affecting foreign affairs between the two world wars may be examined under the broad headings of isolationism or noninterventionism, and internationalism or interventionism. Then and later, Americans used the terms loosely. They were misleading if one defined them literally.

Isolationists did not want the United States to cut itself off from the rest of the world or even from Europe. Furthermore, most isolationists were not pacifists. American pacifists generally were internationalists, though as a matter of short-term expediency many of them cooperated with isolationists in the decade before Pearl Harbor. When isolationists objected to military preparedness programs (they particularly criticized naval construction), they did so on the grounds that the particular forces were not in their view, essential for the foreign policies they considered desirable for the United States.

Central themes in isolationist attitudes were "unilateralism" and "noninterventionism." As "unilateralists" they opposed "entangling alliances." They did not believe the United States could prevent wars through cooperation with European states. They feared that international commitments would involve the United States unnecessarily in the wars that inevitably swept other parts of the world. They determined to maintain maximum freedom of action for the United States. Most of them opposed membership in the League of Nations and World Court. They had faith in the "power of example." That is, they believed the United States could do more for the world by building and maintaining its own prosperity and freedom under democracy than it could through internationalism and military force.

As "noninterventionists" they believed the United States could and should have stayed out of World War I. That noninterventionist theme ran through the neutrality laws of the 1930's. From 1939 to 1941 noninterventionists believed it was more important for the United States to stay out of the European war than it was to assure a British victory over the Axis. Their noninterventionist attitudes toward Europe, however, were not necessarily extended to Latin America, the Pacific area, or the Far East. Isolationism and expansionism were not necessarily incompatible. Isolationism included nationalism, though nationalism generally affected spokesmen for other points of view as well. It included xenophobia and Anglophobia. Many isolationists in the 1930's blamed urban big businessmen, munitions manufacturers, and international financiers for involving the United States in foreign wars and overseas imperialism to serve their selfish economic interests.

Isolationist leaders included such diverse figures as Senator Henry Cabot Lodge of Massachusetts, chairman of the Senate Foreign Relations Committee from 1919 until his death in 1924, and Senator William E. Borah of Idaho, chairman of that committee from 1924 to 1933. They included the LaFollettes of Wisconsin, father and sons. There were Senators Hiram Johnson of California, Burton K. Wheeler of Montana, Gerald P. Nye of North Dakota, and Arthur H. Vandenberg of Michigan. Raymond Moley, George N. Peek, and Hugh Johnson, early New Dealers, were isolationists. In 1939–1941 the most colorful and controversial isolationist was the famed aviator, Charles A. Lindbergh.

There were isolationists in all parts of the country, but they were most powerful in the Middle West and least so in the South. Ethnically, German-Americans, Irish-Americans, and many Italian-Americans tended to be isolationists. In terms of religious affiliations they were particu larly numerous among Roman Catholics and Lutherans. Isolationism was stronger in rural and small-town America (outside of the South) than in cities. In economic terms isolationism won wide support from farmers and farm leaders, especially in the upper Mississippi Valley, and from agrarian progressives. One encountered isolationism in western mining states, in service businesses, among retailers, and in light-goods manufacturing.

Politically there were more isolationalists in the Republican Party than in the Democratic Party. Nevertheless, many urban Republicans were internationalists and some Democrats such as Burton K. Wheeler were isolationists. Isolationists included both liberals and conservatives. In the 1920's and early 1930's liberal and progressive isolationists used an economic interpretation to blame wars on the selfish profit seeking of big business, shipbuilders, munitions makers, and international financiers. During the five years before Pearl Harbor, however, isolationists gradually refocused away from economic considerations toward political explanations. As they became increasingly critical of presidential power in general and of President Roosevelt in particular, they gradually became more conservative. Throughout most of the period from 1918 to 1941 a very large percentage of the American people adhered to variations of the isolationist point of view.

In contrast, internationalists believed that because of America's great power and the interdependence of the world the United States could not avoid involvement in world politics. The United States had not and probably could not stay out of world wars. Wars and major power shifts abroad inevitably affected American interests and security. Consequently, internationalists believed the United States in cooperation with other like-minded states should throw its power and influence against potential aggressor states to prevent wars. If, in spite of such cooperative efforts, war began, internationalists believed the United States should aid the victims of aggression, at least with aid short of war. They urged membership in the League of Nations and the World Court. Most of them emphasized the importance of Anglo-American cooperation in world affairs. Though pacifists generally were internationalists, most internationalists were not pacifists.

After World War II began in Europe, the term "interventionist" applied to those who believed that a British victory over the Axis was absolutely essential to American security. They believed it was more important to assure a British victory than it was to keep the United States out of the European war. A minority of those interventionists, such as Secretary of War Henry L. Stimson, believed the United States would have to become a full belligerent against Germany to accomplish that essential defeat of the Axis. But most so-called interventionists before Pearl Harbor, following President Roosevelt's leadership, wanted to limit American support to aid short of war. Just as some noninterventionists were not isolationists, so some interventionists were not internationalists.

Notable among internationalist leaders, of course, was President Woodrow Wilson. Another was President Roosevelt's Secretary of State Cordell Hull of Tennessee. Though quite different, Henry L. Stimson of New York, Secretary of State under Hoover and Secretary of War under Franklin D. Roosevelt beginning in 1940, was an internationlist.

Among Senate internationalists were Tom Connally of Texas, James Byrnes of South Carolina, and Carter Glass of Virginia. Mayor Fiorello La Guardia of New York City was an energetic internationalist. And President Franklin D. Roosevelt was an internationalist. From 1932 to 1935 he sometimes seemed like an isolationist. Under pressure from William Randolph Hearst, Roosevelt in 1932 said he no longer favored American membership in the League of Nations. The early New Deal was a nationalistic approach to the problem of the depression. The World Economic Conference in London in 1933 failed partly because Roosevelt refused to cooperate in any international monetary stabilization agreement. And Roosevelt signed the isolationist neutrality legislation of the 1930's. Nevertheless, in his personal convictions he was an internationalist. In his second and third terms as President his actions in foreign affairs increasingly (though imperfectly) coincided with his convictions.

Support for the internationalist view came from all parts of the country, but the Northeast was the most consistently internationalist section and the South was the most vehemently interventionist section. Ethnically, Anglo-Saxons probably were more internationalist than the country as a whole. In terms of religious affiliations internationalists were relatively numerous among Episcopalians and Jews. Economically, southern cotton producers generally were internationalists. Heavy industry (including owners, management, and workers) tended to be internationalist. General Motors and General Electric, for example, were in the internationalist camp very early. Large eastern financiers and bankers, including the House of Morgan, were internationalist. So were many large eastern newspapers and news publications such as the *New York Times, New York Herald Tribune,* and the Luce publications. People in urban areas were more likely to be internationalist than those in rural areas and small towns.

Politically there were more internationalists in the Democratic Party than in the Republican, though many Republicans were internationalists, including Secretary of War Stimson, Secretary of the Navy Frank Knox, Wendell Willkie, and others. Professional classes, educators, and people with college degrees were more likely to be internationalists than those with less education. Many liberals supported the internationalist view, particularly urban liberals. But in the late 1930's and before Pearl Harbor, a growing number of conservatives were internationalists. They included southern Democrats who had not liked Roosevelt's New Deal and conservative business and financial leaders who benefited from appropriations for defense, Lend-Lease, and aid to Britain. Roosevelt could not have implemented his internationalist and aid-short-of-war policies without the support he got for those policies from many who had opposed his New Deal. Most of the time from 1918 to 1941 internationalists were in a minority. That was particularly true in the middle of the 1930's.

According to public opinion polls, from 1939 to 1941 the American people and their leaders held two seemingly irreconcilable views. More than 85 percent of them wanted a British victory over the Axis (very few wanted an Axis victory). At the same time, approximately 80 percent of those same Americans opposed a declaration of war on the Axis to accomplish that British victory. After the fall of France and the Battle of Britain, in contrast to earlier patterns, the majority believed it was more important to assure the defeat of the Axis than it was to keep the United States out of the war. And most of them supported Roosevelt's steps to aid Britain short of war. To that extent the internationalists had won the upper hand even before Pearl Harbor.

Americans earnestly debated the foreign policy issues all the way from the President's Cabinet and Congress down to every bar and barber shop in the country. A colorful and important part of that controversy was the role of organized pressure groups, the "battle of the committees." They tried to arouse support for or opposition to particular policies by means of advertisements, pamphlets, radio speeches, rallies, and motion pictures. They also tried to influence government policy makers through lobbying, petitions, and letters. Many such pressure groups from 1918 to 1941 may be analyzed in terms of the ideological controversies between isolationists and internationalists.

During the fifteen months preceding the attack on Pearl Harbor the most powerful isolationist or noninterventionist pressure group was the America First Committee. It began as a student organization at Yale University under the leadership of R. Douglas Stuart, Jr., a young law student. By September, 1940, it had expanded to become a national pressure group with its headquarters in Chicago. Its national chairman was General Robert E. Wood, head of Sears, Roebuck and Company. At its peak in 1941 it had around 850,000 members, with its greatest strength in the Middle West. Its most prominent speakers were Charles A. Lindbergh, Senator Burton K. Wheeler, and Senator Gerald P. Nye. Its sources of support roughly coincided with those of the noninterventionist movement as a whole, except that its main leadership and financial backing came from middle western businessmen. It was a more conservative coalition than the isolationist movement as a whole. Some anti-Semites and pro-Nazis supported America First, but the committee's leadership tried to bar such unsavory elements. They represented only a tiny part of its total membership. America Firsters believed it was more important for the United States to stay out of the European war than to assure a British victory over the Axis. The committee leaders feared that Roosevelt's steps to aid Britain short of war would prove to be steps to war for the United States. America First vigorously opposed Lend-

Lease, use of the American Navy to escort convoys to Britain, and repeal of the vital provisions of the Neutrality Act in 1941. It suffered defeat in each of those efforts, however, and it collapsed with the Japanese attack on Pearl Harbor.

There were also numerous internationalist and interventionist pressure groups. The League to Enforce Peace urged creation of the League of Nations at the close of World War I. Between the two world wars the League of Nations Association urged American membership and support for the League. During the year and one-half before Pearl Harbor the two most powerful interventionist pressure groups were the Committee to Defend America by Aiding the Allies, and Fight for Freedom, Incorporated. The Committee to Defend America by Aiding the Allies grew partly out of a suggestion by President Roosevelt to William Allen White, a Republican newspaper editor from Emporia, Kansas. White was national chairman of the committee when it was organized in May, 1940, and it was often called the White Committee. Clark Eichelberger was executive director. In 1940 and the first months of 1941 committee leaders consulted frequently with Administration policy makers. The White Committee believed that it was more important for the United States to assure a British victory over the Axis than it was for the United States to stay out of the European war. Like the President, the White Committee opposed a negotiated peace and favored all-out aid short of war. It conducted major campaigns for the destroyer deal in 1940, for Lend-Lease, and for convoys. It continued in existence until after Pearl Harbor, but its influence declined after White resigned as chairman early in 1941. Many interventionists became convinced that the White Committee's short-of-war approach would not be enough to defeat the Axis.

That trend in interventionist thinking led to the organization of Fight for Freedom, Incorporated, in April, 1941. Bishop Henry W. Hobson, Episcopal Bishop of southern Ohio, was national chairman and Senator Carter Glass of Virginia was honorary chairman. Among its speakers were Douglas Fairbanks, Jr., Robert E. Sherwood, Dorothy Thompson, and Wendell Willkie. Leaders of Fight for Freedom agreed with Stimson and Knox in the President's Cabinet that aid short of war would not be sufficient and that the United States should enter the European war as a full belligerent on the side of Great Britain.

Those pressure groups on both sides helped to clarify issues and crystallize existing attitudes. They helped to inform the public, organize public opinion, and make it vocal. They helped to convert general attitudes into demands for action on particular measures. In that sense they were agencies for the democratic process in the formulation of American foreign policies.

MILITARY FORCES

American military forces helped defeat Germany in World War I. By November, 1918, the American Expeditionary Force in Europe had nearly two million men. American combat contributions and losses were not nearly as great as those of other major belligerents, but they did help break the stalemate on the Western Front.

After the armistice the United States quickly dismantled its military forces. Servicemen and their families insisted on rapid demobilization. Economy-minded congressmen and taxpayers would not provide the funds needed to maintain large military forces. With the defeat of Germany, there did not appear to be any direct military threat to American security requiring the maintenance of massive armed forces. Americans agreed on the necessity for defense of North America, including Alaska, Hawaii, and Panama. But opinions differed on whether South America and the Philippines should be included in defense planning. And the widespread disillusionment with the results of World War I made most Americans determined that the United States should never again become a belligerent in "foreign wars" on distant continents.

The attitudes of American military leaders were not greatly different from civilian views. Much big-navy propaganda in the decade after World War I pointed with alarm at the British Navy, though a war between the United States and Great Britain was most unlikely. Army thinking had not advanced much beyond pre-World War I levels. General William Mitchell's quixotic efforts on behalf of air power won headlines (and a court-martial) but did not convert many generals, admirals, or civilians to his cause.

Most of the time between the two world wars the Army had fewer than 150,000 men in uniform. Reserve and National Guard units found it impossible to fill their authorized ranks. Much of their "modern" equipment dated from World War I.

The Navy fared better than the Army, but it had its difficulties. The Navy General Board resolved to implement prewar plans to build and maintain a "navy second to none," meaning a Navy at least as large as Britain's. The Washington Conference of 1921–1922 and economy-minded congressmen and taxpayers blocked those plans. Under the leadership of Secretary of State Charles Evans Hughes, the delegates to the Washington Conference concluded the Five Power Naval Treaty in 1922. It provided for a ten-year holiday in the construction of capital ships. It limited battleships to 35,000 tons and to 16-inch guns. It called for a 5–5–3–1.7–1.7 ratio in capital ships between Great Britain, the United States, Japan, France, and Italy. Those limitations, however, did not extend to light cruisers, destroyers, or submarines. The agreement compelled the scrapping of certain ships in being or under construction. In the years that followed, Congress did not even provide funds for naval construction permitted under the treaty. Naval officers from the United States and other countries helped to prevent subsequent disarmament conferences from effectively extending the naval limitations to smaller vessels.

Those general patterns continued through most of the depression years of the 1930's. Nevertheless, under the leadership of President Franklin D. Roosevelt the United States very slowly began to enlarge and modernize its Armed Forces, particularly after 1938. Roosevelt was an enthusiastic advocate of naval power. He had been influenced by Mahan's ideas and had served as Assistant Secretary of the Navy under President Wilson before and during World War I. In 1934 he began to use Public Works Administration funds for naval construction. When the naval limitations agreements expired in 1936 and Japan built beyond those limits, Roosevelt urged Congress to provide funds to expand the American Navy. The United States Navy was by no means small or weak when Japan attacked Pearl Harbor. As war in Europe drew nearer, Roosevelt also persuaded Congress to provide large appropriations for the Army Air Corps. The land forces remained small and weak throughout the 1930's, but in September, 1940 (after the fall of France and during the Battle of Britain), Congress adopted the first peacetime selective service law in American history. Under that law young men were drafted to serve for twelve months in the Western Hemisphere. In the summer of 1941 Congress extended that period of service to eighteen months, though that extension passed the House of Representatives by a margin of only one vote. Under Roosevelt's leadership the United States rapidly enlarged and modernized its land, sea, and air forces.

At the same time, defense planning began to broaden its horizons. Continental concerns became hemispheric. In the face of Nazi Germany's terrifying military successes, by 1940–1941 American military planners shifted from their earlier focus on the Pacific to a "Europe-first" orientation.

Despite rapid military preparations from 1939 to 1941, and despite changes in strategic planning, the United States was not militarily prepared to meet the fantastic requirements for victory over the Axis when Japan attacked Pearl Harbor on December 7, 1941.

SUPPLEMENTARY READINGS

Adler, Selig. *The Isolationist Impulse: Its Twentieth-Century Reaction.* London and New York: Abelard-Schuman, Ltd., 1957.

Bailey, Thomas A. *The Man in the Street: The Impact of American Public Opinion on Foreign Policy.* New York: Macmillan Co., 1948.

Beard, Charles A. *The Idea of National Interest: An Analytical Study in American Foreign Policy.* New York: Macmillan Co., 1934.

Chadwin, Mark L. *The Hawks of World War II.* Chapel Hill: University of North Carolina Press, 1968.

Cole, Wayne S. *America First: The Battle Against Intervention, 1940–1941.* Madison: University of Wisconsin Press, 1953.

_____. *Senator Gerald P. Nye and American Foreign Relations.* Minneapolis: University of Minnesota Press, 1962.

Curti, Merle. *Peace or War: The American Struggle, 1636–1936.* Boston: J. S. Canner & Co., 1959.

Divine, Robert A. *American Immigration Policy, 1924–1952.* New Haven, Conn.: Yale University Press, 1957.

Gardner, Lloyd C. *Economic Aspects of New Deal Diplomacy.* Madison: University of Wisconsin Press, 1964.

Johnson, Walter. *The Battle Against Isolation.* Chicago: University of Chicago Press, 1944.

Jonas, Manfred. *Isolationism in America, 1935–1941.* Ithaca, N.Y.: Cornell University Press, 1966.

Leuchtenburg, William E. *Franklin D. Roosevelt and the New Deal, 1932–1940.* New York: Harper & Row, Publishers, 1963.

_____. *The Perils of Prosperity, 1914–1932.* Chicago: University of Chicago Press, 1958.

Millis, Walter. *Arms and Men: A Study in American Military History.* New York: G. P. Putman's Sons, 1956.

Mitchell, Broadus. *Depression Decade: From New Era through New Deal, 1929–1941.* New York: Rinehart & Co., Inc., 1947.

Rauch, Basil. *The History of the New Deal, 1933–1938.* New York: Creative Age Press, 1944.

Schlesinger, Arthur M., Jr. *The Age of Roosevelt: The Coming of the New Deal.* Boston: Houghton Mifflin Co., 1958.

_____. *The Age of Roosevelt: The Crisis of the Old Order, 1919–1933.* Boston: Houghton Mifflin Co., 1956.

_____. *The Age of Roosevelt: The Politics of Upheaval.* Boston: Houghton Mifflin Co., 1960.

Shannon, David A. *Between the Wars: America, 1919–1941.* Boston: Houghton Mifflin Co., 1965.

Soule, George. *Prosperity Decade: From War to Depression, 1917–1929.* New York: Rinehart & Co., Inc., 1947.

Williams, Benjamin H. *Economic Foreign Policy of the United States.* New York: McGraw-Hill Book Co., 1929.

30

The United States and the Versailles Treaty

The peace settlements ending World War I fell short of the hopes and best thinking in Europe and America. The peace treaties did not implement all of President Woodrow Wilson's Fourteen Points. Some analysts questioned the adequacy of his proposals even if they had all been adopted. Nevertheless, the peace treaties included most of Wilson's Fourteen Points. The League of Nations Covenant provided international machinery for peacefully correcting flaws in the settlements. For all its shortcomings, the Versailles settlement was not necessarily foredoomed to failure. Its subsequent failure and the eruption of World War II two decades later resulted from the conduct at home and abroad of the parties to the treaty during the years that followed. And the failure of the peace was due partly to the refusal by the United States to approve the treaty, join the League of Nations, and assume its share of the responsibilities for guarding that peace.

The central figure for the United States in the peace settlements was President Woodrow Wilson. He led the nation before, during, and after World War I. He helped formulate the ideological rationale for American participation in that war and for the peace settlement that followed. Wilson headed the five-man peace commission representing the United States at Versailles, and he played the leading role in the negotiations. He battled unsuccessfully to get Senate approval of the Versailles Treaty.

Most of Wilson's views on international affairs and peace were not original with him. Scholars, statesmen, and diplomats both in Europe and America had been developing those ideas for many years. Wilson simply drew the ideas together, converted them into appealing language, popularized them, and used his position as President of the United States in his efforts to implement them. Wilson was aware of the role of power and security considerations in international affairs, but he tended to translate such matters into moral terms. His peace views were rooted in his Calvinist, Anglo-Saxon, Victorian, nineteenth-century liberal value system. He believed in the capacity of informed men to solve their problems (domestic and international) through democratic processes. He believed in the essential goodness or perfectability of man. He rejected radicalism and shared the general economic attitudes of laissez-faire, free-trade, nineteenth-century liberals. Wilson was not a doctrinaire pacifist, but he preferred diplomacy, conciliation, and arbitration to more violent methods in international affairs.

The President summarized his major proposals for the postwar peace settlement in the Fourteen Points presented in his message to Congress on January 8, 1918. Several of his points dealt with general matters, including "open convenants of peace, openly arrived at," freedom of the seas in peace and war, removal of trade barriers, reduction of armaments, and impartial adjustment of colonial claims. Eight points applied the doctrine of self-determination to political settlements in specific parts of Europe, such as Russia, Belgium, Alsace-Lorraine, Italy, Serbia, Turkey, Poland, and Austria-Hungary. Most of his proposals dealt with political, rather than economic, aspects of the peace settlement. Three of his Fourteen Points had economic connotations: freedom of seas in peace and war, removal of economic barriers so far as possible, and impartial adjustment of colonial claims. But none of those three satisfied radicals (then or now), and none was accomplished in practice. The fourteenth point (and the one on which Wilson placed his greatest hopes) urged the formation of a "general association of nations" to afford "mutual guarantees of political independence and territorial integrity to great and small states alike."

For years American scholars and statesmen assumed that Wilson's ideas were sound. They blamed the failure of the peace settlement on the fact that it did not sufficiently conform to the principles President Wilson outlined. More recently, however, there has been growing criticism, not only of the failure to implement his Fourteen Points but of the adequacy of Wilson's ideas even if they had been fully put into practice. Leftists criticized Wilson's ideas for neglecting the economic bases for world peace and order. Professors Arno J. Mayer, N. Gordon Levin, and others found Wilson, his moderate progressivism, his Fourteen Points, and his performance at Versailles quite inadequate in terms of worldwide socioeconomic distress and revolutionary ferment after the War, and in the face of the radical challenge and alternative represented by the bolshevik revolution in Russia. The so-called realists, on the other hand, led by Hans J. Morgenthau and George F. Kennan, criticized Wilson for not being sufficiently alert to the role of power in international affairs. They found him too idealistic and utopian.

As the Western armies advanced in the late summer and fall of 1918, German military leaders urged their government to seek an armistice. Field Marshall Paul von Hindenburg and General Erich Ludendorff hoped for an arrangement that would allow them to regroup their forces and prepare for more effective military operations in the future if a satisfactory peace settlement were not forthcoming. Believing that Wilson might be easier to handle than France's Georges Clemenceau or Britain's David Lloyd George, the German government approached the American President early in October, 1918. Wilson did hope for an armistice that would leave Germany strong enough to prevent the Allies from insisting on a Carthaginian peace that would not endure. Nevertheless, Wilson did not allow himself to become a German pawn. In the prearmistice negotiations he maneuvered the Germans into acknowledging defeat and ousting the Kaiser. The belligerents agreed, with two qualifications, that the Fourteen Points would be the basis for the peace negotiations. At Britain's insistence "freedom of seas" was ruled out of the negotiations. And France required that the door be left open for reparations payments in the peace settlement. The military provisions of the armistice detailed by Marshall Foch left the Germans powerless to resume effective combat against the Allies. Concluded on November 11, 1918, the armistice was, in effect, a surrender, and both the civilian and military leaders of Germany realized that at the time.

In the congressional elections just before the armistice the Republicans won slim majorities in both houses of Congress. In a parliamentary system of government the election would have removed Wilson from his position as head of the government. Nevertheless, President Wilson determined to lead the American peace delegation himself. In addition to the President, the five-man delegation included Secretary of State Robert Lansing, Colonel Edward M. House, General Tasker H. Bliss, and Henry White. White was the only Republican. He was an experienced diplomat, but he had little standing in the Republican Party. The delegation did not include any of the leading Republican statesmen, though some of them (such as Taft and Root) shared many of Wilson's peace views. It included no senator from either party. In actual practice, Colonel House was the only delegate that Wilson consulted very much. The President's party that sailed on the S. S. *George Washington* on December 4, 1918, included many technical advisers and some members of the Inquiry that had prepared numerous reports on matters to be considered at the peace conference.

Wilson arrived nearly a month before the peace conference began and won enthusiastic acclaim from huge crowds in England, Italy, and France. That encouraged his hopes, but it also inflated Wilson's already exaggerated messianic feelings and self-righteousness. Similarly, it encouraged utopian expectations among the European people that no human could have fulfilled.

The conference began on January 12, 1919. Earlier, Wilson had called for a "peace between equals," but the victors negotiated the Versailles Treaty. When they had decided on the terms, they presented the treaty to the Germans, who had no practical alternative but to protest and sign it almost unchanged.

The plenary sessions were too cumbersome, so the Big Four did most of the negotiations. They included Wilson for the United States, David Lloyd George of Great Britain, Georges Clemenceau for France, and Vittorio Orlando from Italy. When they considered Asian matters the Japanese representative made it five. Russia was not represented at the conference. The Big Four issued brief news releases, and the completed treaty was made public, but they conducted their negotiations in closed sessions.

Much of that was contrary to principles Wilson had advanced earlier. It was a dictated peace negotiated by the victors and imposed on the vanquished. It was an open convenant, but it was not "openly arrived at." And the actual negotiators represented only the great powers, hardly democracy in international affairs. But as with so much of the whole story, it was not necessarily what Wilson wanted, and it was not within his power to control. Though he had become convinced of the necessity for the defeat of Germany, he would have preferred a stronger Germany in 1919 to moderate the more extreme demands by the victors. He wanted more open negotiations than the others would allow. Moreover, most professional diplomats and academic specialists believe that diplomatic negotiations conducted in the public eye are less likely to accomplish desirable results than those in closed sessions where there may be greater freedom to bargain and give and take. And finally, Realists point out that though states may have equal rights, they do not have equal power. France, Britain, the United States, and, to a lesser extent, Italy and Japan commanded the power that defeated the Central Powers. They were powerful enough to determine the peace terms. And because of their power they were the states on which the success or failure of the peace most depended.

The statesmen at Versailles faced incredibly difficult tasks. The war had devastated vast areas, destroyed millions of lives, ravished productive facilities, dislocated economies, and changed the power relations among them. The bolshevik revolution in Russia left the menacing specter of communism challenging all if the peacemakers failed. The negotiators understood the magnitude of their tasks and responsibilities. In some respects all of them, including Wilson, shared common values and goals. Despite his personal dislike for Wilson, Lloyd George agreed with the President on many important issues in the negotiations. The Big Four agreed on the preservation of national sovereignty and the multi-state system. All defended the existing economic systems and neglected economic bases for international friction and war. As Professor Richard Hofstadter phrased it, "Wilson's struggle with Clemenceau and Lloyd George . . . was not a struggle between an Old Order and a New Order, but merely a quarrel as to how the Old Order should settle its affairs."

Nevertheless, Wilson did differ from the others in important respects. His Fourteen Points aimed at a more hopeful peace settlement than any of the leading European statesmen were prepared to suggest. Harsh and punitive as the treaty was, it would have been harsher without his influence. Wilson was responsible for including the Covenant of the League of Nations in the Versailles Treaty.

To accomplish as much as he did required great ability and heroic effort. Lloyd George and Clemenceau were tough and wily adversaries at the bargaining table. If their own views and abilities were not formidable enough, the political and public opinion influences in each of their countries forced them to reject some of Wilson's proposals. Commitments made earlier, in the so-called secret treaties, further stiffened resistance to the President's efforts. The European victors had poured years of effort, millions of men, and vast sums of money into the war against the Central Powers. Even Wilson could not persuade Europeans to forgo the fruits of victory. After suffering so terribly at the hands of the Germans, they were not willing to trust their future security to the as yet unformed and untried League of Nations. At Versailles Wilson worked long, hard, and successfully to master the details of the negotiations. He was a tough and resourceful bargainer. He got much of what he sought in the negotiations, including the League of Nations. But he faced obstacles and difficulties that even superhuman talents and efforts could not have overcome entirely.

When completed the Versailles Treaty was a complex, book length document. It left Germany as an independent state with its own government. Germany had to return Alsace-Lorraine to France. Germany lost some eastern areas to Poland and Czechoslovakia. Denmark and Belgium received small territorial gains. The treaty provided for French occupation of the Rhineland until 1935. Germany lost all of its overseas colonies. Ultimately they were assigned to victorious states to be administered as mandates under the League of Nations. Germany was disarmed except for a 100,000-man army. In Article 231 Germany had to accept sole responsibility for the war. It had to pay reparations for both direct and indirect war damages to the Allies. Contrary to Wilson's wishes, the treaty did not specify either amounts or time limits for those reparations. The Reparations Commission in 1921 set the figure at $33 billion. About one third of that amount represented direct damages to Allied property, and one half to two thirds represented indirect costs such as pensions and widow's allowances. And the treaty included the League of Nations Covenant. The German delegates blanched at the treaty and cried "foul," but had to settle for only minor changes. After the formal signing ceremonies in the Hall of Mirrors at Versailles on June 28, 1919, Wilson returned to the United States to battle for Senate approval.

Most assumed that the United States Senate would approve the Versailles Treaty, including the League Covenant, perhaps with clarifying reservations. Most Americans approved the treaty in general. Even its opponents operated from that assumption about public opinion. The President recognized the treaty's many imperfections, but he saw it as the world's best hope for a peaceful future. After having been compelled to compromise so much at the conference table, Wilson was in no mood to yield further. He resolved to fight for his treaty. With ringing determination the President insisted: "The Senate is going to ratify the treaty."

Nevertheless, opposition began to form long before he presented the treaty to the Senate on July 10, 1919. Many liberals and liberal publications that had supported the President earlier were disillusioned and critical because it fell so far short of their idealistic expectations. German-Americans thought it was too harsh on Germany. Italian-Americans complained that it did not give Italy all it had been promised earlier. Irish-Americans thought it was too favorable to Britain. Countless other Anglophobes, including the Hearst newspapers, shared that view. Widespread isolationism and nationalism assured objections to the League Covenant, and particularly to its crucial Article X. Postwar disillusionment developed rapidly among returning servicemen and their families. Part of the opposition was partisan politics. Wilson had, in effect, invited political opposition by appealing for the election of a Democratic Congress in 1918, by failing to name any leading Republican to the peace commission, and by personally heading the delegation to France. And some, led by Senator Henry Cabot Lodge, simply hated Wilson personally. Clearly the Versailles Treaty would not go unopposed in the United States.

The United States Senate would cast the crucial vote. And it gave the President ominous warnings of things to come even before he formally presented the treaty for its consideration. On March 4, when Wilson was in the United States briefly during the peace conference, Senator Lodge presented his "Round Robin" signed by more than one third of the Senators. That group, large enough to block Senate approval, warned that the League Covenant "in the form now proposed" was not acceptable.

Despite some subsequent modifications of the covenant, most of the dissenters remained unappeased. The Democrats in the Senate had the advantages of a good cause, Wilson's leadership, and good party discipline. But they were in a minority. The minority leader, Senator Gilbert M. Hitchcock of Nebraska, earnestly tried to win approval for the treaty, but he was no match for the oratorical, political, and parliamentary talents of his adversaries in the Senate.

The Senate Republicans were stronger but they were by no means united. They included about a dozen mild reservationists, such as Frank B. Kellogg of Minnesota, who favored approval with certain clarifying reservations. There were fourteen irreconcilables who opposed the treaty and League Covenant in any form. They filled six seats in the Foreign Relations Committee and included some of the most powerful men in the Senate, such as William E. Borah of Idaho, Hiram Johnson of California, and Robert M. LaFollette of Wisconsin. The most able among them were agrarian progressives who, in part, saw the war, the treaty, and the League as products of selfish profit seeking by urban big business and finance. And finally, there were about twenty strong reservationists led by Senator Henry Cabot Lodge of Massachusetts, chairman of the Foreign Relations Committee. They professed to favor the League but wanted strong reservations to guard American sovereignty and congressional authority in foreign affairs. Even now one cannot be certain whether they really wanted the treaty with protective reservations or whether they simply used the reservations and a "yes but" approach as tactics to destroy what they did not really want. Given public opinion approval for the treaty, the close balance between parties in the Senate, the divisions in Republican ranks, and Wilson's already demonstrated leadership abilities, the treaty was by no means a lost cause when the contest began.

Senator Lodge deliberately prolonged committee consideration of the treaty to allow time for the people to weary of the subject and for opposition to build. He consumed two weeks reading the 264-page document in committee. Sixty witnesses testified on the subject. That may have been a democratic effort to give every view a hearing; it was also part of Lodge's delaying tactics. As time dragged on and disaffection grew, President Wilson tried to win support and favorable action by conferring individually at the White House with Republican senators. He met with the Foreign Relations Committee for three hours on August 19, to explain and defend the agreement. He was willing to accept certain explanatory reservations if they were not subject to approval by other states. He secretly gave Hitchcock four reservations he would have accepted if necessary. But his patience wore thin, and he feared the treaty's chances were fading with the passage of time.

Finally, he resolved to go to the people. He persuaded himself that what he wanted was what the people wanted. If he could explain the issues and arouse popular concern, the voters might force the Senate to act favorably. Wilson was an unusually able speaker with a cause he believed to be not only right but essential. His physician warned that such a strenuous effort might endanger his already frail health, but Wilson considered the cause more important than life itself. He left Washington by special train on September 3, traveled through the Middle West and on to the West Coast, and returned. His biographer, Arthur S. Link, wrote: "In all he traveled 8,000 miles in twenty-two days and delivered thirty-two major addresses and eight minor ones. It was not only the greatest speaking effort of Wilson's career, but also one of the most notable forensic accomplishments in American history." He moved vast audiences with his lucid and earnest appeals. But his great effort probably did not change a single vote in the Senate. At every stop he was followed by senators who effectively attacked the treaty in addresses before large crowds.

The President fell ill after his speech in Pueblo, Colorado, and was rushed back to Washington where he suffered a paralytic stroke on October 2, 1919. Though his mind remained clear, the President was near death for days, and he never fully regained his health during the year and a half that remained of his administration. For a time Mrs. Wilson determined who and what matters should be brought to her sick husband's attention. Even Senator Hitchcock found it difficult to get audiences with him. Wilson might not have compromised with Lodge even if his health had been unimpaired. But his illness isolated him from the realities and from political advisers. It may have stiffened his determination to yield no further.

On September 10, 1919, the Foreign Relations Committee voted out the treaty but recommended forty-five amendments and four reservations. The Senate defeated those committee amendments and also Hitchcock's reservations. Instead, Lodge introduced fourteen reservations on November 6. One of them would have allowed the United States to determine whether it had fulfilled the necessary obligations for withdrawal from the League. Another said the United States would not have to accept a mandate territory under the League of Nations without congressional approval. The Lodge reservations further guarded domestic matters and the Monroe Doctrine from League authority. Another aimed to please Irish-Americans and Anglophobes by insisting that the United States would not be bound by Britain's six votes (that is, including the votes of Commonwealth states).

But the most important of the Lodge reservations dealt with Article X of the League Covenant. It was the heart of the whole system and stated:

The Members of the League undertake to respect and preserve as against external aggression the territorial integrity and existing political independence of all Members of the League. In case of any such aggression or in case of any threat or danger of such aggression the Council shall advise upon the means by which this obligation shall be fulfilled.

Wilson had repeatedly pointed out that the United States would have a veto in the Council. He insisted that Article X was a moral rather than a legal obligation and that Congress would retain its exclusive authority to declare war. Nevertheless, the second Lodge reservation said that the United States would assume

no obligation to preserve the territorial integrity or political independence of any other country . . . under the provisions of article 10, or to employ the military or naval forces of the United States under any article of the treaty for any purpose, unless, in any particular case the Congress . . . shall by act or joint resolution so provide.

Observers then and later disagreed on whether the Lodge reservations would or would not have destroyed the League's chances for success. Professor Thomas A. Bailey concluded that they would not. He believed the League of Nations would have had a better chance for success with the United States in (even with the Lodge reservations) than with the United States out. Top British and French leaders shared that view at the time, and those states probably would have acquiesced in the Lodge reservations as the price for American participation in the League of Nations. Professor Arthur S. Link appears to share or at least sympathize with President Wilson's opposite view. In any event, Wilson believed that the Lodge reservations, particularly the one dealing with Article X, would destroy the League's chances for preserving world peace. On that matter he would not compromise.

The Senate voted on the Versailles Treaty on November 19, 1919. When it included the Lodge reservations the Democrats under Wilson's control and the irreconcilables combined to defeat it. When they voted on it without the Lodge reservations, the irreconcilables and strong reservationists combined to defeat it. A later effort to win approval with the reservations on March 19, 1920, failed by a margin of seven votes. The treaty and membership in the League of Nations were dead so far as the United States was concerned.

Wilson hoped to make the presidential election of 1920 "a great and solemn referendum" on the League of Nations. Despite his poor health and the two-term tradition, he even considered the possibility of running for a third term to battle for American membership in the League. Cox and Roosevelt did their best for the cause, but went down to defeat at the hands of Harding's equivocation and popular desires for "normalcy." After his inauguration President Harding ignored his earlier talk of an association of states. In 1921 the United States made a separate peace with Germany in an agreement much like the Versailles Treaty but without the League of Nations Covenant.

Largely because of conditions in other parts of the world, Woodrow Wilson failed to get the kind of peace treaty he wanted. Largely because of influences within the United States, he failed to get Senate approval of the Versailles Treaty and American membership in the League of Nations. No one can know for certain what might have happened if the United States had approved the treaty and joined the League. But obviously the League did not prevent World War II without American participation. Many then and later believed a constructive role by the United States in the League of Nations might have increased the chances for enduring peace. Woodrow Wilson thought so anyway, and he battled with all his strength for that belief.

Then and later Wilson was the subject of bitter hatred and worshipful adoration. England's John Maynard Keynes and Harold Nicolson railed at him in their books and articles. Professor Hans Morgenthau and other "realists" made him the symbol for the worst in American attitudes toward foreign affairs. Professor Richard Hofstadter wrote that Wilson

> . . . appealed for neutrality in thought and deed, and launched upon a diplomatic policy that is classic for its partisanship. He said that American entrance into the war would be a world calamity, and led the nation in. He said that only a peace between equals would last, and participated in the *Diktat* of Versailles. He said that the future security of the world depended on removing the economic causes of war, and did not attempt even to discuss these causes at the Peace Conference. . . . He wanted desperately to bring the United States into the League, and launched on a course of action that made American participation impossible.

Professor Thomas A. Bailey advanced the shocking but probably correct view that "If he had died [after his great speaking tour] the United States probably would have entered the League, and the League might have been more successful." As Bailey saw it, "The genius of a Sophocles or a Shakespeare never created a tragedy more poignant than that of Woodrow Wilson." But Wilson's sympathetic biographer, Professor Arthur S. Link saw it differently:

> And so it was Wilson the prophet, demanding greater commitment, sacrifice, and idealism than the people could give, who was defeated in 1920. It is also Wilson the prophet who survives in history, in the hopes and aspirations of mankind and in whatever ideals of international service that the American people still cherish. One thing is certain, now that men have the power to sear virtually the entire face of the earth: The prophet of 1919 was right in his larger vision; the challenge that he raised then is today no less real and no less urgent than it was in his own time.

SUPPLEMENTARY READINGS

Adler, Selig. *The Isolationist Impulse: Its Twentieth-Century Reaction.* London and New York: Abelard-Schuman, Ltd., 1957.

Baker, Ray Stannard. *Woodrow Wilson and World Settlement.* 3 vols. Garden City, N.Y.: Doubleday & Co., Inc., 1923–1927.

Bailey, Thomas A. *Woodrow Wilson and the Great Betrayal.* New York: Macmillan Co., 1945.

_____. *Woodrow Wilson and the Lost Peace.* New York: Macmillan Co., 1944.

Bartlett, Ruhl J. *The League to Enforce Peace.* Chapel Hill: University of North Carolina Press, 1944.

Birdsall, Paul. *Versailles Twenty Years After.* New York: Reynal and Hitchcock Co., 1941.

Buehrig, Edward H. *Woodrow Wilson and the Balance of Power.* Bloomington: Indiana University Press, 1955.

Fleming, Denna F. *The United States and the League of Nations, 1918–1920.* New York: G. P. Putnam's Sons, 1932.

Gelfand, Lawrence E. *The Inquiry: American Preparations for Peace, 1917–1919.* New Haven, Conn.: Yale University Press, 1963.

Hofstadter, Richard. *The American Political Tradition and the Men Who Made It.* New York: Alfred A. Knopf, Inc., 1948.

Keynes, John Maynard. *The Economic Consequences of the Peace.* New York: Harcourt, Brace & Co., 1920.

Levin, N. Gordon Jr. *Woodrow Wilson and World Politics: America's Response to War and Revolution.* New York: Oxford University Press, Inc., 1968.

Link, Arthur S. *Wilson the Diplomatist: A Look at His Major Foreign Policies.* Baltimore: Johns Hopkins Press, 1957.

Mayer, Arno J. *Politics and Diplomacy of Peacemaking: Containment and Counterrevolution at Versailles, 1918–1919.* New York: Alfred A. Knopf, Inc., 1967.

Morgenthau, Hans J. *In Defense of the National Interest.* New York: Alfred A. Knopf, Inc., 1951.

Notter, Harley. *The Origins of the Foreign Policy of Woodrow Wilson.* Baltimore: Johns Hopkins Press, 1937.

O'Grady, Joseph P. (ed.). *The Immigrants' Influence on Wilson's Peace Policies.* Lexington: University of Kentucky Press, 1967.

Smith, Daniel M. *The Great Departure: The United States and World War I, 1914–1920.* New York: John Wiley & Sons, Inc., 1965.

Smith, Gene. *When the Cheering Stopped: The Last Years of Woodrow Wilson.* New York: William Morrow & Co., Inc., 1964.

Stromberg, Roland N. *Collective Security and American Foreign Policy from the League of Nations to NATO.* New York: Frederick A. Praeger, Inc., 1963.

Tillman, Seth P. *Anglo-American Relations at the Paris Peace Conference of 1919.* Princeton, N.J.: Princeton University Press, 1961.

Vinson, John C. *Referendum for Isolation: Defeat of Article Ten of the League of Nations Covenant.* Athens: University of Georgia Press, 1961.

Yates, Louis A. R. *United States and French Security, 1917–1921.* New York: Twayne Publishers, Inc., 1957.

31

The Good Neighbor Policy

The United States expanded its interests and modified its methods in Latin America from 1918 through 1941. During the decade following World War I, the United States continued its Dollar Diplomacy and Big Stick policies in the Caribbean and Central America. Beginning a bit under President Calvin Coolidge and developing impressively under Presidents Herbert Hoover and Franklin D. Roosevelt, the United States began to abandon its strong-arm methods and experimented more with goodwill tactics. Various considerations caused the change. Both urban and rural anti-imperialists spoke to the American conscience when they contrasted the nation's ideals with its practices in Latin America. Some businessmen and statesmen began to realize that the coercive methods hurt American interests by provoking anti-American emotions and policies. The need for foreign markets during the depression and the desire for friendly governments in the face of the growing Axis menace persuaded many that conciliatory methods might serve the United States better in Latin America than coercion.

World War I increased United States influence without altering its methods. Generally Latin Americans favored the Allies over the Central Powers, but they worried about the menace from the United States more than they did about the threat from Germany. The war diverted British and European trade and capital; businessmen and financiers from the United States eagerly filled the gap. Circumstances compelled the Latin

Americans to look to the United States for leadership in the defense of neutral rights from 1914 to 1917.

When the United States declared war in 1917, President Wilson urged Latin-American states to follow suit. Most of them did not do so. Of the twenty countries, only eight declared war. Seven of the eight were in the Caribbean and Central America. The United States had its Marines in Haiti and Nicaragua when those states joined the war. Brazil was the only South American state (and the only large Latin-American country) to declare war. Five other Latin-American countries broke relations with Germany. The remaining seven (including the major states of Mexico, Argentina, Chile, and Colombia) remained neutral throughout the war. None of the Latin-American belligerents provided more than token military contributions.

Eleven Latin-American countries sent delegations to the Paris Peace Conference after World War I, and ten of them ratified the Versailles Treaty. Initially, they enthusiastically supported the League of Nations. At one time or another all of the Latin-American states belonged to the League, though not all at the same time. Their motives varied, but many hoped the League would protect them from the United States. They saw the Monroe Doctrine as a unilateral policy designed to serve the United States, not Latin America. Many of them considered the regional Pan American Union as little more than a tool for the United States. Perhaps the League of Nations might serve Latin America better. When it did not, their enthusiasm languished. By World War II only nine of them remained in the League, and most of those were inactive. The League had not effectively guarded their interests, and the Good Neighbor Policy made the United States seem less ominous.

In the 1920's American businessmen increased their trade and investments in Latin America. During that decade of prosperity Latin America absorbed about one sixth of American exports and provided one fourth of its imports. The United States sold manufactured goods and bought minerals and tropical products such as sugar and coffee. Britain continued its commercial lead south of the equator, but America's proportion there grew. In Central America and the Caribbean the United States pushed far into the lead. The United Fruit Company, incorporated under Minor Keith's leadership in 1899, controlled much of the trade and productive capital in several states. Since those tropical countries relied heavily on their exports of one or two main products, changes in the American market or policies drastically affected their domestic prosperity and politics. By 1929 Americans had loaned and invested over $5.5 billion in Latin America, about the same as Britain. Most British capital was south of the equator; two thirds of American investments in Latin America were north of the equator, particularly in Cuba and Mexico. Businessmen, traders, and financiers in the 1920's easily got assistance from the United

States government, particularly from Secretary Herbert Hoover's Department of Commerce. That economic activity benefited many Latin Americans, but they resented their dependence on the American economy, and they feared the power behind that economic penetration.

In the 1920's no European or Asiatic states endangered the security of the United States in Latin America. Nevertheless, American troops stayed in Haiti and in 1927 returned to Nicaragua. The United States retained its treaty rights to intervene in such countries as Cuba, Panama, and Nicaragua. It maintained customs receiverships in Caribbean and Central American states. It continued to use the *de jure* theory of recognition to spank governments that displeased the United States.

With no external threats to force them to turn to the United States for protection, with continued evidence of the Big Stick policy, and with increasing American economic penetration, anti-Americanism grew rapidly in Latin America. Newspapers, politicians, and authors savagely denounced "Yankee Imperialism." Latin-American governments adopted tariffs and taxes discriminating against American businesses. The Pan Latin and Pan Hispanic cultural movements added to the general anti-American atmosphere. Statesmen at the Pan American Conference in Santiago, Chile, in 1923 criticized American policies. At the Conference in Havana, Cuba, five years later, denunciations of the United States reached unprecedented levels. Additional economic and military coercion by the United States promised to increase hostility and resistance. Consequently, for both practical and ideological reasons some Americans began to doubt the wisdom of the Big Stick policy. Late in the 1920's self-interest and ideology began to turn the United States away from the Big Stick toward what became the Good Neighbor Policy.

The United States' treatment of Colombia provided an early example of the relation between economic self-interest and conciliatory policies. That South American state still rankled at the loss of Panama, which it blamed on President Theodore Roosevelt and the United States. The Democratic administration of Woodrow Wilson offered a settlement and apology, but Theodore Roosevelt would admit to no wrongdoing, and his Republican friends in the Senate blocked action. With Roosevelt's death in 1919 more Republicans joined Democrats on the issue. But the final element in the compound was the economic interest of American oil companies. Persuaded that the Colombian government would discriminate against them in favor of British oil interests if the United States failed to assuage Colombian feelings (and finances), the oil companies urged a settlement. Consequently, in 1921 the United States paid Colombia $25 million, the amount it had wanted when it rejected the Hay-Herran convention nearly twenty years earlier. There was no formal apology, but it was implied. Anti-imperialist ideology, Democratic partisanship, and economic self-interest all helped to do the job. With Colombia appeased, American capitalists got access to the oil.

President Coolidge and his Secretaries of State, Charles Evans Hughes and Frank B. Kellogg, did not repudiate the methods of their predecessors, nor did they promise not to use coercion in the future. Nevertheless, they edged a bit away from the Big Stick. In 1924 the United States took its Marines out of the Dominican Republic, and temporarily removed them from Nicaragua the following year. The United States continued to hold out against Mexico's claims under Article 27 of its Constitution of 1917, which barred foreigners from owning subsoil minerals and petroleum. The United States insisted that Article 27 should not apply to oil lands obtained by American companies before the adoption of the Constitution. But the oil companies were not America's only economic interests in that state. In 1927 the administration sent Dwight W. Morrow of J. P. Morgan and Company to resolve the differences with Mexico. Morrow did not abandon business and financial interests, but he did use tact and suasion. American oil interests prevailed, but Morrow's methods improved relations.

Herbert Hoover had had far more experience in foreign affairs than his two predecessors in the White House. As Secretary of Commerce in the 1920's he had actively supported American businessmen in Latin America. But his Quaker beliefs made him unenthusiastic about the use of force, and his varied experiences abroad made him alert to the harmful diplomatic and economic effects of Big Stick methods. More than any of his twentieth-century predecessors, Hoover worked to improve relations with Latin America, though he did not abandon American economic interests there. Between his election in 1928 and his inauguration in 1929 Hoover made a goodwill tour of ten Latin-American countries. He referred in friendly terms to Latin America in his inaugural address and a few weeks later said, "It never has been and ought not to be the policy of the United States to intervene by force to secure or maintain contracts between our citizens and foreign States or their citizens."

In 1930 Hoover and his Secretary of State, Henry L. Stimson, abandoned Wilson's *de jure* theory of recognition in Latin America and returned to the *de facto* theory the United States had pursued during the eighteenth and nineteenth centuries. That is, under Hoover the United States stopped basing recognition on the grounds of morality or legality. Instead, the administration reverted to the older practice of extending recognition when a government was clearly in control of the state and could bind that state in its dealings in international affairs. Hoover and Stimson did not, however, extend that *de facto* theory to Central America, where a multilateral treaty specified other standards for recognition.

The Hoover administration removed the last of the Marines from Nicaragua in January, 1933. It would have taken them out of Haiti, too, except that Haiti rejected the terms for withdrawal. The administration turned its back on Americans who urged new interventions in one or another of the Latin-American states. And in 1930 the President authorized publication of the memorandum on the Monroe Doctrine prepared two years earlier by J. Reuben Clark, Jr., in the Department of State. Clark concluded that the Roosevelt Corollary was not justified by the Monroe Doctrine. He contended that the United States could not properly justify intervention in the internal affairs of a Latin-American state under the terms of the Monroe Doctrine. Hoover was not rejecting the right of intervention, but he did reject intervention in the name of the Monroe Doctrine.

The Great Depression destroyed Hoover's popularity in the United States, but his policies won approval in Latin America. When he sought reelection in 1932, Latin Americans generally preferred him over the Democratic nominee, Franklin D. Roosevelt. Latin Americans not only liked Hoover's policies, but they worried about Roosevelt. The Democratic candidate's name reminded them of his cousin's earlier Big Stick policies. Furthermore, as Assistant Secretary of the Navy under President Wilson, Franklin D. Roosevelt had helped with the interventionist policies in Haiti, the Dominican Republic, and elsewhere. The Democratic platform rejected "interference in the internal affairs of other nations," and it urged "cooperation with nations of the Western Hemisphere to maintain the spirit of the Monroe Doctrine." But the Republican platform had similar planks. In his first inaugural address on March 4, 1933, President Roosevelt said: "In the field of world policy, I would dedicate this nation to the policy of the good neighbor." He did not specifically focus that statement toward Latin America, however, and it was only a tiny part of the address.

If Latin Americans were less than ecstatic about Roosevelt's election, his administration's initial policies toward Cuba did not ease their misgivings. General Gerardo Machado had ruled Cuba ruthlessly since 1925. Violence erupted in 1931, and the depression increased disaffection. President Roosevelt acknowledged the importance of the developments when he named Sumner Welles to represent the United States in Cuba. In August, 1933, an army revolt ousted Machado. The next month Dr. Ramón Grau San Martín became President. A surgeon and professor at the University of Havana, Dr. Grau favored social and economic changes for the benefit of the poor. He denounced the privileged position of foreign business and capital.

Despite his earlier and later identification with goodwill methods, Welles urged military intervention by the United States (a course permitted under the Platt amendment). Some members of Roosevelt's Cabinet had financial interests in Cuba and favored Welles's recommendations. Roosevelt and Secretary of State Hull decided not to land Marines, but they did bring pressure against Dr. Grau. The United States refused to recognize his government. It became apparent that the American market for Cuban sugar might shrink if Dr. Grau remained. The President sent American naval vessels to Cuban waters. The real power behind Dr. Grau's administration, Colonel Fulgencio Batista and the army, saw the advantages of going along with American wishes. Batista abandoned Dr. Grau and supported his more conservative successor, Colonel Carlos Mendieta. That new government quickly won American recognition. The United States did not land troops in Cuba, but when he was deposed in January, 1934, Dr. Grau contended that he "fell because Washington willed it." Most Latin Americans agreed with him.

Though the beginnings were not promising from the Latin-American point of view, President Roosevelt and Secretary of State Hull soon made the Good Neighbor Policy their own. Roosevelt's Latin-American policies divided into two broad overlapping phases. From 1933 to 1938 the Roosevelt administration concentrated on eradicating remaining vestiges of the old Big Stick policies. From 1936 until Roosevelt's death in 1945 the United States built on the growing goodwill to lead Latin America to unity against Axis threats to the peace and security of the Western Hemisphere. The Great Depression had had disastrous effects on American economic relations with Latin America. Trade declined sharply, Latin-American debtors defaulted, investments went bad, and new private capital from the United States stopped going south. Nevertheless, through both phases of Roosevelt's Good Neighbor Policy America's relative position in the Latin-American economy grew.

In December, 1933, Secretary Hull set the tone for what was to follow when he personally headed the American delegation to the Seventh Pan-American Conference at Montevideo, Uruguay. Anti-Americanism was much in evidence, and few were sanguine about the results of the Conference. Hull, however, set about trying to convince the Latin Americans of the friendly intentions of the United States under its new President. The Latin Americans introduced a Convention on Rights and Duties of States that included a clause renouncing the right of any state "to intervene in the internal or external affairs of another." It aimed at the United States, and the Latin Americans expected Hull to oppose it. Instead, to their surprise and pleasure, Hull supported the Convention, reserving only such rights as the United States had by "the law of nations as generally recognized and understood." On his return trip to the United States, Hull visited a half-dozen Latin-American countries, where he emphasized America's goodwill and friendship. The Montevideo Conference did not erase the memory of the Big Stick, but it encouraged Latin Americans to hope that the Roosevelt administration was in fact dedicated to the policy of a Good Neighbor in the Western Hemisphere.

The Roosevelt administration concluded an executive agreement that led to the removal of American Marines from Haiti in 1934, nearly twenty years after they first went in. American treaty rights to intervene in Haiti expired in 1936. In 1941 the United States and Haiti signed an agreement that would end the customs receivership there by 1947. In 1934 the United States extended its *de facto* recognition policy to Central America, just as Hoover had earlier extended it to the rest of Latin America. In that same year the Roosevelt administration signed a treaty with Cuba abrogating the Platt amendment, except for the right to maintain a base at Guantanamo Bay. The United States gave up its treaty rights to intervene in Cuba and its several legal controls over Cuban sovereignty. Two years later the United States abandoned its treaty rights to intervene in Panama. At the Inter-American Conference at Buenos Aires, Argentina, in 1936, the United States renounced the right to intervene in the internal affairs of other American states and did not attach the reservation Hull had included at Montevideo three years before. In 1937 the United States abandoned its rights to use military force to protect transit across the Isthmus of Tehuantepec in southern Mexico.

After enactment of the Reciprocal Trade Agreements Act in 1934, the United States negotiated trade agreements with thirteen Latin American states by the end of 1941. The agreements were not as effective economically as Hull had hoped, but they were part of the general effort represented by the Good Neighbor Policy. Similarly, the Export-Import Bank created by the government in the middle of the 1930's provided loans for economic development and trade expansion in Latin America. Its operations were very limited at first but grew as World War II approached. At the same time, both government and private sources published much goodwill propaganda.

The supreme test for Roosevelt's Good Neighbor Policy came in 1938 when Mexico invoked Article 27 of its Constitution and expropriated foreign oil holdings. The action grew directly out of the refusal of the oil companies to meet workers' demands for substantial pay raises and various nonwage benefits. Under President Lázaro Cárdenas the Mexican government supported the workers' demands. When the oil companies refused to yield, President Cárdenas, on March 18, 1938, announced the expropriation of the oil properties. Mexicans united in cheering their government's action. Foreign companies exhausted every possible legal device in the futile effort to regain their holdings. They hired Donald Richberg, a former New Deal administrator, to represent them in negotiations with the Mexican government. They spent huge sums on propaganda to support their position. They boycotted the nationalized oil industry so that Mexico found it difficult to get technicians, equipment, tankers, and markets for its petroleum. The British government strongly supported the claims of the Royal Dutch Shell Oil Company and even broke diplomatic relations with Mexico. They and the American companies urged the United States government to throw its weight against the Mexican action. Some in the State Department favored a firm policy, and for a short time the United States stopped its purchases of Mexican silver.

President Roosevelt, however, rejected military intervention and acknowledged Mexico's right of expropriation. The United States government insisted only that Mexico pay adequately and promptly for the properties seized. Even that position left room for sharp differences. Mexico wanted ten years to pay and insisted that the price be based on the actual capital invested. The oil companies demanded that Mexico also pay for the petroleum still in the ground. In 1940 the Sinclair Oil Company reached a settlement with Mexico. And less than a month before Japan attacked Pearl Harbor, the United States and Mexico concluded an agreement on the matter. In the final settlement Mexico paid about one tenth the amount sought by the American companies. The settlement infuriated the oil firms. With the Roosevelt administration unwilling to back their demands, however, they had to take what they could get. The Roosevelt administration's performance further convinced Mexicans and other Latin Americans that the United States had in fact abandoned the old interventionist policies. The Good Neighbor Policy passed its most severe test.

The second phase of Roosevelt's Good Neighbor Policy began about 1936. Built on the accumulating goodwill, it emphasized multilateral responsibility for maintaining the peace and security of the Western Hemisphere, particularly in the face of the Axis menace. Prior to the 1930's the Monroe Doctrine was exclusively a unilateral United States policy; from 1936 onward the United States began to work with Latin-American countries to guard peace and security.

A quarter of a million Japanese lived in Latin America, particularly in Brazil and Peru. About six million persons of Italian ancestry lived in Latin America in the 1930's, more than any European nationality except for the Spanish and Portuguese. The Latin-American countries quickly and easily assimilated the Italians. Neither Japan nor Italy seriously endangered the United States or Latin America in the Western Hemisphere.

The threat from Nazi Germany, however, was more formidable. Nearly two million Germans lived in Latin America, and many of them retained their German citizenship. They concentrated particularly in southern Brazil, northern Argentina, and southern Chile. Not easily assimilated, many continued to use the German language and retain ties with the fatherland. Nazi Germany directed much propaganda toward Germans in Latin America. Furthermore, Hitler's Minister of Economics, Hjalmar Schacht, used barter arrangements, blocked currency, and aggressive sales techniques to challenge American and British economic supremacy there. Those efforts competed with Hull's multilateral reciprocal trade program, and they met with disturbing successes. The Nazis made little headway in the Caribbean and Central America, but south of the equator their growing penetration was alarming. In Colombia a German airline operated close to the Panama Canal until 1939. With the victories of German military forces under General Erwin Rommel early in World

War II, Americans worried about the closeness of West Africa to Brazil. Many exaggerated Nazi strength in Latin America, but they could not overlook the danger. So long as Roosevelt's efforts concentrated on hemispheric neutrality and security they could gain support from isolationists as well as internationalists.

On the initiative of President Roosevelt, the United States and Latin America held a special Inter-American Conference for the Maintenance of Peace at Buenos Aires, Argentina, in December, 1936. Secretary Hull led the American delegation, and President Roosevelt personally delivered an opening address there. The Conference agreed that the American states should consult in the event of war among them or in the event of a war outside the Western Hemisphere that might endanger hemispheric peace or security. The Conference did not provide the machinery for consultation, but the agreement to consult was the first major step in building multilateral responsibility for enforcing the Monroe Doctrine.

By the time of the eighth regular Pan-American Conference in Lima, Peru, two years later, the world situation had grown more alarming. Japan had renewed its aggression in China. Franco's Fascist forces were gaining control of Spain. Hitler's Nazi Germany had taken over Austria and part of Czechoslovakia. The Pan-American Conference approved the Declaration of Lima, which reaffirmed the agreement to consult and also provided the machinery for consultation. Under the Declaration of Lima any American state could call a meeting of the foreign ministers of the American states to consider threats to peace and security.

As a consequence of the Declaration of Lima, the First Meeting of Foreign Ministers of American Republics gathered in Panama City three weeks after Germany invaded Poland in September, 1939. The meeting approved a General Declaration of Neutrality. It created an Inter-American Financial and Economic Advisory Committee to consider economic problems caused by the war. In the Declaration of Panama it created a safety zone around the Western Hemisphere and warned belligerents not to conduct military operations within that zone.

In July, 1940, after the fall of France and during the Battle of Britain, the Western Hemisphere had a Second Meeting of Foreign Ministers in Havana, Cuba. Delegates there worried that Nazi Germany might seize Caribbean colonies of the European countries it had conquered. In the Act of Havana the Foreign Ministers agreed that if Germany threatened the colonies of France or the Netherlands in the Western Hemisphere, one or more American states could take them over and administer them while the danger lasted. They also agreed that an attack on any American state by a non-American state would be considered aggression against all.

The safety zone authorized at Panama was ineffective, and it was never necessary to invoke the Act of Havana. Nevertheless, those and other less publicized arrangements signaled an unusually cooperative pattern in inter-American relations. The Latin-American countries helped the United States in many ways before Pearl Harbor. For example, in 1939 the Dominican Republic offered the United States use of its territory for continental defense. In the spring of 1941 Panama gave the United States permission to use bases on its soil for hemispheric defense. At the same time, Mexico agreed to allow American military airplanes to fly over its territory. United States military advisers replaced German advisers in eleven Latin-American countries before Pearl Harbor. Latin-American governments cooperated in ousting Germans and Italians from commercial airline operations there. Several Latin-American countries agreed to sell most of their production of vital raw materials to the United States for defense production. At the same time, the United States tried to cushion the harmful effects of the war on the Latin-American economies.

With the Japanese attack on Pearl Harbor, nine Caribbean and Central American countries declared war on the Axis powers immediately. In addition, Mexico, Colombia, and Venezuela broke relations with the Axis by the end of December; all three had remained neutral in World War I. At the Third Meeting of Foreign Ministers at Rio de Janeiro, Brazil, in January, 1942, they agreed to recommend that all countries in the Western Hemisphere break relations with the Axis powers. The United States had hoped for a stronger resolution, but eighteen of the twenty Latin-American countries severed relations with the Axis before or shortly after the Rio Conference. Only Argentina and Chile refused to do so at that time. Similarly, most Latin-American countries cooperated in suppressing subversive activities and in severing economic ties with the Axis. With the conspicuous exception of Argentina, the Latin-American countries provided splendid cooperation and assistance to the United States during World War II. The Good Neighbor Policy, inspired as it was by a mixture of ideological, economic, and security considerations, served the interests of the United States in World War II far better than the Big Stick could have.

SUPPLEMENTARY READINGS

Bemis, Samuel Flagg. *The Latin American Policy of the United States: An Historical Interpretation.* New York: Harcourt, Brace & Co., 1943.

Brandes, Joseph. *Herbert Hoover and Economic Diplomacy: Department of Commerce Policy, 1921–1928.* Pittsburgh: University of Pittsburgh Press, 1962.

Cline, Howard F. *The United States and Mexico.* Rev. ed. Cambridge, Mass.: Harvard University Press, 1963.

Cox, Isaac J. *Nicaragua and the United States, 1909–1927.* Boston: World Peace Foundation, 1927.

Cronon, E. David. *Josephus Daniels in Mexico.* Madison: University of Wisconsin Press, 1960.

DeConde, Alexander. *Herbert Hoover's Latin American Policy.* Stanford, Calif.: Stanford University Press, 1951.

Dozer, Donald M. *Are We Good Neighbors? Three Decades of Inter-American Relations, 1930–1960.* Gainesville: University of Florida Press, 1959.

Duggan, Lawrence. *The Americas: The Search for Hemisphere Security.* New York: Henry Holt & Co., 1949.

Ellis, L. Ethan. *Frank B. Kellogg and American Foreign Relations, 1925–1929.* New Brunswick, N.J.: Rutgers University Press, 1961.

Ferrell, Robert H. *American Diplomacy in the Great Depression: Hoover-Stimson Foreign Policy, 1929–1933.* New Haven, Conn.: Yale University Press, 1957.

Gardner, Lloyd C. *Economic Aspects of New Deal Diplomacy.* Madison: University of Wisconsin Press, 1964.

Guerrant, Edward O. *Roosevelt's Good Neighbor Policy.* Albuquerque: University of New Mexico Press, 1950.

Hull, Cordell. *The Memoirs of Cordell Hull.* 2 vols. New York: Macmillan Co., 1948.

Martin, Percy A. *Latin America and the War.* Baltimore: Johns Hopkins Press, 1925.

Mecham, J. Lloyd. *The United States and Inter-American Security, 1889–1960.* Austin: University of Texas Press, 1961.

Olson, Paul R., and Hickman, C. Addison. *Pan American Economics.* New York: John Wiley & Sons, Inc., 1943.

Parks, E. Taylor. *Colombia and the United States, 1765–1934.* Durham, N.C.: Duke University Press, 1935.

Perkins, Dexter. *A History of the Monroe Doctrine.* Rev. ed. Boston: Little, Brown & Co., 1963.

Rippy, J. Fred. *Latin America and the Industrial Age.* 2d ed. New York: G. P. Putnam's Sons, 1947.

————. *Latin America in World Politics.* 3d ed. New York: F. S. Crofts & Co., Inc., 1938.

Smith, Robert F. *The United States and Cuba: Business and Diplomacy, 1917–1960.* New York: Bookman Assoc., 1960.

Wood, Bryce. *The Making of the Good Neighbor Policy.* New York: Columbia University Press, 1954.

————. *The United States and Latin American Wars, 1932–1942.* New York: Columbia University Press, 1966.

32

The United States and Europe, 1921-1941

During the two decades between World War I and World War II, Americans and their leaders heatedly debated various alternatives for the United States in world affairs. America groped for its proper role as a powerful state in an unstable and insecure international situation. In the 1920's, and particularly in the 1930's, millions of Americans favored continentalism, unilateralism, nonintervention in Europe, and opposed commitments for joint action with European states. Nevertheless, the transient isolationist triumphs in those decades constituted a rearguard action, a dying gasp for American isolationism. Fundamental developments both on the world scene and within the United States were destroying the bases for isolationism. Externally, the increasing interdependence of the world, the erosion of the old power balances, the rise of the Axis challenge, and the development of increasingly mobile and destructive weapons provided a world environment that challenged the adequacy of isolationist policies for American interests and security. Similarly, within the United States the growth of industry and finance, the rise of the city, and the decline of rural and small-town America weakened the domestic bases for isolationism.

RELATIONS WITH EUROPE IN THE REPUBLICAN ERA

During the Republican administrations of Warren G. Harding, Calvin Coolidge, and Herbert Hoover the United States negotiated numerous agreements with European states. The United States participated in international conferences and approved multilateral pacts on various matters. American businessmen and financiers actively expanded trade and investments all over the world, including Europe. The federal government supported that overseas business expansion. The United States did not literally isolate itself from the rest of the world. Many Americans in both parties urged internationalism and collective security policies. Nevertheless, through it all the United States refused to commit its power to the defense of peace and security in Europe. Even the multilateral pacts the United States approved aimed at making American involvement less necessary. Those patterns prevailed in political, military, and economic relations with Europe.

In the 1920's American relations with Britain and France cooled a bit, while relations with Germany improved. The United States did not establish diplomatic relations with the Soviet Union at all. The Democratic Wilson administration withheld recognition from the communist government of Russia, and the three Republican administrations continued that nonrecognition policy.

The United States sent observers to sessions of the League of Nations. It participated in nonpolitical conferences sponsored by the League or its specialized agencies. The United States never joined the League, however, and it never assumed collective security responsibilities in cooperation with the League.

Similarly, the United States did not join the World Court. Presidents Wilson, Harding, Coolidge, Hoover, and Roosevelt all favored American adherence to the protocol of the Permanent Court of International Justice. Many scholars and statesmen supported their position. In January, 1926, the Senate voted 76 to 17 to join the World Court; however, it attached five reservations. One would have prohibited the Court from giving an advisory opinion in any case involving the United States without American consent. Other members of the Court refused to accept that reservation. Compromise on the issue failed. In January, 1935, President Franklin D. Roosevelt and Secretary of State Cordell Hull tried to win Senate approval for American adherence to the protocol. They failed. The Hearst newspapers and Father Charles E. Coughlin of Michigan, among others, aroused massive opposition. A majority in the Senate voted for adherence, but fewer than the necessary two thirds. The United States never became a member of the Permanent Court of International Justice.

The United States participated in various armaments limitations conferences, but the results did not preserve peace and security. Americans and their leaders had many different attitudes toward disarmament. Some were doctrinaire pacifists. Others were progressives and radicals who believed that big business in general and munitions makers in particular promoted armaments races for their own profits. They saw patriotic and security arguments for military preparedness as either cynical or naïve camouflage for big-business profiteering. Millions believed that military preparations provoked international insecurity, arms races, friction, and war. Disarmament would reduce taxes and government expenditures. Americans hoped that armament limitations would make involvement abroad less necessary and less likely by reducing the military power of potential foreign adversaries.

Appropriately, the Washington Conference of 1921–1922 grew partly out of a disarmament resolution introduced by an isolationist, Senator William E. Borah of Idaho. Secretary of State Charles Evans Hughes seized the initiative, however, and shocked the delegates at the Conference into action with his dramatic disarmament proposals. The resulting Five Power Naval Treaty of 1922 limited the tonnage of capital ships of Great Britain, the United States, Japan, France, and Italy to a 5–5–3–1.7–1.7 ratio. That made it unnecessary for the United States to build beyond those limits. At the same time, the Four Power Pact ended the Anglo-Japanese Alliance of 1902 and to that extent made it less necessary for the United States to maintain a navy strong enough to fight those two naval powers at the same time (a most unlikely possibility anyway). The agreements concluded at the Washington Conference did not apply to smaller ships. They had no enforcement provisions. And they did not bind the United States to share security responsibilities either in Europe or Asia. Indeed, Secretary Hughes carefully shaped the treaties to make them acceptable to the Senate, including Borah's isolationists.

The Geneva Naval Conference of 1927 was even less successful. The United States, Great Britain, and Japan sent delegations, but France and Italy refused to participate. The Conference dealt with limiting cruisers and smaller ships to supplement the capital ship limitations in the earlier Five Power Pact. Technical Navy spokesmen in the British and American delegations set the tone for the negotiations. Britain, with its worldwide empire and long sea routes, wanted an agreement that would allow construction of numerous relatively inexpensive light cruisers with 6-inch manually operated guns. The United States, in contrast, with less extensive commitments and with much greater wealth, insisted on fewer but heavier cruisers mounting 8-inch mechanically operated guns. The Japanese tried to work out a compromise, but with naval officers dominating the proceedings both countries refused to yield. British and American officers thought partly in terms of a possible war between those two states. Undoubtedly military and diplomatic planners must anticipate every possible contingency, but fear of an Anglo-American war bordered on the ridiculous. In any event, compromise failed. Neither

Britain nor the United States would yield. With the collapse of the Geneva negotiations, a race in the construction of crusiers and other smaller vessels developed.

In 1930 at the London Naval Conference the Anglo-American differences on cruisers persisted. The Japanese demanded more than they had at Geneva. France insisted that it could not consider any armament limitations unless Britain and the United States agreed to consultative or collective security pacts to guard French security against Germany. Both Great Britain and the United States refused to make binding commitments to France. The naval officers of the several states continued to use technical arguments to obstruct agreement. The final treaty, in general, extended the Five Power Pact ratio to smaller naval vessels until 1936. It authorized equality in submarines. It included an escalator clause that allowed construction beyond treaty levels if any one of the states felt endangered by another country's naval expansion. The agreement disappointed the Japanese and strengthened extremists there. Unable to get security commitments from the United States and Great Britain, France refused to sign the treaty. When France would not sign, neither would Italy.

The World Disarmament Conference in Geneva beginning in 1932 wrestled with efforts at limiting both land and sea armaments. Fifty-nine countries, including the United States, sent delegations. But it quickly floundered on France's obsession with security, and on Britain's and America's unwillingness to commit themselves to consultative security pacts. As Professor Robert H. Ferrell phrased it: "The conference quickly reached the familiar impasse, of French demands for disarmament through security and American demands for security through disarmament." The Soviet Union urged complete disarmament, but the Conference did not seriously consider the idea. President Hoover proposed reducing armaments by one third, but nothing came of the suggestion. The Conference failure probably weakened moderates in Germany and played into the hands of Hitler's Nazis.

The Pact of Paris or Kellogg-Briand Pact of 1928 fitted into the same general pattern. It had the appearance of internationalism, but it did not bind the United States or any other country to responsibilities for enforcing the Pact. In April, 1927, French Foreign Minister Aristide Briand proposed that the United States and France sign a bilateral treaty outlawing war. He hoped such an agreement might commit the United States to the security of France against Germany. Senator William E. Borah, chairman of the Foreign Relations Committee, urged expanding the proposal to include all peaceful countries. That expansion would dilute and nullify Briand's original objective. Secretary of State Frank Kellogg took up the multilateral idea and pushed it vigorously. The Pact of Paris, signed in August, 1928, renounced war as an instrument of national policy. The Senate quickly approved it. Eventually most of the countries of the world ratified it, including Germany, Japan, and the Soviet Union. Some then and later insisted that the Pact of Paris, by outlawing war, made neutrality obsolete and obligated peace-loving states to enforce the Pact against warring states. Kellogg, Borah, and the Senate Foreign Relations Committee emphatically rejected that view. They insisted that by binding states to renounce war as an instrument of national policy (except for self-defense) it made armaments less necessary and war less likely.

The United States also demonstrated its unwillingness to assume responsibilities in Europe by its handling of the war debt controversy. During and immediately after World War I the United States government loaned over $10 billion to European governments. The largest loans went to the leading Allies, Britain, France, and Italy. Under the refunding agreements concluded in the 1920's, the European states were obligated to pay the United States government more than $22 billion in principal and interest over a period of sixty-two years.

The United States had entered World War I late, and its total military contribution was small relative to those of the European belligerents. Consequently, Europeans contended that the war debts were simply America's contribution to the common task of winning the war, and they should be canceled. Similarly, in the 1920's Europeans emphasized the economic relation between the reparations Germany owed the Allies and the war debts the Allies owed the United States government. They insisted that any reduction of reparations must be matched by lowering war debts. They further pointed out that they did not have gold enough to pay the debts, and America's protective tariffs made it impossible for them to pay through exports to the United States.

Americans rejected all of those arguments. They insisted the loans were business arrangements and must be paid. To cancel the debts would simply transfer the financial burden from Europeans to American taxpayers. So long as European governments found money to build armaments and finance welfare programs, Americans believed they could find the means for paying the war debts. Furthermore, the United States consistently refused to admit any relationship between reparations and war debts. And the tariff, according to Americans, was a domestic matter of no concern to European governments. Ironically, private American loans and investments helped Germany pay reparations to the Allied governments. Those reparations payments, in turn, helped European governments to pay on their war debts to the United States. When the Great Depression temporarily ended American loans and investments abroad, the whole structure came tumbling down.

In 1931 President Hoover belatedly tried to check the financial avalanche with a one-year moratorium on intergovernmental debts. It applied to both reparations and war debts. It did not cancel the obligations, but suspended payments on them for one year. Hoover hoped the moratorium would check financial collapse in Europe and, to that extent, restore world (and American) prosperity. More specifically, Americans had made substantial loans and investments in Germany. If German banks closed, those loans (and the banks and creditors that made them) could be wiped out. Nevertheless, the moratorium was "too little and too late." It did not prevent financial collapse in Central Europe. It did not restore European prosperity. It did not prevent many Americans from losing on their loans and investments in Germany. It did not restore prosperity in the United States. And it did not prevent the desperate German people from turning reluctantly to Adolf Hitler and his National Socialists as they sought a way out of their difficulties.

PRESIDENT ROOSEVELT AND EUROPE

Franklin D. Roosevelt became President in March, 1933. He was one of the most powerful personalities in American political history. By temperament he was outgoing and an activist. Roosevelt was not doctrinaire. He tended to improvise and experiment. He was an extremely talented politician. He was keenly alert both to the practical possibilities and the limitations of circumstances at home and abroad.

In more specific terms, Roosevelt was an internationalist, not an isolationist. During his first term he concentrated mainly on domestic matters related to the depression. That priority forced him to compromise with isolationists to win essential support for his New Deal program. That was particularly essential since many of the western agrarian progressives whose support he needed for New Deal measures were isolationists on foreign affairs. Under pressure from William Randolph Hearst in 1932 Roosevelt said he no longer favored American membership in the League of Nations. The New Deal's National Recovery Administration and Agricultural Adjustment Administration were in tune with economic nationalism. His influence on the London Economic Conference in 1933 was not on the side of internationalism. He signed the several neutrality acts into law.

Then and later, some believed that the President exaggerated isolationist strength. They believed he could have moved the nation toward internationalism more quickly and effectively if he had battled the isolationists more aggressively and directly. But Roosevelt never forgot that President Wilson had tried that after World War I and had lost. Roosevelt's one-sided victory over Republican Alf M. Landon in 1936 led the President to overconfidence. Consequently, he suffered a succession of reverses. Congress refused to adopt his court-packing proposal early in 1937. The President worried about isolationist denunciations of his

Quarantine speech in October, 1937. IIis efforts to purge conservative Democrats in the 1938 Democratic primaries failed. And in the congressional elections of 1938, voters substantially cut the Democratic majorities in both houses. As a result of the growing opposition, the President virtually stopped building his domestic New Deal program. And in foreign affairs he moved more slowly and cautiously than he would have preferred, and more slowly and cautiously than many of his internationalist advisers thought desirable and necessary.

Though an internationalist, Roosevelt was not utopian. The President realistically knew it took much more than words to accomplish goals in both domestic and world politics. He emphasized the need for cooperation among the great powers, particularly Anglo-American cooperation. Roosevelt loved the sea, was a disciple of Mahan, and had served as Assistant Secretary of the Navy. He considered sea power particularly essential to American security.

In analyzing President Roosevelt's approach to world affairs it is essential to distinguish between his general ideas on the one hand and his methods for implementing them on the other. In 1932 he spoke of "a difference between ideals and the methods of attaining them." He contended that "Ideals do not change, but methods do change with every generation and world circumstances." In his ideals Roosevelt was always a dedicated internationalist. In his methods he was more hesitant, uncertain, and ambiguous, and less candid.

Both external and internal conditions accounted for that uncertainty and groping on methods and tactics. On the world scene he did not know just what actions by the United States under his leadership might contribute most to world peace and security. Part of his difficulty was the timidity and division within and among European states. With France torn internally, with Britain dedicated to appeasement, and with the League of Nations floundering, Roosevelt could not find anything substantial to work with in Europe. He considered appeals to European leaders, offers to mediate, and consultative pacts. Roosevelt liked the idea of economic methods. He sometimes pursued actions parallel to, but independent of, those by European states and the League of Nations. On the domestic scene New Deal requirements and the power of isolationism forced the President to be cautious and ambiguous. Isolationism and the requirements of his domestic program compelled him to reject certain alternatives and to acquiesce at times in isolationist policies that he did not really want.

From 1939 onward, however, the circumstances changed both at home and abroad. In important ways those changes alarmed and disturbed the President. In Europe, World War II erupted, Nazi Germany attacked its neighbors, France fell, Britain fought off disaster in the Battle of Britain, and in the Russo-German War Nazi Germany overran Eastern Europe. Within the United States, conservative political opposition brought the New Deal to a standstill. Isolationist opposition grew more strident.

In other ways, however, those external and internal developments simplified the President's methodological difficulties. The countries that fought against the Axis in Europe no longer equivocated or wavered. When Winston Churchill took over the reins in May, 1940, Britain determined to resist Hitler's assaults and defeat the Axis adversaries. When Nazi Germany attacked the Soviet Union in June, 1941, Joseph Stalin made it clear that Russia would fight to the last. Both Britain and the Soviet Union were doing all they could to resist the Axis aggressors. Both sought all the help they could get from any source, including the United States. Europe provided both the urgent need and the opportunity to add America's power to the forces checking Axis aggression and trying to restore world peace and security.

Within the United States isolationist opposition provided very real difficulties for the President. Most Americans continued to oppose a declaration of war against the Axis until December 7, 1941. Nevertheless, in certain respects the President's position strengthened. Most Americans favored Britain over the Axis. Most considered the defeat of the Axis powers essential for American security and vital interests. Western agrarian progressives who had supported the New Deal now broke with the President. At the same time, however, conservative southern Democrats and conservative Republican businessmen in the East who had opposed the New Deal now rallied to the support of Roosevelt's foreign policies. The President was by no means a free agent in foreign affairs. Isolationist strength, opposition to a declaration of war, and Roosevelt's own political caution, kept him from being very bold and candid. Nevertheless, by 1940–1941 both the world and domestic situations enabled the President to develop his "all-out aid short of war" formula. It provided less aid to the states fighting the Axis than they wanted or needed. It was not enough to assure defeat of the Axis. But it helped sustain resistance. It was not utopian either at home or abroad. It was realistic in the sense that it provided the maximum assistance against the Axis abroad within the limits set by domestic circumstances in the United States.

Roosevelt's role in the World Economic Conference in 1933 illustrated the impact of isolationism and the requirements of the early New Deal. Operating on the assumption that the causes and solutions for the depression were largely on the world scene, the Hoover administration shared in planning a World Economic Conference to meet in London. In 1933 Roosevelt and Hull went along with the plans for the Conference. The states agreed to exclude war debts and reparations from consideration. The main topics were to be monetary stabilization and tariffs. Roosevelt was interested in international approaches, but in 1933 he con-

sidered them secondary to the establishment of a sound national economy. He would not endanger his domestic recovery program by entering
into sweeping international understandings. The President authorized
the American delegation headed by Secretary of State Hull to consider
bilateral trade agreements subject to Senate approval. Conceivably the
delegates might consider a temporary stabilization agreement. But the
President did not authorize them to conclude general tariff or monetary
stabilization agreements.

Except for a silver agreement negotiated by Senator Key Pittman of
Nevada, the Conference failed. Each country stressed different issues.
Each proposed different (even irreconcilable) solutions. The gold standard countries, led by France, clashed with those that Britain led. Each
wanted a stabilization agreement that would give it a special advantage
over the others in international exchange. In the midst of the confusion
President Roosevelt sent Raymond Moley on a much-publicized special
mission to the London Conference. Moley negotiated a joint statement
with Britain and the gold bloc countries that they would try to stabilize
currencies within the limits of their individual situations. President
Roosevelt promptly responded with his famous "bombshell" message rejecting the Moley statement and any other stabilization agreement at
that time. According to the President, the states should first stabilize
their internal economies before attempting international monetary
agreements. The Conference probably would have failed with or without
Roosevelt's message, but it provided the *coup de grâce*. Economic nationalism carried the day, and all the major states (including the United
States) shared the responsibility for the failure.

A particularly vivid expression of, and force for, isolationism from
1934 to 1936 was the Senate Investigation of the Munitions Industries
headed by Senator Gerald P. Nye of North Dakota. The investigation
emerged from disillusionment with the results of World War I. It grew
out of a passionate determination to prevent the United States from becoming involved in any future European wars. In addition, however, the
Nye committee emerged from domestic considerations within the United
States. It was part of the antibusiness attitudes widely shared in the depression years. In 1934 the probe was as antibusiness as it was antiwar.
In other words, partly it grew out of the same general attitudes that
spawned the New Deal. The Nye committee acknowledged the importance
of noneconomic causes for wars, but it believed the drive for profits
played a large role in involving the United States in foreign wars. It
focused its attacks on shipbuilders, munitions manufacturers, and international bankers, but it insisted that war prosperity affected the foreign
policy attitudes of many in all sectors of the population.

In 1935–1936 the investigation also began to attack the warmaking potential of the executive branch of the government. It criticized the War

Department, the Navy Department, the Department of Commerce, and the Department of State. And it also began to see the President as part of the compound. At first it considered the President an unfortunate victim of irresistible pressures from urban economic interests. By the latter part of the 1930's, however, Nye and others began to see the President as a force for war quite as dangerous as munitions makers and international bankers.

After extensive and widely publicized hearings, the Nye committee proposed the enactment of laws to restrict the warmaking potential of both urban economic groups and the executive branch of the government. It urged government ownership of munitions industries and wanted to tax the profits out of war. Congress did not enact most of its proposals. Those that Congress adopted were not as rigid as the committee wanted. And those Nye committee proposals that became law were all repealed before the United States became a belligerent in December, 1941. Nevertheless, the Nye committee publicized and popularized isolationist views. And from 1935 to 1937 it helped lead to the enactment of a series of neutrality laws designed to insure that the United States would never again enter a European war.

Most political leaders in the 1930's said they favored neutrality legislation, but they differed widely on the kind of legislation they wanted. Internationalists led by Roosevelt and Hull wanted discretionary authority for the President to discriminate against aggressor states in support of the victims of aggression. They hoped such discretionary authority might help prevent wars and check aggressors. Traditionalists, led by Senators William E. Borah of Idaho and Hiram Johnson of California, wanted to defend conventional neutral rights, including the right to trade with belligerents in noncontraband goods. Isolationists, led by Senators Gerald P. Nye, Arthur H. Vandenberg of Michigan, and Bennett Champ Clark of Missouri, wanted mandatory legislation to restrict both the President and urban economic groups. They thought the discriminatory authority sought by internationalists would put the United States on one side in a war and would inevitably bring the nation into that war. They did not think neutral rights were worth defending if that defense put the United States in a war. They wanted to abandon neutral rights on the high seas and to bind the President to treat all belligerents alike in the interests of noninvolvement. The laws actually enacted fell short of the desires of isolationists, but they were closer to their views than to those of the internationalists or traditionalists.

Though technically not neutrality legislation, the Johnson Act of 1934 fitted the general pattern. It specified that governments that defaulted on war debt payments to the United States could not borrow from private American citizens or firms. It defined default to include both nonpayment and partial payment of amounts due at a particular time. If it hoped to pressure European governments to pay on their war debts, it failed. Britain had been making partial payments, but it stopped all payments after the Johnson Act. The law probably was more of an angry nationalistic slap at Europeans than any real effort to win further payments. Many isolationists hoped it would prevent the development of financial ties that might involve the United States in European wars.

Congress adopted the first Neutrality Act in August, 1935. A temporary measure, Congress amended and extended it in February, 1936. The Neutrality Act of 1936 expired in May, 1937. And President Roosevelt signed the so-called "permanent" Neutrality Act on May 1, 1937. The details in the three laws varied, but they had general characteristics in common. All of them reflected the rationale of the Nye munitions investigation. All three Neutrality Acts included a mandatory arms embargo that prohibited the sale of munitions to all belligerents. The President could not discriminate against an aggressor in applying the ban. That arms embargo was consistent with the theory that profits and prosperity from the sale of munitions to belligerents had helped involve the United States in World War I. The Neutrality Acts of 1936 and 1937 included a ban on private loans to all belligerents. It supplemented the Johnson Act and fitted the theory that the United States had entered World War I partly because of its financial involvement on the side of the Allies. In one form or another each of the three Neutrality Acts prohibited American citizens from traveling on belligerent ships. That provision aimed to prevent incidents such as the sinking of the *Lusitania* in World War I, when the loss of American lives on that British merchant ship helped to arouse anti-German interventionist sentiment in the United States. And finally, the Neutrality Act of 1937 included cash-and-carry provisions until May 1, 1939. They specified that belligerents buying nonembargoed goods in the United States must pay cash and carry those products away in non-American ships. Belligerent destruction of those ships and cargoes might be less likely to arouse interventionist responses in the United States than if they were American owned and manned.

In January, 1937, in separate legislation, Congress extended the arms embargo to both sides in the Spanish Civil War. Ironically, the Roosevelt administration urged that action and eventually Senator Nye opposed it. The administration's policy, in effect, worked to the advantage of the fascist forces of General Franco in Spain. The President may have acted partly to appease the largely urban Catholic voters in the United States. His course also paralleled the noninterventionist policies of France and Great Britain.

Through quiet behind-the-scenes inquiries and explorations in the 1930's, President Roosevelt tried to find ways to preserve peace in Europe, but those efforts failed. Not until 1939 did he begin to battle aggressively to lead the nation to internationalist steps short of war to check Axis aggression. Even then he was more cautious and less frank than many internationalists preferred. As war drew near in 1939 Roosevelt and Hull would have liked complete repeal of the Neutrality Act. Since that was not possible politically, they tried to persuade Congress to repeal the arms embargo and reenact the cash-and-carry provisions, which expired on May 1, 1939. The British and French would control the seas in any European war, so such a law would operate to their advantage and against the Axis. Despite every effort, however, the administration failed. Even a dramatic White House conference between the President, Hull, and Senate leaders failed to break the jam. When war in Europe began on September 1, 1939, the Neutrality Act of 1937 (including the arms embargo) was still binding—except that the cash-and-carry provisions had expired four months before. But Roosevelt's failure to win revision of the Neutrality Act in the spring and summer of 1939 was the last defeat he suffered at the hands of isolationists in Congress. After the European war began, the isolationists never again defeated an administration proposal in Congress.

With the coming of war, President Roosevelt proclaimed American neutrality, but he did not appeal for neutrality in thought as Wilson had done. The President called a special session of Congress and urged repeal of the arms embargo and reenactment of cash-and-carry. Still fearful of isolationist strength, however, neither Roosevelt nor Hull publicly based those recommendations on the ground of protecting American security by helping Britain and France. In his message to Congress the President said: "I give you my deep and unalterable conviction . . . that by the repeal of the embargo the United States will more probably remain at peace than if the law remains as it stands today. I say this because with the repeal of the embargo, this Government clearly and definitely will insist that American citizens and American ships keep away from the immediate perils of the actual zones of conflict." In that key passage the President was citing the merits of cash-and-carry as an argument for repealing the arms embargo—even though the two were not causally related except in a political sense.

Since most Americans wanted cash-and-carry, the main debate centered on repeal of the embargo. Isolationists or noninterventionists insisted that repeal would be an unneutral attempt to aid the Allies, that it would be a step to war for the United States, and that the Allies were not fighting for democracy but for the defense of their empires and power dominance. Internationalists or interventionists contended that the embargo helped the Axis against the democratic Allies, that repeal would not involve the United States in the war, and that it would enable the United States to expand the munitions manufacturing facilities essential for national defense. Like the President, most who urged repeal of the embargo did not explicitly justify it in terms of aiding the allies against the Axis. After heated debate Congress passed and the President signed the Neutrality Act of November, 1939. It was a compromise between isolationism and internationalism, but its total effect helped the struggle against Nazi Germany. With the repeal of the embargo Americans could now sell munitions to Britain and France. Reenactment of cash-and-carry appeased isolationists, but under its terms the British and French, who controlled the seas, could get products in the United States while Germany could not.

Hitler's blitzkrieg had crushed Poland by the time the embargo was repealed. During the winter of 1939–1940 there was a temporary lull in the fighting. The headlines did not go to Hitler but went instead to the war between the Soviet Union and Finland. American sympathies were wholly with the Finns ("who paid their war debts to the United States") against communist Russia. But Americans were no more eager to get involved there than in Western Europe. The United States provided some material aid for Finland, but it was "too little and too late." Inevitably the Soviet Union triumphed over Finland.

The winter lull did not last long. In April, 1940, Adolf Hitler's forces overwhelmed Denmark and Norway. On May 10, the German armies drove into the Netherlands, Belgium, and Luxembourg. Within a few days the blitzkrieg was rolling into northern France. Less than a month after the attack began, the British army in Europe was driven into the sea at Dunkirk. With France reeling from the blows of the German assault and from its own internal weakness, Italy chose to attack the unhappy nation from the south. Finally, with the Germans in control of their capital city and considerably over half of their area, the French under Marshall Petain signed an armistice with Hitler on June 22, 1940. Even before the fall of France the German *Luftwaffe* began its assault on the British Isles. By August and September of 1940 the Battle of Britain was well under way. At the same time, the German submarines took a heavy toll of British shipping. The outlook for the Western democracies in Europe was indeed dismal in 1940.

Those alarming developments added to the earnestness and the passions of the foreign policy debate in the United States. The noninterventionist America First Committee and the interventionist Committee to Defend America by Aiding the Allies provided leadership and forums for that heated debate. But public opinion polls indicated that with the fall of France and the Battle of Britain the President's aid-short-of-war approach won the upper hand and isolationists slipped to a minority status. From the middle of 1940 onward, the polls consistently showed that most Americans believed it was more important for the United States to assure a British victory over the Axis than it was for the United States to stay out of the European war. While the election did not provide voters with clear alternatives on foreign affairs, President Roosevelt's election in November, 1940, to an unprecedented third term freed him to move ahead more rapidly with his efforts to arm America and to aid the victims of aggression.

In June, 1940, Roosevelt appointed Henry L. Stimson to be Secretary of War and Frank Knox to be Secretary of the Navy. Both were militant interventionists. Since both were Republicans, the appointments gave the appearance of bipartisanship to Roosevelt's defense and foreign policies. On September 3, 1940, the administration announced an executive agreement that provided for the transfer of fifty overaged American destroyers to Great Britain in exchange for bases in British possessions in the Western Hemisphere. Britain needed the destroyers to guard its supply lines from German submarines and airplanes. American bases in its colonies would relieve Britain of security burdens there, while helping the United States with hemispheric defense. On September 16, 1940, President Roosevelt signed the first peacetime military conscription law in American history.

After the election of 1940 the question of America's course when Britain could no longer pay cash came increasingly under consideration. In a long letter to President Roosevelt on December 8, Prime Minister Winston Churchill described Britain's needs and warned that the time was coming when England would "no longer be able to pay cash." He also pointed out that if Great Britain were "divested of all saleable assets" it would cause "cruel privations" in Britain and "widespread unemployment in the United States" after the war. Reminding the President "that the defeat of the Nazi and Fascist tyranny is a matter of high consequence to the people of the United States and to the Western Hemisphere," Churchill expressed confidence that Roosevelt would find the "ways and means" to cope with the crisis. At his press conference on December 17, 1940, President Roosevelt described his plan "to eliminate the dollar sign" in aiding Great Britain. In his fireside chat on December 29, he vividly portrayed the disastrous consequences to American security if Britain fell or agreed to a negotiated peace. He called upon Americans to make the United States "the great arsenal of democracy." In his message on January 6, 1941, the President urged Congress to pass legislation to implement his lend-lease idea.

During the next two months the United States witnessed one of the most spirited and important debates in the history of American foreign affairs. In and out of Congress, Americans argued the need, the merits, and the dangers of the President's proposal. The White Committee and America First threw their full resources into the contest. On February 8, the House of Representatives passed H.R. 1776 by a vote of 260 to 165. The Senate approved it a month later, 60 to 31. The measure Roosevelt signed into law on March 11, 1941, authorized him to "sell, transfer title to, exchange, lease, lend, or otherwise dispose of" any "defense article" to "the government of any country whose defense the President deems vital to the defense of the United States."

Revision of the Neutrality Act in 1939 enabled Britain and its allies to buy American goods (including munitions) on a cash-and-carry basis. The Lend-Lease Act resolved the problem of financing and allocating aid to Britain and other countries. Much of the foreign policy controversy from March through November, 1941, focused on the "carry" part of cash-and-carry. Lend-Lease materials would not help Britain's struggle against the Axis if German submarines sent them to the bottom of the ocean.

In the spring of 1941 Secretary of War Henry L. Stimson and other interventionists urged the President to use the American Navy to escort British convoys. Isolationists vigorously opposed, believing that convoys would mean war for the United States. Roosevelt decided not to seek congressional authorization for convoys, fearing that he would be defeated in a vote on the issue. Instead, he ordered naval "patrols" designed to render maximum aid to Britain, short of actual convoys, against Axis raiders in the western Atlantic. In April, 1941, American warships began to trail German submarines in areas outside the war zones and report their positions to British convoys and airplanes. In that same month the United States occupied Greenland and declared that the Red Sea was no longer a war zone.

In an address on May 27, 1941, President Roosevelt said: "The delivery of needed supplies to Britain is imperative. This can be done; it must be done; it will be done." He announced the extension of American patrols but did not call specifically for convoys. In his address the President reasserted the doctrine of freedom of the seas and proclaimed a state of unlimited national emergency. Early in July, 1941, the United States took over the defense of Iceland. Subsequently the American Navy extended its patrols and convoyed American and Icelandic ships as far as Iceland.

The policies of the American and German governments combined to prevent incidents involving American ships on the Atlantic Ocean during the first twenty months of the European war. No ship flying the American flag was sunk by a German submarine until May 21, 1941, when the Germans sent the *Robin Moor*, an American merchant vessel, to the bottom of the South Atlantic with no loss of life. During the last half of 1941 the number of shooting incidents increased, but no Americans lost their lives on any ship flying the American flag until October, 1941. On August 17, the *Sessa*, an American-owned merchant ship under Panamanian registry, was torpedoed near Iceland. One casualty was an American. On September 4, a German submarine missed with two torpedoes fired at the *Greer*, an American destroyer. The *Steel Seafarer*, flying the American flag, was bombed in the Red Sea on September 5, with no loss of life. German subs torpedoed three other American-owned ships flying the flag of Panama later in September.

As a consequence of the attacks on American ships, on September 11, 1941, President Roosevelt delivered his famous "shoot-on-sight" address. He accused the German submarine of firing on the *Greer* first "without warning and with deliberate design to sink her." He labeled this "piracy legally and morally." (He neglected to mention that the *Greer* had been trailing the submarine for hours before the submarine finally fired upon its pursuer.) He warned of Hitler's plan to control the oceans. The President ordered the American Navy to attack German and Italian ships wherever found within the patrol zones without waiting for them to attack first. In the undeclared naval war that followed, a German submarine torpedoed the *Kearny*, an American destroyer, on October 17, with the loss of eleven lives.

On October 9, 1941, President Roosevelt urged Congress to repeal the "crippling provisions" of the Neutrality Act. Specifically, he wanted to permit arming of American merchant ships and to allow them to enter combat zones. That meant repeal of the "carry" part of cash-and-carry. The President said the changes would "not leave the United States any less neutral than we are today, but will make it possible for us to defend the Americas far more successfully, and to give aid far more effectively against the tremendous forces now marching toward conquest of the world." As before, Americans in and out of Congress heatedly debated the issue. Isolationists led by the America First Committee insisted that repeal of the vital provisions of the Neutrality Act would be a long step toward war for the United States. But once again the administration's short-of-war formula prevailed. Public opinion polls showed that a majority of Americans approved the President's proposals. Both houses of Congress adopted the revisions, and they became law with Roosevelt's signature on November 17, 1941.

Within limits, President Roosevelt's European policies in 1939–1941 succeeded. By the end of November, 1941, he had authority to do almost everything to aid Great Britain and the Soviet Union against Germany except send the American Army and Air Force into the battle. He could supply Lend-Lease aid. His "shoot-on-sight" policy was an undeclared naval war on Axis ships in the western Atlantic. With the repeal of the vital provisions of the Neutrality Act, armed American merchant ships protected by the American Navy could carry goods all the way to England. And a majority of Americans in and out of Congress supported those actions. That aid short of war helped sustain resistance to Axis aggression.

Nevertheless, aid short of war was not enough to defeat the forces of Hitler and Mussolini in Europe. Stimson, Knox, and others in the President's Cabinet emphasized that inadequacy, and so did Fight for Freedom, the interventionist pressure group. They urged Roosevelt to speak frankly to the American people and to ask Congress to vote a declaration of war on Germany. In 1941 the President probably realized that aid short of war would not be enough to crush the Axis. He feared defeat in Congress, however, if he abandoned his short-of-war approach. He may have been right. According to public opinion polls, approximately 80 percent of Americans opposed a declaration of war by the United States before the Japanese attacked Pearl Harbor. Isolationist opposition in Congress increased. In the summer of 1941 the House of Representatives adopted draft extension by a margin of only one vote. Less than a month before Pearl Harbor the vote against the administration on repeal of the vital provisions of the Neutrality Act was greater than the opposition vote had been against repeal of the arms embargo in 1939 or against Lend-Lease early in 1941. A shift of ten votes in the House of Representatives would have prevented revision of the Neutrality Act in the fall of 1941.

President Roosevelt and most Americans saw the Axis led by Hitler's Nazi Germany as a terribly dangerous and evil external threat to American (and world) peace, security, and freedom. The President believed his policies gave the maximum assistance the American people were willing to provide for the struggle against the European Axis before Pearl Harbor. Despite pressure from Secretary Stimson and others, Roosevelt's fear of noninterventionist strength prevented him from putting the issue of war or peace squarely before Congress until after Japan attacked Pearl Harbor. As Stimson wrote later, "the impasse into which America had thought herself in 1941 might have continued indefinitely if that had been the will of the Axis." Japan's attack on December 7, 1941, broke that impasse.

SUPPLEMENTARY READINGS

Adler, Selig. *The Uncertain Giant, 1921–1941: American Foreign Policy Between the Wars.* New York: Macmillan Co., 1965.

Barnes, Harry Elmer (ed.). *Perpetual War for Perpetual Peace: A Critical Examination of the Foreign Policy of Franklin Delano Roosevelt and Its Aftermath.* Caldwell, Idaho: Caxton Printers, Ltd., 1953.

Beard, Charles A. *American Foreign Policy in the Making, 1932–1940.* New Haven, Conn.: Yale University Press, 1946.

————. *President Roosevelt and the Coming of the War, 1941: A Study in Appearances and Realities.* New Haven, Conn.: Yale University Press, 1948.

Cole, Wayne S. *Senator Gerald P. Nye and American Foreign Relations.* Minneapolis: University of Minnesota Press, 1962.

Current, Richard N.   *Secretary Stimson: A Study in Statecraft.* New Brunswick, N.J.: Rutgers University Press, 1954.

Divine, Robert A.   *The Illusion of Neutrality.* Chicago: University of Chicago Press, 1962.

_____. *The Reluctant Belligerent: American Entry into World War II.* New York: John Wiley & Sons, Inc., 1965.

Drummond, Donald F.   *The Passing of American Neutrality, 1937–1941.* Ann Arbor: University of Michigan Press, 1955.

Ellis, L. Ethan.   *Frank B. Kellogg and American Foreign Relations, 1925–1929.* New Brunswick, N.J.: Rutgers University Press, 1961.

Ferrell, Robert H.   *American Diplomacy in the Great Depression: Hoover-Stimson Foreign Policy, 1929–1933.* New Haven, Conn.: Yale University Press, 1957.

_____. *Peace in Their Time: The Origins of the Kellogg-Briand Pact.* New Haven, Conn.: Yale University Press, 1952.

Hull, Cordell.   *The Memoirs of Cordell Hull.* 2 vols. New York: Macmillan Co., 1948.

Langer, William L., and Gleason, S. Everett.   *The Challenge to Isolation, 1937–1940.* New York: Harper & Bros., 1952.

_____. *The Undeclared War, 1940–1941.* New York: Harper & Bros., 1953.

Moulton, Harold G., and Pasvolsky, Leo.   *War Debts and World Prosperity.* Washington, D.C.: Brookings Institution, 1932.

O'Connor, Raymond G.   *Perilous Equilibrium: The United States and the London Naval Conference of 1930.* Lawrence: University of Kansas Press, 1962.

Pratt, Julius W.   *Cordell Hull.* 2 vols. New York: Cooper Square Publishers, Inc., 1964.

Sherwood, Robert E.   *Roosevelt and Hopkins: An Intimate History.* New York: Harper & Bros., 1948.

Stimson, Henry L., and Bundy, McGeorge.   *On Active Service in Peace and War.* New York: Harper & Bros., 1948.

Tansill, Charles C.   *Back Door to War: The Roosevelt Foreign Policy, 1933–1941.* Chicago: Henry Regnery Co., 1952.

Tate, Merze.   *The United States and Armaments.* Cambridge, Mass.: Harvard University Press, 1948.

Trefousse, Hans L.   *Germany and American Neutrality, 1939–1941.* New York: Bookman Associates, 1951.

Vinson, John C.   *The Parchment Peace: The United States Senate and the Washington Conference, 1921–1922.* Athens: University of Georgia Press, 1955.

Wiltz, John E.   *In Search of Peace: The Senate Munitions Inquiry, 1934–1936.* Baton Rouge: Louisiana State University Press, 1963.

33

The road to Pearl Harbor

The attack on Pearl Harbor culminated long-term trends and tendencies in relations between the United States and Japan. For half a century after Commodore Matthew C. Perry visited Japan in 1853–1854 the two countries generally had satisfactory relations. But Japan's impressive triumphs in the Russo-Japanese War of 1904–1905 marked a turning point in Japanese-American relations. From 1905 until the end of World War II American and Japanese interests in East Asia and the western Pacific often conflicted. Leaders in both countries worried about the threat represented by the growing power of the other. Japan's opportunism in using World War I to strengthen its position in China increased American fears. President Wilson tried unsuccessfully to block Japanese demands at the Versailles Conference. Relations improved during the prosperity decade of the 1920's, but they sharply worsened during the depression of the 1930's. The various patterns led to war by the end of 1941.

Numerous considerations aroused American concern about Japanese expansion. Annexation of the Philippines in 1899 gave the United States a territorial "Achilles heel" in the western Pacific that Japanese expansion endangered. America's greatest interest and activity in East Asia had been in northern China, Korea, and Manchuria, where Japan (and the Soviet Union) were most active and powerful. Consequently, Japanese expansion there alarmed the United States more (and Great Britain and France less) than if Japan had concentrated on other parts of Asia. In the 1930's the danger increased as Japan moved into accord with Nazi Germany and Fascist Italy. By 1940–1941 the three Axis powers loomed as a terrifying totalitarian combination aimed at conquering the world. With the European states either conquered or fighting for survival against Germany and Italy, the United States was the only major power capable of challenging Japanese conquest of East Asia.

In addition, attachment to the Open Door policy in China affected American responses to Japanese moves. The Open Door policy aimed at equality of opportunity in China. It also urged maintenance of Chinese independence and territorial integrity. When enunciated by Secretary Hay in 1899–1900, the Open Door policy was a weak verbal effort to guard American economic, missionary, and security interests against the ambitions and power of imperialistic states active in East Asia. The United States lacked the power and the will to enforce the Open Door, but the idea seized the imaginations of Americans and their leaders. Their dedication to the Open Door stiffened American opposition to Japanese ambitions in China. Secretary Hull, particularly, translated Japanese-American differences into the moralistic terms of the Open Door, the right of self-determination, the sanctity of treaties, and the immorality of aggression.

Both external and internal considerations prompted Japanese expansion in Asia and the Pacific area. Japan determined to guard its national security against external threats. As Chiang Kai-shek and his Kuomintang gave leadership and power to Chinese nationalism and antiforeign sentiments by the latter part of the 1920's, Japan feared the Chinese challenge to its special interests in East Asia. Later the growing power of Chinese Communists in northern China added to Japanese security concerns there. Russian and Japanese interests had chronically conflicted in northeast Asia. The consolidation of political power by the Communists under Lenin and Stalin, the industrial development under Stalin's five-year plans, and eventually the increasing military might of the Soviet Union portended future dangers to Japanese interests and security. By 1939–1941 the Axis triumphs in Europe made Great Britain, France, the Soviet Union, and the Netherlands too weak to block Japanese expansion. Japanese leaders believed that Chinese and Russian power posed threats to Japan; the preoccupation of European states elsewhere gave Japan a splendid opportunity to win the dominant position it considered essential for its vital interests and national security in East Asia and the western Pacific. Only China and the United States stood in Japan's way.

In addition to external reasons for Japanese expansion, there were also internal explanations. Part of the domestic influences arose from intense Japanese nationalism and hostility to European (and American) imperialism in Asia. Some of the bases lay in Japanese ideologies comparable to American Manifest Destiny ideas earlier. The Japanese believed Japan had a natural right to a special position in the Far East much like the special position of the United States in North America. Some called for a Japanese Monroe Doctrine for Asia. The military in general and the Army in particular provided an additional domestic influence behind Japanese expansion. Top military officers often came from the same families that included business and political leaders. In the 1920's the civilians generally had the upper hand, but in the crises of the 1930's military initiative and control grew. Most of the more disturbing (and tragic) Japanese actions in foreign affairs (including the attack on Pearl Harbor) grew out of military influence, particularly Army influence.

In addition, economic problems and aspirations encouraged Japanese expansion in the 1930's. Japan's economic difficulties emerged from enduring conditions within its home islands. It had a relatively small area, and much of that was not suitable for agriculture. Japan's dense population could not survive on the soil and sought employment in urban workshops and factories. Its industries grew, but they were handicapped by capital shortages, inadequate supplies of raw materials, and by tiny home markets. The world depression of the 1930's made those internal economic problems acutely serious. The depression cut the ability and willingness of other countries to buy Japanese products. Many countries (including the United States) discriminated against Japanese goods with increased tariffs and import restrictions. Japan's foreign trade dropped 50 percent from 1929 through 1931. If Japan could not sell abroad, it could not buy the raw materials its factories required. It could not sustain an acceptable standard of living for its growing population. And it could not build and maintain the wealth and military forces believed essential for its power, prestige, and security. Japanese leaders hoped to guard national security and restore economic prosperity through expansion in East Asia and the western Pacific. By building a Greater East Asia Co-Prosperity Sphere Japan could assure access to essential raw materials needed for its industrial production and military machine. It could control markets for its industrial products and surplus capital. It could find outlets for its surplus population. And the military preparations and actions to accomplish that Greater East Asia Co-Prosperity Sphere could themselves stimulate prosperity.

Given those external security considerations and domestic influences, most leaders believed it essential to expand and guard Japan's special position in Manchuria, Korea, and China. Though there was little disagreement on the general goals, the Japanese differed on methods for accomplishing those goals. Civilians in general, Baron Shidehara in the 1920's, and Prince Konoye later, favored a friendly and flexible approach. The Army in general, General Baron Tanaka in the 1920's, and General Tojo later, favored more positive and militant methods.

During the prosperity decade of the 1920's Japanese moderates won the upper hand and relations between the United States and Japan improved. Prosperity helped moderates persuade the Japanese that their interests could be served by peaceful trade and amicable diplomacy. Like Stresemann in Germany at the same time, Baron Shidehara as Japan's Foreign Minister from 1924 to 1927 and from 1929 to 1931 won support for his conciliatory policies.

Japan's role in the Washington Conference of 1921–1922 fitted that general pattern. In the Five Power Naval Treaty Japan accepted the short end of a 5–5–3 ratio in capital ships, and agreed not to fortify further island bases in the Pacific. In the Four Power Treaty Japan, Great Britain, the United States, and France agreed to respect each other's insular possessions in the Pacific and to consult concerning any threat to the status quo there. That treaty ended the Anglo-Japanese Alliance. In the Nine Power Treaty Japan and other signatory states endorsed the Open Door policy. The states agreed to respect China's independence and territorial integrity. They called for equality of economic opportunities and agreed not to seek additional special privileges in China. Shortly after the Washington Conference Japan agreed to terminate the Lansing-Ishii Agreement in which the United States had recognized Japan's special interests in China. In spite of irritations aroused by the American immigration quota law of 1924 that did not give any quota to Japan or China, the moderates and their conciliatory foreign policies prevailed in Japan most of the time in the 1920's.

In the depression decade of the 1930's, however, extremists gained strength. Relations between the United States and Japan deteriorated. The Manchurian incident of 1931–1933 set the tone. The Japanese military used an explosion on the South Manchuria Railway north of Mukden in September, 1931, as an excuse for a full-scale military assault on Manchuria. Early in 1932 Japan also took military action against China near Shanghai. Americans sympathized with China but were not willing to risk war to check Japan in Manchuria. Preoccupied with the depression in the United States, President Hoover initially left the matter to his Secretary of State. At first Stimson did, not favor vigorous actions by the United States. He hoped America's restraint might enable Japanese moderates to check the military. That approach did not last long, and it did not succeed.

In January, 1932, Secretary of State Stimson announced the United States policy in the crisis. Though issued by the Secretary of State and called the Stimson Doctrine, President Hoover originally suggested the idea, and he determined its limits. In the Stimson Doctrine the United States charged that the Japanese action in Manchuria violated the Kellogg-Briand Pact of Paris that Japan had ratified. The United States would not recognize changes brought about in China or Manchuria in violation of existing treaties. Secretary Stimson believed in collective security and considered nonrecognition as the first in what could become a series of increasingly coercive actions against an aggressor state. He envisaged the possibility of economic sanctions against Japan and hoped for European and League of Nations support. President Hoover, however, considered nonrecognition as simply an expression of America's moral disapproval of the Japanese action. He saw nonrecognition as a substitute for (not a prelude to) stronger actions. He believed economic sanctions could lead to war. Neither he nor the American people were willing to risk war to block Japanese aggression in Manchuria. Furthermore, he saw the Stimson Doctrine as a unilateral United States policy. In actual practice the European states and the League of Nations were no more willing to risk war than the United States was. The League voted nonrecognition but would go no further. The Stimson Doctrine indicated America's disapproval of Japan's course, but neither it nor the League's action inhibited the Japanese in Manchuria. Japan simply withdrew from the League of Nations and proceeded as it had before.

From 1933 to 1937 Japan and the United States went their separate ways. President Roosevelt concentrated on domestic economic and political matters. Insofar as he concerned himself with foreign affairs, he looked more to Europe and to Latin America than to Asia. The administration wanted to avoid war with Japan. At the same time, Japan consolidated its control of the puppet kingdom of Manchukuo that it organized in Manchuria.

In 1937, however, an undeclared Sino-Japanese war erupted that did not end until the United States and its allies crushed Japan in 1945. A minor shooting skirmish between Japanese and Chinese troops at Marco Polo Bridge near Peiping on July 7, 1937, triggered the developments. Japan used the incident as an excuse to begin an all-out assault on China, though neither side declared war. China under Chiang Kai-shek fought back, but it was a losing battle. Japanese forces overran much of China, including the Yangtze Valley and China's seaports and larger cities. The fall of France made it easy for Japan to move into northern parts of French Indochina in September, 1940. The Axis Tripartite Pact of September, 1940, tried to use the collective security formula to warn the United States against interfering. In July, 1941, after the Russo-German War in effect safeguarded Japan against the Soviet Union in the North, Japan swept over the rest of Indochina. Japan never completely crushed Chinese military resistance, but its military successes endangered the interests of all states active in the Far East.

In the United States Americans overwhelmingly sympathized with China. Japanese abuse and even murder of American missionaries, businessmen, and others in China inflamed American emotions. The Japanese bombing of the *Panay*, an American gunboat, in December, 1937, aroused American fears and anger. Nevertheless, neither the administration nor the American people would risk war to check Japan. The government urged Americans to leave China or remain at their own risk. Even the *Panay* incident did not arouse Americans to a war fever. The Roosevelt administration and most Americans considered Nazi Germany and Fascist Italy in Europe to be more serious dangers than Japan was. After the European war erupted in September, 1939, President Roosevelt wanted to avoid a Pacific war that might interfere with the main task of defeating Hitler and Mussolini in Europe.

As the months and years passed, the United States under the leadership of Roosevelt and Hull took various steps short of war to help China and check Japan. Mild individually, those American actions gradually became tougher, especially after the fall of France and the Axis Tripartite Pact in 1940. Their cumulative and potential effects alarmed both moderates and extremists in Japan. President Roosevelt never invoked the Neutrality Act in the Sino-Japanese War. Technically he declined to do so because neither side declared war (though he had earlier invoked the Neutrality Act in the undeclared war between Italy and Ethiopia). His real reasons included his correct belief that the arms embargo and cash-and-carry would hurt China more than Japan. Hence his decision was the first of many efforts to throw America's weight against Japanese aggression.

In a major address in Chicago on October 5, 1937, Roosevelt called for a "quarantine" of aggressors. He did not name Japan, but he had that country in mind. The quarantine address was part of the President's groping for a way to preserve peace and guard national security in a troubled world. It was also an effort to lead Americans away from isolationism. Isolationists denounced the speech, but internationalists in the South and in the cities of the Northeast praised it. In June, 1938, the government sent letters to American manufacturers and exporters of airplanes, airplane parts, and aerial bombs asking them not to sell to any country bombing civilian populations. That "moral embargo" aimed mainly at Japan. Most of the companies voluntarily cooperated, partly because failure to do so might endanger their chances for winning government defense contracts.

In July, 1939, Secretary Hull sent notice that the United States would terminate its trade treaty with Japan on January 26, 1940. Ending that treaty did not stop trade with Japan, but it left Japan uncertain about America's future course. Conceivably, if Japan's actions displeased or harmed Americans enough the United States might, after ending the treaty, invoke drastic trade restrictions or bans. Beginning in July, 1940, the government made all exports of aviation fuel and high-grade scrap iron and steel subject to federal license and control. In September, 1940, after Japanese troops moved into northern Indochina, President Roosevelt announced an embargo on the export of scrap iron and steel to Japan. Officially the administration acted to safeguard needed supplies of those vital materials for American defense needs, but it tightened the economic screws on Japan. At the same time, the United States loaned China $25 million and added another $100 million in November. In 1940–1941 the United States based its Navy fleet at Pearl Harbor, Hawaii, to serve as a deterrent to aggressive Japanese actions in the western Pacific.

Early in 1941 top British and American military leaders began staff conferences to make preliminary plans in the event the United States entered the war against the Axis in Europe and Asia. During 1941 America lengthened its list of commodities subject to export license control. The United States began to extend Lend-Lease aid to China. In April, 1941, President Roosevelt signed an executive order that made possible the famed "Flying Tigers" under the command of Colonel Claire L. Chennault. The President allowed officers and men to resign from American armed forces to fight in Chennault's Volunteer Air Force for China against Japan. The United States also provided Curtiss P–40 fighters and other equipment essential for that operation.

On July 25, 1941, after Japanese forces had swept over the rest of Indochina, President Roosevelt announced his most drastic action. He froze all Japanese assets in the United States. That placed financial and trade relations with Japan under the control of the United States government. At the same time, the British and Dutch governments also froze Japanese assets. So far as Japan was concerned, the freeze particularly hurt with regard to oil. If Japan could not get the oil it needed for its military forces, it would not be able to settle the "China incident" and establish its Greater East Asia Co-Prosperity Sphere. It could not long sustain its power and prestige in Asia and the western Pacific. As Herbert Feis phrased it: "From now on the oil gauge and the clock stood side by side. Each fall in the level brought the hour of decision closer."

In August, 1941, President Roosevelt and Prime Minister Churchill met secretly at sea off the coast of Newfoundland. The most famous product of that conference was the eight-point Atlantic Charter that spelled out common Anglo-American ideological goals, including "the final destruction of the Nazi tyranny." They and their advisers also discussed many other matters, including policies toward the Sino-Japanese war. Churchill wanted the United States to warn Japan that it faced war if it invaded Malaya or the Dutch East Indies. President Roosevelt would not go that far, and Secretary Hull opposed anything approaching a war ultimatum. Nevertheless, after his return from the Atlantic Conference, Roosevelt on August 17, 1941, told the Japanese Ambassador that if Japan took "any further steps in pursuance of a policy or program of military domination by force or threat of force of neighboring countries" the United States would "take immediately any and all steps which it may deem necessary toward safeguarding the legitimate rights and interests of the United States and American nationals and toward insuring the safety and security of the United States."

President Roosevelt and his advisers hoped that America's aid short of war would help China resist Japanese aggression and prevent the Sino-Japanese war from further endangering American interests and security. The United States wanted to preserve China and cause Japan to withdraw from the areas it had conquered since 1931, or at least since 1937. In other words, the Roosevelt administration hoped to establish the Open Door against the Japanese challenge.

The United States paralleled its short-of-war actions with diplomatic efforts to win a peaceful settlement of differences with Japan. America's Ambassador Joseph C. Grew pursued those efforts in Tokyo. During 1941 Secretary Hull conducted some forty or fifty conferences with the Japanese Ambassador Kichisaburo Nomura. In November Japan sent Saburo Kurusu on a special mission to assist Nomura. The United States had successfully deciphered Japanese diplomatic codes, so Hull had the advantage of knowing in advance Japan's instructions to its emissaries in Washington. All of those diplomats from both countries wanted to prevent war between the United States and Japan. Nevertheless, the diplomats, the governments, and the citizens of both countries insisted on terms that irreconcilably conflicted with those of the other. The particular item on which compromise proved impossible was China. While willing to compromise on other matters, Japan insisted on a free hand in China. In contrast, the United States under certain circumstances would remove its economic restrictions and make trade concessions, but it would not abandon China to the Japanese.

There were divided counsels in both the United States and Japan. Some Americans believed economic coercion might force Japan to compromise and restrain its ambitions. Others feared short-of-war methods might drive Japan to use military power to gain access to the resources it needed. Conceivably Japan might strike at its American tormentor, the only country able to block Japanese ambitions by the latter months of 1941. But no one in the administration was willing to acquiesce in Japanese domination of China. Similarly, Premier Konoye and some officers in the Japanese Navy feared American economic and military might. They wanted to exhaust every possible diplomatic device to win acceptable concessions from the United States. The Army, led by General Hideki Tojo, however, doubted the willingness of the United States to yield to diplomatic efforts, and banked on Japan's military superiority in East Asia and the western Pacific. Both moderates and extremists considered Japanese dominance in China to be absolutely essential and not subject to compromise. As diplomatic efforts floundered on the rock of China, as America's stand stiffened in July and August, and as the Japanese Army under Tojo grew more impatient, Prime Minister Konoye in desperation proposed a personal meeting with President Roosevelt. Persuaded that Konoye could not or would not make meaningful concessions at such a meeting, the United States rejected the proposal.

In effect, United States diplomacy and short-of-war policies confronted Japan with the alternatives of backing down or fighting. It could either stop its moves south and abandon its efforts to settle the "China incident," or it could fight to break American and Chinese opposition to its goals. Neither the moderates nor the extremists in Japan would accept the former alternative. When the moderates failed to persuade the United States to relax its controls and give Japan a free hand in China, Prince Konoye's government fell from power. In October, 1941, General Tojo headed a new and more militant government.

As early as July, 1941, the Japanese government decided to establish its Greater East Asia Co-Prosperity Sphere and settle the "China incident" even if that meant war with the United States. Japanese military forces began secret training for the attack on Pearl Harbor. By September Japanese military leaders insisted that if they did not soon fight and break American opposition, oil and other shortages would prevent them from winning such a war. By September 6, 1941, Japan decided on war with the United States unless America yielded to Japan's minimum demands.

On November 20, 1941, Nomura placed Japan's final terms before Secretary Hull. In those proposals, Japan agreed not to expand further south. Japan proposed that the United States and Japan cooperate to get the supplies each needed in the Netherlands East Indies. Each would restore normal commercial relations with the other. The United States was to supply oil for Japan. And the United States was not to interfere with relations between Japan and China (that is, the United States was to give Japan a free hand in China).

Roosevelt and Hull briefly considered proposing a *modus vivendi*, but strong Chinese objections and Churchill's misgivings helped kill the idea. Instead, on November 26, 1941, Secretary Hull presented Nomura and Kurusu with the American terms. They were as unacceptable to Japan as the Japanese proposals had been to the United States. The Secretary insisted that Japan endorse Hull's principles of conduct in international affairs. The United States called on Japan to withdraw all its military forces from China and Indochina. Japan was to support the Nationalist Government of China and, in effect, end its commitments to the European Axis. The United States would remove its economic restrictions, conclude a trade treaty, and cooperate with Japan in assuring equality of access to raw materials and markets in Asia. In those proposals Hull wanted to make the American position clear, but he and the other American civilian and military leaders knew that Japan would reject the terms.

On December 6, 1941, as the tensions mounted, President Roosevelt sent a message to Emperor Hirohito of Japan urging him to preserve peace. On instructions from their government, Nomura and Kurusu arranged an appointment with Secretary Hull at one o'clock in the afternoon on Sunday, December 7, 1941, to present Japan's reply to America's proposals of November 26. Because of delays in decoding and typing the fourteen-part reply, the emissaries arrived at the State Department an hour late. It was a formality anyway. Since America had broken Japan's secret diplomatic code, Hull and the President already knew the contents of the Japanese reply. As President Roosevelt said when he saw the first thirteen parts, "This means war."

The real Japanese reply, however, came nearly an hour before Hull coldly received the Japanese diplomats at 2:20 P.M. A little before eight o'clock in the morning, Hawaiian time, Japanese airplanes attacked Pearl Harbor. The bursting bombs and torpedoes left 3,500 dead and wounded Americans. Much of the American fleet at Hawaii was converted into a mass of twisted metal, while military aircraft went up in flames without even getting into the air against the enemy.

The attack on Pearl Harbor was a brilliant tactical military success for Japanese sea and air forces. It temporarily destroyed America's striking power in the Pacific. In broader strategic and power terms, however, the attack on Pearl Harbor (an action demanded by Japan's professional military leaders) doomed Japan to defeat. American leaders knew in advance that Japanese forces were under way and that war was imminent. They had sent war warnings to the American military commanders in Hawaii and the Philippines. But they expected Japan to strike at British and Dutch possessions in Southeast Asia and the southwest Pacific. They did not expect the attack on Pearl Harbor. If Japan had by-passed American territories and forces, the United States probably would have declared war anyway. But the President might have had a divided and weakened nation behind him. The attack on Pearl Harbor aroused the American people. It ended the foreign policy debate between isolationists and interventionists. It destroyed the America First Committee and the isolationism for which it spoke. Americans united behind their President and determined to crush their assailants. On December 8, with only one dissenting vote, Congress voted to declare war on Japan. When Germany and Italy then declared war, Congress on December 11, 1941, promptly and without dissent voted war against the European Axis powers.

With the relatively inexact methods and incomplete data at his command, the historian can only make semi-informed guesses concerning the motives, causes, and wisdom of pre-Pearl Harbor decisions. Despite the tremendous importance of President Franklin D. Roosevelt and his civilian and military advisers, neither the "great man theory of history" nor the "devil theory of history" is very helpful. A broader view chronologically and topically is essential, including careful consideration of world developments abroad and domestic influences within the United States and within the other countries involved. Externally, the power and security threats posed by Nazi Germany, Fascist Italy, and militarist Japan brought war to the United States. British, Chinese, and Russian needs in the face of the Axis challenge, and the diplomatic and propaganda efforts by Winston Churchill, Chiang Kai-shek, Joseph Stalin, and their associates helped draw the United States to their side. Domestically, the dominant economic, political, ethnic, religious, ideological, and emotional considerations moved the United States in the same direction. The interventionist South was prominent among those domestic influences. But even more important were the needs and desires of the growing urban society associated with the rise of American industry and finance. Among the many consequences of United States participation in World War II from 1941 to 1945 was the spectacular expansion of America's military, diplomatic, economic, and ideological influence in other parts of the world. The United States never went back to the more limited role it had played in world affairs before December 7, 1941.

SUPPLEMENTARY READINGS

Barnes, Harry Elmer (ed.). *Perpetual War for Perpetual Peace: A Critical Examination of the Foreign Policy of Franklin Delano Roosevelt and Its Aftermath.* Caldwell, Idaho: Caxton Printers, Ltd., 1953.

Beard, Charles A. *President Roosevelt and the Coming of the War, 1941: A Study in Appearances and Realities.* New Haven, Conn.: Yale University Press, 1948.

Borg, Dorothy. *American Policy and the Chinese Revolution, 1925–1928.* New York: Macmillan Co., 1947.

————. *The United States and the Far Eastern Crisis of 1933–1938.* Cambridge, Mass.: Harvard University Press, 1964.

Borg, Dorothy and Okamoto, Shumysei (eds.). *Pearl Harbor as History: Japanese-American Relations, 1931–1941.* New York: Columbia University Press, 1973.

Current, Richard N. *Secretary Stimson: A Study in Statecraft.* New Brunswick, N.J.: Rutgers University Press, 1954.

Divine, Robert A. *The Reluctant Belligerent: American Entry into World War II.* New York: John Wiley & Sons, Inc., 1965.

Feis, Herbert. *The Road to Pearl Harbor: The Coming of the War Between the United States and Japan.* Princeton, N.J.: Princeton University Press, 1950.

Ferrell, Robert H. *American Diplomacy in the Great Depression: Hoover-Stimson Foreign Policy, 1929–1933.* New Haven, Conn.: Yale University Press, 1957.

Griswold, A. Whitney. *The Far Eastern Policy of the United States.* New York: Harcourt, Brace & Co., 1938.

Hull, Cordell. *The Memoirs of Cordell Hull.* 2 vols. New York: Harper & Bros., 1948.

Langer, William L., and Gleason, S. Everett. *The Challenge to Isolation, 1937–1940.* New York: Harper & Bros., 1952.

———. *The Undeclared War, 1940–1941.* New York: Harper & Bros., 1953.

Millis, Walter. *This is Pearl! The United States and Japan, 1941.* New York: William Morrow & Co., Inc., 1947.

Morison, Samuel E. *The Rising Sun in the Pacific, 1931–April 1942.* Boston: Little, Brown & Co., 1948.

Neumann, William L. *America Encounters Japan: From Perry to MacArthur.* Baltimore: Johns Hopkins Press, 1963.

Rappaport, Armin. *Henry L. Stimson and Japan, 1931–1933.* Chicago: University of Chicago Press, 1963.

Schroeder, Paul W. *The Axis Alliance and Japanese-American Relations, 1941.* Ithaca, N.Y.: Cornell University Press, 1958.

Stimson, Henry L., and Bundy, McGeorge. *On Active Service in Peace and War.* New York: Harper & Row, Publishers, 1948.

Tansill, Charles C. *Back Door to War: The Roosevelt Foreign Policy, 1933–1941.* Chicago: Henry Regnery Co., 1952.

Trefousse, Hans L. (ed.). *What Happened at Pearl Harbor? Documents Pertaining to the Japanese Attack of December 7, 1941, and Its Background.* New York: Twayne Publishers, Inc., 1958.

Wohlstetter, Roberta. *Pearl Harbor: Warning and Decision.* Stanford, Calif.: Stanford University Press, 1962.

PART VI

The nuclear age
1942-1973

34

The bipolar world and the challenge of the Third World: External influences on American foreign relations, 1942-1973

If World War I and the Great Depression severely jolted nineteenth-century international patterns, World War II shattered them by the time it ended in 1945. The human, economic, and emotional tragedies of World War II in Europe, Asia, and elsewhere are beyond the capacity of the human mind to comprehend. Some may be inspired by its drama and heroics; none should forget its inhumanity, destructiveness, and horror. It destroyed Hitler's Nazi Germany, Mussolini's Fascist Italy, and militarist Japan. But it also destroyed much more, including much of irreplaceable value.

The war cost the United States government around $350 billion, not including continuing indirect costs. Americans suffered more than a million casualties, including 300,000 military deaths. The war affected the lives of most Americans who lived through it, often tragically. Nevertheless, the United States emerged from World War II stronger and wealthier than ever before. Most belligerents were not so fortunate.

One writer estimated that the total worldwide costs of the war, including government expenses and the value of property destroyed, exceeded four trillion dollars. Perhaps forty million persons, civilians and soldiers on both sides, lost their lives as a result of World War II. Hitler's Nazis murdered six million Jews. Killed in the military forces of the belligerents during World War II were approximately eight million Russians, three million Germans, one and a half million Japanese, 250,000

385

British troops, 80,000 Italians, and 200,000 Frenchmen. In Hiroshima and Nagasaki on August 6 and 9, 1945, more than 100,000 Japanese men, women, and children died when American airplanes dropped atomic bombs on those cities. Dresden and Tokyo suffered comparable losses in conventional and incendiary bombings. And those cold figures do not begin to hint at the countless personal tragedies and shattered lives caused by the war. Nor do they adequately suggest the economic devastation and suffering.

So far as international power relations were concerned, World War II helped create a bipolar arrangement with most states in varying degree bound to and dependent upon one or another of the two superpowers, the United States and the Soviet Union. The war destroyed the power of the former Axis states, Germany, Italy, and Japan. Despite their victories, the war drastically weakened the former dominant states of Western Europe, notably Great Britain and France. It devastated the economies and institutions of Europe, Asia, and elsewhere. For some the acute economic hardships made communism with its utopian promises seem more attractive than it might have in less desperate circumstances.

By arousing nationalism in colonial areas and by weakening the capacity of the imperial states to control their colonies, World War II speeded the disintegration of the old European empires in Asia and Africa. On that issue Americans were torn between their ideological dedication to the rights of revolution and self-determination on the one hand, and their common security and economic interests with Britain, France, and the other colonial powers on the other hand. The Soviet Union faced no such dilemma. Ideologically, Communists saw imperialism as part of capitalist efforts to stave off inevitable collapse. In security terms Soviet leaders saw anticolonialism in Asia and Africa as weakening their adversaries in the power struggles of the cold war.

Many states, great and small, contributed to the common task of defeating the Axis in World War II. But the victory could not have been accomplished without the tremendous economic and military power of the United States and the Soviet Union. Their military successes and economic miracles dramatized their unprecedented might and rewarded them with the power that comes with prestige. The United States quickly dismantled its huge wartime military forces in 1945–1946, but (along with Great Britain) for a few years it commanded a monopoly on atomic weapons. The Soviet Union maintained much of its wartime military strength, and it mastered the techniques for making nuclear weapons by 1949.

The role of urbanization in those developments should not be overlooked. Urban commerce, industry, science, technology, and finance helped make the world more close-knit and interdependent. Germany, Japan, and Russia developed the power to challenge old security arrangements as they built urban industrial economies. Both fascism and communism were, in part, totalitarian efforts to grapple with opportunities and problems created or intensified by industrialization. And the unbelievable destructiveness of modern war would be impossible without the complex weapons manufactured, financed, and delivered by urban industrial economies.

The United States and the Soviet Union had cooperated sufficiently from 1941 to 1945 to accomplish the victory over the Axis. For a multitude of reasons they were unable to continue that cooperation successfully after the war. Both the United States and the Soviet Union had had long histories of expansion; the cold war was the clash of those two expanding states and systems. Ideologically, the leaders of the Soviet Union crusaded for what they believed to be the inevitable triumph of world communism; Americans envisaged the spread of democracy, preferably democratic capitalism. Most religious groups in the United States felt an almost sacred obligation to oppose atheistic communism wherever it was. Nationalism in both countries reinforced the ideological and emotional bases for conflict. Until his death in 1953, Joseph Stalin's distrust of the West evolved into pathological paranoia; many people in the United States developed comparable obsessions with regard to the communist menace. As in all states, the leaders of the United States and the Soviet Union worried about national security, including security against possible revived Axis powers and against the other superpower. Each resolved to make certain that Germany, Japan, and Italy would never again threaten world peace and security. Each determined to guard against threats from the other superpower. Those ideological and security considerations and the dispersion of their military and economic resources provided the felt need and opportunities for the United States and the Soviet Union to expand their influence and control into the power vacuums left at the end of World War II. As Ronald Steel wrote in his provocative book, *Pax Americana,* "The crusade that was the war against fascism gave way to the new crusade that was the cold war against communism."

The Soviet Union converted Eastern European states into communist satellites. It made lesser gestures toward the Middle East and northeast Asia. Though the Soviet Union played only a small role in the development, China fell to communist domination in 1949. And Communist Parties elsewhere responded to the wishes of the Soviet leaders. At the same time, the United States expanded its power and influence directly and indirectly in much of the noncommunist world by means of the Truman Doctrine, the Marshall Plan, the North Atlantic Treaty Organization, the Organization of American States, the Southeast Asia Treaty Organization, numerous military alliances, foreign aid programs, trade, investments, and various military actions, including those in Korea from 1950 to 1953 and in Vietnam in the 1960's and until 1973.

In the devastation left by World War II and in the developing cold war, most countries needed one or the other of the superpowers for their reconstruction, security, and survival. None of those weaker states (communist or noncommunist) really wanted it that way; each would have preferred to be the master of its own destiny and beholden to no other state. But that was not practical. Millions on both sides of the Iron Curtain worried that the giants might start a nuclear war that would destroy the superpowers and everyone else as well. Many on both sides had serious doubts about the wisdom and responsibility of the superpowers. Nevertheless, after World War II most leaders and citizens of weaker states were convinced that they must have the aid and support of the United States or the Soviet Union, particularly if they were threatened by the other of the giants. In a choice between unpleasant alternatives, most of the world reluctantly cooperated with (or submitted to) one or another of the giants in the cold war, the United States or the Soviet Union.

Even the United Nations organization could not successfully prevent or end the cold war between the communist and noncommunist worlds. Millions all over the world hoped that the United Nations, formed by the victors at the close of World War II, would succeed where the earlier League of Nations had failed. The United Nations had the advantage of support from all the victorious states, including the United States and the Soviet Union. On numerous occasions in the 1940's and 1950's it helped prevent war: in Iran, Indonesia, Korea, Palestine, Trieste, the Congo, and elsewhere. Through its Economic and Social Council and its commissions and specialized agencies, the United Nations tried to improve the soil for world peace through economic and humanitarian reforms and development.

Nevertheless, the United Nations system was torn by cold war tensions and cleavages. Its Charter assigned the "primary responsibility for the maintenance of international peace and security" to the Security Council. But both conviction and political realities led the authors of the United Nations Charter to base the peace-keeping functions of the Security Council on the principle of unanimity among the great powers. They gave each of the five permanent members (the United States, the Soviet Union, Great Britain, France, and China) authority, by a negative vote, to veto substantive matters before the Security Council. They included the veto because the great powers (including both the United States and the Soviet Union) would not have approved the Charter without that authority. Furthermore, many believed that in a practical sense the United Nations could not preserve peace without the effective cooperation (or at least the acquiescence) of the great powers. The United Nations was not designed to be a world government, and it was not expected to be able to prevent aggression by a great power. Consequently, the growing cold war between the noncommunist states led by the United States and the communist world led by the Soviet Union destroyed the premise on which the peace-keeping functions of the United Nations and its Security Council originally were based.

As the breach widened, the United States and the Soviet Union used contrasting methods in the United Nations. With the communist states in a minority, the Soviet Union frequently vetoed actions by the Security Council that it considered contrary to its interests. Checked there, the United States from 1947 to the 1950's tried to bypass the veto by increasing the peace-keeping functions of the General Assembly, where the veto did not apply. That tactic served American interests on some issues for a time. But as the membership of the United Nations and General Assembly sharply increased with the addition of the newly independent states of Asia and Africa, the United States found the method less effective. Most of the new members of the United Nations were not communist-controlled, but most of them did not share America's preoccupation with the cold war. Both the United States and the Soviet Union continued their membership in and support for the United Nations. But the tensions of the bipolar world immobilized that great world organization on many crucial issues.

In the 1950's and 1960's, bipolar cold war patterns persisted, but certain developments began to blur those patterns. Notable among those newer tendencies were the recovery of Europe, the Peace Offensive, and the growth of nationalism all over the world.

By the third quarter of the twentieth century, the European states had substantially rebuilt their shattered cities and industries. Production and standards of living in West Germany, France, Great Britain, and other states surpassed prewar levels. Though still weak compared to the United States and the Soviet Union, they were strong and prosperous relative to their immediate postwar conditions. The United States contributed greatly to that revival through its government loan to Britain, the Marshall Plan, and private loans, investments, and technology. But the Europeans owed even more to their own impressive individual and cooperative efforts. By the 1950's and 1960's the states of Western and Eastern Europe no longer needed the economic assistance of the United States or the Soviet Union as much as they had earlier. And as their national military forces grew and as the Peace Offensive developed, many in those states doubted whether they even needed the security support of a superpower as much as they had earlier. Those patterns did not completely free the European states from dependence on either the United States or the Soviet Union, but they did encourage more independent inclinations within them. Many Europeans began to fear and resent their particular superpower as much as they did the one on the other side of the Iron Curtain.

Beginning a bit in 1953 and developing irregularly in succeeding years, the Soviet Union inaugurated a so-called Peace Offensive. Emphasis on "peaceful coexistence" overlaid the continuing cold war patterns.

Numerous variables helped account for the Soviet Peace Offensive. The death of Joseph Stalin in March, 1953, and the emergence of new leadership formed part of the explanation. Stalin's death led to an internal struggle for power within the Communist Party and the Soviet government. Some of his successors had emerged from backgrounds much like his. More of them, however, grew out of the developing political, industrial, and military bureaucracy of the Soviet Union. The Communists claimed to have created a classless society, but in fact a new middle class developed in the Soviet Union. It generally wanted stability, order, growth, efficiency, and respectability much as middle classes did in the noncommunist world. The leaders of the Soviet Union after 1953, such as Georgi Malenkov, Nikita Khrushchev, Nikolai Bulganin, Aleksei Kosygin, and Leonid Brezhnev, were dedicated Communists. But some of them had backgrounds and temperaments so different from those of Lenin, Trotsky, Stalin, and Molotov that they could not be expected to follow domestic and foreign policies like those of their predecessors.

Difficulties within the Soviet Union and the communist world encouraged the Peace Offensive. After the sacrifices and hardships of World War I, the revolutions, the five-year plans, and World War II, even the patient and long-suffering Russians wanted more butter and less guns. Farmers in particular were restive. Titoism in Yugoslavia in 1948, the 1953 riots in East Germany, the uprisings in Poland and Hungary in 1956, and the schism with Communist China, all required the attention of Soviet leaders and left them less free to attempt adventuresome forays against the noncommunist world. Despite the Soviet Union's continued preponderance of power, its control over Communist Parties and states outside its own borders eroded. The term "bloc" became less appropriate than it had been earlier and the term "polycentrism" was a comparatively more accurate description of the communist world. With roots deep in geography, history, ideology, and power considerations, the cleavage between the Soviet Union and the People's Republic of China assumed major porportions in the 1960's and 1970's. That rift between the two leading communist states portended fundamental consequences in world affairs.

The nuclear stalemate also contributed to the Peace Offensive. The Soviet Union had ended America's monopoly on atomic weapons in 1949. The United States successfully demonstrated a hydrogen or thermonuclear weapon in 1952, but the Soviet Union made the same weapon the following year. Each country had intercontinental bombers capable of delivering those fantastically destructive weapons and exploding them on the cities of the other. Each country developed intercontinental missiles capable of carrying nuclear and thermonuclear warheads at fantastic speed and accuracy to the population centers of the other. Leaders in both the United States and the Soviet Union knew that neither could win or survive a total thermonuclear war. In addition, each of the superpowers commanded conventional land, sea, and air forces more powerful than those in any previous war. Both the United States and the Soviet Union would fight (even with thermonuclear weapons) if they believed survival were at stake. But the certainty of mutual destruction in such a war forced rational persons in both countries to demonstrate greater restraint and moderation than they might have in other circumstances.

Initially, most Americans believed that the Peace Offensive did not represent any fundamental change in the objectives of Soviet foreign policies. Like Stalin, his successors continued to guard the security and power of the Soviet Union. They hoped to avoid World War III with the West if that were possible without destroying Soviet security. And they continued to promote the spread of communism. They shifted methods rather than goals. In many respects the new policies were more difficult for the United States to handle effectively than the old Stalin policies had been. But the Peace Offensive and the Western responses did make possible the solution of some cold war problems. The Austrian Peace Treaty of 1955, the Nuclear Test Ban Treaty in 1963, and the Strategic Arms Limitation agreement of 1972 were among the consequences of the changing world environment.

In addition to Europe's revival and the Peace Offensive, in the 1950's and 1960's the bipolar cold war patterns were modified by the further growth of nationalism in Asia, Africa, Latin America, and Europe. The most powerful ideological and emotional force in world affairs after World War II was neither communism nor democracy. It was nationalism. World War II and its aftermath helped extend that spirit of nationalism to the "Third World," Asia, Africa, and Latin America. Former colonial peoples determined to throw off all vestiges of the old colonialism. And the postwar weakness of the old imperial states gave those nationalistic and anticolonial aspirations the opportunity to succeed. By 1950 nationalism had carried the day in Asia; by the 1960's it had prevailed in Africa. Changes in the composition of the United Nations illustrated the political success of those nationalistic aspirations. By 1974 the original membership of the United Nations had more than doubled. When the United Nations originally formed at the close of World War II, most of its member states were parts of Western civilization in Europe and the Western Hemisphere. By 1974 the states from Africa, Asia, and the Near East outnumbered and outvoted those Western states in the General Assembly.

Most of the new countries of Asia and Africa were not communist-dominated. Most of them did not individually command much power.

They often disagreed sharply among themselves. But they did agree in their determination to throw off outside domination. Their hostility against the former imperial states was partly economic. Despite their industrial goals and accomplishments, the developing states of the Middle East, Asia, Africa, and Latin America largely produced agricultural and mineral products. Even in the 1970's, foreign capital controlled much of that production. Prosperity continued to depend very much on markets in the industrialized states. In Populist terms, those economically underdeveloped areas had a relation to the North Atlantic metropolis or to the Soviet Union similar to that of rural North Dakota to the urban Northeast in an earlier phase of American history. And the people of those developing areas felt the same hostility and resentment against the industrial-financial states that western farmers in the United States once felt against Wall Street in New York City. In Marxian terms, the challenge of the Third World was a projection into the international arena of the class struggle between the rich and the poor, with both the United States and the Soviet Union in the role of the rich. Nationalism also had racial aspects, as Orientals in Asia and blacks in Africa threw off white domination.

As a relatively new development, the nationalism in Asia and Africa was particularly spectacular and important. But nationalism also grew in Europe. When Marshal Tito led Yugoslavia out of the Soviet Union's bloc in 1948, he did not break with communism. Tito as a Communist and a nationalist objected to Stalin's nationalistic and imperialistic attempts to keep Yugoslavia, in effect, a colonial satellite of the Soviet Union. Similarly, the uprisings in Poland and Hungary in 1956 were not, for the most part, directed against communism. They were primarily nationalistic rebellions against Soviet domination and imperialism in Eastern Europe. The same was true of developments that brought Soviet military intervention in Czechoslovakia in 1968.

General Charles de Gaulle's rise to power in France in 1958 was a further expression of increasing European nationalism. De Gaulle's nationalism antagonized those who hoped to build a united Europe and a North Atlantic system. Nevertheless, many who disliked de Gaulle found satisfaction in having a European leader talk back to the United States. He evoked empathy among many who sympathized with his chauvinistic challenge to the bipolar patterns. The United States and the Soviet Union continued to be much more powerful than any other states; outlines of the bipolar patterns persisted. Nevertheless, the revival of Europe and the Peace Offensive encouraged many in Europe, Asia, Africa, and Latin America to believe that they could safely go on their own without help and protection from either of the superpowers.

In providing a more flexible and fluid international situation, those developments may have helped preserve world peace and avoid a suicidal

World War III. But those new patterns also complicated America's tasks in world affairs. Indeed, America's many military commitments could involve the United States in local conflicts encouraged by the greater nationalism and independence of the many states. The proliferation of nuclear weapons among additional states could make that unstable situation even more dangerous. Efforts to guard peace and security in that explosive world atmosphere spectacularly expanded United States power and influence over much of the earth during and after World War II.

SUPPLEMENTARY READINGS

Albrecht-Carrié, René. *A Diplomatic History of Europe Since the Congress of Vienna.* New York: Harper & Bros., 1958.

Bloomfield, Lincoln P. *The United Nations and U.S. Foreign Policy: A New Look at the National Interest.* Boston: Little, Brown & Co., 1960.

Dallin, David J. *Soviet Foreign Policy After Stalin.* Philadelphia: J. B. Lippincott Co., 1961.

Gatzke, Hans W. *The Present in Perspective: A Look at the World since 1945.* 3d ed. Chicago: Rand McNally & Co., 1965.

Holborn, Hajo. *The Political Collapse of Europe.* New York: Alfred A. Knopf, Inc., 1961.

Kennan, George F. *Russia and the West under Lenin and Stalin.* Boston: Little, Brown & Co., 1961.

Lukacs, John. *A History of the Cold War.* Garden City, N.Y.: Doubleday & Co., Inc., 1961.

Morgenthau, Hans J. *Politics Among Nations: The Struggle for Power and Peace.* 3d ed. New York: Alfred A. Knopf, Inc., 1961.

Mosely, Philip E. *The Kremlin and World Politics.* New York: Vintage Books, Inc., 1960.

Robertson, Charles L. *International Politics since World War II: A Short History.* New York: John Wiley & Sons, Inc., 1966.

Shirer, William L. *The Rise and Fall of the Third Reich: A History of Nazi Germany.* New York: Simon and Schuster, Inc., 1960.

Schuman, Frederick L. *Russia since 1917: Four Decades of Soviet Politics.* New York: Alfred A. Knopf, Inc., 1957.

Steel, Ronald. *Pax Americana.* Rev. ed. New York: Viking Press, 1970.

Ulam, Adam B. *Expansion and Coexistence: The History of Soviet Foreign Policy, 1917–1967.* New York: Frederick A. Praeger, Inc., 1968.

35

The triumph and travail of the city: Domestic influences on American foreign relations, 1942-1973

During and after World War II urbanization, with its accompanying growth of science, industry, and finance, affected and even dominated most other patterns on the domestic scene. The rise of the city, with its many economic, social, ethnic, racial, religious, educational, and ideological ramifications, directly and indirectly affected all parts of the country. And that urbanization, in its broadest sense, further promoted the expansion of American interests, activities, and power in other parts of the world.

THE PEOPLE

The population of the United States increased from about 134 million in 1942 to around 210 million in 1974. That gave America the fourth largest population of any country in the world, after China, India, and the Soviet Union.

The rural-urban distribution became overwhelmingly urban and suburban. Rural and small-town America dwindled to less than a third of the total population, and its influence and power declined even more. In most states, including such traditionally farm states as Iowa and Nebraska, urban population exceeded rural. Only about five percent of Americans made their livings directly as farmers, and many of those got parts of their incomes from nonfarm sources. Farmers and farms not only declined in numbers, they also changed greatly. Science and technology revolutionized farming methods just as they affected urban manufacturing. Commercial farms grew strikingly in size, capitalization, mechanization, and production. The enlarged operations, in addition to marketing difficulties, inspired sophisticated managerial innovations that often gave the producer, processor, and distributor a community of interest cutting across rural-urban lines. Furthermore, the modes of living for twentieth-century commercial farmers often differed little from those of persons on comparable social and economic levels in the cities. Automobiles, highways, airplanes, radio, television, mass-circulation newspapers and magazines, schools and universities, commercial recreational facilities, and mass-produced consumer goods were available to farmers as they were to city people. Those developments did not wholly eliminate differences between rural and urban interests and views on domestic and foreign affairs, but they did reduce many of those differences.

About one American in five lived in the "supermetropolis" extending almost continuously for nearly 500 miles along the northeastern seaboard. That huge concentration of people, talent, industry, and capital exerted an influence on American thought, taste, education, national politics, and foreign policy that far exceeded its proportion of the population. The center of the nation's population continued to move west, and California replaced New York as the most populous state. But that movement took people off the farms and out of small towns in the South and Middle West and into cities and suburbs, particularly on the coasts.

Americans of Anglo-Saxon, Germanic, and Scandinavian origins (that is, from northern and western Europe) continued to be more numerous than other ethnic groups within the white population of the United States. Nevertheless, Americans of Latin and Slavic descent from southern and eastern Europe and from Latin America constituted a growing proportion, particularly in cities. Their economic, social, educational, and political status generally improved relative to that in earlier decades.

As America's main adversary in world politics shifted from Germany to the Soviet Union, ethnic attitudes on foreign affairs also changed. Most of those changes weakened isolationist strength. German-Americans had tended to be isolationist before World Wars I and II, but those tendencies evaporated when the Soviet Union became the danger. As Samuel Lubell asked: "If Germany is overrun, will German-Americans vote 'isolationist'?" Similarly, Irish-Americans generally have turned away from their earlier isolationism. Refugees who fled from Eastern European countries to escape Nazi persecution during World War II and Soviet domination after the war often sympathized with efforts to end foreign domination of their original homelands. Hungarians and Poles who fled to the United States when the Soviet Union crushed the 1956 uprisings often voiced those sentiments.

The 23 million American blacks increasingly crowded into cities, including northern cities. Long the victims of discrimination and unequal opportunities, even Roosevelt's New Deal in the 1930's did little to improve their status. War and prosperity increased their opportunities, and President Harry S. Truman and his successors supported demands for greater racial equality in federal employment and the armed forces. In athletics and the arts, blacks gradually won the recognition that their talents warranted. In the 1950's and 1960's, the United States Supreme Court threw the weight of its decisions against segregation and discrimination. The civil rights movement emerged from very real humanitarian and idealistic concern for human rights and dignity. In its early phases, however, it focused primarily on the status of black people in the South. To that extent initially it was partly a product of growing urban dominance and urban hostility to rural and small-town America (in that instance, in the South). Gradually, however, even Northerners could not continue to ignore the debased condition of blacks in northern cities. Only then did talk about the "white backlash" gain much attention. To some degree the civil rights movement and criticism of American policies in Vietnam merged. The continued failure to win full equality with whites made some nonwhites unwilling to support the war in Vietnam. Nevertheless, the proportion of blacks in American military forces exceeded their proportion in the total population. Blacks fought bravely and skillfully for their country. Probably on the whole the foreign policy attitudes in the Afro-American population did not differ greatly from the foreign policy views of the white population of the United States.

The secularization of American thought continued in the last third of the twentieth century. As before, the majority of Americans with religious affiliations belonged to one or another of the Protestant denominations. Nevertheless, the patterns changed in degree. The Roman Catholic Church was the largest single religious organization in the United States. Anti-Catholic prejudice continued and sometimes took vicious forms in opposition to the nomination and election of Catholic John F. Kennedy to the Presidency in 1960. Nevertheless, Kennedy's election won support from most liberals, and his responsible conduct as President helped destroy the myth that the church would control his actions as chief executive. Revelations of the fantastically inhuman massacre of European Jews by Hitler's Nazis helped discredit all forms of anti-Semitism. One could still encounter anti-Semitism and no Jew won the Presidency, but discrimination against Jews declined substantially. At the same time anti-Protestant prejudice grew. Critical comments about Baptists, Methodists, or Calvinists became more commonplace and respectable. Careful scholars used the term WASP (white Anglo-Saxon Protestant) accurately and unemotionally. But in popular usage it was often a term of denigration. Those patterns, too, in some degree reflected the dominance of the city, with its large Catholic and Jewish populations, and the decline of the predominantly Protestant rural and small-town America.

Communism's explicit atheism and materialism made it easy for leaders and members of most religious groups to add their weight to the struggle against the Soviet Union, though some pacifist faiths such as the Quakers and some with a more secular emphasis such as the Unitarians may have been exceptions. The opposition of Catholicism to communism probably encouraged interventionist rather than noninterventionist attitudes toward the cold war. The Calvinist clergyman who said that the cold war was fundamentally a struggle between Christianity and atheism probably was voicing a view shared by millions. Growing evidence of anti-Semitism in the Soviet Union as well as its support for Arab states against Israel also brought American Jews into the religious alignment against the Soviet Union.

American Jews were not all Zionists, but Jewish opinion and political strength in the major cities was one of the important domestic influences behind President Harry S. Truman's support for and recognition of the new state of Israel in 1948. Most American Jews also wanted the United States government to back Israel against the Arab challenges led by Egypt's Gamal Nasser in 1956 and 1967.

Developments in transportation, communication, and education reduced the significance of geographic remoteness and inadequate information as bases for isolationism. Television was added to such older media as books, newspapers, radio, and motion pictures. For all its trivia, television brought news and information on world affairs into the homes of most Americans. Through television the most remote farmer, the provincial villager, and the urban worker could all sit in on interviews and discussions by top political, diplomatic, and military officials from the United States and other countries. Thirst for knowledge, drive for economic gain, a high level of prosperity, and the belief that it was "the thing to do" led a growing proportion of young people to continue their formal educations beyond levels achieved by their parents. The combination of improved transportation facilities and economic prosperity enabled growing numbers to visit foreign lands. The farmer or small businessman making the "grand tour" of Europe was not as unusual as he would have been a generation earlier. Students, teachers, and scholars found abundant opportunities to travel, study, teach, and do research in other lands. Private business, government aid programs, and military forces took many Americans abroad each year. Opportunity and exposure to broader horizons did not assure immunity to provincialism, but they may have contributed to its decline and to the growth of internationalism.

THE ECONOMY

World War II ended America's great depression. Despite fluctuations and many who did not share the prosperity, the years from 1942 to 1974 were the most productive and prosperous in American history. Though agriculture and commerce were important, industry and finance dominated, and they continued to promote activity and expansion overseas.

The magnitude of American industrial production and financial growth during World War II and the cold war was unprecedented. Many feared that the end of the war would bring an economic slump and a return of the depression. Instead business expenditures for conversion to peacetime production, a backlog of consumer needs and desires, and wartime savings helped extend wartime prosperity into the immediate postwar years. Gross national product grew from around $150 billion in 1942 to over $1,000 billion in 1974, twice the GNP of the Soviet Union. With about 5 percent of the world's population, the United States produced nearly two thirds of the world's manufactured goods. Despite impressive gains by the Soviet Union and other states, no country in the world came close to equaling America's total industrial production. The United States government and American businesses had more capital at their disposal than any state had ever had before.

Despite its size, the domestic market in the United States could not absorb all the goods, services, and capital turned out by the American economy. Foreign markets were helpful for many sectors of the economy, and they were essential for others. Every state and city in the United States, as well as most counties and smaller communities, produced goods that found their way into foreign markets and into American military forces. Conventional trade arrangements and business investments absorbed part of America's output, but they did not operate unaided during World War II and the cold war. Government appropriations during World War II sent guns, airplanes, ships, bombs, ammunition, and food to American military forces all over the world and to all the countries fighting the Axis. The value of lend-lease aid alone totaled $50 billion. Government expenditures for foreign aid programs (both military and nonmilitary) since World War II have totaled $120 billion. Appropriations for foreign aid and military preparedness provided vastly larger government subsidies to American prosperity than the prewar New Deal had. Foreign aid programs and growing private loans and investments abroad in effect helped subsidize foreign markets for American goods and services. During the cold war military appropriations steadily increased until annual appropriations of $50 billion for preparedness became commonplace. The fighting in Vietnam pushed those figures even higher.

During World War II and the cold war, the external need for American aid and military preparedness was very real and very great. By happy coincidence that external need provided the occasion for equally necessary government subsidies for markets for the tremendous output of the American economy. To paraphrase a statement on a different subject, if there had not been a foreign need and threat, Americans might have found it necessary to invent one. The American people and their elected representatives in Congress supported the large appropriations partly because of humanitarian compassion for those who needed help and partly because the military forces were considered essential to guard national security against the threat from communist states. In addition, however, both Republican and Democratic administrations found it easier to get support for their adventures overseas because of the economic advantages those appropriations provided for millions of Americans (and because of the fear that ending aid programs, military appropriations, and subsidized foreign markets would shatter the economic well-being of most Americans). Even if communism, the Soviet Union, China, and Vietnam had not existed, continued American prosperity would have required the United States to be active and expansionist in other parts of the world. And all Americans in varied degree were tied directly or indirectly to that industrial economy. Some suggested that private enterprise could sustain economic prosperity through its own efforts unaided (or unobstructed) by the federal government. Others contended that the United States could maintain a prosperous economy largely through government planning within American boundaries, essentially self-containment. In practice, however, Americans did not have sufficient opportunity or inclination to attempt either alternative during World War II and the cold war.

Most American economic activity occurred within the boundaries of the United States. But the part that overflowed into other areas of the world was gigantic. America's annual exports were only about 4 percent of its gross national product, but the value of those exports exceeded the total annual GNP of all but nine countries of the world. American goods and services went to every continent, to every country, and to many millions of homes abroad. American private investments abroad grew spectacularly from the 1950's onward. By 1974 American direct investments abroad totaled more than $80 billion, four times the foreign investments from the second-ranking capital exporting country and 60 percent of all worldwide direct foreign investments. The largest investments went to the developed countries of Canada, Great Britain, and Western Europe, but investment capital went all over the world, including the countries of Asia, Africa, the Middle East, and Latin America. Huge American corporations such as International Business Machines and General Motors, and various conglomerates and American-dominated multinational firms commanded greater wealth, resources, and economic power than most sovereign countries and their governments. American dollars, products, technicians, and businessmen went to every continent and to most countries. And the United States government (under both Democratic and Republican administrations) did its energetic best to help and support business enterprises abroad. Radicals saw that activity as economic imperialism and exploitation. New Left scholars saw it as "Open Door Imperialism." Recipient countries and peoples worried that Americans were taking over. Foreign businessmen feared American competition. But whether one saw the development as evil and exploitative, whether one saw it as simply "good business," or whether one saw it as contributing to peace and prosperity, American foreign trade and investments were an extremely important part of United States expansion in Europe, the Western Hemisphere, Asia, Africa, and the Middle East after the end of World War II. It was no fiendish conspiracy, as radicals would have one believe, and many millions all over the world benefited from it. But it was intimately related to America's active internationalism and concern with developments abroad. And any substantial curtailment of that economic activity abroad would have major economic, political, and diplomatic repercussions at home and abroad.

MILITARY FORCES

The United States built and maintained larger and more powerful military forces during World War II and the cold war than ever before in its history. Those forces grew out of both external security needs and out of domestic influences. They affected world affairs, and they influenced domestic developments within the United States. American military forces helped crush the Axis. They became a major deterrent to war and a guardian of the peace; they also developed the capacity to destroy all human civilization. They were instruments for guarding freedom and democracy against the fascist and then the communist menace; they were also a domestic influence that many feared endangered American democracy at home. In tune with tradition, the Armed Forces of the United States were subject to civilian control and were used to accomplish goals defined by civilian leaders; in practice top military officers helped shape the nation's policies and goals, both foreign and domestic.

Even before the Japanese attack on Pearl Harbor on December 7, 1941, the United States had increased its land, sea, and air forces. With that attack the United States built, equipped, trained, and used the largest and most powerful military forces in its history. Approximately fifteen million Americans had served in the nation's Armed Forces by the end of the fighting in August, 1945. Only the forces of the Soviet Union played a larger role in defeating Nazi Germany. And despite the major roles of Great Britain and others, no country contributed as much as the United States to the defeat of the other Axis powers, Italy and Japan. Under General Dwight D. Eisenhower, America and its Allies invaded North Africa in November, 1942; defeated Mussolini's Italy by September, 1943; waged an air war over Europe; invaded Western Europe at

Normandy on D-Day, June 6, 1944; and helped force the final surrender of Germany on V–E Day, May 8, 1945. In the Pacific under Admiral Chester W. Nimitz and General Douglas MacArthur, American military forces checked the Japanese advance in naval battles of the Coral Sea, Midway, and Guadalcanàl; successfully island-hopped toward the Philippines and Japan; triumphed in the bloody conquest of the Philippines, Iwo Jima, and Okinawa in 1945; bombed Tokyo and other Japanese cities into flaming infernos; dropped atomic bombs on Hiroshima and Nagasaki; and forced the Japanese surrender that was formally signed aboard the U.S.S. *Missouri* in Tokyo Bay on V–J Day, September 2, 1945.

Responding to the cries of "bring the boys home" and to economy moves, the United States quickly dismantled its military forces at the close of World War II. At its lowest point, in 1947–1948, the United States had about one and a half million men in its Armed Forces, more than ever before in peacetime and more than had served in most of its wars.

With the cold war, Americans and their leaders in both political parties supported appropriations to enlarge the Armed Forces. The Air Force, in particular, found it easy to win ever larger appropriations. The United States increased its military manpower to around two and a half million, and the requirements of the Korean war and the fighting in Vietnam pushed the figures to more than three million. With atomic weapons, thermonuclear weapons, intercontinental bombers and missiles, nuclear-powered submarines, and improved conventional weapons, American military forces commanded destructive power unknown to any country's military forces in peace or war. Those forces helped to give the United States the power to support its worldwide diplomacy and commitments.

At the same time, those military forces exerted unprecedented peacetime influence on domestic developments within the United States and on foreign policies. Wars (past, present, and future) accounted for most of the national debt that passed the $400 billion mark. Most of America's taxes and government expenditures also went to pay for its Armed Forces. In the early years of the cold war, President Truman limited military appropriations to "only" $15 billion per year. With the Korean war, military expenditures skyrocketed, and appropriations of $40 to $50 billion a year became commonplace. With the fighting in Vietnam the figures pushed even higher. All those amounts were much greater than total expenditures for nonmilitary purposes, including diplomacy. The Department of Defense became America's largest consumer. Whole sectors of the economy depended upon and eagerly sought defense contracts. Millions of Americans benefited directly in wages and profits from defense expenditures; indirectly every American felt the effects of those expenditures. Understandably, retired military officers found their way onto the boards of directors of most corporations seeking government contracts.

The military influence was not limited to economic matters. Former top-ranking military officers filled such positions as President of the United States, Secretary of Defense, Secretary of State, and many other high civilian posts in the federal government. Like other departments, the Defense Department used propaganda to influence the minds of soldiers, ROTC cadets, and civilians. Through the National Security Council and other government organs, military officers directly affected American foreign policies. When Secretary of Defense Robert S. McNamara under Presidents Kennedy and Johnson did not sufficiently defer to the wishes of professional military officers, the anguished cries of generals and admirals were striking evidence of their restiveness under effective civilian control. The fighting in Vietnam enabled military officers to increase their influence on American foreign policies.

In 1961, after a career as a professional Army officer and after eight years as President of the United States, Dwight D. Eisenhower in his Farewell Address said:

> This conjunction of an immense military establishment and a large arms industry is new in the American experience. The total influence—economic, political, even spiritual—is felt in every city, every State house, every office of the Federal government. We recognize the imperative need for this development. Yet we must not fail to comprehend its grave implications. . . . In the councils of government, we must guard against the acquisition of unwarranted influence, whether sought or unsought, by the military-industrial complex. . . . We must never let the weight of this combination endanger our liberties or democratic processes.

So long as man is imperfect, so long as men and states feel conflicts of interests, so long as America faces dangerous challenges from such states as the Soviet Union and China, and so long as there is no world government, the United States must maintain powerful military forces. The close relationship between military power and foreign affairs requires consultation with military authorities in formulating and implementing foreign policies. But the leading "realist," Professor Hans J. Morgenthau, probably was correct when he wrote:

> To surrender the conduct of foreign affairs to the military . . . is to destroy the possibility of compromise and thus surrender the cause of peace. . . . A foreign policy conducted by military men according to the rules of the military art can only end in war. . . . the instrument of foreign policy should not become the master of foreign policy.

POLITICAL PATTERNS

Like nearly everything else in the United States from 1942 to 1974, politics reflected urban industrial and financial dominance in a war and cold war environment. On the national level, in the last half of the twentieth century, struggles for political dominance within and between parties were contests largely between different sectors of the urban population. Rural and small-town America could be little more than supplementary makeweights in close contests between contending urban factions.

The cities generally controlled both major parties. Wendell Willkie's nomination for President in 1940 was a victory for the urban-internationalist wing of the Republican party, and so were the nominations of Governor Thomas E. Dewey of New York in 1944 and 1948, and of General Dwight D. Eisenhower in 1952 and 1956. The choice of Richard M. Nixon in 1960, 1968, and 1972 broke the pattern, but his service as Vice President gave him a special advantage. He made his peace with business, but much of the urban establishment eagerly seized on the Watergate scandals to bludgeon his administration. Senator Barry Goldwater of Arizona in 1964 did not fit the pattern, but he did not win election either.

President Franklin D. Roosevelt molded an increasingly urban coalition to accomplish his reelection in 1936, and the cities reigned in the Democratic party from that time until the death of President John F. Kennedy in 1963. The policy of choosing vice presidential running mates from another section and sector of the country made it possible for Harry S. Truman of Missouri and Lyndon B. Johnson of Texas to gain the Presidency. The election of Truman in 1948 was one of the political miracles of the century, and the Republicans helped Johnson's election in 1964 by choosing a nominee who was unacceptable to much of urban America. Insofar as they reflected urban interests and values, President John F. Kennedy of Massachusetts and his Democratic administration had more in common with Federalist Alexander Hamilton than with Thomas Jefferson, the founder of Kennedy's party. Kennedy and Hamilton differed in many important respects, of course, but they (and their foreign policy views) shared an urban orientation that contrasted sharply with the agrarianism of Thomas Jefferson or William Jennings Bryan.

The power and prestige of urban wealth revealed itself in the number of successful businessmen and heirs of "robber barons" who won high places in political life. W. Averell Harriman, son of E. H. Harriman, the railroad financier; Governor Nelson A. Rockefeller of New York, grandson of John D. Rockefeller; President John F. Kennedy of Massachusetts, Senator Robert F. Kennedy of New York, and Senator Edward M. Kennedy of Massachusetts, sons of Joseph P. Kennedy; and Governor George Romney of Michigan, former head of American Motors, are just a few of many examples. Similarly, Secretaries of State since 1944 have often come from business or corporation law backgrounds, including Edward R. Stettinius of United States Steel, Dean Acheson, John Foster Dulles, and Christian A. Herter. Republican President Eisenhower appointed a top General Motors Corporation executive, Charles Wilson, to be his first Secretary of Defense; the Democratic Kennedy-Johnson administrations placed a top Ford Motor Company executive, Robert S. McNamara, in that Cabinet post.

Social welfare legislation grew largely out of urban needs and thought. Much of it was benevolent capitalism that did not really challenge industrial-financial dominance; it was not radical and often it was not even terribly liberal. The civil rights movement (like the Civil War in 1861–1865) was partly an earnest and honest struggle for human rights; initially it was also (like the Civil War) part of the continuing efforts by urban America to strike at the older leadership of rural and small-town America. Both the domestic needs of the cities and the foreign policy requirements of World War II and the cold war necessitated "big government" far beyond the needs or desires of earlier less complex circumstances within the United States and on the world scene.

IDEOLOGICAL PATTERNS

For Americans World War II was partly an ideological struggle for democracy and freedom against totalitarian fascism and Nazism. The cold war was partly an ideological crusade for democracy and capitalism against the challenge from totalitarian communism. Without minimizing other bases for those conflicts, most Americans felt the ideological aspects very deeply.

Developments both at home and abroad destroyed American isolationism. Within the United States urbanization, the related growth of industry and finance, and the educational and propaganda efforts of internationalists eroded the domestic bases for isolationism. Externally the Axis menace, the Japanese attack on Pearl Harbor, and the growing power of the Soviet Union provided the *coup de grâce*. Those developments shattered the public careers and reputations of most isolationists who refused to repudiate their pre–Pearl Harbor stance. The stigma attached to isolationism and the necessity for unity in the struggle against the Axis silenced prewar isolationists and provided impressive bipartisan support for Roosevelt's leadership of the war effort. During and after World War II, leaders in both political parties resolved that the United States would not revert back to isolationism as it had after World War I. Senator Arthur H. Vandenberg of Michigan helped lead the Republican party to bipartisan support for internationalism, the United Nations, and containment. Bipartisanship in foreign policy ideally meant that leaders and members of both major political parties helped shape and support those policies. In practice more often it meant endorsement of the foreign policies of the administration in power. From 1942 until 1949, there was little effective dissent from internationalism in responsible circles of either major party or in any part of the country.

Isolationism under that name never recovered from the Japanese attack on Pearl Harbor. In fragmentary forms under other guises, however, one could find remnants of it within a minority of the population after 1942. Though they generally remained silent on foreign affairs during World War II, most of the leading prewar isolationists, such as Charles A. Lindbergh, Burton K. Wheeler, and Gerald P. Nye, continued to believe that they had been right before Pearl Harbor. With the fall of China to the Communists in 1949, the beginning of the Korean war in 1950, and the presidential election campaign of 1952, bipartisanship in foreign affairs broke down. Herbert Hoover and Senator Robert A. Taft called for a continentalism or "Fortress America." Senator Joseph McCarthy of Wisconsin charged the State Department with harboring Communists and Communist sympathizers. In contrast to the Europe-first orientation of most internationalists, many within the Republican party criticized President Truman and Secretary of State Dean Acheson for neglecting Asia. They denounced the administration for "losing" China to the Communists, either through bungling or Communist influence. Widespread support for the Bricker amendment expressed dissatisfaction with presidential authority and would have increased congressional restraints on the President in foreign affairs. Growing opposition to foreign aid programs fitted the same general pattern. Many became more critical of America's NATO allies in Europe, including Great Britain. The United Nations came under growing attack. The "massive retaliation" policy that Secretary of State John Foster Dulles announced in 1954 seemed to attach greater importance to America's own unilateral nuclear capability in restraining the Soviet Union than it did to the limited-war capability of the United States and its allies using conventional weapons. While using the language of internationalism and collective security, American policies in Korea, Formosa, and Vietnam in effect backed into unilateralism. Such echoes of an older isolationism did not disappear. Nevertheless, the dominant view after World War II in both the Democratic and Republican parties was internationalist rather than unilateralist and noninterventionist toward Europe.

In leadership circles in the 1950's and early 1960's, the Realist school of thought provided a more sophisticated challenge to internationalist ideas. The leading Realists in the United States after World War II included Professor Hans J. Morgenthau of the University of Chicago, George F. Kennan of the Department of State and later at the Institute for Advanced Study at Princeton, and the columnist Walter Lippmann. They rejected isolationism, but they directed their main fire against utopian internationalists such as Woodrow Wilson and Cordell Hull. In their view idealistic crusades for utopian and unlimited goals could not succeed, and they made compromise, accommodation, and peace impossible. As Morgenthau phrased it: "The objectives of foreign policy must be defined in terms of national interest and must be supported with adequate power." The Realists emphasized limiting America's goals in foreign affairs to those that could be accomplished with the power available. They did *not* contend that "might makes right," but they did insist that right (or foreign policy goals of any sort) could not prevail without sufficient supporting power broadly defined. In that sense they emphasized that though America's power was great, it was not unlimited. The Realists generally gave priority to European developments, were not impressed by the power of the newly emerging states of Asia and Africa, and did not want to commit America to major wars in Asia that would leave it vulnerable elsewhere. The Realist school had much influence on professional diplomats, administration advisers, and academic specialists in international affairs.

Americans often differed sharply among themselves on specific issues such as Communist China, Korea, Cuba, and Vietnam. Until the latter part of the 1960's, however, there was a wide area of agreement among the American people on foreign affairs, particularly where the cold war with the Soviet Union was concerned. That consensus extended to both political parties, to all sections of the country, and to most social and economic groups. During World War II, nearly all Americans agreed that the Axis powers must be defeated and crushed. During World War II and the cold war, most Americans recognized that developments in other parts of the world inevitably affected American interests and security, that the United States could not isolate itself from world affairs. They agreed that because of its great power the United States could not avoid affecting world affairs whether it wanted to or not, and that it therefore had a special responsibility to use its power wisely. They knew that the United States was powerful. But they also realized that it was not all-powerful, and that the limits of its power made it essential for the United States to cooperate with other like-minded states to guard peace and security. Most Americans agreed that the main threats to peace and security came from the communist bloc headed by the Soviet Union and China. And finally, from 1947 onward most Americans in both parties supported the containment of Soviet expansionist tendencies. During the two and a half decades following the Japanese attack on Pearl Harbor, consensus was more striking than diversity in American attitudes toward foreign affairs.

Challenges from both the right and the left forced modifications of the consensus from time to time, but it proved to be remarkably stable over the years. The trauma of the more extreme of those challenges strained the fabric of American society and raised serious fears about the survival of American freedom and democracy. Those extremist challenges did not prevail, however, and even when the requirements of party and election politics moderated the challenges substantially, they failed to triumph in presidential contests.

In the early 1950's Senator Joseph R. McCarthy of Wisconsin spearheaded a major challenge from the right with his charges that the Democratic Roosevelt-Truman administrations had been "soft on communism" both at home and abroad. In more moderate terms, that theme affected the Republican presidential campaign in 1952, though Dwight D. Eisenhower as President conducted American foreign affairs within the framework of the established consensus. The Republican Party's attempt to challenge the consensus from the right with the nomination of Senator Barry Goldwater of Arizona in 1964 had little effect beyond demonstrating once again the strength of that consensus. Most American historians wrote from a liberal-internationalist-realist frame of reference; the challenges from the right won little following and no respectability among diplomatic historians.

There were also challenges from the left. Some denounced American imperialism whether of the Big Stick, dollar diplomacy, or Open Door variety. Henry A. Wallace and his Progressive Party criticized America's anti-Soviet policies in the presidential election of 1948, but he failed to win any electoral votes. That general view won little support in the "placid decade" of the 1950's.

In the latter part of the 1960's, however, the growing unpopularity of American military involvement in Vietnam provided a much more receptive environment for that challenge. Young people (including many college students and young faculty members) whose memories did not extend back to the tense international crises of the early cold war found it difficult to see the Soviet Union and communism as so oppressive and aggressively fearsome as their elders had contended. Seared by the ordeals of the Great Depression and World War II, older Americans had experienced "doing without" and were reconciled to compromises with perfection in their personal lives, in domestic affairs, and in foreign relations. In contrast, middle class young people on college and university campuses had been reared in an atmosphere of prosperity, permissiveness, and peace. They had had little personal experience with deprivation and tended to be impatient with a world, a society, a government, and an older generation that failed to provide "instant utopia." New Left scholars (many quite young themselves) found ready acceptance for their critical "revisionist" interpretations that blamed the origins of the cold war on American expansion and on unjustified hostility to communist Russia.

Those scholars also attacked the Vietnam policies of Presidents Johnson and Nixon. Criticisms, however, did not come only from the left. Some criticisms of American policies in Vietnam in the late 1960's and early 1970's came from most of the various ideological groups: internationalists, realists, pacifists, neoisolationists, radicals, and from "hawks" and militarists who thought the government was not being aggressive enough in prosecuting the war. Those challenges to the foreign policy consensus and to the war in Vietnam reached peaks in 1968–1970, when they forced Lyndon B. Johnson to abandon any plans for seeking an additional term as President, when they undercut Vice President Hubert H. Humphrey's bid for the White House, and when in the spring of 1970 widespread violence erupted on college and university campuses in response to President Richard Nixon's decision to send American troops into Cambodia. With traditional bonds and loyalties seemingly snapping, growing numbers felt alienated from America, from the "establishment," and from government policies at home and abroad.

Some predicted a resurgence of American isolationism. And indeed (though most of them were unaware of the similarities and were quick to deny or explain away the parallels) Vietnam critics did advance lines of reasoning used earlier by isolationists before Pearl Harbor. Like prewar isolationists, Vietnam critics denounced secrecy in government, excessive presidential power in foreign affairs, too much influence by the military and big business, and involvement in wars abroad that were not essential to America's vital interests and security. Like prewar isolationists, they charged that involvement abroad diverted attention and money away from pressing problems at home. They urged limiting presidential power in foreign affairs, increasing popular control over foreign policies, curtailing American expansion abroad, and concentration on domestic reforms. But those who talked in such terms by the early 1970's generally were not the same people or spokesmen for the same groups that had urged noninterventionist policies before Pearl Harbor. The most notable critics of American involvement in Vietnam had been Europe-first internationalists in World War II or spoke for groups (including urban groups) that had been internationalists at that time.

Campus violence, noisy radicals, critical news media, and political partisanship provided an exaggerated portrait of the degree of breakdown of the foreign policy consensus. In the election of 1972 the relatively moderate Democratic Party challenge from the left with the presidential candidacy of George McGovern was even less successful than the Republican Party challenge from the right with Barry Goldwater had been eight years earlier. The foreign policy consensus prevailed.

To a limited degree, however, the domestic challenges and changed circumstances abroad did modify that consensus. McCarthyism and the Republican campaign tactics in 1952 hurried President Eisenhower's efforts to end the fighting in Korea in 1953. And the anti-Vietnam agitation and the Democratic campaign tactics in 1972 hurried President Nixon's moves to end the fighting in Vietnam. Furthermore, developments abroad and changes at home led the Nixon administration beginning in 1969 to inaugurate modifications of American foreign policies. Externally the Soviet Peace Offensive, the rupture between China and Russia, the growing strength and independence of European states, the increasing hostility of Third World states, and the unpopularity abroad of America's involvement in Vietnam, all encouraged limiting America's role in world affairs. Similarly within the United States the unfavorable balance of payments and the alienation of important domestic groups (blacks, ethnics, youths, women, radicals, intellectuals, and urban news media) from government, party, and foreign policy leadership made it expedient to consider more limited roles for the United States abroad. The Nixon Doctrine, first announced in July, 1969, did not repudiate the major policies the United States had pursued in foreign affairs since World War II. It did not abandon American commitments in Europe and elsewhere. It did not turn away from containment and internationalism, and it did not embrace isolationism. But it did envisage a lower profile for the United States in Asia, and it called on other states to assume larger shares of the manpower and financial responsibilities for guarding their interests and security than before. The Nixon Doctrine adjusted to changing conditions at home and abroad, and it sustained more of the postwar foreign policy consensus than extremists on either the right or the left would have preferred.

THE ADMINISTRATION AND CONDUCT OF FOREIGN RELATIONS

In an earlier and simpler time the frontier farmer found it both necessary and possible to be a jack-of-all-trades. When democracy was "spelled with a small d," most Americans feared and distrusted elites of almost any sort. They expected "citizen soldiers" to fight and win their wars. They expected the man-next-door to enact or administer laws if he were elected to public office. They expected amateur "shirt-sleeve diplomats" to serve American interests in dealings with other countries. And they wanted close congressional control over it all. That faith in the amateur and generalist was not always misplaced, just as distrust of elites was not always unjustified.

Nevertheless, the active role of the United States in the increasingly complex and dangerous world of the twentieth century required the services of individuals whose qualifications extended beyond contributing time and money to the right political party or candidate. The increasingly complex urbanized society of the twentieth century put a premium on specialization and placed the generalist at a disadvantage. That pattern contributed to the development of a more professional military force. It led to a more professional career foreign service to conduct American diplomacy. And it increased the administration's freedom and authority in the conduct of foreign affairs.

The United States Congress in the twentieth century continued to have important powers in foreign affairs, particularly negatively. The Senate still had to approve treaties before they bound the United States.

Diplomatic appointments continued to be subject to Senate approval. Congress continued to have exclusive authority to declare a formal state of war. Congressional investigations (or threats of congressional investigations) could inhibit an administration's course in foreign affairs. And Congress' power to appropriate funds and levy taxes became more important to American foreign policies than ever before. Foreign aid programs, powerful modern military forces, and undeclared military actions would not be possible if Congress refused to provide the funds. When filled by an able person, the post of chairman of the Senate Foreign Relations Committee continued to be one of the more powerful government positions relating to foreign affairs. Nevertheless, in general the powers of Congress in foreign affairs declined relative to those of the President.

From the beginning of American constitutional history the powers of the President in foreign affairs tended to increase. That growth was most striking in the twentieth century, and it evolved during both Democratic and Republican administrations. Numerous circumstances and tactics enhanced that presidential power. The need for secrecy or consistency discouraged Presidents from taking Congress or the people into their confidence on certain matters. Presidents used executive agents for certain missions to bypass the Senate's authority to approve (or reject) regular diplomatic appointees.

Presidents increasingly used executive agreements to avoid the Senate's power in the treaty-making process. Executive agreements were not subject to Senate approval. Theoretically they bound only the administration that signed them, not subsequent Presidents. Theoretically, also, executive agreements dealt with less important matters than treaties. In practice, however, Presidents considered themselves bound by executive agreements concluded by earlier administrations. And in practice they often dealt with very important matters. The Yalta and Potsdam agreements were executive agreements, not treaties. Executive agreements could not be used as peace treaties formally ending wars, but they served for armistices and truces.

Science and technology increased the President's direct role in diplomacy. With modern transportation facilities he or his Secretary of State could quickly fly to meet with foreign leaders and conduct negotiations personally. Radio and telephone enabled him to consult at any moment with American diplomats abroad and with heads of other states. Radio and television enabled the President or his Secretary of State to speak directly to the people at home and abroad on foreign policies.

Presidents used many tactics to win congressional support in foreign affairs. They appointed Senators to commissions negotiating agreements, with the expectation that those legislators would then help persuade the Senate to approve the agreement. For example, Senators Tom Connally and Arthur H. Vandenberg, both members of the Foreign Relations Committee, were among the American delegates who helped draft the United Nations Charter in San Francisco in 1945. Presidents often consulted with Senate and House leaders and committees to win their support for foreign policies. Presidents of both parties used their control of patronage to win needed votes. In moments of crisis Presidents (including both Eisenhower and Johnson) sought and got congressional resolutions endorsing their course of action, thus enabling the chief executive to move ahead with greater freedom and effectiveness than might have been the case without that vote of confidence.

Under the President the Department of State has the main responsibility for implementing American foreign policies. The Secretary of State is the top member of the President's Cabinet. The position was always a political appointment, but after World War II the men named to that post had had previous experience in foreign affairs more often than had usually been the case earlier. George Marshall, Dean Acheson, John Foster Dulles, and Dean Rusk, for example, had had substantial experience in foreign affairs before becoming Secretaries of State.

The relative influence of the President and his Secretary of State on American foreign policies varied according to the temperaments and abilities of the two men. Franklin D. Roosevelt, John F. Kennedy, and Richard M. Nixon played dominant roles in foreign affairs and were often, in effect, their own Secretaries of State. In contrast Dean Acheson under President Truman and John Foster Dulles under President Eisenhower generally provided the ideas and initiative that then won presidential support.

The Department of State remained one of the smaller departments of the government. Nevertheless, in the twentieth century it grew spectacularly in comparison with its tiny, informal structure in the eighteenth and nineteenth centuries. In 1974 the Department of State was a highly complex organization in huge quarters with something like 8,000 persons on its payroll in Washington. In the postwar era it had to handle a steadily growing number and variety of problems in American relations with an increasing number and variety of foreign states.

In recognition of the wide variety of interests and concerns in foreign affairs, the National Security Council created in 1947 brought together the Secretary of State, the Secretary of Defense, and other top administration officials to consult and advise the President on national security matters. It languished in the Kennedy and Johnson administrations, but was given renewed importance by President Nixon. Under the President, National Security Adviser Henry A. Kissinger upstaged Secretary of State William P. Rogers in the diplomacy and policy making of Nixon's administration.

In the eighteenth and nineteenth centuries, American diplomats and consuls abroad generally were political appointees. Very often they had had no previous experience in foreign affairs and did not know either French (the diplomatic language) or the language of the country to which they were assigned.

Late in the nineteenth century and early in the twentieth century, Presidents Grover Cleveland and Theodore Roosevelt tried to give greater weight to ability and experience in making diplomatic appointments. The Rogers Act of 1924 was a major step forward. It merged the consular and diplomatic services into a single Foreign Service. It strengthened merit provisions for entering the Foreign Service through very rigid examinations. It increased the pay for Foreign Service officers. Though most diplomatic posts continued to be filled by political appointees, it became possible for career men to move up through the ranks and eventually become ministers and ambassadors.

Drawing on the experience under the Rogers Act, Congress adopted the Foreign Service Act of 1946. Under that law as subsequently amended and modified, young men and women between the ages of 21 and 31 could begin careers in the Foreign Service by passing rigid written, oral, and medical examinations and by obtaining satisfactory security clearance. Pay scales steadily improved to attract able individuals. The Department of State drew its Foreign Service officers from all over the country and from many different colleges and universities. Foreign Service ranks include women and blacks. The new Foreign Service officer was trained in the Department of State Foreign Service Institute and other schools. The law provided for a "promotion-up or selection-out" system to weed out individuals who did not mature sufficiently to assume the greater responsibilities of higher grades. In addition, the Department of State appointed individuals with needed specialties as Foreign Service Reserve officers for limited terms. American Foreign Service officers might serve in any one of some 120 diplomatic posts abroad or in any of approximately 150 consular posts. Most of America's ambassadors in 1973 were career officers rather than political appointees.

The system was not perfect, of course. McCarthyism in the 1950's severely damaged the Foreign Service and destroyed the professional careers of individual officers—particularly China experts. The Defense Department and National Security Advisor Kissinger in the White House overshadowed the State Department and Foreign Service officers on many important foreign policy matters. The system produced some officers who were not adequate for the responsibilities they faced. Nevertheless, for the most part the Foreign Service included intelligent, well-educated, dedicated career officers with diverse backgrounds, personalities, and temperaments. If the United States ought to have even better representatives abroad, perhaps some among the more able who read this book may consider dedicating their talents and lives to that worthy service.

SUPPLEMENTARY READINGS

Goldman, Eric F. *The Crucial Decade—And After: America, 1945–1960.* New York: Vintage Books, Inc., 1960.

Graebner, Norman A. *The New Isolationism: A Study in Politics and Foreign Policy since 1950.* New York: Ronald Press Co., 1956.

Johnson, Lyndon B. *The Vantage Point: Perspectives of the Presidency, 1963–1969.* New York: Holt, Rinehart & Winston, Inc., 1971.

Johnson, Walter. *1600 Pennsylvania Avenue: Presidents and the People, 1929–1959.* Boston: Little, Brown & Co., 1960.

Lubell, Samuel. *The Future of American Politics.* 2d ed. rev. Garden City, N.Y.: Doubleday & Co., Inc., 1956.

McCamy, James L. *Conduct of the New Diplomacy.* New York: Harper & Row, Publishers, 1964.

Millis, Walter. *Arms and Men: A Study of American Military History.* New York: G. P. Putnam's Sons, 1956.

Mills, C. Wright. *The Power Elite.* New York: Oxford University Press, Inc., 1959.

Morgenthau, Hans J. *In Defense of the National Interest.* New York: Alfred A. Knopf, Inc., 1951.

————. *Politics Among Nations: The Struggle for Power and Peace.* 4th ed. New York: Alfred A. Knopf, Inc., 1967.

Plischke, Elmer. *Conduct of American Diplomacy.* 3d ed. Princeton, N.J.: D. Van Nostrand Co., Inc., 1967.

Schlesinger, Arthur M., Jr. *A Thousand Days: John F. Kennedy in the White House.* Boston: Houghton Mifflin Co., 1965.

Servan-Schreiber, J.-J. *The American Challenge.* New York: Atheneum Publishers, 1968.

Steel, Ronald. *Pax Americana.* New rev. ed. New York: Viking Press, 1970.

Whyte, William H., Jr. *The Organization Man.* Garden City, N.Y.: Doubleday & Co., Inc., 1956.

36

Soviet-American
relations to 1945

Substantial conflicts of interests and ideas developed in relations between the United States and czarist Russia late in the nineteenth century, long before the Bolsheviks came to power. The triumph of the Communists under Lenin and Trotsky in the fall of 1917 made a bad situation worse. The United States withheld diplomatic recognition from the communist government of the Soviet Union until 1933. Relations improved when the two countries fought common enemies in World War II, but they were never really cordial. After World War II, the cold war between the communist bloc led by the Soviet Union and noncommunist states led by the United States dominated world politics. Peaceful coexistence in the 1950's and 1960's modified the friction and hostility but did not end it.

From 1914 to 1917 Americans found it difficult to consider the Allied cause a struggle for democracy when one of the Allies was autocratic Russia under Czar Nicholas II. The revolution in March, 1917, that ended the czarist era and established a provisional government under Prince Lvov and later under Alexander Kerensky, briefly improved Russian-American relations. The United States Ambassador to Russia was David R. Francis, an elderly St. Louis businessman and politician. Encouraged by his reports, the Wilson administration and most Americans believed that the Russians had thrown off their shackles and had turned to democracy on the Western model. They hoped the new provisional govern-

414

ment would prosecute the war against the Central Powers more successfully than the czarist regime had. The United States quickly recognized
the provisional government, on March 20, 1917, and authorized loans of
$325 million to that government. Probably most Russians wanted "bread,
peace, and land." The provisional government failed to satisfy the hopes
of either the Russians or the Americans. In incredibly chaotic circumstances, the Russian government could neither feed its people nor win
military battles. It fell before the Bolshevik revolution in the autumn
of 1917.

The revolution in November, 1917, took the Wilson administration and
the American people by surprise. David Francis insisted (incorrectly)
that Lenin and Trotsky simply were agents of the German government
whose assignment was to take Russia out of the war. He contended that
the Bolsheviks had little support and would soon be overthrown. He advised the American government not to recognize the new communist
regime in Russia. At the same time, Francis actively encouraged counter-
revolutionary activity against the Bolsheviks. President Wilson's moralistic attitudes, Secretary of State Lansing's conservatism, and the
requirements of the war against Germany all helped make American
leaders receptive to Francis' advice. American hostility to the Bolsheviks
increased in March, 1918, when Lenin's government signed and ratified
the Treaty of Brest-Litovsk ending Russia's war with Germany. In that
peace treaty Russia lost one fourth of its population, vast natural resources, and much of its manufacturing capacity. But with economic and
military conditions hopelessly demoralized and with no recognition or
help from the West, Lenin and Trotsky believed they had no practical
alternative but to accept the harsh German terms.

If economic desperation, military defeat, revolution, counterrevolution, and a cruel peace settlement were not difficulties enough, the Russians also faced intervention by military forces from Japan, Great Britain, France, and the United States. Britain and France particularly
urged those Allied interventions. The official reasons for intervention
were to protect large stocks of war supplies, to help 45,000 Czechoslovak
troops get out of Russia to fight against Germany on the Western Front,
and to help reestablish an Eastern Front against the Central Powers.
Though not officially admitted, other reasons included the desire to restrain Japanese ambitions in Manchuria and Siberia, and to encourage
counterrevolutionary overthrow of the Bolsheviks and establishment of
a government that would continue the war against Germany. In 1918
Allied forces landed at Archangel and Murmansk in North Russia as well
as in Siberia. The United States under President Wilson participated in
the interventions but did so only reluctantly and with serious misgivings. The President explicitly ordered American forces not to meddle in
Russian domestic matters. The United States did not remove its troops

from North Russia until July, 1919, and American soldiers remained in Siberia until April, 1920.

The military interventions in Russia failed to accomplish any of the official objectives. The Czech troops got to Vladivostok, but would have gotten there without Allied intervention. World War I ended before they could be sent into combat on the Western Front. The supplies scattered and had no influence on the outcome of the war. Intervention did not re-establish an Eastern Front. The Japanese did not withdraw from Siberia until long after American and British troops had left. Contrary to Wilson's wishes and orders, the Allied interventions did encourage counter-revolutionary forces, particularly those under Admiral A. V. Kolchak in Siberia. But neither the direct nor the indirect effects of the interventions caused the Communists to fall. The Bolsheviks crushed Kolchak's efforts early in 1920. The Allied interventions further convinced the Bolsheviks that capitalist states led by Britain, France, the United States, and Japan were their mortal enemies. Though they probably would have believed that even without the interventions, those military movements provided the Communist leaders with handy propaganda that they used against the West effectively inside and outside the Soviet Union.

The United States continued to withhold diplomatic recognition from the communist government throughout the remainder of the Democratic Wilson administration and through the three Republican administrations that followed. Not until several months had passed in the Roosevelt administration did the United States finally agree to exchange diplomatic representatives with the Soviet Union.

In addition to the original reasons for nonrecognition, numerous influences helped prolong that policy for sixteen years. Newspapers in the United States got most of their information from anti-Bolshevik sources. They consistently portrayed the Communists in hostile terms. The slanted press coverage affected public opinion. Churches (particularly Roman Catholic and Orthodox Catholic) opposed recognition because of the atheistic, antireligion, and antichurch policies of the Bolsheviks. Many clergymen in Russia suffered persecution, imprisonment, exile, or death at the hands of the Bolsheviks. American businessmen gained more political influence after World War I and in the 1920's. Understandably, they opposed communism as a revolutionary challenge to capitalism. More specifically, some American firms had made loans to the czarist or provisional governments; the Bolsheviks refused to acknowledge or pay those debts. Some American businesses had owned property in Russia that the Bolsheviks destroyed or confiscated. The "Red Scare" that swept the United States at the close of World War I and in the early 1920's further stiffened opposition to recognition.

A few Americans favored recognition, but they got little support in the 1920's. Most prominent among them were western agrarians led by

Senators William E. Borah of Idaho, Burton K. Wheeler of Montana, and Robert M. LaFollette of Wisconsin. They were progressives, but they were not Communists or even fellow travelers.

The American people never urgently demanded recognition of the Soviet Union. Nevertheless, by the early 1930's some of the bases for opposing recognition weakened and support for recognition increased. Both internal and external influences operated, but the domestic ones were the more decisive. The Great Depression made Americans desperate for anything that might help restore prosperity. Trade with Russia had never been great, but it continued in the 1920's despite the absence of diplomatic relations. Some (including heads of conservative business corporations) hoped that recognition and a trade treaty might increase markets in the Soviet Union and to that extent promote profits and prosperity. General Electric, Standard Oil, Ford Motor, and American Locomotive were among the corporations in the United States that did business with the communist government of the Soviet Union in the 1920's and hoped recognition would help that business. Furthermore, some American firms had made financial settlements with the Soviet Union for property they had lost in Russia, so that basis for opposing recognition was weaker than before. Ideologically, the Red Scare had faded by 1933. Most Americans were less worried about the danger of a Communist take-over than they had been a dozen years before.

In addition, certain external developments encouraged recognition or at least reduced opposition to it. The Soviet Union sought recognition. Great Britain, France, and Italy had extended recognition in 1924, and Japan did so a year later. Lenin died in 1924, and Trotsky and his followers were exiled or executed. Joseph Stalin was a dedicated Communist, but he seemed to be less of a world revolutionist and more of a nationalist than his predecessors and opponents in Russia. Efforts at Communist revolutions outside of Russia had failed. And despite the intensity of the Great Depression, most people in America and elsewhere did not turn to communism. The Soviet Union still refused to pay debts contracted by earlier Russian governments. But by 1933 most countries that owed war debts to the United States government were defaulting, so the Soviet Union was not much worse on that issue than many other states with which the United States had diplomatic relations. American delegates had participated in conferences that included representatives from the Soviet Union and had signed multilateral treaties that included the Soviet Union. Consequently, the United States had, in effect, already extended a *de facto* level of recognition. The Axis was not yet a reality and most could not predict the course to World War II. Nevertheless, Mussolini's Fascists had been in power in Italy since 1922, Japan had already taken over Manchuria, and Hitler and his Nazis had gained control in Germany in January, 1933. Some in the Soviet Union and the United

States hoped that recognition might facilitate cooperation against Japan in Asia and Germany in Europe. International law experts pointed out that recognition would not imply approval of communism. And by 1933 most Americans realized that David Francis was mistaken in 1917 when he had predicted an early collapse of the communist regime in Russia. Some in the United States continued to oppose recognition, including church groups, the American Federation of Labor, and the American Legion. Nevertheless, by 1933 the reasons for opposing recognition did not seem quite so persuasive, and arguments for recognition became more convincing.

In October, 1933, the Roosevelt administration proposed that the two countries initiate conversations to consider arrangements for establishing formal diplomatic relations. Foreign Commissar Maxim Litvinov represented the Soviet Union in those negotiations. Friendly and genial, he did not look at all like the bearded, bomb-carrying Bolshevik that some Americans may have expected. The negotiations got little publicity, but in November, 1933, President Roosevelt announced a recognition agreement in the form of an exchange of letters between the two governments. The Soviet Union waived all claims against the United States for damages growing out of American participation in the Allied interventions during World War I. The Soviet Union agreed to discuss the debt problem with the United States. It also promised to refrain from revolutionary propaganda in the United States and to restrain persons under its control from such activities. Americans were to enjoy the right of freedom of worship while living or traveling in the Soviet Union. With that exchange of letters, President Roosevelt named William C. Bullitt to be America's first Ambassador to the Soviet Union.

Unfortunately, recognition did not lead to cordial relations, and the results were not nearly as satisfactory as the more optimistic had hoped. Trade did not increase enough to affect the depression in the United States. Negotiations on intergovernmental debts broke down completely by the end of 1935. The Soviet Union never paid the debts owed to the United States by earlier Russian governments. The Communist International continued to promote revolutionary propaganda in the United States. And the United States and the Soviet Union were not able to work together against the Axis powers until both were drawn into the war in 1941.

In the 1930's, both countries focused most of their attention and energies on domestic matters rather than on foreign affairs. Furthermore, the methods each used to deal with the Axis menace worked at cross-purposes. Until Munich in 1938, the Soviet Union urged collective security with the West to block Axis aggression. At the same time, Americans embraced isolationism to guard against involvement in any foreign wars. The United States did not cooperate with the Western European democracies against Hitler and Mussolini; it certainly would not work with Communist Russia.

By 1939 President Roosevelt was leading the United States away from isolationism toward collective security of the aid-short-of-war variety. By that time, however, the Soviet Union had abandoned its seemingly futile efforts to cooperate with the West against the Axis. The Soviet Union had inaugurated its own isolationist policies toward Axis aggression and war in Europe and Asia. Through the Russo-German Nonaggression Pact of 1939, the Soviet Union appeased Hitler and opened the door to Germany's attack on Poland that started World War II. The Russo-Finnish War of 1939–1940 was part of the Soviet Union's efforts to build its defense arrangements against future assault by Nazi Germany. In April, 1941, the Soviet Union concluded a Neutrality Pact with Japan, the Asian member of the Axis. Each of those actions, particularly the Russo-Finnish War, further alienated Americans. Most people in the United States did not like Communist Russia any more than they did Nazi Germany. Those Soviet arrangements with the Axis, coming at the same time as Americans were awakening to the dangers of the Axis menace, infuriated millions in the United States. In the minds of most Americans the Axis powers were more to be hated and feared than the Soviet Union, mainly because at that particular time they were more powerful and aggressive.

Not until Hitler started the Russo-German War on June 22, 1941, and Japan attacked Pearl Harbor on December 7, 1941, did the United States and the Soviet Union finally draw together in a struggle for survival against a common enemy. American isolationists saw the Russo-German War as one more reason why the United States should stay out of the European war. They ridiculed the idea of fighting on the side of "bloody Joe." Senator Bennett Champ Clark of Missouri asked if anyone could "conceive of American boys being sent to their deaths singing 'Onward Christian Soldiers' under the bloody emblem of the Hammer and Sickle." Charles A. Lindbergh said he "would a hundred times rather see my country ally herself with England, or even with Germany with all her faults, than with the cruelty, the godlessness, and the barbarism that exist in Soviet Russia." They wanted the United States to sit back and let Nazi Germany and Communist Russia destroy each other.

American Communists, on the other hand, abruptly changed from isolationists to fervent interventionists. On June 21, they insisted that Britain was simply fighting to preserve its ill-gotten empire. They denounced Roosevelt as a "warmonger" and urged the United States to stay out of the war. With the beginning of the Russo-German War, however, American Communists immediately reversed themselves, urged the United States to declare war on Germany, and denounced isolationists as traitors and fascists.

The Roosevelt administration, the interventionists, and the majority of the American people continued to believe that the Axis powers were still the most dangerous threat to American peace and security. Most Americans approved when Roosevelt added the Soviet Union to the list of countries receiving aid short of war. The President did not apply the Neutrality Act to the Russo-German War, so American ships could carry products all the way to Russian ports. Lend-Lease aid went to the Soviet Union as it did to Great Britain, China, and other states.

As Hitler's blitzkrieg smashed deeper into Russian territory, most Americans (including most experts on Russia) expected Germany to crush the Soviet Union just as it had every other continental European country it had attacked. Many assumed that Stalin's purge of the military in the 1930's had deprived the Soviet Union of essential officers. As the Russians fought bravely and effectively to defend their country, however, and with the help of "Generals November and December" successfully checked the German armies at the gates of Moscow, Americans came to admire the Russian courage and fighting ability.

In the whole period from June 22, 1941, when the Russo-German war began, until September 2, 1945, when the last of the Axis powers surrendered, relations between the United States and the Soviet Union were fairly good, better than they had been at any time since the Communists came to power in 1917. But they were not nearly as cooperative as those between the United States and Great Britain. There was much friction and irritation. Each country was reluctant or unwilling to share military secrets with the other. The Soviet Union would not allow American observers on the fighting fronts in Eastern Europe. The United States and Great Britain worked together in developing the atomic bomb, but they did not inform the Russians officially until the Potsdam Conference shortly before Hiroshima. The United States and Great Britain established a Combined Chiefs of Staff, but they did not create one with the Soviet Union. The United States and Great Britain trucked supplies for the Soviet Union through Iran, but they experienced annoying difficulties in their dealings with Russian officials and officers there. Late in the war, American and British airplanes began shuttle bombing operations. That is, they took off from Britain or Western Europe, dropped their bombs on targets in Germany, and landed at air bases in Russian-controlled territory for more fuel and bombs. Then they dropped bombs on German targets on their return trips. Though directed against the common foe, Americans and British encountered much difficulty making arrangements with the Russians for shuttle bombing.

The issue that most angered Soviet leaders was the delay in establishing a second front against Germany in Western Europe. Except for the Italian campaign and isolated raids, from June, 1941, until June, 1944, the Soviet Union was the only country fighting on land against the Axis armies on the European continent. Stalin repeatedly urged the Western powers to establish a second front to relieve the military pressure on the Soviet Union and to speed Hitler's final defeat. Roosevelt assured him there would be a second front in 1942, and Churchill told him he could expect one in 1943. When both years passed with no Anglo-American invasion of Western Europe, Stalin's deep distrust of his noncommunist allies increased. Anglo-American forces invaded North Africa in 1942, they knocked Italy out of the war in 1943, and they pushed north against German forces in Italy. American and British bombers made ever more massive and destructive air attacks on Hitler's Europe. Nevertheless, Stalin insisted that those actions did not significantly reduce German strength in Eastern Europe and could never crush the Axis. He and other Russian leaders became convinced that the Western powers were deliberately postponing a second front until Hitler's forces had destroyed themselves and the Russians in Eastern Europe.

Though the Soviet Union, Great Britain, and the United States all were dedicated to the unconditional defeat of Nazi Germany, they differed on the methods for accomplishing that defeat. Stalin and the Russians were not concerned about minimizing Anglo-American losses; they did want to reduce and end very quickly the terrible sacrifices the Soviet Union was making. For a variety of reasons Great Britain under Winston Churchill either hoped a massive cross-channel invasion would not be necessary or wanted to delay it until all necessary preparations assured its success. Britain's terrible casualties in World War I, the near catastrophes of Dunkirk and Dieppe, and its limited power and resources, made Churchill's Britain hesitate to risk the losses that even a successful second front in Western Europe might entail. For many years Britain had had vital interests in the Mediterranean area and attached greater importance to military operations against the Axis there than the United States or the Soviet Union did. In World War I, Churchill had urged the Gallipoli campaign in the eastern Mediterranean, and despite its failure he never lost his obsession for the general idea. Churchill worried about and hoped to limit Russian expansion in the region. In World War II, he wanted to strike at Hitler's "soft underbelly" by way of the Mediterranean.

Most Americans and their leaders believed that the Axis defeat in Europe required a second front. Their greater power and limited experience made them more optimistic about the outcome and less fearful of the costs than the British were. American military leaders wanted a massive cross-channel invasion of Western Europe not later than 1943, with a possible smaller preliminary operation in 1942. Even the Americans, however, could not overlook the very great risks involved nor the tremendous preparations essential for success. The persistent arguments by British military and civilian leaders, and President Roosevelt's eventual

support for the British position, gave priority to Anglo-American campaigns in North Africa, Sicily, and Italy, and delayed the second front.
Not until nearly three years after the Russo-German war began and two
and a half years after Pearl Harbor did Allied forces invade France on
June 6, 1944, D–Day, and establish the second front against Nazi Germany
that Stalin had sought for so long.

Despite continued friction, however, relations between the United
States and the Soviet Union did improve during World War II. On January 1, 1942, representatives from the United States, the Soviet Union,
Great Britain, and other countries fighting the Axis signed the Declaration of the United Nations. That executive agreement was the alliance
against the Axis. The signatory powers agreed to all-out war and promised not to make a separate peace with the enemy. They accepted the
principles of the Atlantic Charter drafted by Roosevelt and Churchill in
August, 1941.

The United States gave $11 billion worth of Lend-Lease aid to the
Soviet Union, more than to any other country except Great Britain.
Americans delivered most of that aid. Both government and private
propaganda in the United States lauded the Russians (though not communism). Hollywood motion pictures used Englishmen, Chinese, and
Russians as heroes, and Germans and Japanese as villains. Pro-Russian
movies included "Mission to Moscow" and "Song of Russia." Conservative newspapers and news magazines found kind things to write about
Russians fighting the Nazis. Similarly, Soviet propaganda provided a
more favorable portrait of the United States and the West than usual.
In 1943 the Russians abolished the Comintern. There was some return
lend-lease. And the Soviet Union eventually allowed American and British planes to use bases on its soil.

Soviet-American cooperation and friction manifested itself in a series
of top-level conferences at Moscow and Teheran in 1943, and at Yalta and
Potsdam in 1945. In those conferences and others certain patterns
evolved. Winston Churchill of Great Britain, Joseph Stalin of the Soviet
Union, and Franklin D. Roosevelt of the United States all were dedicated
to guarding the security and vital interests of their respective countries.
All agreed on the necessity for crushing the Axis. All gave priority to
immediate military considerations in the early critical phases of the war.
All determined to destroy German capacity to endanger peace and security in the future. To that end all wanted the defeat, denazification, and
decartelization of Germany. Once the danger of imminent defeat passed
and it became apparent that Hitler and his allies would not triumph,
both Churchill and Stalin gave greater attention to postwar arrangements than Roosevelt did. More than the others, Roosevelt wanted to
postpone decisions on such matters until victory was accomplished.

Stalin's attitudes and emotions emerged from long and personal experience with violence, intrigue, revolution, and war. He did not trust Communists close to him in the Soviet Union, he feared the Axis powers, and he distrusted leaders of capitalist countries in the West. Stalin determined that the Soviet Union would dominate Eastern Europe. That determination grew out of Russian historical habits, concern for security against Germany and the West, Russia's military dominance there at the close of World War II, and the desire to spread communism. Churchill, the aristocrat, journalist, soldier, and conservative politician, in his own way was as tough-minded as Stalin. He was dedicated to guarding British national and imperial interests. He welcomed the Soviet Union's help in the struggle against Nazi Germany, but he distrusted Soviet ambitions in the postwar world.

President Roosevelt, too, was a realist. He did not envisage a utopian postwar era of sweetness and light. Like the others, he understood the role of national power in international affairs. Roosevelt believed that peace and security depended on the ability of the great powers (the United States, the Soviet Union, Great Britain, and China) to work together in the postwar period as they did during the war. He realized that cooperation among the great powers would not be possible unless the security, vital interests, and reasonable ambitions of those states and their peoples were safeguarded. Roosevelt was aware of the deeply engrained Russian fear and distrust of the West. Nevertheless, the President hoped that if the West were conciliatory and sympathetic toward the Soviet Union's security concerns, it might be possible for the United States, the Soviet Union, and Great Britain to cooperate for world peace. He thought it worth the effort. And he had a not entirely unjustified confidence in his own ability to win the cooperation of others through the power of his personality.

In October, 1943, the aging Secretary of State Cordell Hull represented the United States at a meeting in Moscow with Britain's Anthony Eden and with the Soviet Union's Molotov. At that conference of foreign ministers, the British and Americans assured the Russians of a second front in 1944. The three states established a European Advisory Commission to consider problems in areas liberated from Hitler's domination. Hull persuaded the conference to adopt a four-power declaration (including China) calling for unconditional surrender of the Axis powers and for the creation after the war of "a general international organization, based on the principle of sovereign equality of all peace-loving states, and open to membership by all such states, large and small, for the maintenance of international peace and security." At the close of the conference, Stalin told Hull that the Soviet Union would go to war against Japan after the defeat of Nazi Germany.

424 *An interpretive history of American foreign relations*

In November, 1943, building on the groundwork laid in Moscow, Roosevelt and Churchill met with Chiang Kai-shek in Cairo, and then went on to a four-day conference with Stalin at Teheran, Iran. Roosevelt did not want to travel so far from the United States at that time, but Stalin would not go any further than Teheran so the President reluctantly agreed. Though Churchill had visited Stalin earlier, Roosevelt and Stalin met for the first time at Teheran. Much of the conference dealt with planning the final military defeat of Nazi Germany. Roosevelt and Churchill reaffirmed plans for invading Western Europe in 1944. Stalin again indicated that the Soviet Union would attack Japan after the European war ended, though he indicated that Russia would expect territorial compensation in northeast Asia. They reached no firm agreements on nonmilitary matters, but the three leaders informally discussed numerous postwar political and territorial problems, including Germany, Poland, and colonial areas. Roosevelt was dedicated to the importance of Anglo-American cooperation. Nevertheless, in his efforts to win Stalin's confidence at Teheran, the President sided with the Soviet leader in opposition to Churchill on particular issues.

While the Teheran Conference confidently planned major military actions to crush Nazi Germany, the Yalta Conference in February, 1945, met when those successful military assaults had nearly accomplished their task. In three months Hitler would be dead and Nazi Germany beaten. As in 1943, Stalin would not travel far. Consequently, despite their own responsibilities at home and despite the President's failing health, Churchill and Roosevelt made the long journey to Yalta in the Crimea. It was the last such conference that Roosevelt attended before his death on April 12, 1945. From the American frame of reference, the most important goals at Yalta were to assure continued cooperation between the Soviet Union, Great Britain, China, and the United States in the postwar era; to obtain firm commitments from the Soviet Union that it would attack Japan after Germany surrendered; to win Russian support for the United Nations organization; and to plan postwar arrangements in Germany, Poland, and elsewhere.

Russian national interests and its military control of the area assured the Soviet Union's dominant position in Eastern Europe at the close of World War II. Nevertheless, at Yalta Roosevelt and Churchill won Stalin's commitment to use "democratic means" in the areas liberated from Nazi domination and "the earliest possible establishment through free elections of governments responsive to the will of the people." At the same time, the Soviet Union agreed that the provisional or Lublin government of Poland that it controlled would "be reorganized on a broader democratic basis with the inclusion of democratic leaders from Poland itself and from Poles abroad." That government should then "be pledged to the holding of free and unfettered elections as soon as possible on the basis of universal suffrage and secret ballot." They agreed that the eastern boundary of Poland would generally follow the Curzon line. That, in effect, transferred lands in eastern Poland to the Soviet Union. To compensate for those territorial losses, Poland was to get additional lands in eastern Germany, though the Yalta agreement did not define that new western Polish boundary.

At Yalta the leaders of the three states renewed their determination to force the unconditional surrender of Nazi Germany. They resolved to destroy Nazism and militarism "to ensure that Germany will never again be able to disturb the peace of the world." Germany was to be disarmed, its general staff dissolved, its war industries eliminated, and war criminals punished. They insisted that they did not propose "to destroy the people of Germany, but only when Nazism and militarism have been extirpated will there be hope for a decent life for Germans, and a place for them in the comity of nations." Churchill blocked the dismembering of Germany, but the Yalta agreement provided that the Soviet Union, the United States, Great Britain, and France would each occupy a separate area (the French zone to be carved out of the British and American zones). They approved German reparations in kind. They could not agree on a specific amount of reparations, so the question was referred to a reparation commission that would use "as a basis for discussion" the Soviet demands for $20 billion reparations, with half of it going to Russia. Churchill argued for a less harsh treatment of Germany than Stalin and Roosevelt wanted. He had no love for Germany, but he feared that its complete destruction would leave a vacuum that would enhance the power and danger of the Soviet Union in Europe. Roosevelt did not want Russian domination of Europe, but by sympathizing with Soviet fears of a revived Germany he hoped he might win Stalin's confidence and cooperation for peace after the war.

The statesmen at Yalta discussed the preliminary plans for an international organization for peace and security that had been drafted at Dumbarton Oaks in 1944. They considered at length the great-power veto, Soviet demands for including the Ukraine and Byelorussia as members, and trusteeship arrangements. They agreed that the conference to draft the United Nations charter would meet in San Francisco on April 25, 1945. Attendance at that conference would be limited to representatives from states that had declared war on the Axis.

And finally, in a secret agreement signed at Yalta, the Soviet Union promised to go to war against Japan within two or three months after Germany surrendered. In return the United States and Great Britain supported Stalin's demands for the return of territory in Asia taken from Russia in the Russo-Japanese War of 1904–1905. The southern part of Sakhalin Island, the Kuril Islands, and the lease of Port Arthur as a naval base would be restored to Russia. The port of Dairen would be inter-

Occupation Zones in Germany and Austria 1945-46

U.S.   RUSSIAN   BRITISH   FRENCH

BERLIN AND VIENNA UNDER FOUR POWER OCCUPATION

nationalized, with "the preeminent interests" of Russia there "safe-guarded." Subject to Chiang Kai-shek's concurrence, Outer Mongolia was to remain under Soviet domination and Russia's earlier control in Man-churian railroads was to be restored. For its part the Soviet Union agreed to conclude "a pact of friendship and alliance" with Nationalist China to help liberate China from the Japanese. American civilian and military leaders (including General Douglas MacArthur) wanted the Soviet Union to join the fight against Japan to end that war quickly and save American lives. The United States and Great Britain had not yet perfected the atomic bomb. The United States planned to invade Japan in the fall of 1945. Given the suicidal Japanese resistance in the south-west Pacific and the heavy losses inflicted on American forces, military leaders expected around 500,000 casualties in the conquest of Japan's home islands. The Soviet Union might reduce those losses and speed the Japanese surrended by tying down Japanese military forces on the Asi-atic mainland. Not love of the Soviet Union, but an eagerness to save American lives and end the war quickly, guided Roosevelt and his mili-tary advisers on that matter.

President Roosevelt's optimism about the possibility of working ami-cably with the Soviet Union began to fade before his death two months after the conference. Nevertheless, the Americans left the Crimea per-suaded that they had helped make important progress toward arrange-ments for enduring peace and security after the final defeat of the Axis powers.

The Yalta agreements (executive agreements, not treaties) and Presi-dent Roosevelt later were subjected to vehement criticism in the United States and elsewhere. In the 1940's and 1950's many on the right accused Roosevelt of "selling out" to the Russians, and blamed Yalta for the op-pressive Soviet and Communist domination of Eastern Europe. Historians generally rejected that view, however, and insisted that Roosevelt had won as much in the way of Soviet concessions to democracy and self-de-termination for the people of the area as Soviet national interests and military domination in Eastern Europe would permit. Realists charged Roosevelt with being utopian, moralistic, and naive in his dealings with the tough-minded Stalin. More recently, New Left and revisionist schol-ars have attacked the agreements and Roosevelt from the opposite direc-tion. They provide a sympathetic portrait of Stalin and the Soviet Union, while at the same time portraying the United States and the West as ag-gressively attempting to expand into areas of legitimate Soviet concern in Eastern Europe.

On April 25, 1945, two weeks after Roosevelt's death and less than two weeks before the German surrender, delegates from all the countries fighting the Axis gathered in San Francisco to draft the United Nations Charter. Signed on June 25, 1945, that Charter provided for an international organization consisting of a General Assembly, a Security Council, a Secretariat, a Social and Economic Council, a Trusteeship Council, and an International Court of Justice. All members were to be represented in the General Assembly and each state was to have one vote. It could discuss problems and make recommendations. A two-thirds vote was required for important matters and a majority vote for others. The Security Council, composed of five permanent members (the United States, the Soviet Union, Great Britain, France, and China) and six temporary members elected by the General Assembly for two-year terms, was to have primary responsibility for the maintenance of international peace and security. Procedural matters were to require a vote of any seven members of the Security Council. Decisions on substantive matters, including actions to settle international disputes, would require a vote of seven including all of the permanent members voting. A negative vote by any one of the permanent members would block action. In practice, abstention from voting was not interpreted as a veto. Though the Soviet Union was later criticized for its use and abuse of the veto, all of the five states that were to be permanent members of the Security Council (including the United States) insisted on the veto power and probably would not have approved the Charter without that provision. With careful advanced planning in the United States by the administration, congressional leaders, and private groups, the circumstances that led the United States to reject membership in the League of Nations after World War I were not repeated. The Senate quickly approved the United Nations Charter by the overwhelming vote of 89 to 2.

In July, 1945, at Potsdam near Berlin in Germany, leaders of the Big Three met for the last time during World War II. Stalin again represented the Soviet Union. Harry S. Truman had succeeded Roosevelt in the American Presidency. And elections in Great Britain brought Clement Attlee to replace Churchill in the midst of the conference. Russia's methods in Poland and elsewhere in Eastern Europe seemed to violate the spirit and even the letter of the Yalta agreements. Through the Soviet military presence, transient coalition goverments, rigged elections, economic penetration, control of Communist Parties, and other tactics, the Soviet Union was assuring its domination of Eastern European states by methods that Americans considered undemocratic and in violation of the Yalta agreements. For the people of Eastern Europe who had survived, the ordeal of World War II simply shifted them from their own autocratic regimes to domination by Hitler's Nazi tyranny to postwar oppression at the hands of Communist Russia. Truman was not as patient with the Russians as Roosevelt had been. Increasingly his advisers, including Secretary of the Navy James V. Forrestal, Ambassador W. Averell Harriman, and James F. Byrnes, who became Secretary of State shortly before Potsdam, saw Stalin and the Soviet Union in the same light as Churchill did. Discussions on Germany and Poland went less smoothly at Potsdam than they had at Yalta.

By the time the Potsdam conference began, the United States and Great Britain had successfully exploded an atomic weapon in New Mexico, and were preparing to use it against Japan. Japan's navy and air force were mostly destroyed. Its defeat was inevitable. The Soviet Union's military involvement against Japan no longer seemed as essential or even desirable as it had a few months earlier at Yalta. But that decision had already been reached. In the Potsdam Declaration of July 26, 1945, the United States, Great Britain, and China demanded Japan's unconditional surrender and warned that the "alternative for Japan is prompt and utter destruction." President Truman informed Stalin of the development of the atomic bomb, but the Soviet leader did not seem surprised or impressed by the information.

When the Soviet Union notified Japan of its decision for war on August 8, 1945, the United States had already dropped an atomic bomb on Hiroshima and was preparing to drop another on Nagasaki the next day. According to a study by Gar Alperovitz, the United States may have used the bomb at that time partly to impress and inhibit the Soviet Union. Japanese leaders were already discussing peace, and on August 10 Japan offered to surrender, provided it could keep its Emperor. By August 14, 1945, the two countries had agreed on terms and with the signing of the surrender on September 2, 1945, V–J Day, the fighting ended. The United States, the Soviet Union, Great Britain, and their allies had together successfully accomplished the defeat of the Axis powers in World War II. But that war had not yet ended when alarming evidences of the pending cold war with the Soviet Union began to appear. Russian forces continued to advance southward in Asia after August 14, and many Americans believed Soviet ambitions rather than Japanese resistance inspired that advance. World War II had destroyed the fearsome Axis challenge. In the years following that war, the United States and the Western powers would face a different and more powerful challenge from the Soviet Union and the communist states.

SUPPLEMENTARY READINGS

Alperovitz, Gar. *Atomic Diplomacy: Hiroshima and Potsdam.* New York: Vintage Books, Inc., 1967.

Bailey, Thomas A. *America Faces Russia: Russian-American Relations from Early Times to Our Day.* Ithaca, N.Y.: Cornell University Press, 1950.

Browder, Robert P. *The Origins of Soviet American Diplomacy.* Princeton, N.J.: Princeton University Press, 1953.

Butow, J. C. *Japan's Decision to Surrender.* Stanford, Calif.: Stanford University Press, 1954.

Byrnes, James F. *Speaking Frankly.* New York: Harper & Bros., 1947.

Churchill, Winston S. *Triumph and Tragedy.* Boston: Houghton Mifflin Co., 1953.

Clemens, Diane Shaver. *Yalta.* New York: Oxford University Press, 1970.

Deane, John R. *The Strange Alliance: The Story of Our Efforts at Wartime Cooperation with Russia.* New York: Viking Press, 1947.

Dulles, Foster Rhea. *The Road to Teheran: The Story of Russia and America, 1781–1943.* Princeton, N.J.: Princeton University Press, 1945.

Feis, Herbert. *Churchill, Roosevelt, Stalin: The War They Waged and the Peace They Sought.* Princeton, N.J.: Princeton University Press, 1957.

————. *The Atomic Bomb and the End of World War II.* Rev. ed. Princeton, N.J.: Princeton University Press, 1966.

————. *Between War and Peace: The Potsdam Conference.* Princeton, N.J.: Princeton University Press, 1960.

Fleming, D. F. *The Cold War and Its Origins.* 2 vols. Garden City, N.Y.: Doubleday & Co., Inc., 1961.

Gaddis, John L. *The United States and the Origins of the Cold War, 1941–1947.* New York and London: Columbia University Press, 1972.

Kennan, George F. *Russia and the West under Lenin and Stalin.* Boston: Little, Brown & Co., 1960.

Kolko, Gabriel. *The Politics of War: The World and United States Foreign Policy, 1943–1945.* New York: Random House, 1968.

McNeil, William H. *America, Britain and Russia: Their Cooperation and Conflict, 1941–1946.* London: Oxford University Press, 1953.

O'Connor, Raymond G. *Diplomacy for Victory: FDR and Unconditional Surrender.* New York: W. W. Norton & Co., Inc., 1971.

Rose, Lisle A. *After Yalta.* New York: Charles Scribner's Sons, 1973.

Smith, Gaddis. *American Diplomacy during the Second World War, 1941–1945.* New York: John Wiley & Sons, Inc., 1965.

Snell, John L. *Illusions and Necessity: The Diplomacy of Global War, 1939–1945.* Boston: Houghton Mifflin Co., 1963.

————. *Wartime Origins of the East-West Dilemma Over Germany.* New Orleans: Hauser Press, 1959.

Stettinius, Edward R., Jr. *Roosevelt and the Russians: The Yalta Conference.* Garden City, N.Y.: Doubleday & Co., Inc., 1949.

Williams, William Appleman. *American-Russian Relations, 1781–1947.* New York: Rinehart & Co., Inc., 1952.

37

Cold war and
peaceful coexistence

After 1945 the separate efforts by the United States and the Soviet Union to guard their respective vital interests and national security evolved into a terrifying cold war that repeatedly threatened to erupt into World War III. In the nuclear age such a total war would mean mutual and worldwide destruction far surpassing anything before in the history of human conflict.

Most American scholars in the 1940's and 1950's blamed the cold war on Soviet and communist expansion. "Realists," led by George F. Kennan and Hans J. Morgenthau, saw the Soviet Union as a formidable adversary, but criticized the moralistic-legalistic-universal emphases of American foreign policies. Most traditional historians of the cold war, such as Herbert Feis, believed that the United States under President Harry S. Truman and Secretaries of State George C. Marshall and Dean Acheson generally demonstrated laudable statesmanship in leading the United States to internationalism, collective security, and containment by means of the Truman Doctrine, Marshall Plan, NATO, and the limited Korean war. The containment policy (particularly in Europe) was seen as a responsible, restrained, and generally successful response to the Soviet and communist challenges.

In the 1960's and 1970's, however, traditional and realist interpretations faced growing challenges from "revisionist" historians, who advanced more sympathetic analyses of Soviet policies and more critical

431

views of American containment policies. Revisionists, including William A. Williams, Walter LaFeber, and Gabriel Kolko, differed among themselves, but generally they placed the main responsibility or blame for the cold war, not on the Soviet Union, but on the United States. They criticized American expansion and containment policies as unjustified, unwise, and warlike threats to the Soviet Union, to China, to the Third World, and to world peace.

The interpretation advanced in this chapter sees the cold war as the clash of two expansionist and self-righteous systems and powers—the Soviet Union and the United States. Each, when judged by its own interests and ideologies, felt justified in its course. The consequences of the activities of both superpowers was an alarming cold war that threatened the survival of the whole world. But those consequences also included successful avoidance of a thermonuclear war. Given the explosive international crises since World War II and the available technological capacity for worldwide destruction by either or both of the superpowers, avoidance of a World War III for so many years has been no small accomplishment. And if it did nothing more, it enabled the world to survive long enough for younger and hopefully wiser people in America and abroad to try their hands at accomplishing that better and more peaceful world that mankind has sought over so many thousands of years.

Soviet-American relations from the end of World War II until 1974, for purposes of analysis, may be divided into three overlapping periods: the era of dwindling hope and growing tension in 1945–1946; cold war and containment from 1947 onward; and the era of "peaceful coexistence" beginning around 1953.

FROM HOPE TO RESIGNATION

During the immediate postwar years many Americans clung to the rapidly fading hope that it might be possible to work with the Soviet Union for peace as it had been possible earlier to work with that country to defeat the Axis. The spirit that guided President Roosevelt's policies toward the Soviet Union did not entirely disappear. The United States quickly dismantled its wartime military forces. The United Nations began to function. The victors began the negotiation of peace treaties.

Nevertheless, even before the fighting stopped in 1945, distrust, friction, and conflicts of interests and ideas began to disrupt relations between the West and the Soviet Union. The world learned quickly that the postwar era was to be shaken by recurring crises and war scares fully as alarming as those that preceded and accompanied World War II. Emboldened by the American monopoly on atomic weapons, President Truman and his Secretary of State James F. Byrnes were firmer, less conciliatory, and less trusting in their dealings with the Soviet Union than Roosevelt and Stettinius had been. Journalists on the West Coast and elsewhere began to drum up a war scare with the Soviet Union as early as August, 1945. A major crisis erupted in the winter of 1945–1946 when Russia attempted unsuccessfully to convert the northern province of Azerbaijan in Iran into an autonomous area, presumably under Soviet domination. Friction developed between the communist and noncommunist states in the United Nations. Finding itself consistently in a minority, the Soviet Union began uninhibited use of its veto in the Security Council to guard its interests there. American efforts to get agreement on an effective international control of atomic energy along the lines of the Baruch plan floundered on Russia's objections to the inspection and enforcement provisions demanded by the West. Speaking in Fulton, Missouri, in March, 1946, Winston Churchill said that "from Stettin in the Baltic to Trieste in the Adriatic an Iron Curtain has descended across the continent."

Americans were shocked when the Soviet Union proceeded to convert Eastern European states into Communist satellites without following democratic procedures. Stalin all along had demanded the establishment of governments in Eastern Europe that would be friendly to the Soviet Union; the United States and Great Britain had insisted that those governments must represent the democratic wishes of the people there. According to Western leaders those elected governments would not necessarily be unfriendly to the Soviet Union. Stalin, however, said, "A freely elected government in any of these East European countries would be anti-Soviet, and that we cannot allow." There was friction in the negotiations of peace treaties for Italy and the Eastern European states.

The Soviet Union, France, Great Britain, and the United States were completely unable to reach agreement on peace treaties for Germany and Austria. In effect, the Soviet Union wanted treaties that would destroy the capacity of Germany and Austria to endanger Soviet security and would either neutralize those states or put them in the Communist bloc. The United States and Great Britain determined to end Nazism and militarism in Germany and Austria but wanted treaties that would assure their place with the West.

In terms of the conflicting expansion of Russia and America in Europe, the United States saw Stalin's demands as efforts to expand Soviet domination into Eastern and Central Europe (or, more accurately, to maintain in the postwar period control of the areas its armies had overrun while defeating Nazi Germany). At the same time Stalin saw the Anglo-American demands in Germany and Eastern Europe as hostile efforts by the capitalist countries to expand their influence to the very borders of the Soviet Union and into areas freed from Nazi domination at the cost of millions of Russian lives.

Many in the United States continued to hope that mutually satisfactory cooperation with the Soviet Union was possible and criticized American policies for the deteriorating relations. Secretary of Commerce Henry A. Wallace was one of those. When Wallace spoke out in an address at Madison Square Garden in September, 1946, Secretary Byrnes insisted that the President must choose between the two cabinet members. One of them had to go. Truman promptly fired his Secretary of Commerce. By the end of 1946, most Americans and their leaders in both parties were convinced that friendly relations with the Soviet Union on horonable terms were not possible and that they must thenceforth consider Communist Russia as an adversary rather than as a partner in international affairs. The principle of unanimity among the great powers on which Roosevelt had based his hopes and on which the United Nations security system was based had been shattered.

COLD WAR AND CONTAINMENT

With the open acknowledgment of the cold war, the United States in 1947 formulated and began to implement the containment policy toward the communist bloc led by the Soviet Union. From 1947 onward, under both Democratic and Republican administrations, the United States pursued a containment policy in its dealings with the communist states.

Many individuals helped develop and implement the idea, but the immediate author of containment was George F. Kennan, a career foreign service officer and the State Department's leading expert on the Soviet Union. In 1946, while serving in the American embassy in Moscow, he outlined his views in a long cable to the Department of State. General George C. Marshall, who became Secretary of State in January, 1947, made Kennan the Policy Planning Adviser in the Department of State. Kennan's ideas that were already shaping American policies toward the Soviet Union were spelled out publicly in a major article entitled, "The Sources of Soviet Conduct," published in the July, 1947, issue of the journal *Foreign Affairs*. The article was signed "X," but the author was George Kennan. It was a seminal analysis of the assumptions underlying American policies toward the Soviet Union.

In that article Kennan contended that the two principal sources of Soviet conduct were Russian historical experience and communist ideology. On the basis of that experience and ideology, Soviet leaders firmly believed that communism and capitalism were inevitably antagonistic and incompatible, that there could not be any relaxed peaceful coexistence. They were convinced of the inevitable overthrow of capitalism by a revolution of the proletariat. There was no deadline by which it must or would be accomplished, so communists could afford to be patient in the confident conviction that the collapse was inevitable.

Kennan concluded that as a result of those convictions the government of the Soviet Union would not drop its basic antagonism against the capitalist countries. It would, he believed, constantly maintain pressures designed to spread communist power and undermine capitalism. He wrote that "the United States cannot expect in the foreseeable future to enjoy political intimacy with the Soviet regime. It must continue to regard the Soviet Union as a rival, not a partner, in the political arena."

Building on that analysis in his article, Kennan contended: "The main element of any United States policy toward the Soviet Union must be that of a long-term, patient but firm and vigilant containment of Russian expansive tendencies." Nevertheless, he did not close on quite such a negative tone:

> The United States has it in its power to increase enormously the strains under which Soviet policy must operate, to force upon the Kremlin a far greater degree of moderation and circumspection than it has had to observe in recent years, and in this way to promote tendencies which must eventually find their outlet in either the break-up or the gradual mellowing of Soviet power. For no mystical, Messianic movement—and particularly not that of the Kremlin—can face frustration indefinitely without eventually adjusting itself in one way or another to the logic of that state of affairs.

In the years that followed, many different analyses of Soviet-American relations emerged from both official and nonofficial sources. Kennan's article was not often quoted by the 1960's and 1970's. Kennan himself became critical of many of the ways containment was invoked. In his *Memoirs* he contended that he had meant only political containment, not military. Furthermore, he did not favor containing Soviet expansion everywhere in the world, but mainly wanted to prevent the United States, the United Kingdom, the Rhine Valley, and Japan from falling under communist control. He believed containment "lost much of its rationale with the death of Stalin and with the development of the Soviet-Chinese conflict." Most Americans who implemented the policy, however, were more doctrinaire and universal in their conceptions of containment than he was. In practice American policies toward the Soviet Union and the other communist states from 1947 onward generally coincided with the assumptions and the analysis in that article, broadly defined.

The specific actions of the United States in implementing its containment policy varied depending upon the particular circumstances abroad and the particular individuals and groups dominant within the United States. Nevertheless, certain general patterns evolved with substantial consistency through the years. The United States implemented containment through foreign aid programs, through nominal support for the United Nations, through regional organizations and alliances, through massive military preparations and limited military actions, generally through a Europe-first emphasis, and through negotiations from strength. Each of those requires elaboration and illustration.

Foreign aid programs were the earliest major containment actions by the United States because in the chaos following World War II the economic needs were the most immediate and pressing. The specific patterns in American foreign aid varied over the years as the circumstances changed at home and abroad. Initially, American aid was largely economic assistance to Europe. As the European economies steadily recovered, late in the Truman administration and on into the Eisenhower administration, the United States gave relatively less priority to economic assistance and more to military aid. Similarly, as Europe recovered and as anticolonialism grew in Asia, Africa, and Latin America, American aid programs began to refocus away from Europe toward those economically less developed areas of the world.

Domestically, America's foreign aid programs grew out of very real ideological and humanitarian compassion for peoples in other parts of the world. They also, in part, grew out of the expectation by economic groups in the United States that those aid programs would benefit American economic prosperity and growth. Externally, American foreign aid programs from 1946 onward were inspired largely by the conviction that the aid was essential to guard peace and security against the alarming spread of communism in general and Soviet power in particular.

In 1946 the United States government loaned Great Britain $3.75 billion to help save that major ally from bankruptcy. In February, 1947, Great Britain notified the United States that because of its acute economic difficulties it could not continue aid to Greece and Turkey after March 31. The British warned that without substantial aid the communist guerrillas might triumph in Greece, and Turkey might succumb to Soviet pressures. Consequently, in a major address before a joint session of Congress on March 12, 1947, President Truman asked for $400 million to aid Greece and Turkey. In his key statement the President said: "It must be the policy of the United States to support free peoples who are resisting attempted subjugation by armed minorities or by outside pressures." Though he did not explicitly denounce the Soviet Union, his Truman Doctrine aimed against the dangers of a communist takeover in those eastern Mediterranean states. Congress debated the issue at length, but with bipartisan support both houses voted the necessary funds by more than two-thirds majorities. Though the Greeks and Turks were primarily responsible for the course of events in their countries, Truman Doctrine aid helped crush the guerrillas by the middle of 1949 and helped buoy up Turkish strength.

As economic distress, human suffering, and political restiveness grew in postwar Europe, the Truman administration recognized an increasingly urgent need to extend long-term constructive assistance. The result was the Marshall Plan or European Recovery Program worked out by George Kennan and his policy planning staff and proposed by Secretary of State Marshall in an address at Harvard University on June 5, 1947. It was a comprehensive plan by the United States to assist European economic recovery on the basis of self-help and mutual assistance. In his address Marshall said it was "directed not against any country or doctrine, but against hunger, poverty, desperation, and chaos. Its purpose should be the revival of a working economy . . . so as to permit the emergence of political and social conditions in which free institutions can exist." It was offered to all European states, including the Soviet Union and its satellites.

European representatives quickly met to plan their own contributions to recovery and to estimate their requirements from the United States. Their initial requests were much larger than the United States could or would provide. They were promptly scaled down to more manageable levels. Stalin considered the proposal an anti-Soviet action by the United States. Consequently, the Soviet Union refused to participate and prevented its satellites from doing so. The Communist *coup d'état* in Czechoslovakia in February, 1948, inadvertently increased support for the plan in the United States. With former isolationist Arthur H. Vandenberg leading the fight in the Senate, Congress approved the Economic Cooperation Act in the spring of 1948 and eventually provided some $17 billion for the plan over a four-year period. Appropriately, the President named an industrialist, Paul Hoffman, to head the European Cooperation Administration that administered the plan for the United States.

The European people accomplished most of the huge task of rebuilding their war-torn economies, but through the European Recovery Program the United States speeded and constructively aided that recovery. In terms of external considerations, through the Marshall Plan the United States tried to sustain free, viable, and independent European states and thereby prevent the spread of communism and Soviet domination. Domestically, the Marshall Plan appealed to American ideological dedication to democracy in opposition to totalitarian communism. It represented compassionate humanitarian desires to reduce human suffering. And it won support from many who realized that European bankruptcy would destroy profits and prosperity in the United States as well. Though generally lauded in the 1940's and 1950's, more recently critics at home and abroad have seen the Marshall Plan in sinister terms as an instrument for American imperialism in Europe, a selfish scheme to prevent a postwar depression in the United States, and a device to stave off the collapse of American and world capitalism.

By 1949 the Truman administration gradually began to modify its foreign aid programs in two major ways. It extended increasing economic aid to Asia, Africa, and Latin America, and it allocated more to military assistance programs. The Point IV program for technical assistance to developing states that President Truman proposed in 1949 was part of the first change. Similarly, most of the aid under the Agency for International Development went to those developing states. The Alliance for Progress in Latin America and the Peace Corps, both initiated by the Kennedy administration, fitted the same general pattern. The United States provided much military equipment to the states most willing to cooperate in opposing communist expansion, including South Korea, Pakistan, and West Germany.

Though foreign aid continued in the 1950's and 1960's, American opposition to both kinds increased. Critics of aid to developing states contended that it was a costly drain on American taxpayers, that much of it was wasted, that the recipients continued to be unappreciative and critical of the United States, and that it helped build competition for some sectors of the American economy. Critics of military assistance (often not the same people who criticized economic aid) contended that it encouraged arms races and even war among the states of Asia, the Middle East, Africa, and Latin America. They charged that the arms often went to undemocratic regimes whose principal virtues were their capacity to maintain order and their opposition to communism. By 1974 foreign aid continued, but changing circumstances abroad and growing opposition within the United States relegated those programs to a smaller part of the total American effort in world affairs.

In addition to foreign aid, the United States also tried to implement its containment policy through the United Nations. The United States played a major role in the origins and continued history of the United Nations. The United States provided more money for the operation of the United Nations than any other country. All the presidential administrations (both Democratic and Republican) after World War II reaffirmed their support for the United Nations. With American cooperation that organization helped settle international disputes peacefully and was responsible for many constructive economic, social, and cultural programs.

In terms of the cold war and containment, however, the United Nations was not as effective as Americans had hoped. Indeed, since it was based on a unanimity among the great powers that did not exist by 1947, the very foundations of its security system disappeared almost as soon as it came into existence. The United States often bypassed the United Nations with its containment policies. The Truman Doctrine and the Marshall Plan were early examples of American actions in the cold war that avoided the United Nations. The United States also tried to modify the United Nations peace-keeping procedures to serve American interests better in the cold war. In practice, however, the modifications did not make the United Nations into an effective vehicle through which the United States could oppose communist expansion.

The U.S. Faces the Soviet Union

COMMUNIST STATES

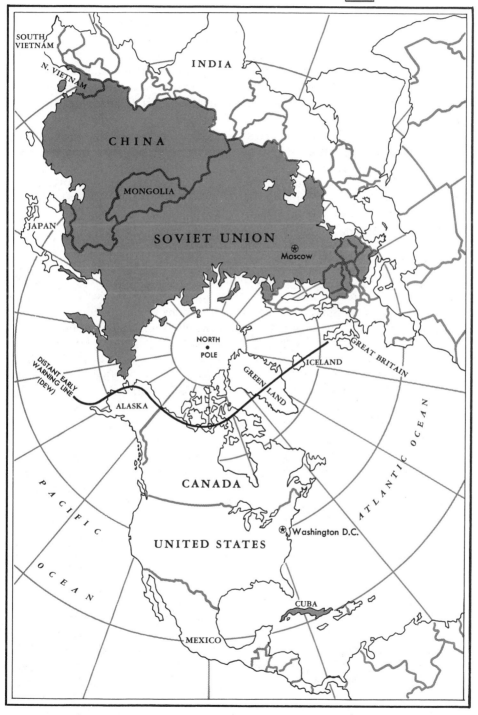

Partly because of the cold war cleavages, the United Nations was not able to develop its own independent military forces. The cold war often disrupted United Nations social and economic efforts. And the Soviet veto repeatedly blocked actions desired by most of the rest of the Security Council members led by the United States. The Security Council was able to act against aggression by North Korea in June, 1950, only because the Soviet Union at that time was boycotting United Nations organs that seated representatives from Nationalist China. The Russian representative was not present to cast his veto.

As early as 1947, the United States began to bypass the Soviet veto in the Security Council by helping to increase the peace-keeping powers of the General Assembly, where the veto did not apply. At the suggestion of Secretary of State Marshall, the General Assembly in 1947 created an Interim Committee or "Little Assembly" to meet when the General Assembly was not in session. More important was the Uniting for Peace Resolution urged by Secretary of State Dean Acheson and adopted by the General Assembly in the fall of 1950. That resolution authorized calling the General Assembly into session on 24-hour notice if the Security Council were prevented by a veto from effectively handling a threat to the peace. The resolution created a Peace Observation Commission to observe and report on situations of international tension. It recommended that United Nations members maintain military units within their armed forces that could be made available promptly for use on the recommendation of the Security Council or the General Assembly. The Uniting for Peace Resolution helped increase the effectiveness of the United Nations in the Suez crisis of 1956 and later in the Congo.

By the 1960's, however, the United States no longer found the General Assembly very satisfactory as a substitute for the Security Council on cold war issues. The original membership of the United Nations had more than doubled and most of the new members were former colonies in Asia and Africa. Most of them were not communist-dominated. Nevertheless, most of them did not share America's preoccupation with containing communist expansion. Many were as critical of the United States and its policies as they were of the Soviet Union. As relatively poor and weak states, they felt no great affection for either of the wealthy superpowers. Consequently, while most of the countries represented in the General Assembly did not line up with the Soviet Union on cold war issues, neither could the United states depend on their support on such issues.

With the "tyranny of the veto" preventing the Security Council from serving American interests in the cold war, and with the "tyranny of numbers" having a comparable effect in the General Assembly, the United States began to favor increased powers for the Secretary General of the United Nations. Each of the first four men who served as Secretary General (Trygve Lie from Norway, Dag Hammarskjold from Sweden, U Thant of Burma, and Kurt Waldheim of Austria) in varied ways increased the peace-keeping functions of the office. Dag Hammarskjold, in particular, expanded and effectively used his limited authority to preserve or restore peace. He was an unusually able, patient, and persistent diplomat. In 1961 his death in an airplane crash in Africa while on another of his many diplomatic missions brought U Thant to the Secretary General's post. Equally dedicated to the United Nations and world peace, he shared many of the sentiments of the Afro-Asian critics of both the Soviet Union and the United States. Most Americans and their leaders in both parties continued to support the United Nations. So far as the cold war and containment were concerned, however, the United States generally found it necessary to work outside the framework of that world organization.

In addition to foreign aid programs and efforts to work through the United Nations, the United States implemented its containment policy through regional organizations and alliances. Articles 51 and 52 of the United Nations Charter permitted that method. According to Article 51, "Nothing in the present Charter shall impair the inherent right of individual or collective self-defense if an armed attack occurs against a Member of the United Nations, until the Security Council has taken the measures necessary to maintain international peace and security."

Most important among the regional organizations through which the United States worked were the North Atlantic Treaty Organization (NATO), the Organization of American States (OAS), and the Southeast Asia Treaty Organization (SEATO). The OAS had substantial nonmilitary functions and the others envisaged possible nonmilitary activity, but NATO and SEATO were primarily military arrangements to block communist expansion.

Great Britain, France, and the Benelux countries had concluded a fifty-year Brussels Pact in 1948, but the creation of NATO in 1949 acknowledged that those Western European states were not strong enough to defend themselves against the Soviet Union without help from the United States. It recognized that changing economic and power patterns in the 1940's made a North Atlantic grouping more viable when dealing with the Soviet Union than any European group could be. Initially, NATO had twelve members, including the United States and Canada in North America. Greece and Turkey were added in 1951 and West Germany in 1955. The countries agreed to consult whenever the "territorial integrity, political independence or security" of any one of them was threatened. Article V provided that "an armed attack against one or more of them in Europe or North America shall be considered an attack against them all" and that in the event of such an attack they would "assist the party or parties so attacked by taking forthwith, individually

United States Collective Defense Arrangements

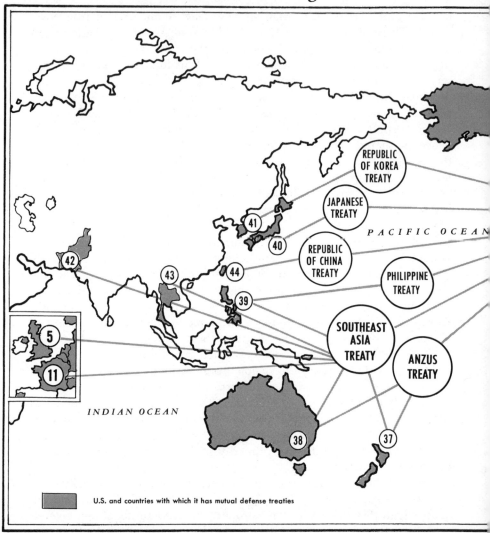

U.S. and countries with which it has mutual defense treaties

NORTH ATLANTIC TREATY (NATO)

1 UNITED STATES	9 LUXEMBOURG
2 CANADA	10 PORTUGAL
3 ICELAND	11 FRANCE
4 NORWAY	12 ITALY
5 UNITED KINGDOM	13 GREECE
6 NETHERLANDS	14 TURKEY
7 DENMARK	15 FEDERAL REPUBLIC
8 BELGIUM	OF GERMANY

RIO TREATY

1 UNITED STATES	26 COLOMBIA
16 MEXICO	27 VENEZUELA
17 CUBA	28 ECUADOR
18 HAITI	29 PERU
19 DOMINICAN REP.	30 BRAZIL
20 HONDURAS	31 BOLIVIA
21 GUATEMALA	32 PARAGUAY
22 EL SALVADOR	33 CHILE
23 NICARAGUA	34 ARGENTINA
24 COSTA RICA	35 URUGUAY
25 PANAMA	36 TRINIDAD AND TOBAGO

ANZUS TREATY

1 UNITED STATES
37 NEW ZEALAND
38 AUSTRALIA

PHILIPPINE TREATY

1 UNITED STATES
39 PHILIPPINES

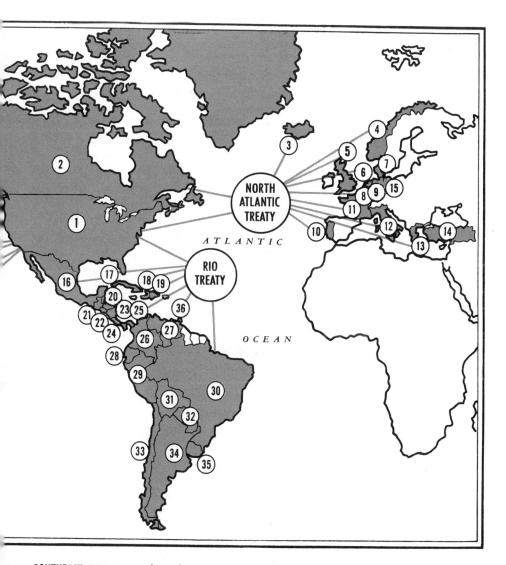

SOUTHEAST ASIA TREATY (SEATO)

1 UNITED STATES
5 UNITED KINGDOM
11 FRANCE
37 NEW ZEALAND
38 AUSTRALIA
39 PHILIPPINES
42 PAKISTAN
43 THAILAND

JAPANESE TREATY

1 UNITED STATES
40 JAPAN

REPUBLIC OF CHINA TREATY

1 UNITED STATES
44 REPUBLIC OF CHINA

REPUBLIC OF KOREA TREATY

1 UNITED STATES
41 REPUBLIC OF KOREA

and in concert with the other parties, such action as it deems necessary, including the use of armed force, to restore and maintain the security of the North Atlantic area." NATO developed complex organizational and planning machinery that a simple alliance did not provide.

NATO was never without its difficulties. Americans complained that the European states did not contribute enough military force and equipment. European states insisted that internal economic and political circumstances made it impossible to provide as much as the United States urged. Some Europeans worried whether the United States would really stand firm in a showdown with the Soviet Union or whether it would revert to its prewar isolationism. Many debated whether NATO could really stop and throw back a Soviet military assault, or whether it would only serve as a "trip wire" that would bring America's massive military power (including nuclear weapons) into the defense of Europe. If it were the latter, continental Europeans envisaged the possible loss and reinvasion of Europe by the United States and Great Britain. That view (repeatedly denied by the United States) did not arouse enthusiasm among Europeans who remembered the horrors of World War II. The military weakness of NATO was the major reason for the Paris Pacts signed in 1954 and ratified in 1955. They allowed West German rearmament up to twelve divisions or 500,000 men, and added West Germany's power to NATO. The United States further supplemented manpower shortages by assigning tactical nuclear weapons to its forces in Europe.

Though cold war considerations were involved, the Organization of American States, established in 1947–1948, built on the groundwork of the older Pan American Union dating back to 1889–1890. It included the United States and all Latin-American countries.

More feeble and ineffective than NATO and the OAS was the Southeast Asia Treaty Organization, created through the efforts of Secretary of State John Foster Dulles in 1954–1955. Designed to do for Southeast Asia what NATO tried to do for Europe, SEATO had the appearance of power without much real substance. Only three of its eight members (Pakistan, Thailand, and the Philippines) were actually Asiatic countries. The other five were Great Britain, France, Australia, New Zealand, and the United States.

In addition to those regional organizations, the United States concluded bilateral and multilateral alliances. By the 1970's the United States had military ties and commitments to nearly forty-five countries scattered over five continents. The United States supplied military equipment and advisers to most of those states. That pattern was a striking demonstration of American expansion since its "no entangling alliances" days less than a generation before.

America's foreign aid programs, its activities in the United Nations, and its role in regional organizations and alliances, all reflected the realization that American peace and security depended partly on the prosperity, strength, and cooperation of other countries. Nevertheless, the United States never depended exclusively or even primarily on the power and actions of foreign countries and international organizations. In defending its interests and security the United States relied mainly on its own resources, including its own military power. Its monopoly of atomic weapons gave it tremendous power at the close of World War II. From 1948 onward the United States slowly expanded and modernized both its conventional and nuclear military forces. The Korean war beginning in 1950 accelerated that buildup, and the fighting in Vietnam in the 1960's and early 1970's pushed military budgets even higher. Secretary of State John Foster Dulles' talk of "massive retaliation" in 1954 put a premium on the deterrent power of Strategic Air Command intercontinental bombers armed with thermonuclear bombs. The development of intercontinental missiles and Polaris submarines further increased America's capacity to wage total war. At the same time, the United States maintained conventional military forces equipped with ever greater firepower, and under Presidents Kennedy and Johnson the American capacity to fight limited wars further increased.

The United States did not use its nuclear and thermonuclear weapons against the communist world, and as the Soviet Union developed a comparable capacity for total war in the 1950's and 1960's both superpowers realized that a total thermonuclear war would result in mutual destruction with no victor and few survivors. Nevertheless, both countries considered the maintenance of those fantastically costly and destructive weapons essential for national security, to deter aggression by the other. Ironically, the thermonuclear sword of Damocles helped rational men prevent a third world war in the third of a century following World War II.

There were, however, numerous limited wars, and the United States used its conventional military forces in many parts of the world. American troops, first as occupation forces and later as allies, remained in Germany, Japan, and elsewhere after World War II. When Stalin in 1948–1949 tried to force the West out of Berlin, located deep within East Germany, the United States and Great Britain responded by successfully airlifting supplies into the beleaguered city until the Soviet Union lifted the blockade in May, 1949. American forces under the auspices of the United Nations fought to stop aggression in Korea from June, 1950, until the armistice there three years later. The American Seventh Fleet guarded the waters between Formosa and the Chinese mainland. The United States landed troops in Lebanon in 1958 and in the Dominican Republic in 1965. American U–2 aircraft photographed the Soviet Union, China, and other communist areas from incredibly high altitudes. The Central Intelligence Agency departed from the theory that it was an information rather than an action organ by contributing to changes of government in Guatemala and elsewhere. A partial blockade by the American Navy in 1962 forced Soviet removal of missiles from Cuba. And in 1965, President Johnson committed American land, sea, and air forces to military actions in Vietnam. Maintenance and use of powerful military forces was a vital part of America's containment policy.

In human affairs one can rarely know for certain "what might have been" if alternative courses of action had been followed. The containment policy may or may not have been necessary or wise; most Americans at the time thought it was both. If one judged it by its own assumptions, the containment policy was impressively successful in Europe. After 1947 the Soviet Union added only one more European state to the communist bloc, Czechoslovakia in February, 1948. Marshal Tito's Yugoslavia remained communist, but it successfully broke from Soviet domination that same year. Poland and Hungary tried unsuccessfully to break the Soviet hold in 1956. At the same time, the noncommunist states in Central and Western Europe gained substantially in power, prosperity, and independence.

Containment was less effective in Asia. Despite American aid, in 1949 the Nationalist government of China under Chiang Kai-shek fled from the mainland to Formosa and the Communists under Mao Tse-tung gained control of China. Only major military efforts by the United States and other countries prevented South Korea and South Vietnam from falling to communist domination. Soviet support for the Arab states against Israel helped lead to a brief war in 1967.

In Asia economic difficulties, political instability, and anticolonial hostility made the communist task easier and the American task there more difficult. In addition, despite the major military campaigns in Korea and Vietnam, American leaders generally considered Europe more vital to American interests than Asia. Guided by that Europe-first emphasis, the United States would fight limited wars with conventional weapons in Korea and Vietnam, but would risk total nuclear war to defend Western Europe.

Theoretically the United States was always willing to negotiate honorable settlement of its differences with the Soviet Union and other communist countries. But from 1947 onward most Americans and their leaders believed that such negotiations would not have acceptable results unless their diplomats were backed by awesome power. From 1947 until 1953, the United States and its allies concentrated most of their efforts in international affairs on building and organizing that power. Though there was much negotiation on each side of the Iron Curtain and much name-calling for propaganda purposes, there was little serious negotiation across the Iron Curtain from 1947 to 1953.

THE PEACE OFFENSIVE

The Soviet Peace Offensive and the "peaceful coexistence" that developed irregularly and imperfectly from 1953 onward provided encouraging opportunities for peaceful settlements in relations between the communist and noncommunist worlds. But they also created special new problems and intensified old ones for both the Soviet Union and the United States. If the Soviet Union after 1953 was in fact ceasing to be an aggressive military threat to the peace and security of the United States and the noncommunist world, and if it had irrevocably turned to peaceful competition with the West, then the Peace Offensive was a desirable development. In that event Americans should have welcomed the opportunity to compete with the Soviet Union in efforts to demonstrate which of the two systems could more effectively provide the "good life" for people all over the world. On the other hand, if the Soviet Peace Offensive were simply a cynical shift in tactics designed to speed the communist triumph by dividing and softening the noncommunist world, then it made the Soviet Union a more difficult adversary than it had been earlier under Stalin. It was not hard to arouse Americans and people in other noncommunist states to sacrifice and unity when confronted by a fearsome and aggressive adversary; it could be extremely difficult to win that sacrifice and unity at home and abroad if the powerful Russian bear successfully made itself look like a lovable teddy bear.

In practice, both the Soviet Union and the United States had difficulty deciding what the new patterns meant and in adjusting to the consequences of those patterns. Soviet leaders were not agreed on the best course in world affairs, nor on their estimates of the probable reactions in the communist and noncommunist worlds to the various alternatives considered. Responses in other communist states troubled Soviet leaders. In 1956 many in Poland and Hungary interpreted the new Soviet image as an offer of greater autonomy. The results were uprisings in those satellite states and their forceful suppression by Soviet military forces. Communist leaders in China and Albania increasingly denounced the Soviet Peace Offensive as a bourgeois compromise with capitalism and as an abandonment of the idealistic crusade for world communism. In other words, the Soviet Union had difficulties after 1953 because leaders and citizens in other communist states believed the Peace Offensive propaganda. The Soviet Union also ran into difficulties with the United States because so many Americans did not believe the propaganda.

Many variables affected American responses to the Peace Offensive. Some of the patterns could be identified in the differing responses by President Dwight D. Eisenhower from 1953 to 1961, and by his Secretary of State John Foster Dulles. The general-turned-President greatly respected his experienced and able Secretary of State. Both men insisted that their foreign policy views were identical. Nevertheless, their backgrounds and temperaments differed greatly. The intervals when the President's health prevented him from personally directing foreign affairs provided opportunities to contrast his approach with that of his Secretary of State. The small-town boy from Abilene, Kansas, made his way to the White House by way of West Point and a long and distinguished career as a professional Army officer. But his greatest talent was not as a battle commander, as a tactician, or as a strategist. He excelled most in his ability to get along with people and in persuading dissimilar individuals to put aside differences and work together for a common cause. He was not vindictive. He did not hold grudges. He looked for the best in others and preferred not to dwell on personal unpleasantries. Those were among his more valuable characteristics as commander of Allied forces during World War II, as Chief of Staff from 1945 to 1948, and as Supreme Allied Commander of NATO forces in Europe from 1950 to 1952. He was anticommunist and did not believe that the Peace Offensive was any more than a change in Soviet tactics. Nevertheless, as President he welcomed and eagerly sought opportunities to ease tensions between the communist and noncommunist worlds. He earnestly sought "peace with justice."

John Foster Dulles emerged from the same general background that had earlier produced such men as John Jay, Elihu Root, Charles Evans Hughes, and Henry L. Stimson. He was born into a wealthy and distinguished eastern family, and his grandfather and uncle had previously served as Secretaries of State. Dulles was a Phi Beta Kappa at Princeton. He was long a member of the New York law firm of Sullivan and Cromwell, and his practice specialized in international business and finance. He was a devout and active Presbyterian. His long and distinguished career in diplomacy and international affairs began at the second Hague Conference in 1907, and included a place at the Versailles Conference in 1919 and the key role in negotiating the peace treaty in 1951 ending the war with Japan.

Understandably, Dulles favored an active role for the United States in world affairs. His professional and religious background heightened his moralistic-legalistic approach in foreign affairs. Given his very great ability, his long experience in foreign affairs, and his self-righteousness, one could understand his tendency to run a "one-man show" when he headed the Department of State from 1953 to 1959. He was as dedicated to peace as President Eisenhower was, but he was highly skeptical of the Soviet Peace Offensive. Dedicated Communists saw no hope for real peace until world communism prevailed; Dulles saw little hope for amicable relations with the Soviet Union until democracy prevailed in Moscow. His temperament and values were in tune with the cold war atmosphere of the Stalin era, though he criticized negative containment and called for a rollback of communist power. In his view the "neutralism" of Afro-Asian states was immoral in a struggle between democracy and totalitarian communism.

The President steadfastly backed his able Secretary of State. But Eisenhower's background and temperament made him eager to explore the peaceful possibilities of the post-Stalin foreign policies; Dulles' background and temperament made him distrustful of the new Soviet image. Eisenhower's poor health, McCarthyism, and various developments abroad frustrated his hopes for a more peaceful world. Dulles generally set the tone for American foreign policies, a tone that was not in tune with the Peace Offensive. At the same time, however, Dulles' tendency to talk tough to European allies and his lack of empathy with the independent foreign policies of Afro-Asian states helped loosen America's ties with many noncommunist states and to that extent played into the hands of the Soviet Union.

Despite divided counsels in both the Soviet Union and the United States, from 1953 onward kid gloves often covered the iron fists in the cold war. And the results were often helpful. The United Nations successfully negotiated a truce in Korea in 1953. The following year the chronic Trieste controversy was resolved. A Geneva agreement in 1954 arranged a truce for Indochina. After a decade of failure, the powers successfully concluded a peace treaty for Austria in 1955. In July, 1955, a summit conference in Geneva brought together Eisenhower for the United States, Bulganin for the Soviet Union, Eden for Great Britain, and Faure for France. They did not conclude agreements on specific issues, but the conference provided a hopeful spirit devoid of mutual recriminations and name-calling. (The Foreign Ministers Conference in the fall of 1955 dominated by Dulles and Molotov did not continue that amiable atmosphere.) The United States and Communist China began informal conversations at the ambassadorial level in Poland in August, 1955. There were numerous exchanges of cultural, athletic, and economic delegations between the United States and the Soviet Union. In September, 1959, Premier Nikita Khrushchev toured the United States and ended his visit with an amiable conference with the President at Camp David. In that "spirit of Camp David" Eisenhower tried to use the time remaining to him as President to improve international relations in a series of visits to foreign lands where he generally won enthusiastic receptions.

The President's heart attack in September, 1955, Soviet suppression of the Polish and Hungarian uprisings in 1956, and the Suez crisis of that same year all helped check the momentum of Soviet-American peace efforts in Eisenhower's first term. In 1958 Khrushchev gave Great Britain, France, and the United States six months to make arrangements for turning West Berlin over to East Germany or for making it a neutralized and disarmed "free city." Failing that, Khrushchev threatened to make a separate peace with communist East Germany and turn the responsibility for access to Berlin over to the East German government (which the United States did not recognize). The deadline passed with the West standing firm in Berlin, and Khrushchev did not carry out his threat. But in 1960 he again talked of making a separate peace with East Germany.

Both the United States and the Soviet Union considered the divided Germany in Central Europe a threat to peace. Both urged negotiation of a German peace treaty. But each wanted a treaty that would work to its power and security advantage. The United States wanted a German government chosen by free elections. The government of the united Germany should then be allowed to make its own security arrangements. The United States believed such a peace settlement would lead to an anticommunist German government committed to the West and to NATO. The Soviet Union would not permit that. It insisted on German unification through negotiations between the existing governments of East and West Germany, with the resulting state excluded from both NATO and the communist Warsaw Pact. Such an arrangement would weaken the Western position in Europe. The powers scheduled another summit conference to meet in Paris in May, 1960. Two weeks before that conference, however, the Soviet Union shot down an American U–2 airplane on a photo reconnaissance flight over Russian territory. Khrushchev used that incident as the excuse for scuttling the summit conference. Despite certain accomplishments, the Soviet Peace Offensive and President Eisenhower's own peace efforts failed to end the cold war.

Neither of the Democratic administrations that followed (that of President John F. Kennedy in 1961–1963 and that of President Lyndon B. Johnson in 1963–1969) substantially altered the general outlines of Soviet-American relations. When it began construction of the wall between East and West Berlin in August, 1961, the Soviet Union, in effect, confessed a partial failure of its policies in Eastern Europe. And the wall also symbolized a failure of the Peace Offensive. President Kennedy's conversations with Premier Khrushchev in Vienna in 1961, and President Johnson's discussions with Premier Aleksei Kosygin at Glassboro, New Jersey, in 1967 did not alter the general patterns.

At the same time, as the cold war continued, states on both sides of the Iron Curtain grew bolder in trying to pursue policies independent of the superpowers. The Soviet Union faced uprisings in Hungary and Poland and a widening rift with Communist China. In 1958 Charles de Gaulle came to power in France. A French nationalist, he denounced America's influence in Europe and Europe's dependence on the United States. When he blocked Britain's efforts to join the Common Market in 1963, he justified his action partly on the ground that Britain would be the instrument for American imperialism in Europe. He developed France's independent nuclear force, contending that Europe could not depend upon the United States in a real emergency. He urged emphasis on Europe rather than on North Atlantic groupings that included the United States. And he took France out of NATO and in 1967 forced NATO's headquarters and military forces out of France. Many in the communist world rejected the extremism of Communist China, while at the same time seeking greater autonomy for their countries. Millions of people in Western Europe and Great Britain criticized de Gaulle, but at the same time hoped he was right in believing that Europe could shape its own destiny independent of the United States.

Despite erratic fits and starts, the Peace Offensive did not entirely erase the cold war under Presidents Eisenhower, Kennedy, Johnson, and Nixon. The strategic arms race continued. Disturbing conflicts of interests and crises continued to plague Soviet-American relations. Nevertheless, by the early 1970's, nearly twenty years after the first hesitant beginnings of the Peace Offensive, important new initiatives encouraged renewed hope for significant improvement in Soviet-American relations. By 1974 circumstances domestically within the United States and the Soviet Union, and external developments on the world scene, facilitated easing cold war tensions.

Within the United States the widespread alienation of young people, blacks, women, ethnics, news media, intellectuals, and others, from the cold war and Vietnam policies of both Presidents Johnson and Nixon greatly intensified domestic political pressures for winding down not only the war in Vietnam but the cold war with the Soviet Union and with the People's Republic of China as well. President Nixon's long record as a conservative Republican and "cold warrior" helped protect him from charges of being "soft on communism" or "appeasing the Reds," and left him more free to conclude compromise agreements than a liberal Democratic President might have been. Furthermore, his substantial experience in foreign affairs while serving as Vice President under President Eisenhower, his talent for the art of political compromise at home and abroad, his able National Security Assistant Henry A. Kissinger, and the abilities of the Department of State's Foreign Service career men, all facilitated the developments. The Nixon administration tried "to move from confrontation to negotiation." In comparison with the Eisenhower initiatives, the Nixon administration attached comparatively less importance to improved spirit in the relationship, and worked more through quiet, hard-nosed negotiation of specific differences troubling relations between the countries.

Externally changes in the communist, noncommunist, and Third World countries tended to encourage easing bipolar cold war tensions. The growing strength of noncommunist states such as Germany, France, Great Britain, and Japan encouraged their increased independence. The expansion of the European Community to include Great Britain, Ireland,

and Denmark was part of those developments, as were West Germany's Berlin and Moscow accords with the Soviet Union and East Germany. Similarly in the communist world the increased independence of national communist parties and policies (despite the Soviet military invasion of Czechoslovakia in 1968) paralleled the growing strength and autonomy among Western states. The major cleavage between the Soviet Union and the communist government of the People's Republic of China represented a serious problem for the Soviet Union and an encouraging opportunity for the United States. And the growing alienation of the Third World states of Africa, Asia, and Latin America from both the United States and the Soviet Union further blurred bipolar patterns in world affairs. In Vietnam, the Middle East, and South Asia, old-fashioned cold war crises persisted, but by the 1970's the internal and external environment seemed more receptive to (or more insistent upon) new peace initiatives than at any time since the early months of the Eisenhower-Khrushchev years.

Early in 1972 those circumstances at home and abroad culminated in the unprecedented presidential missions by Richard M. Nixon to China and Moscow. Among the agreements emerging from the latter visit (agreements patiently pounded out by career diplomats in prolonged negotiations long before the President's trips) were the important SALT or Strategic Arms Limitations agreements. And in 1973 Leonid Brezhnev, first secretary of the Communist Party in the Soviet Union, conferred in the United States with President Nixon.

Whether those summit meetings were precursors of continued and solid improvement of American and Western relations with the Soviet Union, the People's Republic of China, and other communist states remained to be seen. But the changes internally and externally suggested that they were rooted in substantial developments and were not simply surface manifestations.

SUPPLEMENTARY READINGS

Acheson, Dean. *Present at the Creation: My Years in the State Department.* New York: W. W. Norton & Co., Inc., 1969.

Bloomfield, Lincoln P. *The United Nations and U.S. Foreign Policy: A New Look at the National Interest.* Rev. ed. Boston: Little, Brown & Co., 1967.

Bohlen, Charles E. *Witness to History, 1929–1969.* New York: W. W. Norton & Co., Inc., 1973.

Eisenhower, Dwight D. *Mandate For Change, 1953–1956: The White House Years.* Garden City, N.Y.: Doubleday & Co., Inc., 1963.

————. *Waging Peace, 1956–1961: The White House Years.* Garden City, N.Y.: Doubleday & Co., Inc., 1965.

Feis, Herbert. *From Trust to Terror: The Onset of the Cold War, 1945–1950.* New York: W. W. Norton & Co., Inc., 1970.

Ferrell, Robert H. *George C. Marshall.* New York: Cooper Square Publishers, Inc., 1966.

Gaddis, John L. *The United States and the Origins of the Cold War, 1941–1947.* New York and London: Columbia University Press, 1972.

Gardner, Lloyd C. *Architects of Illusion: Men and Ideas in American Foreign Policy, 1941–1949.* Chicago: Quadrangle Books, 1970.

Geyelin, Philip L. *Lyndon B. Johnson and the World.* New York: Frederick A. Praeger, Inc., 1966.

Graebner, Norman A. *Cold War Diplomacy: American Foreign Policy, 1945–1960.* Princeton, N.J.: D. Van Nostrand Co., Inc., 1962.

Johnson, Lyndon B. *The Vantage Point: Perspectives of the Presidency, 1963–1969.* New York: Holt, Rinehart & Winston, Inc., 1971.

Jones, Joseph M. *The Fifteen Weeks, February 21–June 5, 1947.* New York: Harcourt, Brace & World, Inc., 1964.

Kennan, George F. *Memoirs, 1925–1950.* Boston: Little, Brown & Co., 1967.

————. *Russia and the West under Lenin and Stalin.* Boston: Little, Brown & Co., 1960.

Kissinger, Henry A. *The Necessity for Choice: Prospects of American Foreign Policy.* New York: Harper & Bros., 1960.

Kolko, Joyce and Gabriel. *The Limits of Power: The World and United States Foreign Policy, 1945–1954.* New York: Harper & Row, Publishers, 1972.

LaFeber, Walter. *America, Russia, and the Cold War, 1945–1971.* 2d. ed. New York: John Wiley & Sons, Inc., 1972.

Maddox, Robert J. *The New Left and the Origins of the Cold War.* Princeton, N.J.: Princeton University Press, 1973.

Nixon, Richard. *U.S. Foreign Policy for the 1970's: Shaping a Durable Peace.* Washington: U.S. Government Printing Office, 1973.

Schuman, Frederick L. *The Cold War: Retrospect and Prospect.* Baton Rouge: Louisiana State University Press, 1962.

Truman, Harry S. *Memoirs.* 2 vols. Garden City, N.Y.: Doubleday & Co., Inc., 1955–56.

Williams, William Appleman. *The Tragedy of American Diplomacy.* Rev. ed. New York: Delta Book, 1962.

38

The United States and Latin America since 1942

During the 400 years preceding the twentieth century, international politics largely involved relations among European states and their expansion in other parts of the world. By the middle of the twentieth century that pattern no longer prevailed. Neither of the two superpowers after World War II was in Western Europe. Though culturally part of Western civilization, geographically the United States was 3,000 miles from Europe. The Soviet Union was only partly European; most of its territory and many of its people were in Asia. But the geographic dispersal of the multistate system and of international politics was not limited to the rise of the United States and the Soviet Union.

Most of the world's people do not live in Europe and North America, and by the 1970's most of the world's states were not on those two continents. Most people in the world are neither Christians nor Jews. Most people do not have white skins. Most people are illiterate or very nearly so. Most people in the world are incredibly poor by European and American standards. And many of those people only recently won their independence from European imperial dominance. International diplomacy was difficult when conducted largely within Western civilization; it became vastly more difficult when it broadened to include the non-Western peoples of Asia, Africa, and the Middle East.

The most powerful ideological and emotional force in international affairs after World War II was neither democracy nor communism. It was, instead, nationalism and anticolonialism. Nationalism had long been powerful in Europe and the Western Hemisphere, and it continued to be. But during and after World War II it spread to Asia, the Middle East, and Africa. Though the newly emerging states of the Third World did yet command as much strength as the superpowers or Western Europe, their potential was awesome. Despite the importance of the cold war, developments in Latin America, Asia, Africa, and the Middle East could very possibly have even greater consequences. Increasingly the United States had to turn its attention toward those developing states.

Though Latin America was part of Western civilization, in many respects its general problems, attitudes, and place in world politics corresponded to those in Asia, Africa, and the Middle East. Under President Roosevelt's administration the Good Neighbor policy greatly improved relations between the United States and Latin America. Building on that groundwork, nearly all Latin-American countries cooperated effectively with the United States in the war against the Axis. That cooperative atmosphere survived long enough to permit creation of the Organization of American States at the close of World War II. The United States government and private American institutions continued to expand their influence and power in Latin America.

Nevertheless, from 1945 onward United States relations with Latin American countries cooled. With the exception of Cuba and Chile, the Latin-American states did not turn to communism, but neither did they wholly approve of American policies. The United States did not explicitly repudiate the earlier Good Neighbor policy, but it allowed it to languish through neglect. Though many in the United States bemoaned the neglect, it took crises in Guatemala, Cuba, and the Dominican Republic, and growing fears about the Communist threat there to arouse the government of the United States to reexamine and revitalize its policies toward Latin America. And even then the results were not very satisfactory either to the United States or to the countries of Latin America.

With the exception of Argentina, the Latin-American countries provided excellent cooperation in the struggle against the Axis during World War II. Nine Central American and Caribbean states declared war within four days after the United States did, and three others broke relations with the Axis in December, 1941. In January, 1942, the Third Meeting of Ministers of Foreign Affairs gathered in Rio de Janeiro, Brazil. The American delegation, led by Sumner Welles, did not urge the states to declare war, but it did want them to break relations with the Axis powers. Opposition from Argentina prevented the United States from getting exactly what it wanted. The resolution adopted at Rio simply "recommended" that the states break relations. The conference approved arrangements to combat subversive activities by Axis agents, recommended severing economic ties with the Axis, and planned hemispheric economic mobilization for the war effort. It also initiated studies for development of the inter-American system after the war.

The resolutions and understandings concluded at Rio were quickly translated into effective cooperative action. By the end of the conference, eighteen Latin-American states had broken relations with the Axis powers. All of them declared war before the middle of 1945 (though Argentina did so only reluctantly and under much pressure). Brazilian soldiers fought ably in Italy, and a squadron of the Mexican Air Force went to the Philippines and got into combat shortly before Japan surrendered. Other Latin-American countries offered military forces, though the United States War Department declined those offers. Brazil, Panama, Cuba, Ecuador, Peru, and Chile all allowed the United States to build military bases on their territory. The United States sent Lend-Lease aid to eighteen Latin-American countries, largely in the form of military airplanes and naval vessels. Most of that aid went to Brazil, Chile, and Mexico. Except for Argentina, most Latin-American governments cooperated with the Emergency Advisory Committee for Political Defense in combating enemy propaganda and subversive activities.

Latin America increased its production of essential raw materials and channeled them to the United States and its allies. Latin America exported large quantities of quinine, copper, tin, sugar, rubber, and oil for the war effort, with Cuba, Chile, Mexico, Brazil, and Bolivia providing the most. At the same time, the United States tried to help their economies during the war. American purchases helped sustain their prosperity. The war cut Latin-American access to most European products, so the United States channeled more consumer goods to Latin America to help fill that void. Price controls in the United States kept the cost of those goods relatively low for Latin-American importers (though inflation there pushed prices up before they reached consumers). The Export-Import Bank loaned $275 million to a dozen Latin-American countries during the war, much of it for transportation facilities and development of natural resources. The largest loans went to Brazil, Chile, Mexico, Uruguay, and Peru. All those developments were part of the joint war effort. They also reduced British, German, and other European influences in Latin America and, at the same time, increased American economic and diplomatic expansion there.

Before the end of World War II the states in the Western Hemisphere began to plan reorganization of the inter-American system. The Organization of American States, created after the war, was based on three multilateral agreements: the Inter-American Treaty of Reciprocal Assistance of 1947, the Pact of Bogota of 1948, and the Charter of the OAS. Drafted at a special Inter-American conference at Rio de Janeiro in 1947, the Inter-American Treaty of Reciprocal Assistance provided that an attack on one American state in the Western Hemisphere would be viewed as an attack on all, whether the aggressor was an American or non-American country. A two-thirds vote of representatives of American states could impose sanctions on the aggressor. Those sanctions would bind all members, except that no state could be required to use its military forces without its consent. The treaty also required that disputes among states in the Western Hemisphere be submitted to the inter-American system before going to the United Nations. The United States Senate unanimously approved the treaty and it went into operation in 1948.

The Ninth International Conference of American States in Bogota, Colombia, in 1948 adopted the American Treaty on Pacific Settlement, or Pact of Bogota. It provided for various peaceful methods of settling disputes, including conciliation, mediation, arbitration, and use of the International Court of Justice. Several countries, including the United States, signed the Pact with reservations because they would not accept compulsory arbitration. The Bogota conference also drafted the Charter of the Organization of American States. Under that charter inter-American conferences met every five years to decide general policies. Meetings of Consultation of Ministers of Foreign Affairs could be called to handle urgent problems and crises. The Council served as the permanent executive and policy organ of the OAS, and the old Pan American Union was the general secretariat. In addition the OAS included an Inter-American Economic and Social Council, an Inter-American Council of Jurists, an Inter-American Cultural Council, an Advisory Defense Committee, and other commissions. Member states supplied funds according to their wealth and population (a formula under which the United States provided the greater part of the money for the organization). The Organization of American States became one of the more important regional organizations. Its activities and conferences extended into economic, social, cultural, and legal matters. From the point of view of the United States the three multilateral agreements continued, expanded, and improved the prewar efforts to multilateralize the Monroe Doctrine.

In addition, all Latin-American countries (including Argentina) sent representatives to the San Francisco Conference that drafted the United Nations Charter in 1945. Their spokesmen generally lined up with the smaller states who disliked the great-power veto in the Security Council. In contrast to their views on the League of Nations after World War I, in 1945 the Latin-American states attached greater importance to regional organizations than to the United Nations with its veto. All the Latin-American states ratified the United Nations Charter by the end of 1945. Latin-American representatives were included on the Security Council and other organs of the United Nations. Though they were not always united, generally they voted with the United States on cold war issues.

Despite wartime cooperation, creation of the Organization of American States, and frequent accord in the United Nations, relations between the United States and Latin America began to cool even before the end of World War II. The Good Neighbor policy lost its momentum and its priority in American foreign policies. Leaders in both Democratic and Republican administrations continued to emphasize goodwill and mutual interests in relations with Latin America. Inter-American conferences abounded with felicitous speeches. Nevertheless, various developments undermined the Good Neighbor policy.

Despite its multilateral emphasis, during World War II and the cold war the United States often decided major policies in world affairs without consulting leaders of Latin-American countries. The position of Assistant Secretary of State for Latin American Affairs changed hands frequently during and after World War II. Some, such as Sumner Welles and Nelson Rockefeller, were interested and able. Others, such as Spruille Braden from 1945 to 1947, led Latin-Americans to fear a revival of the Big Stick policy. President Franklin D. Roosevelt symbolized the Good Neighbor policy to millions of Latin Americans. Many of them feared that the Good Neighbor policy might not survive his death in April, 1945.

During World War II the United States gave priority to developments in Europe and Asia; it continued to do so during the cold war. Latin Americans thought their problems deserved more consideration than the United States gave them. During World War II the Latin Americans sold their products to the United States at controlled prices and built large dollar reserves. When they spent those dollars after the war, however, they had to pay inflated prices. The credits rapidly dwindled and generally went for consumer products rather than for capital items that might have increased Latin-American productivity. Reciprocal trade agreements generally had reduced Latin-American tariffs on manufactured goods from the United States and lowered American rates on minerals and agricultural products. After the war Latin Americans wanted to diversify their economies and increase their manufacturing capacities. The United States discouraged tariff protection for Latin-America's infant industries, a policy that some considered part of America's "Open Door Imperialism." After World War II the United States directed its largest foreign aid programs toward Europe. Asia was second and Latin America a poor third. Given the widespread poverty in Latin American countries, their leaders insisted that they needed a Marshall plan fully as much as the Europeans did. Private American capital generally found ample investment opportunities within the United States at the close of World War II. When American capital ventured abroad more in the 1960's and 1970's, it often found safer and more profitable outlets in Europe and Canada than in Latin America. Legislation in Latin-American countries that discriminated against (or even expropriated) foreign businesses discouraged many American businesses from venturing south.

And finally, America's preoccupation with blocking communist expansion in the cold war placed Latin America low on America's foreign policy priorities after World War II. Despite the extreme poverty there, the sharp contrasts between the rich and the poor, and the weakness of the middle classes, Latin Americans generally were not attracted to communism. Their traditions, culture, values, and religion more often inclined to the right than to the left. Radical movements there generally were distinctly Latin-American developments. Partly to appease the United States and partly out of conviction, many Latin-American countries outlawed the Communist Party. Though Communists were numerous and active in such states as Brazil, Guatemala, and Venezuela, only in Cuba and Chile did they gain control of governments. Neither propaganda nor trade efforts by the Soviet Union met with much success there. At inter-American conferences Latin-American delegates approved resolutions opposing communist efforts to penetrate the Western Hemisphere.

Nevertheless, most Latin Americans were not as obsessed with the communist menace as the United States was. Their own internal economic and political problems seemed far more important to them. And they worried that the United States might use the communist threat as an excuse for intervening in Latin America. Despite America's official rejection of unilateral intervention in the internal affairs of Latin-American countries, the fears south of the border were not entirely unjustified. Argentina's refusal to cooperate during World War II evoked American economic pressures in 1944–1945. The growing power of Juan D. Peron and his efforts to make Argentina the leader of Latin America against American domination further alienated the United States. Under Spruille Braden's influence the State Department actively and publicly opposed Peron's election as President of Argentina in 1946. But the voters in that South American country, reacting against American meddling, voted Peron into office. Not until 1955 did Argentina overthrow his dictatorship. In 1954 the American Ambassador and the Central Intelligence Agency helped engineer the overthrow of the pro-communist regime of President Jacopo Arbenz in Guatemala. American diplomats and dollars also influenced developments in other Latin-American countries. But the most spectacular crises occurred in Cuba during the Kennedy administration and in the Dominican Republic during the Johnson administration.

In 1959 Fidel Castro successfully overthrew the Cuban dictator, Fulgencio Batista. Castro was a colorful nationalist and radical who promised revolutionary social and economic changes. Though he was not a Communist, some of his closest advisers were. Initially, many in the United States sympathized with the bearded rebel and were glad the brutal Batista regime ended. Very quickly, however, relations between the

United States and Cuba deteriorated. Chauvinism and radicalism moved Castro to direct his ire against American imperialism. He railed against the United States in fiery speeches and television appearances, and his government began to expropriate American property and businesses in Cuba. Castro began to turn to the Soviet Union for trade and aid. The United States retaliated with economic restrictions such as ending American imports of Cuban sugar. In January, 1961, two years after Castro seized power, President Eisenhower broke diplomatic relations with Cuba. When John F. Kennedy became President, the Central Intelligence Agency's plans for overthrowing Castro were already well advanced. Urged on by his military and CIA advisers, the President approved the plan, provided it would not be necessary to use United States military forces. The resulting Bay of Pigs invasion in April, 1961, was a fiasco for the new Kennedy administration. Castro's forces quickly destroyed and captured the invaders (mostly Cuban nationals secretly trained and equipped by the United States).

That disturbing situation became far more alarming in October, 1962, when American intelligence sources (including U–2 aerial photographs) revealed the presence of Soviet medium-range missiles in Cuba capable of striking at the United States. Though some of the President's advisers urged more forceful actions, Kennedy demanded removal of the missiles and imposed a naval "quarantine" or blockade stopping offensive military equipment from reaching Cuba. The crisis was a direct confrontation between the two thermonuclear powers. Though the United States and Soviet governments alone decided their policies in the crisis, a misstep by either of them could have set off a thermonuclear war. Most of the world's people were in the role of helpless onlookers whose survival was at stake as the two giants stalked each other. Fortunately reason prevailed. President Kennedy's actions were firm but limited. Khrushchev correctly concluded that the Soviet Union's vital interests were not directly involved and declined to risk nuclear war. The Soviet Premier backed down, the missiles and jet bombers were removed, and the crisis passed. Increased economic and diplomatic pressure from the United States forced Castro to depend largely on the Soviet Union and other communist states for the trade, aid, and equipment Cuba needed. Thousands of refugees fled to the United States. But despite the difficulties caused partly by United States opposition, Castro's regime survived as a communist island in the Western Hemisphere.

Though less terrifying, a more massive and less justified American intervention occurred in the Dominican Republic in 1965. President Rafael Trujillo was assassinated in 1961. After more than three decades of his rule, the death of the dictator inevitably led to instability, struggles for power, and changes of government in that Caribbean country. Revolutionary violence in April, 1965, endangered American lives and property.

The Johnson administration feared that the Communists would make the Dominican Republic another Cuba. Consequently, the President ordered United States Marines into the Dominican Republic to protect lives, restore order, and prevent a communist take-over. Subsequent reports suggested that the communist danger was not as great as the administration believed, and the number of American troops landed there seemed embarrassingly excessive. The intervention violated America's noninterventionist promises during the preceding thirty years. The Tenth Meeting of Consultation of Ministers of Foreign Affairs of the OAS quickly authorized an Inter-American Force to assume responsibility for maintaining order in the Dominican Republic. That face-saving action enabled the United States to remove its troops. It also converted the operation into a multilateral arrangement that was more accceptable to the Latin Americans than the original unilateral United States intervention had been. Both in Cuba and in the Dominican Republic the United States acted unilaterally before turning to the Organization of American States.

Despite America's preoccupation with the cold war, its neglect of the Good Neighbor policy, and the widespread anti-Americanism in Latin America, the United States was not entirely insensitive to the needs and aspirations of the people there. From 1945 through 1967 United States aid to Latin America (including loans) totaled more than $8 billion. The Point IV technical assistance program inaugurated by President Truman in 1949 was part of that aid. Dr. Milton S. Eisenhower, after missions through Latin America for the President in 1953 and again in 1958, recommended expanded American aid for economic and social development there. Countries obtained developmental loans through the Export-Import Bank, the Inter-American Development Bank, and the World Bank. By 1974, private American investments in Latin America totaled over $12 billion, about one sixth of American investments abroad.

Under the leadership of President John F. Kennedy, the Peace Corps and Alliance for Progress provided constructive help. On the initiative of the United States a special meeting of the Inter-American Economic and Social Council at Punta del Este, Uruguay, in August, 1961, adopted the Declaration and Charter of the Alliance for Progress. Through that program the United States promised more than $10 billion over a ten-year period to aid economic and social development, on the condition that the Latin-American states made needed reforms and planned constructive use of their own resources and of outside aid. It was, in effect, a belated Marshall plan for Latin America. Millions of Latin Americans benefited from government and private assistance from the United States.

The low-profile emphasis of the Nixon Doctrine beginning in 1969 affected America's course in Latin America as well as in Asia. In an agreement concluded in 1971, the United States formally gave up its treaty rights to construct an interocean canal across Nicaragua. The United

States continued aid programs in Latin America, but increasingly preferred to channel that aid through multilateral organizations. There was more emphasis on "helping the Americas to help themselves," on shifting from "a relationship of predominance to one of partnership," and encouraging Latin American governments "to take the initiative, and to share responsibilities in dealing with the problems of the hemisphere." American trade and private investments increased, particularly in Mexico, Brazil, and Panama, but they were not nearly as large as in Canada and Western Europe. And the same Third World nationalism, restiveness, and alienation that the United States encountered in Asia, Africa, and the Middle East, also increasingly complicated its relations with Latin America.

Latin America remained an acute problem for itself and for the United States. The wealthy minority that controlled most states would not make the sweeping reforms essential if the Alliance for Progress were to succeed. Nationalism, poverty, and national weakness fostered hatred for the rich and powerful neighbor in North America. In such a setting extremist demagogues of the right and the left found receptive listeners when they denounced American imperialism and blamed the United States for their miseries.

Whether United States policies in Latin America were wise or unwise, effective or ineffective, conditions abroad and within the United States greatly expanded American power there. Externally, World War II destroyed the German challenge in the Western Hemisphere and sharply reduced Britain's trade and investments. In the face of the Axis and communist challenges, the United States officially shifted from a unilateral to a multilateral approach to hemispheric security. In doing so, however, the United States did not decrease its influence on the policies of the Latin-American governments. The United States was committed to the defense of the states in the Western Hemisphere. American military advisers served in most Latin-American countries. American industries manufactured most of the military equipment in Latin-American armed forces.

Latin America was second only to Western Europe in American foreign trade. Latin America bought nearly one fourth of American exports and sold nearly half of its exports to the United States. Some countries sold more than three fourths of their exports in the United States. American investments in Latin America far exceeded those from any other country. Latin Americans studied in American universities, and American military officers, technicians, engineers, scientists, economists, and businessmen advised Latin-American governments and businesses. American expansion and influence often benefited Latin Americans. But it was expansion just the same, and it grew out of both international and domestic influences. The Latin-American countries were not colonies of the United States. They could and did shape their own domestic and foreign policies. They could and did criticize America and Americans. But the extent of American expansion and influence south of the border was so great that the peace, security, and well-being of millions of people there depended very much on what the United States did and did not do.

SUPPLEMENTARY READINGS

Abel, Elie. *The Missile Crisis*. Philadelphia: J. B. Lippincott Co., 1966.

Alexander, Robert J. *Communism in Latin America*. New Brunswick, N.J.: Rutgers University Press, 1957.

Berle, Adolf A., Jr. *Latin America: Diplomacy and Reality*. New York: Harper & Row, Publishers, 1962.

Dozer, Donald M. *Are We Good Neighbors? Three Decades of Inter-American Relations, 1930–1960*. Gainesville: University of Florida Press, 1959.

Dreier, John C. *The Organization of American States and the Hemisphere Crisis*. New York: Harper & Row, Publishers, 1962.

Duggan, Laurence. *The Americas: The Search for Hemisphere Security*. New York: Henry Holt & Co., Inc., 1949.

Guerrant, Edward O. *Roosevelt's Good Neighbor Policy*. Albuquerque: University of New Mexico Press, 1950.

Meyer, Karl, and Szulc, Tad. *The Cuban Invasion: The Chronicle of a Disaster*. New York: Frederick A. Praeger, Inc., 1962.

Lieuwen, Edwin. *U.S. Policy in Latin America: A Short History*. New York: Frederick A. Praeger, Inc., 1965.

Pachter, Henry M. *Collision Course: The Cuban Missile Crisis and Coexistence*. New York: Frederick A. Praeger, Inc., 1963.

Perkins, Dexter. *A History of the Monroe Doctrine*. Boston: Little, Brown & Co., 1963.

_____. *The United States and Latin America*. Baton Rouge: Louisiana State University Press, 1961.

Rippy, J. Fred. *Globe and Hemisphere: Latin America's Place in the Postwar Foreign Relations of the United States*. Chicago: Henry Regnery Co., 1958.

Schlesinger, Arthur M., Jr. *A Thousand Days: John F. Kennedy in the White House*. Boston: Houghton Mifflin Co., 1965.

Schneider, Ronald M. *Communism in Guatemala: 1944–1954*. New York: Frederick A. Praeger, Inc., 1958.

Smith, Robert F. *The United States and Cuba: Business and Diplomacy, 1917–1960*. New York: Bookman Associates, 1960.

Sorensen, Theodore C. *Kennedy*. New York: Harper & Row, Publishers, 1965.

Whitaker, Arthur P. *The United States and Argentina*. Cambridge, Mass.: Harvard University Press, 1954.

_____. *The Western Hemisphere Idea: Its Rise and Decline*. Ithaca, N.Y.: Cornell University Press, 1954.

39

The United States and the Afro-Asian states since 1942

Geographically Europe is a relatively small peninsula extending from the huge "world island" that includes Asia and Africa, the two largest continents in the world. Though long under European domination, those two continents contain more than half of all the people in the world, and their populations are increasing very rapidly. The histories of their great civilizations extend back thousands of years. Asia and the Middle East produced the world's great religions. Though extremely heterogeneous, most of the people and states of Asia and Africa shared certain general characteristics after World War II. Nearly all were swept by change and revolution. Fervent nationalism and anticolonialism developed. They determined to win racial equality. In their "revolution of rising expectations" the people in Asia and Africa determined to increase their industrial productivity, raise standards of living, provide educational opportunities, and improve health and medical facilities.

Most of them won their independence from European domination during the two decades following World War II. Outside of China, most of them were not Communists or under communist rule. They were determined not to allow foreign domination or control—not by Western European states, not by the Soviet Union or China, not by their Afro-Asian neighbors, and not by the United States. With a few exceptions such as Nationalist China on Formosa, South Korea, Japan, the Philippines, Thailand, and South Vietnam, most Afro-Asian states rejected binding commitments with the United States in opposition to communist expansion. Similarly, most of them refused blandishments that might have brought them under the domination of the Soviet Union or Communist China. Though they differed sharply among themselves, most Afro-Asian states determined to pursue active independent foreign policies. Westerners often referred to them as neutralist vis-à-vis the cold war, but the Afro-Asians preferred the terms nonaligned or independent. Most of their leaders insisted that they were neither pro-American nor pro-Russian; they were pro-Africa or pro-Asia. They often sought and welcomed outside assistance from communist or noncommunist sources but would not compromise their new independence to get that aid.

Prior to the twentieth century, the United States had little interest in Central Asia, the Middle East, and Africa. Great Britain, France, the Netherlands, Belgium, and other European states dominated there economically, politically, and militarily. Not until the twentieth century, and particularly during and after World War II, did the United States direct much attention toward those areas. Even in East Asia the United States had not been as active and powerful as Britain and France. In the 1940's and to a less extent later, ideological dedication to the right of self-determination caused Americans to sympathize with Afro-Asian struggles for independence. American leaders pressured European states to provide self-government and independence for their colonies. The ideological commitment of Presidents Woodrow Wilson and Franklin D. Roosevelt to self-determination caused friction with the British and French. At the same time, American traders, investors, and manufacturers hoped the elimination of European rivals would open opportunities for them to expand economically into Asia, the Middle East, and Africa.

As the cold war developed, however, American attitudes and policies began to change. The United States needed the power and cooperation of European states to contain Soviet expansion. If American anticolonial policies helped destroy their empires, the United States might find those European states less cooperative. Independence in Asia and Africa would separate European states from colonies, peoples, and resources that had contributed much to their wealth. That would reduce the power those states could contribute to blocking communist expansion.

Though most leaders in Asia and Africa were not Communists, the Soviet Union and Communist Parties successfully identified themselves with anti-imperialism. Americans worried that the instability and violence that often accompanied independence in the new states would give Communists the chance to take over even if most people in those countries did not want that. Chauvinism and anticolonialism in Asia and Africa increasingly aimed at the United States. Nationalism, anticolonialism, instability, violence, and poverty made many new countries less inviting (and less profitable) for American business expansion than Europe and Canada were. Sympathy for Israel against the challenges led by Egypt's Nasser reduced American empathy with Arab nationalism.

In the eighteenth century the United States emerged from violence and revolution to independence and democracy. By the middle of the twentieth century, however, the United States was established, wealthy, and powerful. Like the poor boy who climbed to fame and fortune, it was more difficult to sympathize with the trials and tribulations of the lowly after one had risen to wealth, power, and respectability. Forgetting their own revolutionary and violent past, many Americans were shocked by the travail in Asia and Africa. Some Americans began to suspect that those people lacked qualities essential for orderly and responsible self-government. American belief in the right of self-determination did not disappear, but doubts about it increased. In any event, by the 1960's and 1970's many in Asia and Africa (both Communists and non-Communists) considered the United States the leading defender of the remaining vestiges of colonialism and a threat to their independence and freedom.

THE UNITED STATES AND EAST ASIA

During most of the nineteenth century, American interests were better served in China than the weakness of the United States might have led one to expect. From the 1890's onward, however, United States policies toward China were among the nation's least successful. The future of China was the specific issue that the United States and Japan were unable to compromise before Pearl Harbor. The diplomatic log jam on that issue led to war between the United States and Japan. From 1941 to 1945 the United States spent billions of dollars and thousands of lives fighting to defeat the Japanese challenge to China's survival as an independent sovereign state.

Less than four years after the final defeat of Japan, however, the Chinese Communists under Mao Tse-tung defeated Chiang Kai-shek's armies and drove them off the mainland to Formosa. China's territorial integrity was largely intact, but the United States did not recognize the communist government. China was closed to American businessmen, missionaries, and diplomats more completely than it might have been if Japan had triumphed. The huge communist bloc led by the Soviet Union and China seemed to be a more fearsome threat to American interests in East Asia and the Western Pacific than Japan had been. For more than twenty years after the communist triumph in China the United States withheld diplomatic recognition from that government of a state containing more than 800 million people. American soldiers fought against Chinese troops in Korea from 1950 to 1953. Representatives of the Nationalist government continued to fill China's seats in the Security Council and General Assembly of the United Nations, though that government did not control one square foot of mainland China. And propaganda from Communist China viciously denounced American imperialism and aggression in Asia.

Many in the United States, particularly in the Republican party, blamed the Roosevelt and Truman administrations for the triumph of the Chinese Communists in 1949. Senator Joseph McCarthy charged that Communists and fellow travelers influenced the China policies of the Democratic administrations. Those themes were repeated with many variations throughout the McCarthy era and during the presidential campaign of 1952. Senator McCarthy and his followers failed to prove Communist influence on the State Department's course in East Asia. Conceivably, if it had been willing to marshal its manpower, industrial capacity, and financial resources, the United States might have been able to shore up Chiang Kai-shek's regime and defeat the Chinese Communists. But it might have received little help from the Chinese people. And it might have involved the United States in a major war on the mainland that Asian experts and military leaders had long warned against.

In contrast to the views advanced by their critics, President Truman and Secretary of State Dean Acheson insisted that the United States had done all it properly could to help save China from communism and that Chiang Kai-shek's Kuomintang fell because of circumstances in Asia that were beyond the power of the United States to control. American economic and military assistance to the Chinese Nationalists during and after World War II was very great. The Soviet Union under Stalin lived up to its agreement to recognize Chiang Kai-shek's government, and it concluded a Sino-Soviet pact in 1945 consistent with the Yalta agreement. Except for captured Japanese military equipment left behind for advancing Communist Chinese armies, the Soviet Union gave little help to Mao Tse-tung.

In 1937 the Kuomintang and the Communists agreed to a truce so both could concentrate on fighting the Japanese aggressors, but that truce largely broke down by 1941. During the remainder of the war, the Communists and Nationalists generally neglected the task of fighting Japan and renewed their older struggle against each other for control of China. At the same time, Chiang Kai-shek's regime grew more inefficient, corrupt, and authoritarian. Urgent appeals for reforms had no significant results. With the Communists too strong to ignore or defeat with available forces after World War II, American diplomatic representatives General Patrick J. Hurley and General George C. Marshall tried to work out a compromise between the Chinese Nationalists and Communists. Those efforts failed. Both sides sought only the defeat of the other.

Though China was the second largest country in the world after the Soviet Union and though it had many natural resources, both its area and its resources were insufficient for its huge and rapidly growing population. Too many people with too little food resulted in chronic suffering and famine. That situation was made even worse by several decades of civil strife and foreign war. Perhaps no government could successfully have satisfied the needs of the Chinese people in such difficult circumstances (the Chinese Communists did not do so after they gained control in 1949). In any event, the reactionary regime of Chiang Kai-shek could not do it. The Chinese disagreed sharply on the kind of government they wanted, but by 1949 most of them agreed that they did not want the Kuomintang. Chiang Kai-shek fell partly because the Chinese people abandoned him.

And finally, the Generalissimo overextended his military forces in major efforts to crush the Chinese Communists and, as General Marshall had warned, suffered disastrous defeats as a result. The Chinese Communists under Mao Tse-tung triumphed in 1949 because of their own strength and efforts, because of the corruption and ineffectiveness of the Chinese Nationalists, and because the Kuomintang failed to satisfy the needs of the Chinese people. The Nationalists fell in spite of substantial assistance from the United States.

In a China White Paper released by the Department of State in 1949, Secretary of State Dean Acheson defended the administration's policies and blamed the fiasco on circumstances in China and on Chiang Kaishek's regime. Though not explicit, the tacit implications of the White Paper pointed toward American recognition of the Communist government of China. But both internal and external developments soon blocked that course of action. President Truman firmly backed his Secretary of State. Nevertheless, internally the breakdown of bipartisanship, the renewed "great debate" on American foreign policies in general and on China policies in particular, Senator McCarthy's charges of Communist influences in the State Department, and growing political opposition to the Democratic administration for being "soft on communism" made it politically dangerous for Truman and Acheson to recognize the new government of China. Externally the Korean War and the massive involvement of Red China's troops in that war in 1950 strengthened American opposition to recognition. As the historian Foster Rhea Dulles wrote, the hardening of United States policies toward the Communist government of China and America's increasing support for the Nationalist government on Formosa "was a natural consequence of the direct clash between American and Chinese Communist troops on the Korean battlefield; it also reflected the impact of domestic politics."

Japan had controlled Korea from 1905 until its defeat in World War II forty years later. During that war China, Great Britain, the Soviet Union, and the United States committed themselves to Korean independence. In 1945 Soviet troops accepted the surrender of Japanese forces north of the thirty-eighth parallel in Korea, and the United States did so south of that line. Ostensibly a temporary division for that specific purpose, it became permanent. The divided Korea in East Asia symbolized and aggravated the cold war cleavages much as the divided Germany did in Europe. Bilateral, multilateral, and United Nations efforts failed to resolve the problem, and both the Soviet Union and the United States consolidated their positions and formed separate governments in their respective spheres of Korea. Then both the Soviet Union and the United States withdrew most of their troops in 1948–1949. In January, 1950, Secretary Acheson publicly traced America's "defensive perimeter" in terms that excluded Korea and Formosa. On June 25, 1950, North Korean military forces crossed the thirty-eighth parallel and attacked South Korea.

The United States and the United Nations acted promptly and decisively. On the initiative of the Truman administration an emergency session of the Security Council ordered a cease fire and withdrawal of North Korean forces to the thirty-eighth parallel. It also urged all states in the United Nations "to render every assistance to the United Nations in the execution of this resolution and to refrain from giving assistance to the North Korean authorities." Only its boycott of United Nations organs that seated representatives from Nationalist China prevented the Soviet Union from vetoing that U.N. action. When North Korean forces continued their advance, the Security Council further strengthened its opposition. In Korea General Douglas MacArthur became commander in chief of United Nations forces drawn largely from South Korea and the United States. In the fall of 1950, United Nations troops checked the North Korean advance, drove them back to the thirty-eighth parallel, pushed into North Korea, and advanced toward the Yalu River that separated North Korea from China.

Contrary to estimates in General MacArthur's intelligence reports, the United Nations drive to the Yalu brought Chinese military forces into the fray. Using their unlimited manpower to supplement their limited firepower, the Chinese and North Koreans checked the United Nations advance and once again invaded South Korea. Though they had allowed MacArthur's forces to invade North Korea, the United Nations and the Truman administration carefully limited the fighting to Korea and authorized only conventional weapons. General MacArthur and his more militant supporters wanted to expand the war by blockading China, having the Chinese Nationalists invade the mainland, and bombing bases in China north of the Yalu. When MacArthur persisted in urging those actions in opposition to his civilian superiors in the United States and the United Nations, President Truman relieved the General of his command in April, 1951. Most Americans cheered the General and denounced the President. The frustrations of fighting a limited war for

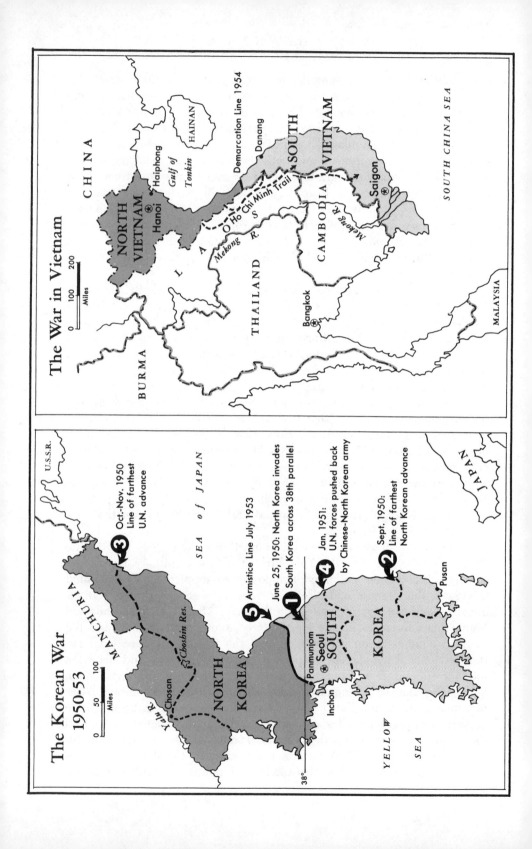

The War in Vietnam

CHINA

NORTH VIETNAM
⊛ Hanoi

Haiphong

Gulf of Tonkin

HAINAN

Demarcation Line 1954

Danang

SOUTH VIETNAM

L A O S

Ho Chi Minh Trail

Mekong R.

CAMBODIA

Mekong R.

Saigon ⊛

BURMA

THAILAND

Bangkok ⊛

MALAYSIA

SOUTH CHINA SEA

0 100 200
Miles

The Korean War 1950-53

U.S.S.R.

MANCHURIA

Yalu R.

Chosan

Chosbin Res.

NORTH KOREA

SEA of JAPAN

3 Oct.-Nov. 1950:
Line of farthest
U.N. advance

5 Armistice Line July 1953

1 June 25, 1950: North Korea invades
South Korea across 38th parallel

4 Jan. 1951:
U.N. forces pushed back
by Chinese-North Korean army

2 Sept. 1950:
Line of farthest
North Korean advance

Panmunjom

Seoul ⊛

Inchon

SOUTH KOREA

Pusan

JAPAN

YELLOW SEA

38°

0 50 100
Miles

limited goals were not nearly as thrilling and inspiring as MacArthur's contention that "in war there is no substitute for victory."

In the final analysis, however, Truman's will prevailed. United Nations forces suffered heavy casualties, but they successfully checked military advances by North Korea and China. After prolonged negotiations (and after the death of Stalin in Russia and the inauguration of Eisenhower in the United States), United Nations negotiators concluded a truce with the Chinese and North Koreans in July, 1953. Determined to settle for nothing less than unification of Korea, South Korea's President Syngman Rhee threatened to renew hostilities. But he and his government were so dependent upon economic and military support from the United States that he reluctantly acquiesced in the continued division of his country. Altogether, more than 50,000 Americans died during the Korean War from 1950 to 1953, nearly 35,000 of them killed in combat. Casualties were greater than in any previous American conflict, except the Civil War, World War I, and World War II.

Just as the cold war led to the rearming of West Germany in Europe, so the Communist triumph in China and the conduct of the Korean War led the United States to change its postwar policies toward Japan. Initially, the United States and its allies determined to demilitarize Japan, prosecute and punish Japanese leaders responsible for the war and atrocities, break the power of the Zaibatsu or huge business combines, inaugurate economic reforms, and train the Japanese in the ways of peaceful political democracy. General Douglas MacArthur as Supreme Commander of the Allied Powers directed those occupation policies. In 1946 Japan adopted a constitution that provided for a parliamentary system of government and a bill of rights and prohibited Japanese military forces. Despite opposition from the Soviet Union, John Foster Dulles negotiated a peace treaty for Japan that went into effect in 1952.

Gradually, however, Japan began to depart from the patterns outlined during the occupation period, and the United States actively encouraged some of those departures. American military forces stayed on in Japan to contribute to common defense. With American encouragement Japan began to build new land, sea, and air forces. The United States supplied military equipment and in 1954 concluded a Mutual Assistance Agreement with Japan. Prewar industrial and financial houses such as Mitsubishi revived. The International Military Tribunal for the Far East (like the War Crimes Tribunal in Nuremberg in Germany) tried, convicted, and sentenced to death General Tojo and other leaders. But many other wartime officers led Japan's new military forces. Civilians who had been purged from political activity during the occupation filled many high government offices, including that of premier. Japanese pacifists and Marxists denounced those developments and America's role in them. Japan was not included in the Southeast Asia Treaty Organization in

1955, but it was a valued member of the anticommunist coalition the United States organized, aided, and led in East Asia.

In 1960 the two countries concluded a Treaty of Mutual Cooperation and Security. Japan became (after the United States and the Soviet Union) the third-ranking industrial state in the world. It was second only to Canada as an export market for American products, though both Canada and Japan sold more in the United States than they bought there. The United States and Japan removed a major irritant in their relations when they agreed to the return of Okinawa to Japanese control in 1972. Conflicting economic interests, including America's unfavorable trade and exchange balances with Japan, strained relations, and America's improved relations with mainland China added another complication. But in the early 1970's Japan was America's best customer and most valued ally in Asia.

Despite its failure in China, Chiang Kai-shek's Nationalist government on Formosa had many enthusiastic friends in the United States, particularly in the Republican party. Due largely to the influence of the United States, representatives from the Kuomintang continued to fill China's seats in the United Nations. Some in the United States and many in other parts of the world would have settled for a "two-China" policy in and out of the United Nations. But the governments of Communist China and Nationalist China both emphatically rejected such an arrangement. American criticisms of the Chinese Communists were exceeded only by the violent denunciations of the United States by Mao Tse-tung's government.

No presidential administration would actively support an attempt by Chiang Kai-shek's forces to reinvade the Chinese mainland. But from July 1950 onward America's Seventh Fleet guarded the Formosa Strait against any attempt by Communist China to destroy the Nationalist stronghold there. The United States provided military equipment and advisers for Chiang Kai-shek's forces.

In 1954–1955 an alarming crisis developed as artillery from the Chinese mainland shelled the Nationalist-held offshore islands of Quemoy and Matsu. Of limited significance of themselves, their seizure could foreshadow and facilitate a full-scale attempt to take Formosa. The United States under President Eisenhower and Secretary of State Dulles warned against any Communist effort to capture those offshore islands as a part of any general assault on Formosa. In December 1954, the United States and Nationalist China concluded a mutual defense treaty. In February 1955, at Eisenhower's request, both houses of Congress provided nearly unanimous approval of the Formosan Resolution supporting the President's authority to use American military forces if necessary to defend Formosa. Some around the President favored strong military action by the United States, including possible use of nuclear weapons, if necessary to defend Formosa against mainland China. Eisenhower was not prepared to abandon Chiang's government, but he rejected the advice of his more militant counselors. From the frame of reference of most Americans at the time, the United States was attempting to "contain" further Chinese Communist expansion; from mainland China it appeared that the United States was expanding by interfering in a Chinese internal matter as the government of China sought to exercise its authority over its people and territory in Formosa. By mid-summer of 1955 tensions eased a bit, and the United States and Communist China began talks at the ambassadorial level in Geneva. Neither side accepted the position of the other, but China did not move militarily against Formosa, an informal truce developed, and by early 1956 that particular crisis passed.

Renewed shelling of Quemoy in 1958 by mainland artillery revived the controversy. Again ambassadorial talks (moved to Warsaw, Poland) failed to resolve differences. The United States and Communist China were no more able to reach agreement than before, but each reluctantly acquiesced in the existing situation in preference to the alternative of war. A third crisis over Quemoy erupted briefly in 1962 during the Kennedy administration. Though individual Democrats heatedly denounced the Eisenhower-Dulles policies, President Kennedy and his Secretary of State Dean Rusk continued to follow essentially the same nonrecognition and containment policies that their Republican predecessors had pursued toward Communist China.

Relations did not improve during the Johnson administration from 1963 to 1969. The Warsaw talks continued intermittently, but did not result in agreement. Mainland China perfected an atomic bomb in 1964, and three years later added hydrogen bombs to its arsenal. China had not yet developed systems for delivering those weapons on targets in the United States, but its nuclear and thermonuclear power and potential increased concern both in the United States and in the Soviet Union. The roles of the United States and Communist China in Vietnam further exacerbated relations. Both the United States and China wanted to avoid the sort of direct military clash they had had in Korea, but the risk of such a conflict seemed very great.

But during the Nixon administration beginning in 1969, even that part of the cold war began to thaw a bit. The United States relaxed its trade and travel bans slightly, and made it clear that it would not be impervious to diplomatic initiatives from China. Secret missions to Peking by the President's Assistant for National Security Affairs, Dr. Henry Kissinger, in July and October, 1971, paved the way for President Nixon's unprecedented trip to Peking in February, 1972. That visit did not immediately produce concrete agreements of fundamental import. But it did open communications at the highest level and encouraged cautious hope for continued progress. The issue of the future of Nationalist China on Formosa continued to bar the establishment of full normal diplomatic relations between the United States and the People's Republic of China (President Nixon first referred to Communist China by that name in October, 1970). But the Chief of the American Liaison Office in Peking was an ambassador in everything but name, and President Nixon indicated the great importance he attached to the post when he named the able and distinguished David K. E. Bruce to that position in 1973.

The thaw in Chinese-American relations resulted from both external and domestic developments. In Asia the growing hostility between the Soviet Union and the People's Republic of China encouraged each of those communist states to improve their relations with the United States. From the American standpoint, the task of ending or preventing conflicts in Southeast and Central Asia needed China's cooperation. Similarly, China's nuclear accomplishments and its huge military manpower made that country an essential part of arms limitations considerations. And more than twenty years after the Nationalist Chinese were driven from the mainland, the aging Chiang Kai-shek's pretensions to speak for China were wearing a bit thin. Within the United States President Nixon's status as a conservative, anti-Communist Republican made him politically less vulnerable to charges of appeasing the Communists and consequently more free to undertake initiatives with "Red China" than a liberal Democratic President might have been. Even his administration's support for United Nations membership for the People's Republic of China, and the failure of American efforts to prevent the expulsion of Nationalist China, evoked surprisingly little political uproar within the United States.

THE VIETNAM WAR

In Southeast Asia the United States found it difficult to contend with the dual challenges of nationalism and communism. War and civil war inflamed Indochina and Vietnam almost continuously from 1940 onward, and the United States was deeply affected and involved. Japan's military forces occupied northern Indochina in 1940 and took over the rest of that French colony in July, 1941. That triggered the American decision to freeze all Japanese assets a few days later. By cutting Japan off from its essential oil supplies, that American action helped lead to the Japanese attack on Pearl Harbor. French military efforts after World War II to reestablish control over Indochina and to crush the Vietminh under Communist Ho Chi Minh cost heavily in money, equipment, and manpower. The Truman and Eisenhower administrations provided much aid and equipment for the French, but most Americans had little sympathy for the French difficulties until their surrender at Dien Bien Phu in 1954.

The Geneva agreements in July, 1954, called for cessation of hostilities in Indochina. Cambodia and Laos were to be independent and neutralized. Provisionally, Vietnam was divided at the seventeenth parallel, and in 1956 there were to be elections to unify Vietnam. An International Commission for Supervision and Control was to oversee implementation of the agreements. At the same time, the United States representative at Geneva called for United Nations supervision of the elections to assure their freedom and fairness.

In October, 1954, President Eisenhower promised Prime Minister Ngo Dinh Diem of South Vietnam that the United States would help develop and maintain "a strong, viable state, capable of resisting attempted subversion or aggression through military means." The United States provided economic assistance and military equipment. It sent a military Assistance Advisory Group to help organize and train the military forces of South Vietnam.

The autocratic Diem regime faced incredibly difficult problems in South Vietnam. Decades of war and civil strife left acute social and economic problems. Buddhists in South Vietnam increasingly opposed the policies of Catholic Diem's government. Diem did not allow the elections in 1956 that the Geneva agreements called for. He really did not believe in (or practice) democracy. He contended that conditions in North Vietnam would not permit honest elections, and he (and American leaders) believed the Communists could win such an election even if it were conducted fairly. The South Vietnamese Communists (Viet Cong) stepped up their guerrilla warfare against the Diem regime and those who supported it. In 1960 the Viet Cong organized the National Liberation Front, and Ho Chi Minh's North Vietnam government increased its aid to the Viet Cong. As the Viet Cong gained strength and the Diem regime lost ground, the Kennedy administration shifted priorities from economic assistance to more military aid. At the same time, the United States increased its military forces in South Vietnam. When Eisenhower left office in 1961, the United States had less than 1,000 officers and men in South Vietnam; at the time of Kennedy's death in November, 1963 (not long after Diem was ousted from power and killed), the United States had more than 15,000 troops there.

In 1964–1965 the civil war between the government of South Vietnam and the Viet Cong continued. But with increasing soldiers and supplies from Ho Chi Minh's Communist government of North Vietnam, with military equipment from Red China and the Soviet Union, and with soldiers and supplies from the United States, it became more and more of an international cold war conflict. In August, 1964, after North Vietnamese torpedo boats attacked American destroyers in the Gulf of Tonkin off Vietnam, President Lyndon B. Johnson requested and got a joint congressional resolution authorizing him "to take all necessary steps, including the use of armed force, against aggression in Southeast Asia." Only two Senators voted against the resolution, and no one in the House of Representatives opposed it. Incident followed incident; each act of violence on one side led to greater violence by the other. In February, 1965, American Air Force planes began bombing selected targets in North Vietnam. In March American ground forces went into combat against the Viet Cong and troops from North Vietnam. Navy warplanes based on carriers at sea attacked roads, bridges, and supply lines in North Vietnam. More and more North Vietnamese troops entered the fray, and American leaders called for ever larger reinforcements. At the end of January, 1968, in the midst of the Vietnamese Tet holiday season, the Viet Cong and North Vietnamese forces launched an all-out surprise offensive on most of the cities of South Vietnam, including Saigon. The Tet offensive caused very heavy casualties. It emboldened opponents of the war in the United States and elsewhere. But South Vietnam and United States military forces struck back with devastating effectiveness, blunting the offensive and destroying some of the best of the Viet Cong and North Vietnamese units. By 1969 nearly 550,000 American troops were in South Vietnam and the American commander there, General William C. Westmoreland, wanted more. Despite escalation of the war, neither the Viet Cong, North Vietnam, nor Communist China gave any evidence that they were ready to quit (or even ready to negotiate). Premier Nguyen Cao Ky's government, headed by military officers, and later the government under President Nguyen Van Thieu, retained power partly because of the support they got from the United States.

President Johnson, Secretary of State Dean Rusk, and Secretary of Defense Robert McNamara repeatedly insisted that the American objective was to defend South Vietnam against communist aggression from North Vietnam supported by equipment from Communist China and the Soviet Union. The Johnson administration repeatedly indicated its willingness and even eagerness to negotiate a peaceful settlement that would allow the South Vietnamese to shape their own destiny free from outside coercion. Ho Chi Minh's government, however, insisted that there could be no negotiations and no peace until the United States took its military forces out of Vietnam. North Vietnam also demanded the establishment in Saigon of a coalition government including the Viet Cong.

America's massive involvement in the fighting in Vietnam aroused much criticism in the United States and in other parts of the world. Some critics (particularly conservative Republicans and members of the armed forces) said the United States should either make an all-out effort to win the war or should get out of Vietnam. Other critics (largely from the President's own Democratic party) insisted that the conflict was largely a civil war between South Vietnamese, that North Vietnam had provided few soldiers and little equipment for the Viet Cong, and that the Vietnamese (North and South) were as determined to prevent Chinese domination there as the United States was. There were heavy casualties and many atrocities on all sides in the conflict. The "Mylai massacre" of villagers by a platoon under Lt. William Calley got the most publicity, but critics of America's involvement had no difficulty discovering examples of women and children who had been cremated by American napalm bombs, or disfigured or killed by American shells.

Senator J. William Fulbright, Democratic chairman of the Foreign Relations Committee, was one of the more able critics of the administration's policies. He stressed the role of nationalism in Southeast Asia. He described Ho Chi Minh as a dedicated Communist and also a fervent nationalist who opposed domination by any outside power whether that power be France, China, or the United States. Unfortunately for the United States, Ho Chi Minh spoke for both communism and nationalism, and America's crusade against communism there made the United States appear as the aggressive and imperialistic enemy of Vietnamese nationalistic aspirations. Most critics insisted that America's vital interests and security were not at stake in Vietnam. They contended that America's massive involvement there weakened the United States in more important parts of the world and disrupted peaceful efforts to improve Soviet-American relations.

With the escalation of both the fighting abroad and the protests at home, the Johnson administration almost desperately sought an honorable way out of the debacle. But American and South Vietnamese military forces were unable either to crush their opponents or to force them to negotiate an acceptable settlement. Military escalation sufficient to defeat the enemy would risk involving China directly in the war and would have aroused increased opposition within the United States and from people all over the world. For the United States to withdraw its military forces and equipment unilaterally (without comparable actions by North Vietnam's sources of supply) seemed likely to result in North Vietnamese control over all of Vietnam and the triumph of communism in Southeast Asia. And though discussions with North Vietnamese representatives got underway in Paris in 1968, they made little headway. That impasse essentially ruined President Johnson's administration and led to his decision in 1968 not to seek another term in the White House.

The shift from the Democratic Johnson administration to the Republican Nixon administration in 1969 did not immediately resolve the problem either at home or abroad. The Nixon administration sought a settlement through diplomatic negotiations—both at the formal Paris peace talks and through Henry Kissinger's secret peace efforts. But through most of Nixon's first term as President those efforts floundered. The North Vietnamese insisted on terms that, in the administration's view, would have entailed not only total withdrawal of American military forces, equipment, and aid from South Vietnam, but would also essentially have handed South Vietnam over to domination by the Communist-led government of North Vietnam. Fearing the consequences in Vietnam, in Southeast Asia, and in other countries to which the United States had made commitments, the Nixon administration found the North Vietnamese terms unacceptable.

Paralleling its diplomatic efforts was the Nixon administration's Vietnamization policy, preparing the South Vietnamese to defend themselves while scaling down the direct United States military role there. It also included a brief but much criticized military incursion into Cambodia in 1970 to destroy North Vietnam bases and sanctuaries there, American support for a South Vietnam drive into Laos in 1971, and renewed American air attacks on North Vietnam and the mining of North Vietnamese harbors in 1972. Those actions were designed to guard the shrinking American forces still in Vietnam and to weaken the military opposition that the South Vietnamese would have to contend with as they took over the ground war responsibilities. By the end of 1972 the Nixon administration had reduced America's military forces in Vietnam by nearly half a million men from their peak of nearly 550,000 early in 1969. And the United States had removed the last of its ground fighting forces.

President Nixon's diplomatic efforts and Vietnamization policies until the end of 1972 were no more acceptable to most critics of the war at home and abroad than President Johnson's had been. The incursion into Cambodia in particular provoked widespread and often violent protests and demonstrations—especially on college and university campuses during the spring of 1970. Despite the continued unpopularity of the Vietnam war, however, the majority of the American people reluctantly shared the administration's contention that under the circumstances the United States had certain responsibilities that it should not abandon by total unilateral withdrawal from South Vietnam. The frustrating inconclusiveness of the fighting abroad and the strong protests at home against the war encouraged a reversal of American expansion into Southeast Asia. But the probable ideological, political, military, and power consequences abroad of a unilateral United States withdrawal and the continued strength of collective security, anticommunist, and containment sentiments at home made the majority of the American people and their leaders in both parties reluctant to reverse that expansion. They wanted to get off the tiger's back but were afraid of the consequences of doing so. President Nixon's reelection in November, 1972, to a second term in the White House suggested that his course in the difficult situation in Southeast Asia was more widely approved under the circumstances than the alternatives urged by Democratic Senator George McGovern, by activists on college campuses, and by much of the news media.

In October, 1972, during the final stages of the American presidential campaign, a breakthrough occurred in Kissinger's secret negotiations in

Paris. On October 8, the North Vietnamese agreed to treat the military issues separately from the political issues in South Vietnam, dropping their demand for a coalition government in Saigon. For the first time negotiations progressed rapidly and appeared to be approaching a mutually acceptable conclusion. Before reaching that point, however, Hanoi radio broadcast on October 26 that a nine-point peace agreement had been reached and could be signed on October 31. That break in the secrecy forced an American response. Dr. Kissinger confirmed the essential accuracy of the Hanoi announcement. He said that certain differences remained to be resolved, but that agreement could come quickly. Nevertheless, both October 31 and the election day passed without the conclusion of an agreement. Negotiations deadlocked and broke off in mid-December. The United States then resumed bombing of North Vietnam. For nearly two weeks B-52 heavy bombers pounded Hanoi, Haiphong, and other targets with unprecedented ferocity. And through it all President Nixon and Dr. Kissinger maintained a silence that provided neither the American people nor the world with an explanation for the developments. But on January 8, 1973, Kissinger resumed his talks with North Vietnamese representative. On January 15, President Nixon ordered suspension of the bombing because of the negotiating progress. On January 23, he announced the successful conclusion of the negotiations. And on January 27, 1973 the agreements were signed ending the longest war in American history.

President Nixon's critics predictably explained the administration's gyrations in terms of cynical political opportunism before the election, a cold-blooded viciousness during the bombings, and a contempt for Congress and public opinion during his silence prior to January 23. Until the documents in the United States and Vietnam become available to scholars in the future, one cannot be certain of the truth. The most critical theories conceivably may prove to be correct. But there are other possible explanations. Given the strength of peace sentiment in the United States, the North Vietnamese may have considered the weeks before the American election to be the most advantageous time to conclude a settlement. By October 26 the negotiations had progressed as far as the North Vietnamese wanted them to go. Consequently they made the preliminary terms public in an effort to avoid further concessions in the negotiations. They believed that the Nixon administration would not hazard the loss of the election by holding out on the remaining issues. But the North Vietnamese were mistaken. With a formidable lead in the campaign (according to public opinion polls) and with most of the criticisms coming from those who would vote for Senator McGovern anyway, Nixon felt no pressing political need to yield to the North Vietnamese tactic. It is also possible that the President may have considered American national interests, "peace with honor," and the long-term verdict of history to be of greater importance than the immediate political benefits of a peace settlement before election day. With Nixon's overwhelming election victory in November (only Massachusetts prevented him from winning the electoral votes of all fifty states), the chances for an early softening of the United States position in the negotiations evaporated. The bombings were the administration's heavy-handed way of suggesting to the North Vietnamese that they might derive certain benefits from resuming serious negotiations.

The peace agreement signed on January 27, 1973, provided for an internationally supervised cease-fire in South Vietnam. It required release of all military prisoners and withdrawal of all United States and allied military forces within sixty days. The United States agreed to remove the mines from North Vietnamese waters. An International Commission composed of members from Canada, Indonesia, Hungary, and Poland, and Joint Military Commissions would control and supervise implementation of the agreement. It provided that there should be no military alliances for either North or South Vietnam, and no foreign military bases or advisers on the territory of either. There should be no use of bases in Laos or Cambodia to endanger South Vietnam, and all foreign military forces would withdraw from Laos and Cambodia. In the political portions of the agreement the United States and North Vietnam called for self-determination for the people of South Vietnam. The agreement provided for free general elections in South Vietnam under international supervision and for future peaceful reunification of Vietnam through Vietnamese negotiations. The United States agreed to contribute to the postwar reconstruction of Indochina, including North Vietnam.

There were violations and charges of violations in the implementation of the agreement. Its success and duration can be determined only with the passage of time. But the agreement did make practicable the withdrawal of American military forces from the Vietnam quagmire. It did return American prisoners of war, some of whom had been in captivity for as much as eight or nine years. It provided a reasonable hope that the people of South Vietnam might choose their own government, independent both of the United States and of North Vietnam. And it did end, for the United States, its longest and one of its most traumatic wars.

Though Congress never formally declared war, the costs of the Vietnam conflict for the United States and Southeast Asia were huge. Some two and a half million Americans served in the armed forces in Vietnam. Over 55,000 of them died there, more than lost their lives in the Korean War, and more Americans than died in any other wars except the Civil War and the two World Wars. Fighting in an essentially preindustrial peasant society, the United States used the most sophisticated communications systems and powerful weapons of war ever. Though it did not use its nuclear and thermonuclear weapons, American military planes dropped more tons of explosives on targets in Vietnam than they had used on the three Axis powers during World War II. The costs of the war, direct and indirect, exceeded those of any American war except World War II, and they will continue to grow long into the future. If the losses for the United States were great, they were vastly greater for the Vietnamese, North and South. In addition, for millions of people all over the world, the Vietnam War shattered an earlier more attractive and optimistic image of the United States. The American people themselves were torn internally, their self-image and self-esteem badly tarnished. Instead of the knight in shining armor riding off to save damsels in distress by fighting evil dragons, the United States had become the villain, the oppresser, the imperialist. Those new images may be distortions, too, but the images formed just the same. Perhaps one wishes to retain one's childlike idealism and purity; the trauma of adjusting to human imperfections and limitations is never pleasant—either for individuals or for nations. But if out of all that the American people, and their government and its foreign policies, can gain maturity, restraint, humility, and wisdom to more wisely guide America's future role in world affairs, the ordeal could have more beneficial side effects than may seem apparent at the moment.

THE MIDDLE EAST AND AFRICA

The Middle East was and is one of the most important areas in the world. Its ancient civilizations were highly developed when Europeans and North Americans were still little more than savages. Important roots of Western civilization may be traced to the region, and it produced three of the world's great religions: Judaism, Christianity, and Islam. In addition to its cultural and religious importance, the Middle East was and is important strategically. Key transportation routes pass through the area, and for centuries powers struggled to control it. Since it borders on the Soviet Union, it was inevitably included in cold war calculations. And finally, in addition to its cultural-religious and strategic importance, economically it was a trade link between Europe and Asia, and it floats on the world's largest oil reserves.

The Middle East was dominated by various powers during its long and complicated history: the Persians, the Greeks, the Romans, and the Turks, among others. In the twentieth century, Great Britain and France gained control of much of the area.

Though a few Americans reached there before the American Revolution, the United States gave relatively little attention to the Middle East until the twentieth century and particularly after World War II. Externally, the power vacuum left by the decline of British and French power after the war and the danger of Soviet expansion forced American attention to the Middle East. Arab nationalism and hostility toward Israel chronically threatened to erupt into wars that could spread to other parts of the world. The Suez Canal was vital to the power and prosperity of America's British and French allies. And Middle Eastern oil enhanced the power of any states that controlled it. Internally, American interest and activity in the Middle East grew partly out of profits to be obtained by American oil companies. And American Jews and many others were greatly concerned about the creation, success, and security of the state of Israel.

Jews had long wanted to re-create a homeland in Palestine. In obtaining a mandate over Palestine, the British formally accepted the 1917 Balfour Declaration pledging support for establishing ultimately a homeland for the Jews, while at the same time assuring protection for the interests of Arabs in the area. Nazi persecution of European Jews forced many to flee to other parts of the world. Those refugees and displaced persons made the creation of a Jewish state seem even more urgent. The whole movement won powerful financial and political support from the organized Zionist movement in the United States and elsewhere. The Truman administration actively supported creation of a Jewish homeland in Palestine.

In 1947 the United Nations General Assembly voted to partition Palestine between an Arab and a Jewish state. The state of Israel came into existence in May, 1948, and President Truman promptly extended diplomatic recognition. To Arab nationalists, however, creation of Israel was an extension of Western imperialism in an area they had held for centuries. They waged war in an unsuccessful effort to prevent it. America's Ralph Bunche, serving as United Nations mediator, arranged a truce and helped negotiate four armistice agreements between Israel and Egypt, Jordon, Lebanon, and Syria in 1949. But the Arab states never reconciled themselves to the existence of Israel. Arab refugees who fled from their lands in Israel remained as an enduring symbol of Arab resolve to destroy Israel and to regain those lands. Though Arabs could agree in their opposition to Israel, they disagreed on most other matters. And until 1955 they got little encouragement or support from the Soviet Union.

The Eisenhower administration supported Israel, and Secretary of State John Foster Dulles made it clear that he did not like Afro-Asian "neutralist" policies. Nevertheless, the Republican administration was slightly less enamored of Israel than the Democratic Truman administration had been and slightly more tolerant of other states in the Middle East. The Jewish vote was more important to Democratic political strength in northeastern cities than it was to the Republican party. Similarly, American oil interests were more likely to support the Republican than the Democratic party. It was only a difference in degree, but it may have helped account for the contrast between the Eisenhower-Dulles policies in the Arab-Israeli crisis of 1956, and the Truman policies in 1948–1949 and the Johnson policies in 1967.

In the summer and fall of 1956, a succession of developments inflamed the smoldering embers in the Middle East. When Egypt's Gamal Abdel Nasser made a cotton-for-arms deal with Communist Czechoslovakia and negotiated for Russian aid, Secretary of State Dulles countered by withdrawing proffered American (and British and World Bank) financial aid for the construction of Egypt's high Aswan dam on the Nile. Nasser then promptly nationalized the Suez Canal and boasted he would use canal revenues to finance construction of the dam. France and particularly Great Britain under Prime Minister Anthony Eden considered Suez vital to their economies and security. When diplomacy failed, they used force. Without informing the United States, the states of Israel, Great Britain, and France attacked and defeated Egypt's armies. Most Americans did not like Nasser and sympathized with Israel, Britain, and France. They wanted their most valued European allies to be prosperous, strong, and cooperative. At the same time, however, the United States opposed aggression by one state against another. Though there was Egyptian provocation, in the Suez crisis the Eisenhower administration saw Israel, Britain, and France as aggressors. Pressure from the United States, the Soviet Union, Commonwealth countries, and the United Nations caused the British, French, and Israelis to withdraw their military forces without accomplishing their objectives of ousting Nasser and regaining control of the canal. A small United Nations Emergency Force patrolled the border areas. The fiasco ended Eden's political career. It painfully dramatized Great Britain's declining power and its dependence on the United States. Despite its military defeat, Egypt retained control of the canal and Nasser emerged stronger than before. The Suez crisis turned some Arab states more toward the Soviet Union than before, and the Soviet Union provided increasing economic and military assistance to them.

The Soviet Union's growing interest and activity in the Middle East moved the United States under President Eisenhower and Secretary of State John Foster Dulles to extend its containment policy to that area. With encouragement from the United States, in 1955 Great Britain, Turkey, Iraq, Iran, and Pakistan created the Middle East Treaty Organization. Geographically METO bordered the Soviet Union in the Middle East and lay between NATO in Europe and SEATO in Asia. Turkey to the west was a member of both NATO and METO, Pakistan to the east belonged to both SEATO and METO, and Great Britain was in all three of those regional organizations. The United States did not formally join METO, but it was the leading member of NATO and SEATO and supported METO states against the Soviet Union. On paper NATO, METO, and SEATO ringed the Communist world and blocked further expansion by Communist states. In practice METO (like SEATO) lacked effective power.

Responding to the President's request, Congress in 1957 adopted a resolution authorizing him to extend military and economic assistance to any Middle East country that requested such aid to resist armed communist aggression. Acting under that "Eisenhower Doctrine" the United States briefly sent 13,000 Marines into Lebanon in the summer of 1958 to cope with an uprising encouraged by the newly formed United Arab Republic under Nasser. When Iraq withdrew from METO in 1959 the United States helped its remaining members organize the Central Treaty Organization or CENTO to oppose Communist expansion.

For a decade after the Suez crisis of 1956 the United Nations Emergency Force helped maintain an uneasy peace between Israel and its neighbors. Nevertheless, numerous incidents endangered that peace, and neither the Israelis nor the Arabs considered the arrangement satisfactory or permanent. Egypt successfully operated the Suez Canal but closed it to Israeli ships. Though Nasser suppressed Communists in Egypt, the Soviet Union helped finance construction of the Aswan Dam to which Nasser attached such great importance. The Soviet Union also supplied large amounts of modern military equipment to cooperative Arab states, particularly to the United Arab Republic.

In May, 1967, emboldened by military equipment and diplomatic support from the Soviet Union, President Nasser demanded removal of the United Nations Emergency Force. Secretary General U Thant promptly complied, and Egyptian troops moved into the Gaza Strip, Sharm el-Sheikh, and other areas. Nasser closed the Gulf of Aquaba to ships bound for Israel's gulf port. Incidents grew more frequent and tensions mounted. Secretary General U Thant rushed to the area and urged a "breathing spell," but his efforts to prevent war failed. On June 5, 1967, fighting erupted between Israel and Egypt, Syria, and Jordan. As in the two previous military contests, Israel's forces quickly and easily crushed the Arabs despite the military equipment and advisers that Russia had provided. With the active leadership and support of the United States, the United Nations Security Council unanimously and repeatedly called for a cease-fire. But by the time the fighting actually stopped, six days after it began, Israeli forces were completely victorious. They had swept over the Gaza Strip, the Sinai Peninsula, and advanced to the Suez Canal. They had driven into Syria and Jordan. And they had seized that part of Jerusalem that had been in Jordan.

Despite its support for the Arab states, the Soviet Union (like the United States) was not willing to risk a nuclear war over the issue. Nevertheless, when its military equipment proved insufficient against the Israelis, Soviet prestige required that it make a major diplomatic effort to turn back the Israeli advance. The Soviet Union urged the Security Council to adopt a resolution condemning Israel's aggression and insisting that Israel withdraw to the positions it had held before the fighting started. The United States under President Lyndon B. Johnson helped block the Soviet resolution in the Security Council. Then the Soviet Union invoked the Uniting for Peace Resolution to get a special session of the General Assembly to deal with the matter. Most Afro-Asian leaders considered Israel the instrument of Western and American imperialism, so Russia's chances (and Nasser's) appeared better in the General Assembly, where the Afro-Asian states commanded a large number of votes. The Soviet Union again urged that Israel be condemned as an aggressor and that it withdraw its forces from the territory it had overrun.

Throughout the whole crisis the United States repeatedly insisted on preserving the independence and territorial integrity of all states in the Middle East. It urged justice for refugees there. It insisted that Egypt had no right under international law to close the Gulf of Aquaba to Israel. It denied the right of Israel unilaterally to extend its jurisdiction over the Old City of Jerusalem. But the United States also insisted that simply restoring conditions to their prewar status would lead to continuing difficulties and future wars. The United States promised support for any negotiations inside or outside of the United Nations that offered hope for an enduring solution to the friction between Israel and the Arab states. A majority in the General Assembly voted for the Soviet resolution, but most of the states in Western Europe and in the Western Hemisphere opposed it. The resolution did not win the necessary two-thirds vote.

Israel continued to occupy and develop lands it had conquered in 1967; the Arab states demanded the return of those lands. The Suez Canal remained closed. Since Nasser did not have the military power necessary to dislodge Israeli troops, and since the Soviet Union or other countries would not do it for him, he could not salvage political and diplomatic victory from Egypt's military defeat as he had done a decade earlier. Nasser's death in 1970 did not fundamentally change the patterns. Palestinian refugees and terrorists repeatedly exacerbated the explosive situation both for the Arab governments and for Israel. Airplane hijackings and the murder of Israeli athletes at the Munich Olympics in 1972 were conspicuous parts of the whole tragic compound.

The United States and the Soviet Union were both wary of allowing the Middle East crises to erupt into a great power nuclear war, but neither would allow the other to gain control there. Egypt's ouster of Soviet advisers in 1972 did not end the Soviet power or presence. United States initiatives in 1970 led to an uneasy cease-fire and attempted negotiations, but no agreement was forthcoming. During the 1972 presidential campaign leaders of both American political parties tried to outdo each other in professing their support for Israel, but no administration cared to risk war in the Middle East. With no settlement in sight the region remained a dangerous trouble spot.

Africa was the world's second largest continent, with an area nearly four times that of the United States. Its rapidly growing population exceeded the population of the United States by some 100 million. In the second half of the twentieth century no major part of the world changed more rapidly than Africa. Despite sharp differences among them on specific issues and personalities, Africans shared with the people of Asia, the Middle East, and Latin America intense nationalism, anticolonialism, determination to assure racial equality, and the "revolution of rising expectations." In 1950 there were only four independent African states: Egypt, Ethiopia, Liberia, and the Union of South Africa. By 1973 that number had multiplied ten times. In brief decades much of Africa was trying to make social, economic, educational, political, and international changes that took Europe centuries to accomplish. At the same time, most Africans determined to retain the best in their own cultures and to shape their own futures independent of Western civilization. But Africa was extremely varied, and its people and leaders were by no means agreed on the kind of future they wanted to build, nor on who should govern it and how.

American interests in Africa extended back to the eighteenth century. Trade and treaties with the Barbary States of North Africa, colonizing freed slaves in West Africa, and the slave trade were conspicuous parts of America's early activities there. Nevertheless, America's role was always small relative to that of European states. The United States often followed and supported Great Britain's lead as that country dismantled its empire and tried to help the Africans in the difficult early stages of independence.

Partly because its own power and prosperity were not so directly involved, the United States urged self-determination and independence for colonies in Africa more consistently than it did in Asia. Americans hoped the transition from colonialism to self-government could be accomplished in an orderly manner, but they considered the transition inevitable and generally desirable. Both the United States government and private institutions provided much economic, technical, and educational assistance to the newly independent peoples and states in Africa. American businessmen saw in the resources and markets of Africa profitable opportunities for trade and investment. With American trade there annually exceeding two billion dollars and with investments totaling more than two billion, United States economic expansion began to gain on European entrepreneurs. Though Americans worried about the danger of communist triumphs, most Africans and their leaders rejected communism.

The decades after World War II witnessed the end of the old colonial empires in Asia, the Middle East, and Africa. The United States variously encouraged that development or resigned itself to it. When cold war requirements seemed pressing, the United States sometimes backed into opposing nationalistic movements in Asia and Africa that seemed to advance communism as well. Most states in the Third World did not individually command the elements essential for great power in world politics. Most of them never would. There continued to be sharp cleavages within and among the Afro-Asian states. The future forms of their societies, economies, political systems, and international policies continued to be uncertain. The capacity of the United States to influence those developments was decidedly limited. Nevertheless, great challenges, opportunities, and dangers for the United States in international affairs in the future lay in the Afro-Asian world. And the United States would be well advised to meet them creatively and constructively in tune with the best aspirations of the people there, aspirations that are not necessarily incompatible with America's own best values.

SUPPLEMENTARY READINGS

Acheson, Dean. *Present at the Creation: My Years in the State Department.* New York: W. W. Norton & Co., 1969.

Barnett, A. Doak. *Communist China and Asia: Challenge to American Foreign Policy.* New York: Harper & Bros., 1960.

Bloomfield, Lincoln P. *The United Nations and U.S. Foreign Policy.* Rev. ed. Boston: Little, Brown & Co., 1967.

Blum, Robert. *United States and China in World Affairs.* New York: McGraw-Hill Book Co., 1966.

Cooper, Chester L. *The Lost Crusade: America in Vietnam.* New York: Dodd, Mead & Co., 1970.

Dulles, Foster Rhea. *American Foreign Policy Toward Communist China, 1949–1969.* New York: Thomas Y. Crowell Co., 1972.

Eisenhower, Dwight D. *Mandate for Change, 1953–1956: The White House Years.* Garden City, N.Y.: Doubleday & Co., Inc., 1963.

_____. *Waging Peace, 1956–1961: The White House Years.* Garden City, N.Y.: Doubleday & Co., Inc., 1965.

Emerson, Rupert. *Africa and United States Policy.* Englewood Cliffs, N.J.: Prentice-Hall, Inc., 1967.

Fairbank, John K. *China: The People's Middle Kingdom and the U.S.A.* Cambridge, Mass.: Harvard University Press, 1967.

_____. *The United States and China.* New ed. Cambridge, Mass.: Harvard University Press, 1958.

Fall, Bernard B. *The Two Viet-Nams: A Political and Military Analysis.* Rev. ed. New York: Frederick A. Praeger, Inc., 1964.

Finer, Herman. *Dulles Over Suez.* Chicago: Quadrangle Books, Inc., 1964.

Fulbright, J. William. *The Arrogance of Power.* New York: Random House, Inc., 1966.

Graebner, Norman A. *The New Isolationism: A Study in Politics and Foreign Policy Since 1950.* New York: Ronald Press Co., 1956.

Johnson, Lyndon B. *The Vantage Point: Perspectives of the Presidency, 1963–1969.* New York: Holt, Rinehart & Winston, Inc., 1971.

McKay, Vernon. *Africa in World Politics.* New York: Harper & Row, Publishers, 1963.

————. *African Diplomacy.* New York: Frederick A. Praeger, Inc., 1966.

Nixon, Richard. *U.S. Foreign Policy for the 1970's: Shaping a Durable Peace.* Washington: U.S. Government Printing Office, 1973.

Palmer, Norman D. *South Asia and United States Policy.* Boston: Houghton Mifflin Co., 1966.

Polk, William R. *The United States and the Arab World.* Cambridge, Mass.: Harvard University Press, 1965.

Reischauer, Edwin O. *The United States and Japan.* 2d ed. Cambridge, Mass.: Harvard University Press, 1957.

Rostow, W. W. *The Diffusion of Power: An Essay in Recent History.* New York: Macmillan Co., 1972.

Safran, Nadav. *The United States and Israel.* Cambridge, Mass.: Harvard University Press, 1963.

Schlesinger, Arthur M., Jr. *The Bitter Heritage: Vietnam and American Democracy, 1941–1966.* Boston: Houghton Mifflin Co., 1967.

Sheehan, Neil; Smith, Hedrick; Kenworthy, E. W.; and Butterfield, Fox. *The Pentagon Papers as Published by The New York Times.* New York: Bantam Books, Inc., 1971.

Spanier, John W. *American Foreign Policy Since World War II.* 6th ed. New York: Frederick A. Praeger, Inc., 1973.

————. *The Truman-MacArthur Controversy and the Korean War.* Cambridge, Mass.: Belknap Press, 1959.

Speiser, Ephraim A. *The United States and the Near East.* 2d ed. Cambridge, Mass.: Harvard University Press, 1950.

Steel, Ronald. *Pax Americana: The Cold War, Empire and the Politics of Counter-Revolution.* New rev. ed. New York: Viking Press, 1970.

Truman, Harry S. *Memoirs.* 2 vols. Garden City, N.Y.: Doubleday & Co., Inc., 1955–1956.

40

Possibilities for the future

America's historical role in world affairs becomes meaningful partly in terms of external and internal influences. It follows, therefore, that any fundamental foreign policy changes in the future will require modification of the world and domestic circumstances affecting American foreign relations.

More than most people, Americans have believed confidently in their ability to accomplish "the impossible" in their personal lives and in the domestic and foreign policies of their government. The talents and initiative of the men and women who were bold enough to leave the Old World and build lives in the New World inspired that optimism. The abundant resources and opportunities available in America justified that attitude for many. Fortunate circumstances abroad and growing American power helped extend that confidence into the realm of foreign affairs.

"Realists" deride American idealism and utopianism. They point to the discrepancies between idealistic foreign policy slogans and the harsh realities of international politics. Realists urge the United States to limit its goals and commitments in foreign affairs to those that are essential to national interests and that the United States can accomplish with the power available for those purposes. Their guidance is perceptive and helpful.

Nevertheless, the "realists" and skeptics are not always correct, and the "idealists" are not always wrong or unrealistic. Individuals and states

489

have often accomplished "the impossible." The timid can generally find reasons for resigning themselves to circumstances that the more imaginative and bold might convert into creative accomplishments. If American foreign policies have sometimes aimed at unattainable goals, others have often too readily acquiesced in unsatisfactory circumstances. Many Englishmen in the twentieth century pride themselves on a national talent for being practical, for realistically adjusting to circumstances that cannot be changed. But that "practical" and "realistic" attitude might have made the great accomplishments of Elizabethan or Victorian England impossible. Dedicated "idealists" have often been "realists" in practice, and "realists" often underestimate man's creative capacities. Americans would do themselves and the world an injustice if they were to forgo idealism in foreign affairs and resign themselves and their country to goals that the more "practical" would consider attainable. Great leaders and great people can still accomplish miracles that their more skeptical critics will never realize.

At the same time, however, the wise idealist should weigh the domestic and international circumstances that enhance or inhibit the foreign policies of the United States. The most brilliant leaders and the most artful diplomats must operate within limits that circumstances at home and abroad impose. And they cannot always alter those circumstances as easily or as drastically as some might wish.

Many individuals, when looking in their mirrors, tend either to approve what they see or to believe it too difficult to change what they see. Similarly, many Americans find it easy to approve or rationalize much of what they see in American society, economy, government, ideals, and practices. What they dislike they find difficult to change. If one believes that the United States should follow substantially different foreign policies, one must consider the possibility that the alternative policies might require drastic changes within the United States.

Individuals often wish that the attitudes and actions of their friends and associates were different. But their capacity to change the persons around them is decidedly limited. That is also true for states. Using its thermonuclear weapons the United States could destroy civilization, but it lacks the power to remake the world in its own image even if it chose to do so. In the second half of the twentieth century, America's capacity for creative changes in the international community is more limited than its capacity for destruction.

In considering what is desirable or undesirable in the foreign policies of the United States one must examine the value and consequences of American expansion. In some circumstances continued expansion could culminate in an American world empire. In the thermonuclear age continued expansion could result in total war and total destruction for the United States, its allies, its enemies, and for neutrals. Continued American expansion could undermine the independence, freedom, and uniqueness of other states and peoples. On the other hand, stopping American expansion could leave the initiative to other states and systems. It could abandon millions to a communist domination beyond their power to escape. Reversal of American expansion, turning to "self-containment," could invite developments abroad, including possible expansion by the Soviet Union and China, that could endanger the peace and security of the whole noncommunist world. To limit or reverse expansion could force important domestic political and economic changes within the United States. In any event, substantial modification or reversal of that expansion pattern would require changes abroad or within the United States or both. And neither kind of change is likely to be accomplished easily.

Whatever paths Americans may choose for the United States in world affairs, whatever changes they may seek at home or abroad, whatever conclusions they may reach about the wisdom of American expansion, there are certain domestic developments that all should earnestly seek for Americans and their leaders. These include increased knowledge, wisdom, self-discipline, and sense of responsibility in both domestic and international matters. The peace, security, welfare, and survival of humanity may well depend upon those qualities within the United States.

INDEX

Index

495

Trist, Nicholas P., 137–39
Troppau-Laibach, Conference of, 86
Trotsky, Leon, 235, 303, 307, 415
Trujillo, Rafael, 460
Truman, Harry S., 396, 397, 401, 407, 428–29, 431–46, 466–71, 482
Truman Doctrine, 436
Tunis, 51
Turkey, 436, 441
Turner, Frederick Jackson, 172–73
Twenty-One Demands, 281
Tyler, John, 96, 118–20, 153

U

Ukase of 1821, 109–10
Unitarians, 93
United Fruit Company, 343
United Nations, 388–89, 422–28, 438–41, 457–58, 469–71, 474, 483–85
United Nations Declaration, 422
United States-Nicaraguan Concession, 263
United States Steel Corporation, 165, 239, 403
Uniting for Peace Resolution of 1950, 440, 485
Upshur, Abel P., 118
Urbanization in America, 19, 23, 49–50, 93, 118–19, 168–69, 200–201, 241, 246, 285–86, 312, 320–21, 324, 386–87, 394–409
Uruguay, 456
Utrecht, Treaty of, 14
U-2, 450, 460

V

Van Buren, Martin, 96, 118, 123
Vancouver, George, 126
Vancouver Island, 127–29
Vandenberg, Arthur H., 322, 362, 404, 411, 437
Vanderbilt, Cornelius, 142–43
Venezuela, 193–94, 260–61
Vergennes, Count de, 37
Vermilion iron range, 125
Verona, Conference of, 86
Versailles Treaty, 302–4, 307–8, 330–35, 343
Veto, in United Nations, 428, 440
Vicksburg, Fall of, 186
Viet Cong, 475–81
Vietnam War, 401, 407–8, 446, 452, 474–81
Vietnamization, 478
Villa, Francisco, 265–66
Virgin Islands, 201
Virginius episode, 203–4

Visit and Search, 288
V-J Day, 429

W

Waldheim, Kurt, 441
Walker, J. G., 257–58
Walker, William, 143
Walker Commission, Second, 257–58
Wall Street Journal, 221
Wallace, Henry A., 407, 434
Wanghia, Treaty of, 154–55
War Debts, 362–63, 357–58
War of 1812, 16, 26–28, 71–79, 80–81
War Hawks, 77–78
Warsaw Pact, 450
Washington, George, 22–23, 49–52, 55
Washington, S. S., 332
Washington, Treaty of, 191–92
Washington Conference of 1921–22, 327–28, 374
Wayne, Anthony, 54
Webster, Daniel, 95, 104, 121–24, 132, 153–56, 201, 204, 273
Webster, Noah, 26
Webster-Ashburton Treaty of 1842, 122–25, 152
Weimar Republic, 302–3
Weinberg, Albert K., 99–101
Wellborn, Fred W., vii
Welles, Gideon, 182
Welles, Sumner, 346, 458
West, 46, 66–70, 76–81, 93–94, 96, 114–15, 118, 127–30, 132–33, 145–46, 284; *see also* Middle West
West Indies, 42–43, 52–54, 104–5, 149
Westmoreland, William C., 476
Westward movement, 19–21, 92–93, 165, 168
Weyler, Valeriano, 214–15
Whaling interests, 132, 152
Wheeler, Burton K., 322, 325, 405, 417
Whig Party and American foreign relations, 95–96, 99, 115, 118, 123, 129–30, 132, 135–36, 141, 145–46, 153–56
White, Henry, 332
White, William Allen, 326
White Committee, 326
White Man's Burden ideas, 229, 246
Whitman, Marcus, 126
Wilkes, Charles, 180
Wilkinson, James, 47, 106
William II, 162, 190, 194, 227–28, 230–32, 289–94
Williams, William A., 275, 432
Willis, Albert S., 210
Willkie, Wendell, 320, 324, 326, 403
Wilmot Proviso, 145–46

This book is set in 10 and 9 point Caledonia, leaded 2 points. Part numbers are 18 and 36 point Baskerville. Chapter numbers are 36 point Baskerville. Part and chapter titles are 24 point Baskerville. The size of the type page is 27 × 45½ picas.